THE MEASURE OF AMERICA 2010–2011

MAPPING RISKS AND RESILIENCE

THE MEASURE OF AMERICA 2010–2011

MAPPING RISKS AND RESILIENCE

Kristen Lewis
Sarah Burd-Sharps

FOREWORD BY
Jeffrey D. Sachs

A joint publication of the **Social Science Research Council**
and **New York University Press**

NEW YORK UNIVERSITY PRESS
New York and London
www.nyupress.org

Library of Congress Cataloging-in-Publication Data

Lewis, Kristen.
The Measure of America 2010–2011 : Mapping Risks and Resilience american human development project / Kristen Lewis and Sarah Burd-Sharps ; with foreword by Jeffrey D. Sachs.
p. cm.
Includes bibliographical references and index.
ISBN 978-0-8147-8379-5 (cl : alk. paper) — ISBN 978-0-8147-8380-1 (pbk: alk. paper) —
ISBN 978-0-8147-8381-8 (e-book)
1. United States—Social conditions—21st century—Statistics. 2. Quality of life—United States—Statistics. 3. Social indicators—United States—Statistics. I. Burd-Sharps, Sarah. II. Title.

HN59.2.L495 2010
306.0973'090512—dc22 2010028834

New York University Press books are printed on acid-free paper, and their binding materials are chosen for strength and durability.

Printed in the United States of America

Designed by Humantific | UnderstandingLab, Inc.

c 10 9 8 7 6 5 4 3 2 1
p 10 9 8 7 6 5 4 3 2 1

Team for the preparation of The Measure of America 2010–2011: Mapping Risks and Resilience

LEAD AUTHORS
Kristen Lewis and Sarah Burd-Sharps
American Human Development Project Co-Directors

CHIEF STATISTICIAN
Patrick Nolan Guyer

RESEARCHER AND CONTRIBUTING WRITER
Ted Lechterman

ADVISORY PANEL
Ivye Allen, Foundation for the Mid South
Craig Calhoun, Social Science Research Council
Dalton Conley, New York University
Sheldon Danziger, University of Michigan
Frank Furstenberg, University of Pennsylvania
Carla Javits, REDF
Jerome Karabel, University of California, Berkeley
Ichiro Kawachi, Harvard University
Gary King, Harvard University
Ellen Levy, LinkedIn
Jeff Madrick, The New School
Katherine Newman, Princeton University
Adela de la Torre, University of California, Davis

SENIOR STATISTICAL ADVISOR
Neil Bennett, City University of New York

EDITING
Francis Wilkinson, Substantive Editor
Bob Land, Copyeditor

DESIGN
Humantific | Understanding Lab, Inc.

Contents

Boxes, Figures, Maps, and Tables

Foreword

by Jeffrey D. Sachs

Bravo to the American Human Development team for another breakthrough volume. *The Measure of America 2010–2011* could not be more timely. As poverty is rising and high unemployment is causing searing pain across society, we need an accurate understanding of America's diverse and complex conditions. No other publication comes close to this one in documenting and explaining America's disparate socioeconomic realities, especially the vast differences across regions and social groups and the alarming shortfall of America's performance compared with other high-income countries.

The United States today is a country of great and increasing socioeconomic inequality, with unimagined wealth living side by side with entrenched poverty. The report's rigorous and revealing maps, graphs, tables, and flowcharts open new and valuable perspectives on America's fast-changing and crisis-ridden society. The insightful analysis in *The Measure of America 2010–2011* describes the key factors driving these changes.

Stunning data hit us between the eyes. Of America's 435 congressional districts, the very richest and the very poorest are near neighbors in New York City: Manhattan's East Side and the South Bronx, respectively. That kind of cheek-to-jowl inequality offers a metaphor for America as a whole—the paradox of a society of profound divisions struggling to find common ground and understanding.

For far too long, America coasted on an unexamined boast of being "number one," with superlatives in every sphere of life. Only now, after the bursting of the financial bubble, are we waking up to a far more somber reality. Persistent inequalities of opportunity scar a country in which yawning gaps in income, educational attainment, and life expectancy far exceed those in any other high-income democracy, and insecurity is greater and more widespread. Moreover, most Americans are not fully aware of the interwoven social, political, and economic factors that tend to keep some groups and regions stuck in deep poverty, poor health, and low educational attainment.

The Measure of America opens our eyes and bids us to reconsider some basic realities. The report's data powerfully depict the enormous differences in socioeconomic conditions across regions (including by states, congressional districts, and metropolitan areas), race and ethnicity, and gender. Asian Americans are generally the highest earning, healthiest, and best educated of the racial and ethnic groups studied in the report, followed by whites—with Latinos, African Americans, and Native Americans trailing far behind in terms of well-being and access to opportunity. In general, the South still lags the rest of the nation in key socioeconomic indicators, but the report describes the tremendous diversity found within every region.

Like previous studies of the American Human Development Project, the report holds America up to a revealing comparison with European and other high-income countries. The comparative findings are deeply troubling and should give all Americans pause about our priorities and policy assumptions. America lags our peer countries on crucial dimensions of well-being, ranking as the worst or near-worst with regard to life expectancy, child mortality, health-care costs, obesity, science and math literacy, child poverty, carbon emissions per person, violent crime, and voter participation.

The current report does not carry much happy news, but its powerful messages are all the more urgent. Our society is divided deeply; income, health, and educational outcomes are under dire threat, and roads to opportunity are littered with obstacles for far too many Americans.

The report's crucial positive news is that America remains highly productive and innovative, two characteristics that are vital for America's economic, social, and political recovery. America's challenge, the report strongly implies, is to find a new pathway to broad social cooperation, one that encourages us once again to think, act, and solve problems as a united society in common pursuit of a better future for all Americans.

Jeffrey D. Sachs
Director of the Earth Institute at Columbia University and
Special Advisor to United Nations Secretary-General Ban Ki-moon

Acknowledgments

Words cannot express our profound gratitude to those who have supported this project. We are grateful to our funders for believing in this initiative and for their steadfast support and encouragement. They include: the Conrad N. Hilton Foundation—Steven M. Hilton, Ed Cain, and Bill Pitkin—and the Lincy Foundation—Jeff Wilkins and Sothida Tan. We owe special thanks to the Social Science Research Council—particularly to our colleagues Craig Calhoun, Mary McDonnell, and Paul Price—for their support of the Project's work.

We are deeply indebted to our Advisory Panel, an engaged group that, acting in their personal capacities, provided invaluable guidance at every stage of the project, and to our Senior Statistical Advisor, Neil Bennett, for his expert advice. Responsibility for all errors, however, lies with us alone.

We greatly appreciate the written contributions of Jeffrey D. Sachs and Darell Hammond.

The report benefited from background papers commissioned from the following sectoral or thematic experts and researchers: Taylor Owen (human security), Jan Pierskalla and Erik Wibbels (natural resource curse), Radha Duggal Pennotti (health security), and Ted Lechterman (risks and resilience).

In addition to suggestions from the Advisory Panel, Richard Arum, Richard Cebula, Josh DeWind, Pawanpreet Dhaliwal, John B. Johnson IV, Joe Karaganis, Walter W. McMahon, Will Nicholas, Joan Sanger, Eugene Steuerle, and Christiana Stoddard provided detailed and extremely helpful comments on various components of the manuscript. Neva Goodwin, Ken Prewitt, and Rob Wood engaged us with thoughtful conversation, for which we are truly grateful. Special thanks to Shareen Hertel for her subtitle suggestion. For statistical advice and assistance, many thanks to John Blodgett, Richard Hendra, David Lamoureux, Hannah Yang Moore, Jack Norton, and Sanjay Reddy. Hannah Burd, Sairah Husain, and Anne Tatlock provided valuable research support. Diana Tung provided vital assistance in the homestretch with good cheer and great attention to detail.

At the Social Science Research Council, the following individuals provided critical support to various aspects of the project's administration, finances, and communications: Sara Acosta, Jolanta Badura, Jennifer Carroll Blackman,

Sara Duvisac, Melissa Goss, Lisa Henderson, John Koprowski, Gail Kovach, Ebony Livingston, Zach Menchini, Diane Nasella, Siovahn Walker, Lisa Yanoti, and Zach Zinn.

For their professional expertise, we owe tremendous thanks to: David Greenbaum, Keith Woodman, George Chaclas, and Glenn Pudelka of Edwards Angell Palmer & Dodge LLP (legal); Jim Brasher, Becky Castle, and Pam Wuichet of Project Resource Group (fundraising); Michael Gordon, John Keaten, and Sam Nagourney of Group Gordon (communications); Jamie Kennard and the team at Krate (web development); and Rosten Woo, Sha Hwang, and Zach Watson of RMW Design (maps).

To the talented professionals who turned the manuscript into an actual book, we owe a huge debt of gratitude; a thousand thanks to Frank Wilkinson, Bob Land, and the Humantific | UnderstandingLab team of Elizabeth Pastor, Garry VanPatter, Michael Babwahsingh, and Valentina Miosuro, who have once again outdone themselves. In discovering within a flat manuscript limitless dimensions of meaning, Humantific turned text and digits into a work of both art and sense. Thanks to Ilene Kalish, Despina Gimbel, Charles Hames, Aiden Amos, Betsy Steve, and the team at NYU Press for their excitement about and confidence in this project from the beginning, and their perseverance in seeing it through.

As for the two other members of our core team, the dynamic duo of Patrick Nolan Guyer and Ted Lechterman, it's difficult even to know where to start. Patrick's statistical expertise, methodological rigor, and gentle but firm insistence on not letting the interpretation get ahead of the data kept the analysis on solid ground, and his gracious professionalism and good cheer were always in evidence. Ted's research prowess, lovely writing, and keen analytical sense were a tremendous boon; he made crucial substantive contributions, not least of which was his fine work on the education chapter, all the while keeping the day-to-day operations on track with an almost uncanny level of productivity.

We are enormously grateful for the enthusiastic, generous support of our dear parents, siblings, in-laws, extended families, and friends, many of whom are no doubt less spellbound by the results of the American Human Development Index than they kindly pretended to be. And last, but certainly not least, we must thank our husbands and children: David, Dalia, and Sophie Sharps and Paul, Zoë, Sophie, and Benjamin Lewis Ewing. We know too well that the intense periods of work associated with this book sometimes had negative impacts on their human development levels, to say the least, and are grateful beyond words for the many ways, large and small, that their love, good humor, understanding, and unflagging support both grounded and buoyed us.

thank you!

THE MEASURE OF
AMERICA
2010–2011
MAPPING RISKS AND RESILIENCE

Key Findings

"You manage what you measure." Among management consultants, this phrase has become something of a mantra. With the rapid advance in recent years of computerization and digital networks, the capacity of businesses, universities, governments, and other institutions to measure results has grown exponentially. You can see the thesis at work in school districts across the United States, where administrators are now measuring student achievement and adjusting pedagogy and resources on the basis of test results. They are managing what they measure.

This Human Development Report is the second produced for the United States, following the inaugural 2008–2009 report. It provides a gauge of core areas of well-being, or human development, across the nation, with data broken down by state, congressional district, race, gender, and ethnicity. **Three areas in particular form the basic building blocks of human development and contribute the data used to calculate the American Human Development Index:** health (the capacity to live a long and healthy life), education (access to knowledge), and income (the capacity to maintain a decent standard of living).

Americans are one people, but given **vast gaps** in human development among them, they face starkly different challenges.

As America's economy, educational infrastructure, and health-care system have expanded and evolved over many years, the average income, educational attainment, and life expectancy of Americans have risen. But they have sometimes risen in wildly divergent fashion for different people in different places. The typical Asian American in New Jersey lives one quarter century longer, is eleven times more likely to have a graduate degree, and earns $33,149 more per year than the typical Native American in South Dakota, whose earnings are below the median American earnings of 1960. This is what is meant by a "gap" in human development; measured on the American Human Development Index, the gap between Asian Americans in New Jersey and Native Americans in South Dakota translates into an entire century of progress in health, education, and living standards.

Americans are one people, but given vast gaps in human development among them, they face starkly different challenges. This report provides measurements of some of the most important indicators of human development in the hope that such data will lead to better management of the conditions that create, or contribute to, those outcomes. **Particularly in times of budget cuts and hard choices, good data**

are indispensable for wise decisions. By presenting measurements of well-being beyond the narrow confines of Gross Domestic Product (GDP) and other economic indicators, this report offers a tool to pinpoint areas, some chronic, that will require sustained attention if America is to realize the promise of genuine opportunity for all its citizens. Furthermore, a more holistic analysis of which groups are surging forward and which are stalled or left behind is essential to helping the most vulnerable develop the resilience necessary to prevail in the face of financial crisis, recession, environmental catastrophe, or other challenges.

Indeed, the theme of this year's report is Mapping Risks and Resilience. In the wake of Hurricane Katrina, the financial crash of 2008, and the BP oil spill in the Gulf, it is clear that the capacity to weather difficult times is crucial. Yet tens of millions of Americans lack even the most rudimentary shelter from a storm, be it meteorological or financial. Decreasing the risks Americans face and increasing their resilience in the face of adversity are keys to advancing human development.

We have included a number of **new features** since publication of the first human development report, *The Measure of America 2008–2009*:

- **New American Human Development Index scores and rankings** for states and congressional districts to facilitate comparisons with data in the first report
- **New analysis of race and ethnicity by state**
- **Encouraging examples of what is working** to address stubborn social and economic problems
- **A Dashboard of Risks,** a supplement to the American HD Index that measures risk in ten areas of health, education, and income. The Dashboard features faster-changing indicators to highlight pervasive risk factors, from low-birth-weight babies and children not enrolled in preschool to housing insecurity and those not counted in unemployment figures because they have stopped looking for work (see pages 34-35)
- **An appendix of indicators** for further analysis, including comparisons of the United States and other OECD nations

Along with these new features, the report and Index contain a wealth of data and analysis on human development to provide:

- Answers to questions of policy makers, teachers and students, journalists, and others;
- A roadmap of needs and vulnerabilities to guide philanthropies, government agencies, concerned citizens, and others to populations that are falling behind;

Decreasing the risks Americans face and increasing their resilience in the face of adversity are keys to advancing human development.

- A more comprehensive framework for diagnosing underlying causes of disadvantage and discussing poverty, encompassing noneconomic factors that both contribute to and define poverty.

KEY FINDINGS OF THE AMERICAN HUMAN DEVELOPMENT INDEX:

- Americans born today can expect to live 78.6 years on average, nearly nine years longer then in 1960.
- Eighty-five percent of adults have at least a high school education, and overall school enrollment is higher than at any other point in history.
- Once-rapid progress in median earnings of adults since 1960 has slowed to a crawl since 2000.
- Some of the largest gaps in well-being are found within a single city or among population groups living within a few miles of one another.

A Long and Healthy Life

The unprecedented attention to the nation's health-care structure over the last two years overlooked the country's most alarming health problem: huge disparities in health outcomes for different population groups. The most pervasive threats to health—everyday hazards such as tobacco, alcohol, poor diet, and lack of exercise—are often bundled together with environmental, social, and economic stresses, resulting in chronic illness and premature death. While we tend to credit medical research and advanced treatments for increased life expectancy, gains made in recent decades are due to a decrease in the risk of premature death. Decreasing risks and increasing resilience almost certainly remain the surest and most achievable path to improved health and longer lives for Americans.

There are huge disparities in health outcomes for different population groups.

KEY FINDINGS OF THE REPORT AND INDEX:

- Life expectancy in the United States is 78.6 years, on par with Chile, though Chile spends one-tenth what the United States spends on health care.
- In the country as a whole, Asian Americans live, on average, thirteen years longer than African Americans, more than twelve years longer than Native Americans, more than eight years longer than whites, and nearly four years longer than Latinos.
- The eleven states with the shortest life spans are in the South.
- Whites in Washington, DC, live, on average, twelve years longer than African Americans in the same city.
- Life expectancy in Virginia's Eighth Congressional District, in suburban Washington, DC, is a decade longer than life expectancy in West Virginia's Third Congressional District, in the rural southern part of the state.

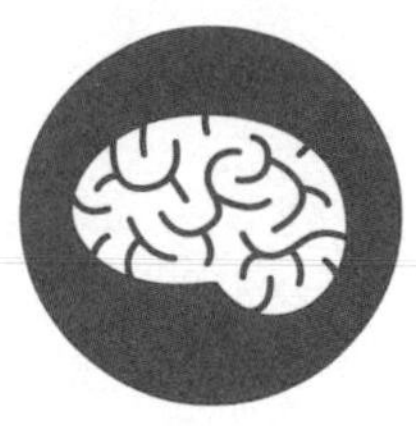

More education correlates to better, healthier, happier, and longer lives as well as higher incomes.

Access to Knowledge

More education correlates to better, healthier, happier, and longer lives as well as higher incomes. In a knowledge economy, education provides a bulwark against economic downturns and disruptions, is a key factor in expanding opportunity, and remains a long-term source of resilience in the face of adversity. In the 2007–9 recession, college graduates faced a combined unemployment and underemployment rate of 10 percent; those with only a high school education faced rates twice as high, while 35 percent of high school dropouts were either unemployed or underemployed.

KEY FINDINGS OF THE REPORT AND INDEX:

- Washington, DC, scores highest on the Education Index developed for this report; 85.8 percent of adult residents are high school graduates, and 26.7 percent have graduate or advanced degrees. Arkansas ranks last, with 82 percent and 6.3 percent, respectively.
- The top five states in the Education Index spent an average of over $14,500 per K–12 pupil. The bottom five spent under $9,000 per pupil.
- In California's Thirtieth Congressional District (Hollywood, Beverly Hills, Santa Monica, and Malibu), nearly three in five adult residents are college graduates, and more than one in four have advanced degrees. A few miles west in California's District 34 (downtown Los Angeles), only three in one hundred residents have advanced degrees.
- In every ethnic and racial group studied except Asian Americans, women have higher educational attainment and enrollment than men.
- More than 90 percent of white adult women today are high school graduates; more than 40 percent of Latino men are not.
- More than a quarter of high school freshmen do not graduate in four years—if they graduate at all.

A Decent Standard of Living

Personal earnings, the measure employed in the American HD Index to represent standard of living, have risen from the median income of $23,000 in the mid-1970s to nearly $30,000 today. But the rise has been anything but even across diverse populations. Female earnings doubled in constant dollars, from $12,800 to $24,700, while male earnings rose by only $2,500. Perceptions that the rich have gotten richer while the poor have gotten poorer are borne out—emphatically—by the data. And finally, while we frequently measure and devote policy attention to salaries and wages, wealth, or net worth, is vital for building long-term economic security and acts as a cushion when income is disrupted. Efforts to help those with few assets build greater economic security and set their children on a trajectory of opportunity and choice have received relatively less attention.

Personal earnings have risen from the median income of $23,000 in the mid-1970s to nearly $30,000 today.

KEY FINDINGS OF THE REPORT AND INDEX:

- The wealth of the top 1 percent of households rose, on average, 103 percent (to $18.5 million per household) from 1983 to 2007. The poorest 40 percent of households experienced a 63 percent decline in wealth during the same period (to $2,200 per household).
- Washington, DC, has the highest median earnings, at $40,342; Arkansas has the lowest, at $23,471.
- By the end of the 2007–9 recession, unemployment among the bottom tenth of U.S. households was 31 percent, which is higher than unemployment during the worst year of the Great Depression; for households earning $150,000 and over, unemployment was just over 3 percent.
- Between 2005 and 2008, median earnings for men in Michigan fell more than 12 percent—from $39,000 a year to $34,000.
- The wealthiest 20 percent of U.S. households have slightly more than half of the nation's total income. The poorest 20 percent have 3.4 percent of total income.
- The wealthiest congressional district in the United States is NY-14 on Manhattan's East Side, with median earnings of $60,000; the poorest is NY-16, a few subway stops away in the Bronx, with median earnings of $18,000.

Just as the data in this report enable us to pinpoint problems in specific communities, they also point the way toward better outcomes.

Advancing Human Development

American history is frequently portrayed as a march of progress, as ever larger numbers of Americans claim their civil rights, advance through education and hard work, and secure unimpeded access to the American Dream. But progress on many fronts is growing more elusive and, for some Americans, has assumed the character of myth.

Incomes have been stagnant for a decade, and high unemployment due to the Great Recession has undermined the security of tens of millions of Americans. Chronic health problems associated with poor diet and lack of exercise, including diabetes and obesity, consume a disproportionate amount of health-care spending while condemning millions to poor health and sapping their income-earning potential, reducing their quality of life, and shortening their lives. Educational failure is epidemic in countless American cities and towns, relegating millions of American youth to a life of dead-end jobs, poverty, and social exclusion.

These problems are not new or unknown. Likewise, while their remedies may be complex and perhaps incompletely understood, they are not abject mysteries. Just as the data in this report enable us to pinpoint problems in specific communities, they also point the way toward better outcomes.

In **health**, we must address the **"Fatal Four"**—the risk factors that are the most significant contributors to premature death, namely, **smoking, poor diet, physical inactivity, and drinking to excess.** Part of the answer is personal responsibility. But health strategies built around personal responsibility alone are proven recipes for failure. People live their lives within a social context; to optimize health outcomes, we must change the attitudes and environments that undermine health—from senseless risk-taking among men who feel obligated to conform to masculine norms to environments in which sugary, salty, fatty foods are sometimes the only options.

In **education**, research shows that **quality preschool** is the single most decisive means to prepare disadvantaged children for elementary school. Providing universal access to quality preschool should be a national goal. Similarly, **high school graduation** is essential to lifetime success, yet the rate of on-time high school graduation has been fundamentally unchanged for three decades. Raising the compulsory age of education to 18 in states where it is earlier is an obvious way to improve the education prospects—and thus the life prospects—for millions of teens who would otherwise drop out, thereby all but ensuring lives of severely limited opportunities and low incomes.

In **income**, endemic poverty puts tens of millions of families at risk and strips them of the resilience they need to weather hard times. The negative consequences of this extend to health and education, as stress, poor diet, and other factors associated with poverty wear down health and chronic lack of resources undermines educational attainment. To build resilience, we must make basic financial literacy a part of high school curricula and enact programs like automatic enrollment in retirement plans that help low-income Americans build up assets.

***

This book concludes with a set of recommendations for priority actions required in order to improve scores on the American HD Index. The report provides a wealth of data on issues critically important to social policy. But knowing about problems and addressing problems are very different things. The information is at hand. The will to apply it is yet to be summoned.

INTRODUCTION

Human Development in America Today

In the chronicling of the American story, the human development approach seeks to shift focus from the financial sphere of growth and profits to the human sphere of opportunity and freedom.

IN THIS SECTION:

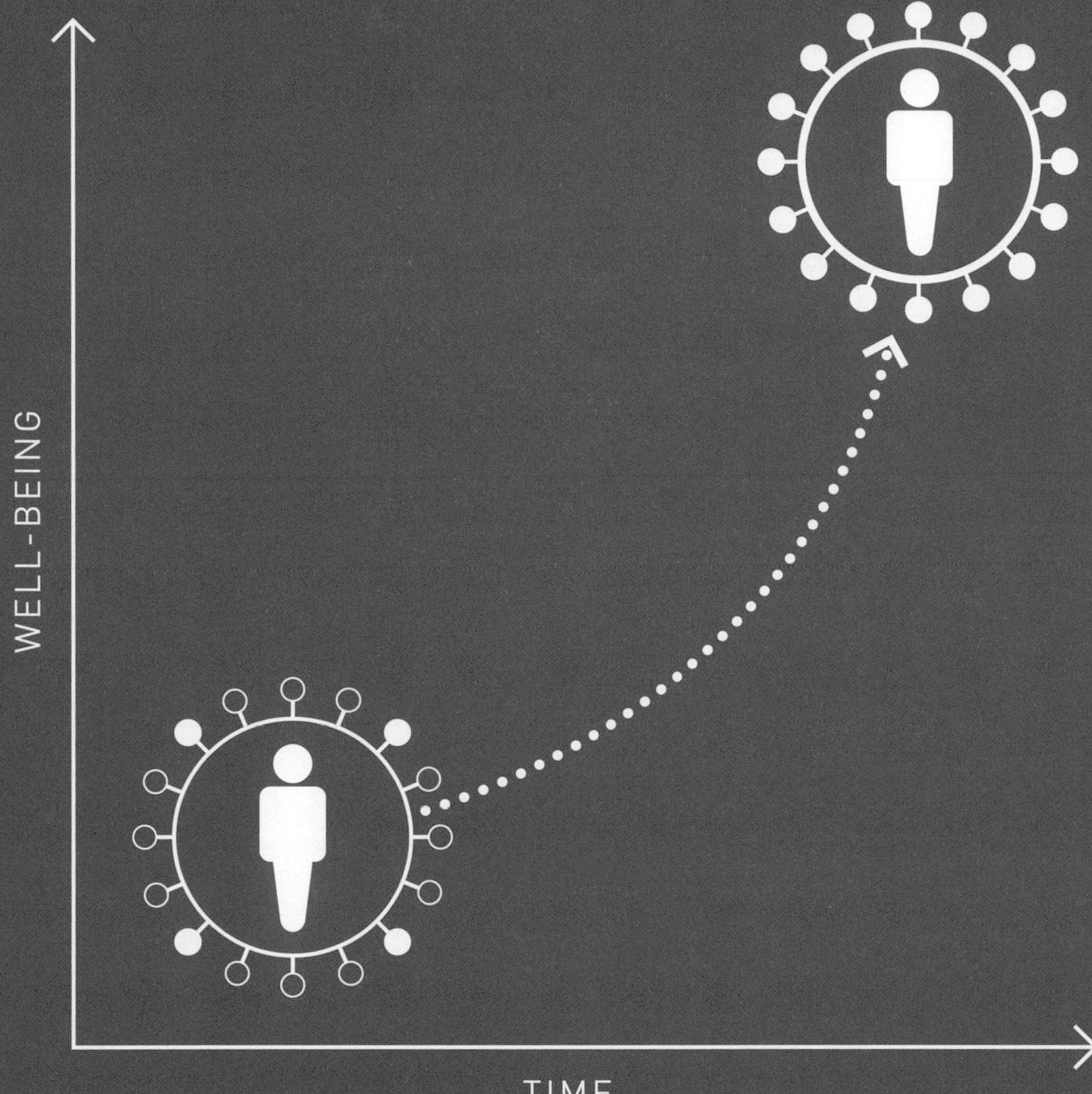
WELL-BEING
TIME

Introduction

> "The success of an economy and of a society cannot be separated from the lives that members of the society are able to lead . . . We not only value living well and satisfactorily, but also appreciate having control over our own lives."
>
> **AMARTYA SEN,** *Development as Freedom*, 1999

Human development is the process of enlarging people's opportunities and improving their well-being.

America's ability to fulfill its promise as a nation that offers everyone a fair chance relies on broadly shared freedom and opportunity. And today more than ever, raising our standard of living depends upon effective competition in the global marketplace. How are we faring in these two missions?

For too long, we have looked to the Gross Domestic Product (GDP) to answer these and other crucial questions, tacitly equating market growth with progress. In December 2009, home foreclosures were still on the rise, and unemployment was holding steady at nearly 10 percent—only the second time since the Great Depression that the unemployment rate had reached double digits. Yet even as the bottom was falling out for countless American families, GDP was on the rise.

We won't know the full extent of the damage, the degree to which the recession upended the foundations of daily life for millions of Americans, until at least 2011. Why? Because **while economic indicators—inflation, construction, retail trade, wholesale inventories, commodity prices, and much more—are released at least every quarter, vital signs of human well-being, such as the percentage of babies born with low birth weights or the number of young children living in extreme poverty, are measured annually at best, and released after a two- or three-year delay.**

Thus, we knew in January 2010 how much money Americans spent on their health in the fourth quarter of 2009. But we won't know how long they were living in 2009—until 2012. We knew in July 2010 how many new houses were built, bought, and sold from April to June 2010. But we won't know how many families had no home at all until late 2011.

Human well-being depends on the success of the economy, as measured by GDP and other economic indicators. But these indicators tell us only part of the American story—a part that for many reads as a footnote beneath the chapters of our daily lives. **In the chronicling of the American story, the human development approach seeks to shift focus from the financial sphere of growth and profits to the human sphere of opportunity and freedom.** Human development is the process of enlarging people's opportunities and improving their well-being. Human development is dedicated not to how big an economy can swell, but to what ordinary people can do and what they can become. Human development explores the real-world opportunities people have to live in ways they themselves value and freely choose, and the extent to which they are able to realize their potential to the fullest. By placing people at the center of analysis on well-being, this people-centered approach redefines the way we think about and address human—and national—progress.

The human development approach was developed at the United Nations in the late 1980s, born of the frustration that economic progress in developing countries was not translating fully into human progress: healthier children, more literacy, greater political participation, cleaner environments, more widely shared prosperity, or greater freedom. Dr. Mahbub ul Haq, an economist who had worked at the World Bank and served as finance minister in his native Pakistan, developed the approach in response to the human lives he saw "shriveling even as economic production was expanding."[1] He insisted that while **money and economic growth are essential means to an end, they are not ends in themselves.** Human beings are not inputs to economic growth in his view; rather, the opposite is true. Economic growth is only valuable if it enables more people to live long and healthy lives, more children to go to school, and more women to decide for themselves how to live. To Dr. Haq, the only development end worth seeking is the flourishing of human life.

Under Dr. Haq's leadership, the first *Human Development Report,* a study of conditions affecting human well-being around the world, was published in 1990. Over the last two decades, the United Nations Development Programme (UNDP) has commissioned and released twenty such global reports.

Two Approaches to Understanding Progress in America

The American Human Development Project

The American Human Development Project released its first report, *The Measure of America: American Human Development Report 2008–09,* in July 2008, and followed in 2009 with state human development reports for Mississippi and Louisiana, both of which had fared poorly on the 2008–2009 state rankings. A California report is due out in early 2011.

Reports in the American Human Development Report series have spurred a national conversation about access to opportunity among Americans in different parts of the country. In 2010 the Department of Health and Human Services awarded multimillion-dollar grants to develop health-care infrastructure in Jackson, Mississippi, and Fresno, California, based in part on evidence presented in these national and state reports of the obstacles these communities face.

As the human development approach continues to gather momentum in the United States, communities can be expected to leverage these publications to guide business and other investments.

Each year, the report takes on a new topic, ranging from climate change and globalization to political participation, gender equality, and cultural diversity. **More than any other product of the United Nations, the Human Development Report series has shaped the global development debate.** It championed the now-unremarkable idea that better lives for people should be the aim of the international community's efforts.

Starting in 1992, developing countries began to adopt this approach, using national human development reports to explore how people were faring in their own countries and to confront sensitive issues—including corruption, AIDS, and economic gulfs between religious or ethnic groups. Researchers in nearly 150 countries have produced national human development reports, leading to impressive results in the policy realm (see **BOX 1**). *The Measure of America: American Human Development Report 2008–2009*—this book's predecessor—was the first such report ever published for an industrialized country (see sidebar on page 13).

BOX 1 National and Regional Human Development Reports

This volume is only the second human development report prepared for the United States—the only affluent country to have a report. But *The Measure of America* has plenty of company: more than seven hundred regional, national, and subnational human development reports have been produced since Bangladesh first established the national model in 1992. **The world over, human development reports serve as a springboard for debate over development priorities, spurring discussion on sensitive development issues and strengthening the capacity of policy makers and citizens to understand and employ data and analysis.**[2]

In **Uganda**, the 2002 national human development report explored the cultural and traditional factors fueling the AIDS epidemic and demonstrated the economic benefits of improved health care for those living with HIV. The report led to a national conference on HIV/AIDS, which in turn resulted in a program to provide universal access to antiretroviral therapy. The 2000 HDR in Botswana had a similar effect, breaking taboos that had hindered awareness and weakened response to the disease. The report paved the way for a national program providing life-saving treatments.

In **Mexico**, the federal government allocates special resources to indigenous municipalities with the lowest Mexican human development index scores. Antipoverty efforts in the poorest state, Chiapas, are guided using the national HD index.

In **Brazil**, an HD index calculated for the country's five thousand municipalities is a chief mechanism for determining resource allocation, regardless of which political party is in power. During the Cardoso administration, the HD index was used to select states, municipalities, and families for four main federal projects, including one that reached 36 million people living in poverty. Since the start of the Lula administration the index has been used to target social programs for youth and adult education, electricity for all, basic sanitation, food security, and efforts to keep adolescents ages 15 to 17 in school.

The *Arab Human Development Report* series has been an invaluable tool for recognizing sensitive regional issues, such as governance, women's rights, and human insecurity. Regional experts and research institutions write the report, giving it regional legitimacy and opening a window through which the rest of the world can view the region's challenges as understood by the people who live there. Regional and international media highly regard the series, which attracts extensive coverage in the *Economist*, *the New York Times*, and *Time*, and on the BBC, among many other media outlets.

Part I: Understanding Human Development

The Ideas behind Human Development

THE CAPABILITY APPROACH

The concept of human development rests on a conceptual framework that was derived from Harvard economist Amartya Sen's seminal work on capabilities.[3] **Simply put, capabilities determine what a person can do and become. Capabilities shape the real possibilities open to people and determine the freedom they have to lead the kind of lives they want to live.**

Someone rich in capabilities has a full toolkit for making his or her vision of a "good life" a reality. Someone with few capabilities has fewer options, fewer opportunities; for such a person, many rewarding paths are blocked. What we can be and do—our capabilities—are expanded (or constrained) by our own efforts, by our family circumstances, and by the institutions and conditions of our society. Because different people value different things, no comprehensive, universal list of capabilities applies to everyone. In the human development framework, a central concept is the freedom to decide for oneself how to live; a good life is a life of genuine choice. Nonetheless, some basic and widely valued capabilities[4] include being able to:

- Avoid premature death, live a life of normal length, and enjoy good health and physical safety
- Have access to knowledge, including a formal education
- Have adequate nutrition and shelter
- Have access to public space, and retain the ability to move from place to place freely and without fear
- Enjoy freedom of conscience, religion, and belief
- Be treated and protected fairly by the law
- Participate in decisions that affect one's life and have voice and influence in the democratic process
- Hold property, seek employment, and participate in markets
- Be treated with respect, and enjoy independence and equality
- Form personal relationships and a family
- Enjoy recreational activities and pleasurable experiences

What Is Human Development?

Human development is about the real freedom ordinary people have to decide who to be, what to do, and how to live. These diagrams illustrate the central ideas of human development and visually depict how we measure it using the American Human Development Index.

CONCEPT

Human development is defined as *the process of enlarging people's freedoms and opportunities and improving their well-being.*

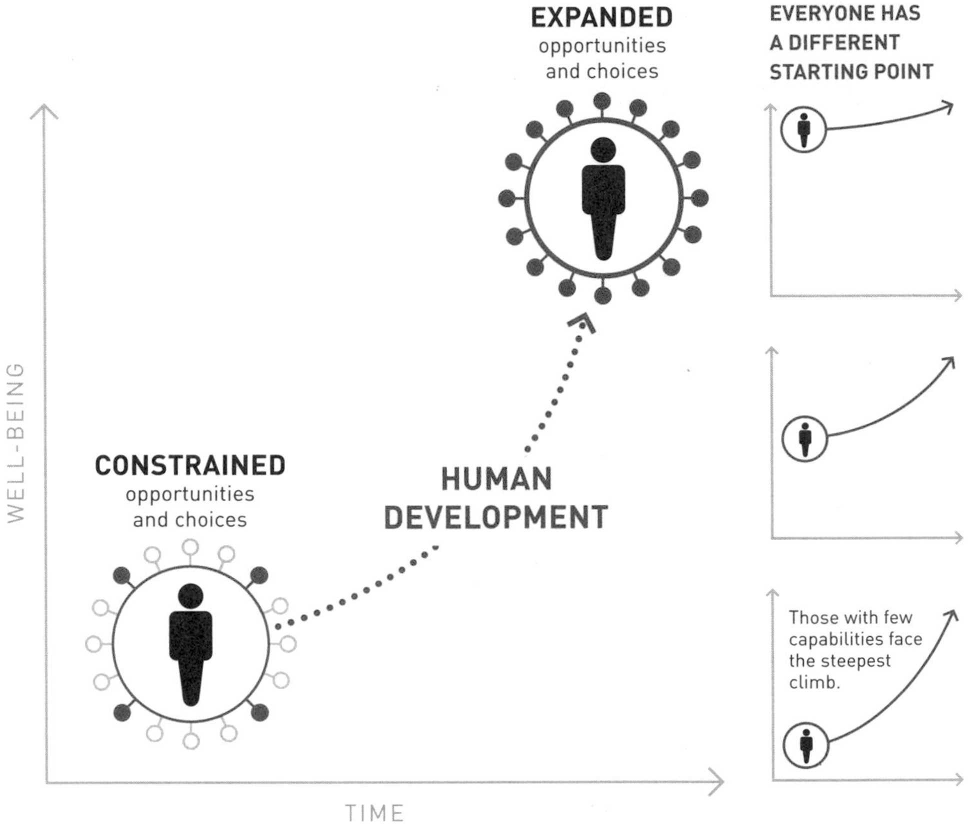

EXPANDED opportunities and choices

CONSTRAINED opportunities and choices

HUMAN DEVELOPMENT

WELL-BEING

TIME

EVERYONE HAS A DIFFERENT STARTING POINT

Those with few capabilities face the steepest climb.

JOURNEY

Human development can be understood as a journey. Even before one's life begins, *parents* play a role in setting the trajectory of one's human development. Numerous factors and experiences alter the course of one's journey through life, *helping* or *hindering* one's ability to live a life of choice and value.

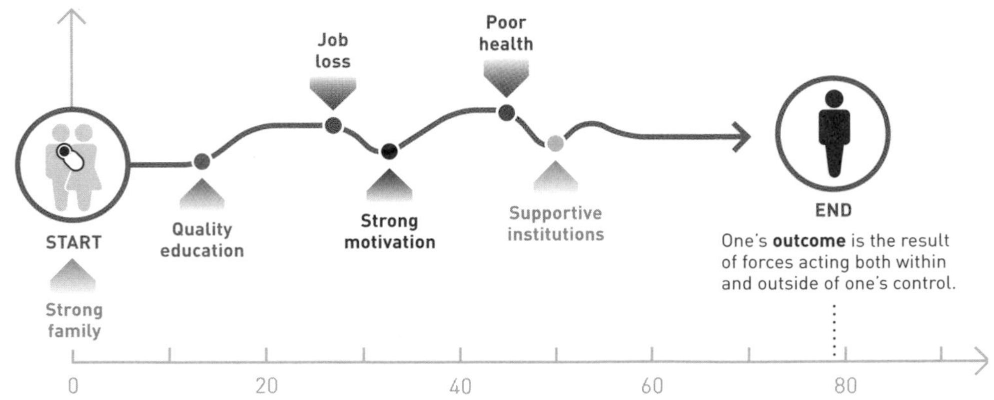

CAPABILITIES

Capabilities—*what people can do and what they can become*—are central to the human development concept. Many different capabilities are essential to a fulfilling life.

Our capabilities are expanded both by our own efforts and by the institutions and conditions of our society.

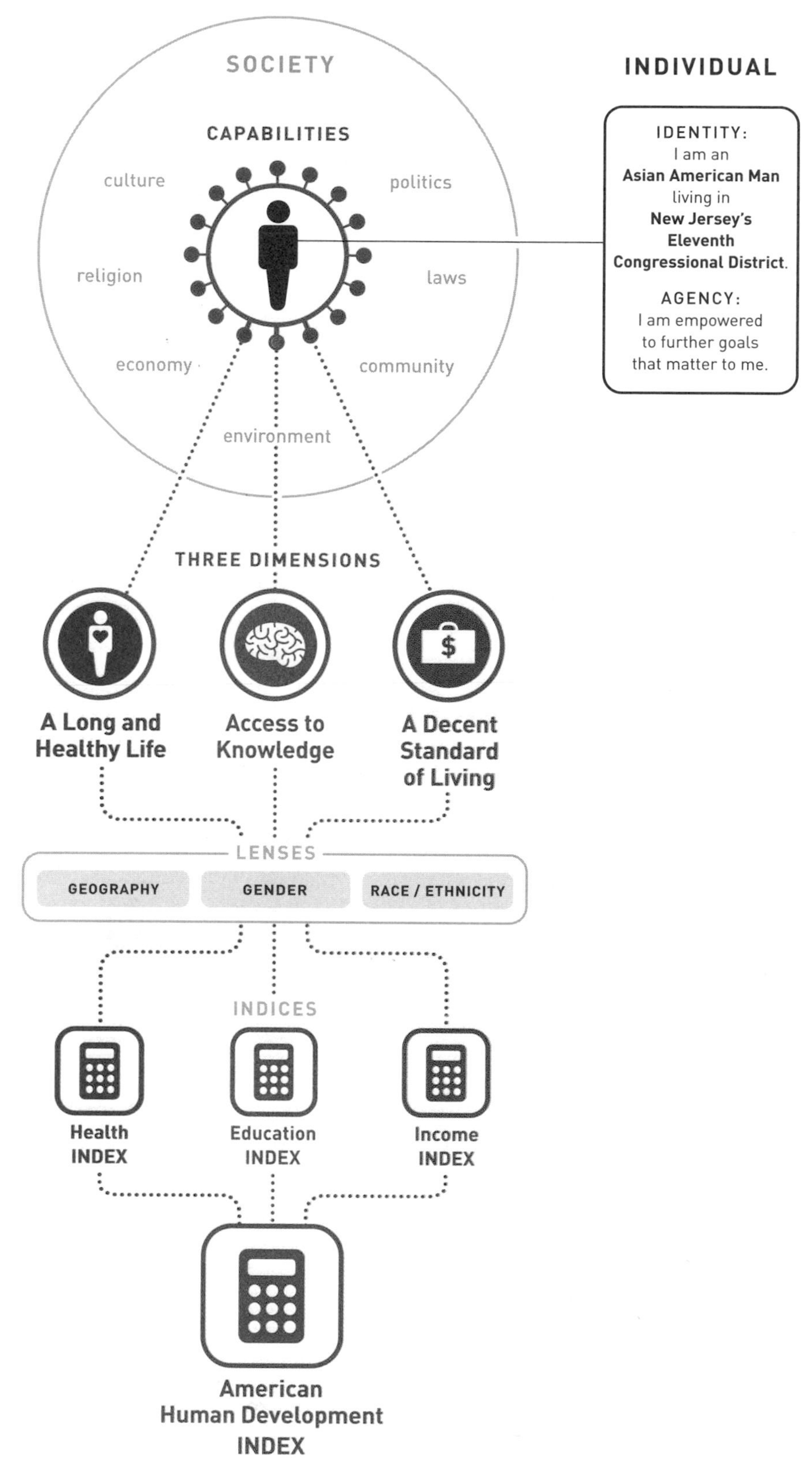

DIMENSIONS

Of all the capabilities, this report focuses in-depth on just *three*, all of which are relatively easy to measure. They are considered core human development dimensions.

LENSES

The results of the American Human Development Index reveal variations among regions, states, and congressional districts; between women and men; and among racial and ethnic groups.

INDEX

The modified American Human Development Index measures the same three basic dimensions as the standard HD Index, but it uses *different indicators* to better reflect the U.S. context and to maximize use of available data. The Index will serve as a *baseline* for monitoring future progress.

People may value many other things that are not on this list. One person may value the capability to hold political office, for instance, whereas another may value the capability to enjoy personal privacy. And there are capabilities on this list that a person might willingly forgo in pursuit of a different freely chosen objective, such as a religious person who chooses to go without food during a fast. An individual may freely choose to pursue a career like firefighting that heightens one's risk for premature death and thus threatens the most fundamental human capability, to be alive, if service to others is central to that person's vision of what it means to lead a valuable life.

In addition, **not all capabilities are measured easily.** Assessing some, such as adequate housing or access to primary education, can be straightforward. Many others, such as societal respect or feelings of control and agency, are tricky to gauge. But they are no less important.

HUMAN AGENCY

Like all people, Americans differ in which needs they consider most basic, and the goals that they wish to pursue in life. For this reason, the capability approach places strong emphasis on **human agency—people's ability to act, individually or collectively, as agents of change in their own lives to further the goals that matter to them.**

In the United States, agency is considered so important that its denial is one of the most severe punishments doled out by our criminal justice system. Prisoners have their basic needs for food, clothing, and shelter met, yet they are denied the agency to make fundamental decisions for themselves about how to live.

The ability to exercise autonomous choice depends on the decisions we make, as well as the circumstances into which we are born and raised and the institutions that govern our lives. Consider Ana, a 12-year-old girl who wants to play dodgeball after school with her friends on her block. But her parents will not let her play outside in her neighborhood without adult supervision because they fear she may be mugged or worse. Gerry, an extremely overweight man, knows getting to work would be less taxing and finding a girlfriend easier if he could slim down. But with nothing in his neighborhood but fast-food restaurants, no sidewalks or parks nearby, and no spare money to join a gym, getting his weight under control is not at all easy despite his best intentions.

> The ability to exercise **autonomous choice** depends on the decisions we make, as well as the circumstances into which we are born and raised.

Agency is critical; we bear responsibility for our actions, and absent determination, ambition, and hard work, valuable choices and opportunities are closed to us. Yet individuals are seldom entirely to blame for their failures—or deserving of all the credit for their successes. **Capabilities are expanded or restricted by the circumstances into which we are born and raised, by the conditions in our communities and workplaces, by the decisions and actions of others, and by politics and policies.**

EFFECTIVE FREEDOM

Straight-A students from poor families go to college at the **same rate** as academic underachievers from affluent families.

The hard-won formal freedoms that nearly all Americans enjoy today are necessary but not sufficient for developing people's capabilities. Consider a bright teenager whose local high school did not prepare her adequately for college studies and whose family lacks either the resources to pay for college or the knowledge required to navigate the admissions and financial aid process. She has the same formal freedom as a well-educated child of affluent professionals, but she does not have the real-life *effective freedom* to make her college dream a reality. Likewise the would-be entrepreneur whose lack of material assets keeps him from qualifying for a business loan, or the dynamic local leader who is shut out of the formal political process by well-financed special interests—both have the rights to try, but not the opportunities to succeed. President Lyndon Johnson was drawing just this distinction between formal freedom and effective freedom when he said, "We seek not just freedom but opportunity. We seek not just legal equity but human ability, not just equality as a right and a theory but equality as a fact and as a result."

There are always exceptions—a child from meager means who becomes a billionaire—but often they are just that, exceptions. Research shows that straight-A students from poor families go to college at the same rate as academic underachievers from affluent families;[5] that the U.S. Congress has forty-four times as many millionaires as the general U.S. population;[6] and that the average wealth of the bottom 40 percent of households is $2,200.[7] These statistics reflect what too many Americans experience—while in principle they have the formal freedom and personal ambition to pursue their goals, they lack the effective freedom necessary to achieve them. Avenues of opportunity are closed to them, despite their hard work and big dreams.

PERSPECTIVES ON POVERTY

Poverty rates fell rapidly between 1964 and 1973, but the official poverty rate has yet to fall below that 1973 level since.[8] For nearly four decades, poverty reduction has stalled. **A significant theoretical advance of the human development and capability approach is a wider definition of poverty that considers the full spectrum of factors, including but not limited to lack of money, that define what it means to be poor.**

Human poverty is the denial of capabilities and opportunities for living a decent life. This definition includes capabilities to have good health, access to knowledge, and a decent material standard of living, but also other capabilities that make life worth living: dignity, self-esteem, fairness in the justice system, and many more. These capabilities are critical to enable people to participate fully in the economic, political, and social life of their communities.

Thirty-seven percent of single women with children had trouble putting food on the table in 2008.

"By necessaries I understand, not only the commodities which are indispensably necessary for the support of life, but whatever the customs of the country renders it indecent for creditable people, even of the lowest order, to be without. A linen shirt, for example, is, strictly speaking, not a necessary of life. The Greeks and Romans lived, I suppose, very comfortably, though they had no linen. But in the present times, through the greater part of Europe, a creditable day-labourer would be ashamed to appear in public without a linen shirt, the want of which would be supposed to denote that disgraceful degree of poverty which, it is presumed, nobody can well fall into without extreme bad conduct. Custom, in the same manner, has rendered leather shoes a necessary of life in England."

Adam Smith
An Inquiry into the Nature and Causes of the Wealth of Nations, 1776

While many people consider the basic physical necessities (such as food and shelter) of a higher order when addressing poverty, those who experience poverty are as likely to speak about the isolation, powerlessness, and mistrust they feel as they are about lack of money or material things. Often the loss of dignity that accompanies poverty stems from the overall conditions of one's life and a sense of powerlessness to change them. Reducing income poverty is a valuable goal, but the challenges the poor often face in bargaining or having the power and confidence to change their situation can be as insurmountable as material deprivations.

Today, measures used to assess poverty focus on assessing levels of income and consumption. These measures are vital for an objective assessment of income poverty, and they are used almost exclusively to determine eligibility for support in a variety of areas. Human poverty is generally harder to identify and measure than income poverty, but it is no less a burden on poor families and a drain on society.

A second perspective on poverty relates to the concept of **relative poverty.** Accepting that extreme poverty still exists in the United States can collide with our intuitions and daily observations. Except in situations of extreme neglect or abuse, no one starves to death. Emergency rooms are required to provide life-saving care to all comers, primary and secondary school are free, and even most low-income families possess material goods that within living memory were the exclusive privilege of the rich. Newer innovations like cell phones and video games are a fact of life for people up and down the income spectrum.

In fact, however, fundamental material deprivations are actually tragically widespread. While almost no one is dying of hunger, thirty-seven percent of single women with children had trouble putting food on the table in 2008, and 15 percent of U.S. households were unable to afford a nutritionally adequate diet at times.[9] Some 1.6 million Americans lived in homeless shelters, transitional housing, or on the streets at some point in 2008, and 6 percent of Americans did not get vital medical care because of cost.[10]

What it means to be poor or rich is radically different through time and from place to place. In 1945, male life expectancy was sixty-four years. Few would argue that 64 is a ripe old age today. Prior to the 1930s, electrical appliances, from irons to refrigerators, were rare in most homes. That electrical appliances are universal today, however, does not mean that everyone who has one is necessarily rich. The intrinsic relativity of poverty means that there is no bright line one can draw to delineate the boundaries separating the poor and the nonpoor. Even the father of modern economics, Adam Smith, recognized that what is "necessary" is socially and historically contingent (see sidebar). Smith observed that **it is not sufficient to have what we need to survive; we also need to have what is required such that we can walk in public without shame.** For his time, those required items were leather shoes and a linen shirt; for modern Americans, the required item may be a mouth with no visibly missing teeth or knowing how to use the Internet.

Only by considering this broader set of perspectives on poverty can we begin to understand which individuals and groups have the capabilities they need to invest in themselves and their families and to become productive, fulfilled members of society. **A more comprehensive definition of poverty is a requirement for more successful policies to fight poverty.**

Measuring Human Development

THE HUMAN DEVELOPMENT INDEX

The hallmark of the human development approach is the Human Development Index. The human development approach is extremely broad, encompassing the wide range of economic, social, political, psychological, environmental, and cultural factors that expand or restrict people's opportunities and freedoms. But the Human Development Index is comparatively narrow, a composite measure that combines a limited number of indicators of human well-being into a single number.

The hallmark of the human development approach is the **Human Development Index.**

The HD Index developed for publication by UNDP's annual human development report includes three variables. **The premise is that although a host of variables must be considered to paint a full picture of human well-being and progress, these three encompass the basics: the ability to lead a long and healthy life, to have access to knowledge, and to have a decent material standard of living.** People the world over generally agree that these goals are the minimal set of worthwhile gauges of human progress.

The American Human Development Index is a modification of UNDP's global index. The modifications address some of the limitations of the global index; for instance, one criticism of the UNDP HD Index is that it leaves unanswered questions about the distribution of income within a country, a weakness addressed in the American HD Index by using median personal earnings rather than GDP per capita as a proxy for living standards. The modifications also allow a more nuanced portrait of the variation in well-being within the United States. The global index was designed to apply to more than one hundred countries, from highly industrialized, affluent countries like Norway, Australia, and Iceland to deeply impoverished countries like Afghanistan, Sierra Leone, and Niger, where people can expect to live between forty-three and fifty years, and where more than 60 percent of adults cannot read. The global index must not only encompass an enormous range of conditions, it must also use indicators reliably available for all countries. In the data-rich United States, the choice of indicators is much wider.

THE AMERICAN HUMAN DEVELOPMENT INDEX

The modified American Human Development Index measures the same three basic dimensions as the standard HD Index, but it uses different indicators to better reflect the U.S. context and to maximize use of available data (see sidebar and **TABLE 1**). All data come from official U.S. government sources. The most recent year for which data are available is 2008, owing to the typical lag in government publication time of two to three years. (For full details, see the Methodological Notes on page 272.)

Calculating the American Human Development Index

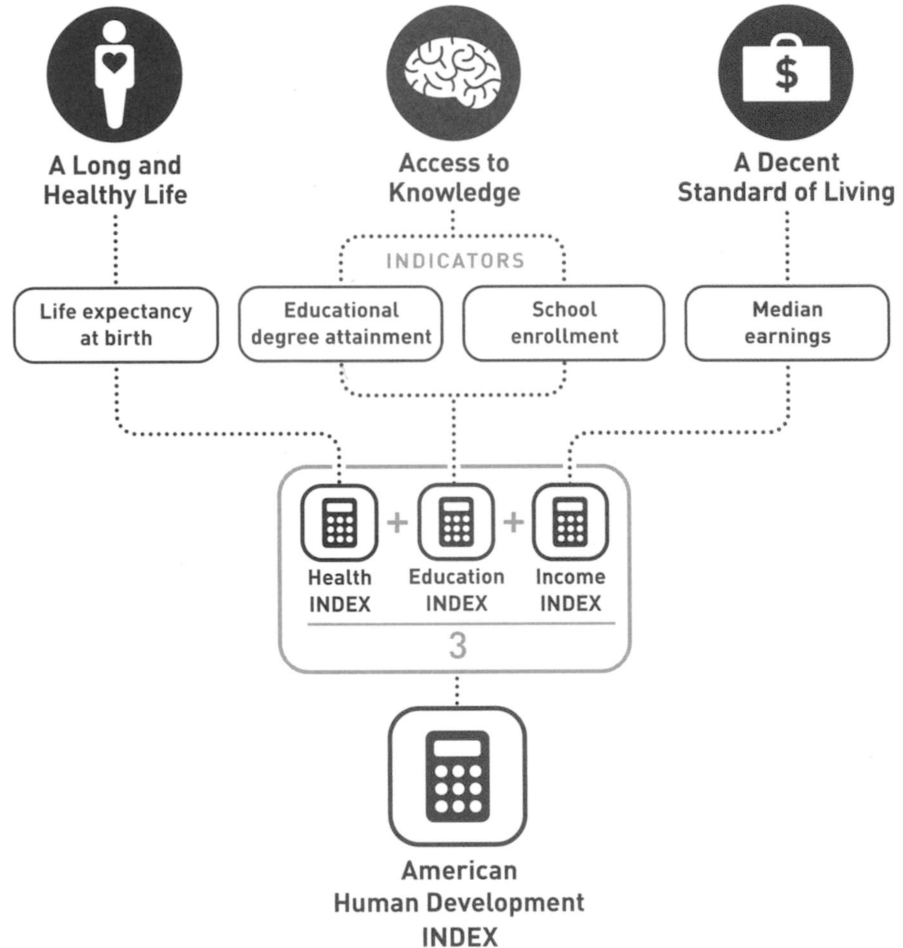

A Long and Healthy Life is measured using life expectancy at birth, calculated from mortality data from the Centers for Disease Control and Prevention, National Center for Health Statistics 2007, and population data from the CDC WONDER database.

Access to Knowledge is measured using two indicators: school enrollment for the population age 3 and older, and educational degree attainment for the population 25 years and older. A one-third weight is applied to the enrollment indicator and a two-thirds weight is applied to the degree attainment indicator. Both indicators are from the American Community Survey, U.S. Census Bureau, 2008.

A Decent Standard of Living is measured using median earnings of all full- and part-time workers 16 years and older from the American Community Survey, U.S. Census Bureau, 2008.

For more details on sources and methods, see the Methodological Notes on page 272.

BOX 2 A Primer on the American Human Development Index

Why do we need an American Human Development Index?
Because national well-being cannot be measured by GDP alone. The American HD Index offers a more comprehensive and nuanced picture of the state of the nation.

What indicators does the American HD Index include?
The American HD Index is a composite measure of three basic areas of human development: health, knowledge, and standard of living. Health is measured by life expectancy. Knowledge is measured by a combination of educational attainment and school enrollment. Standard of living is measured using median personal earnings. All data are from official U.S. government sources.

Why these three components?
Most people would agree that a long and healthy life, access to knowledge, and a decent material standard of living are basic ingredients of a decent life. These are the three ingredients measured by the global HD Index produced by the United Nations Development Programme and by national HD indices in countries ranging from Albania to Zambia, an indication that these core capabilities are universally valued around the world. In addition, measurable, intuitively sensible, and reliable indicators exist to represent these areas.

Can a single indicator measure complex concepts like health, access to knowledge, and standard of living?
People studying large populations use simple, easy-to-collect proxy indicators to represent complex phenomena that cannot be measured directly. Researchers assessing school readiness among children might use as a proxy the number of books in the child's home, or how many shapes and colors she can name. Doctors rely on blood pressure and body temperature as proxies to gauge a person's health. While these proxies hardly capture the full complexity of a child's knowledge or a person's health, they do reveal some important information. Similarly, for large populations, life expectancy is a generally accepted proxy for health; degree attainment and school enrollment are reasonable stand-ins for the broad and elusive concept of knowledge; and earnings are a valuable indicator of living standards.

How can the American HD Index be used?
The American HD Index is a tool for assessing the relative socioeconomic progress of groups of Americans and of different regions of the country. It provides a snapshot of where different groups stand today and sets a benchmark for evaluating progress in the future. Since the release of the first *Measure of America* in 2008, many philanthropic organizations and social service providers have adopted the Index as a way of assessing need, setting priorities, and tracking change over time. Political officeholders and candidates have used the Index to lobby for resources and to assess conditions. College teachers and students are using the Index in classes on American society. Journalists have used the Index to help readers understand social and economic conditions and to explore opportunity and progress in the United States.

What are the American HD Index's limitations?
The Index does not capture information about important areas of human development beyond health, education, and income. In addition, because some of its indicators do not change quickly, the Index cannot be used to measure the short-term impacts of economic fluctuations or policy changes. Consequently, we have added to this volume a "dashboard" of more sensitive indicators to serve as an early-warning system of extreme deprivation. This Dashboard of Risks can be found on page 34. Like all indicators, composite or otherwise, the Index is only as reliable as the data upon which it is based.

Since the release of the first *Measure of America* in 2008, many organizations have adopted the Index as a way of assessing need, setting priorities, and tracking change over time.

The Index facilitates **critical analysis** of how and why policies succeed or fail, and it helps to **focus attention** on which groups are moving forward and which are falling behind.

TABLE 1 Differences between UNDP HD Index and American HD Index

VARIABLE	AMERICAN HD INDEX—INDICATOR USED	UNDP HD INDEX—INDICATOR USED	REASON FOR MODIFICATION
A Long and Healthy Life	Life expectancy at birth	Life expectancy at birth	—
Access to Knowledge	Degree attainment and school enrollment (preschool and above)	Adult literacy and school enrollment (elementary school and above)	• Adult literacy is not sufficiently demanding for an advanced industrialized nation, shows little variation, and is not collected systematically in the United States. • Quality preschool education serves a vital function for cognitive, emotional, and social development.
A Decent Standard of Living	Median personal earnings	Gross Domestic Product per capita	• Refocuses attention from market activity to the wages of a typical worker. • Enables analysis of different access to income between men and women. • Allows comparisons among states and congressional districts as well as among racial and ethnic groups.

See Methodological Notes for more details.

Policymakers, researchers, and the general public today have access to a wealth of reliable data on social, political, environmental, and economic indicators of conditions in the United States. These indicators are invaluable for exploring the multifaceted dimensions of societal well-being, and for tracking progress in specific areas. Yet a composite index that weaves these separate strands of data into a straightforward, easily grasped barometer of well-being is essential. Such an index enables a common frame of reference for political and policy discussions. The American Human Development Index provides such a barometer.

Because its indicators are comparable across geographic regions and over time, the American Human Development Index permits apples-to-apples comparisons from place to place and from year to year. The American Human Development Index facilitates critical analysis of how and why policies succeed or fail, and it helps to focus attention on which groups are moving forward and which are falling behind. The Index thus enables broader analysis of the interlocking factors that fuel advantage and disadvantage, create opportunities, and determine life chances.

BOX 3 Racial and Ethnic Categories in *The Measure of America 2010–2011*

The chapters that follow present the American HD Index by state, congressional district, metropolitan area, racial and ethnic group, and gender. Presenting the Index by geography is relatively straightforward. Presenting it by racial and ethnic groups presents a number of challenges.

The White House Office of Management and Budget (OMB) sets guidelines for the categorization of people by race and ethnicity in government data, and both the U.S. Census Bureau and the Centers for Disease Control and Prevention—the two data sources from which the American HD Index is calculated—follow these conventions. The OMB guidelines include five major racial groups (American Indian or Alaska Native; Asian; Black or African American; Native Hawaiian or Other Pacific Islander; and White) and two ethnicities (Hispanic or Latino; and Not Hispanic or Latino).[11] Although the OMB recognizes Native Hawaiians and Other Pacific Islanders separately from Asians, this group is too small (approximately 0.1 percent of the population)[12] to enable the calculation of reliable life expectancy estimates. Regrettably, this report is thus unable to provide full data on Native Hawaiians and Other Pacific Islanders.

For simplicity, in this report the names of racial and ethnic groups have been abbreviated in accordance with common usage. People who identify themselves as "Black or African American" in Census Bureau surveys are referred to as African American; people who identify as "White" and "Not Hispanic or Latino" are referred to as white, while people who identify as "White" and "Hispanic or Latino" are referred to as Latino.[13] Additionally, the term "Native American" in this report refers to both American Indians and Alaska Natives. This report does not specifically address the human development levels of people who identify as "two or more races" or "some other race," categories that are extremely internally diverse. **FIGURE 1** presents the names and population counts of the racial and ethnic groups to which this report refers.

FIGURE 1 U.S. Population by Racial and Ethnic Group, 2008

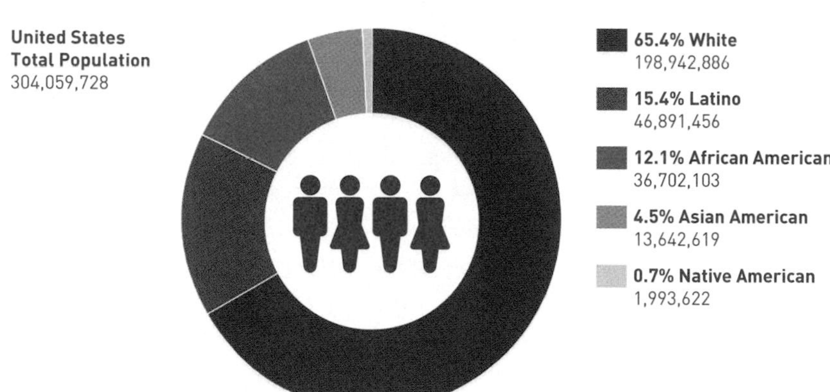

Source: U.S. Census Bureau, American Community Survey, 2008 One-Year Estimates. In 2008, an additional 5,186,219 people (1.7 percent) identified as two or more races, and 701,823 (0.2 percent) identified as some other race.

These categorizations are clearly imperfect, masking enormous differences within groups, an issue that is discussed further in the next chapter.

SUBJECTIVE MEASURES OF WELL-BEING: HAPPINESS AND LIFE SATISFACTION

> *"There are no conditions of life to which a man cannot get accustomed, especially if he sees them accepted by everyone around him."*
> **Leo Tolstoy** *(Anna Karenina, 1877)*

Research into subjective well-being has consistently demonstrated what common wisdom has told us all along: **money does not necessarily buy happiness.**

The American HD Index assesses the well-being of different populations by looking at observed outcomes in health, education, and income. The HD Index is therefore a measure of objective well-being.

Another approach to gauging well-being is to ask people how satisfied they are with their lives. These subjective well-being measures have gained traction in recent years. Using public opinion polls such as the General Social Survey[14] in the United States and the World Values Survey[15] and the Gallup World Poll[16] internationally, social scientists have collected data on happiness and life satisfaction. Composite indexes like the Happy Planet Index have incorporated objective measures of environmental impact and life expectancy with subjective measures of life satisfaction to measure the average years of "happy" life enjoyed in any given place per unit of natural resources consumed.[17]

These measures and others have yielded some fascinating observations about how people assess their own lives. However, they can also lead to some counterintuitive conclusions that deserve more careful scrutiny.

Though most people want (or think they want) to be richer, the impressive increase in material well-being most Western countries experienced in the last sixty years has not let loose a deluge of happiness; reported happiness has remained virtually the same during this period.[18] Research into subjective well-being has consistently demonstrated what common wisdom has told us all along: money does not necessarily buy happiness.[19] Living in a developed nation increases subjective well-being, but gains in income within developed nations do not necessarily increase levels of happiness.[20] It would be a mistake to conclude, however, that having access to basic material resources is unnecessary for well-being. In fact, one interpretation of the Easterlin Paradox (named for the economist who established this inconsistent relationship between money and happiness) is that material resources increase happiness up to the point at which people can meet their basic needs. Beyond a certain minimum threshold, the relationship between further increases in money and happiness tails off.[21]

A second example of self-perceptions of well-being that can run contrary to intuition is related to life-changing events. Some research suggests that people's responses to these events are remarkably fluid and adaptable. For example, people who experience a disabling accident tend to rebound to a baseline level of happiness within a few months. The same feature tends to hold for people who experience positive events: lottery winners experience an initial surge of exuberance, only to fall back to their prelottery state of mind not long thereafter.[22] Despite this return to equilibrium, it is difficult to say that, all things being equal, an accident victim and a lottery winner have the same opportunities at their disposal.

A related notion is the idea that people curb their expectations in response to the limits around them. The query, "Are you happy?" begs the question, "Compared to what or whom?" Adaptation coupled with the natural tendency of people to compare themselves to those closest to them—H. L. Mencken famously said that wealth is an annual income at least one hundred dollars more than the income of one's brother-in-law—suggests that a positive assessment may simply be the result of being resigned to one's lot, with little apparent possibility of change, and the conviction that others nearby are in even worse shape.

Other research has revealed some curious mismatches between objective and subjective states of well-being. For example, a widely cited 2008 study across several countries found that people's satisfaction with the state of their health and with their lives in general showed little correlation to actual health data on life expectancy or HIV/AIDS prevalence.[23] A 2009 study of happiness in U.S. states found that people express higher life satisfaction in certain states where levels of educational attainment, life expectancy, and income are lowest; people in certain states with higher levels of these objective features expressed lower degrees of happiness.[24] Indeed, if policymakers were to allocate resources to states according to a happiness quotient, they might find themselves providing more funds to relatively wealthy states at the expense of relatively poor ones.

The Declaration of Independence asserts the right to life, liberty, and the pursuit—though not necessarily the achievement—of happiness. The qualification of happiness underscores the elusive nature, and relativity, of happiness. Researchers continue to debate how best to study and draw conclusions about happiness and life satisfaction and about what drives people to feel better or worse about their lives. This is not a focus of the American HD Index. The Index attempts to approximate the capabilities, choices, and opportunities that different groups of people have using objective data. To what extent people are able to convert those resources into happiness is a vital, but ultimately separate, question.

The Declaration of Independence asserts the right to life, liberty, and the **pursuit**—though not necessarily the **achievement**—of happiness.

Part II:
Reducing Risks, Increasing Resilience

A set of major recent incidents, including 9/11, the catastrophic impacts of Hurricane Katrina, the financial crisis, and the BP oil spill, compel us to consider threats as well as opportunities, particularly the pervasive perils and often-preventable reversals in our everyday lives that thwart progress in well-being and the expansion of opportunity for all.

This volume focuses on the theme of risks and resilience.

While every generation arguably views the threats it faces as uniquely hazardous, new complexities of today's world arguably call for a wider understanding of and appreciation for protection and prevention.

The first volume of *The Measure of America* series focused chiefly on introducing the human development idea to a U.S. audience. Beginning with this volume, we address questions of human development in the context of a single theme central to American economic and social life. This volume focuses on the theme of **risks and resilience.** In the following chapters, we look at pervasive threats to human well-being in the United States: events and conditions that chronically hamstring the development of fundamental capabilities, as well as those that erode the capabilities that people already have. The report deals with risks and resilience within the framework of the three basic dimensions of human development measured by the Index: a long and healthy life, access to knowledge, and a decent material standard of living.

Capabilities are, in essence, the tools that a person can employ in a freely chosen life of value. Human development is about *expanding* those capabilities, thus maximizing a person's real-world freedom to *decide* for herself what to be and do in her life. But **expansion requires safeguarding the capabilities we already have and overcoming barriers in order to gain capabilities we lack.**

FIGURE 2 **Understanding Risks and Resilience: The Tale of Meg and Dawn**

SCENARIO 1:
Meg

Meg owns a store that sells hiking and camping gear. She lives in Boulder, Colorado.

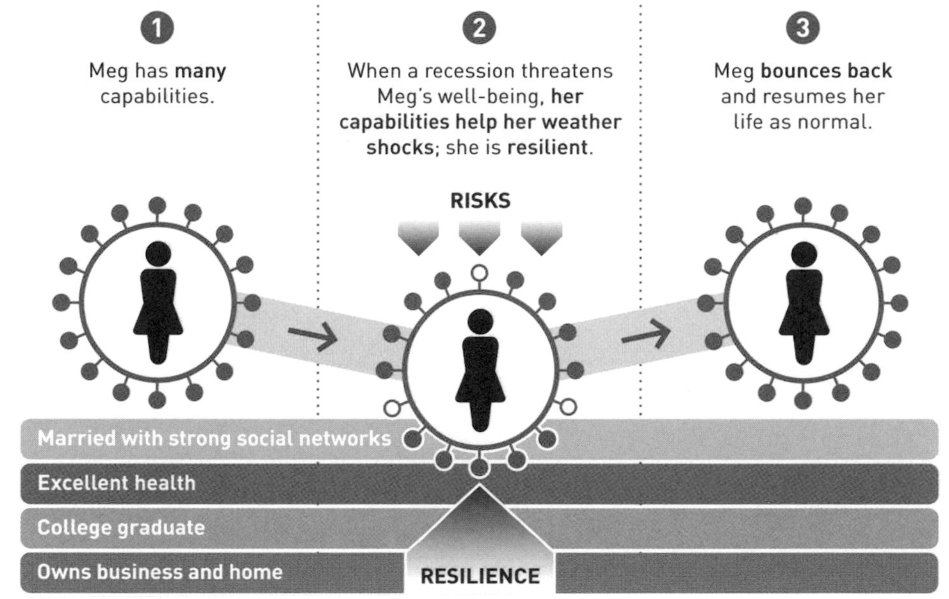

SCENARIO 2:
Dawn

Dawn works in a high school cafeteria. She lives in Cape Girardeau, Missouri.

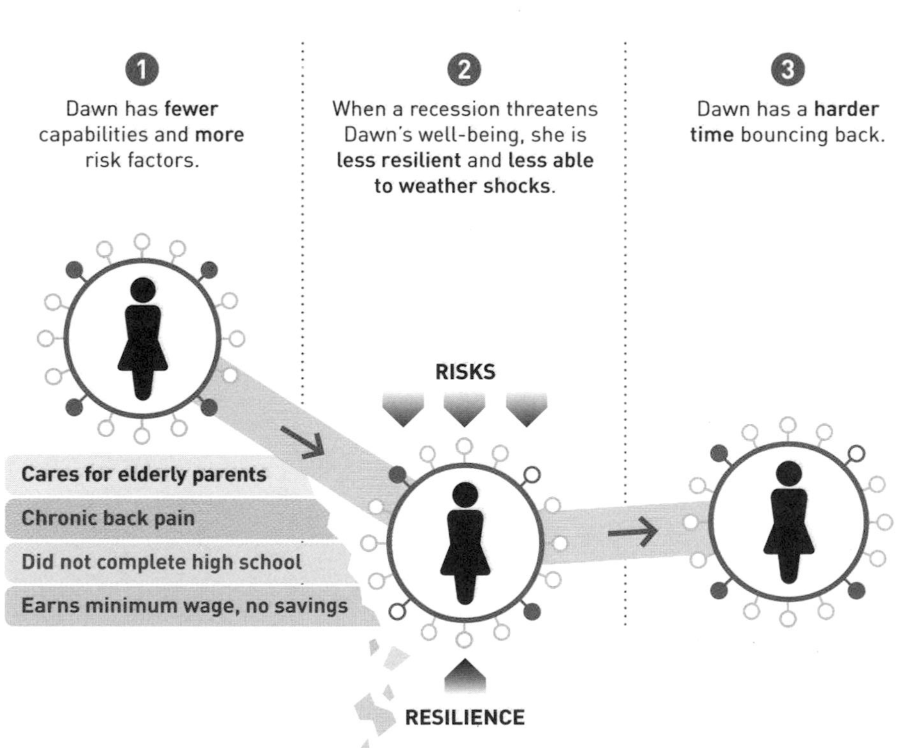

Safeguarding the Capabilities We Have

When the August 29, 2005, breech of the Seventeenth Street Canal levee sent the waters of Lake Pontchartrain coursing through New Orleans, the people trapped on rooftops were not investing their energies in furthering their educations, building secure livelihoods, or saving for retirement; they were just trying—literally—to keep their heads above water. Families whose jobs and savings vanished when the economy crashed in late 2007 shifted their focus from the future to the immediate present, from investing in a better tomorrow to making ends meet day-to-day. As this book goes to press, millions of gallons of oil are gushing into the Gulf of Mexico daily, a result of a calamitous drilling rig explosion just off the fragile Louisiana coast. Eleven men perished. Fisherfolk, those in the tourism industry, coastal residents, and others whose livelihoods and way of life depend on the unique ecosystems of the Gulf Coast could only watch helplessly as one of the worst environmental disasters in American history imperiled family and community capabilities generations in the making.

Preventing, mitigating, and helping people cope with sudden threats are **prerequisites** for human development.

Preventing, mitigating, and helping people cope with sudden threats, whether they result from human actions, forces of nature, or a combination of the two, are prerequisites for human development. **When the vital core of survival, livelihood, and dignity are at risk, human development ceases.** Thus, if we as a society are concerned with expanding opportunity, we must be equally concerned with preempting threats before they materialize and mitigating the effects when catastrophe strikes.

Human development does not move in only one direction; it can stall or even reverse course under trying circumstances. Thus, to advance human development we must *safeguard* capabilities from critical and pervasive threats—particularly those capabilities fundamental to survival, basic health, and bodily integrity; to achieving enough knowledge to participate meaningfully in economic, political, and social life; and to sustaining a minimal standard of living that affords the material necessities for a dignified life. **Human development calls for, as Nobel Laureate Amartya Sen puts it, "growth with equity." But it also requires "downturns with security."**

Overcoming Barriers to Access

Few Americans emerged from the Great Recession of 2007–09 unscathed. Carefully incubated nest eggs cracked as stock markets sank and corporate giants collapsed. Unemployment and underemployment reached alarming levels from which they have only begun to recede, and some of the impacts on the labor market may linger for years to come. Just as the private sector furiously jettisoned costs—often in the form of employees—to keep business afloat, so did the public sector reduce services and cut programs. States slashed budgets for health care and education. Hospitals shut their doors; public schools shed teachers; community colleges and state universities hiked tuitions.

Unemployment/ underemployment, October-December 2009

7.1% of workers with graduate degrees

35.1% of workers without high school degrees

Although everyone felt the effects of this national crisis, some people came out of the battle unbowed while others slipped into debilitating poverty. With rare exceptions, those who weathered the downturn with security benefited from access to fundamental capabilities prior to the collapse. Those with access to health insurance could by and large obtain the medical services they needed, while many uninsured were forced to make untenable choices between groceries and health care. In the fourth quarter of 2009, a shocking 18.2 percent of American workers were either unemployed or underemployed. Among workers with graduate degrees, the rate was 7.1 percent. But among workers without a high school diploma or its equivalent, the rate of un- and underemployment was an astounding 35.1 percent—five times higher.[25] **Workers in the bottom 10 percent of income distribution faced an unemployment rate of 31 percent at the end of 2009,** ten times higher than the rate of workers in the top 10 percent of earners (3.2 percent).[26]

Few have capabilities so extensive as to inoculate them against all risks, financial or otherwise. **But people who have already secured access to fundamental capabilities stand a better chance of weathering shocks and maintaining an upward trajectory through life.** In the United States, people who escape the risks of premature death and chronic disease, attain at least a high school education, and earn income at or above the median tend to have capabilities on which they can draw in hard times. Expanding access to such capabilities will make more people more resilient. But such expansion requires that we remove barriers to achieving basic access.

Workers in the **bottom ten percent** of the income distribution faced an unemployment rate of **thirty-one percent** at the end of 2009.

For some fifteen years, under the rubric of **"human security,"**[27] scholars, statesmen, and experts in foreign policy have explored ways to reduce risks to human populations and to build resilience against threats. The idea of human security focuses not on the security of the state but on the security of individuals within the state, emphasizing human freedom as well as human life. Some development economists have termed efforts to mitigate risks from globalization and other forces **"social risk management."**[28] Social risk management applies concepts from business management and engineering to economic and social conditions, focusing on ways to avert threats and reduce vulnerability to poverty.

If human development is understood as *people's freedom to*—to choose what to do and who to be—human security and social risk management can be understood as *people's freedom from*—from fear and want, from violations of rights, and from chronic and sudden threats to life and livelihood. These concepts are embedded in canonical national and international pronouncements on social protection, from President Franklin D. Roosevelt's "Four Freedoms" address to Congress to the call in the Universal Declaration of Human Rights for freedom from fear and freedom from want.

The richness of rhetoric and universality of thought on human security and social risk management underscore the intuitive power of the desire to protect individuals from harm or the threat of harm. Human development is people-centered and multidimensional, and concerned not only with the aspirations, needs, and rights of humankind but also with the fears of humankind.

Human development is concerned not only with the aspirations, needs, and rights of humankind but also with the fears of humankind.

This second volume of the American Human Development Report series evaluates both **increasing** human development by expanding the capabilities we have, and **protecting** human development by safeguarding existing levels of achievement and removing barriers to the realization of core capabilities. This volume focuses on risks to building lives of choice and on how to prevent, mitigate, and cope with risks by fostering greater resilience.

This report restricts its analysis to societal risks that are severe, frequent, and pervasive. (Terrorism, pandemics, and the like are beyond the scope of this discussion.) The chapters that follow analyze how risks are distributed across the American population. Risks to health are explored chiefly with regard to variations in vulnerability among racial and ethnic groups as well as between men and women. Given the role of state and local governments in education, risks to access to knowledge are conceived largely in geographic terms. The chapter on income examines vulnerability over the life cycle, since people of different age groups face different risks to their standard of living.

Conclusion

Human development is an expansive, hopeful concept that values, above all, human freedom—the freedom of women and men to decide for themselves what to do and who to become. Real, effective freedom

- Rests on legally enshrined, formal freedoms;
- Is expanded or constrained by people's capabilities—the tools or equipment they have for living a life of choice and value;
- Requires that women, men, and children have security in their daily lives—that they are protected from grave threats to their lives, livelihoods, dignity, and freedom, whether sudden or chronic.

An expansive vision of human development rests on a stable foundation. A person who feels that the underpinnings of her life might give way at any moment cannot plan, invest, or build. Prevention is nearly always less costly, more effective, and more humane than intervention after a crisis takes hold. While some catastrophes cannot be prevented, we can always try to prepare for them.

Prevention is nearly always less costly, more effective, and more humane than intervention after a crisis takes hold.

This second volume of the American Human Development Report series explores what the American HD Index reveals about the distribution of effective freedom, opportunity, and well-being in the United States today. It then examines in greater depth the three subcomponents of the American HD Index—the Health Index, the Education Index, and the Income Index—and discusses the chief reasons that different groups of Americans experience such strikingly different outcomes across these fundamental domains of human well-being. An exploration of the most severe and pervasive risks that imperil the basic capabilities of Americans in general as well as those of Americans of different geographic areas, racial and ethnic groups, age groups, and sexes is central to each chapter.

This book concludes with **a set of recommendations** for priority actions required to improve scores on the American HD Index across the board, to close the gaps that separate groups, and to build the resilience of people against the inevitable vicissitudes of life and the sudden, severe shocks that destroy capabilities years in the making. **Throughout history, difficult times are often those periods during which new ideas and extraordinary leadership can yield long-lasting solutions. It is our hope that this work can contribute to these ideas and help to illustrate the American story with a greater understanding of the opportunities and constraints of ordinary people. After all, they are the real wealth of our nation.**

The following pages contain a "Dashboard of Risks" with ten indicators that signal direct threats to human development progress. Each chapter contains a mapping of the top and bottom states at risk in the relevant indicators.

Dashboard of Risks

The ten indicators presented here track risk factors that may slow or reverse human development progress and which pose direct threats to the expansion of people's capabilities and freedoms.

The indicators measure outcomes that can change relatively quickly, and are thus more responsive to new policies in the short term than the composite American Human Development Index. Taken together, the Dashboard indicators help the user unpack factors fueling gaps in the Index scores of different population groups, craft solutions to address pervasive threats, and better assess the impact of various interventions in the near term.

RISKS TO A LONG AND HEALTHY LIFE

The percentage of newborn babies with **low birth weight** (less than 5.5 pounds) is a sensitive indicator of population health—in particular, women's health and access to medical care. Compared to babies born with normal weight, low-birth-weight babies face a higher risk of infant death, developmental delays, and physical and cognitive impairments.[29]

Diabetes rates track the prevalence of this chronic disease, a leading cause of death.[30] Obesity and physical inactivity contribute significantly to diabetes.

The **trauma-related death rate** captures the number of preventable deaths due to homicide, suicide, and unintentional injury, such as car crashes or workplace accidents.

RISKS TO ACCESS TO KNOWLEDGE

The percentage of **3- and 4-year-olds not enrolled in preschool** is an important indicator of school readiness and life chances. Children without access to quality early-childhood education are at higher risk of repeating grades and eventually dropping out than children who attend preschool.[31]

An important measure of student achievement is the percentage of **fourth-graders not demonstrating reading proficiency** on the National Assessment of Educational Progress test. Reading proficiency is a strong predictor of school performance.[32]

Students who do not graduate from high school on time are at a higher risk of never graduating, not going on to higher education, and neither working nor attending school in early adulthood than those who graduate on time.[33]

RISKS TO A DECENT STANDARD OF LIVING

Children under 6 living in households with incomes below the poverty line are vulnerable to a range of risks to healthy cognitive and emotional development, which, in turn, is associated with a host of poor outcomes later.

Marginally attached workers are adults who are available to work, but have stopped trying to find employment. These individuals, who have looked for work within the past year but not in the prior four weeks, are not included in standard unemployment counts.

Renters with severe housing-cost burdens spend more than half of their household incomes on rent and utilities. Such renters are at risk of having to forgo other essential goods and services.

Elderly poverty engenders a host of risks to the well-being of adults over 65. While Social Security can reduce these risks, too many elderly individuals face trade-offs in such essential areas as medical care, home-care services, energy consumption, and food security.

STATE	LOW-BIRTH-WEIGHT INFANTS (%) 2007[34]	PEOPLE AGE 18 AND OLDER WITH DIABETES (%) 2008[35]	DEATH RATE DUE TO TRAUMA (per 100,000) 2007[36]	CHILDREN AGES 3 AND 4 NOT ENROLLED IN PRESCHOOL (%) 2008[37]	4TH-GRADERS READING BELOW PROFICIENT (%) 2009[38]	HIGH SCHOOL FRESHMEN NOT GRADUATING AFTER 4 YEARS (%) 2007[39]	CHILDREN UNDER 6 LIVING IN POVERTY (%) 2008[40]	MARGINALLY ATTACHED WORKERS (per 10,000)* 2009[41]	RENTERS WITH SEVERE HOUSING-COST BURDEN (%) 2008[42]	ELDERLY POVERTY (%) 2008[43]
Alabama	10.5	11.2	78.1	53.1	71.8	32.9	25.8	96.5	20.9	12.1
Alaska	6.0	6.7	86.4	57.0	72.8	30.9	13.4	106.3	13.9	3.7
Arizona	7.1	7.8	75.5	67.6	75.3	30.4	23.0	92.1	22.5	8.6
Arkansas	9.1	9.5	71.8	50.2	71.2	25.6	28.7	79.7	21.1	12.5
California	6.8	8.5	49.6	49.2	76.3	29.3	20.1	123.6	26.6	8.7
Colorado	9.0	6.0	66.3	51.1	59.8	23.4	18.0	66.4	23.2	8.4
Connecticut	8.0	6.8	47.4	35.6	57.6	18.2	14.3	100.4	24.9	7.6
Delaware	9.3	8.3	52.3	52.7	64.9	28.1	14.2	94.0	23.0	7.7
District of Columbia	11.3	8.0	63.1	26.4	83.2	45.1	25.7	120.3	23.7	15.2
Florida	8.7	9.5	68.8	48.4	64.2	35.0	21.3	106.4	27.3	10.4
Georgia	9.5	9.9	64.4	49.1	70.7	35.9	23.6	92.1	22.4	11.9
Hawaii	8.1	8.2	46.5	45.4	74.3	24.6	12.2	113.8	26.6	6.8
Idaho	6.8	7.0	63.1	63.4	67.7	19.6	19.6	78.5	16.7	7.6
Illinois	8.5	8.3	49.6	44.0	67.7	20.5	20.0	90.8	24.1	9.2
Indiana	8.2	9.6	58.1	59.8	66.3	26.1	22.3	85.7	22.5	8.3
Iowa	7.0	7.0	51.0	49.4	65.8	13.5	17.7	57.2	21.0	8.3
Kansas	7.2	8.1	60.3	52.5	64.9	21.1	17.9	68.0	19.7	8.1
Kentucky	9.0	9.9	76.3	51.5	63.8	23.6	27.6	93.4	21.2	13.8
Louisiana	11.3	10.7	83.4	45.0	81.7	38.7	29.5	70.6	22.7	13.5
Maine	6.7	8.3	58.8	60.9	64.5	21.5	19.5	96.1	23.4	9.2
Maryland	9.3	8.7	46.5	48.3	62.9	20.0	11.5	81.6	21.9	8.2
Massachusetts	7.9	7.2	42.2	37.7	52.8	19.2	13.3	70.5	23.3	10.2
Michigan	8.3	9.1	55.6	50.7	70.3	23.0	22.2	118.1	26.9	8.7
Minnesota	6.5	5.9	52.5	53.7	62.8	13.5	13.2	78.3	21.5	8.6
Mississippi	12.0	11.3	86.6	45.5	78.3	36.4	33.0	126.7	22.6	16.9
Missouri	8.1	9.1	70.0	57.0	64.3	18.1	22.6	70.7	20.0	9.3
Montana	7.2	6.5	84.3	62.8	65.4	18.5	23.6	55.0	18.9	8.9
Nebraska	7.0	7.8	50.9	55.0	65.2	13.7	16.3	58.8	17.5	9.8
Nevada	8.2	8.6	76.2	71.6	76.0	48.0	17.3	79.6	21.5	8.6
New Hampshire	6.9	7.2	52.4	48.5	58.7	18.3	10.6	83.9	19.9	8.3
New Jersey	8.4	8.4	39.3	32.7	59.8	15.6	14.2	93.6	24.0	7.9
New Mexico	8.6	7.9	97.9	57.1	80.2	40.9	29.1	67.5	22.0	13.4
New York	8.3	8.4	37.2	39.9	64.0	31.2	20.0	108.6	25.8	11.8
North Carolina	9.1	9.3	69.0	50.5	67.8	31.4	22.5	84.1	20.9	11.4
North Dakota	6.6	7.6	57.2	62.4	65.2	16.9	19.1	50.0	17.3	13.1
Ohio	8.7	9.9	59.0	53.7	64.3	21.3	22.7	102.7	22.6	8.8
Oklahoma	8.1	10.1	81.6	54.0	72.3	22.2	25.9	64.8	19.7	10.9
Oregon	6.1	6.9	60.7	56.3	69.1	26.2	21.2	92.7	24.0	8.7
Pennsylvania	8.4	8.8	59.6	50.3	63.4	17.0	19.5	86.2	22.8	9.3
Rhode Island	7.9	7.4	47.3	43.5	64.4	21.6	17.2	97.1	23.0	10.9
South Carolina	10.2	10.1	74.9	51.1	72.4	41.1	25.9	106.5	20.9	12.1
South Dakota	6.8	6.6	57.6	61.9	67.2	17.5	21.9	58.2	17.2	10.3
Tennessee	9.4	10.4	74.8	55.5	72.0	27.4	26.0	82.9	21.9	11.4
Texas	8.3	9.7	59.6	57.0	72.4	28.1	25.8	70.0	20.9	12.2
Utah	6.8	6.1	53.4	59.5	69.0	23.4	11.4	74.5	18.0	6.8
Vermont	6.5	6.4	62.9	44.6	58.6	11.4	15.0	80.0	22.9	8.5
Virginia	8.3	7.9	56.0	50.5	61.5	24.5	15.8	64.1	20.7	8.4
Washington	6.3	6.9	57.8	56.8	66.6	25.2	16.7	92.9	21.3	8.2
West Virginia	9.5	11.9	87.7	67.8	74.3	21.8	29.7	81.8	20.4	10.5
Wisconsin	7.0	7.2	61.8	54.7	67.3	11.5	15.7	85.5	20.3	8.4
Wyoming	8.7	7.4	80.7	59.3	67.4	24.2	14.2	56.2	14.9	7.3

* Working-age adults

See sources on page 284.

CHAPTER 1

What the American Human Development Index Reveals

IN THIS SECTION:

- Introduction
- Historical Trends: A Half Century of Development Progress
- Presenting American Human Development Index Scores
- Conclusion

How Do We Stack Up?

Human Development Index

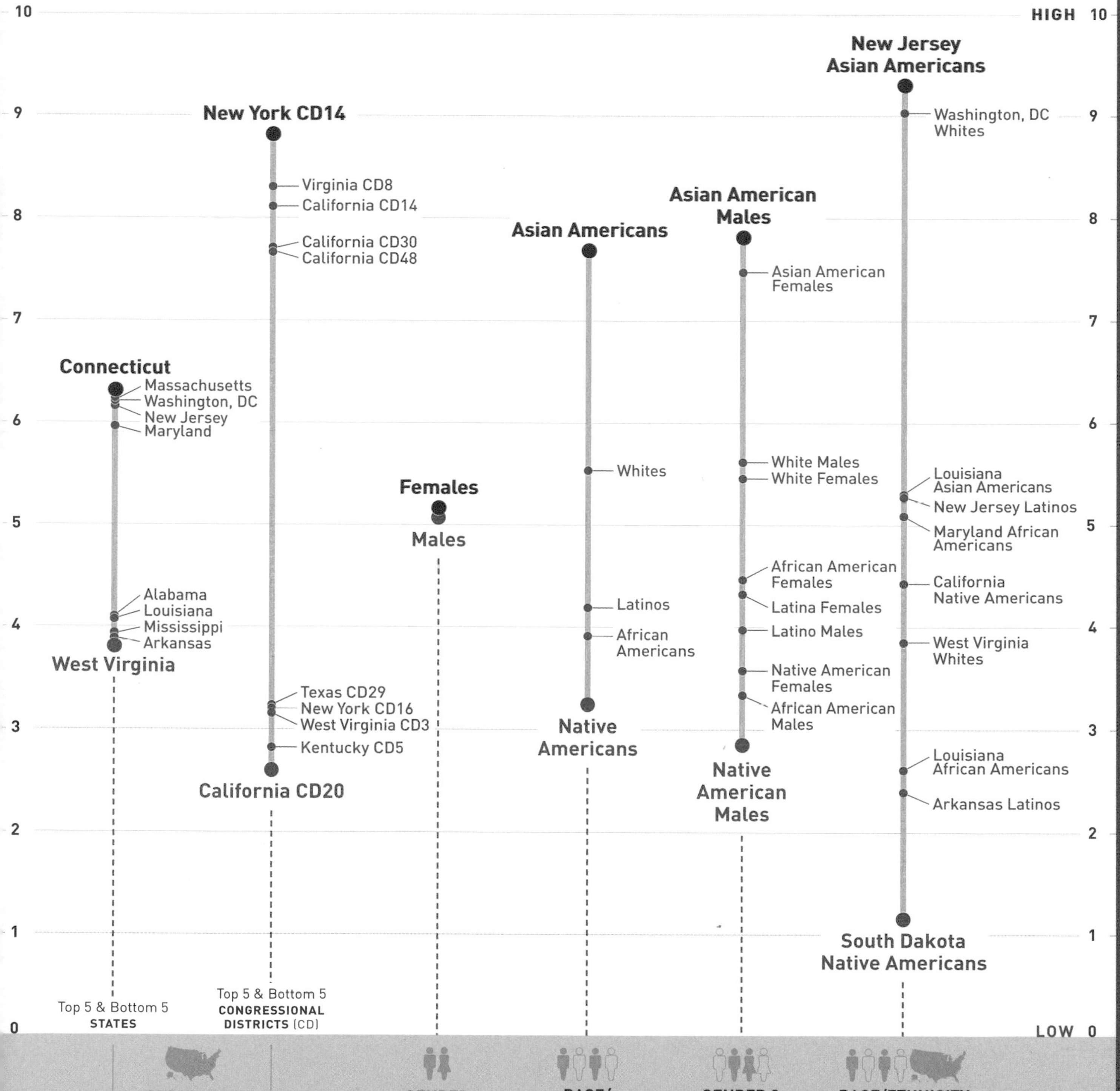

Introduction

> "Our gross national product . . . if we should judge America by that—counts air pollution and cigarette advertising, and ambulances to clear our highways of carnage. It counts special locks for our doors and the jails for those who break them. It counts the destruction of our redwoods and the loss of our natural wonder in chaotic sprawl. . . . Yet the gross national product does not allow for the health of our children, the quality of their education, or the joy of their play. . . . It measures neither our wit nor our courage; neither our wisdom nor our learning . . . . it measures everything, in short, except that which makes life worthwhile. And it tells us everything about America except why we are proud that we are Americans."
>
> **ROBERT F. KENNEDY,** 1968

What we don't measure, we don't address.

Gross domestic product (GDP) is a vital measure. Tracking the expansion and contraction of market activity and production tells a crucial part of a nation's story—but an incomplete one. Complementing GDP with data on the health, education, and income of the typical American along with information about who among us has—or lacks—access to the basic building blocks of opportunity allows for a richer, more comprehensive understanding of how we are faring.
By using only GDP growth and other strictly economic metrics to gauge societal success, we risk overlooking significant disparities in fundamental areas of human well-being. Without a more comprehensive assessment of human development, we can fall short of our goals without even knowing it. On several important gauges, including the infant death rate, the child poverty rate, and the on-time high school graduation rate, America has slipped behind other countries in recent years. But our relatively high GDP has enabled policymakers to downplay these troubling realities. What we don't measure, we don't address.

To expand opportunities for people to lead lives that are long, healthy, safe, and free, with the capabilities to thrive rather than merely to survive, we must first understand how ordinary people are doing.

The American Human Development Index:

- **Paints** a far more detailed portrait of well-being and opportunity throughout the United States than does GDP alone, and this portrait. . .
- **Enables** us to better analyze the interlocking factors that fuel advantage and disadvantage, create opportunities, and determine life chances. Because it uses easily understood indicators that we can compare across geographic regions and over time, it. . .
- **Provides** a standard frame of reference, enabling us to make apples-to-apples comparisons from place to place and from year to year.

The American HD Index is expressed in numbers from 0 to 10. The Index score for the whole country is 5.17, a moderate upward tick from 5.05 in *The Measure of America 2008–2009.* The overall Index score comprises scores related to the human condition in different states, congressional districts, and major metropolitan areas, broken down by race, ethnicity, and sex. Some populations enjoy levels of well-being near the top of the 10-point scale, others fall slightly above or below the U.S. average, and some have levels of health, education, and earnings that place them near the bottom of the Index.

Connecticut is the top-ranked state, with an HD Index score of 6.30. If current national trends continue, we would expect the U.S. national score to reach Connecticut's level in the year 2022. Connecticut was the top-ranked state in the 2008–09 Index as well. But not all states have progressed at the same pace. Arkansas, for example, dropped two places in the state rankings. It is now the next-to-last state, with human development levels roughly equivalent to well-being conditions in America nearly two decades ago. If we compare Arkansas to Connecticut, we see a gap in human development of about three decades; in other words, more than a generation of human progress separates Connecticut from Arkansas.

The Index enables us to make apples-to-apples comparisons from place to place and from year to year.

The good news is that some Americans are experiencing the longest life spans in human history while expanding their choices through high levels of educational attainment and earning incomes that make comfortable and secure living standards possible for themselves and their families. Asian Americans in New Jersey are living, on average, nearly ninety-two years. Two in three adult Asian Americans have earned a bachelor's degree or higher, and their median personal earnings are 68 percent above the national median.

The bad news is that many Americans do not enjoy equivalent levels of well-being. If current trends continue, the country as a whole will not reach the levels of health, education, and income prevalent among Asian Americans in New Jersey for another fifty years. Decades of progress in health, education, and earnings have bypassed certain groups. For instance, Native Americans in South Dakota lag almost a half century behind the rest of the nation in the categories measured by the American HD Index, living, on average, sixty-six years, and earning less than the typical American did in 1960. **The typical Asian American in New Jersey lives an astonishing quarter of a century longer, is eleven times more likely to have a graduate degree, and earns $33,149 more per year than the typical Native American in South Dakota.** The gap in incomes exceeds the entire median earnings of American workers (about $30,000). Separating Native Americans in South Dakota and Asian Americans in New Jersey is a century of human development progress. The category "Asian American" can include people who trace their heritage to a wide range of countries. See **BOX 1** for further discussion of important differences within various racial and ethnic groups.

This chapter introduces the American HD Index using 2007 and 2008 data, the most recent years for which the required data are available nationally. In addition, this chapter provides detailed findings about variations in human development based on analysis by geography, gender, race, and ethnicity. Subsequent chapters explore the reasons behind these variations, considering health, education, and income, and the interplay of these three basic areas in terms of the freedoms and opportunities they afford for different groups of Americans.

BOX 1 Broad Racial and Ethnic Labels Mask Considerable Diversity

The American Human Development Index is calculated using official government data and the racial and ethnic categories defined by the White House Office of Management and Budget. While these data sources and categorizations make possible reliable comparisons across the nation, they limit our ability to reflect the vast diversity that exists within racial and ethnic groups.

Broad categories like "Asian American" or "Latino" include people from wildly disparate origins. For instance, the category "African Americans" includes descendants of slaves as well as newly arrived immigrants from Africa or parts of the Caribbean. Asian Americans are descendants of peoples originating in East Asia, Southeast Asia, or the Indian subcontinent. Latinos trace their ancestry to countries throughout the Americas and parts of Europe. Whites range from descendants of passengers on the Mayflower to recently arrived Bosnian refugees.

This point is best illustrated with a concrete example. Asian Americans are sometimes touted as a "model minority" to which other racial and ethnic groups should aspire. This stereotype tends both to undervalue the opportunities and constraints with which immigrant groups arrive in the United States and to overemphasize the homogeneity of the Asian American category.

Two in three Asian Americans are foreign-born,[1] a notably higher proportion than for other major racial and ethnic groups, and considerable variation in human development outcomes exists depending upon country of origin.

Cambodians, Laotians, and Hmong register far lower on many human development dimensions than Indians and Japanese, for example. While fewer than 7 percent of Japanese adults lack a high school diploma, a full 40 percent of Hmong have not graduated high school.[2] Median family income for Indians in 2008 was nearly $100,000 and for Japanese families, it was $83,500, compared to $60,000 for Vietnamese families, less than the median family income for the United States as a whole.[3] Human development levels also vary considerably by gender among Asian Americans in general and within different Asian ancestral groups.

Even when the differences in starting points for Asian Americans of different origins are held constant, however, **Asian Americans generally best other groups on a wide array of human development outcomes**, a reality that poses interesting questions for researchers.[4]

Race and ethnicity offer just one lens through which to examine opportunity and freedom. But although the differences within groups can be as large as those between them, the chasms in human development revealed by comparing U.S. racial and ethnic groups present strong evidence that these categories retain great salience in assessing well-being.

Historical Trends: A Half Century of Development Progress

In recent decades, human development has improved dramatically in the United States (see **TABLE 1**). The average American today lives nearly nine years longer than an American in 1960, is twice as likely to have graduated from high school, is almost four times as likely to earn a bachelor's degree, and earns nearly twice as much (adjusted for inflation).

However, once-rapid progress has slowed to a crawl in this first decade of the twenty-first century. Between 2005 and 2008 the HD Index value for the United States as a whole rose 0.12 points—from 5.05 to 5.17. The improvement from 2005 to 2008 was driven mostly by an encouraging increase of over eight months in life expectancy and small gains in educational attainment. Median personal earnings have stagnated since 2000. During an earlier three-year period, from 1995 to 1998, earnings increased by almost $2,000. Americans' earnings today are not enabling living standards to rise.

TABLE 1 Historical Trends in Human Development, 1960–2008

YEAR	AMERICAN HD INDEX	LIFE EXPECTANCY AT BIRTH (years)	AT LEAST HIGH SCHOOL DIPLOMA (%)	AT LEAST BACHELOR'S DEGREE (%)	GRADUATE OR PROFESSIONAL DEGREE (%)	SCHOOL ENROLLMENT (%)	MEDIAN EARNINGS (2009 dollars)
2008	5.17	78.6	85.0	27.7	10.2	87.3	29,755
2005	5.05	77.9	84.2	27.2	10.0	86.8	29,994
2000	4.67	77.0	80.4	24.4	8.9	82.8	30,085
1990	3.82	75.4	75.2	20.3	7.2	80.8	25,451
1980	2.86	73.7	66.5	16.2	5.6	71.9	23,548
1970	2.10	70.8	52.3	10.7	3.6	73.3	22,648
1960	1.23	69.7	41.1	7.7	2.5	76.9	17,285

Source: American Human Development Project calculations. See Methodological Notes for more details.

A Long and Healthy Life is measured using life expectancy at birth, calculated from mortality data from the Centers for Disease Control and Prevention, National Center for Health Statistics 2007, and population data from the CDC WONDER database.

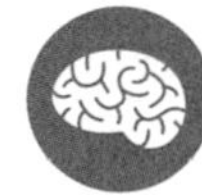

Access to Knowledge is measured using two indicators: school enrollment for the population age 3 and older, and educational degree attainment for the population 25 years and older. Both indicators are from the American Community Survey, U.S. Census Bureau, 2008.

A Decent Standard of Living is measured using median earnings of all full- and part-time workers 16 years and older from the American Community Survey, U.S. Census Bureau, 2008.

For more details on sources and methods, see the Methodological Notes on page 272.

Presenting American Human Development Index Scores

COMPARISONS BY STATE

Top HD ranking:
1. Connecticut
2. Massachusetts
3. Washington, DC

Bottom HD ranking:
49. Mississippi
50. Arkansas
51. West Virginia

As was the case in the 2008–09 Index, Connecticut tops the state HD ranking, followed by Massachusetts, Washington, DC, and New Jersey. Mississippi, Arkansas, and West Virginia score the lowest (see **MAP 1** and **TABLE 2**). States at the top tend not to have straight As across the board; instead, they do relatively well in several categories. For example, well-rounded Connecticut ranks fifth on the Health Index, third on the Education Index, and fourth in terms of earnings.

Along with West Virginia and Arkansas, the Gulf states of Mississippi, Louisiana, and Alabama make up the bottom five states. Life expectancies in these states today are roughly on par with the average American's life span two decades ago. Fewer than one in five adults in West Virginia, Mississippi, and Arkansas have a college degree, compared to one in four adults nationally. Residents of top-ranked Connecticut are more than twice as likely as residents of bottom-ranked West Virginia to have a master's or professional degree.

In measuring differences in human development between states, the HD Index reveals that money alone does not tell the whole story. For example, Oregon and Texas each have about the same median earnings—around $27,300

FIGURE 1 Same Income, Different Human Development Level

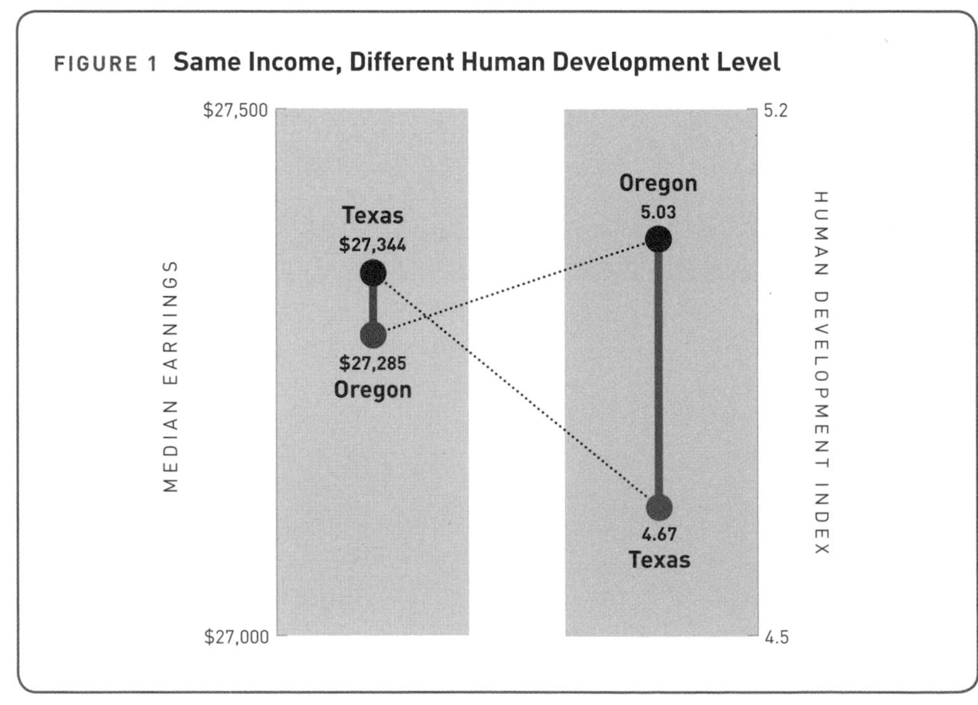

MAP 1 American Human Development Index by State

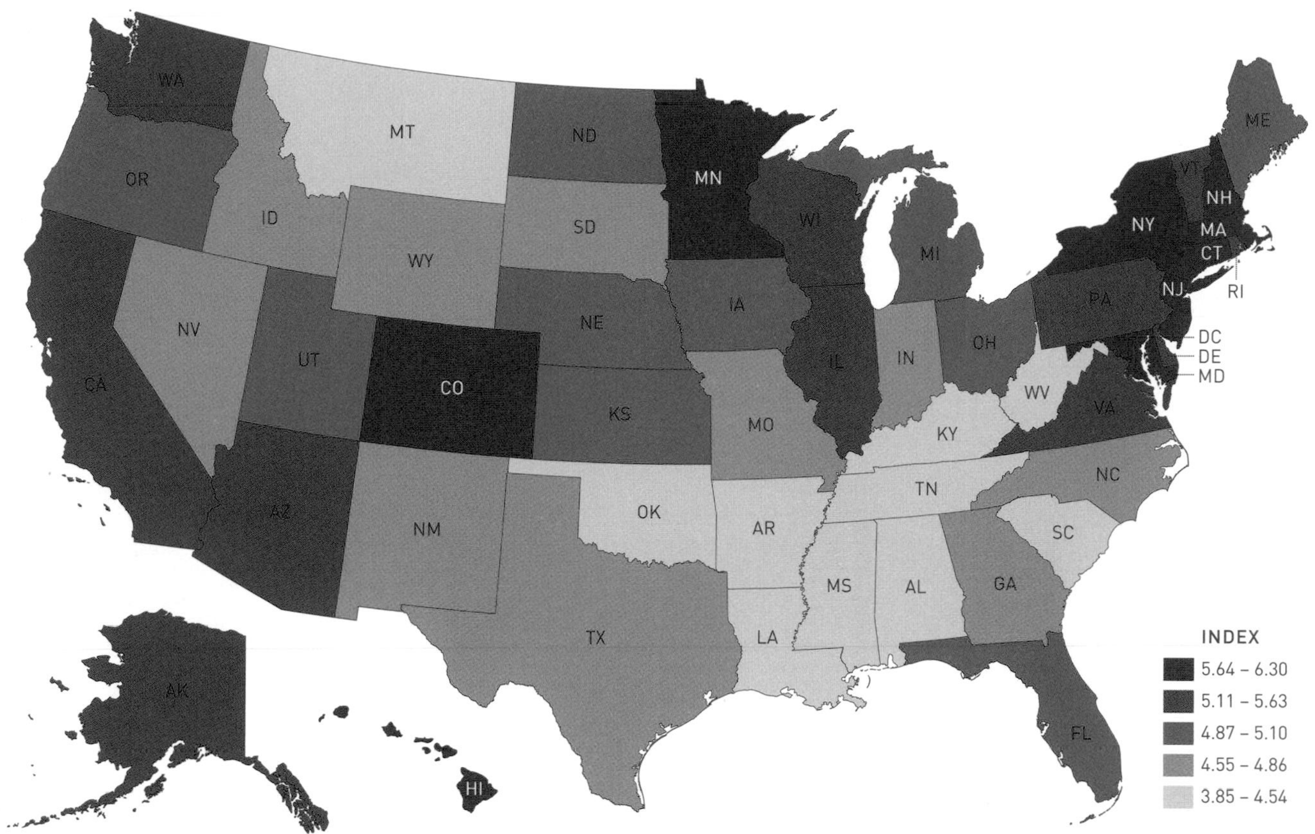

per person. Yet these earnings afford very different levels of well-being for their citizens. Oregonians today live on average about three-quarters of a year longer than Texans. While nearly 90 percent of adults in Oregon have earned at least a high school diploma, in Texas fewer than 80 percent have. Oregonians earn bachelor's degrees and professional degrees at higher rates as well. These higher levels of education and longer lives put Oregon significantly ahead of Texas on the state ranking of the HD Index, and demonstrate that the same income is buying two different levels of human well-being (see **FIGURE 1**).

Residents of states with higher earnings do not necessarily live longer.

Looking at the relationship between earnings and health outcomes, Maryland is third in terms of personal earnings, behind only Washington, DC, and New Jersey. Yet Maryland ranks only thirty-third in life expectancy among the states. Utah, in the top ten in longevity, ranks near the bottom (thirty-ninth) among the states on earnings. **Thus, states that are not the most affluent can achieve a superior record on health; conversely, residents of states with higher median earnings do not necessarily have longer lives** (see **FIGURE 2**).

Scores on the HD Index are averages for the categories they describe, whether

FIGURE 2 **Relationship between Earnings and Life Expectancy, by State**

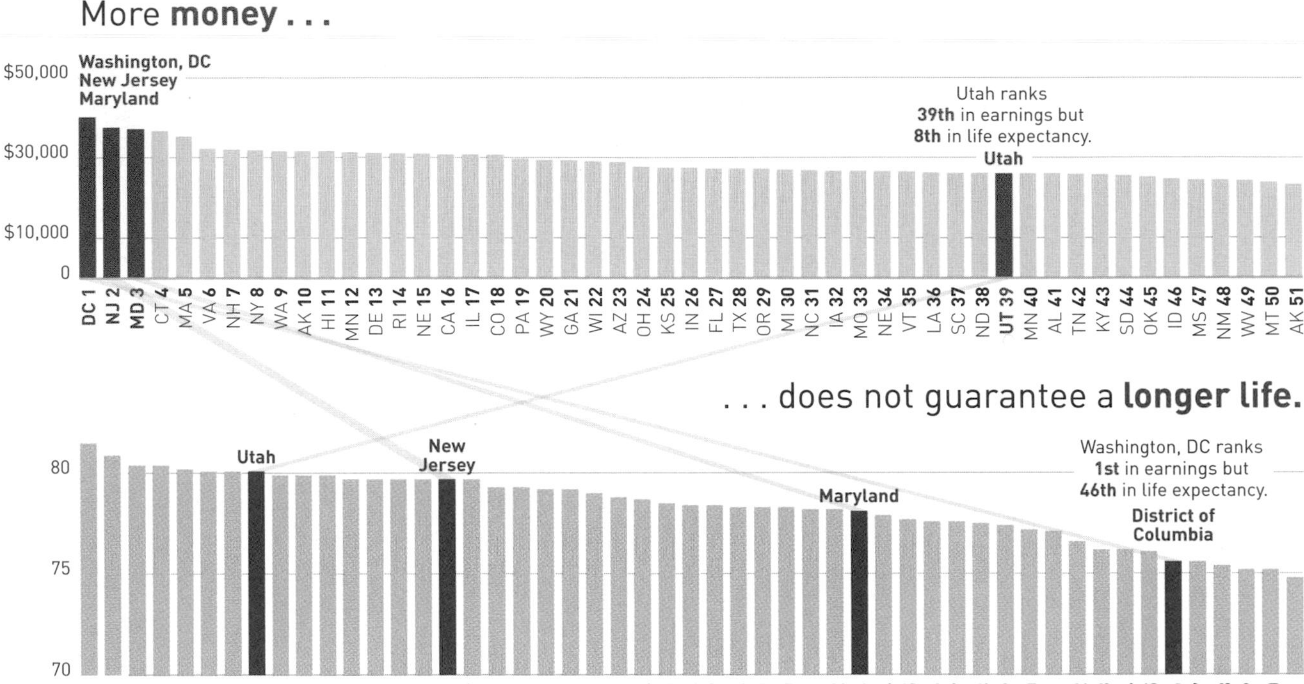

states, congressional districts, or racial/ethnic groups; like all averages, they mask variation within the groupings. For example, Connecticut's Index score is the average for all adults within that state; this average glosses over large contrasts between different parts of the state, between different racial and ethnic groups within the state, and between women and men. The well-being score for whites in Connecticut (6.77) is higher than the well-being score for Latinos (4.72), for instance, and typical earnings in the state differ between the congressional districts that make up Connecticut by as much as $6,600. A more comprehensive understanding of how different groups fare within states requires a look at smaller geographical areas and at racial, ethnic, gender, and other disparities.

Some people question why the Index does not reflect differences in the cost of living in different parts of the United States. While the relative costs of basic goods and services, especially the cost of housing, vary across the country, adjusting for the cost of living introduces its own sets of complications and inaccuracies. For that reason, we have not made such an adjustment here. See **BOX 2** for a discussion on cost-of-living adjustments.

TABLE 2 American Human Development Index by State

RANK	STATE	AMERICAN HD INDEX	LIFE EXPECTANCY AT BIRTH (years)	AT LEAST HIGH SCHOOL DIPLOMA (%)	AT LEAST BACHELOR'S DEGREE (%)	GRADUATE OR PROFESSIONAL DEGREE (%)	SCHOOL ENROLLMENT (%)	MEDIAN EARNINGS (2009 dollars)
	United States	5.17	78.6	85.0	27.7	10.2	87.3	29,755
1	**Connecticut**	6.30	80.2	88.6	35.6	15.2	92.1	36,827
2	**Massachusetts**	6.24	80.1	88.7	38.1	16.4	91.5	35,533
3	**District of Columbia**	6.21	75.6	85.8	**48.2**	**26.7**	**92.7**	**40,342**
4	**New Jersey**	6.16	79.7	87.4	34.4	12.8	90.8	37,707
5	**Maryland**	5.96	78.1	88.0	35.2	15.4	90.3	37,320
6	**New York**	5.77	80.4	84.1	31.9	13.8	89.7	31,963
7	**Minnesota**	5.74	80.9	91.6	31.5	10.0	87.0	31,442
8	**New Hampshire**	5.73	79.7	90.9	33.3	12.0	88.1	32,207
9	**Hawaii**	5.73	**81.5**	90.3	29.1	9.9	85.0	31,766
10	**Colorado**	5.65	79.9	88.9	35.6	12.7	87.5	30,853
11	**Rhode Island**	5.56	79.3	83.7	30.0	11.3	91.5	31,179
12	**California**	5.56	80.4	80.2	29.6	10.8	89.5	31,008
13	**Virginia**	5.53	78.5	85.9	33.7	13.8	87.8	32,467
14	**Washington**	5.53	79.7	89.6	30.7	10.9	85.7	31,812
15	**Illinois**	5.39	78.8	85.9	29.9	11.2	88.6	30,964
16	**Delaware**	5.33	78.3	87.2	27.5	10.8	88.4	31,320
17	**Alaska**	5.27	78.3	91.6	27.3	9.7	84.9	31,774
18	**Vermont**	5.27	79.7	90.6	32.1	12.2	87.9	26,627
19	**Wisconsin**	5.23	79.3	89.6	25.7	8.6	87.1	29,168
20	**Pennsylvania**	5.12	78.2	87.5	26.3	10.0	87.0	29,891
21	**Arizona**	5.11	79.9	83.8	25.1	9.2	84.2	29,049
22	**Utah**	5.08	80.1	90.4	29.1	9.4	85.2	26,126
23	**Florida**	5.07	79.7	85.2	25.8	9.0	86.9	27,366
24	**Iowa**	5.06	79.7	90.3	24.3	7.3	87.3	26,857
25	**Kansas**	5.06	78.4	89.5	29.6	10.1	87.2	27,690
26	**Nebraska**	5.05	79.2	90.1	27.1	8.6	87.6	26,659
27	**Oregon**	5.03	79.0	88.6	28.1	10.1	85.8	27,285
28	**Michigan**	4.99	77.9	88.1	24.7	9.4	91.2	27,125
29	**North Dakota**	4.92	80.1	89.6	26.9	6.6	82.8	26,224
30	**Maine**	4.89	78.7	89.7	25.4	8.9	87.3	26,120
31	**Ohio**	4.87	77.5	87.6	24.1	8.7	88.5	27,805
32	**Georgia**	4.86	77.1	83.9	27.5	9.7	86.1	29,453
33	**South Dakota**	4.82	79.9	90.3	25.1	7.3	82.5	25,717
34	**Wyoming**	4.80	77.6	**91.7**	23.6	7.9	**81.6**	29,507
35	**Nevada**	4.78	77.6	83.5	21.9	7.0	81.9	31,122
36	**Indiana**	4.74	77.7	86.2	22.9	8.1	85.9	27,677
37	**Missouri**	4.68	77.4	86.5	25.0	9.1	85.9	26,801
38	**Texas**	4.67	78.3	**79.6**	25.3	8.3	84.2	27,344
39	**Idaho**	4.65	79.2	87.9	24.0	7.4	83.9	24,776
40	**North Carolina**	4.64	77.2	83.6	26.1	8.6	86.5	26,943
41	**New Mexico**	4.56	78.2	82.4	24.7	10.7	86.6	24,495
42	**Montana**	4.49	78.4	90.9	27.1	8.4	81.8	24,033
43	**South Carolina**	4.36	76.6	83.2	23.7	8.5	84.1	26,247
44	**Tennessee**	4.33	76.2	83.0	22.9	8.0	85.7	26,044
45	**Kentucky**	4.23	76.2	81.3	19.7	7.9	85.5	25,861
46	**Oklahoma**	4.15	75.6	85.5	22.2	7.2	84.5	25,283
47	**Alabama**	4.09	75.2	81.9	22.0	7.7	83.6	26,112
48	**Louisiana**	4.07	75.4	81.2	20.3	6.5	83.3	26,357
49	**Mississippi**	3.93	**74.8**	79.9	19.4	6.8	86.7	24,620
50	**Arkansas**	3.87	76.1	82.0	18.8	**6.3**	83.0	**23,471**
51	**West Virginia**	3.85	75.2	82.2	**17.1**	6.7	83.7	24,404

* The **highest** and **lowest** performers are in color. **Note:** American HD Index Scores have been rounded to two decimal places. The resulting values may therefore appear to be tied in several instances. The rankings reflect the original values that result from calculation of the Index.

BOX 2 Accounting for Cost-of-Living Differences

The cost of essential goods and services varies across the nation and within distinct regions. **However, we currently have no reliable way to factor these variations into the HD Index without introducing biases and inaccuracies.** First, no official measurement of a nationally comparable cost of living currently exists; and second, cost-of-living variations within compact regions, such as states or cities, are often more pronounced than variations between states and regions.

The **Consumer Price Index (CPI)**, calculated by the U.S. Bureau of Labor Statistics (BLS), helps us understand changes in the purchasing power of the dollar over time. The CPI is sometimes mistaken for a cost-of-living index, but in fact it is best used as **a measure of the change in the cost of a set of goods and services over time in a given place.** Measuring differences across region and place is far more complicated. For example, the percentage of a budget spent on particular items can vary significantly (e.g., air conditioning in Texas versus Alaska). Collecting timely data on the prices of a wide variety of goods and services in many different localities is also very costly and time-consuming. The BLS once produced a cost-of-living measure called the Urban Family Budgets series but this was discontinued during the 1980s due to the high costs associated with producing it.

Unofficial measures such as the **American Chamber of Commerce Research Association (ACCRA) Cost of Living Index** are regularly updated and widely cited. However, this index suffers from several serious problems, chiefly that it only takes into consideration the living costs incurred by urban households in the wealthiest fifth of the income distribution. The ACCRA index thus leaves out the middle class, the poor, and residents of rural areas. While these omissions could be addressed, this would be a costly and time-consuming exercise requiring significant expertise and resources.

Existing cost-of-living measures are also heavily influenced by housing costs, but **the simple conclusion that people are worse off because of high housing costs is misleading.** The cost of housing in turn reflects less quantifiable factors such as the quality of public services, the security of neighborhoods, and the cleanliness of local environments. Demand for housing is often greater in places where residents enjoy a higher quality of life, therefore inflating housing prices and causing the costs of living to rise.

Finally, cost-of-living variations within states or compact areas such as major cities are sometimes far starker than variations between states or regions. Within Manhattan, which common perceptions and the ACCRA index both suggest is one of the most expensive places to live in the United States, the average monthly rent for a two-bedroom apartment in a non-doorman building in April 2010 ranged from $6,437 in the island's southwest Tribeca neighborhood to $1,910 in northern Manhattan's Harlem.[5] The combined prices of three basic supermarket items (milk, rice, and diapers) were 33 percent more expensive in southern Manhattan than in Harlem.[6] These variations within the same city attest to just how misleading generalizations about the cost of living at almost any level of geography can be.

COMPARISONS BY CONGRESSIONAL DISTRICT

The 436 congressional districts (CDs) in the United States[7] afford a more intimate view of variations in development than the fifty states. Each congressional district contains roughly 650,000 residents; consequently they are more numerous in densely populated areas. Seven states—Alaska, Delaware, Montana, North Dakota, South Dakota, Vermont, and Wyoming—have only one congressional district each. However, most states have several districts, and California has fifty-three (as of 2010)—the most of any state.

The American HD Index allows for tracking change over time. What has changed since 2005, the year from which data for the first American HD Index were drawn, in terms of well-being by congressional district? Texas is home to several noteworthy improvements in human development. In fact, of the ten districts that show the greatest progress, half are in Texas; four are in the greater Houston metro area, and a fifth is in the west central part of the state. Congressional Districts Eight, Eleven, Fourteen, Eighteen, and Twenty-nine all moved up in the rankings, largely on the strength of higher earnings. Despite the fact that these

MAP 2 American Human Development Index by Congressional District

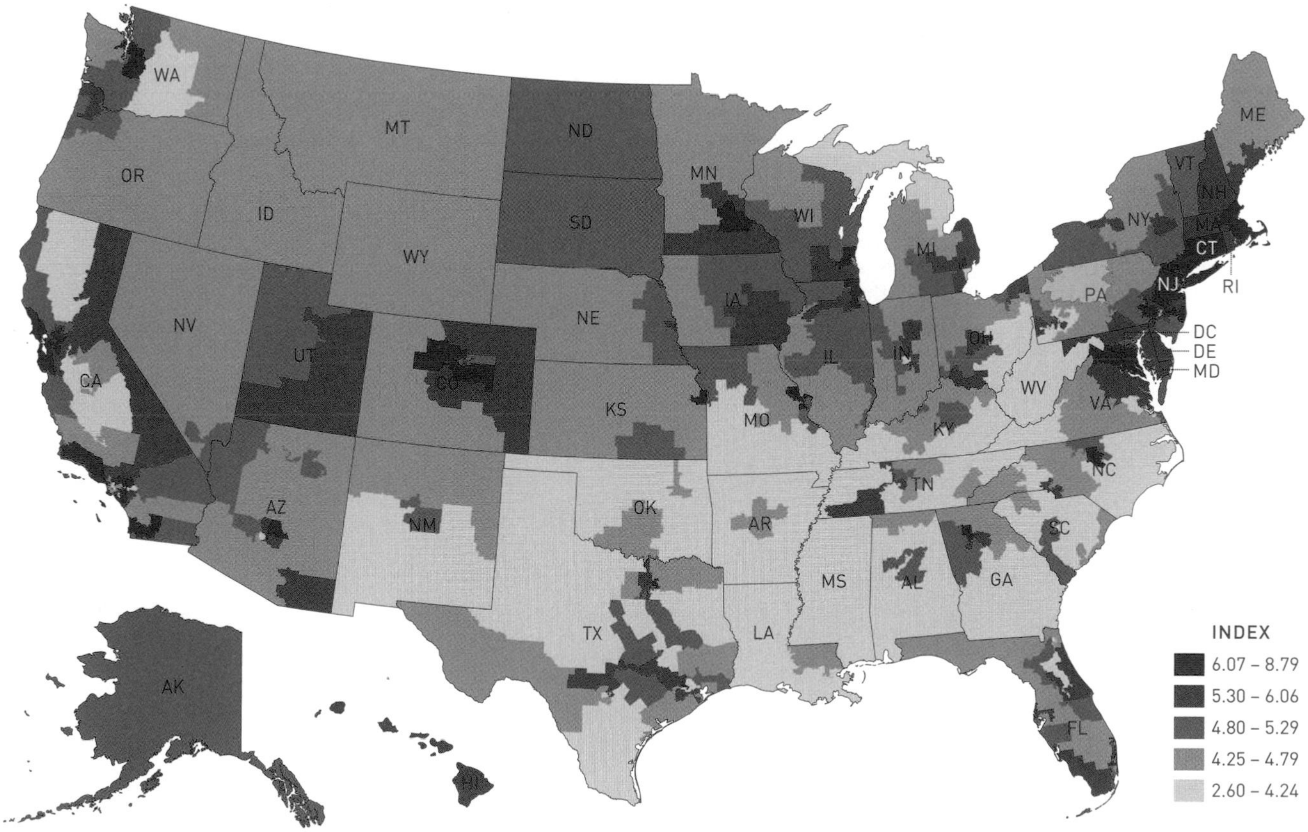

A **seventy-five-year gap** in human development separates the top- and bottom-ranked districts.

data were collected in the middle of the recession, the earnings of the typical worker increased by over $2,000 in each of these five districts, a remarkable gain considering that during this same time period earnings in over 75 percent of districts decreased.

The range in HD Index scores among congressional districts is much wider than the range of scores among states (see **TABLE 3**). **While state scores range from 6.30 in Connecticut to 3.85 in West Virginia, congressional district scores range from 8.79 in New York's Fourteenth District (Manhattan's East Side) to only 2.60 in California's Twentieth District (the Central Valley around Fresno).** Human development in New York's Fourteenth District is about where the country as a whole will be, if current trends continue, in forty years, while human development in California's Twentieth District is comparable to the United States as a whole in the late 1970s. **A seventy-five-year gap in human development thus separates the top- and bottom-ranked districts.** A resident of California's Twentieth District is more than five times as likely to lack a high school diploma or its equivalent, is about seventeen times less likely to have a master's degree, and, on average, makes less than a third of the median earnings of a resident of New York's Fourteenth District.

HD Index scores among congressional districts exhibit wide variations even within one state (see **TABLE 3**). New York's Fourteenth District, which tops the rankings for both the overall HD Index and for earnings, is situated only a few miles from New York's Sixteenth District, the poorest district in the nation in earnings and fourth-to-last overall on the American HD Index. The Fourteenth District consists of Manhattan's East Side, Roosevelt Island, and parts of western Queens. The Sixteenth is just over two miles away in the South Bronx. Despite their proximity, nearly seventy years of human development—more than two generations—separate these two sections of New York City.

The states with the most congressional districts exhibit the widest ranges in HD Index scores (see **TABLE 4**). California and New York have the greatest ranges between their top and bottom districts.

TABLE 3 Top and Bottom Twenty Congressional Districts on the American Human Development Index

RANK	DISTRICT	AMERICAN HD INDEX	LIFE EXPECTANCY AT BIRTH (years)	AT LEAST HIGH SCHOOL DIPLOMA (%)	AT LEAST BACHELOR'S DEGREE (%)	GRADUATE OR PROFESSIONAL DEGREE (%)	SCHOOL ENROLLMENT (%)	MEDIAN EARNINGS (2009 dollars)
TOP 20 Congressional Districts								
1	**CD 14, New York**	8.79	82.8	91.3	**65.7**	**30.3**	100.5	**60,099**
2	**CD 8, Virginia**	8.30	**83.7**	89.6	58.9	29.3	97.1	51,260
3	**CD 14, California**	8.11	82.9	90.6	57.2	28.4	99.9	47,879
4	**CD 30, California**	7.71	80.8	93.8	57.6	25.6	97.7	46,977
5	**CD 48, California**	7.66	82.1	92.9	51.7	20.4	99.0	44,803
6	**CD 15, California**	7.60	83.1	88.7	45.3	19.2	95.5	46,751
7	**CD 8, Maryland**	7.57	83.2	89.3	55.2	29.6	94.3	41,263
8	**CD 11, Virginia**	7.51	81.6	91.4	52.7	24.0	93.2	46,680
9	**CD 8, New York**	7.48	82.0	85.6	52.9	25.0	95.3	44,706
10	**CD 8, California**	7.47	82.6	83.2	50.0	19.4	**104.3**	42,815
11	**CD 12, California**	7.44	82.9	90.3	45.1	17.8	98.9	41,990
12	**CD 11, New Jersey**	7.33	80.6	92.0	47.7	19.3	95.4	46,761
13	**CD 7, New Jersey**	7.31	80.7	92.1	45.9	19.2	95.1	46,891
14	**CD 12, New Jersey**	7.28	80.0	93.2	48.0	21.9	95.6	46,142
15	**CD 46, California**	7.17	81.8	89.7	41.7	15.6	100.5	40,927
16	**CD 18, New York**	7.12	81.9	87.4	48.1	25.6	90.7	42,141
17	**CD 10, Virginia**	7.12	80.8	89.9	49.1	20.2	91.7	44,732
18	**CD 6, Colorado**	7.11	81.3	**96.6**	48.3	16.3	93.7	41,346
19	**CD 5, New Jersey**	7.11	81.0	93.6	43.2	15.7	92.6	45,395
20	**CD 4, Connecticut**	7.06	81.4	88.8	46.6	20.8	92.9	42,100
BOTTOM 20 Congressional Districts								
416	**CD 3, Alabama**	3.61	74.7	78.6	19.4	7.7	84.3	22,560
417	**CD 2, Georgia**	3.55	74.6	78.0	15.4	5.6	80.8	24,296
418	**CD 1, North Carolina**	3.53	75.0	76.7	13.4	4.1	86.9	21,997
419	**CD 5, Louisiana**	3.52	75.0	78.9	17.2	5.6	80.1	23,299
420	**CD 6, South Carolina**	3.52	75.3	78.8	15.9	5.5	82.7	22,154
421	**CD 4, Arkansas**	3.50	75.1	80.3	15.0	4.3	84.1	21,856
422	**CD 9, Virginia**	3.50	75.7	76.1	16.6	6.3	82.6	21,599
423	**CD 4, Tennessee**	3.50	75.9	77.7	13.4	4.7	79.5	22,898
424	**CD 1, Kentucky**	3.50	75.5	78.4	13.1	5.4	80.7	22,924
425	**CD 7, Alabama**	3.46	74.7	79.5	16.8	5.5	82.7	22,125
426	**CD 1, Arkansas**	3.39	74.8	78.8	13.3	4.2	82.8	22,153
427	**CD 4, Alabama**	3.37	74.3	75.0	13.2	5.0	77.5	25,153
428	**CD 2, Mississippi**	3.34	73.6	76.4	18.6	6.1	87.2	20,962
429	**CD 2, Oklahoma**	3.33	74.5	82.0	14.4	4.9	80.7	21,913
430	**CD 8, Missouri**	3.24	75.1	77.2	14.5	5.8	80.3	21,103
431	**CD 29, Texas**	3.23	78.2	53.8	**6.8**	2.0	76.8	22,932
432	**CD 16, New York**	3.20	79.0	58.4	10.6	2.9	84.3	**17,995**
433	**CD 3, West Virginia**	3.16	**72.9**	77.2	13.8	5.3	80.6	23,206
434	**CD 5, Kentucky**	2.82	73.6	68.6	10.6	4.7	80.1	21,031
435	**CD 20, California**	2.60	77.5	**53.8**	7.0	**1.8**	**75.5**	18,616

* The **highest** and **lowest** performers are in color.
Source: American Human Development Project calculations. See Methodological Notes for more details.
Note: Enrollment can be over 100 percent if adults 25 and older are enrolled in school.

The ten largest metropolitan areas are home to about **one-quarter** of the country's total population.

TABLE 4 Range of Congressional District Index Scores on the American Human Development Index by State

RANK	STATE	NUMBER OF DISTRICTS	AMERICAN HD INDEX RANGE	MINIMUM AMERICAN HD INDEX SCORE	MAXIMUM AMERICAN HD INDEX SCORE
1	**New York**	29	5.59	3.20	8.79
2	**California**	53	5.51	2.60	8.12
3	**Virginia**	11	4.80	3.50	8.30
4	**Texas**	32	3.47	3.23	6.69
5	**Georgia**	13	3.24	3.55	6.79
6	**North Carolina**	13	3.15	3.53	6.68
7	**Illinois**	19	3.04	3.80	6.84
8	**Missouri**	9	3.00	3.24	6.24
9	**Michigan**	15	2.80	3.95	6.75
10	**Pennsylvania**	18	2.72	3.86	6.58
11	**Washington**	9	2.65	4.24	6.89
12	**Arizona**	8	2.60	3.71	6.31
13	**Florida**	25	2.44	3.87	6.31
14	**Colorado**	7	2.38	4.73	7.11
15	**Maryland**	8	2.35	5.22	7.57
16	**Kentucky**	6	2.28	2.82	5.10
17	**New Jersey**	13	2.19	5.14	7.33
18	**Minnesota**	8	2.04	4.65	6.69
19	**Kansas**	4	1.99	4.24	6.22
20	**Alabama**	7	1.93	3.37	5.31
21	**Wisconsin**	8	1.92	4.35	6.28
22	**Tennessee**	9	1.90	3.50	5.40
23	**Ohio**	18	1.79	3.98	5.77
24	**Oregon**	5	1.64	4.26	5.90
25	**Indiana**	9	1.53	4.22	5.75
26	**South Carolina**	6	1.53	3.52	5.05
27	**Oklahoma**	5	1.32	3.33	4.64
28	**Massachusetts**	10	1.30	5.52	6.82
29	**Louisiana**	7	1.26	3.52	4.79
30	**New Mexico**	3	1.23	3.95	5.18
31	**Nebraska**	3	1.12	4.44	5.56
32	**Nevada**	3	1.02	4.26	5.28
33	**Arkansas**	4	1.00	3.39	4.39
34	**West Virginia**	3	0.99	3.16	4.16
35	**Connecticut**	5	0.98	6.09	7.06
36	**Mississippi**	4	0.89	3.34	4.23
37	**Iowa**	5	0.85	4.62	5.47
38	**Utah**	3	0.72	4.81	5.53

Note: States with two or fewer congressional districts not included (Alaska, Delaware, District of Columbia, Hawaii, Idaho, Maine, Montana, New Hampshire, North Dakota, Rhode Island, South Dakota, Vermont, and Wyoming).

TABLE 5 American Human Development Index, by Major Metro Area

RANK	GREATER METRO AREA	AMERICAN HD INDEX	LIFE EXPECTANCY AT BIRTH (years)	AT LEAST HIGH SCHOOL DIPLOMA (%)	AT LEAST BACHELOR'S DEGREE (%)	GRADUATE OR PROFESSIONAL DEGREE (%)	SCHOOL ENROLLMENT (%)	MEDIAN EARNINGS (2009 dollars)
	United States	5.17	78.6	85.0	27.7	10.2	87.3	29,755
1	Washington, DC	6.94	80.3	89.3	**46.8**	**21.9**	92.4	**42,556**
2	Boston	6.55	80.5	**89.9**	41.9	18.6	**92.7**	37,138
3	New York	6.26	81.0	83.8	35.3	14.5	90.9	36,466
4	Philadelphia	5.70	**77.7**	87.6	32.1	12.6	90.4	35,523
5	Chicago	5.61	79.0	85.5	33.0	12.5	88.7	32,618
6	Los Angeles	5.60	**81.1**	76.8	29.9	10.5	90.6	30,349
7	Atlanta	5.53	78.5	87.4	34.6	11.9	88.4	32,173
8	Miami	5.46	81.0	82.7	29.5	10.6	88.9	**28,443**
9	Dallas	5.11	78.5	81.2	29.6	9.5	84.9	30,834
10	Houston	5.02	78.2	**80.1**	**28.2**	**9.3**	**84.4**	31,079

* The **highest** and **lowest** performers are in color.
Source: American Human Development Project calculations. See Methodological Notes on page 272 for more details.

COMPARISONS BY MAJOR METROPOLITAN AREA

The ten largest metropolitan areas in the nation are home to almost 80 million residents, roughly one-quarter of the country's total population. They are Boston, New York, Philadelphia, and Washington, DC, in the East; Los Angeles in the West; Atlanta, Dallas, Houston, and Miami in the South; and Chicago in the Midwest. Rather than restrict analysis to the formal boundaries of municipalities, the Index considers Metropolitan Statistical Areas, as defined by the White House Office of Management and Budget, in order to analyze core cities and surrounding counties as unified metro areas (see **TABLE 5**). The Methodological Notes on page 272 contain further details on metro areas.

Since metropolitan areas are large and densely populated, they provide rich data that enable a more comprehensive look at the different populations within them. By analyzing their constituent congressional districts (see **MAP 2**), we can observe additional layers. For example, **many metro areas reveal major gaps between the HD Index of racial and ethnic groups.** In the Dallas metropolitan area, Asian Americans have the highest HD Index (8.09) and Latinos the lowest (3.87). Although life expectancies for both groups are well above the average for the metro area as a whole, less than half (48.5 percent) of all Dallas-area Latinos had a high school diploma or its equivalent, while more than half (54.9 percent) of all Dallas-area Asian Americans had a bachelor's degree or higher. Median earnings for Dallas-area Asian Americans were more than $15,000 higher than median earnings for their Latino neighbors. **All together, more than fifty years of human development separate these two Dallas-area communities.**

More than fifty years of human development separate Asian Americans and Latinos in the Dallas area.

COMPARISONS BY GENDER

One of the most striking differences in well-being between women and men in America is the earnings gap between them. Women topped men on the HD Index in 2008 due to the fact that the average American woman can expect to live more than half a decade longer than the average American man (see **TABLE 6**) and that a higher percentage of girls and women are enrolled in school. Female education scores, especially on enrollment, have crept up in recent years while other indicators have remained largely stable, allowing women to take the lead in the overall HD Index by a small margin. Yet despite this, **men typically earn about $11,000 more than women.** Subsequent chapters explore fully the causes of this yawning earnings divide.

COMPARISONS BY RACE AND ETHNICITY[8]

Asian Americans and whites enjoy the highest levels of human development, and **Native Americans** the lowest.

Asian Americans and whites enjoy the highest levels of human development in the United States, and Native Americans the lowest (see **TABLE 7**). Asian Americans have the longest life expectancies of any group, nearly nine years longer than the national average. They also have more advanced degrees, higher enrollment rates, and higher earnings than other Americans. Using the most recent available data, the average Asian American lives an eye-opening thirteen years longer than the average African American, earns about $13,000 more per year than the typical Native American, and is almost five times as likely to have a master's or professional degree as the average Latino. The HD Index was not calculated for groups with fewer than fifty thousand people (such as African Americans in twelve states), due to the statistical instability of survey-based estimates for small populations.

COMPARISONS BY RACE, ETHNICITY, AND GENDER

Human development levels between men and women by race and ethnicity show many of the same results as described above except that African American women, Latina women, and Native American women do much better on the HD Index than their male counterparts, mostly on the strength of their longer life expectancies (see **TABLE 8**). Here, the differences between groups are particularly striking. For example, life expectancy variation between Asian American women, who enjoy the longest life expectancies of all, and African American men, who live the shortest lives on average, is an astounding nineteen years. In 2008, Asian American men made almost $23,000 more per year than Latina women, the least well-paid group. Important differences in well-being also exist between people of different age groups, and the American Human Development Project is exploring ways to assess them (see **BOX 3**).

TABLE 6 American Human Development Index by Gender

RANK	GENDER	AMERICAN HD INDEX	LIFE EXPECTANCY AT BIRTH (years)	AT LEAST HIGH SCHOOL DIPLOMA (%)	AT LEAST BACHELOR'S DEGREE (%)	GRADUATE OR PROFESSIONAL DEGREE (%)	SCHOOL ENROLLMENT (%)	MEDIAN EARNINGS (2009 dollars)
	United States	5.17	78.6	85.0	27.7	10.2	87.3	29,755
1	**Women**	5.15	**81.2**	**85.6**	27.0	9.6	**90.8**	23,997
2	**Men**	5.07	76.0	84.3	**28.4**	**10.8**	84.0	**35,170**

* The **highest** performer is in color.
Source: American Human Development Project calculations. See Methodological Notes for more details.

TABLE 7 American Human Development Index by Racial and Ethnic Group

RANK	GROUP	AMERICAN HD INDEX	LIFE EXPECTANCY AT BIRTH (years)	AT LEAST HIGH SCHOOL DIPLOMA (%)	AT LEAST BACHELOR'S DEGREE (%)	GRADUATE OR PROFESSIONAL DEGREE (%)	SCHOOL ENROLLMENT (%)	MEDIAN EARNINGS (2009 dollars)
	United States	5.17	78.6	85.0	27.7	10.2	87.3	29,755
1	**Asian American**	7.68	**87.3**	85.1	**49.7**	**19.9**	**102.1**	**34,835**
2	**White**	5.53	78.7	**90.1**	30.7	11.4	88.6	31,932
3	**Latino**	4.19	83.5	**60.8**	12.9	4.0	**79.7**	21,936
4	**African American**	3.91	**74.3**	80.7	17.5	6.0	88.6	24,792
5	**Native American**	3.24	75.1	75.6	**12.7**	**3.9**	80.4	**21,744**

* The **highest** and **lowest** performers are in color.
Source: American Human Development Project calculations. See Methodological Notes for more details.
Note: Enrollment can be over 100 percent if adults 25 and older are enrolled in school.

TABLE 8 American Human Development Index by Gender and Racial/Ethnic Group

RANK	GROUP	AMERICAN HD INDEX	LIFE EXPECTANCY AT BIRTH (years)	AT LEAST HIGH SCHOOL DIPLOMA (%)	AT LEAST BACHELOR'S DEGREE (%)	GRADUATE OR PROFESSIONAL DEGREE (%)	SCHOOL ENROLLMENT (%)	MEDIAN EARNINGS (2009 dollars)
1	**Asian American Men**	7.81	84.6	87.5	**53.0**	**23.9**	100.7	**40,815**
2	**Asian American Women**	7.47	**89.7**	83.0	46.8	16.4	**103.2**	29,133
3	**White Men**	5.61	76.2	89.7	32.1	12.2	85.3	40,157
4	**White Women**	5.46	81.2	**90.4**	29.4	10.6	91.9	25,531
5	**African American Women**	4.45	77.6	81.8	19.0	6.7	94.4	22,874
6	**Latina Women**	4.29	86.3	62.5	13.8	4.2	82.6	**18,178**
7	**Latino Men**	3.94	80.6	**59.2**	12.1	3.9	77.0	24,849
8	**Native American Women**	3.60	78.1	77.9	14.1	4.2	83.6	19,560
9	**African American Men**	3.33	**70.7**	79.2	15.8	5.2	83.4	26,644
10	**Native American Men**	2.84	72.1	73.2	**11.2**	**3.7**	**76.2**	24,095

* The **highest** and **lowest** performers are in color.
Source: American Human Development Project calculations. See Methodological Notes for more details.
Note: Enrollment can be over 100 percent if adults 25 and older are enrolled in school.

TABLE 9 American Human Development Index for Racial and Ethnic Groups by State

GROUP/STATE	AMERICAN HD INDEX	LIFE EXPECTANCY AT BIRTH (years)	AT LEAST HIGH SCHOOL DIPLOMA (%)	AT LEAST BACHELOR'S DEGREE (%)	GRADUATE OR PROFESSIONAL DEGREE (%)	SCHOOL ENROLLMENT (%)	MEDIAN EARNINGS (2009 dollars)
United States	5.17	78.6	85.0	27.7	10.2	87.3	29,755
States Where Each Racial and Ethnic Group Scores **Highest**							
Asian American—New Jersey	9.30	91.8	91.8	66.8	27.6	98.3	50,069
White—District of Columbia	9.03	83.1	98.9	88.2	51.4	103.4	60,232
Latino—New Jersey	5.28	87.0	69.4	16.1	5.0	81.5	25,440
African American—Maryland	5.09	74.7	85.8	23.9	9.4	92.3	34,446
Native American—California	4.42	81.4	71.5	12.8	3.8	82.7	24,488
States Where Each Racial and Ethnic Group Scores **Lowest**							
Asian American—Louisiana	5.30	82.3	69.3	35.4	15.9	96.4	22,094
White—West Virginia	3.85	75.1	82.2	16.9	6.7	82.8	24,797
African American—Louisiana	2.60	72.1	74.1	12.0	3.9	82.1	19,434
Latino—Arkansas	2.49	79.2	43.2	8.5	2.9	69.7	18,434
Native American—South Dakota	1.15	66.0	78.3	10.3	2.4	74.2	16,920

Source: American Human Development Project calculations. See Methodological Notes on page 272 for more details.

COMPARISONS BY RACE AND ETHNICITY BY STATE

Variations in human development outcomes between racial and ethnic groups at the state level reveal a stark contrast in the experiences of different groups in different parts of the country (see TABLE 9). Whites and Asian Americans in top-ranked states such as Connecticut and New Jersey enjoy human development levels decades ahead of the nation as a whole, while African Americans, Latinos, and Native Americans in lower-ranking states have HD Index levels comparable to those of the United States as a whole in the 1970s or even earlier. Human development among Native Americans in some states is the most troubling. HD Index levels for Native Americans in South Dakota are comparable to the United States as a whole in the late 1950s, more than a half century ago.

There is also remarkable variation when measuring levels of development of one race across several states. African Americans in Maryland have the highest HD Index scores of African Americans of any state, while African Americans in Louisiana have the lowest. African Americans in Maryland, on average, live two and a half years longer, and earn over $15,000 more than African Americans in Louisiana. While South Dakota Native Americans have the lowest Index value of any group in any state, the human development levels of California Native Americans are almost four times those of South Dakota, with well-being levels similar to that of the United States as a whole in the late 1990s. The HD Index values for racial and ethnic groups by state are displayed on pages 213-218.

BOX 3 Does the American Human Development Index Measure Child Well-Being?

The American HD Index captures important information about child well-being and the environments in which children grow into adulthood. However, children under the age of 5 are markedly vulnerable to a range of development challenges and have a distinct set of needs. Their well-being merits special attention both for ethical reasons and because research shows that constraints to the development of adolescents and adults—such as poor school performance, health risk behaviors, and incarceration—are rooted in early childhood experiences of poverty, malnutrition, abuse or neglect, and family instability. If basic needs are unmet in the early years, a child is set, some say irrevocably, on a disadvantageous life trajectory.

Assessing well-being in early childhood thus requires age-appropriate metrics. For this reason, the American Human Development Project is currently developing a "Tots' Index" to gauge the well-being of infants and children from birth to age 5.[9]

In addition to the three basic human development dimensions of health, education, and income that are the pillars of the American HD Index, this proposed index will also include measures of the extent to which small children are protected from harm and given the appropriate stimulation and emotional support they need to achieve a healthy start in life.

Indicators such as low birth weight or child injury rates are important for a comprehensive understanding of the health of children under age 5. Education indicators for this group include measures of preschool enrollment, child reading or storytelling, and the educational level of parents. The Tots' Index can help direct our attention toward the fundamental needs of very young children and build support for collective investment in their well-being—investment that research shows will pay for itself many times over in higher rates of economic productivity and lower rates of various costly social ills.

Conclusion

That significant gaps separate Americans of different racial and ethnic groups is common knowledge—though the size of the gaps often surprises people unfamiliar with the data. Less well known is the tremendous variation within racial and ethnic groups from state to state.

Many existing indicators measure health, education, or income alone for these groups. However, **the HD Index provides a uniquely comprehensive framework in which to analyze the interlocking factors that fuel opportunity, advantage, or disadvantage.** The Index enables us to gain a better understanding of areas where complex challenges intersect, opening the way to more comprehensive, lasting solutions. Ultimately, we hope it helps citizens, advocates, and policymakers develop a more objective, shared analysis of where we stand today and where we want to be tomorrow.

America has made amazing progress since 1960 in the key human development areas of health, education, and income. In many respects, far more opportunities are available to the average resident of this country today than were available five decades ago. However, behind the averages lurk massive variations in well-being defined by geography, gender, and race/ethnicity. Different factors contribute to strikingly different outcomes. We'll turn our attention to these factors in the following chapters.

America has made amazing progress since 1960 in the key human development areas of health, education, and income.

The Building Blocks of the American Human Development Index

A Long and Healthy Life

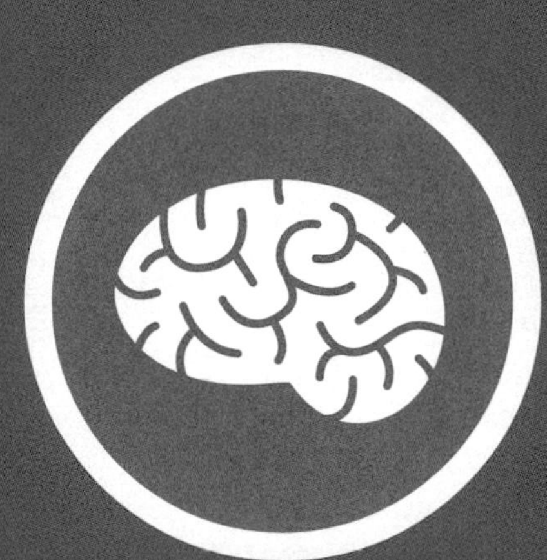

Access to Knowledge

A Decent Standard of Living

CHAPTER 2

A Long and Healthy Life

IN THIS SECTION:

How Do We Stack Up?

Life Expectancy at Birth

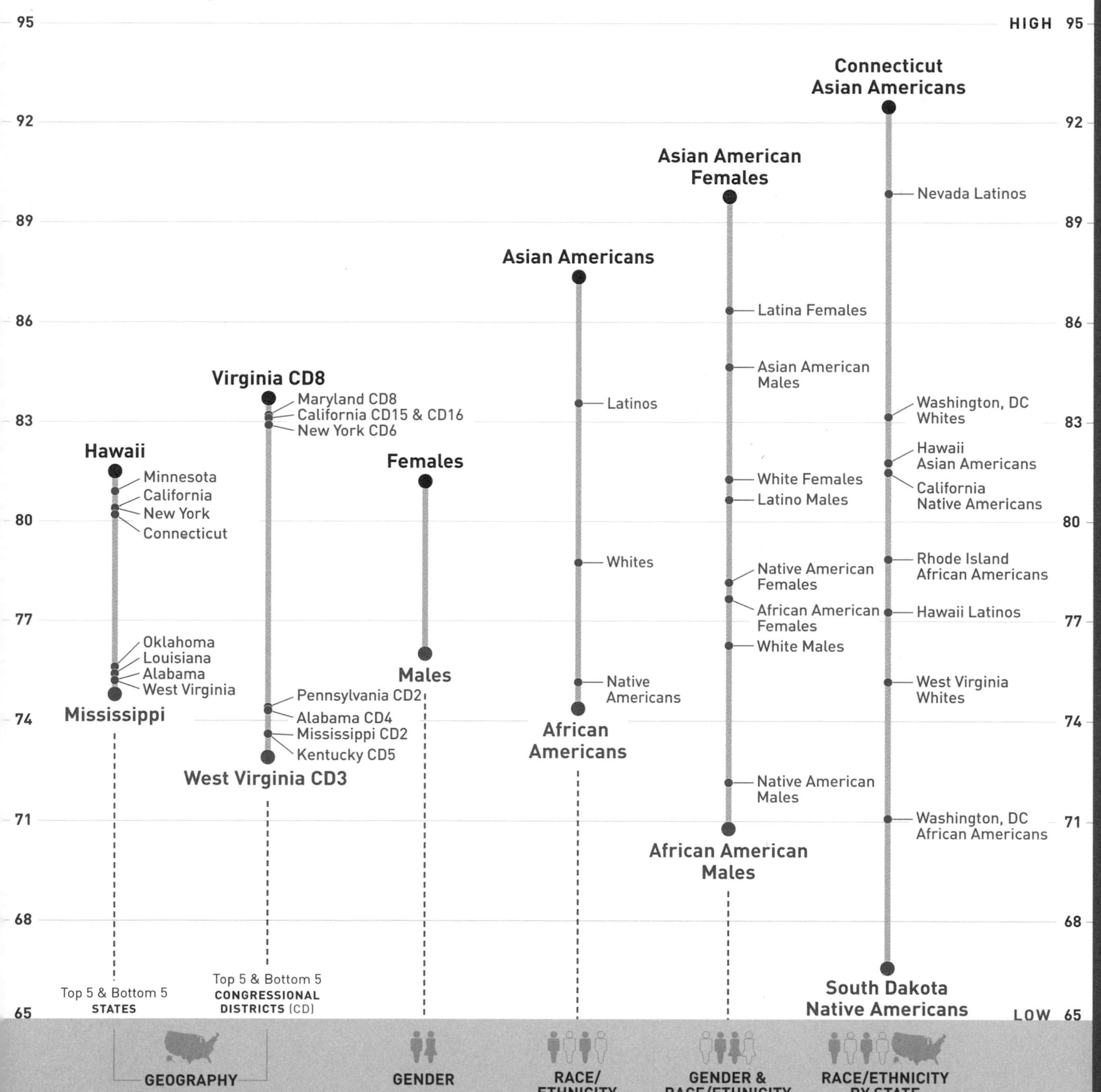

Introduction

"The microbe is nothing, the soil is everything."

LOUIS PASTEUR on his deathbed in 1895

The unprecedented attention to the nation's health care structure overlooked the country's most alarming health problem: **huge disparities in health outcomes for different population groups.**

On March 23, 2010, after a year of bare-knuckled, highly partisan debate, President Barack Obama signed the Patient Protection and Affordable Care Act. The law requires that all Americans have health insurance by 2014 and forbids insurance companies from denying coverage based on preexisting conditions.

The intensity of the health-care reform debate—in political circles, on cable TV, in town hall meetings, and at workplace water coolers and kitchen tables—testified to Americans' deep concern about their ability to access affordable, quality care. In a poll commissioned by the American Human Development Project and conducted in October 2009,[1] health insecurity topped the list of issues that most worry Americans when they think about the future.

In the run-up to the health bill's passage, every angle of health care and health insurance was explored: Why is health care so expensive? Who should run the health-care system? Who will pay for it, and what will it cost? What about competition? What services should be covered? What will happen to the coverage people already have? What about Medicare, mandates, and medicines? Beneath all these questions was an even more fundamental one: who will win and who will lose?

However, the emphasis on politics obscured what is arguably the key issue in health care today: what is making Americans sick in the first place? Research shows that deficiencies in the health-care system cause only 10 percent of premature death, while another 30 percent is attributable to people's genetic predispositions to certain maladies. The bulk of premature death—60 percent—stems from preventable environmental, social, economic, and behavioral health risks.[2] Chief among them are smoking, poor diet, physical inactivity, and alcohol.

The unprecedented attention to the nation's health-care structure overlooked the country's most alarming health problem: **huge disparities in health outcomes**

for different population groups. Asian Americans in Connecticut live, on average, twenty-six years longer than Native Americans in South Dakota. Whites in Washington, DC, live, on average, a dozen years longer than African Americans in the same city. A baby born today in Virginia's Eighth Congressional District can expect to live a decade longer than a baby born today in West Virginia's Third Congressional District.

Analysis of two factors—the social determinants of health and the social gradient—reveals that the freedom to live a flourishing life and enjoy good health is not accessible to everyone.

In the United States, people at the bottom of the social ladder face a risk of premature death **three times greater** than those at the top.

Social determinants of health. Although access to medical care, quality of treatment, and affordability often dominate the discourse on health care, the main drivers of health disparities are divergent patterns of risk and resilience rooted in the social determinants of health. The World Health Organization defines the social determinants of health as:

> The circumstances in which people are born, grow up, live, work, and age, as well as the systems put in place to deal with illness. These circumstances are in turn shaped by a wider set of forces: economics, social policies, and politics.

To eliminate the preventable differences in disease prevalence and death among different population groups, we must improve the conditions of people's daily lives, accounting for the unequal distribution of resources, power, and money that structure them. Such improvement is less a function of access to MRI machines and surgical interventions than to **safe neighborhoods, grocery stores, healthy school lunches, and employment that offers dignity and agency.** Technology plays little part in the health-care divide.

Social gradient. Around the world, health follows what is known as a social gradient: **life expectancy is tied to social position.** People of higher socioeconomic status, as measured by indicators such as occupational prestige, level of educational attainment, and income, have better health, on the whole, than people of lower socioeconomic status. More affluent people flourish and thrive; less affluent people do not. In the United States, people at the bottom of the social ladder face a risk of premature death three times greater than those at the top.[3]

The social determinants of health and the effects of the social gradient are varied; racial and socioeconomic disparities in health outcomes are significant across a range of conditions. People of lower socioeconomic status as well as African Americans and Native Americans die at a higher rate than others from nearly every cause, making the task of remedying these disparities appear Herculean. Yet only a few conditions—all of them amenable to change—account for the bulk of these disparities. For instance, people with less education die sooner chiefly because they smoke more; African Americans die sooner primarily due to hypertension, HIV, diabetes, and trauma (unintentional injuries and violence).[4]

The Indicator for Health Is Life Expectancy at Birth

The most valuable capability people possess is to be alive. Advancing human development requires, first and foremost, expanding the real opportunities people have to avoid premature death by disease or injury, to enjoy protection from arbitrary denial of life, to live in a healthy environment, to maintain a healthy lifestyle, to receive quality medical care, and to attain the highest possible standard of physical and mental health.

In the American HD Index, life expectancy at birth stands as a proxy for the capability to live a long and healthy life. Life expectancy at birth is the average number of years a baby born today is expected to live if current mortality patterns continue throughout his or her lifetime. The most commonly used gauge of population health the world over, life expectancy at birth represents one-third of the overall American HD Index.

One obstacle to longer lives is complacency about the dangers inherent in habitual behavior. Our focus is instead drawn to highly publicized hazards that, in general, undermine the health of relatively few people. The salmonella outbreak from peanuts (January 2009) and the cookie dough E. coli infections (June 2009) shook people's confidence in the safety of the food supply. Concern about the safety of imports, particularly those from China, is at an all-time high following the 2008 discovery of toxins in toy trains and China's contaminated milk scandal, in which the industrial chemical melamine sickened more than fifty thousand Chinese children. Likewise, the H1N1 flu pandemic and concern about the country's preparedness for a major disease outbreak alarmed Americans. The government has a regulatory responsibility to protect Americans from unsafe products and to contain epidemics, and people themselves should take precautions to keep safe. But these instances of grave and immediate peril are mercifully rare.

The more consequential health threats are hidden in plain sight—in our everyday lives. Fear of dying in a plane crash is more common (and anxiety-producing) than fear of a far more likely possibility: dying behind the wheel of one's own car. The exotic swine flu raised nationwide alarms, but seasonal influenza, which kills about thirty-six thousand Americans every year, proves to be the greater killer. Shark attacks animate our fears, but more people die in backyard pools. The mundane risks that we ignore—eating fast food, drinking soda, talking on a cell phone while driving—may be the most difficult to address.

There are two ways to address illness: prevent it from happening and treat it once it arrives. Both are essential, but the former can save more lives more cheaply and more humanely.

This chapter identifies—by state, congressional district, gender, and racial and ethnic group—life expectancy gaps and the fatal four risk behaviors that are, for most Americans, the "real" causes of death. The chapter then evaluates leading health risks for the population as a whole and for groups with the shortest life expectancies, concluding with recommendations for building greater health resilience.

Part I: What the Health Index Reveals

Historical Trends

Life expectancy at birth in the United States in 2007, the most recent year for which data are available, was 78.6 years, a nearly nine year increase since 1960 and an eight-month improvement over the 2005 life expectancy of 77.9 years.

Improvements in American life expectancy over the last half century are smaller than those in other industrialized countries over the same time period. For instance, in 1987 only seven countries had a higher life expectancy than the United States, and the United States shared eighth place with eight others; today, all of those countries, plus about a dozen more, surpass the United States in projected life span.[5] People in Australia and Italy, for example, countries tied with the United States in 1987, can now expect to live to age 81, two and a half years longer than Americans.

In addition, progress within the United States has been highly uneven. **Life expectancy in several congressional districts in West Virginia, Kentucky, and Mississippi is comparable to American life expectancy as a whole in the late 1970s.** Life spans in these districts are less than 74 years, even as many Americans elsewhere routinely live into their 80s and 90s.

U.S. life expectancy is **78.6** years.

International Comparisons

The United States ranks thirtieth among the world's nations in life expectancy at birth. **Why does one of the world's richest and most technologically advanced nations perform so poorly compared to other countries,** falling below not just affluent nations such as Japan and Switzerland, but also middle-income Costa Rica?

The problem isn't lack of spending; more than 16 percent of U.S. GDP goes to health care.[6] In fact, residents of twenty-nine countries live longer lives, on average, than Americans do, while spending as little as one-eighth as much per capita on their health. U.S. life expectancy at birth—78.6 years—is on par with that of Chile, a country that spends one-tenth of what the United States spends. Combined public and private health-care spending in the United States amounts to more than $7,500 per person annually. For less than half the price, citizens of Japan, San Marino, Iceland, Italy, Australia, Spain, Sweden, and Israel outlive Americans by between four years (Japan) and two years (Israel).[7]

When it comes to the survival of the youngest Americans, the picture is worse: the United States ranks thirty-ninth in the world for infant survival. A baby born today in Slovakia, Poland, Hungary, Croatia, or Cuba has a better chance of living to

Residents of twenty-nine countries **live longer** than Americans do, while spending as little as **one-eighth as much per person** on their health.

Delaware and Cuba have roughly the same life expectancy (about 78 years), but Cuba spends **one-ninth** per person on health.

celebrate his or her first birthday than does a baby born in the United States.

Some have argued that comparing the United States—with its large, diverse population and a federalized system that assigns significant responsibility for health care to the states—to other affluent countries, especially smaller European and Nordic countries, is unfair. This argument rests in part on a view that other affluent countries are extremely homogeneous. But Australia, Canada, and New Zealand are, like the United States, highly diverse nations of immigrants. In fact, the foreign-born population in these three countries, as well as in Luxembourg and Switzerland, today stands near or above 20 percent. In Austria, Germany, the Netherlands, and Sweden, approximately 12 percent of the population is foreign-born, about the same percentage as in the United States, and in Belgium, France, Greece, and Ireland, more than one in ten residents are foreign-born.[8] Immigrants hailing from Africa, Asia, Latin America, and the Caribbean are racial minorities in their new countries. Furthermore, these figures include only the foreign-born themselves; adding to this group those we think of in the United States as "second-generation immigrants"—the children of immigrants—would swell these numbers considerably, revealing far more racial and ethnic diversity than many Americans associate with our peer nations.

The American Human Development Project calculated life expectancy at birth as well as infant death rates for each of the fifty states plus Washington, DC, enabling comparisons between U.S. states as well as between states and foreign countries in terms of expenditures and results. **Which states perform better—or worse—using health dollars to maximize years of human life?** The analysis, conducted in late 2009 and using the most recent data available at that time, yielded the following information:

- Life expectancy in Hawaii (81.5 years) trails that of top-ranked Japan (82.7 years), but Japan spends roughly half of what Hawaii does (see **BOX 1**).
- Delaware and Cuba have nearly the same life expectancy (about 78 years), but Cuba spends one-ninth per person.
- Life expectancy in Alabama (75.2 years) and Louisiana (75.4 years) is comparable to that of Ecuador, yet spending in Ecuador is about one-thirteenth of those U.S. states.
- Albanians live longer than residents of seven U.S. states (Alabama, Arkansas, Kentucky, Louisiana, Mississippi, Oklahoma, and West Virginia) and Washington, DC, but those jurisdictions spend twelve to twenty-one times more than Albania.
- Washington, DC, which has the highest infant mortality rate in the nation (12.1 infant deaths per 1,000 live births), does only marginally better than Belarus (12.4), despite spending thirteen times more on health care.

All of the twenty-nine countries whose people live longer lives than Americans have universal or near-universal coverage for a core set of health services. The ways in which this coverage is delivered differ widely, from employer-based coverage to government-run, single-payer plans. At the time of this report, shortly after Congress's March 2010 passage of the health-care reform law, the United States did not yet have affordable health coverage for all. **There are still 47 million Americans without health insurance of any kind, while 80 million more lack it intermittently over a given two-year period.** Still others have inadequate coverage that renders unaffordable important aspects of health care.[9]

The crazy-quilt structure of the American health-care system is one reason that the United States is an outlier among affluent nations in terms of cost. Hospital care and outpatient care are both significantly more costly in the United States than in peer nations. The contributing factors are numerous:[10]

- **High input costs.** U.S. health care is characterized by higher salaries for medical professionals, pricier drugs and medical devices, and large profits that chiefly benefit private providers in the system.
- **Perverse incentives.** The fee-for-service nature of remuneration leads to more medical tests, visits, and procedures.
- **Administrative and marketing costs.** High costs stem from the complexity of the system, inefficiency, the large number of entities involved, differing state regulations, and, for private insurance companies, the costs associated with sales and marketing.

Gains in life expectancy have come less from advances in medical treatment than from **public health measures** that lower the risk of premature death.

Unlike the cost gap, lower life expectancy in the United States is not entirely a result of the U.S. health-care system. Research shows that the United States compares well with other affluent Organisation for Economic Cooperation and Development (OECD) countries "in terms of screening for cancer, survival rates from cancer, survival rates after heart attacks and strokes, and medication of individuals with high levels of blood pressure or cholesterol."[11] Yet gains in life expectancy have come less from advances in medical treatment than from public health measures that lower the risk of premature death. Readers of the *British Medical Journal* chose "the sanitary revolution"—the introduction of systems for clean water and sewage disposal—as the greatest medical advance since 1840, edging out antibiotics and anesthesia and handily besting the discovery of the structure of DNA. Thanks to warnings on cigarettes, greater regulation, changing social norms, and higher taxes on cigarettes, between 1970 and 2000 the United States experienced the largest drop in the number of cigarettes consumed per adult of any country in the world, leading to sharp declines in deaths due to lung cancer and cardiovascular disease. (From the mid-1930s to the mid-1980s the United States had the highest rate of cigarette consumption in the developed world.[12]) Litigation also played a role; the 1998 Master Settlement Agreement between the United States and seven tobacco companies, which mandated changes in the marketing of tobacco products and a $206 billion settlement to states, was followed by a drop in smoking prevalence from 24.1 percent of the population in 1998 to 20.6 percent in 2008.[13]

Despite this success, life expectancy in the United States remains lower than in other OECD countries, largely, it seems, due to the greater prevalence of chronic disease—higher rates of heart disease, lung cancer, AIDS deaths among the young and middle-aged, infant mortality, and trauma (unintentional death, homicide, and suicide) as well as the extremely poor health of Native Americans and African Americans, which is addressed later in this chapter.

Inequality adversely affects the health of those at the bottom of social hierarchies; the steeper the social ladder, the worse the health effects on those on the bottom rungs.

BOX 1 What Can We Learn from Japan?

Japanese today live the longest lives of any national population in recorded history, 82.7 years on average. At the same time, they spend significantly less on health than most other industrialized countries. Some factors that contribute to these long lives at a bargain price are as follows.

Universal health coverage coupled with tight price regulation. Since 1961, Japan has had a mandatory public health insurance system and centralized price controls for medical treatments and drugs, resulting in affordable health care for all.

A highly educated population. Japan has a well-educated population, and education is linked throughout the world to physical and mental health and longer lives. Better-educated people tend to practice healthier behaviors, are more informed consumers of medical services, and are more likely to adhere to treatment regimes.

Good nutrition. Japan has a low rate of heart disease. The Japanese diet is high in fish (a low-fat, low-calorie protein), low in comparatively fatty livestock products (East Asians consume less than 40 kilograms per year per capita of such products, compared to an average 88 kilograms per year per capita for all industrialized countries[14]), and high in vegetables. Obesity rates are below 5 percent.[15] It is widely accepted that this traditional low-fat, low-cholesterol, vegetable-rich diet lowers the risk of heart disease and other chronic diseases.

Low levels of inequality. Japan has a low Gini index,[16] which indicates comparatively low levels of income inequality within the country. Inequality adversely affects the health of those at the bottom of social hierarchies; the steeper the social ladder, the worse the health effects on those on the bottom rungs.[17]

Analysis by State, Congressional District, Gender, Race, and Ethnicity

COMPARISONS BY STATE

Americans live, on average, 78.6 years. The gap between Hawaii, where longevity is greatest (81.5 years), and Mississippi, where it is shortest (74.8 years), is just shy of seven years, a difference comparable to the gap between Switzerland and Oman or Panama.

The states in which Americans live the longest are Hawaii (81.5), Minnesota (80.9), California (80.4), New York (80.4), Connecticut (80.2), Massachusetts (80.1), North Dakota (80.1), and Utah (80.1) (see **MAP 1**).

The states whose residents can expect the shortest lives are Mississippi (74.8), West Virginia (75.2), Alabama (75.2), Louisiana (75.4), Oklahoma (75.6), Arkansas (76.1), Kentucky (76.2), and Tennessee (76.2). Regionally, the South is home to the bottom eleven states in terms of life span, and only two (Florida and Virginia) that are in the top half.

Top ranking:
1. Hawaii
2. Minnesota
3. California

Bottom ranking:
49. Alabama
50. West Virginia
51. Mississippi

MAP 1 Life Expectancy by State

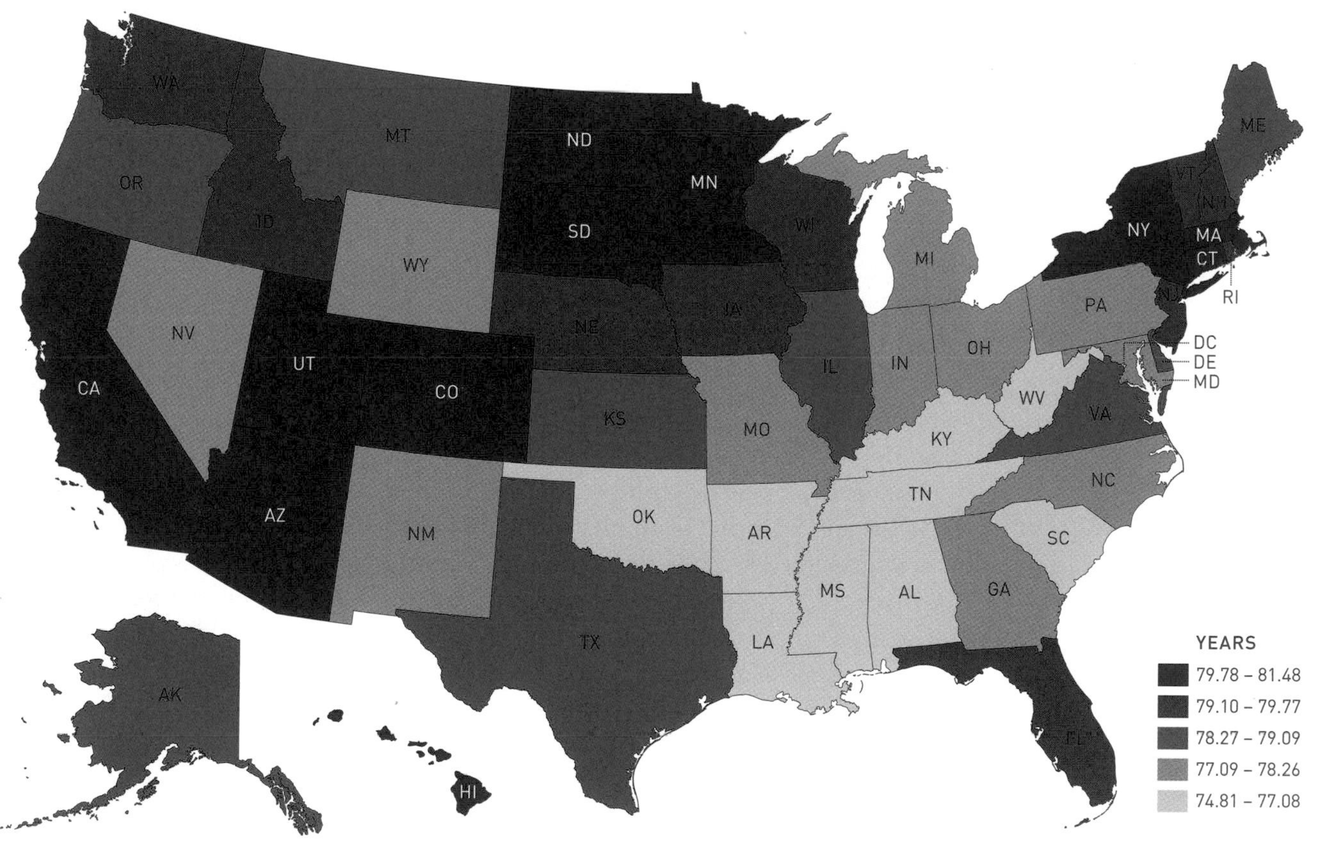

FIGURE 1 How Do They Kill Us? Let Us Count the Ways.

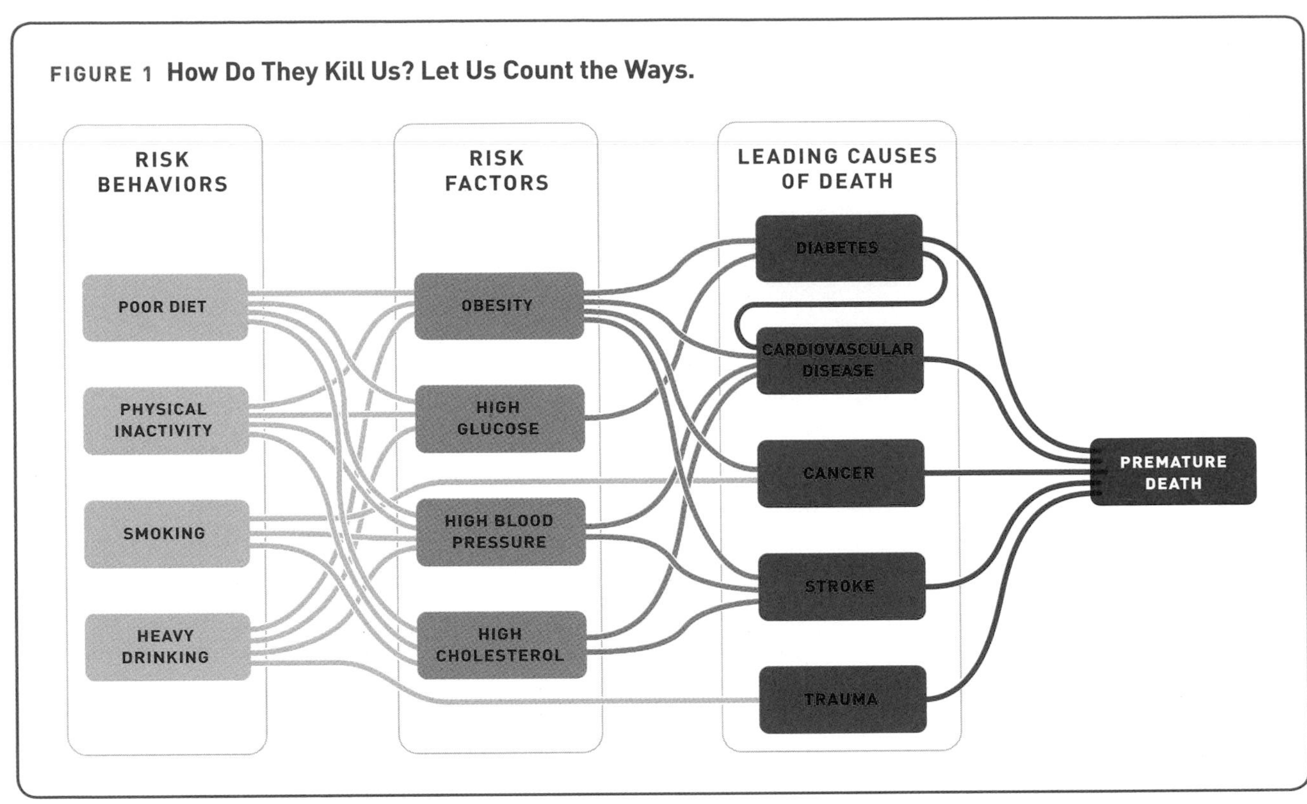

What accounts for the differences in life expectancy among U.S. states? The answer is largely different rates of chronic disease, the leading killer of Americans. Chronic diseases, including heart disease and stroke, cancer, and diabetes, kill seven in ten Americans and are responsible for 75 percent of health-care costs.[18]

However, these incurable, costly, and debilitating conditions are largely preventable. In fact, four modifiable risk factors are responsible for the lion's share of premature death and disability caused by chronic disease: smoking, unhealthy diet, physical inactivity, and excessive drinking.[19] These "fatal four" risk behaviors tend to cluster, with chronic diseases typically stemming from multiple risk factors that overlap[20] (see **FIGURE 1**).

Not everyone who dies from a chronic disease has engaged in high-risk behavior. For example, some 10 percent of men and 20 percent of women with lung cancer never smoked.[21] Diabetes risk factors include not just obesity and sedentary lifestyles but also genetics and family history. Exposure to secondhand smoke can cause lung cancer, coronary heart disease, and stroke.[22] People who "do everything right" can still die prematurely from chronic disease; no magic formula guarantees longevity, but much can be done to reduce risk and improve the odds. Tackling the fatal four through policy interventions, public health campaigns, and supportive neighborhood, school, and work environments would yield longer, healthier lives for millions of Americans and lower health costs for the nation as a whole.

BOX 2 Health: More than a Matter of Personal Choice

Personal responsibility for health is a popular idea that makes intuitive sense. It rests on the notion that risk behaviors are freely chosen, the result of personal choice. Smoking, drinking, unhealthy diet, and lack of exercise—the fatal four behavioral risks—are by this light entirely the result of the exercise of free will. One can "just do it" ("it" being exercise) or "just say no" (to smoking, drinking, and eating junk food).

But reality is more complicated. **The environments in which people are raised and live their lives shape the decisions—good and bad alike—that people make about their health.** These environments, in turn, result from the distribution of power, money, and knowledge in society; political processes; policies on education, health care, home ownership, and public safety; and the regulatory system.[23] Encouraging people to take greater personal responsibility for their health is a key element of reducing risk behaviors, but health strategies built around personal responsibility alone are proven recipes for failure.

How "voluntary" is cigarette smoking, for example, a practice of one in five American adults and the country's leading cause of preventable mortality and morbidity? Nine of ten smokers began to smoke during adolescence. Research shows that the earlier smoking starts, the more likely the smoker is to become addicted to nicotine.[24] During adolescence, susceptibility to peer, role model, and advertising influences is high, and decision making, risk assessment, and impulse control are not fully developed. Society's understanding that young teens do not have the capacity to make major life decisions is reflected in laws that regulate the age at which a person can legally enter into a binding contract, leave school, work full-time, get married, or consent to sex. The chemically addictive nature of nicotine also challenges the notion that cigarette smoking is a freely chosen behavior in adults; once the habit takes hold, abandoning it is extremely difficult. Children exposed to the tobacco smoke of their parents are clearly not acting voluntarily,[25] yet these passive smokers nonetheless face elevated risk of heart and lung diseases while observing a powerful role model for smoking. In 2007 more than half of all smokers ages 18 to 24 and nearly four in ten smokers ages 25 to 64 tried—and failed—to quit smoking at least once over the course of the year.[26]

Why have smoking rates declined so sharply, down from four in ten adults in 1965 to two in ten adults today?[27] Personal agency and free choice are surely part of the answer. But after decades of steady declines, cigarette use remained flat from 2004 to 2006. According to the Office on Smoking and Health of the Centers for Disease Control, funding for comprehensive state programs for tobacco control and prevention decreased by 20 percent from 2002 to 2006, while "tobacco-industry marketing expenditures nearly doubled from 1998 ($6.7 billion) to 2005 ($13.1 billion)." The increased marketing was targeted at youth and at Americans with low incomes and educational levels, who smoke in disproportionately high numbers. Significantly, eight of ten tobacco-industry marketing dollars went to discounting, including coupons or two-for-one offers, which reduced the unit price of tobacco. Tax policies that increase the cost of cigarettes have accelerated declines in smoking and also proved useful in deterring youth from smoking in the first place.[28]

Seven in ten obese patients report being stigmatized even by their doctors.

A high degree of stigma is attached to many of these risk factors, particularly to poor diet, physical inactivity, and their common consequence, obesity. This stigma is both unkind and unproductive; studies have found that stigma and the shame, stress, and social isolation it spurs can actually intensify risk behaviors.[29] At the root of the stigma is the prevailing view that health risk behaviors are entirely matters of personal choice, and that bad choices represent an individual moral failure[30] (see **BOX 2**). With drinking and, to a lesser degree, smoking, this stigma is fading somewhat, thanks to the dissemination—through public health campaigns, the willingness of people suffering from addiction disorders to share their experiences, and the rise of groups like Alcoholics Anonymous and other twelve-steps programs—of information on the chemically addictive nature of nicotine and alcohol. Not so with obesity—even though most Americans are overweight themselves. Though jokes rooted in racial and ethnic stereotypes are increasingly taboo, it's open season on the obese, who are stereotyped as lazy, lacking in self-control, and weak-willed. Remarkably, seven in ten obese patients report being stigmatized even by their doctors.[31] Yet evidence increasingly suggests that Americans' neighborhood environments and the structure of our everyday lives play a significant role in the obesity epidemic.

Our analysis shows that state rates of diabetes, obesity, smoking, and physical activity are strongly correlated with state scores on the health index. Correlations also exist between state life expectancy and rates of health insurance coverage and Medicaid eligibility limits for parents, a finding consistent with decades of research indicating that early detection and effective disease management, which health insurance makes more likely, reduce premature death from chronic disease.

Rates of diabetes, smoking, and uninsurance all remain statistically significant predictors of life expectancy at the state level even when controlling for variations in personal earnings, health expenditures, and the distribution of the population between rural and urban areas. Rates of smoking, diabetes, and uninsurance all tend to be higher in states with lower life expectancies and lower in states with higher life expectancies.

Of these three variables, diabetes rates had the largest effect, followed by rates of smoking and uninsurance. These three factors together account for two-thirds of the variation in life expectancy among U.S. states, according to our analysis.

Fairly modest improvements in the health profile of a state population are associated with impressive gains in life expectancy. For instance, a 10 percent reduction in diabetes in a state is associated with six additional years of life; a 10 percent reduction in smoking with one-and-one-third additional years of life; a 10 percent increase in the percentage of people covered by health insurance with ten additional months of life.[32]

BOX 3 A Tale of Two States: Life Expectancy in Minnesota and Mississippi.

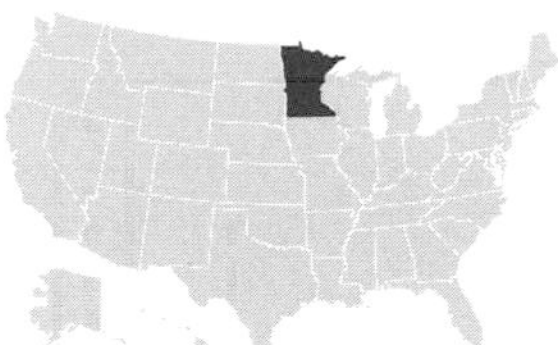

Minnesota has the second-highest life expectancy in the United States (80.9 years), a life span comparable to that found in France, Sweden, and Spain. Evidence suggests that many factors contribute to the longevity of Minnesotans. For instance, 91.5 percent of Minnesotans have health insurance, a higher percentage than in any other state but Hawaii and Massachusetts. Minnesotans also smoke less than the national average. Spending in Minnesota on preventative public health measures (as opposed to medical treatments), such as childhood immunization, food safety, and cancer screening clinics, is well above the national average. Minnesota, along with Utah, has the lowest rate of obese and overweight children. In Minnesota, over 90 percent of adults have at least a high school degree; the state ranks third in the proportion of adults who have completed high school.

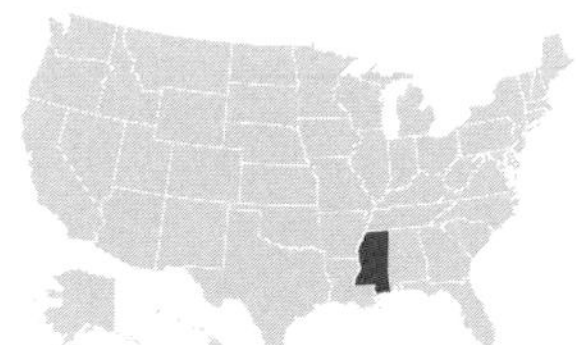

Mississippi has the nation's lowest life expectancy (74.8 years). People in Mississippi live shorter lives than people in Mexico, where health expenditure per capita is one-sixth the amount. Nearly one in five Mississippians lack health insurance, a higher percentage than all but seven other states. Mississippi is second only to West Virginia in diabetes diagnoses, and the prevalence of adult obesity in the state, where one-third of adults are obese, is 25 percent higher than the national average and the greatest of any state.[35] The state also has the highest rate of childhood obesity; 44 percent of children ages 10 to 17 are obese or overweight.[36] Mississippians are also less likely to exercise regularly than the residents of any other states except Tennessee and Louisiana. Finally, Mississippi has, after Texas, the highest rate of adults over the age of 25 who did not complete high school. Education and good health are strongly correlated, and parents with more education tend to be more effective in supporting healthy outcomes for their children.

An analysis of state life expectancy and total state expenditures on health (combining public and private spending) revealed no relationship between higher health spending and better health outcomes in the United States.[33] (This is not the case with education, as discussed on page 141.) Small increases in health-care expenditures are associated with large changes in life expectancy in very poor countries, since roughly a third of deaths in such places are among children who die for lack of low-cost interventions like immunizations and safe water; water-related diseases alone account for 80 percent of the burden of disease in developing countries.[34] In affluent countries, the relationship between spending and outcomes evaporates. In West Virginia, life expectancy is about 75 years, and the combined public and private expenditures per person on health care exceed $6,000 per year; in Utah and California, life expectancy tops 80 years, but spending is much less—$4,100 and $4,800, respectively, in part due to lower rates of smoking and diabetes. The examples of Minnesota and Mississippi, detailed in **BOX 3**, highlight some of the factors that influence health in the United States, where chronic diseases have overtaken communicable diseases as the leading causes of death.

COMPARISONS BY CONGRESSIONAL DISTRICT

Variation in life expectancy by congressional district is extremely large (see **MAP 2**). Five congressional districts register life expectancies of at least 82.9 years, a full decade longer than the life expectancy found in the lowest congressional district, West Virginia's Third District, at 72.9 years.

The districts in which Americans are living the longest are two suburbs of Washington, DC, Virginia's Eighth and Maryland's Eighth; residents of these areas live more than 83 years, on average. All of the next twenty-one districts save two are in either in the San Francisco metro area or in the New York City metro area, with life expectancies around 82 years (see **TABLE 1**).

Americans are living the shortest lives in parts of West Virginia, Kentucky, Mississippi, Alabama, Oklahoma, and Pennsylvania—specifically, in several predominantly African American neighborhoods of Philadelphia. The gap between the overall HD Index score and the life expectancy score stands out in

TABLE 1 Congressional Districts with the Longest and Shortest Life Spans

CONGRESSIONAL DISTRICT	DESCRIPTION	AMERICAN HD INDEX	LIFE EXPECTANCY
Longest Life Span			
CD 8, Virginia	Northern Virginia suburbs of DC	8.30	83.7
CD 8, Maryland	Maryland suburbs of DC	7.57	83.2
CD 15, California	Silicon Valley	7.60	83.1
CD 16, California	Santa Clara County, San Jose County	6.27	83.1
CD 6, New York	Southeastern Queens including Jamaica and Far Rockaway	5.90	82.9
CD 12, California	Portions of San Francisco and Northeastern San Mateo counties	7.44	82.9
CD 14, California	Portions of San Mateo, Santa Cruz, and Santa Clara counties	8.11	82.9
CD 14, New York	Manhattan's East Side, Astoria, and western Queens	8.79	82.8
CD 5, New York	Northeastern Queens, suburban Long Island	6.30	82.7
CD 15, New York	Upper Manhattan and parts of the Bronx	5.87	82.6
CD 8, California	Most of San Francisco	7.47	82.6
CD 9, New York	Portions of Queens and Brooklyn	6.57	82.4
Shortest Life Span			
CD 8, Tennessee	Northwestern Tennessee—Jackson, Millington, Union City	3.69	75.0
CD 1, Arkansas	Northeast Arkansas—Jonesboro, Newport, Wynne	3.39	74.8
CD 7, Louisiana	Heel of Louisiana—Sulphur, Lake Charles, Lafayette, Crowley	3.87	74.8
CD 7, Alabama	West Central Alabama—Demopolis, Selma, Tuscaloosa	3.46	74.7
CD 3, Alabama	Eastern Alabama—Piedmont, Anniston, Auburn, Tuskegee	3.61	74.7
CD 2, Georgia	Southwest Georgia—Americus, Albany, Cairo	3.55	74.6
CD 1, Pennsylvania	Central and South Philadelphia, parts of Delaware County	3.56	74.5
CD 2, Oklahoma	Eastern Oklahoma, abutting Arkansas	3.33	74.5
CD 2, Pennsylvania	West Philadelphia, North Philadelphia, Northwest Philadelphia	4.81	74.4
CD 4, Alabama	Northern Alabama—Decatur, Gadsden	3.37	74.3
CD 2, Mississippi	Mississippi Delta—Clarksdale, Greenville	3.34	73.6
CD 5, Kentucky	Eastern Kentucky—Corbin, Pikeville, Somerset	2.82	73.6
CD 3, West Virginia	Southern West Virginia—Huntington, Williamson, Beckley	3.16	72.9

MAP 2 Life Expectancy by Congressional District

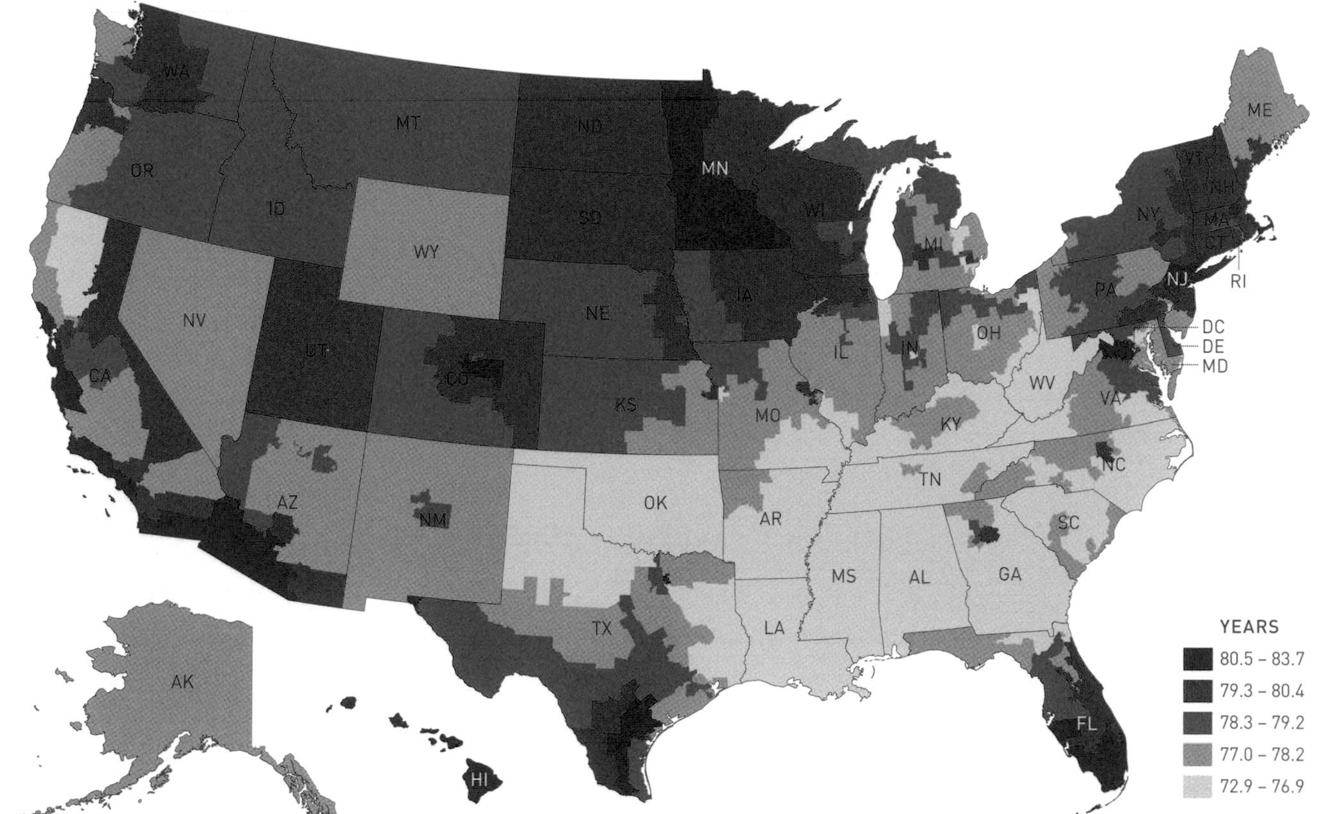

Pennsylvania's Second District, inner-city Philadelphia; residents in this district are doing far better in terms of income and education than they are in health. Philadelphia has one of the highest homicide rates in the country, a topic to which we return later in this chapter. The other congressional districts in this group have high rates of diabetes and obesity.

COMPARISONS BY GENDER

Globally, female life expectancy is about four and a half years higher than male life expectancy.[37] More baby boys are born than baby girls, but girls and women have a survival advantage at every age. This global phenomenon was long thought to be rooted in biological or genetic differences between females and males. **Today, however, a consensus is emerging that some of the difference is rooted in the social determinants of health—in this case, what it means to behave as a man or a woman in a given society.** The life expectancy gap between women and men in Russia widened after the collapse of the Soviet Union, for instance, as male risk behaviors, particularly risky drinking, spiked in a precipitously transformed economic system. Yet during the same period (1990–2005), the gap between the sexes narrowed in most European countries, as increasing proportions of men abandoned harmful practices, especially smoking. In OECD countries, the purported female biological or genetic advantage combines with men's and women's differing patterns of health-risk behaviors, preventive health practices, and use of health-care services to yield a six-year life expectancy gap in favor of women.[38]

In the United States, the life-span gap between women and men is five years—slightly smaller than the OECD average. Women report more physical illness and higher levels of depression than men do,[39] but their life expectancy is nonetheless better. The gap widens or shrinks among different population groups. The gender gap in life expectancy is largest among African Americans (women outlive men by nearly 7 years), followed by Native Americans (6 years) and Latinos (5.7 years). The smallest gender gaps are found in Asian Americans (4.9 years) and in whites (5 years).

COMPARISONS BY RACE AND ETHNICITY

With the explosion of genetic research commanding much attention, the notion of developing specific medicines targeted to the genetic makeup of specific racial groups is much in the news. However, a biological basis of race is an idea with scant scientific support, and greater genetic diversity is apparent within races than between them.[40] In addition, the National Human Genomic Research Institute indicates that hereditary factors account for a very small proportion of disease, including endemic conditions like diabetes, high blood pressure, and breast cancer.[41] Little evidence supports the view that racial groupings determined by genetic markers have "clinical or epidemiologic utility" for medical research and practice.[42] **Although races are not genetically distinct in ways that make these categories useful to medical researchers, they are socially distinct in numerous ways that influence health outcomes and longevity.**

Thirteen years of life span, on average, separate the racial groups with the shortest and longest lives in the United States.

Differences at the National Level

Thirteen years of life span, on average, separate the racial groups with the shortest and longest lives in the United States (see **FIGURE 2**). In addition, significant differences exist in the leading causes of death between these groups, as can be seen in **TABLE 2**. Obviously, great variation also exists within groups as well as between them.

In the nation as a whole, Asian Americans live the longest lives (87.3 years), with life expectancies outstripping those of Japan, the top-ranked country in the world, by an impressive 5-year margin. Asian American women live to 89.7, Asian American men to 84.6. Cancer, heart disease, and stroke are the three leading causes of death for this population. Asian Americans have the lowest smoking rates of all ethnic groups, 9.6 percent for all adults and under 5 percent for

FIGURE 2 Life Expectancy by Racial and Ethnic Group

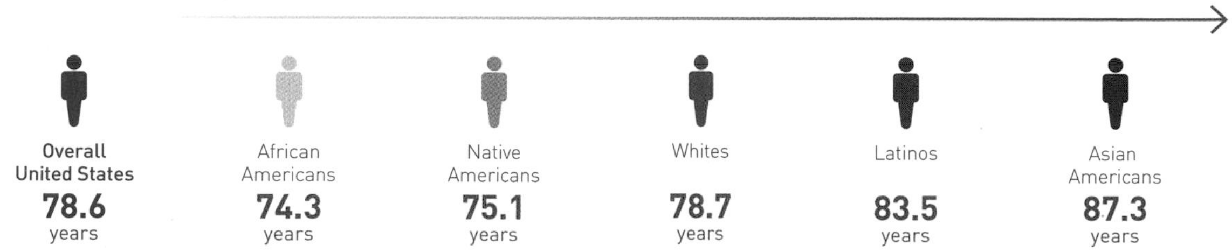

Overall United States	African Americans	Native Americans	Whites	Latinos	Asian Americans
78.6 years	74.3 years	75.1 years	78.7 years	83.5 years	87.3 years

TABLE 2 Leading Causes of Death in the United States, 2006

	OVERALL UNITED STATES	AFRICAN AMERICANS	NATIVE AMERICANS	WHITES	LATINOS	ASIAN AMERICANS
1	**Heart disease**	Heart disease	Heart disease	Heart disease	Heart disease	Cancer
2	**Cancer**	Cancer	Cancer	Cancer	Cancer	Heart disease
3	**Stroke**	Stroke	Unintentional injury	Chronic lower respiratory disease	Unintentional injury	Stroke
4	**Chronic lower respiratory disease**	Unintentional injury	Diabetes	Stroke	Stroke	Unintentional injury
5	**Unintentional injury**	Diabetes	Liver disease	Unintentional injury	Diabetes	Diabetes
6	**Diabetes**	Homicide	Stroke	Alzheimer's disease	Liver disease	Influenza and pneumonia
7	**Alzheimer's disease**	Kidney disease	Chronic lower respiratory disease	Diabetes	Homicide	Chronic lower respiratory disease
8	**Influenza and pneumonia**	Chronic lower respiratory disease	Suicide	Influenza and pneumonia	Chronic lower respiratory disease	Kidney disease
9	**Kidney disease**	HIV	Kidney disease	Kidney disease	Influenza and pneumonia	Suicide
10	**Septicemia**	Septicemia	Influenza and pneumonia	Suicide	*Perinatal period	Alzheimer's disease
11	**Suicide**	Influenza and pneumonia	Homicide	Septicemia	Kidney disease	Hypertension
12	**Liver disease**	*Perinatal period	Septicemia	Liver disease	Alzheimer's disease	Septicemia
13	**Hypertension**	Hypertension	Alzheimer's disease	Parkinson's disease	Suicide	*Perinatal period
14	**Parkinson's disease**	Alzheimer's disease	*Perinatal period	Hypertension	Congenital anomalies	Homicide
15	**Homicide**	Liver disease	Congenital anomalies	Pneumonitis	Septicemia	Liver disease

*Cause of death arising during the perinatal period refers to stillbirths at or beyond 28 weeks' gestation and deaths in the first week of life.
Source: Centers for Disease Control and Prevention, National Center for Injury Prevention and Control, WISQARS Leading Causes of Death Reports, 1999–2006.

BOX 4 The Latino Epidemiological Paradox

Educational attainment, which has a strong positive correlation with life expectancy worldwide, is commonly cited as a chief reason for the exceptionally long lives of Asian Americans. Yet Latinos, who have the lowest levels of educational attainment of any racial or ethnic group in the United States, outlive whites and African Americans, both of whom have more education, by four and eight years, respectively. In addition, Latinos are disproportionately uninsured, and insurance coverage and longevity are linked for other racial/ethnic groups. Latinos face barriers of language, culture, and legal status (immigration) in accessing appropriate medical care; have high rates of poverty; and are concentrated in jobs with poor working conditions and disproportionately high physical risks.

Why, then, do Latinos fare so well on the health index? And why is infant mortality, a highly sensitive indicator of societal health conditions, lower among Latinos than among whites, African Americans, and Native Americans?[44] Two theories attempt to explain the conundrum as a product of measurement error: the "healthy migrant" hypothesis and the "salmon bias" hypothesis.[45] The healthy migrant hypothesis holds that, typically, only people with better-than-average health would contemplate emigration, due to its many risks and uncertainties. Thus, according to this theory, the Latino population is disproportionately healthy because it comprises a high proportion of immigrants. The salmon bias hypothesis posits that Latino immigrants disproportionately return to their countries of origin when they are ill, preferring to die "at home" than in the United States; thus these deaths are not counted in U.S. mortality statistics.

Yet studies show that neither of these theories adequately accounts for the Latino life expectancy advantage.

If the paradox is "real" rather than a measurement fluke, what accounts for it? The prevalence of risk behaviors is one possible explanation. Though Latinos have fewer medical screenings like Pap tests, probably due to their lower rates of insurance coverage, Latinos drink less than non-Hispanic whites and have lower smoking rates (about 15 percent for all Latino adults compared to the national average of 19.8 percent, and 10 percent for women[46]). Smoking and drinking are leading causes of heart disease, stroke, and cancer. Research on the infant mortality advantage among Latinos holds that babies born to Latina mothers are less likely to be of low birth weight and less likely to die before age 1 because aspects of Latino culture, such as social support, family cohesion, and diet, support healthy outcomes for mothers and infants.[47]

More research is needed to determine how these and other protective cultural factors might serve to safeguard adult health. But the fact that Latino health outcomes worsen with acculturation in the United States gives credence to cultural explanations. The majority of the Latino paradox research focuses on more recent immigrants, and more research is needed on the outcomes of second- and third-generation Latinos as well as on different subgroups (e.g., Cuban Americans, Mexican Americans, etc.) to fully understand the impact of cultural assimilation, education, and health.

Despite relatively good health among Latinos, negative health disparities do exist, including a higher rate of death due to unintentional injury, increasing cases of diabetes, and an HIV infection rate for Latina women that is five times higher than the rate for white women.[48]

women.[43] They also have the lowest rates of obesity and the highest levels of educational attainment.

Asian Americans are about four years ahead of Latinos, number two in the rankings with a life expectancy at birth of 83.5 years. Latino women live to 86.3, men to 80.6. Latinos in the United States live longer, on average, than Swiss, Spaniards, and Swedes, who have very high life expectancy. The long life spans of Latinos, who face many socioeconomic challenges in the United States, is a puzzle known in public health circles as the Latino Epidemiological Paradox (see **BOX 4**). For Latinos, heart disease, cancer, and unintentional injuries are the three leading causes of death.

Whites have a life expectancy of 78.7 years, about the U.S. average. White women live, on average, 81.2 years; white men, 76.2 years. Heart disease, cancer, and chronic respiratory disease are the leading killers of white Americans. Whites smoke at slightly higher rates—about 21.4 percent—than the national average.

Native Americans (75.1 years) and African Americans (74.3 years) live the shortest lives; in fact, their life expectancies are comparable to those found in the country as a whole more than a quarter century ago, or in Vietnam, Syria, and Tunisia today. Among Native Americans, women can expect to live 78.1 years; men, 72.1 years. The leading causes of death among Native Americans are heart disease, cancer, and unintentional injuries.

Heart disease, cancer, and stroke are the leading causes of death for African Americans. The largest gender gap, nearly 7 years, is found among African Americans; women live, on average, 77.6 years; men, 70.7 years.

Life Expectancy

92.4
Years
Asian Americans—Connecticut

66
Years
Native Americans—South Dakota

An astonishing **26 years** separates Asian Americans living in Connecticut from Native Americans in South Dakota.

FIGURE 3 **Native American Life Expectancy by State**

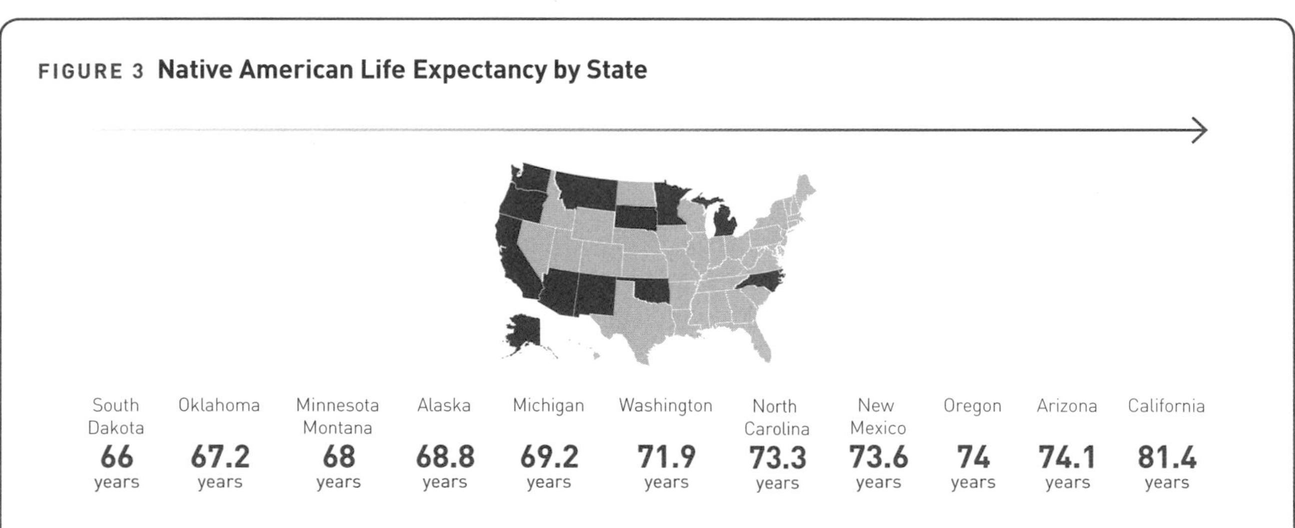

Differences between Racial and Ethnic Groups State-by-State

A race-by-state analysis of the American HD Index shows that the 13-year gap between the life span extremes at the national level doubles for racial and ethnic groups in the best- and worst-performing states. An astonishing 26 years separates Asian Americans living in Connecticut, whose life expectancy is 92.4 years, from Native Americans in South Dakota, who live, on average, only 66 years—less than people in Guyana (66.5), Mongolia (66.2), or Pakistan (66.2).[49] To put this figure in historical perspective, **Native Americans in South Dakota have life spans equivalent to that of the average American in the mid-1940s** (see **FIGURE 3**).[50]

Among the thirty-one states with **Asian American** populations large enough to be considered in this analysis,[51] life spans for these residents were, on average, over 80 years. Asian Americans live the longest lives in Connecticut, Arizona, New Jersey, Colorado, Massachusetts, Illinois, and New York—over 90 years in each. The states in which Asian Americans are living the shortest lives are Tennessee, Louisiana, Oklahoma, and Hawaii (which topped the state rankings for all racial and ethnic groups, but is ranked last for Asian Americans and Latinos).

In all but three states—Alabama, Mississippi, and Hawaii—**Latinos** live longer than the national average. They have the longest lives in a geographically diverse group of states—Nevada, Illinois, Massachusetts, and New Jersey—86 years or more.

Whites live the longest lives, 80.4 years or more, in Washington, DC, Minnesota, South Dakota, North Dakota, Connecticut, and New York. Two of these jurisdictions are home to the lowest life expectancies for other groups: South Dakota is last for Native Americans, and Washington, DC, is last for African Americans (see **BOX 5**). The states at the bottom for whites, with life expectancy below 77 years, are Tennessee, Louisiana, Arkansas, Nevada, Kentucky, Mississippi, Alabama, Oklahoma, and West Virginia. Interestingly, Nevada is among the best states for Latinos; Latinos in Nevada live an average of 13 years more than whites in Nevada.

Only twelve states have populations of **Native Americans** of sufficient size to be included in this analysis; a gulf of 15 years separates life spans in the top and bottom states. Native Americans in five states have life expectancies below 70; they are living shorter lives than people in Azerbaijan or Guatemala.

Life expectancy for **African Americans** is shorter than the national average in every state except Rhode Island and New York. The top states for African Americans, with life spans ranging from 77.3 years to 78.8 years, are Rhode Island, New York, Massachusetts, Oregon, Colorado, Arizona, and Connecticut. The bottom states, with life expectancies less than 72.3 years, are Arkansas, Mississippi, Louisiana, West Virginia, and Washington, DC.

BOX 5 Washington, DC—Best for Whites, Worst for African Americans

A white baby born today in the nation's capital can expect to live 83.1 years, 4 years more than the national average. An African American baby born today in the same city has a life expectancy of 71 years, a dozen years less and about the same as that of the average American baby in the early 1970s.

This yawning gap is evidence of starkly segregated worlds in Washington, DC, where whites experience some of the highest well-being levels in the nation while African Americans live, on average, drastically shorter lives of constrained opportunity. Residential segregation by income, educational attainment, and race in Washington, DC, has created distinct sets of social health determinants for the two groups.

Health disparities are evident from the start. African American infant mortality is triple the white rate (see **TABLE 3**). African Americans in Washington,DC die from homicide at more than forty times the rate of whites.

But African Americans die earlier from all major causes of death, and many of those causes reflect conditions of their daily lives. African Americans are more than three times more likely to be unemployed; those who are employed earn half of what whites earn and are half as likely to be in higher-status managerial or professional occupations. The African American poverty rate is nearly four times higher than the white rate. Whites are half as likely to lack health insurance, three times as likely to walk to work, four times as likely to have a college degree, and five times as likely to have a graduate or professional degree.

The disparity in life chances—including the chance to remain alive—is stark.

TABLE 3 Selected Social Determinants of Health

	AFRICAN AMERICANS	WHITES
Median personal earnings (2009 dollars)	$30,911	$60,232
Poverty rate (all ages)	23.6%	8.1%
Adult population with at least a high school degree or equivalent	80.8%	98.9%
Adult population with at least a bachelor's degree	21.6%	81.6%
Adult population with an advanced degree	9.5%	51.4%
Walked to work	5.3%	18.1%
Employment in management, professional, and related occupations[i]	35.7%	74.1%
Homicide rate[ii]	43.1 per 100,000	too small to report
Infant mortality rate[iii]	16.5 per 100,000	5.4 per 100,000
Rate of uninsured non-elderly	10.2%	5.2%
Percentage of the adult population either overweight or obese	66.3%	38.2%
Adult smoking rate (every day or some days)	22.3%	9.8%
Adult and adolescent AIDS case rate[iv]	263.8 per 100,000	63.4 per 100,000

Source: First seven rows, ACS, 2008 1-Year Estimates. [ii] Homicide: CDC Compressed Mortality File, 2006. Infant mortality: CDC Compressed Mortality File, 2004–6. Last four rows are from KFF State Health Facts: Rate of uninsured non-elderly—Urban Institute and Kaiser Commission on Medicaid and the Uninsured, estimates based on the Census Bureau's March 2008 and 2009 Current Population Survey (CPS: Annual Social and Economic Supplements). Adult obesity/overweight rate—Centers for Disease Control and Prevention, Behavioral Risk Factor Surveillance System Survey Data, 2008, unpublished data. Adult smoking rate—Centers for Disease Control and Prevention, Behavioral Risk Factor Surveillance System Survey Data (BRFSS), 2008, unpublished data. AIDS case rate by race/ethnicity—Centers for Disease Control and Prevention, Division of HIV/AIDS Prevention-Surveillance and Epidemiology, Special Data Request, February 2009.

What Fuels These Gaps?

Different factors contribute to the strikingly different life expectancy gaps between states, congressional districts, and racial and ethnic groups. Among them:

- **Policy and investment at the state level.** Key social determinants of health include public education, the public health infrastructure, health insurance coverage, social services, income supports like state earned income tax credits, and housing.

- **The prevalence of risk behaviors within different geographic, racial, and ethnic population groups.** Risk factors tend to cluster and have cumulative effects across life spans.

Risk factors for premature death tend to cluster and have cumulative effects across life spans.

- **Residential segregation.** Neighborhood residential segregation by race/ethnicity and by income is widespread. Low-income neighborhoods have fewer green spaces, sidewalks, playgrounds, and full-service grocery stores, and more crime, liquor stores, polluting industries, and housing with toxic dangers like lead paint. High-income neighborhoods have more safe and accessible public spaces for exercise and play, twice as many supermarkets per capita,[52] and fewer environmental impediments to healthful living. In addition, high-income residents have the resources to join a gym and pay for high-quality nutrition rather than junk calories.

- **Cultural norms that foster resilience.** Among Latinos, protective cultural factors appear to influence their comparatively low incidence of low-birth-weight babies and low rates of infant mortality. In addition, strong social support and family cohesion may also increase life expectancy. These protective factors could mitigate known health risks, such as low rates of health insurance coverage. Among Asian Americans, high levels of investment in education pay dividends in the form of longer lives as well as higher salaries, as do healthier diets and fewer risk behaviors.

- **The legacy of discrimination and disadvantage.** African Americans and Native Americans have been historically disadvantaged throughout American history. The short lives of Native Americans in South Dakota and Montana, and African Americans in Arkansas, Mississippi, and Louisiana, are rooted in contemporary social determinants of health, which in turn stem at least in part from a legacy of state and federal policies that severed societal and family bonds; suppressed linguistic, spiritual, and cultural freedom; and stripped communities of their resources and rights.

- **Differences within groups.** Long-settled Asian American communities tend to fare considerably better than newly arrived Asian American immigrant communities; this is reflected in the life expectancy gap between Asian Americans in New Jersey and Louisiana. The latter are principally Vietnamese Americans whose incomes and educational attainment are also lower than Asian Americans in New Jersey. Such disparities are common within racial groupings.

Health outcomes are in part dependent on the health risks we face.

Health outcomes are in part dependent on the health risks we face. What are the risks to which different groups of Americans are disproportionately exposed? What protective factors buffer other groups from health threats and bolster their resilience? We turn to these questions in the next section.

A Long and Healthy Life

Dashboard of Risks

The three indicators presented here—**low birth weight**, **diabetes**, and **trauma**—track risk factors that may slow or reverse human development progress and which pose direct threats to people's capability to live a long and healthy life.

Low-birth-weight infants (%), 2004–06[1]

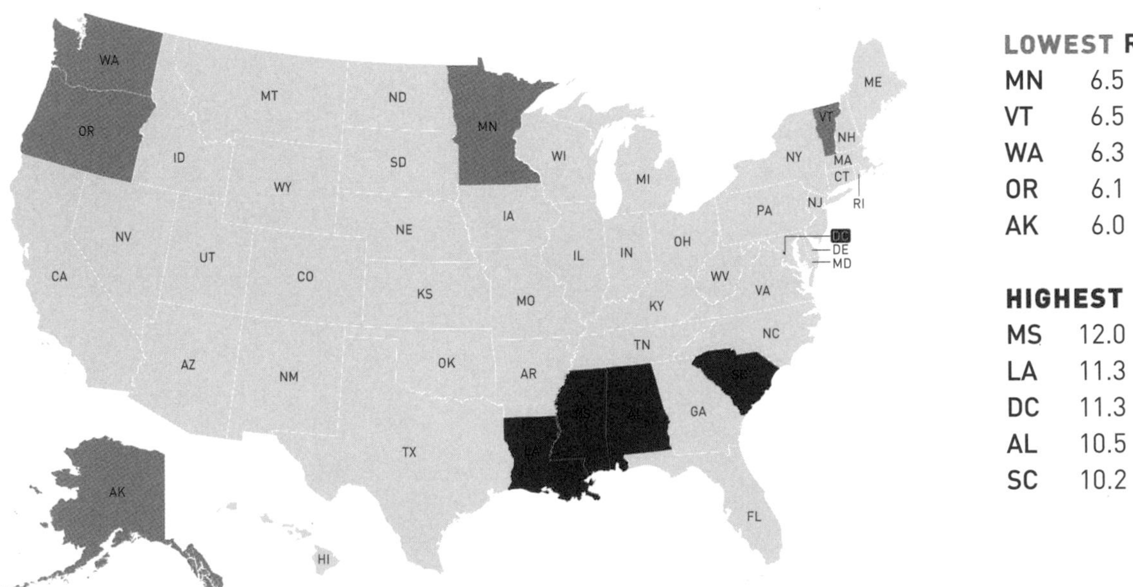

LOWEST RISK

MN	6.5
VT	6.5
WA	6.3
OR	6.1
AK	6.0

HIGHEST RISK

MS	12.0
LA	11.3
DC	11.3
AL	10.5
SC	10.2

[1] Centers for Disease Control and Prevention, Births: Preliminary Data for 2007, 2009. Tables 8 and 13. Percent of live births weighing less than 2,500 grams, or 5.5 pounds.

People age 18 and older with diabetes (%), 2008[2]

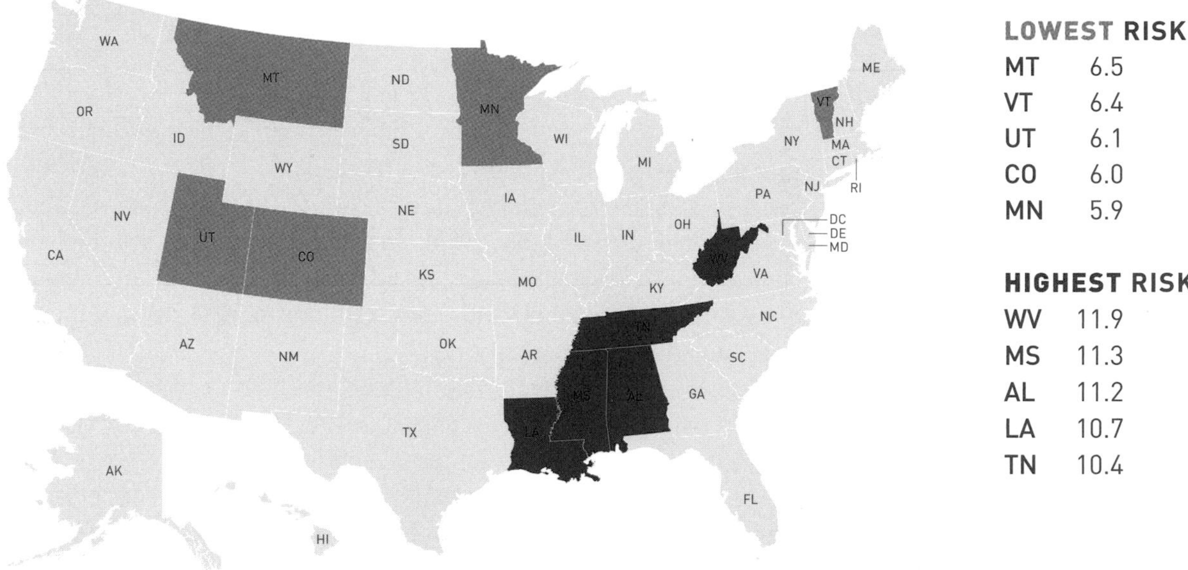

LOWEST RISK

MT	6.5
VT	6.4
UT	6.1
CO	6.0
MN	5.9

HIGHEST RISK

WV	11.9
MS	11.3
AL	11.2
LA	10.7
TN	10.4

Death rate due to trauma—unintentional injury, homicide, and suicide (per 100,000)[3]

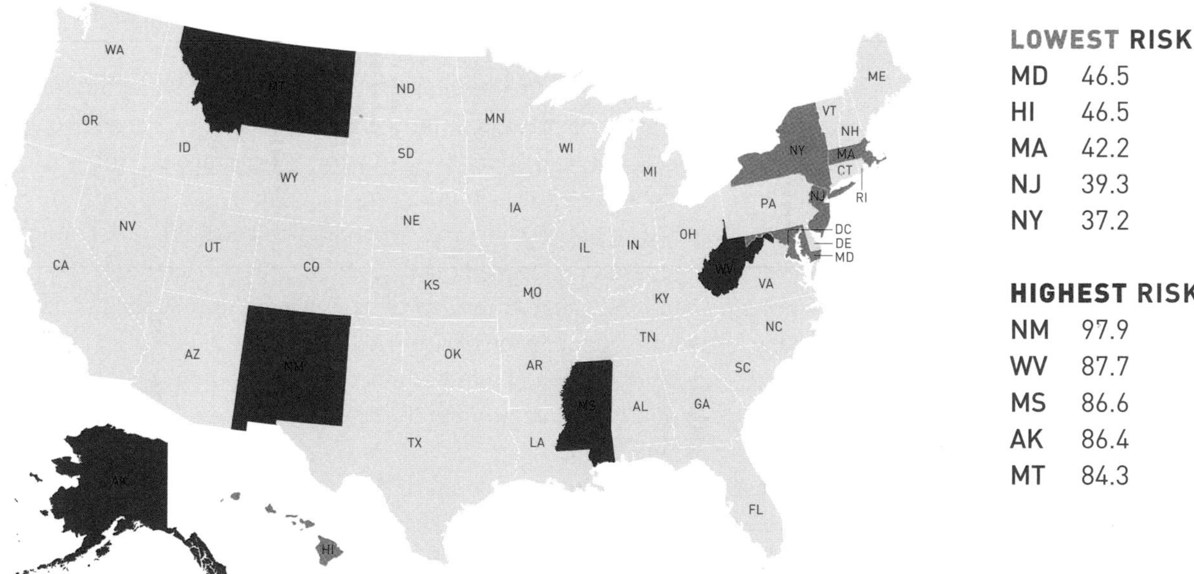

LOWEST RISK

MD	46.5
HI	46.5
MA	42.2
NJ	39.3
NY	37.2

HIGHEST RISK

NM	97.9
WV	87.7
MS	86.6
AK	86.4
MT	84.3

[2] Centers for Disease Control and Prevention, Behavioral Risk Factor Surveillance System, 2008.

[3] American Human Development Project calculations. "Trauma" refers to mortalities resulting from unintentional injury, homicide, and suicide. Mortality counts from WISQARS Leading Causes of Death Reports, Centers for Disease Control and Prevention, National Center for Injury Prevention and Control, and the Multiple Cause of Death Files for 2007 received by agreement with CDC/NCHS and NAPHSIS Vital Statistics Cooperative Program. Population counts are July 1, 2007, bridged-race population estimates from the CDC WONDER Database.

PART II:
Reducing Risks and Increasing Resilience in Health

This section examines two sorts of health risks: those that imperil the health of Americans from all walks of life, including poor nutrition, physical inactivity, and the resulting obesity epidemic; and those that disproportionately imperil the health of distinct groups of Americans, including male adolescents and adult men, people with low socioeconomic status, people with persistent and severe mental illness, Native Americans, and African Americans.

Although poor diet and inactivity threaten the health of Americans from all social groups, these risk behaviors pose a particularly acute threat to certain subgroups. Socioeconomic status, race/ethnicity, gender, and age are not mutually exclusive categories; they interact in ways that heighten health risks for certain groups. Disentangling the effects of place, race, gender, and age is a continuing challenge for researchers and analysts.

The Paradox of Food Insecurity and Obesity

Despite the abundance of food in America, food insecurity—having normal eating patterns disrupted because of lack of food, or not having enough money to eat a varied and nutritious diet—is not uncommon in poor neighborhoods. Somewhat counterintuitively, food insecurity has a complex relationship with obesity.

Food insecurity contributes to weight gain because inexpensive foods are typically more caloric and less nutritious than more costly foods. The link seems strongest for women; adult women who are food insecure are more likely to be obese than women who have steady and sufficient resources for maintaining a healthy diet. For men and children, research has not shown a direct relationship between food insecurity and obesity.[53]

Risks Facing Everyone: Obesity

America is grappling with a new paradigm in human existence: the virtual elimination of food scarcity. Over the past twenty-five years, the perennial preoccupation of humankind—getting enough to eat—has been replaced by another imperative: keeping an avalanche of sugary, fatty, salty foods at bay. Paradoxically, in the shadow of this unprecedented abundance, a surprisingly large number of Americans still struggle to access a nutritionally adequate diet (see sidebar). A simultaneous drop in physical activity has accompanied this revolutionary change. The one-two punch of more food (of worse quality) and a sedentary culture has dramatically transformed the typical American body, threatening decades of gains in life expectancy for the next generation of Americans.

Between 1980 and 2006 the rate of adult obesity more than doubled, increasing from 15 percent to 34.3 percent. In addition to those who are obese, one-third of Americans are now overweight.

With two of every three adults in the United States either overweight or obese, carrying excess weight has become the American norm within a single generation. The rates of obesity and overweight among children rose even more sharply, tripling between 1980 and 2004. One hopeful sign is that the rate of increase in obesity among children stalled between 2004 and 2006. Nonetheless, one in three children are either obese (16.4 percent) or overweight (18.2 percent).[54]

Obesity leads to serious health problems, impairs psychological and emotional well-being, and impedes socioeconomic success by socially stigmatizing and isolating children and by blunting the employment and marriage prospects of adults. Americans have begun to respond to these perils. New attention to school lunches, efforts to ban soft drinks and junk foods in public schools, and First Lady Michelle Obama's "Let's Move" program to address childhood obesity are all elements of a public health response focused on environmental changes as well as on the exercise of individual willpower.

Obesity imperils **physical health** in many ways:

- Obesity shortens life span, correlating to an increase in total mortality among adults from age 35 to 89.[55]
- The seventh-leading cause of death in America, diabetes accounts for 11 percent of all health-care costs. Eighty percent of people with diabetes are overweight; being overweight is the number-one risk factor for the disease. Its complications include blindness, amputation, and heart disease. Once a disease of middle age, Type 2 diabetes is a new epidemic among American children, largely due to the spike in childhood obesity.[56]
- People who are obese are more likely to have high blood pressure, high levels of blood fats, high glucose, and high levels of "bad" cholesterol, all risk factors for heart disease and stroke, the first- and third-leading causes of death. Physically inactive people are twice as likely as normally active people to develop heart disease.[57]
- Obesity also increases the risk of developing certain kinds of cancer; 20 percent of cancer in women and 15 percent of cancer in men are attributed to obesity.[58]
- Babies born to obese women are more than twice as likely to die during their first month of life as babies born to women of normal weight, and obese women face higher rates of maternal mortality than do non-obese women.

Obesity takes a serious toll on the **psychological and emotional well-being** of obese adults and children. Obese adults are significantly more likely to suffer depression, anxiety, stress, poor self-esteem, poor body image, and other mental health disorders than people who are not obese.[59]

Obese children are 60 percent more likely to be bullied than children of normal weight, independent of race, ethnicity, or social class.[60] Obese adolescents are more likely to report feelings of hopelessness and to have contemplated or attempted suicide than adolescents who are not obese.[61]

Type 2 diabetes is a new epidemic among American children, largely due to the spike in childhood obesity.

What Does It Mean to Be Obese or Overweight?

Body mass index (BMI) is a measure of body fat that applies to both women and men. It is calculated by dividing a person's weight in kilograms by his or her height in meters squared.

Obesity is defined as a body mass index of 30 or above. A person who is five-feet-four and weighs 174 pounds (30 pounds overweight) would have a body mass index of 30, as would a person who is five-feet-nine and weighs 203 pounds.

Overweight is defined as a body mass index between 25 and 29.9. A person who is five-feet-four and weighs between 145 and 173 pounds is considered overweight, as is a person who is five-feet-nine and weighs between 169 and 202 pounds.[62]

Stigma and discrimination against people who are overweight or obese can limit their educational, employment, and romantic success, with serious impacts on their **financial well-being:**

- Obese students are less likely to be admitted to college than similarly qualified students who are not obese.[63]
- Obese job applicants receive poorer ratings and are less likely to be hired than non-obese applicants with the same qualifications, and obese employees earn less than other employees.[64]
- Women suffer particular economic harm from being overweight, both because heavier women tend to marry men with lower earnings or to remain single and because overweight women are more likely to find themselves in lower-prestige, lower-paying jobs.[65]

Obesity rates are reaching epidemic levels within all population groups, but are higher in some social and geographic groupings than in others.

GEOGRAPHY

Though the South has higher obesity rates than other regions, **no region is immune.**

According to the Centers for Disease Control, more than 75 percent of the counties in the Appalachian region (Kentucky, Tennessee, and West Virginia) and in parts of the South (Alabama, Georgia, Louisiana, Mississippi, and South Carolina) have dangerously high levels of obesity and diabetes, as do large swaths of tribal lands in the West and in the northern plains.[66] The states with the highest obesity rates are Mississippi, Alabama, West Virginia, Tennessee, South Carolina, Oklahoma, Kentucky, Louisiana, Michigan, Arkansas, and Ohio. Though the South has higher obesity rates than other regions, no region is immune. In only nineteen states is the obesity rate less than 25 percent. **In 1991 every single U.S. state had an obesity rate less than 20 percent, but today, only one does: Colorado.**[67]

FIGURE 4 Obesity and Overweight Rates by Race/Ethnicity

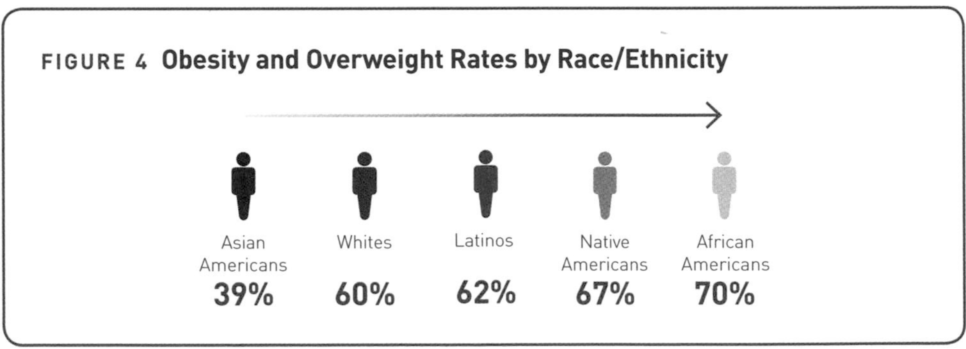

RACE, ETHNICITY, SEX, AND AGE

Obesity rates vary by race and ethnicity (see **FIGURE 4**). Sixty percent of whites are obese or overweight, compared to 70 percent of African Americans, 62 percent of Latinos, and 67 percent of Native Americans. Asian Americans have a much lower rate, at about 39 percent. Considerable variation exists in the data for Native Americans. Studies of Native American tribes in Oklahoma, the Dakotas, Montana, and Arizona have found obesity rates ranging from 30 percent to 65 percent.[68]

Disaggregating obesity rates by sex reveals a more nuanced reality. About one in four American men are obese, with little racial variation (except Native American men, who have higher obesity rates than other men). But four in ten Latina women and five in ten African American women are obese, compared to three in ten white women.[69]

Among children and adolescents, a similar divergence exists. African American girls and female adolescents are twice as likely to be obese as their white counterparts, and Latino boys and male adolescents are more than twice as likely to be obese as their white counterparts.[70] Native American children and adolescents also face high rates of obesity and overweight, ranging from 25 percent to 50 percent; as with adults, obesity rates vary by tribal affiliation, region, and place of residence.[71]

FIGURE 5 Overweight and Obese Adults, by Educational Attainment, 2005

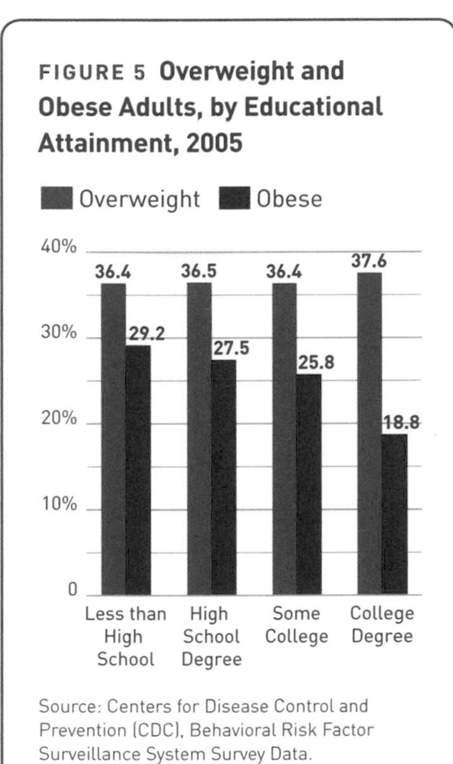

Source: Centers for Disease Control and Prevention (CDC), Behavioral Risk Factor Surveillance System Survey Data.

EDUCATIONAL ATTAINMENT LEVEL

In the early stages of the obesity epidemic, people with less education had higher rates of overweight and obesity than people with more education. For example, from 1991 to 1998, adults who had not graduated high school had obesity rates roughly double those of college graduates.[72] But the protective value of education seems to be eroding. Today, the obesity rate among adults without high school diplomas is 50 percent (rather than 100 percent) higher than the rate among college graduates, and the overweight rate hovers around 37 percent regardless of educational level (see **FIGURE 5**).

The overweight rate of the U.S. population today hovers around **thirty-seven percent** regardless of educational level.

WHAT FUELS THE OBESITY EPIDEMIC?

The doubling of the obesity rate in just twenty-five years results from socioeconomic shifts coupled with the efforts of the food industry to get Americans to buy more food. Overstating the extent of the changes is difficult. Social cues that once limited eating—including set mealtimes, smaller portions, the high cost of food, and a slimmer prevailing body type—now take second billing to signals that encourage overconsumption (see **FIGURE 6**).

Social cues that once limited eating now take second billing to signals that encourage overconsumption.

FIGURE 6 Today's Obesogenic Environment

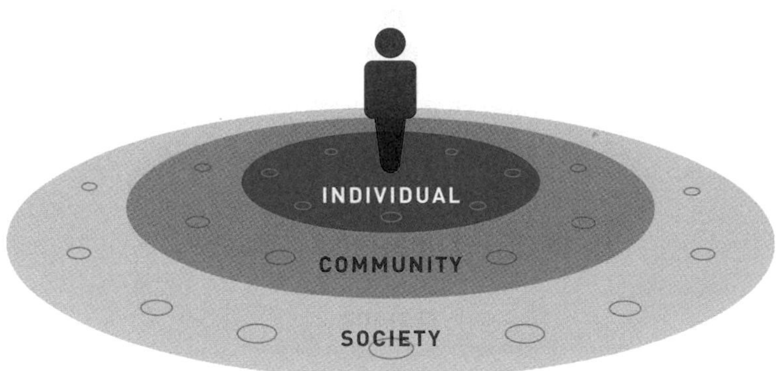

What environmental factors promote **obesity**?

SOCIETY	COMMUNITY	INDIVIDUAL
• More infrastructure for cars than for pedestrians • Prevalence of fast food • Both adults working (no home cooked meals) • All-the-time eating (no set times) • Food industry pushes junk food • Food industry advertising overpowers health messages • Agriculture subsidies • Weak regulatory framework for food	• More corner stores, more liquor stores, fewer grocery stores • Neighborhoods not safe for outdoor exercise • Prevailing body type • No parks or green space • No sidewalks • Junk food at school cafeteria	• Limited time to cook • Limited cooking skills • Lack of information about nutrition • Cannot afford healthy foods • Developed preference for salty, sweet, or fatty foods and drinks • Stress

WHAT HAS CHANGED?

The food supply has increased dramatically, leading to fierce competition among food companies and cheaper prices. America's food supply is sufficient to feed every American twice over and still have plenty left over to export. Excluding exports, the food industry produces thirty-eight hundred calories per capita per day, double what most women need, a third more than most men need, and vastly more than children and elderly people need.[73] The soft drink industry alone produces enough soda to provide every American with fifty-two gallons per year, the equivalent of 557 twelve-ounce cans for every man, woman, and child[74]—more than double the 1970 supply.[75] Whereas in the 1960s food accounted for about one-third of household expenditures, today it accounts for about one-seventh, even though Americans eat out more often, buy more prepared and processed food, and consume more overall.[76] Roughly 80 percent of the cost of food today reflects production and marketing costs—packaging, advertising, and labor. Paradoxically, though processed foods have become extremely inexpensive, lean proteins, whole grains, fruits, and vegetables have become more expensive. A University of Washington study found that **high-calorie foods of little nutritional value cost less than $2 per one thousand calories, whereas low-calorie, healthy foods cost nine times more—more than $18 per one thousand calories.**[77]

The food industry, which employs one in six Americans and makes up 13 percent of GDP, spends more than $11 billion each year on advertising, 70 percent of which promotes fast food, highly processed snack or convenience foods, candy, soft drinks, or alcohol. Former Food and Drug Administration director David Kessler contends that the consumption of processed foods with enormous amounts of fat, sugar, and salt have altered brain chemistry in ways that make people crave them,[78] a hypothesis that a growing body of evidence supports.

Roughly 80 percent of the cost of food today reflects production and marketing costs.

Americans are far more sedentary today than they were a generation ago. The collapse of manufacturing in the United States and the rise of the service sector took a huge swath of the population off its feet and into chairs for much of the day. The movement of employment from walkable central cities to suburban office parks and the need for lengthier commutes has increased driving times. With women entering the labor force en masse, some exchanged a lifestyle of steady physical activity related to childcare and housework for a more sedentary one at an office. The explosion of television viewing, the advent of video games, and heightened concerns about safety and child supervision took children off the streets and plunked them in front of a screen (see **BOX 6**).

Eating norms have changed. With both parents in the workforce, home-cooked meals served at a set time have given way to meals eaten on the fly. Half of family food budgets is spent on food prepared outside the house. Home-cooked food is typically lower in calories, sugar, salt, and fat than fast food, restaurant food, and frozen dinners.[79]

What Happened to My Breakfast?

YESTERDAY TODAY[86]

Coffee with milk and sugar

Medium Latte

Medium Mocha

YESTERDAY TODAY

210 calories

1.5 oz. Muffin

4 oz. Muffin

Children were once admonished not to spoil their dinner with snacks. Today, snacks and sugary drinks are pervasive at all hours and locations. One in three elementary schools, seven in ten middle schools, and nine in ten high schools have a vending machine, school store, or snack bar where students can buy snacks.[80] Obesity rates among children are highly correlated to such easy access to snacks, along with schools' proximity to fast-food outlets.[81]

Portion sizes have increased. Numerous studies show that people eat and drink more when given larger servings, and since the 1970s, portion sizes of all types have ballooned.[82] Carbonated soft drinks, which have become the single biggest source of calories in the American diet, typically came in twelve-ounce cans thirty years ago, but now are sold in a twenty-four-ounce size (with about three hundred calories[83]) that has become, for many, the standard portion. Soft drinks readily promote weight gain because, despite their high calories, people do not compensate for soda drinking by eating less food (as they might, for example, if they ate a slice of pizza, which also has about three hundred calories).[84] The reason that French citizens are generally thinner than Americans is that they eat less, and they eat less in part because their food portions are 25 percent smaller—even in identical chain restaurants like McDonald's and Häagen-Dazs.[85]

Even home-cooked meals are not immune. A study of seven different editions (published between 1936 and 2006) of the cookbook *The Joy of Cooking*[87] found that, of the eighteen recipes that had been published in all seven editions, the average calories per serving had increased for seventeen of them—with an average increase of 63 percent. The rise resulted both from enlarged serving sizes (a dish previously described as feeding six now is described as feeding four, for instance) and changes in ingredients.

Norms about body size have changed. Obesity is called an epidemic in part because it appears to be contagious, spreading through social networks. A recent study showed that someone with an overweight or obese friend—even if the friend lives far away—is 57 percent more likely to become overweight or obese him- or herself.[88] Another study showed that individuals living in neighborhoods in which a high proportion of residents are obese are more likely to be obese themselves, even when controlling for important socioeconomic variables.[89]

BOX 6 Children Who Sit, Sit, Sit, Sit.

"How I wish
we had something to do!
Too wet to go out
and too cold to play ball.
So we sat in the house.
We did nothing at all.
So all we could do was to
Sit!
Sit!
Sit!
Sit!
And we did not like it,
not one little bit!"[90]

Writing in 1957, Dr. Seuss inhabited a world in which children spent the bulk of their free time playing outside. Absent the arrival of an alarmingly anarchic anthropomorphized cat, staying indoors all day was a boring prospect.

Today's children suffer not a lack of something to do indoors but rather a superabundance of passive entertainment options. Indoor media entertainment, from TV to video games, consumes the majority of children's waking hours outside the classroom.

According to a 2009 Kaiser Family Foundation study of 8- to 18-year-olds,[91] the average child spends an astonishing seven hours and thirty-eight minutes per day using various entertainment media—more than fifty-three hours a week. Seven in ten children in the study reported having a television in their bedroom, which is associated with an additional hour and a half of watching TV. Only 30 percent of respondents reported family rules about media use. Children whose families did have such rules reported three fewer screen-time hours per day. Middle school and high school students spent an additional hour and a half per day sending and receiving text messages.

According to the American Academy of Pediatrics, free, unstructured play is essential for physical health as well as social, emotional, and cognitive development. In addition to increasing levels of physical activity, unstructured play also helps kids manage stress, develop social skills, and become resilient. Studies show that children are getting increasingly less unstructured playtime, a trend exacerbated by the 2001 No Child Left Behind Act. The Act pushed schools—low-performing schools in particular—to reduce recess and physical education in order to provide more time for reading and mathematics.[92]

Yet not even summer vacation leads to physical activity. Research has shown that children engage in less physical activity in summer than they do during the school year, becoming less cardiovascularly fit and gaining weight two to three times faster.[93]

The average child spends an astonishing seven hours and thirty-eight minutes per day using various entertainment media—more than **fifty-three hours a week**.

Risks Facing Men

The nation's focus on women's health has increased in recent decades—after a long history of neglect and denial. However, research suggests and experience confirms that males are also exposed to distinct health risks across the life cycle.[94] Men and boys are more likely than women and girls to engage in more than thirty different behaviors that increase their risk of disease, injury, and death.[95] In fact, a man's ideas about what kinds of health-risk and care-seeking behaviors are "normal" for men predict a man's health behaviors, even when key variables like educational level and income are held constant.[96] **In short, men's behavior norms—"acting like a man"—can be dangerous to men's health.** Some examples:

- **Physical risk-taking:** Boys take more physical risks than girls, increasing exposure to accidents and their rate of injury.[97]
- **Stoicism:** Boys learn through peer pressure to "assiduously avoid displays of emotional and physical pain" and associate "tough, stoic self-presentations" with manliness.[98] These childhood lessons bear fruit in the form of the constrained care-seeking behaviors of adult men.
- **Peer influences:** Teenaged boys engage in riskier behaviors than teenaged girls (fast driving, violent conflict resolution, binge drinking). When in groups, this risk taking becomes even more pronounced, underscoring the strong social dimension of this behavior. For instance, teenaged boys drive faster in the presence of other teenaged boys.[99]
- **Reckless driving:** Men account for nearly three-fourths of traffic fatalities. In fatal crashes in which alcohol was a factor, 83 percent of drivers with dangerously high blood alcohol levels were men.[100]
- **Occupational hazards:** Men predominate in occupations with the highest risk of injury (commercial fishing, construction, logging) and account for more than nine of ten workplace deaths.[101]
- **Violence and homicide:** Men are far more likely to be involved, as perpetrators and victims, in violence. Men ages 15 to 24 are more than six times more likely to be victims of homicide than women of the same age range, and men between ages 25 and 34 are five times more likely than women of the same age to be homicide victims.[102]
- **Unintentional injuries:** The male rate of death due to unintentional injuries is more than three times higher during ages 15 to 34[103] and double the female rate over the life course.[104]

Men and boys are more likely than women and girls to engage in more than thirty different behaviors that increase their risk of disease, injury, and death.

- **Suicide:** Suicide is the seventh-leading cause of death for men, who are more likely than women to take their own life at every age—and more than five times as likely between the ages of 15 and 24.
- **"Manly" vs. "girly" behaviors:** Social norms about masculinity often discourage healthful practices associated in the popular imagination with women (eating salads, wearing sunscreen) and encourage harmful practices associated with toughness (drinking to excess, a "weekend warrior" approach to exercise, taking foolhardy risks, fighting).[105] Though men report getting more exercise than women, they eat fewer fruits and vegetables and are more likely to smoke, to be overweight, and to consume alcohol to excess (see **TABLE 4**).
- **Care-seeking:** Men are less likely than women to seek medical and mental health care, to use medical services, and to practice preventative health behaviors;[106] twice as many men as women have no regular provider of medical care.[107]
- **Coping mechanisms for stress:** Men are more likely to deal with stress through harmful behaviors (drinking, smoking, violence, social withdrawal) than women, who are more likely to "tend and befriend" in response to stress, both providing and seeking care and social support[108].
- **Social support:** Strong social networks are proven to be a predictor of good health. Men report smaller, less supportive social networks; fewer and less intimate friendships; and fewer close confidants other than their spouse than do women.[109] Isolation and loneliness are forms of stress, and chronic stress damages the heart and blood vessels.

Men are more likely to deal with stress through harmful behaviors.

TABLE 4 Diet and Exercise, Men and Women, 2008

	MEN	WOMEN
Current smoker (%)	20.6	16.2
Not exercised in past 30 days (%)	23	28
Drank heavily on at least one occasion in the past month 5 drinks or more for men, 4 drinks or more for women (%)	20.3	9.4
Consumes fewer than 5 fruits or vegetables daily (%)	80.4	71.5
Overweight (%)	42	27.9
Obese (%)	27	24.2

Source: Centers for Disease Control and Prevention (CDC), Behavioral Risk Factor Surveillance System Survey Data.

Cultures continually evolve, and gender roles are not fixed. Technological change, economic shifts, new information, government policy, and crises often spur changes in gender norms. The potential for change in social norms is a cause for optimism about our ability to narrow the gap between women and men in health. In recent years, the life expectancy gap between women and men in affluent countries has been narrowing, a change largely attributable to men engaging in fewer harmful practices, particularly smoking and drinking to excess.

Improvements in diet and exercise have great potential to boost men's health, as do changing conceptions about manhood. Driving fast, acting tough, and avoiding the doctor are all learned behaviors. The fact that women do the lion's share of work associated with keeping their families healthy—acquiring greater knowledge about health and the health-care system in the process—has nothing to do with biology and everything to do with social norms about what it means to be a mother, father, daughter, son, wife, or husband.

Risks Facing People with Low Socioeconomic Status

Educational attainment, income, occupational status, and neighborhood characteristics—these four factors combine to produce a person's socioeconomic status, or social ranking. Americans are somewhat allergic to the notion that some groups among us enjoy higher status than others, preferring to think that the ideal of "all men are created equal" applies not just to the law but also to social realities. But decades of research confirm that these differences not only exist but exert a powerful influence on people's choices, opportunities, and well-being.

Studies from around the world demonstrate conclusively that health status moves in step with socioeconomic status; a low social ranking increases mortality risk, and a high social ranking has a protective effect on health. In the United States, those near the top of the social ladder face about half the risk of dying before age 65 than those in the middle of the ladder, and one-third the risk of those near the bottom.[110] The deleterious effects of low social ranking on health start early and accumulate through the life course. Injury, asthma, physical inactivity, and chronic conditions are more prevalent among children from families with low socioeconomic status.[111] Compared to counterparts raised in relative affluence, adults at 50 who lived in poverty as children are at least 40 percent more likely to have heart disease, 46 percent more likely to have asthma, 75 percent more likely to have hypertension, 83 percent more likely to have diabetes, and 225 percent more likely to have experienced a heart attack or stroke.[112] Research shows that poor childhood health influences adult economic status as well as adult health status.[113]

People with low incomes and limited educations are more susceptible to poor diet, smoking, hazardous living environments, inferior access to and quality of health care and education, and psychosocial risk factors associated with low socioeconomic status, including higher levels of stress, anxiety, and depression. All of these factors increase the likelihood of premature death.

Education. Around the world and across the United States, people with less education die earlier than people with more education. Research shows that each additional year of education reduces a person's likelihood of dying in the next 10 years by 3.8 percentage points. Put another way, each additional year of education is associated with 1.2 additional years of life expectancy at age 35.[114]

The life-expectancy gap between those with more and less education has been growing. Between 1990 and 2000, the gap at age 25 between people with a high school diploma or less and people who attended even some college grew by about 30 percent. The life expectancies of men with less education were static during the decade, and the life expectancies of women with less education actually decreased. Meantime, the life spans of the better-educated grew 1.6 years. In 2000, a 25-year-old with a high school diploma or less could expect 50 more years of life,

Low levels of education affect the next generation.

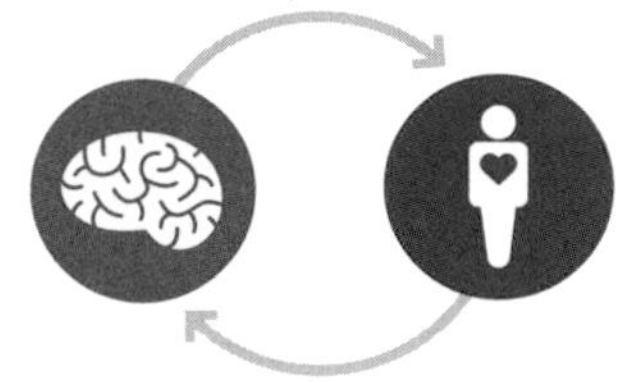

Women who don't graduate from high school run twice the risk of having a low-birth-weight baby, who, in turn, is less likely to graduate from high school on time.

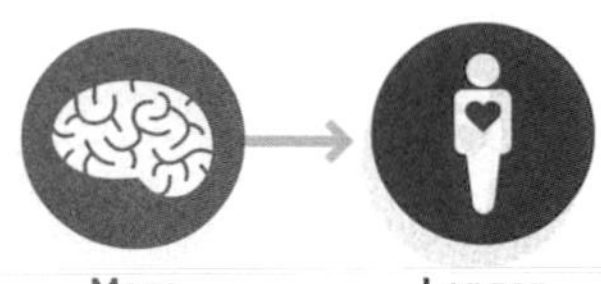

8.4 Years +

25-year-old **African American men** with at least some college live 8.4 years longer than 25-year-old African American men with a high school degree or less.

7.4 Years +

25-year-old **white men** with at least some college live 7.4 years longer than 25-year-old white men with a high school degree or less.

5.4 Years +

25-year-old **African American and white women** with at least some college live 5.4 years longer than 25-year-old African American and white women with a high school degree or less.

whereas a 25-year-old with at least some college could expect 57 more years of life (see sidebar). The growing returns to education in the form of years of life have accrued to men and women, whites and African Americans alike.[115] (Latinos were not included in this study.)

The harmful health effects of low levels of educational attainment extend into the next generation. Women with fewer than twelve years of education are more than twice as likely to have a low-birth-weight baby (5.5 pounds or less) than a woman with thirteen or more years of education.[116] Part of this difference is attributed to higher rates of smoking among people with less education, but even controlling for maternal smoking, less-educated women are 50 percent more likely to have a low-birth-weight baby.[117]

Low-birth-weight babies have twenty times the mortality risk of normal-weight babies and face a heightened risk of developmental delays, cognitive impairments, and physical disabilities like cerebral palsy.

Better-educated people have more access to health care and are more likely to comply with treatment regimens. But low educational attainment also chips away at life expectancy in ways not so obviously linked with health, because low educational attainment is a consequence of and a contributor to low socioeconomic status overall. Low levels of educational attainment thus raise the risk of chronic stress, circumscribe career options, and increase the likelihood of risk behaviors, especially smoking.

Stress and other psychosocial risk factors. Chronic stress "weathers" people, shortening lives and hastening physical and cognitive decline (see sidebar). While stereotypes of stressful situations lean toward the heroic—bases loaded in the bottom of the ninth with two outs and the winning run on base—that kind of cinematic, short-term stress, especially in the context of a life characterized by high status and personal agency, is not hazardous to an otherwise healthy person.

Dangerous chronic stress stems from prolonged lack of control over the conditions of daily work or home life. This kind of unrelenting "toxic" stress leads to physical symptoms from headaches to heart attacks; psychological reactions like anger, anxiety, and depression; and behavioral responses such as overeating, smoking, and interpersonal conflict. It is also the type of stress to which people with inadequate educations and low incomes are disproportionately exposed. Indeed, as educational attainment and incomes rise, the perception of stress decreases.[118]

People who have little education are more often involved in the criminal justice system as perpetrators or victims of crimes and generally live in more dangerous neighborhoods than people with more education. They may live in overcrowded housing. Research shows that people who fail to graduate high school are twice as likely as those with some college education to have a heart attack in response to anger.[119] People with little education are also less likely to marry, forgoing a buffer against loneliness and isolation.

In addition to experiencing chronic stress, people of low socioeconomic status also experience acute stress more often than others. They are more likely to be disabled or seriously ill, to experience the death of a loved one, to be incarcerated or have a family member incarcerated, to be a victim of violent crime, to divorce or separate, to lose a job, to be forced to move, or to be homeless.

Work. Job insecurity and long-term unemployment are chronic stressors in the lives of those with low socioeconomic status, and both have been linked to premature death. In addition, jobs in which workers have little chance to develop or exercise their skills and little autonomy—characteristics of low-level jobs open to people without high school degrees—raise the risk of cardiovascular disease.

Neighborhood. People with similar levels of education and income tend to cluster; this type of residential segregation is growing. Concentrated poverty is often accompanied by a host of social and environmental factors that harm health, such as an absence of grocery stores and parks that make healthy eating and exercise possible; higher rates of crime and violence that cause chronic stress, injury, and death, and which discourage outdoor exercise; weak social support networks; and a high density of fast-food outlets, liquor stores, waste transfer stations, and toxic industries.

Behavioral risks. Lack of physical activity and rates of smoking are far higher among people with less education (see **TABLE 5**). For example, 41 percent of people with a GED smoke—compared to less than 6 percent of people with a graduate degree. About half of all current smokers have educational attainment at or below a high school degree or its equivalent; this is also the group least likely to quit smoking (and those with graduate degrees are the most successful at quitting smoking).[120] People with less education get less physical exercise, are more likely to live in neighborhoods with little access to safe places to exercise, and are less likely to have the resources to join a gym.

How Does Stress Affect Health?

Stress is the body's reaction to what it perceives as frightening, aggravating, or abnormal. The body reacts to stress by releasing stress hormones like adrenaline and cortisol that trigger spikes in heart rate, blood sugar, blood fats, and blood pressure, and which divert blood to muscles. These changes provide a burst of energy and sharpened acuity to enable a person to respond more effectively to a threat—to jump out of the path of an oncoming truck, for example.

But prolonged stress causes excessive wear and tear on the cardiovascular system, speeds up the process of atherosclerosis, redirects resources away from the immune system, and diverts energy from physiological processes that maintain health over the long term.[121]

TABLE 5 Health Risk Factors by Level of Educational Attainment, 2008

	NO PHYSICAL EXERCISE IN PAST 30 DAYS (%)	CURRENT SMOKER (%)	EVER DIAGNOSED WITH DIABETES (%)
Less than high school	41.8	27.8	13.4
High school graduate	32.2	24.2	10.0
Some college	23.7	19.9	8.8
College graduate	15.5	8.8	6.1

Source: Centers for Disease Control and Prevention (CDC), Behavioral Risk Factor Surveillance System Survey Data.

Risks Facing People with Persistent and Severe Mental Illness

People suffering from persistent and severe mental illnesses like schizophrenia, bipolar disorder, and major depression face a greatly elevated risk of premature death, living, on average, twenty-five fewer years than other Americans. The gap appears to be growing; in the early 1990s the life expectancy gap between this group and others was estimated at ten to fifteen years. Between 30 and 40 percent of the excess risk of death stems from higher rates of suicide and death by unintentional injury—preventable trauma illustrating both the destructive power of mental illnesses and the inadequacy of efforts to safeguard the mentally ill. People with serious mental disorders also face a higher probability of premature death from a host of other causes, and three in five will die of chronic disease.[122] Risk factors are detailed below.

People suffering from persistent and severe mental illnesses face a greatly elevated risk of premature death. They live, on average, **twenty-five fewer years** than other Americans.

Medications. People taking "second-generation" antipsychotic medications, which were introduced about twenty years ago, tend to experience dramatic, sustained weight gain, which increases their risk of metabolic syndrome, insulin resistance, diabetes, and cardiovascular disease. While many of these medications ameliorate debilitating symptoms, they also exact health costs of their own.

Addiction disorders. People with schizophrenia, bipolar disorder, and major depression have higher rates of addiction than the general population and thus are more likely to smoke and to use alcohol and drugs. This phenomenon stems partially from efforts on the part of the mentally ill to self-medicate the anxiety, sadness, and isolation their illnesses cause. Three in four people with a mental illness smoke.

Quality of care. People with serious mental illnesses, symptoms of which can include disordered thinking and fearfulness, are not necessarily effective advocates for their own health. But their difficulties are compounded by the fact that they receive the bulk of their medical care from chronically underfunded public systems plagued by poor coordination between medical and mental health care. In general, the care they receive is inferior to that of the general population.

Social exclusion. Many bulwarks against chronic disease—education, meaningful work, friendships, involvement in community life, intimate relationships, agency, and personal freedom—are significantly less available to people with persistent and severe mental illness. Many mentally ill people are homeless, while others receive their psychiatric care in prison. Stigma, fear, and discrimination combine with poverty and dependence to hinder social acceptance of the mentally ill and curtail their full participation in society.

Safe, supportive housing that facilitates medical, psychiatric, and social services while relieving stress on family caregivers provides a lifeline to those fortunate enough to gain access to it. Along with adequate income and treatment for substance abuse, such housing can bring a life of meaning, dignity, and freedom within reach of people with these illnesses.

Risks Facing African Americans

African Americans live some of the shortest lives of all Americans. They die at a higher rate than whites from all leading causes of death, making the challenges of closing the black-white health gap seem almost insurmountable. But research shows that a limited number of conditions account for the shorter life spans of African Americans. Poorly controlled hypertension accounts for 15 percent of the disparity between blacks and whites, HIV for 11.2 percent, diabetes for 8.5 percent, and homicide for 8.5 percent.[123] Thus, efforts to address these four underlying causes of death, which together account for more than 40 percent of the black-white gap, are central to reducing health inequalities.

Socioeconomic status. One reason African Americans suffer more disability and die earlier than whites is that African Americans, on average, have higher rates of poverty and lower rates of educational attainment; thus, the factors that harm the health of people with low socioeconomic status in general (as discussed on page 95) fuel the black-white life-span gap. Wealth disparities exacerbate the gap. The net worth of whites is about six times greater than that of African Americans, allowing more white families to live in safer, more convenient neighborhoods with more amenities that buffer everyday stress.

The babies of college-educated African American women are **more likely to die** than the babies of white high school dropouts.

Discrimination. When income and educational attainment level are held constant, whites still outlive African Americans. The babies of college-educated African American women are more likely to die than the babies of white high school dropouts.[124] Race itself plays a role in the health disparity between whites and African Americans, and evidence suggests discrimination is the cause. Discriminatory lending and housing policies had the effect of pushing African Americans into neighborhoods marked by threats to health. Though residential segregation has declined modestly for African Americans since 1980, it is still higher for African Americans than for any other group, and African Americans living in the most segregated communities are disproportionately poor.[125] Research shows that social and environmental exposure to the ill effects of residential segregation generate mortality risks—even if individual characteristics like sex, race, and income are held constant.[126] In addition, the medical field is less likely to provide life-saving treatments to African Americans than to whites. Finally, the stress of discrimination, from unpleasant social encounters to racial profiling by police, erodes good health.

RISKS FACING AFRICAN AMERICAN WOMEN

HIV/AIDS. African American women account for two in three women in the United States living with HIV/AIDS; they are more than twenty times more likely to be diagnosed with HIV/AIDS than white women, and four times more likely than Latina women. HIV/AIDS is the fourth-leading cause of death for African American women ages 25–34 and the third-leading cause of death in the 35–44 age bracket. The largest number of diagnoses of new HIV/AIDS infections are among women ages 15–24; these young women may have insufficient power in their intimate relationships to negotiate safe sex, particularly if their partners are older than they are. Other factors are lack of knowledge about HIV/AIDS, a lower perception of risk, and unawareness of their partners' risk factors, particularly IV drug use and sex with men.[127] Stigma in the African American community toward gay, lesbian, bisexual, and transgender people drives into the shadows much sexual activity other than that between heterosexuals, making safe-sex education and behavior change a particular challenge.

Obesity. African American women, particularly low-income African American women in the South, are more likely to be obese than women of other racial groups.[128] Consequently, they face a heightened risk of diabetes, a leading cause of death for African Americans, and hypertension, which contributes to both heart disease and stroke.

If the African American infant mortality rate were the same as the Asian American infant mortality rate, approximately **six thousand babies** who died in 2008 would instead have lived to celebrate their first birthdays.

Maternal/child health. Low-birth-weight babies are disproportionately born to African American mothers, and the African American infant mortality rate is more than double the white rate. If the African American infant mortality rate were the same as the Asian American infant mortality rate, approximately six thousand babies who died in 2008 would instead have lived to celebrate their first birthdays. Low birth weight due to intrauterine growth retardation or preterm birth generally stems from the health of the mother. Reducing risk factors affecting maternal health would help reduce the incidence of low birth weights.

RISKS FACING AFRICAN AMERICAN MEN

African American men, as mentioned above, face heightened risk for all causes of death due to both socioeconomic status and race. Adding gender into the mix introduces an additional, and extremely grave, health risk: homicide. In the country as a whole, the homicide rate among African American men ages 20–24 is 50 percent higher than among men of all races of the same age group (2.25 per 1,000 versus 1.5 per 1,000), 66 percent higher among African American men ages 20–34 (2.52 per 1,000 versus 1.49 per 1,000).

Even these dismaying figures fail to reflect adequately the high cost of homicide in some African American communities. In Philadelphia County, Pennsylvania (which encompasses the city of Philadelphia); Jefferson Parish, Louisiana (adjacent to New Orleans Parish); Wayne Country, Michigan (Detroit); and Cook County, Illinois (Chicago), young African American men die by homicide at a rate 300 percent higher than men of all races. **Young African American men in Philadelphia and Jefferson Parish face a higher chance of death by homicide than do military personnel in Iraq during deployment;** in fact, the death rate of military personnel in Iraq, at about 4 per 1,000,[129] is 20 percent lower than the death rate of African American men ages 20–24, about 5 per 1,000, in these communities.

Risks Facing Native Americans

In the country as a whole, Native Americans have a short life span compared to other groups: 75.1 years compared to the national average of 78.6 years. This already low average obscures a still worse reality in several states (see **FIGURE 7**), in which the shortest life expectancies in the United States are found.

About 2.5 million people, representing more than five hundred different federally recognized tribes, are Native American.[130] Approximately 1.7 million live outside Indian Country and Alaska Native villages, with the remainder living on tribal lands.[131] Native Americans on or near tribal lands, which are typically rural and remote, face interrelated health risks distinct from those facing Native Americans in urban and suburban communities. Data suggest that differences in the social determinants of health among tribal groups and reservations can be significant. For instance, 2000 Census data show that while one-third of Navajo speak English at home, about 90 percent of Creek and Iroquois do. The rate of adults age 25 and older who did not graduate high school ranged from a low of 18 percent among the Creek to a high of 37 percent among the Navajo.[132]

Native Americans have **extremely high** rates of diabetes.

According to new research by the authors of the innovative "Eight Americas" study, which analyzed life expectancy and risk factors by race and county group, among Native Americans living chiefly on or near tribal lands or reservations in the West, **one in four men and one in six women who survive to age 15 will die before age 60.** While cardiovascular diseases and cancers account for most of these early deaths, injuries, diabetes, liver cirrhosis, digestive diseases, and alcohol also take a disproportionately high toll on Native Americans.[133] Three in ten adults have a disability.[134] Of particular concern are diabetes, mental health disorders, and unintentional injuries.

FIGURE 7 States Where Native American Life Span Is Under 70

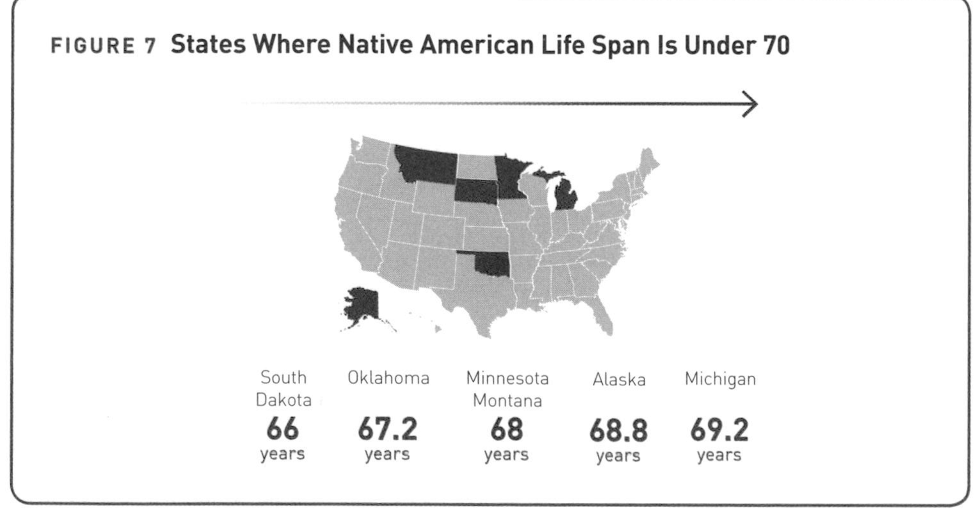

Diabetes. Native Americans have extremely high rates of diabetes, with more than half of the adult populations in some communities, such as the Pima Indians in Arizona, having the disease.[135] It is the fourth-leading cause of death among Native Americans and a contributor to heart disease, the leading cause of death. The incidence of diabetes among children and young adults is rising quickly; the Indian Health Service documented a 54 percent increase between 1996 and 2002 among 15- to 19-year-olds. Obesity rates are higher for Native American men than for men of any other racial/ethnic group, and elevated glucose levels are more prevalent among Native Americans than among all other groups of Americans.[136]

Mental health disorders. Mental health disorders, from addiction to depression and extremely high rates of violence and suicide—the latter even among children—are distressingly common among Native populations. One in three adults smokes,[137] a higher rate than any other ethnic group, and the rate of alcoholism is five times higher than among the general population,[138] leading to a five times greater likelihood of death by liver disease or cirrhosis.[139]

Native American enrollment in higher education has **doubled** in the past twenty years.

Unintentional injuries. Unintentional injuries are the third-leading cause of death for Native Americans, and the leading cause of death for Native Americans under age 44. An extensive research project on the state of the Native American health-care system[140] found that the age-adjusted injury death rate for Native Americans is approximately 250 percent higher than that for the total U.S. population. Native American children died in car crashes at twice the rate of white children. As pedestrians, they were killed by cars at three times the rate of white children. They drown at twice the rate of white children.

A portion of the preventable health risks borne by Native Americans can be attributed to their socioeconomic status. Native Americans, particularly those living on reservations, have high levels of poverty; low levels of educational attainment; high levels of crime, violence, and incarceration; extremely limited career options; and high levels of unemployment. The Pine Ridge Reservation of the Oglala Sioux Tribe in South Dakota has long been identified as one of the poorest communities in the United States.[141] The residential segregation that is a definitional aspect of reservation life means that Native Americans live overwhelmingly among others who struggle against the same obstacles.

However, the policy of self-determination that the federal government and Indian tribes began to implement in the 1970s, which advanced Native sovereignty, appears to have laid a basis for improved conditions. The 1990s saw strong economic growth in Indian Country. While the gaming industry has brought income to many tribes (although not without controversy), even reservations without gaming experienced economic growth in other sectors, such as forestry and tourism. Native American enrollment in higher education has doubled in the past twenty years. These advances may augur lasting improvements in the social determinants of health, leading the way to longer, healthier lives for Native Americans.

Increasing Resilience in Health: What Will It Take?

This chapter has explored the gaps—and sometimes chasms—that separate different groups of Americans when it comes to health. An Asian American baby born today in Connecticut can expect to live a quarter century more than a Native American baby born in South Dakota. A Latina baby girl can expect fifteen more years of life than an African American baby boy. And a white baby born in Washington, DC, will live, on average, seven more years than a white baby born in West Virginia—and a dozen more years than an African American baby born in the same city.

These vastly different outcomes stem primarily not from inequities in the health-care system but from inequities in social, economic, and political systems. They shape the environments into which different groups of Americans are born, define the circumstances in which they grow up, and influence when and how they die. Reducing these disparities requires social change more than medical breakthroughs.

Vastly different health outcomes stem primarily not from inequities in the health-care system but from **inequities in social, economic, and political systems.**

This is not to say that health care and health-care reform are unimportant to human well-being; they are critical. Variations in access to and quality of health care account for about 10 percent of the life expectancy gaps observed in the United States overall, according to an analysis by the Centers for Disease Control.[142] And universal health coverage is vital both to saving lives and to addressing the leading cause of bankruptcy among U.S. households: medical bills. Health insurance contributes to both health security and economic security, essential foundations of a freely chosen life of value.

Though medical treatment is essential once we are sick or hurt, medicine's capacity to prevent chronic disease, the leading cause of death in the United States, pales compared to the power of the environments in which we live, and the thousands of decisions we make, to influence our health.

Specifically, we must address the fatal four risk factors that are the most significant contributors to premature death: smoking, poor diet, physical inactivity, and drinking to excess. Efforts to reduce risky behaviors by altering the environment in ways that optimize health outcomes invariably elicit cries of paternalism. Efforts to protect children are more readily accepted since children are not expected to exercise free choice wisely or otherwise, yet even child-focused health strategies often meet with resistance. Fluoridation of water is widely recognized as a great public health achievement; it is responsible for a tremendous drop in the incidence of child tooth decay[143] and is the chief reason baby boomers approach old age with an unprecedented abundance of teeth. Yet unsubstantiated claims by a wildly misinformed minority derailed fluoridation in many communities, leaving four in ten Americans today living without a fluoridated water supply.[144]

When public health measures elicit outrage about people's right to harm themselves if they so wish and doomsday scenarios about the end of freedom as we know it, behind the loudest voices are often those who stand to lose money from the change. Behind cries in the 1970s that more stringent automobile safety regulations would hurt the little guy in the form of higher car prices was the auto industry, worried about lower profits. Behind the claims that regulating tobacco would usher in an age of nanny-state abnegation of personal freedom or, more recently, that smoking bans in restaurants and bars would kill the hospitality sector? The tobacco industry. And behind opposition to efforts to lessen Americans' exposure to salt, fat, and sugar through greater regulation and use of economic instruments? The food and beverage industries.[145]

Keeping people well and fostering their resilience in the face of health challenges require public health strategies designed to achieve the following:

ADDRESS THE SOCIAL AND ECONOMIC DISPARITIES THAT BREED ILL HEALTH.

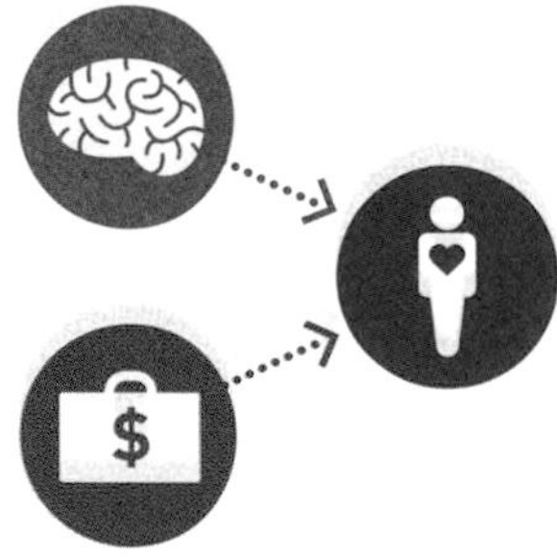

Improvements in the other two subject areas of the American HD Index—education and income—bring improvements in health.

People with very low socioeconomic status, by definition, have no cushion. The fabric of their lives is threadbare. The result is unremitting stress that damages the cardiovascular system, weakens the immune system, and drives high-risk behaviors. For low-income African Americans, discrimination and residential segregation add to the burdens of low socioeconomic status. For Native Americans living on reservations with high poverty rates, isolation and the legacy of destructive federal policies undermine health. For people with persistent and severe mental illness, stigma, isolation, and the absence of supportive, coordinated care in many communities, combined with generally low incomes and levels of educational attainment, push good health out of reach.

Improvements in the other two subject areas of the American HD Index—education and income—bring improvements in health. Education confers well-documented health advantages, making high-quality universal preschool education, quality K–12 education, and greater equity in access to and completion of college education good health policy as well as good education policy. Education enables more fulfilling work with greater stability, control, and freedom, which facilitates longer lives. Likewise, policies that lift families out of poverty and help them build assets—such as the Earned Income Tax Credit, childcare subsidies, food stamps, job training, and increases in the minimum wage—are also policies that foster health resilience by reducing stress and increasing resources available for building wellness. Policies on housing, the built environment, and crime prevention that improve neighborhood safety and walkability and community empowerment efforts that strengthen agency and self-determination also improve health. For people with serious mental illnesses, supportive housing helps unlock both better health and greater participation in society.

MINIMIZE PEOPLE'S EXPOSURE TO HEALTH RISKS.

Smoking, risky drinking, poor diet, and lack of exercise pose grave risks and are, in fact, the leading causes of death in the United States. Minimizing people's exposure to these risks as well as to the risks of trauma (homicide, suicide, and unintentional injury, including car crashes)—which disproportionately takes the life of men, especially male adolescents and men of color—is critical to lengthening the average American life span as well as to closing the gaps that separate population groups. Promising approaches include:

- **Improved food quality in schools.** School breakfasts and lunches should consist of healthy, fresh ingredients, with an emphasis on fruits and vegetables. Soft drinks, candy, fast food, and snack foods should not be sold in schools or on school grounds. Given the importance of early childhood nutrition as well as the fact that food preferences are formed by age 3, regulations should extend to day-care and preschool settings.
- **Greater use of economic instruments to create disincentives for risk behaviors.** Increasing the price of cigarettes through excise taxes has been shown to decrease cigarette consumption, and the price effect is particularly strong for adolescents. Levying such taxes on soft drinks and junk food would reduce people's exposure to sugar, salt, and fat.
- **Expanded bans on smoking in public places.** These bans protect people from secondhand smoke, make it easier for smokers to quit, and reduce the number of cigarettes smokers consume. The United States is unique among affluent nations in not having federal regulations that restrict smoking in public places. The uneven patchwork of state and local regulations has served to widen the disparity in exposure to secondhand smoke.
- **Regulations to limit the amount of fats, salt, and sugar in commercially produced food.** The transfat bans in New York City and Chicago are national models. With little discernible change in taste, such restrictions lower the incidence of high blood pressure, high cholesterol, and heart disease.
- **Lower the blood alcohol limit** for young drivers below the national standard of 0.08 percent, increase penalties, such as fines and license suspensions, for driving while intoxicated, and mandate automatic engine shut-off systems for people with repeat DWI arrests.
- **Raise the driving age and institute graduated drivers' licenses,** which put greater restrictions on the ability of new drivers to drive at night or drive with peers in the car. Teen drivers have four times as many car crashes as adult drivers, and car crashes are the leading cause of death for U.S. teenagers. According to the Centers for Disease Control, in 2008, 3,500

"To cease smoking is the easiest thing I ever did. I ought to know because I've done it a thousand times."

MARK TWAIN

American teens were killed and 350,000 were sent to the emergency room as a result of car crashes. Sixteen-year-olds have higher crash rates than drivers of any age. Research suggests that graduated drivers' license programs reduce fatal injuries by 38 percent among 16-year-old drivers.[146]

- **Improve personal safety in high-crime neighborhoods,** with a view to lowering death rates for young men of color, enabling greater outdoor physical activity, and reducing levels of chronic stress in communities in which people feel unsafe. Altering the built environment—for instance, by adding sidewalks or improving street lighting—is key.
- **Greater regulation of the food industry,** starting with a ban on advertising sugary, salty, fatty snack foods and drinks to children. More than fifty countries have such bans in place.

MITIGATE THE ADVERSE EFFECTS OF HEALTH RISKS.

The food and beverage industry employs top-flight advertising firms and razzle-dazzle messages to sell their products. Government agencies and public interest groups should use this same strategy to foster healthy choices.

Public policy can mitigate health risks in several ways:

- **Counteradvertising.** The tobacco, beverage, and food industries spend hundreds of millions of dollars to get people to consume their products, employing top-flight creative firms, exploiting the potential of new media, and using well-designed, well-tested, appealing images and messages. They are expert in convincing people, especially kids, that their products are cool and fun. The USDA food pyramid and photographs of smokers' lungs simply cannot compete with the razzle-dazzle of commercial advertising. Federal, state, and local governments as well as public-interest groups need to set aside their belief that information alone will foster healthy choices and invest in innovative communications campaigns that really speak to young people.
- **Make mental health care more widely available and less stigmatized.** Chronic stress is toxic to the body and mind alike. The coping strategies that many employ to deal with chronic stress—smoking, use of drugs or alcohol, comforting oneself through food—make health and stress worse. People need support to abandon harmful coping mechanisms and develop new, healthier ones. Most smokers have tried to quit, and failed, as have many alcoholics and drug addicts. Subsidizing tobacco, alcohol, and drug treatment programs for low-income people and requiring insurance plans to cover such programs would help people make healthier choices.

As for obesity, more research is needed to know what actually works. People can lose weight on any diet; the challenge is to sustain the weight loss, which typically requires a whole new way of eating. For those who have tried and failed to shed excess weight, bariatric surgery can, for some, be a good option. Many insurance plans do not cover it, but doing so has the potential to save them money on diabetes care and other treatments for chronic conditions down the road.

Exercise, meditation, relaxation techniques, support groups, and counseling are all proven strategies for reducing stress, yet knowledge of, access to, and acceptance of such strategies are extremely limited in some communities. For too many men, typically masculine behavior creates barriers to adopting healthier coping mechanisms and seeking help. Governments and advocacy groups should support public education campaigns in which male sports stars and others who embody cultural ideals about manhood advocate healthy coping mechanisms and convey the message that asking for help is the strong, not weak, thing to do; boys and male adolescents should be targeted along with adults. In many communities, mental health care remains highly stigmatized. Schools should include relaxation techniques and other coping strategies in health, physical education, and life skills courses.

Coping with stress

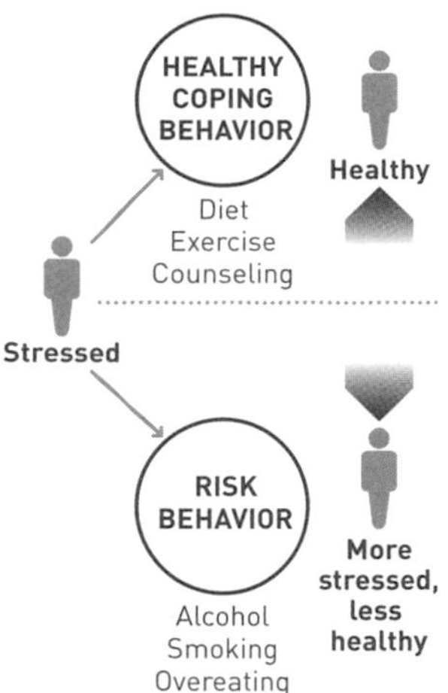

FOSTER GREATER ACCOUNTABILITY FOR REDUCING HEALTH DISPARITIES.

Healthy People 2010 was well-intended—an ambitious government program to promote longer, healthier lives and the elimination of health disparities in our society. But the majority of its targets were not achieved. If we are really serious about reducing health disparities, we need the same focus on bottom-line accountability for health that we have for economic and financial targets. We need to monitor, report, and act on fundamental indicators of health like the infant death rate and the diabetes rate with the same intense focus we as a society apply to the GDP, to the inflation rate, to interest rates, and to gains and losses in the stock market.

For too many men, typically masculine behavior creates barriers to adopting healthier coping mechanisms and seeking help.

CREATE ENVIRONMENTS FOR HEALTHY CHOICES TO BECOME "DEFAULT" CHOICES.

Every school and neighborhood should have a playground; every community should have a park and a full-service grocery store. All Americans should have a place nearby where they can walk, jog, or ride a bike without fear of crime or harassment. That place does not exist for too many people living in poor urban and rural areas. State and local governments should create incentives for grocery stores to set up shop in "food deserts" where little but junk food is available. The private sector should exercise social responsibility by helping low-income people exercise, entering into partnerships with community groups, schools, churches, and neighborhood people to build parks and playgrounds (see **BOX 7**).

Zoning laws should be revised to reduce concentrations of environmental hazards in low-income neighborhoods—from waste transfer stations and polluting industries to liquor stores and fast-food restaurants.

Employers should be encouraged to provide on-site exercise facilities, or to subsidize gym memberships and weight-loss support groups, while limiting junk food in the workplace and offering healthy choices in the cafeteria.

Choice architecture is a promising field devoted to structuring the choices open to a person in a manner that establishes beneficial choices as defaults.[147] Filling vending machines with water, fruit juice, low-fat milk, nuts, and fruits rather than with soda and junk food is an example of choice architecture. If someone wants a snack, the readily available options are healthy ones—yet no one is forced to eat fruit or is prohibited from eating chips. Structuring choices so that the default choice for coffee is low-fat milk rather than whole milk, a recent policy instituted at Starbucks, reduces the level of risk for habitual coffee drinkers, with potentially high benefits in terms of lowered caloric intake over time. Building office buildings in which stairs are convenient and inviting rather than dark and foreboding lowers the barriers to walking a few flights, and thus increasing physical activity and improving health. Moving trash cans with ashtrays away from building entrances and placing them closer to the curb takes secondhand smoke away from a place where people congregate.

Population-based public health strategies save lives.

Individual choices and actions are of, course, critically important. Overcoming addiction, exercising daily, and eating well all require individual agency and effort. **Yet it's hard to make healthy choices in an unhealthy environment. While personal responsibility is a necessary condition for the adoption of new behaviors, it is not, for most people, sufficient.**

Improving children's health requires efforts not just by schools and governments, but by parents. Providing healthy food in sensible portions and rousting children from their stations in front of a TV or video game are essential tasks of parenting. Instituting time limits on screen time seems the bare minimum that parents should do, yet only a minority of families have such limits. The passivity even of educated, advantaged parents who have the resources to create appealing, physically active alternatives for their children is worrisome.

***

Social norms change. People who spent their childhoods in the 1970s sliding around unrestrained in the shotgun seat next to their cigarette-wielding mothers and fathers now conscientiously buckle their own children into car safety seats and avoid secondhand smoke even out-of-doors. The doomsday scenarios of those who warn that public health policies will rob individuals of personal liberty simply don't materialize. Fluoridated water was not, it turns out, a prelude to subjugation by communists. A seat belt is not a prison cell. Cigarette taxes are not tyranny. Population-based public health strategies save lives. And they do so in ways that are both cheaper and more humane than trying to put Humpty Dumpty together again.

BOX 7 Saving Play to Foster a Healthier Generation of Children

Play is on the decline. The Centers for Disease Control reports that only one in five children lives within a half-mile of a park, and half of the children surveyed said that it's difficult to get to a playground or park from their house.[148]

It's not just a matter of making space to play; it's also a matter of making time. One in five elementary schools does not regularly schedule recess for students in all grades.[149] Two studies by the University of Michigan's Survey Research Center—in 1981 and 1997—found that within that time frame, children lost about 12 hours per week in free time, including a 25 percent decrease in play and a 50 percent decrease in unstructured outdoor activities. Meanwhile, children ages 8 to 18 spend an average of 7.5 hours a day in front of a television, computer, or game system screen.[150]

The implications for the health and happiness of our children are grave. The lack of active, outdoor play is contributing substantially to childhood obesity, which has more than tripled in the past thirty years.[151] Rates of childhood obesity are 26 percent higher in neighborhoods with no access to parks or playgrounds.[152] As opportunities for free play decline, rates of attention-deficit disorder, depression and anxiety disorders,[153] and behavioral problems continue to rise.[154]

KaBOOM! is a national organization that strives to counteract these disturbing trends by constructing kid-inspired playspaces and helping communities find, improve, and build playgrounds using online tools. To ensure that children have access to safe, vibrant places to play, KaBOOM! recommends the following activities for members of a community:

- **Adopt a local park** by adding it to an online map of play at http://playspacefinder.kaboom.org/. Communities that adopt a local park can use online tools to organize improvement projects, start play groups, and promote play opportunities with photos and reviews for area parents.
- **Organize a Play Day** (http://playday.kaboom.org)—a chance to gather neighbors, teach children new outdoor games, improve the local park or playground, and participate in a weeklong national Play Day campaign.
- **Build a playground.** KaBOOM!'s online project planner (http://projects.kaboom.org) takes users through every part of the playspace building process, from idea to fund-raising to ongoing maintenance.

With a combination of community empowerment and technological innovation, KaBOOM! hopes to dramatically increase the number of quality playspaces throughout the country.

By: Darell Hammond, CEO and cofounder, KaBOOM!

The lack of active, outdoor play is contributing substantially to childhood obesity, which has **more than tripled** in the past thirty years.

CHAPTER 3

Access to Knowledge

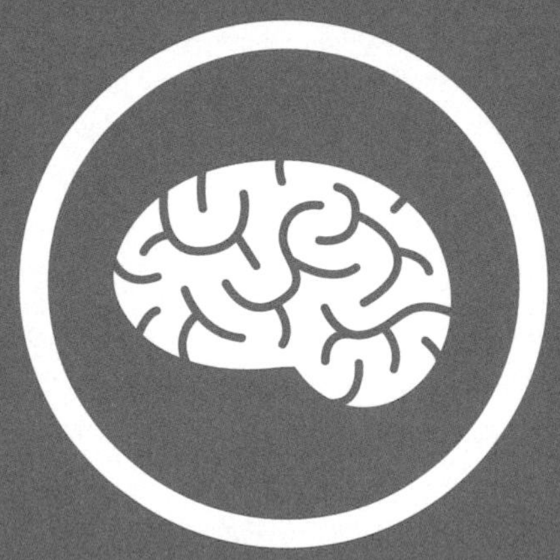

IN THIS SECTION:

How Do We Stack Up?

Educational Attainment and School Enrollment

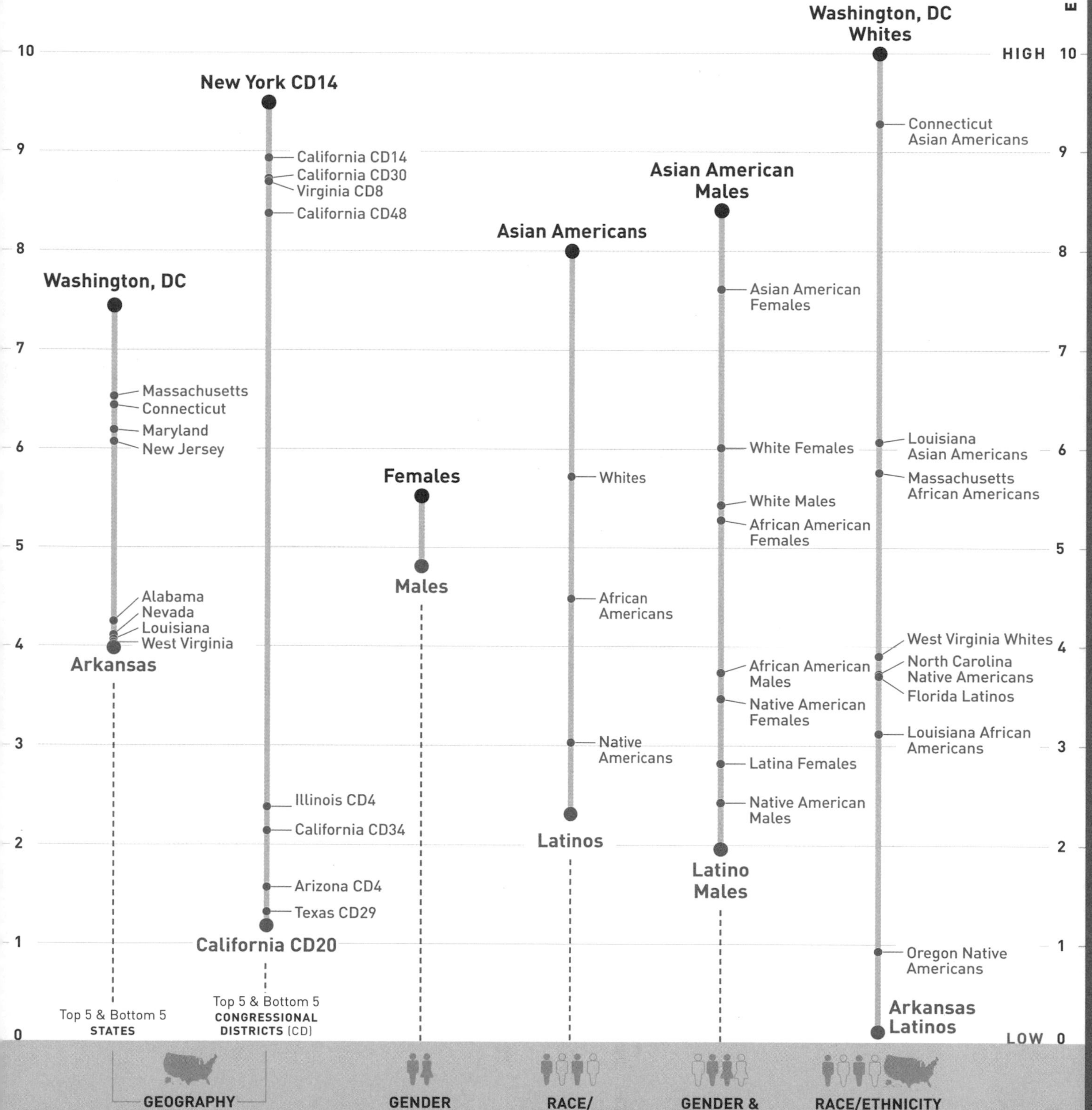

Introduction

> "Let us in education dream of an aristocracy of achievement arising out of a democracy of opportunity."
>
> **THOMAS JEFFERSON**

Education is a wise investment in economic growth and a crucial hedge against uncertainty.

Knowledge is a catalyst for a productive life—for surmounting limitations and for developing and realizing a meaningful existence. Mountains of empirical evidence demonstrate the overwhelming influence that access to knowledge commands over other dimensions of human well-being. For individuals, more education is associated with a longer life, better job prospects, and higher income. The advantages conferred by access to knowledge also ripple out from the individual. At the family level, a parent's educational attainment remains one of the strongest predictors of a child's success. At the community level, more education correlates to less crime, greater tolerance, and increased civic and political participation.

Education is a wise investment in economic growth and a crucial hedge against uncertainty. A globalized, knowledge-based economy demands nimble minds. Recent macroeconomic shocks have exposed how education serves as a buffer against a constricting labor market. In the 2007–9 recession, college graduates faced a combined unemployment and underemployment rate of 10 percent; those workers with only a high school education faced rates twice as high, while a full 35 percent of high school dropouts were either unemployed or underemployed.[1]

Yet for many Americans, basic access to knowledge and the opportunities and security that come with it seem maddeningly elusive. Preliminary evidence suggests that the recession also hindered access to educational resources. By providing $100 billion in education stimulus funds, the American Recovery and Reinvestment Act softened the blow to education budgets in many states, but it failed to fill in all the gaps. California laid off thousands of teachers and postponed buying new textbooks; Delaware and Georgia cut teacher pay; North Carolina reduced state aid to schools by 5 percent;[2] California and Georgia raised tuition at public colleges by more than 30 percent.[3]

Housing instability resulting from sudden unemployment and foreclosures likely caused many children to change schools,[4] a risk factor for diminished educational outcomes.

The Education Index, which summarizes average achievement in access to knowledge, accounts for one-third of the American Human Development Index. The Education Index is computed as a combination of two factors: school enrollment of children ages 3–24 and the educational attainment of adults age 25 and older. The Index thus provides a snapshot of the access to knowledge within a population.

The first part of this chapter presents the findings of the Education Index over time and by place, race, and gender to show how access to knowledge is distributed throughout the country. The second part of the chapter addresses factors that undermine access to knowledge and how we might better safeguard this capability—even in the face of uncertainty.

High School Graduation vs. High School Attainment

High school graduates are those who obtain a traditional high school diploma from an accredited program in a given year. Graduation rates are one important assessment of current school quality and student achievement.

The Education Index used in the calculation of the American Human Development Index uses **high school attainment.** This indicator is the percentage of adults in a population with at least a high school diploma (or its equivalent, such as a GED). While high school graduation rates track the proportion of students who have completed school in a given year, the high school attainment indicator is the level of education for all adults, no matter when they received the degree or whether they secured this credential locally or from elsewhere.

Part I:
What the Education Index Reveals

Historical Trends

The percentage of adults with a bachelor's degree or a graduate degree has **quadrupled** over the past half century.

Since 1960, Americans have made steady progress in obtaining higher levels of educational enrollment and attainment. The percentage of adults with a high school diploma (or its equivalent, such as a GED) has more than doubled, while the numbers with a bachelor's degree or a graduate degree have quadrupled over the past half century. The enrollment ratio is ten points higher now than in 1960. This progress in access to knowledge is a crowning achievement of individual ambition, community mobilization, and public policy.

Between 2005 and 2008 the country as a whole inched further up the Index, albeit at a slower speed than the historical rate evident in **TABLE 1**. As discussed in the second half of this chapter, high school and college graduation rates have leveled off in recent years.

International Comparisons

The United States ranks ninth among Organisation for Economic Co-operation and Development (OECD) countries in terms of educational attainment and school enrollment, sandwiched between Iceland above and Germany below (see **TABLE 2**). The United States ranks far ahead of prominent peers such as Canada, France, and the United Kingdom. It is behind the Nordic countries, Australia, and New Zealand. The United States does better in degree attainment but worse in school enrollment than all of the countries ahead of it (see **BOX 1**).

TABLE 1 Degree Attainment and School Enrollment in the United States

YEAR	LESS THAN HIGH SCHOOL (%)	AT LEAST HIGH SCHOOL DIPLOMA (%)	AT LEAST BACHELOR'S DEGREE (%)	GRADUATE OR PROFESSIONAL DEGREE (%)	SCHOOL ENROLLMENT (%)	EDUCATION INDEX
2008	15.0	85.0	27.7	10.2	87.3	5.15
2005	15.8	84.2	27.2	10.0	86.8	5.04
2000	19.6	80.4	24.4	8.9	82.8	4.25
1990	24.8	75.2	20.3	7.2	80.8	3.54
1980	33.5	66.5	16.2	5.6	71.9	1.91
1970	47.7	52.3	10.7	3.6	73.3	1.10
1960	58.9	41.1	7.7	2.5	76.9	0.82

Source: American Human Development Project calculations based on data from the U.S. Census Bureau.

TABLE 2 Degree Attainment and School Enrollment among Organisation for Economic Co-operation and Development Countries

RANK	COUNTRY	LESS THAN HIGH SCHOOL (%)	AT LEAST HIGH SCHOOL DIPLOMA (%)	AT LEAST BACHELOR'S DEGREE (%)	SCHOOL ENROLLMENT (%)	EDUCATION INDEX
1	Finland	19.5	80.5	20.0	100.8	6.30
2	Sweden	15.4	84.6	22.6	102.0	6.26
3	New Zealand	28.4	71.6	25.3	97.8	5.87
4	Denmark	24.5	75.5	25.0	97.8	5.65
5	Belgium	32.0	68.0	13.5	104.1	5.56
6	Norway	21.1	78.9	31.3	94.1	5.48
7	Australia	31.8	68.2	24.1	97.7	5.39
8	Iceland	35.5	64.5	24.7	99.9	5.29
9	United States	15.0	85.0	27.7	87.3	5.16
10	Germany	15.6	84.4	14.4	87.8	4.59
11	Switzerland	14.0	86.0	18.8	81.0	4.21
12	Hungary	20.8	79.2	17.4	88.9	4.17
13	Netherlands	26.8	73.2	28.3	86.0	4.17
14	South Korea	22.1	77.9	24.4	82.4	4.15
15	Czech Republic	9.5	90.5	13.7	85.1	4.08
16	Poland	13.7	86.3	18.7	84.3	4.03
17	Canada	13.4	86.6	24.6	71.4	3.93
18	France	31.3	68.7	15.3	85.2	3.71
19	United Kingdom	31.7	68.3	21.8	81.8	3.54
20	Spain	49.3	50.7	19.4	89.6	3.49
21	Ireland	32.4	67.6	20.6	80.3	3.33
22	Austria	19.9	80.1	10.4	80.7	3.31
23	Slovak Republic	13.0	87.0	13.1	78.8	3.24
24	Greece	40.4	59.6	15.0	82.3	2.78
25	Italy	47.7	52.3	12.9	87.8	2.68

Source: American Human Development Project calculations. U.S. calculations based on 2008 data from the American Community Survey of the U.S. Census Bureau. International calculations based on 2007 data (except Canada, for which the most recent data are from 2004) from the Organisation for Economic Co-operation and Development, *Education at a Glance 2009*.

In terms of educational attainment and school enrollment, the United States ranks behind the Nordic countries, Australia, and New Zealand.

BOX 1 Do American Schools Prepare American Students for Global Competition?

The strong performance of the United States against several peer nations in educational access can be attributed to the egalitarian ethos that characterizes the American educational system: with the right combination of motivation, ability, and resources, any American child can advance to the highest levels of education, which is not the case in many European countries. In Germany and Austria, for example, students are tracked into different levels of education at early ages and then groomed for particular careers. These formal constraints on access to a degree likely reduce the number of students who graduate from secondary or postsecondary schools and can depress a country's ranking on the Education Index.

Despite the advantages of the United States in enabling access to education, American students nevertheless tend to do relatively poorly in academic achievement. In 2000 the OECD's Program for International Student Assessment (PISA) began conducting tests in math, science, and reading every three years. On the most recently analyzed test, U.S. students performed below the OECD average, ranking twenty-first out of thirty in average science score and twenty-fifth out of thirty in average math score. (Canada, meanwhile, ranked second in science and fifth in math). Nearly one in four American test-takers could not demonstrate basic competency in science, and more than one in four could not demonstrate basic competency in math.[5]

Opinions vary on how well international assessments measure educational achievement, especially when students in different countries—and in different regions of the same country—learn different content at different stages of schooling.[6] Opinions also vary on whether it is useful to compare the United States against peer nations that have far smaller populations.

Many who find the United States' international rankings troubling point to lax and uncoordinated curriculum standards. Each state sets its own curriculum and performance metrics. Not only do curricula vary tremendously among states,[7] but enormous variation also exists in the percentage of students performing at each state's level of proficiency.[8]

A recent proposal to establish and hold states to a set of national standards has touched off a debate in the educational community. As this book goes to print, forty-eight states have signed on to the Common Core State Standards Initiative, a project initiated by the National Governors Association and the Council of Chief State School Officers to align curricula and assessment guidelines across the country. The initiative has received the backing of the Obama administration and several leading companies. A common set of curriculum standards could, in theory, set the bar higher, raising standards in low-performing states and boosting national achievement overall. Critics argue that common standards necessitate a narrowing of curriculum, an increased reliance on standardized tests, inattentiveness to the needs of diverse students, and a chokehold on creative thinking in the classroom.[9] To satisfy both sides, leaders of the common standards movement must set guidelines broad enough to attract consensus but sufficiently—and effectively—narrow to improve student performance across the board.

Analysis by State, Congressional District, Gender, Race, and Ethnicity

COMPARISONS BY STATE

The top five states on the Education Index are the District of Columbia, Massachusetts, Connecticut, Maryland, and New Jersey (see **MAP 1**). The bottom five are Alabama, Nevada, Louisiana, West Virginia, and Arkansas. Eight states declined on the Education Index between 2005 and 2008. The rest showed improvement. Although Washington, DC experienced the greatest decline between 2005 and 2008, it still ranks significantly higher than any of the fifty states.

The states at the top do not perform the best in every category of the Education Index, nor do the states at the bottom perform the worst in every category (see **TABLE 3**).

MAP 1 Education Index by State

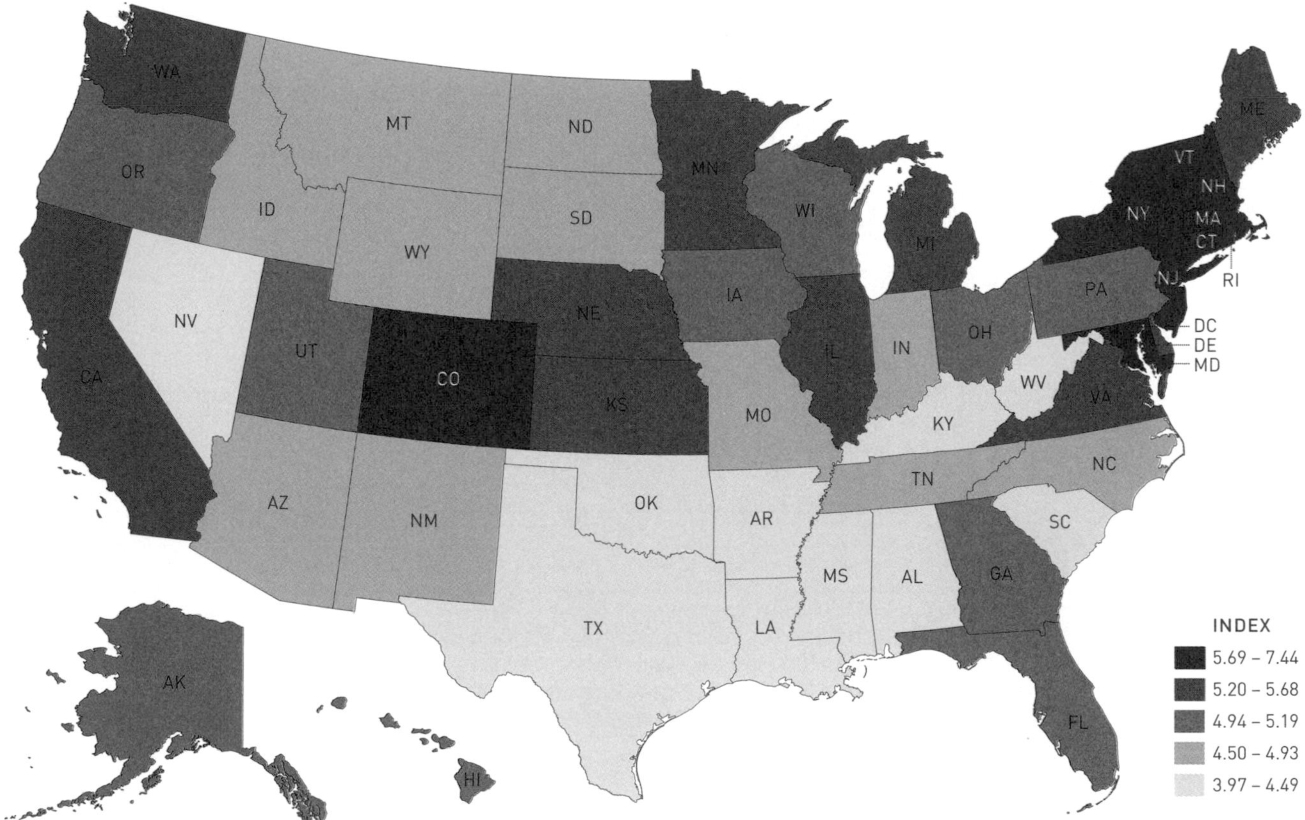

- Wyoming, Alaska, Minnesota, Montana, and New Hampshire have the highest percentage of high school graduates, with more than 90 percent of adults in each state having completed high school. However, none of these states is in the top five on the Index overall.
- Among the top five states with the highest percentage of bachelor's degrees, between one-third and one-half of adults have graduated from college. In the bottom five states, no more than one in five adults have done so.
- The five states with the highest percentage of advanced degrees have more than twice the percentage of advanced degree-holders as the bottom five states.
- Among the top five states in enrollment, Connecticut, Massachusetts, Michigan, Rhode Island, and Washington, DC, more than 90 percent of children and young people are enrolled in school.
- The bottom five states for enrollment are all located in the Mountain West and the Plains—Wyoming, Montana, Nevada, and the Dakotas. Enrollment in these states is closer to eight in ten.

Top ranking:
1. Washington, DC
2. Massachusetts
3. Connecticut

Bottom ranking:
49. Louisiana
50. West Virginia
51. Arkansas

The top five states on the Education Index averaged $14,553 in per-pupil spending in the 2006–7 school year, while the bottom five averaged $8,972.

TABLE 3 Degree Attainment and School Enrollment: Top and Bottom Five States

RANK	STATE	LESS THAN HIGH SCHOOL (%)	AT LEAST HIGH SCHOOL DIPLOMA (%)	AT LEAST BACHELOR'S DEGREE (%)	GRADUATE OR PROFESSIONAL DEGREE (%)	SCHOOL ENROLLMENT (%)	EDUCATION INDEX
Top Five States							
1	District of Columbia	14.2	85.8	48.2	26.7	92.7	7.44
2	Massachusetts	11.3	88.7	38.1	16.4	91.5	6.53
3	Connecticut	11.4	88.6	35.6	15.2	92.1	6.44
4	Maryland	12.0	88.0	35.2	15.4	90.3	6.19
5	New Jersey	12.6	87.4	34.4	12.8	90.8	6.07
Bottom Five States							
47	Alabama	18.1	81.9	22.0	7.7	83.6	4.25
48	Nevada	16.5	83.5	21.9	7.0	81.9	4.10
49	Louisiana	18.8	81.2	20.3	6.5	83.3	4.05
50	West Virginia	17.8	82.2	17.1	6.7	83.7	4.02
51	Arkansas	18.0	82.0	18.8	6.3	83.0	3.98

Source: American Human Development Project calculations based on 2008 American Community Survey.

Degree Producers and Degree Magnets

Some areas of the country produce a large number of educational degrees, while others draw highly educated people in from other places. In Washington, DC, which is treated on the Education Index as a state, less than 40 percent of the population was actually born in the District of Columbia.

Border towns, retirement destinations, and specialized labor market regions like state capitals and high-tech corridors tend to be a magnet for more highly educated individuals than they produce themselves. Comparing the Education Index to indicators that measure the quality of the local schools can help distinguish degree producers from degree magnets.

FIGURE 1 Per-Pupil Spending and State Education Index Score

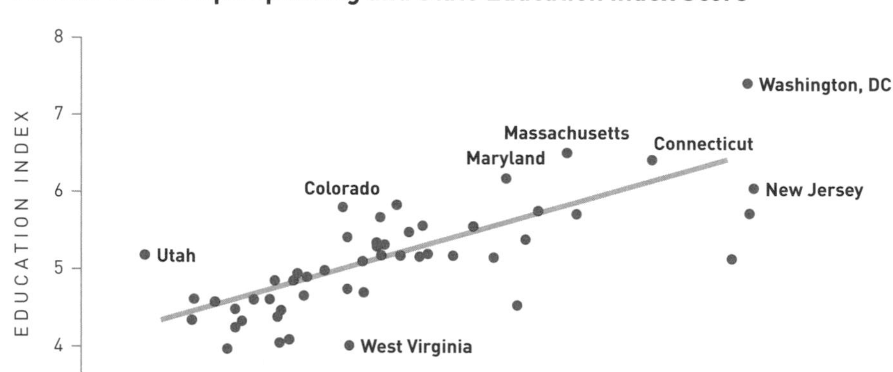

Source: American Human Development Project analysis of U.S. Department of Education, National Center for Education Statistics, Digest of Education 2009, Table 185. The historical average is calculated using constant 2006–7 dollar expenditure levels in 1969–70, 1979–80, 1989–90, 1999–2000, and 2006–7.

BOX 2 The Curious Case of Utah and West Virginia: Per-Pupil Spending and the Education Index

Utah spent $5,918 per student in the 2006–7 school year, an amount lower than any other state. At the same time, Utah still performed above the national average on the Education Index. West Virginia spent $10,087 per pupil in 2006–7, a level slightly higher than the national average, and funding level increases in West Virginia over the past four decades kept pace with the fifty-state average. Today, however, West Virginia still rests at the bottom of the Education Index. **Money in Utah and West Virginia is buying radically different levels of access to knowledge.**

What could explain these persistent disparities? The two states appear fairly similar along certain demographic dimensions: both have small and predominantly white populations. **Major differences between the two states that could affect educational outcomes include the poverty rates, population density, and religious composition.**

West Virginia has a substantially higher percentage of students from poor families and with disabilities. In Utah, 30 percent of students are poor, and 10 percent are disabled. In West Virginia, 50 percent of students are poor, and close to 20 percent are disabled.[12] As discussed later on in this chapter, the federal government estimates that poor students and students with disabilities require more funding to reach state proficiency standards. Thus, even though West Virginia spending matches the national level, the state still may spend less than is necessary to raise attainment and enrollment rates.

Population density exerts a strong pull on indicators of human well-being. West Virginia is one of the most rural states, with over half the population classified as rural by the U.S. Census Bureau. In Utah, only 12 percent live in rural areas.[13] **Rural areas generally show lower rates of high school attendance and college enrollment.** In addition to the challenges of recruiting and retaining qualified teachers in rural areas, the employment opportunities in rural communities less often require degrees beyond a high school diploma.[14]

People with strong social bonds also tend to achieve higher levels of well-being. Utah is the most religiously homogeneous of all U.S. states. A majority of Utahans are Mormon, and Mormons show higher rates of religious activity than people of most other mainstream denominations.[15] The political scientist Robert Putnam has suggested that the Mormon Church, a nexus of social and civic activity for many Utahans, explains why Utah achieves higher outcomes on certain indicators than its demographic profile would seem to imply.[16] Survey research by the Pew Forum on Religion and Public Life confirms that Mormons are more likely than the general population to have graduated from high school.[17]

What explains the variation in Education Index scores across the states? As the Education Index comprises several indicators, no one explanatory factor rises to the top. Nevertheless, states that do comparatively well on the Education Index tend to exhibit higher levels of spending per student in public education over time (see **FIGURE 1**).

Expenditure per student in grades K–12 is strongly correlated with performance on the Education Index. While funding per student increased in every state over the last decade, these increases did not occur at the same rate. In fact, disparities in expenditure per student at the state level were greater in the 2006–7 school year than they were a decade earlier.[10]

The top five states on the Education Index averaged $14,553 in per-pupil spending in the 2006–7 school year, while the bottom five averaged $8,972.[11] The relationship between spending and Index score does not hold across the board, however (see **BOX 2**).

TABLE 4 Top and Bottom Five Congressional Districts in Degree Attainment and School Enrollment

RANK	DISTRICT	LESS THAN HIGH SCHOOL (%)	AT LEAST HIGH SCHOOL DIPLOMA (%)	AT LEAST BACHELOR'S DEGREE (%)	GRADUATE OR PROFESSIONAL DEGREE (%)	SCHOOL ENROLLMENT (%)	EDUCATION INDEX
Top Five Congressional Districts							
1	**CD 14, New York**	8.7	91.3	65.7	30.3	100.5	9.44
2	**CD 14, California**	9.4	90.6	57.2	28.4	99.9	8.93
3	**CD 30, California**	6.2	93.8	57.6	25.6	97.7	8.72
4	**CD 8, Virginia**	10.4	89.6	58.9	29.3	97.1	8.69
5	**CD 48, California**	7.1	92.9	51.7	20.4	99.0	8.33
Bottom Five Congressional Districts							
431	**CD 4, Illinois**	37.4	62.6	20.1	6.8	75.6	2.38
432	**CD 34, California**	46.1	53.9	11.2	2.9	82.1	2.14
433	**CD 4, Arizona**	36.5	63.5	11.9	4.1	72.3	1.57
434	**CD 29, Texas**	46.2	53.8	6.8	2.0	76.8	1.32
435	**CD 20, California**	46.2	53.8	7.0	1.8	75.5	1.18

Source: American Human Development Project calculations based on 2008 data from the American Community Survey.
Note: Enrollment can be greater than 100 percent if adults 25 and over are enrolled in school.

COMPARISONS BY CONGRESSIONAL DISTRICT

The top five congressional districts in terms of educational attainment and enrollment are New York's Fourteenth (Manhattan's East Side), California's Fourteenth (Silicon Valley), California's Thirtieth (Beverly Hills, Malibu, Santa Monica), Virginia's Eighth (Washington, DC, suburbs), and California's Forty-eighth (Orange County around Irvine) (see **TABLE 4**).

The bottom five congressional districts are (from the bottom up) California's Twentieth (the rural Central Valley), Texas's Twenty-ninth (north and east Houston), Arizona's Fourth (inner-city Phoenix), California's Thirty-fourth (downtown Los Angeles), and Illinois' Fourth (downtown Chicago) (see **TABLE 4**). The top-performing congressional districts are located in affluent urban and suburban communities. The bottom five are located in rural and poor urban communities with a majority Latino population.

In the bottom fifth (districts with scores of 4.14 or below), **more than one in five adults** lack a high school education.

In the top fifth of all U.S. congressional districts on the Education Index (districts with scores of 6.16 or above), at least nine in ten adults have completed high school and at least one in three has completed college. More than nine in ten children and young people are enrolled in school. In the bottom fifth (districts with scores of 4.14 or below), more than one in five adults lack a high school education, more than four in five adults lack a college education, and more than one in five children and young people are not enrolled in school.

MAP 2 **Education Index by Congressional District**

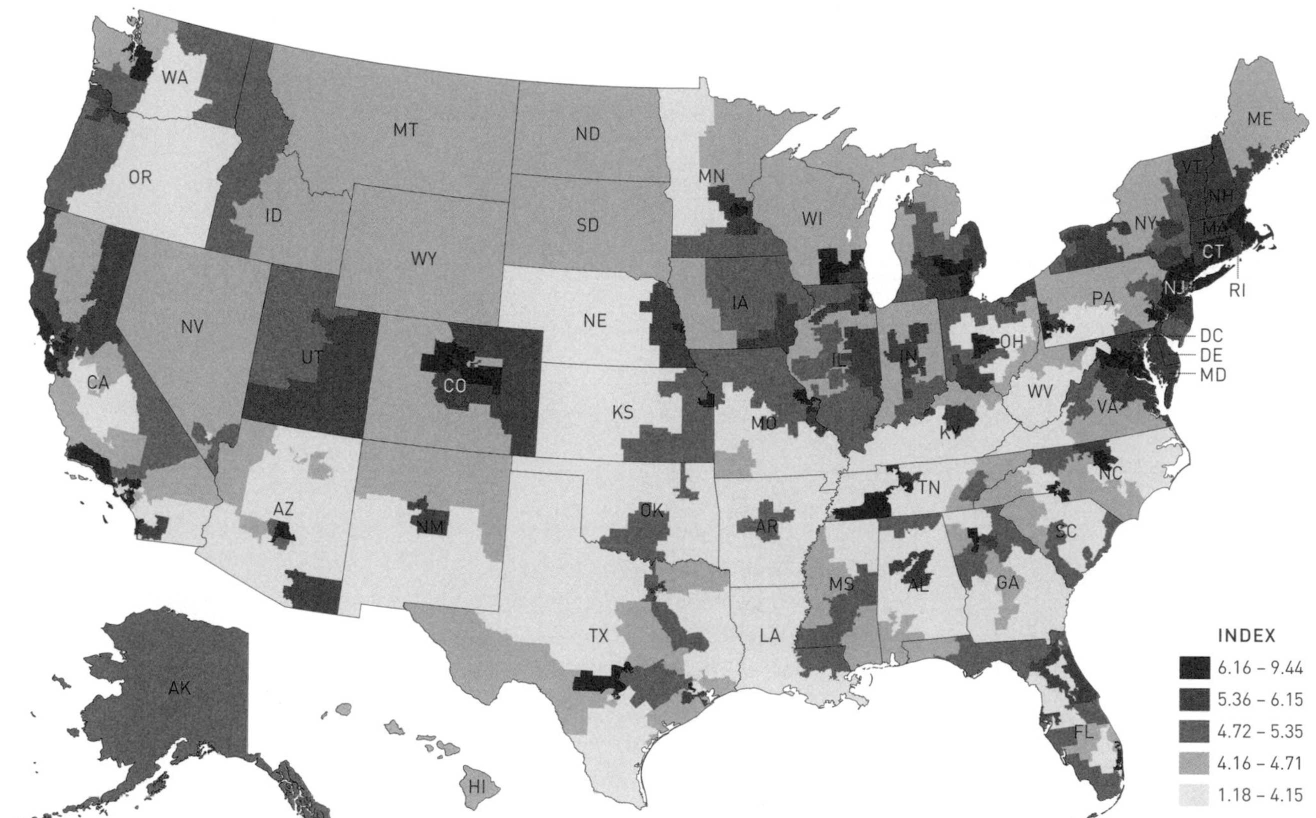

COMPARISONS BY MAJOR METROPOLITAN AREA

The ten most populous metropolitan areas are home to more than one-quarter of the country's population. These metro areas contain enormous diversity, making them resistant to easy categorization. That some of the widest disparities in access to knowledge are observed within metropolitan areas is no coincidence (see **TABLE 5**).

The Los Angeles metropolitan area is home to California's Thirtieth District (CA 30; Santa Monica, Malibu, Beverly Hills), where nearly three in five people have a college education and more than a quarter have advanced degrees. A few miles west is California's Thirty-fourth in downtown Los Angeles, where the chance of encountering someone with an advanced degree is three in one hundred. In terms of access to knowledge, CA 34 is similar to the nation as a whole in the 1980s, while CA 30 is already where the nation as a whole is projected to be in the year 2050, provided current education trends continue. A gap of about seventy years of progress in educational access thus separates these two districts.

As Los Angeles demonstrates, the widest disparities in access to knowledge throughout the country are often to be found between adjacent congressional

TABLE 5 Access to Knowledge by Major Metro Area

METRO AREA	LESS THAN HIGH SCHOOL (%)	AT LEAST HIGH SCHOOL DIPLOMA (%)	AT LEAST BACHELOR'S DEGREE (%)	GRADUATE OR PROFESSIONAL DEGREE (%)	SCHOOL ENROLLMENT (%)	EDUCATION INDEX
Washington, DC	10.7	89.3	46.8	21.9	92.4	7.29
Boston	10.1	89.9	41.9	18.6	92.7	6.98
New York	16.2	83.8	35.3	14.5	90.9	6.03
Philadelphia	12.4	87.6	32.1	12.6	90.4	5.93
Atlanta	12.7	87.4	34.6	11.9	88.4	5.77
Chicago	14.6	85.5	33.0	12.5	88.7	5.68
Miami	17.3	82.7	29.5	10.6	88.9	5.33
Los Angeles	23.2	76.8	29.9	10.5	90.6	5.27
Dallas	18.8	81.2	29.6	9.5	84.9	4.78
Houston	19.9	80.1	28.2	9.3	84.4	4.60

Source: American Human Development Project calculations based on 2008 data from the American Community Survey.

The widest disparities in access to knowledge throughout the country are often to be found between adjacent congressional districts within the same metropolitan area.

districts within the same metropolitan area. **BOX 3** explores some of the dynamics shaping these outcomes.

More than 40 percent of the nation's high school students are located in the fifty largest metropolitan areas.[18] Yet some urban districts graduate only half as many students as their neighboring suburban districts. The urban-suburban gap in the fifty largest metropolitan areas averages 18 percentage points. Philadelphia, Atlanta, Chicago, Columbus, El Paso, and New York all narrowed the gap significantly between the mid-1990s and the mid-2000s.[19] But in the principal school districts in each of these cities, graduation rates span an enormous range—from 31 percent to 77 percent—while averaging just 53 percent.[20]

Why do these gaps exist? American cities have always been dynamic places. However, beginning in 1970, the loss of many urban jobs accompanied the shift from a goods-producing economy to a service economy.[21] Poverty rates in many urban centers began to rise dramatically, as did the number of poor areas. William Julius Wilson, a pioneering sociologist in this field, traces the concentration of poverty in cities to the flight of wealthy residents and the clustering of the less wealthy. These migration patterns largely occurred along racial lines, leaving inner cities overwhelmingly poor and minority, and the uptown and suburban areas overwhelmingly white and wealthy.[22]

Urban districts today face pernicious socioeconomic challenges that even the best-functioning schools struggle to overcome, which is one reason that students from high-poverty neighborhoods are more likely to drop out than students from low-poverty neighborhoods.[23] At the same time, however, education is the primary means by which students from disadvantaged backgrounds break the legacy of disadvantage. Research suggests that this possibility exists for students with the right tools and influences; for example, disadvantaged students in high-achieving schools are more likely to thrive than disadvantaged students in low-achieving schools.[24]

BOX 3 A Tale of Two Districts: High School Disparities in Chicago

New Trier High School, situated in Chicago's North Shore suburbs, is consistently ranked among the best public high schools in the country. Award-winning arts and athletics programs complement top-flight academics.[25] About twenty miles south, just a short drive down Interstate 94, lies J. Sterling Morton High School East, a school of comparable size but notably fewer accolades. At Morton East, 22 percent of students met or exceeded state proficiency standards in 2009, compared to 92 percent at New Trier.[26] Teachers at New Trier also earn an average of $24,000 more than teachers at Morton East.[27]

Illinois' Tenth Congressional District, within which New Trier High School sits, is a majority-white area where 51 percent of adults have bachelor's degrees, and 22 percent have graduate or professional degrees. Morton East falls within Illinois' Fourth Congressional District, a horseshoe-shaped district that wraps through the Latino neighborhoods west of downtown Chicago. Here, only 63 percent of adults have completed high school, 20 percent have a bachelor's degree, and 7 percent have an advanced degree.

Although it made progress between 1980 and 2000, Chicago remains one of America's most residentially segregated cities.[28] In Illinois' Fourth District, 72 percent of the population is Latino, and half of the Latino population are foreign-born. Residents of Illinois' Fourth earn, on average, $13,000 less than residents of Illinois' Tenth. In Illinois' Fourth, children from families struggling with language barriers, fewer economic resources, and fewer years of parental schooling find themselves enrolled in struggling schools—a combination that sharply curbs their access to knowledge.

Immigrant groups often cluster in ethnic enclaves in order to live near family and friends, shop and obtain services in places where their native language is spoken, and take advantage of established labor markets.[29]

Mexican immigrants, who constitute the majority of foreign-born Latinos in Illinois' Fourth District, tend to arrive with fewer educational resources than other immigrant groups today. Part of this disparity stems from Mexico's own highly uneven educational system. The low educational attainment and enrollment of foreign-born Latinos tends to deflate the scores for Latinos as a whole in districts with sizeable contingents of recent immigrants. Low starting points do not seal the fate for access to knowledge in immigrant families, however; Mexican Americans in Chicago today are following the positive trajectory that has long characterized the American immigrant narrative. A study of the 2000 Census found that Chicago Latinos born in the United States attained high school education at double the rate of foreign-born Latinos, and their rate of college attainment was three times higher.[30]

However, a 2005 report found that more than half of the majority-Latino schools in Chicago were designated as struggling, and teachers in these schools received substantially lower salaries, on average, than teachers working in majority-African American or white schools.[31] The progress of U.S.-born Latinos in Chicago is all the more impressive given the obstacles they face in school.

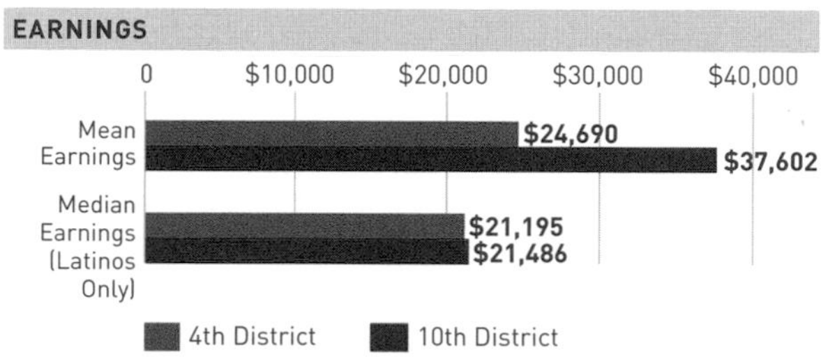

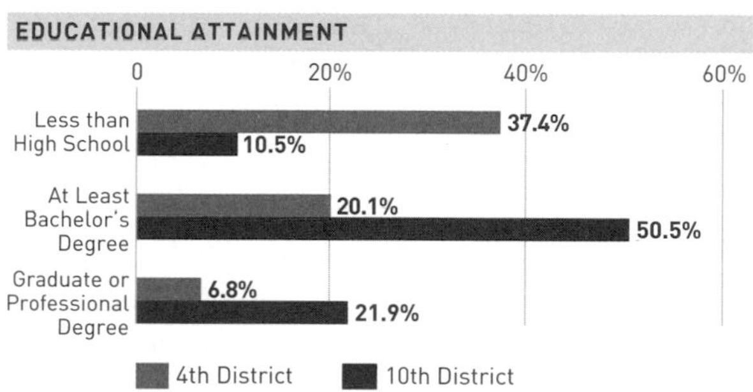

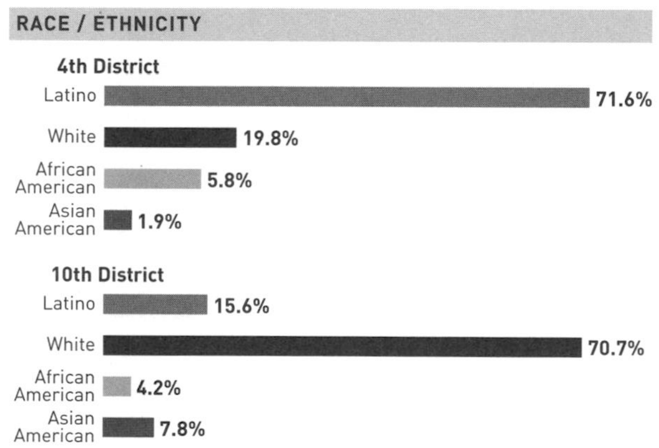

Source: U.S. Census Bureau, American Community Survey 2008 1-Year Estimates. Tables B15002, B20017, B20017I, and C03002.

Closing the Urban-Suburban Education Gap

The Harlem Children's Zone (HCZ) is an example of a promising urban education reform initiative that, in striving to break the link between disadvantaged neighborhoods and disadvantaged students, aims its sights on both at once.

Focused on creating a holistic educational environment, HCZ not only operates four public charter schools in the Harlem neighborhood of Manhattan, but it supplements these formal educational institutions with a wide range of community services: parenting workshops, preschool, after-school activities, and family health and wellness programs.

A recent study suggests that this approach may yield powerful results. By fourth grade, students who attend a Harlem Children's Zone elementary school have eliminated the achievement gap between whites and African Americans in reading and math, and the study authors provide evidence that these improvements result from a combination of neighborhood and school-level investments.[32] Urban education reform efforts, like the Harlem Children's Zone, that address children's academic needs in school and social needs in their neighborhoods show much promise.

COMPARISONS BY GENDER

Nationally, women are more likely to have a high school diploma and to be enrolled in school, but men are more likely to have a bachelor's or advanced degree (see **TABLE 6**).

Washington, DC, is one of only two states where men do better than women in access to knowledge. The other is Utah, where women score 4.84 on the Education Index. In many other states, women do better than men by a full point. Nevada is the worst state for women in terms of educational attainment and enrollment (4.27 out of 10). Arkansas is the worst state for men (3.51).

TABLE 6 shows that women have higher rates of school enrollment and high school completion, but lower rates of college and advanced degree completion. These observations beg the question: is a higher proportion of women than men stopping education after high school? In fact, the answer is no. In 1982 women surpassed men in bachelor's degree conferrals, and women's graduation rates have remained higher than men's ever since. In 2007 women also began to surpass men in graduating with master's and doctoral degrees.[33] Since the Education Index measures the cumulative attainment of the entire adult population, not merely those who graduated recently, it will still be a few years before the proportion of women with bachelor's and graduate degrees exceeds that of men in the population overall.

Gender roles began to shift in the second half of the twentieth century, resulting in higher levels of educational attainment for women than had previously been the norm. These cultural changes can explain why women achieved parity with men, but it leaves unanswered the curious question of why women now consistently exceed men in rates of degree attainment. Some evidence suggests that the motivation to exceed the attainment levels of men stems from the higher financial returns to schooling for women,[34] although evidence is inconclusive as to why this might be. In some cases, it is clear that women calculate that more schooling better equips them to resist wage discrimination, as with a college degree or higher, they can compete for jobs where education is more highly valued, and they can escape traditional low-paying "female" occupations.[35] While the innate abilities of men and women do not seem to differ, women consistently achieve higher grades in school and show higher levels of noncognitive skills.[36]

TABLE 6 Gender Differences in Access to Knowledge

GENDER	LESS THAN HIGH SCHOOL (%)	AT LEAST HIGH SCHOOL DIPLOMA (%)	AT LEAST BACHELOR'S DEGREE (%)	GRADUATE OR PROFESSIONAL DEGREE (%)	SCHOOL ENROLLMENT (%)	EDUCATION INDEX
Women	14.4	85.6	27.0	9.6	90.8	5.52
Men	15.7	84.3	28.4	10.8	84.0	4.81

Source: American Human Development Project calculations based on 2008 data from the American Community Survey.

COMPARISONS BY RACE AND ETHNICITY

Disparities between races in access to knowledge are enormous. Asian Americans top out the Education Index, followed by whites, African Americans, Native Americans, and Latinos (see **TABLE 7**). As **TABLE 7** shows, nearly one in five Asian Americans has a graduate degree; nearly two in five Latinos do not have a high school diploma. Half of all Asian Americans have a bachelor's degree; one-eighth of Latinos and Native Americans do.

Nationwide, more **whites** than any other race have a high school diploma, and in Washington, DC, where whites do best, 99 percent of white adults have completed high school. Nearly nine in ten white adults there have a bachelor's degree, and half of them have advanced degrees. (Only 14 percent of whites living in the District of Columbia, however, were actually born there.[37] The labor market in the nation's capital attracts some of the country's best-educated working-age adults.) Whites do worst in West Virginia.

Nationwide, more whites than any other race have a high school diploma.

African Americans overall have an enrollment rate (88.6 percent) that is higher than the national average (87.3 percent) and equal to whites. Massachusetts is the best state for African Americans in education. There, 97 percent of African American children and young people are enrolled in school, more than four in five adult African Americans have a high school education, and more than one in five have a bachelor's degree. Louisiana is the worst state for African Americans, with more than one-quarter of African American adults today lacking a high school diploma, and fewer than one in eight holding a bachelor's degree.

Asian Americans do best on every aspect of the Education Index except high school completion rates; whites are slightly more likely to have a high school diploma (or equivalent). Virtually all Asian American children are enrolled in school, and nearly half of all Asian American adults have a bachelor's degree. The best state for Asian Americans in education is Connecticut, where nearly two-thirds have bachelor's degrees and nearly one-third have advanced degrees. If current trends continue, that is the level of education projected for the nation

TABLE 7 Racial and Ethnic Differences in Access to Knowledge

RANK	GROUP	LESS THAN HIGH SCHOOL (%)	AT LEAST HIGH SCHOOL DIPLOMA (%)	AT LEAST BACHELOR'S DEGREE (%)	GRADUATE OR PROFESSIONAL DEGREE (%)	SCHOOL ENROLLMENT (%)	EDUCATION INDEX
	United States	15.0	85.0	27.7	10.2	87.3	5.15
1	Asian Americans	14.9	85.1	49.7	19.9	102.1	7.99
2	Whites	9.9	90.1	30.7	11.4	88.6	5.72
3	African Americans	19.3	80.7	17.5	6.0	88.6	4.48
4	Native Americans	24.4	75.6	12.7	3.9	80.4	3.03
5	Latinos	39.2	60.8	12.9	4.0	79.7	2.31

Source: American Human Development Project calculations based on 2008 data from the American Community Survey.

as a whole around the year 2050. Even in Louisiana, where Asian Americans do worst in terms of educational attainment and enrollment, they still surpass the national average.

Native Americans do best in North Carolina, but even there Education Index scores for this group are comparable to the nation as a whole in the late 1980s. Nearly two in five Native Americans lack a diploma in Oregon, and only about one in twenty have a bachelor's degree in Alaska.

Latinos have the weakest performance on every aspect of the Education Index. They do worst in Arkansas, where more than half of Latino adults do not have high school diplomas, only one in twelve has a bachelor's degree, and nearly one-third of children and young adults are not enrolled in school. Latinos in Arkansas are nearly six decades behind the nation as a whole on the Education Index; the educational gulf between Latinos in Arkansas and Asian Americans in Connecticut represents more than a century of progress. Yet in Florida more than a quarter of Latinos have a bachelor's degree, roughly equivalent to the nation as a whole.

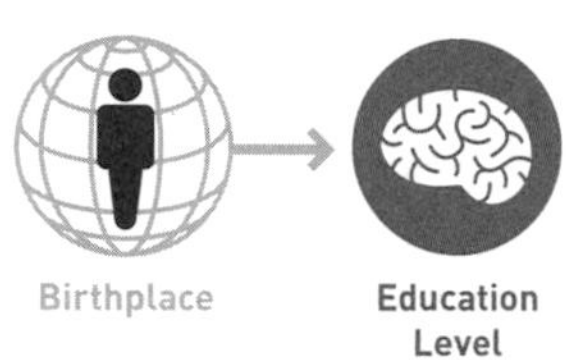

In the United States, native-born Latinos are **19 percent more likely to have higher education** than foreign-born Latinos.

The majority of the current Latino adult population was born abroad. By contrast, the majority of the Latino population under 25 was born in the United States. Native-born Latino adults are much more likely to have attained a high school education than their foreign-born counterparts. The low attainment of foreign-born Latino adults tends to depress Education Index scores for the Latino population as a whole. In fact, if foreign-born Latino adults are temporarily excluded from the calculation, the rate of high school attainment for Latinos jumps nearly eleven points, above 70 percent.

The comparatively low attainment for foreign-born Latinos stems largely from the access to knowledge that they experience in their native countries and the different motivations for and obstacles to immigration encountered by people of different nationalities. In Mexico, the country from which a majority of foreign-born Latinos hail, only one in three adults has completed high school. Cuban Americans, densely concentrated in Florida—where Latinos do best on the Education Index—surpass Latinos from other countries of origin in most human development categories. Twenty-five percent of Cuban Americans ages 25 and older have bachelor's degrees,[38] double the national average for Latinos as a whole. The history of formal resettlement programs for Cuban exiles—policies unavailable to immigrants born in other Latin American countries—likely explains a portion of the relatively higher educational attainment among Cuban Americans.

The educational outcomes and overall socioeconomic status of children are strongly tied to the educational attainment of their parents. Given their lower starting points, the children of many Latino immigrants face particularly high hurdles to enrollment, persistence, and completion in the American education system. In 2008 nearly one in four Latino families with children were living below the poverty line.[39] A survey conducted by the Pew Hispanic Center found that three-quarters of Latino high school dropouts cite the need to support their families financially as a reason for not continuing their own education.[40] Limited English proficiency is also associated with the probability of dropping out of school.[41] Nearly half of Latino children are classified in public schools as learning English as a second language, and Latino children are disproportionately represented in English Language Learner programs.[42] Despite these obstacles, some evidence suggests that, holding constant the constraints of parental background, Latinos are not more likely to drop out of high school than whites, and may even graduate at higher rates.[43]

Added to these challenges are differences in school size and funding. About one-quarter of the country's high schools educate more than 85 percent of the country's Latino children. These schools educate only 29 percent of the country's African American children and 18 percent of the country's white children. The schools that most Latinos attend are also disproportionately large in size, low in resources, located in central cities, and largely confined to just seven states: California, Texas, Florida, New York, Arizona, Illinois, and New Jersey.[44] These states educate almost four in five Latino children; California and Texas alone educate more than half of the nation's Latino children.[45]

Views differ on immigration and naturalization policy, but evidence suggests that citizenship can lift Latino attainment. In a study of Los Angeles children of immigrants, the citizenship status of parents was found to be strongly correlated with their children's educational attainment. More than half of children whose fathers had been naturalized went on to graduate from college, compared to 43 percent of those whose fathers remained legal residents, and 14 percent whose parents remained in the country illegally. Children whose fathers had been naturalized were half as likely to drop out of high school as were children whose fathers had not become citizens.[46]

Despite new laws in many states allowing undocumented young people and the children of immigrants to receive financial aid for college, the dissonance between federal and local policy and the polarization of political debate create difficulties. Undocumented students who qualify for in-state tuition still do not qualify for federal financial assistance; applications that require students to reveal their undocumented status or that of their parents discourage some students from applying.[47] A survey of California Latino young adults found that more than half falsely believed that only U.S. citizens are eligible for financial aid, and more than one-quarter falsely believed that a student's parents must also be citizens in order to qualify for college assistance.[48] If Latinos are to improve in access to knowledge, the United States will have to confront inconsistencies in immigration policy that impose obstacles for many Latino children and impede the nation's ability to draw on the full potential of every person and to compete in a global marketplace in which knowledge is paramount.

The Latino Education "Crisis"

Much attention has been focused on the educational achievement gap between whites and African Americans, while comparatively less research has explored what sets Latinos apart. Latinos consistently show lower levels of degree attainment and school enrollment than other American racial and ethnic groups; in the congressional district rankings, the bottom-ranking districts on access to knowledge tend to be home to large Latino populations.

These findings give the impression of a crisis in access to knowledge among Latinos. Deeper exploration reveals, however, that what appears on the surface to be a crisis is in fact largely attributable to the unique demographic composition of the Latino population. A closer look at factors that influence access to knowledge among Latinos reveals areas of remarkable achievement along with clear opportunities for improvement.

TABLE 8 Degree Attainment and School Enrollment, by Race, Ethnicity, and Gender

RANK	RACE/GENDER	LESS THAN HIGH SCHOOL (%)	AT LEAST HIGH SCHOOL DIPLOMA (%)	AT LEAST BACHELOR'S DEGREE (%)	GRADUATE OR PROFESSIONAL DEGREE (%)	SCHOOL ENROLLMENT (%)	EDUCATION INDEX
	United States	15.0	85.0	27.7	10.2	87.3	5.15
1	Asian American Men	12.5	87.5	53.0	23.9	100.7	8.42
2	Asian American Women	17.0	83.0	46.8	16.4	103.2	7.61
3	White Women	9.6	90.4	29.4	10.6	91.9	6.01
4	White Men	10.3	89.7	32.1	12.2	85.3	5.43
5	African American Women	18.2	81.8	19.0	6.7	94.4	5.27
6	African American Men	20.8	79.2	15.8	5.2	83.4	3.73
7	Native American Women	22.1	77.9	14.1	4.2	83.6	3.56
8	Latina Women	37.5	62.5	13.8	4.2	82.6	2.76
9	Native American Men	26.8	73.2	11.2	3.7	76.2	2.39
10	Latino Men	40.8	59.2	12.1	3.9	77.0	1.89

Source: American Human Development Project calculations based on 2008 data from the American Community Survey.

COMPARISONS BY RACE, ETHNICITY, AND GENDER

For most racial and ethnic groups, women do substantially better than their male counterparts (see **TABLE 8**). Among Asian American males, more than half have a bachelor's degree, although a higher portion of Asian American girls and women are enrolled in school. Among whites, women and girls perform more strongly on the Education Index due to higher enrollment and high school attainment figures, although white men still edge out white women on bachelor's and advanced degrees. In each of the other racial and ethnic categories, women do better than men on every component of the Index. The gender gap in educational attainment is larger for African American women than for any other group; if African American men advance at the country's historical rate of growth on the Education Index, it will take them seventeen years to reach where African American women stand now.

What Fuels These Gaps?

What fuels the gaps in access to knowledge between different elements of the American population today? Since the Education Index comprises several variables, attempts to make broad generalizations necessarily gloss over important nuances. A few factors nevertheless bear mention.

Education and earnings are inextricably linked. A congressional district's standard of living—as measured by median personal earnings—predicts its score on the Education Index more than four times out of five. The relationship appears to work both ways, however, as not only do higher earnings predict higher levels of educational attainment and more widespread school enrollment but also those with higher levels of education tend to command higher earnings.

Geographic location matters. The link between access to knowledge and standard of living can be explained to a certain extent by features of the labor market in different places. For the most part, higher-earning jobs require higher levels of education, and vice versa. Although technology diminishes the importance of geography by allowing people in disparate locations to connect, the availability of high-earning employment opportunities still differs considerably by place. For example, the demand for college degrees is often lower in rural areas, where it is also more difficult to recruit and retain talented educators as well as to continuously enroll school populations that span great physical distances. The economic history of each region of the country varies according to a confluence of features of the natural environment and the choices of individuals, firms, and governments that have accumulated over time. However, by investing in education, regions without prevailing strong economic circumstances can attract business investments and high-wage jobs. That investments in education vary considerably between and within regions of the country is a topic addressed in more depth in the next section.

Parents' education levels shape children's outcomes. As detailed in the next section, parents' levels of educational attainment are among the strongest predictors of their children's educational outcomes. This feature helps to explain some of the persistent disparities between geographic regions and between racial and ethnic groups. This relationship is stronger in the United States than in most peer nations.[49] The intergenerational transfer of assets that allows parents to transmit financial gains to their children also holds for educational attainment. On the one hand, knowing that their efforts can serve as investments in their children's futures can motivate parents to strive for higher levels of educational achievement themselves. On the other hand, as certain families grow ever more educated, children with fewer family resources face greater obstacles to achieve the same educational outcomes as their more advantaged peers. **Women now surpass men on each variable of access to knowledge.** However, not all of these gains, some of which are relatively recent, are reflected in the indicators that compose the Education Index, which takes stock of the entire adult population. Women's superior performance may result from higher wage premiums and lower barriers to educational persistence.

Parents' levels of educational attainment are among the strongest predictors of their children's educational outcomes.

Immigration patterns affect educational outcomes. This section has explored how immigration patterns affect the differential opportunities available to immigrants in terms of education. The appearance of an educational crisis among Latinos—compared with more favorable outcomes among Asian Americans, for example—stems largely from the differences in resources with which each immigrant group arrives in this country and the obstacles they face once they get here. The vulnerabilities of particular groups at different educational access points are the concern of the next section.

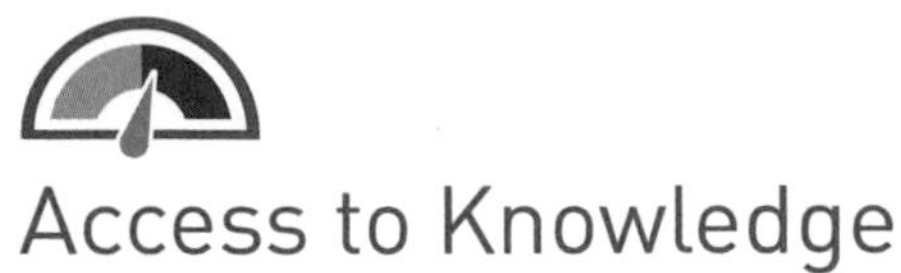

Access to Knowledge

Dashboard of Risks

The three indicators presented here—**preschool enrollment**, **fourth-grade reading proficiency**, and **on-time high school graduation**—track risk factors that may slow or reverse human development progress and which pose direct threats to people's capability to enjoy access to knowledge.

Children ages 3 and 4 not enrolled in preschool (%)[1]

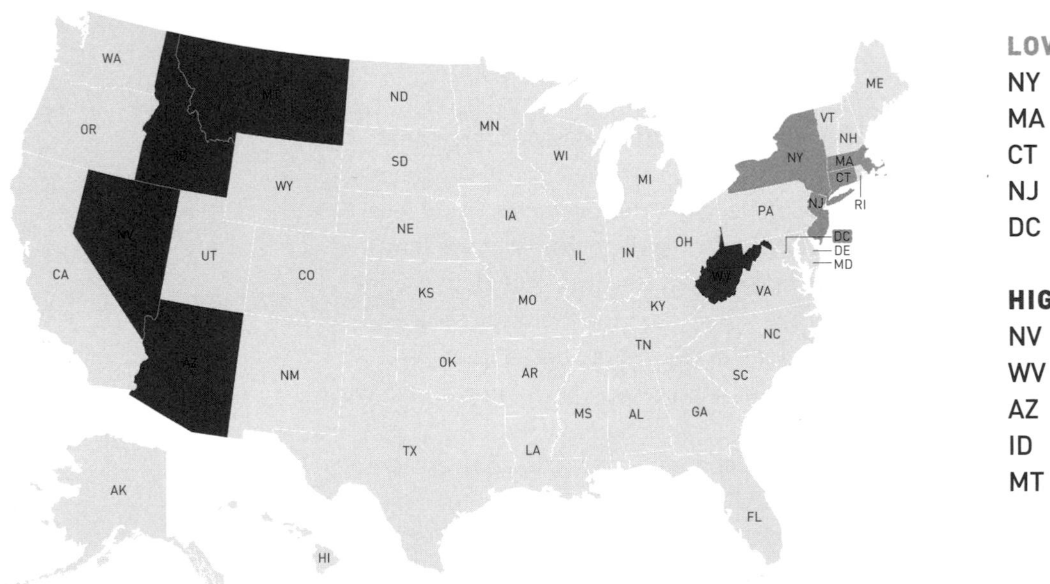

LOWEST RISK

NY	39.9
MA	37.7
CT	35.6
NJ	32.7
DC	26.4

HIGHEST RISK

NV	71.6
WV	67.8
AZ	67.6
ID	63.4
MT	62.8

[1] American Human Development Project calculations based on American Community Survey, 2008 One-Year Estimates, Table B14001.

Fourth-graders reading below proficient (%)[2]

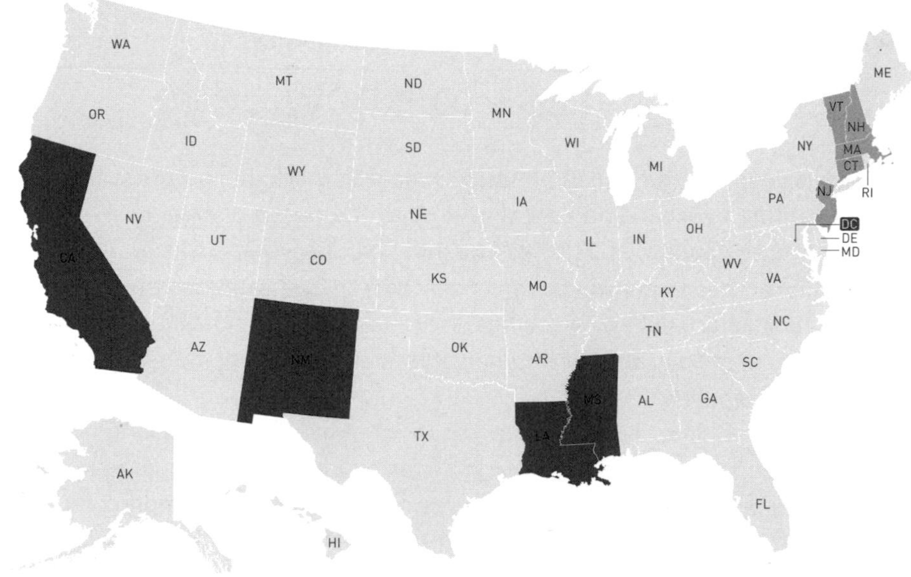

LOWEST RISK

NJ	59.8
NH	58.7
VT	58.6
CT	57.6
MA	52.8

HIGHEST RISK

DC	83.2
LA	81.7
NM	80.2
MS	78.3
CA	76.3

High school freshmen not graduating after four years (%)[3]

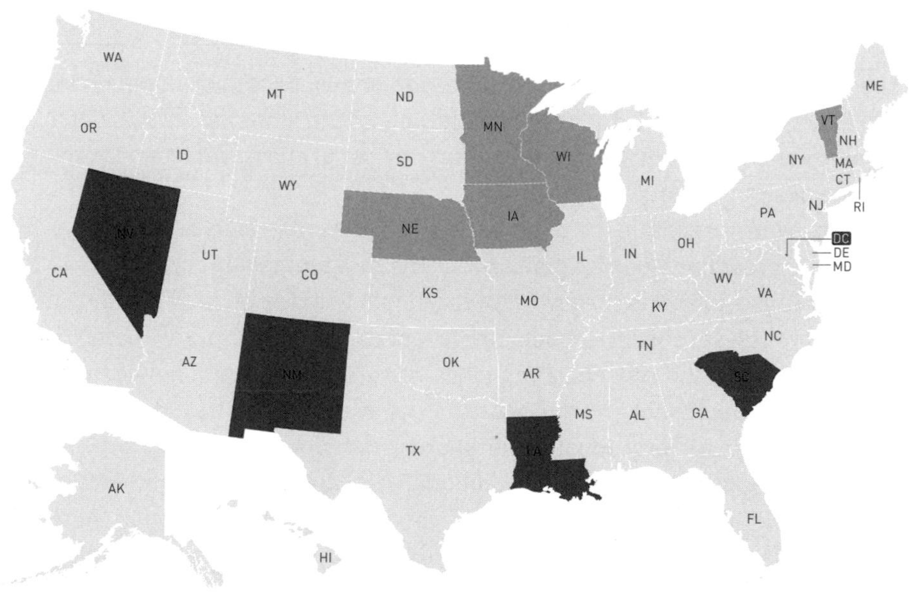

LOWEST RISK

NE	13.7
IA	13.5
MN	13.5
WI	11.5
VT	11.4

HIGHEST RISK

NV	48.0
DC	45.1
SC	41.1
NM	40.9
LA	38.7

[2] American Human Development Project analysis of National Center for Education Statistics, National Assessment of Educational Progress (NAEP), 2009 Reading Assessment.

[3] American Human Development Project analysis of National Center for Education Statistics, Digest of Education Statistics 2009, Table 105. Averaged High School Freshman Graduation Rate.

Part II: Reducing Risks and Increasing Resilience in Access to Knowledge

As previously discussed, the United States has made remarkable progress in the last half century in expanding educational opportunities to a growing and increasingly diverse population. Further investigation uncovers, however, that the expansion of access to knowledge has not occurred evenly across the population, and substantial barriers remain for unlocking the capabilities of all students. This section examines impediments to access at each critical stage of the educational pipeline.

Total Public School Enrollment (Elementary and Secondary), 2007–8

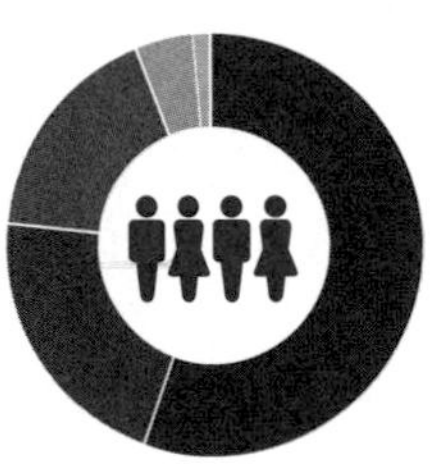

- 56% White 27,062,600
- 21% Latino 10,249,902
- 17% African American 8,267,902
- 5% Asian American 2,348,472
- 1% Native American 587,046

Source: National Center for Education Statistics, Common Core of Data (CCD), "State Nonfiscal Survey of Public Elementary Secondary Education."

Four central premises undergird this discussion. First, in times of crisis or uncertainty, investments in education are tools for resilience. Second, investment and achievement in education in the early years reverberate and multiply throughout later stages. Conversely, investments denied and benchmarks unachieved at earlier stages compound in subsequent years. Third, like so many aspects of human development, the resources afforded by one's family, wealth, neighborhood, immigration status, and culture—collectively termed one's socioeconomic status—powerfully influence one's ultimate access to knowledge in the United States. While acknowledging the power of socioeconomic status, this section attempts to separate immutable individual characteristics from leverage points that respond to policy. Fourth and finally, because education in America is provided, funded, and regulated largely at the state and municipal level, opportunities and outcomes vary tremendously by geography, and local conditions and policies deserve careful scrutiny.

While many factors influence one's access to knowledge (see **BOX 4** for a discussion of broadband penetration), by far the most important is formal education, because school is the *primary* place of knowledge acquisition. In 2008, preprimary through secondary school enrollment consisted of approximately 50 million students in public schools, 6 million in private schools, and between 1 and 2 million in homeschool environments.[50] Just over 12 million students were enrolled in four-year undergraduate institutions (slightly more than half of whom were enrolled in public colleges).[51] An additional 7 million were enrolled in two-year colleges, with the vast majority in public institutions and six in ten of them enrolled on a part-time basis.[52] Slightly more than 2.7 million were enrolled in graduate and professional schools.[53]

BOX 4 Digital Divide Impedes Inclusion

Internet access has become a virtual requirement for full participation in American society, necessary for everything from doing homework to applying for jobs to interacting with health-care providers. Indeed, the Internet is on a trajectory to become the chief way in which people access information, part and parcel of life's essential infrastructure.

Yet not everyone has Internet access or the skills required to reap the benefits of that access. A digital divide separates those who use the Internet for a wide variety of activities and those who do not. Sixty-five percent of American households with incomes below $25,000 per year do not have a broadband connection at home—compared to only 35 percent in the population as a whole.[54]

A recent study commissioned by the Federal Communications Commission (FCC) found that while many of America's most marginalized people struggle to find reliable Internet access, few of them underestimate its role as a prerequisite for inclusion in contemporary life. Although the digital divide is nothing new, the costs of being on the wrong side of the divide are higher today than ever before.

Ten or fifteen years ago, the Internet was, for those who had it, a convenient way to perform many common tasks. Today, however, Internet use is the default expectation for learning, working, banking, dealing with both the private sector and the government, and interacting with each other—with new uses appearing virtually every day. In many cases, the Internet lowers the cost of basic tasks. Employers, even those who do not expect computer literacy on the job, use the Internet as the primary means to publicize job openings, receive applications, and more.[55] Government at all levels is switching to online portals for services ranging from taxes to benefits in housing, childcare, and unemployment. In education, the Internet is increasingly replacing conventional classrooms for job training and continuing education, and schoolchildren, especially those in middle school and older, receive homework assignments online and use the Web to complete the work. It's becoming a standard tool for school communications with parents, and Americans increasingly rely on the Internet for news and to share information.

All this use in turn fuels economic growth. A 2009 study of twenty OECD countries estimated that for every 10-percentage-point increase in broadband connectivity, annual per-capita growth goes up 0.9 to 1.5 percentage points.[56]

With so much at stake and a clear understanding of what they're missing, why are 100 million Americans left offline?[57] **FIGURE 2** shows Internet use by race and educational attainment, based on a survey by the Pew Research Center.

In addition, the U.S. Census Bureau data by state (see U.S. Indicator Table on page 243) shows that Internet access ranges from a high in New Hampshire, where nearly 83 percent of residents live in a household with Internet, to a low in Mississippi, where just over half (52.8 percent) live in a household with Internet.

Not all access has to be at home. But groups that are excluded from participating fully in cyberspace are at risk of being left behind in every arena. Impediments to access include:

- **Home use.** The FCC-commissioned survey found that price is the main constraint—monthly fees but also high installation fees, the upfront cost of hardware, and fear of hidden fees.
- **Public access.** The survey found that the recent recession hit public venues—particularly libraries and other public services in poorer-resourced communities—hard in terms of their ability to meet the surging demand for Internet access for those who lack it at home. Cutbacks in library hours as well as budgets for computers, digital literacy classes, and in-person technical help are widespread.

The good news is that policymakers understand what is at stake. In early 2009 Congress directed the FCC to develop a plan to address the access gap. The resulting revenue-neutral National Broadband Plan, made publicly available in 2010, tasks the government with developing the policies, standards, and incentives to make sure every American has access to broadband capability. The bad news is that the plan relies heavily on the private sector to provide that access. American historical experience, from the rural electrification efforts of the Tennessee Valley Authority to the establishment of water supply and sanitation systems in urban areas across the country, shows that ensuring universal access to basic services often requires some degree of government involvement.

FIGURE 2 Internet Use, by Educational Attainment

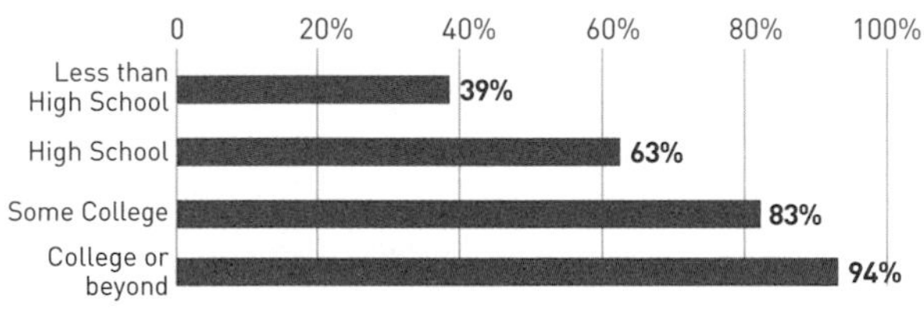

Source: Pew Research Center Internet and American Life Project, Number 30—December 27, 2009 Tracking Survey

Preschool Education: Getting It Right from the Start

Kindergarten is both widely available and nearly universally attended by 5-year-olds.

The United States has achieved remarkable progress over the past fifty years in making kindergarten available and accessible. In 1965 publicly funded kindergarten was available in only eighteen states; today, although attendance is mandatory only in fourteen states, kindergarten is both widely available and nearly universally attended by 5-year-olds.[58]

Progress in extending the benefits of preprimary education to younger children has not kept pace with the advances in kindergarten access, however. Among developed countries today, the United States is a rare exception in not providing universal preschool education for 3-and 4-year-olds—despite overwhelming evidence of the human, community, and national interests that quality preschool education serves (see **FIGURE 3**).

While a few developed countries boast strong educational attainment and achievement in spite of low preschool enrollment figures, most peer nations that

FIGURE 3 Preschool Enrollment among the Thirty OECD Countries*

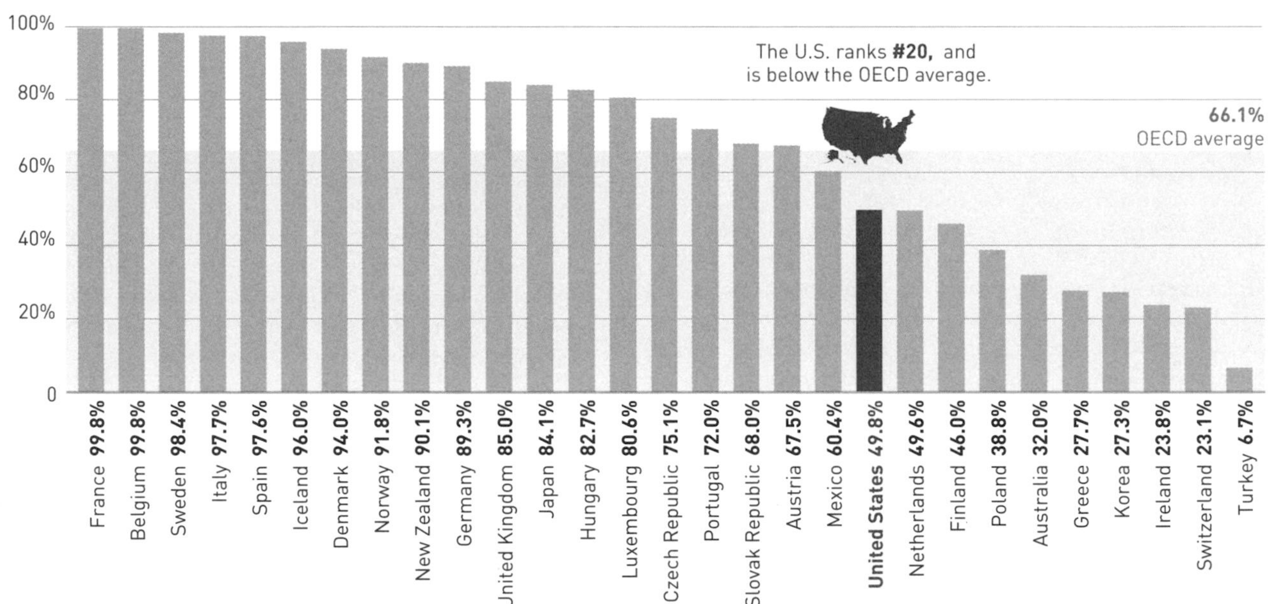

Source: American Human Development Project analysis of UNESCO-OECD-Eurostat (UOE) data collection on education statistics, compiled on the basis of national administrative sources, reported by Ministries of Education or National Statistical Offices, extracted from OECD Stat Extracts, May 2, 2010. *Enrollment data for Canada are not available.

best the United States in other educational measures also show substantially higher rates of preprimary enrollment. Many young children receive care from adults other than their parents, but only one in two American children ages 3 and 4 are enrolled in institutional preschool. Slightly more than half of children in such preschools are in private programs.[59]

Yet proof of the overwhelming benefits of quality preschool education continues to mount. A high-quality early education offers children from disadvantaged backgrounds a chance to start school on equal footing with their more privileged peers—and thus avoid a lowered educational trajectory for the duration of their school careers (see **BOX 5**). An analysis of twenty-six studies of institutional preschool education found that, by early adulthood, those who participated were 31 percent less likely to repeat a grade, 50 percent less likely to be placed in special education, and 32 percent less likely to drop out of high school than nonparticipants.[60] What about education in the earliest years sets children on a positive life trajectory? Surprisingly, effective early childhood education has not been shown with any degree of certainty to increase children's cognitive skills, as measured by IQ tests. Where preschool seems to make the most difference is in social and emotional behavior.[61] In this respect, preschool serves an important purpose in socializing children in how to interact in a social setting, establish and maintain effective relationships, and meet public expectations.

Compelling new evidence suggests that not only is preschool among the most effective educational investments, it may also be the most economically efficient. Compared to other educational investments and interventions, preschool education shows the highest benefit-to-cost ratio. For every dollar invested in high-quality preschool education, a community on average gains between $6 and $10[62] in value in the form of things like reduced costs from incarceration and higher tax revenues from greater earnings later in life. The Brookings Institution

Community Benefits of Preschool

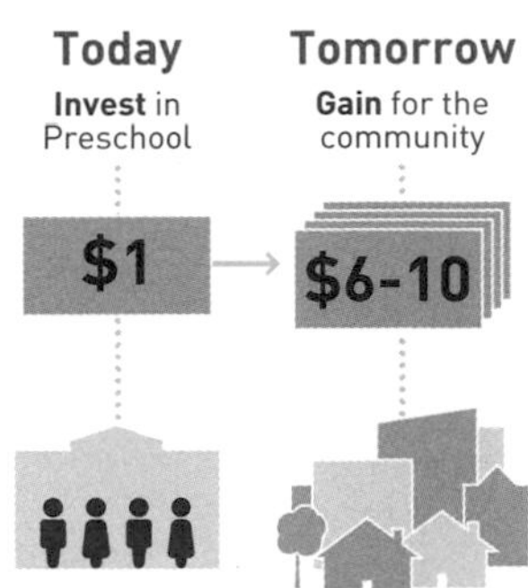

BOX 5 What Makes a High-Quality Preschool Program?

According to the National Institute for Early Education Research,[63] a high-quality preschool program must meet as many as possible of the following ten evidence-based benchmarks:

- Program follows comprehensive learning standards
- Teacher has at least a bachelor's degree
- Teacher has specialized training in early childhood education
- Teaching assistant has a least a certificate in early childhood education
- Teacher undergoes at least fifteen hours of supplementary training per year
- Class size of twenty or fewer children
- Staff-to-child ratio of 1:10 or smaller
- Program provides or is linked to health services of some kind
- Program provides at least one nutritious meal
- Program involves site visits to the child's home

MAP 3 Preschool Enrollment by State

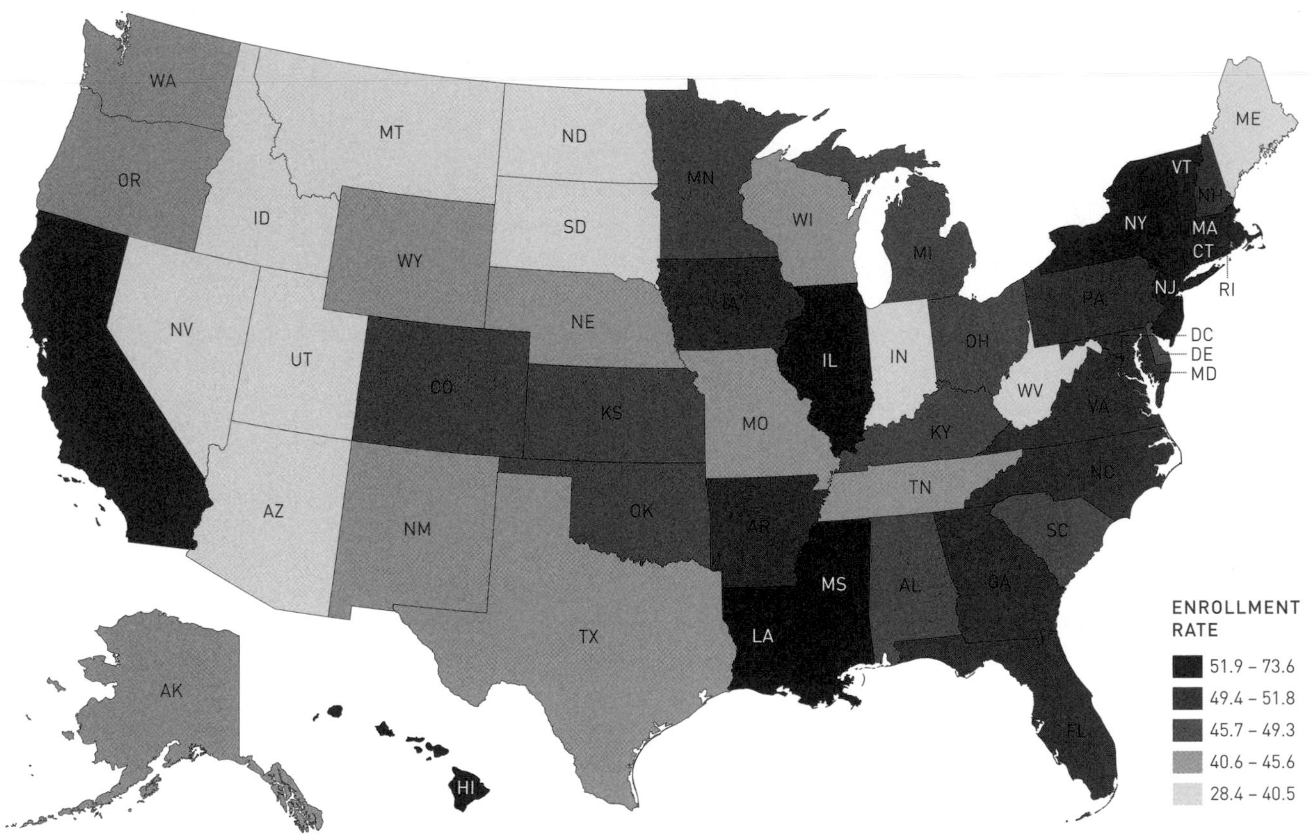

Preschool offers children from disadvantaged backgrounds a chance to start kindergarten on **equal footing** with their more privileged peers.

estimates that a universal preschool program would add over $2 trillion to the United States' gross domestic product (GDP) by 2080.[64]

Recognizing the value of preschool education and the risks posed to those who cannot afford it, in 1965 the United States initiated the Head Start program, a grant to states to provide free preschool for low-income children. In 2008–9, Head Start enrolled approximately 8 percent of all 3- and 4-year-olds,[65] which is half of the more than 2 million children in that age group living in poverty.[66] Unfortunately, because the quality of programs receiving funding through Head Start varies across the country, most participants do not receive the benefits associated with high-quality early childhood education. A recent evaluation of Head Start programs nationwide found overall that children in the program perform better than nonparticipants on a range of metrics while enrolled, but most of those effects disappear by early elementary school.[67]

Nationally, the rate of enrollment in preschool for 3- and 4-year-olds ranges from 28 percent in Nevada to 74 percent in Washington, DC (see **MAP 3**). In 2009, thirty-eight states had policies funding preschool education to some extent. State-funded preschool programs were conspicuously lacking in twelve states (see sidebar). Florida, Georgia, and Oklahoma are the only states with universal preschool, which they provide exclusively to 4-year-olds.

Beyond provision, the quality of state-funded preschool also varies. In 2009 barely half of all state-funded preschool programs required teachers to have a bachelor's degree,[68] despite evidence that low-quality early childhood education can actually damage a child's development.[69]

The vast majority of preschool services available nationwide are private, with 70 percent paid for by parent fees.[70] Employer credits and subsidies, charitable foundation grants and programs, and state subsidies occasionally supplement parents' out-of-pocket expenses.

The lack of a coordinated preschool policy results in access that is fragmented largely according to socioeconomic status. Children whose mothers graduated from college are twice as likely to be enrolled in preschool as those whose mothers did not finish high school, and children from families with earnings at the median or above are one and a half times as likely to be enrolled as children from families with earnings at or below the poverty line.[71]

That the quality of preschool services varies tremendously, both within and between states, is a critical issue. Preschool only confers advantages when it is of high quality, and far too many preschools today, particularly those that serve children from low-income families, badly fail the quality test. Expanding access is necessary but not sufficient; closing the school readiness gap requires that early childhood education settings have qualified teachers and sufficient resources. Currently, work with young children is one of the lowest-paying occupations, something that must change to attract professionals with the necessary skills and training.

States without State-Funded Preschool, 2009

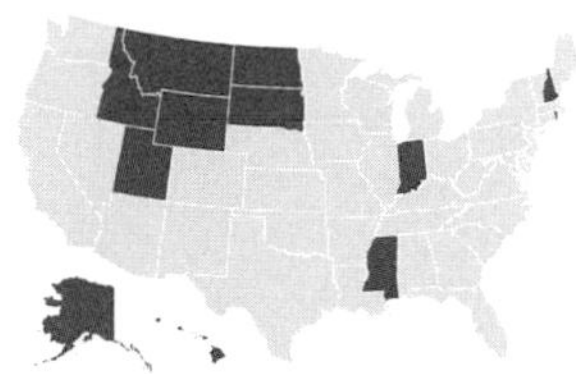

- Alaska
- Hawaii
- Idaho
- Indiana
- Mississippi
- Montana
- New Hampshire
- North Dakota
- Rhode Island
- South Dakota
- Utah
- Wyoming

Source: Barnett et al., *State of Preschool 2009*

Success in High School: The Bare Minimum

GRADUATION RATES AND THE SILENT EPIDEMIC

Whether a student graduates from high school is a reflection of the student's previous educational experiences and a critical indicator of the student's future life prospects. Although the Education Index shows that high school attainment has been rising, and that gaps in attainment by racial and ethnic groups are narrowing, recent research indicates that the percentage of students graduating within four years has plummeted over the past forty years, and the gap in on-time graduation between whites and Asian Americans on the one hand and Latinos, African Americans, and Native Americans on the other hand has remained unchanged.[72]

In 2008, 737,000 students took the test to obtain a General Educational Development (GED) credential,[73] nearly one in four of the high school seniors enrolled that year.[74] Initiated after World War II to allow returning soldiers to complete their education, the GED is a "second-chance" degree that was never intended to replace a high school diploma,[75] and it confers only a fraction of a diploma's benefits. Compared to high school graduates, GED recipients go on to college far less frequently, and they earn substantially less.[76]

The GED is a "second-chance" degree that was never intended to replace a high school diploma.

Nationally, one in three American students do not graduate with a high school diploma after four years; for African Americans, Latinos, and Native Americans, the fraction is closer to one in two.[77] Poor data collection and reporting mechanisms and widespread ignorance of this phenomenon have led one group of researchers to term the rise in dropouts "the silent epidemic."[78]

On-time graduation rates vary considerably by state, ranging from a low of 52.0 percent in Nevada to a high of 88.6 percent in Vermont (see **FIGURE 4**). Not completing high school is associated with a variety of other ills. High school dropouts live an average of seven fewer years than high school graduates,[79] and the gap in life expectancy between dropouts and graduates has been widening over the past three decades.[80] Dropouts earn about a quarter less than high school graduates, are twice as likely to live in poverty, and four times as likely to be unemployed.[81] They are also eight times as likely to be incarcerated.[82]

Students of low socioeconomic status are more likely to drop out of school.[83] Students from disadvantaged backgrounds start school with fewer financial and educational resources; they may be more likely to work jobs in addition to attending school and have higher rates of teen parenthood.[84] Recent immigrants, particularly those who struggle with English, are both less likely to enroll in high school and more likely to drop out after they do enroll.[85] **BOX 6** presents some promising efforts to reduce dropout rates. Students with disabilities also graduate at lower rates than students not classified as disabled.[86]

FIGURE 4 Public High School Graduation Rates, by State, 2006–7

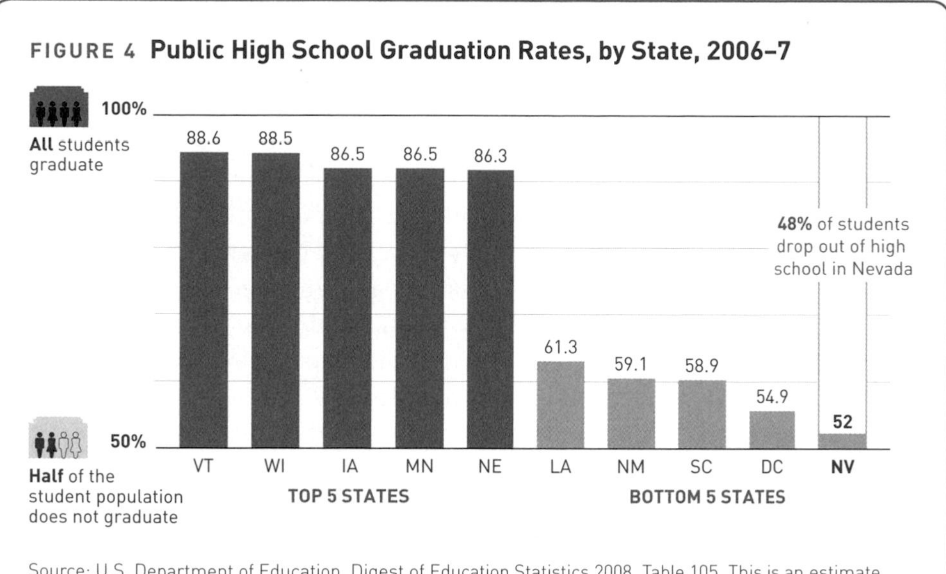

Source: U.S. Department of Education, Digest of Education Statistics 2008, Table 105. This is an estimate of the percentage of an entering freshman class graduating in four years. For all states, see "Access to Knowledge" Indicator Table on page 242.

BOX 6 Successful Approaches for Reducing High School Dropout Rates

Those at risk of dropping out of high school tend to share a common set of warning signs. Students who fail core courses in English or math, achieve low grades, score poorly on assessments, exhibit attendance or discipline problems, or are held back are more likely to drop out.[87] Because many of these warning signs appear long before the high school years, a movement toward developing early warning systems has begun to take root.

By flagging students who exhibit a critical mass of dropout factors, stakeholders can intervene with targeted assistance while students are still likely to benefit from it. Louisiana has instituted a pioneering early warning system that sends emails to teachers and administrators twice a month containing information on students who have exhibited dropout warning signs.[88] For early warning systems to be effective, student tracking must begin early and be accompanied by careful analysis of local factors and by user-friendly technological platforms.

The age at which students are legally required to remain in school varies by state, from 18 to 14. Raising the age of compulsory school attendance has been shown to increase graduation rates[89] and may be a logical place to begin staunching the flood of dropouts.

New Hampshire, Nevada, Colorado, and Illinois have all raised the age of compulsory attendance in recent years. Other states have stepped up enforcement of truancy regulations or have weighted graduation rates more heavily in the systems they use to hold schools accountable for certain benchmarks.[90]

Analyses of dropout intervention programs have revealed mixed results overall.[91] Certain mentoring programs, for example, tend to show small and fleeting positive effects.[92] However, Career Academies, an alternative education program that functions within a traditional school, have achieved robust effects on dropout prevention, graduation rates, and test scores.[93] Career Academies establish partnerships with local employers and combine an academic curriculum with vocational elements. Approximately fifteen hundred Career Academies are operating in the United States.[94]

BUILDING A BETTER NEIGHBORHOOD SCHOOL

Although a hot topic of debate for decades, experts now generally accept that the neighborhood in which a student comes of age exerts the second most powerful influence on life prospects. Family background is the first.[95] Three in five students go to school in one of America's fifty most populous metropolitan areas,[96] where residential segregation remains strong.[97] All else being equal, students from high-poverty neighborhoods are more likely to drop out than students from low-poverty neighborhoods.[98] While the country has eliminated legal barriers to integrated housing markets, and overt and intentional discrimination has dropped dramatically since the 1970s,[99] discrimination nonetheless remains. Nonetheless, a thorough analysis of residential patterns between 1890 and 1990 found that continuing segregation is largely the result of differential spending on housing: whites are willing to pay more to live in affluent neighborhoods than are African Americans with equivalent financial resources.[100]

Teacher quality is, hands down, the most powerful classroom factor influencing student achievement.

Schools tend to be more racially segregated than the neighborhoods in which they are located, as a result of white residents spurning local schools for magnet, charter, or private schools.[101] Yet attempts at correcting this situation can lead to unintended consequences. Holding other factors constant, the racial makeup of a school appears to have little influence on student outcomes. Even among students in racially diverse schools, de facto segregation tends to occur by virtue of the courses students take.[102] In fact, researchers Federico Echenique and Roland Fryer estimate that schools are more socially integrated—that is, minorities interact more closely with whites—when minorities are relatively scarce; once the proportion of a minority population reaches a critical mass of 25 percent, interaction between minorities and whites falls precipitously.[103]

Policy makers are eager to break the link between poor neighborhoods and disadvantaged schools. Unfortunately, researchers have yet to discover a silver bullet, since virtually every type of intervention aimed at changing a student's social context—from neighborhood relocation programs to school vouchers and the public school choice movement—has shown mixed results.[104] For example, despite much excitement about charter schools, which receive public money but are permitted to operate outside of the traditional public school regulatory framework, the overall record of student performance in charters has disappointed even the staunchest advocates for school choice. A 2009 Stanford University evaluation of the country's charter schools found that only 17 percent of charter schools showed gains in student performance that were better than progress made at regular public schools, while 37 percent of charters performed worse than regular schools, and the remainder did no differently.[105]

The mixed findings from various attempts to change students' environments encourage continued innovation, however, especially since explanations for program shortcomings often point not to flaws inherent in the theory that supports the intervention, but to the difficulties in scaling up model programs.

It is useful to explore and attempt to replicate the practices in place at the 17 percent of charter schools that do show significant performance gains, for example. Still, the lack of consensus among researchers calls into question the soundness of policies that place heavy weight on school choice expansion without more attention to quality control.

The Obama administration has called for more parents to be able to choose schools beyond their assigned local public schools. It supports expansion of charter and magnet schools in its blueprint for reauthorizing the Elementary and Secondary Schools Act, the main federal statute that provides funding to states (previously known as No Child Left Behind).[106] As Congress moves toward a vote, legislators must weigh the merits—and ethics—of subjecting students to potentially ineffectual or even damaging experiments against the merits of a perhaps equally alarming alternative: the status quo.

What are some conclusions that can be drawn? Although relocating students has generally been unsuccessful, evidence nevertheless shows that disadvantaged students perform better in high-achieving schools than in low-achieving schools.[107] Capping class size at fifteen students is similarly shown to significantly reduce the gap in test scores between minorities and whites,[108] although the effects of small class sizes are strongest during the first years of primary school.[109] Beyond these and all other factors, however, is the quality of the teacher. Research suggests this is the classroom factor that has the most decisive effect on student achievement.[110] Robust statistical models predict that a modest increase in the quality of teachers (which researchers approximate using teachers' college admissions test scores) in a predominantly minority school will nearly close the achievement gap with a predominantly white school.[111] Teachers with at least three years of experience are also more effective,[112] but because experienced teachers often choose to work in less challenging environments, at-risk youth are more often taught by inexperienced teachers.[113] **BOX 7** addresses emerging research on teacher quality reform.

Capping class size at **fifteen students** is shown to significantly reduce the gap in test scores between minorities and whites.

THE PERSISTENCE OF FUNDING DISPARITIES

A third critical area that influences high school success is funding. Schools are often hamstrung in their efforts to reduce class sizes and recruit quality teachers where they are most needed. A primary impediment is lack of funding, which is determined largely at the state and local levels. Less than 10 percent of public school funding comes from the federal government. States provide schools with half of their revenue, and municipalities raise the balance,[114] subject to constraints that states impose.

In a majority of states, schools with the poorest students receive less funding per pupil than schools with the fewest low-income students. Schools in the bottom fifth as measured by the number of students eligible for free- or reduced-price school lunch received $906 less per pupil (2009 dollars) than schools in the highest

BOX 7 Performance-Based Pay and the Quest for the Elusive Good Teacher

Mounting evidence demonstrates that a high-quality teacher is the single most influential factor in boosting student achievement and reducing disparities among different groups. Despite the evidence, debate rages over the best ways to identify, recruit, prepare, compensate, deploy, and retain the most promising candidates—as well as how to retire teachers who fall short of the high-stakes mission of preparing America's youth. However, key aspects of the teaching profession—salary structures, tenure, education school admissions and curriculum, and teacher certification—clearly need reform.

Measure of America 2008–2009 explored the issue of alternative teacher certification programs like Teach for America, which puts promising young candidates in front of struggling classrooms in exchange for a fast-track teaching credential. Another innovation that has gained steam involves compensating teachers based on performance instead of seniority and degree attainment.

The salary of nearly every American public school teacher is determined by a combination of experience and education,[116] despite the findings that neither advanced degrees nor more than three to five years of teaching experience have much effect at all on student achievement.[117] The use of performance-based compensation to determine bonuses, commissions, and in some cases, entire salaries, is widespread in the private sector. Experiments with compensating teachers according to performance rather than or in addition to years in the classroom have been conducted in several countries around the world (among others, Israel, India, and the United Kingdom) and a growing number of states. In 2007 Texas and Florida were operating statewide performance-based award schemes; at least seventy-eight other school districts across the country were participating in different performance-based programs funded by states, private foundations, or the Department of Education.[118]

Some of these innovations have resulted in tremendous increases in student achievement. The Israeli experiment, for example, centered around providing bonuses of up to half the median teacher salary to teachers based on their students' performance on subject-based high school graduation exams.[119] Performance was gauged according to a value-added model that attempted to separate out how much of the students' score could be attributed to the teacher's own efforts, as opposed to differences in student backgrounds or effort. The experiment also implemented safeguards against test score manipulation. The results found statistically significant gains in student performance across the board, and rather than attempt to game the system, teachers who succeeded in boosting student test scores were found to have experimented with new pedagogical methods and to have spent additional time on instruction. The Israeli experiment may be unique in the rigor of its application, but it points to the potential for well-designed performance-based programs in other locations.

Whether performance-based compensation succeeds in inducing more or more highly qualified teachers into the profession remains to be seen. Measuring the degree to which a teacher actually contributes to a student's outcome has proven notoriously challenging; it requires careful data collection and complex econometric modeling techniques that are not always available. Critics allege further that performance-based compensation mechanisms run several risks: spurring competition and displacing cooperation among teachers, teaching to the test at the expense of broader subject exploration, and turning the teaching profession from a noble calling into a mercenary occupation. Can performance-based initiatives avoid these pitfalls and light the path toward teacher-quality reform? Like most educational reform innovations, the proof will be in the pudding.

Less than 10 percent of public school funding comes from the federal government.

income quartile, for the 2003–4 school year.[115] This disparity is even more alarming given federal guidelines indicating that low-income students require 40 percent more than state average per-pupil spending amounts to achieve proficiency on state standards. In New York and Illinois the gap between high- and low-income schools was $2,467 and $2,047 per pupil, respectively. New Jersey and Alaska, where high-poverty schools receive substantially more funding than affluent schools, are exceptions.

As states determine how school districts disburse funds, access to resources that enable schools to keep class sizes small and to hire the most

effective teachers depends to a large extent on the state in which one lives.
New Jersey provides an important test case for the connection between funding and achievement. In the mid-1980s, high-poverty districts in New Jersey spent over $2,000 less per pupil (in 2009 dollars) than more affluent districts—a disparity that persists in some other states. But after more than twenty years of court battles, poor New Jersey communities finally succeeded in gaining a greater share of state funding. Their schools used the increased funds to hire more support staff, reduce class sizes, and enroll students in preschool. Students responded with dramatic gains in achievement. While achievement scores on state tests increased statewide from 1999 through 2007, the scores of students at schools benefiting from reform showed the greatest gains, narrowing by more than one-third the gap in achievement between students from poor and affluent schools.[120]

In addition to funding disparities, the way money is spent also matters. Personnel costs invariably account for the lion's share of each school district's budget, and this is not surprising given the centrality of the teacher to student achievement. Generous benefits, a growing portion of personnel costs, can cultivate an attractive employment environment for new candidates and ensure well-deserved retirement security for those who have devoted their lives to educating American's youth. However, benefits tilted toward seniority—through which pensioners can sometimes earn as much as double their salary—can create perverse incentives for staff to retire early.[121] In Ohio, a state with a typical teacher pension plan, the median retirement age for teachers is only 58.[122] Beyond rewarding senior staff and retirees for distinguished careers of service, these types of pension schemes common to many states not only fail to attract promising new candidates but they devour resources urgently needed to fill positions in the schools that most need them. A commitment to redressing funding disparities between districts can only succeed alongside a commitment to equitable and efficient compensation policies within districts.

Low-income students require 40 percent more than average pre-pupil spending to achieve proficiency on state standards.

College: Enrollment, Persistence, and Success

The earnings gap between a college graduate and a high school graduate is even larger than the gap between a high school graduate and a dropout. College graduates can expect to earn $750,000 more than high school graduates over the course of their career.[123] Despite historic rises in the number and percentage of high school graduates continuing their education, college students today are taking longer to graduate and are less likely to receive a degree than ever before.[124] Financial aid provisions have been eclipsed by the soaring costs of attending college, and many students are unprepared for college work itself.

BOX 8 Special Education and Disability in American Schools

In the 2007 school year, more than 6 million American public school students, or about 13 percent, were designated as disabled, and the rate of disability diagnosis has been rising over the past four decades.[125] Almost six in ten disabled students are classified as having learning disabilities or impairments in speech or language. The remainder are classified with emotional disturbance, mental retardation, health impairments, or other disabilities (see **TABLE 9**).

TABLE 9 Children 3 to 21 Served by the "Individuals with Disabilities Education Act," by Disability

TYPE OF DISABILITY	TOTAL (thousands)	DISTRIBUTION (%)	PERCENT OF PUBLIC SCHOOL ENROLLMENT (%)
All disabilities	6,606	100.0	13.4
Specific learning disabilities	2,573	39.0	5.2
Speech or language impairments	1,456	22.0	3.0
Mental retardation	500	7.6	1.0
Emotional disturbance	442	6.7	0.9
Hearing impairments	79	1.2	0.2
Orthopedic impairments	67	1.0	0.1
Other health impairments	641	9.7	1.3
Visual impairments	29	0.4	0.1
Multiple disabilities	138	2.1	0.3
Deaf-blindness	2	0.0	0.0
Autism	296	4.5	0.6
Traumatic brain injury	25	0.4	0.1
Developmental delay	358	5.4	0.7

Source: U.S. Department of Education, *Digest of Education 2009*, Table 50.

How Far We've Come

- Once confined to separate classrooms and even separate institutions, students with disabilities today are more likely to spend a large part of their time in a classroom with non-disabled peers. Ninety-seven percent of disabled students spend between 40 and 80 percent of their time in a regular classroom.[126]
- Academic achievement—and potential achievement—varies according to the type of disability and the resources and efforts expended to address it. Overall, students with disabilities do not perform as well on academic assessments, although plenty are able to reach basic, proficient, and even advanced levels of achievement. Students classified as disabled graduate from high school at lower rates than students without designated disabilities, but the gap varies widely from state to state.[127]
- The federal government requires that schools assist disabled students with their transition from school to the next phase of their lives, and many students do make successful transitions. Eight in ten students with disabilities report engaging in some form of education or employment within two years of leaving high school.[128]

And How Far We Still Need to Go

- Native Americans and African Americans are more likely to be diagnosed with a disability than students of other races.[129] Further research is needed to determine to what extent certain groups are in fact at greater risk for disability, and whether minority groups are being unfairly stigmatized.
- The Individuals with Disabilities Education Act (IDEA) authorizes an additional 40 percent of average per-pupil expenditure for each disabled student. Since the act was enacted in 1975, however, Congress has typically allocated no more than 17 percent.[130]
- Students with multiple disabilities (see **TABLE 9**) face challenges that go well beyond gaining a basic grasp of academic fundamentals. Such children, who may experience limited mobility or difficulties communicating, require a far more comprehensive vision of education.
- For severely disabled children with few prospects for independent living, efforts to teach academic skills may be better directed toward creating stable, long-term homes that maximize and sustain emotional connection and dignified, compassionate care.

PREPARING FOR COLLEGE

The expansion of institutions of higher learning was once championed as a way to make college more accessible for more people. Recent evidence points to decidedly mixed results, however. College enrollment has increased alongside shrinking graduation rates. Among four-year college students who enrolled in 2000, only 36 percent graduated within four years, and within six years only an additional 21 percent had graduated. Students at public colleges and universities took longer and graduated at lower rates than students at private schools.[131]

The percentage of students who enroll in two-year colleges (rather than four-year colleges) has grown over the past forty years.[132] Community colleges offer opportunities to those who might not otherwise be able to access postsecondary education, and for those who aspire to careers in certain sectors, the vocational training that some two-year programs provide can promote successful labor market outcomes.[133] However, community colleges do not serve well the strong majority of their students who express an intention to transfer to four-year programs.[134] After three years, four in ten community college students who express the intention to obtain a bachelor's degree have already dropped out of school,[135] and only one in three ever advance to a four-year program,[136] let alone complete one. Even among students with the same high school grades and admissions test scores, those who matriculate directly to a four-year college are ultimately more likely to earn a bachelor's degree.[137] This phenomenon appears to hold true at less selective institutions more generally. A recent study of two hundred thousand students at public universities found that among students with similar characteristics, those who attend a less selective public school instead of a flagship state university are far less likely to graduate from college.[138]

Less selective institutions may have fewer resources to invest in student success. In the case of community colleges, schools may also strive to fulfill several competing missions at once:[139] in addition to preparing students for transfer to bachelor's programs, many community colleges also offer extensive vocational training as well as resources for the local community, such as adult and continuing education opportunities and programs for talented high school students. The diverse student bodies at less selective institutions may include more nontraditional students juggling work and family obligations, as well as many students who arrive at school unprepared for college work by their high school experiences.

Half of all college students lack the reading skills necessary to succeed in college.[140] Increasing numbers of college students must take remedial courses, a consequence of underachievement in high school and a lack of higher-level coursework options in many secondary schools. Three in five students at two-year colleges and one in four students at four-year colleges need one year or more of remedial coursework.[141] By taking remedial courses, students necessarily miss out on other academic opportunities that college provides. Remedial course-taking also severely reduces the likelihood of college completion.

Earnings Gap between High School and College Graduates

The earnings gap between **a college graduate and a high school graduate** is even larger than the gap between **a high school graduate and a high school dropout**.

The most common recommendation for college preparation is to align college standards with high school curriculum, rather than allowing high schools to pass the buck on to colleges for student achievement.[142] Taking advanced math in high school, for example, turns out to be one of the strongest predictors of successful bachelor's degree attainment.[143] The K–12 and college education systems evolved separately, but recent efforts have sought to bring the two closer together. Thirty-eight states have initiated "P–16" and "P–20" councils (prekindergarten through college or prekindergarten through graduate school) to coordinate alignment. However, high schools struggle with students who bring deficiencies from earlier schooling levels, and many schools also grapple with large populations of poor students, disabled students, and students learning English. College outreach programs aim to provide encouragement and resources to supplement high school guidance counselors (see **BOX 9**).

PAYING FOR COLLEGE

Three in five students at **two-year colleges** need one year or more of remedial coursework.

One in four students at **four-year colleges** needs one year or more of remedial coursework.

Between 2000 and 2008 the cost of attending college increased by 30 percent. This includes costs at both four-year and two-year institutions, continuing a long-standing trend.[144] Including room and board, the cost of attending a public university in 2008 averaged over $14,000, about half of median personal income, and the cost of attending a private university averaged about $30,000, surpassing the median income.[145]

The cost of higher education has reached a crisis point. The United States spends a greater proportion of GDP on higher education than any other country,[146] yet the proportion of public money to private money invested in postsecondary education is smaller than in every peer country except Japan and South Korea.[147] American students pay far more for their educations than students in any other developed country.[148] The trend shows no signs of abating. A survey of 863 colleges and universities revealed that endowments lost an average of 23 percent between 2008 and 2009,[149] making continued tuition hikes all but certain.

Increases in financial aid have not kept pace with increases in costs. The federal government established Pell Grants in 1972 to assist low-income students. Thirty years ago, the average Pell Grant covered nearly 80 percent of college costs at a four-year institution, and almost all the costs at a two-year school. Today, with nearly 6 million undergraduates relying on Pell Grants, the award covers only about one-third of the cost of attending a four-year school, and less than two-thirds of the cost of a two-year school. Pell Grant recipients today are less likely than those a decade ago to apply their grants to four-year colleges. They are more likely than ever before to attend commercial, for-profit educational service providers.[150]

Recently a shift has taken place away from need-based aid to merit-based aid. During the past decade, states increased merit aid by more than 200 percent, while increasing need-based aid by 60 percent. Between 2003 and 2007 the amount of aid that research universities granted to students from families earning $80,400 or more increased by more than the amount to students from families earning

BOX 9 Do College Outreach Programs Work?

The quality of information and encouragement available to can make a tremendous difference in their decisions about college. Students in low-achieving districts, where attending college is the exception rather than the norm, too often lack the information and support necessary for the application process, and help with choosing a course of study, applying for aid, and weighing options. These resources tend to be concentrated in suburban districts and urban magnet schools.

To combat this problem, more than one thousand college outreach programs are now operating in the United States, serving 5 percent of all students and 10 percent of all students in poverty.[151] The overall success of college outreach programs is mixed, however.[152]

Upward Bound is a federally funded, locally implemented program that provides college preparation resources to approximately fifty thousand students from low-income families. Resources include college counseling, academic tutoring, and an offsite academic summer retreat. Upward Bound has been shown to increase college enrollment among participants by 6 percent.[153]

Talent Search, which serves close to four hundred thousand low-income students, operates similarly to Upward Bound, except its services are more narrowly focused on providing information on the college search, application, and financial aid processes. An evaluation of Talent Search programs in three states found that Talent Search participants applied to college, sought financial aid, and ultimately enrolled in college at significantly higher rates than nonparticipants. At $375 per participant, Talent Search also costs less than one-tenth of Upward Bound. However, in Indiana, the third state under evaluation, program participants did not show higher rates of enrollment.[154]

GEAR UP, like Talent Search and Upward Bound, is a national grant program for which schools may apply on a competitive basis. Instead of targeting individual students, GEAR UP provides funds to low-income schools to offer college counseling services to students throughout a particular grade level, although participation by individual students is voluntary. Based on a decade of data, a preliminary evaluation of GEAR UP found it had no effect on college enrollment.[155]

$54,000 or less. These shifts in aid at research universities have accompanied increases in enrollments by students from wealthy families and decreases in enrollments by students from poorer families.[156] The rise in tax credits for college expenses and college savings plans has also been shown to favor students from higher income brackets, whose families are more likely to itemize tax deductions.[157]

The gap between available direct aid and the rising costs of college has led to increased reliance on student loans—and a resulting avalanche of student debt. Both the percentage of students graduating with debt and the amount of debt they carry have increased since the mid-1990s. In 1996, fewer than six in ten students graduated with debt, and their debt averaged less than $18,000 (in 2008 dollars). In 2008, the average debt of graduating seniors with loans (two-thirds of all seniors) was $23,200.[158] The federal student loan programs (Stafford and Perkins) regulate the amount of money that students can borrow at any one time and cap interest rates at manageable levels—even deferring interest in certain circumstances. Because the maximum allowable amount that students can borrow through these

Student debt has increased over the past decade.

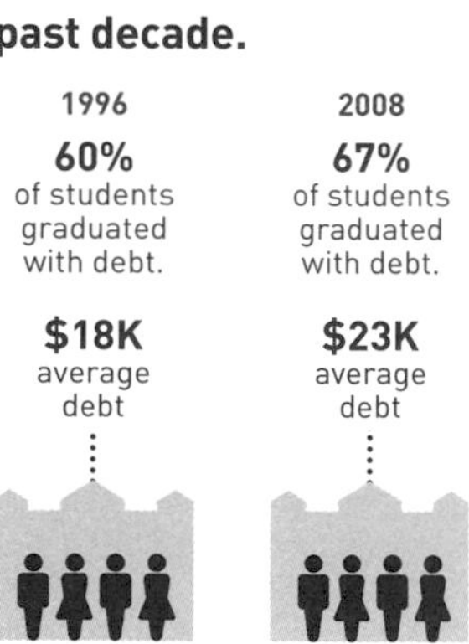

programs has not increased with the increase in college costs, in recent years a booming private student loan market has emerged. Interest rates and lending policies are far less regulated. While one rationale for the existence of loans is for high-income students to make a strategic economic bet against future earnings, low-income students are just as likely to take out private loans—even though they stand at high risk for default.[159]

Increasing Resilience in Access to Knowledge: What Will It Take?

American meritocracy rests, above all, on access to education. Public schools function as a result of a social contract between families and society. Families send their children to school with expectations that they will do their best to succeed. In exchange, schools nurture children's development and prepare them for roles in economic and democratic life. Under the terms of this bargain, hard work, ambition, and talent determine who ascends the ladders of educational attainment, economic security, and social, political, and economic leadership.

Attempts over the past half century to renew America's promise to its children by enforcing this educational contract have been sincere, but reality continues to fall short. While educational achievement remains the chief means by which Americans of humble origins move up the economic ladder, class—the educational qualifications and financial resources of a person's family—substantially predicts success in school. In fact, this correlation is especially strong in the United States. Among thirty peer nations of Europe, Oceania, and East Asia, the link between parental socioeconomic status and student achievement on an international science exam was strongest in the United States.

The educational ladder to success is presently broken. Children from families with limited financial and educational resources are falling behind. To start off, a lost early childhood education is impossible to replace: students who fall behind early often never catch up. Without a family culture of education, including parental expectations of success, and without the financial security to remain enrolled and thriving in high school, many students postpone graduation or give up altogether. For too many who do graduate from high school, the rising costs of college put higher education out of reach, while the labyrinthine application processes for admission and financial assistance can overwhelm those who are first in their families to chart a path to college.

Families matter, but so do neighborhoods and communities. Indeed, access to knowledge varies significantly by geography. Most preschool, elementary, and secondary education policy, curriculum, and funding are determined at the state level, where regulations vary widely. Two students with similar background, ability, and ambition who attend schools in different states can be set on wildly divergent paths. The chance that a 3- or 4-year-old is enrolled in preschool is one-and-a-

College Enrollment Is Outpacing College Readiness

The National Assessment of Education Progress (NAEP), called the Nation's Report Card, tracks trends in educational achievement by testing American students at ages 9, 13, and 17. Since the 1970s, the average scores for 9- and 13-year-olds in reading and math have increased, and gaps in achievement between students of different backgrounds have narrowed considerably.

However, today the scores for 17-year-olds overall are no higher than they were in the 1970s. Despite a growing percentage of students taking higher-level mathematics courses, still only 6 percent of 17-year-olds can solve multi-step problems and apply algebra—rudimentary skills necessary for success in college.

These results suggest that college preparation still has a long way to go to catch up with historically high rates of college enrollment.

Data source: Rampey et al., *NAEP 2008 Trends in Academic Progress.*

half times greater in Massachusetts than in Maine, a thirty-minute drive up I-95. A fourth-grader in Colorado is twice as likely to be a proficient reader as a fourth-grader across the state line in New Mexico. In New York, a high school freshman is twice as likely to delay graduating than a freshman in neighboring New Jersey. And the town or neighborhood in which a student lives sometimes trumps the influence of the state itself: disparities among and within school districts loom large due to residential segregation by income, race, and ethnicity. Funding gaps between schools serving affluent families and those serving poor families are vast; Asbury Park School District in New Jersey spends $30,800 per child while Waterford Unified School District in California spends $4,951.

These trends are not novel. But the cost of extreme stratification is growing. The Great Recession exposed a tectonic shift in the economy. High school dropouts are now less likely to earn a decent living or even to find work at all than ever before. Success in today's labor market requires advanced academic abilities, strong credentials, and transferable skills. People who lack a college education are severely disadvantaged compared to workers with a bachelor's degree. Unless we address the structural weaknesses in our education system, the country's future prosperity, relative standing in the world, and economic security are in jeopardy. Yet recent events and a growing body of research have combined to raise hopes for a turnaround. On the front lines of today's education reform movement is an initiative to establish common curricular standards among the states. Coordinated by the National Governors Association and the state education department heads, the Common Core State Standards Initiative aims to establish clearer, more consistent, and higher expectations for schools across the country. Embraced so far by forty-eight states, the initiative holds promise for students to obtain a consistent and rigorous education no matter where they live.

A fourth-grader in Colorado is **twice as likely** to be a proficient reader as a fourth-grader in nearby New Mexico

Establishing universal standards is a first step toward diminishing these disparities. Common standards do not, however, guarantee the necessary resources to meet the goals, nor that states will be held accountable for their commitments. A shared vision of educational outcomes requires a shared investment in educational resources and a common regulatory framework. Several avenues exist by which governments, private industry, and individuals can pursue improvement in access to quality education immediately.

BUILDING RESILIENCE IN CHILDHOOD

Ensure Universal, Quality Preschool

Overwhelming evidence suggests that education should begin at age 3. In numerous studies of low-income parents and their young children, quality preschool has proved to be the single most decisive and cost-effective intervention—one that sets youth on a path to lifetime success. Despite a solid consensus among researchers about the value of early education, many parents and policy makers remain unaware of just how crucial preschool is. Similarly, they lack the tools to differentiate a high-quality preschool program from a substandard, and potentially harmful, one.

Promoting these research findings and raising awareness among policy makers and parents is essential to achieving the long-advocated goal of universal, quality preschool. With more public support, several options exist for increasing the availability of and enrollment in high-quality preschool. The federal Head Start program could be expanded—but only with quality-control mechanisms and adequate funding in place. Elementary schools could add additional grades. Model private programs could be scaled up and subsidized. Program operators, research groups, advocates, and government agencies must continue to disseminate information about best practices in early childhood education, and to set standards for program delivery to a degree no less rigorous than standard-setting procedures for elementary and secondary education.

BUILDING RESILIENCE IN ADOLESCENCE

More than a quarter of high school freshmen do not graduate in four years—if they graduate at all.

Address the High School Dropout Crisis Head-on

Despite an overall increase in educational attainment over the past thirty years, evidence now shows that the rate of on-time high school graduation has remained essentially unchanged. More than a quarter of high school freshmen do not graduate in four years—if they graduate at all. In most cases, failure to graduate from high school on time forecloses the possibility of college. As a start, by helping preschool children develop noncognitive skills, including persistence and the deferral of gratification in service of a goal, we can lay the foundation for behaviors and habits that will help them succeed in school.

New systems are emerging in many states to identify and engage at-risk youth, which could revolutionize the way schools address the problem. Raising the compulsory age of education to 18 in states where it is earlier is an obvious step. Certain evidence-based programs that have been shown to keep at-risk youth engaged—such as Career Academies and the Harlem Children Zone's community schooling model—should be expanded aggressively, while many other programs that have produced no measurable results should be abandoned. Additionally, intervention programs targeted at particular at-risk populations, such as immigrants and students with disabilities, can help stem the overall tide of dropouts.

Revitalize the Teaching Profession with Highly Qualified, Dedicated, and Adequately Compensated Recruits

As mounting evidence confirms that teacher quality is the single most influential classroom factor influencing student achievement, our nation's schools desperately need bright individuals with the training, commitment, and demonstrated capacity to guide young minds. Too few teachers serving at-risk children—and too few new recruits to the ranks of alternative teacher credentialing programs—possess all three necessary qualities. In revitalizing the teaching profession, ideologically driven and politically expedient efforts must yield to evidence-based solutions. Performance-based pay is one method that, when carefully applied, shows promise for recruiting and retaining excellent educators.

BUILDING RESILIENCE IN YOUNG ADULTHOOD

Offer and Encourage Challenging Coursework in All High Schools

Highly selective, high-cost colleges continue to educate the children of wealth and privilege who, by virtue of family resources and college-oriented high schools, arrive relatively well-prepared. Struggling high schools that have few students with college ambitions generally focus on "back to basics," an emphasis that often limits the higher-level coursework such schools offer and thus access to college. College preparation programs with proven track records include Talent Search and Upward Bound; additional strategies to help high schools manage a dual mission of redressing educational shortcomings and preparing students for college are sorely needed.

Revise the Business Model of Higher Education to Deflate Ballooning Tuition Costs

A college education is less affordable today than ever before. High costs discourage first-generation college applicants and saddle too many college students with unsustainable debt burdens. Legislation passed in 2010 tied Pell Grants to the Consumer Price Index in order to ensure that government aid to students at least keeps pace with inflation, and it established a program to forgive federal student loan debt after twenty years. But these laudable achievements are not enough to close the widening gap between need and aid. At the same time, taxpayers can only contribute so much to the high cost of higher education. It is time to reconsider the financial structure upon which the entire system of higher education operates, with the goal of minimizing barriers to access. Access to knowledge is a capability, not a commodity; no one should be priced out.

Highly selective, high-cost colleges continue to educate the children of wealth and privilege who, by virtue of family resources and college-oriented high schools, arrive relatively well-prepared.

***

Two centuries ago, Thomas Jefferson entreated Americans to "dream of an aristocracy of achievement," one that would arise from a "democracy of opportunity" unique to these shores. It remains not only a noble goal but, in a globalized knowledge economy, an increasingly vital one. This chapter's recommendations—some pragmatic, others idealistic—are based on the best available evidence and are aimed at preserving and expanding this nation's historically high rates of attainment and enrollment. In several areas, we require further study and evaluation. In others, however, for perhaps the first time in history, we have a foundation of research and understanding and the tools required to make real progress toward Jefferson's dream. Like Jefferson, we should continue to dream of democracy's promise and the achievements that are just outside our grasp. But during our waking hours, we must roll up our sleeves and get to work.

CHAPTER 4

A Decent Standard of Living

IN THIS SECTION:

How Do We Stack Up?

Median Earnings of Workers16 and Older

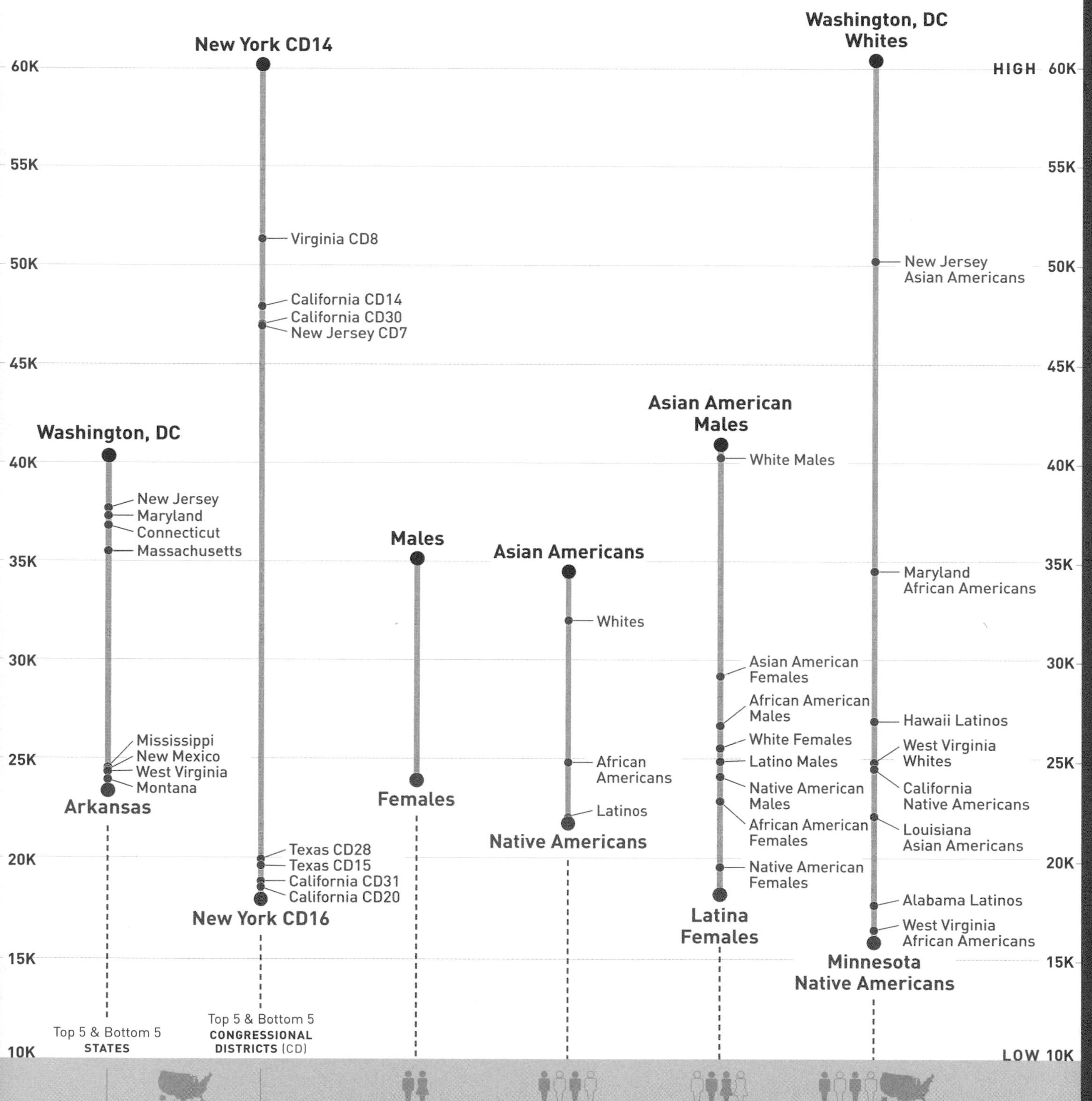

Introduction

"When you have your head in the freezer and your feet in the oven, on average, you are doing okay."

SECRETARY OF LABOR (1962–69) WILLARD WIRTZ,
discussing how workers were doing "on average."

The Great Recession has taken a far heavier toll on **men** than on women and on **workers under 30** than on workers over 55.

The recession that began in the last quarter of 2007 and continued officially through the last quarter of 2009 changed the lives of many and shook the confidence of most, but the financial downturn did not treat all equally. Among those who study labor patterns, one of the most surprising findings was the variation in the recession's impact on different groups.

By the final quarter of the recession, 29 million U.S. workers were unemployed or underemployed. Dividing workers by tenths according to income, those with the lowest earnings (annual household incomes below $12,500) had an unemployment rate of 31 percent—far higher than the worst year of the Great Depression[1] (see **FIGURE 1**). The unemployment rate declined as the income ladder rose, with the top decile (incomes above $150,000) working at what is generally considered to be full employment conditions—3.2 percent unemployment. In sum, the top fifth of households in America experienced small rises in unemployment while those at the bottom of the income ladder[2] experienced devastating levels. The recession took a far heavier toll on men than women, on workers under 30 than on workers over 55, and on those without a high school diploma than on those who are college-educated. The heaviest toll was on African American males.[3]

The human development approach was initially created both to challenge and expand upon the focus on money measures such as GDP and income in interpreting how people are faring. But economic and financial metrics remain a crucial part of the picture. As the data on the recession's impact on different groups show, **income was a powerful predictor of how one would fare during the recession, with the poorest Americans likely to fare the worst.** Because material well-being is a critical ingredient to overall well-being, one-third of the American HD Index measures the capabilities people have to enjoy a decent material standard of living, to have the money necessary to live well, to be well-nourished, to feel secure about the future, to pursue enjoyable leisure activities, and more.

Many different measures help to assess whether people are achieving a decent standard of living. **The American Human Development Index uses median personal earnings as a useful single measure to summarize people's material resources.** **BOX 1** explores other measures that reflect standard of living, including their benefits and drawbacks as analytical tools.

This chapter explores the median personal earnings of various groups—by state, congressional district, metro area, and racial/ethnic group—and analyzes important factors contributing to different levels of earnings. The chapter then evaluates other important measures—such as child poverty, unemployment, assets, and retirement savings—in order to examine the challenges and opportunities faced throughout the life cycle.

FIGURE 1 Unemployment Rates by Household Income, Fourth Quarter 2009 (%)

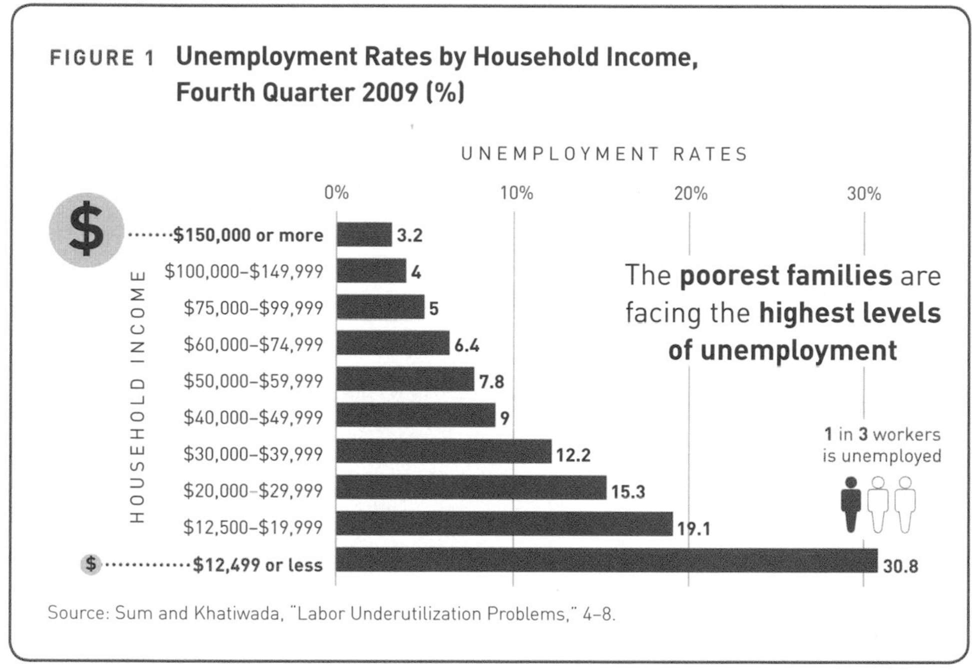

Source: Sum and Khatiwada, "Labor Underutilization Problems," 4–8.

In late 2009, low-income workers had unemployment rates nearly **ten times higher** than those of workers in households earning $150,000 or more.

BOX 1 Median Personal Earnings as the Measure of Standard of Living in the American HD Index

Median personal earnings are the typical amount those working full- or part-time receive from salaries or wages—generally the largest part of overall income. Median personal earnings do not include income from sources other than one's labor, such as interest on savings accounts, rental property income, or government programs such as Social Security.

Why Measure Median Earnings Instead of Mean?
Median earnings are the typical amount earned by an individual or household, obtained by dividing a group into two equal parts and selecting the middle figure. Considering the earnings of a group of ten people, if nine have annual earnings of $50,000 each, and one additional person earns $8 million, median personal earnings are fifty thousand dollars, a sum that accurately reflects earnings for nine of the group's ten members. **Mean earnings,** on the other hand, are average earnings, arrived at by adding up the income of everyone in the group divided by the total number in the group. Mean earnings of this group of ten individuals would be $845,000, a sum that accurately reflects no one in the group. **FIGURE 2** shows median and mean family income in the United States in the period 1998–2007. As is clear, while the increase in income for a typical family was less than $5,000, families with high earnings resulted in a raise in the mean by over $16,000.

FIGURE 2 Comparing Median and Mean Family Income in the United States, 1998–2007

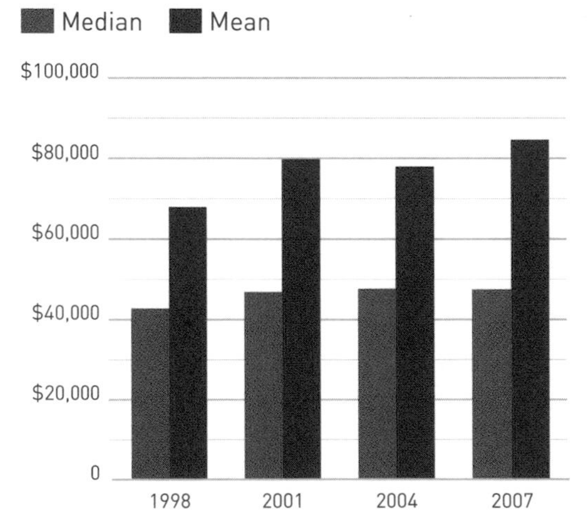

Source: Federal Reserve Board, Survey of Consumer Finances, 2007

In order to understand the situation of everyday Americans, the American HD Index uses median earnings, though analysis of both is helpful to understand the distribution of income in society.

Why Measure Personal Earnings Instead of Household Earnings?
Some people have asked why the American HD Index uses the earnings of an individual when couples in many two-income households pool their income. Household earnings are a useful measure, but personal earnings are critical in order to better understand the varied levels of access to income of men and women in our society.

While household decisions (who does the housework, how finances are organized and spent, etc.) are sometimes made jointly, research shows they are often made unevenly depending on the relative resources each person brings into the relationship.[4] And if the relationship ends in divorce, which is the case in more than 35 percent of marriages,[5] the lower earner generally experiences the biggest decline in standard of living. In addition, women head more than six in ten poor families.[6] Thus, boosting female incomes is one strategy for supporting struggling families and ensuring that children are given a strong start to becoming fulfilled, productive citizens.

Why Not Include Assets or Wealth?
Wealth is vital for building long-term economic security and acts as a cushion when income is disrupted. Ideally, the American HD Index would include wealth measures. However, wealth is more difficult to measure than income, in part because the value of assets like stocks and real estate are constantly in flux, and because the very wealthiest are likely to be missed in random sampling or decline to participate. The Federal Reserve Board, overcoming some of these challenges, produces reliable wealth data on the United States every three years through the Survey of Consumer Finances. However, wealth data are not available for states or congressional districts and thus cannot be incorporated into the American HD Index.

Why Not Adjust for Cost-of-Living Differences?
The cost of goods and services varies across the nation and within distinct regions. However, as discussed earlier, there is currently no official nationwide measure for cost-of-living differences that allows for comparisons from place to place.

Part I: What the Income Index Reveals

Historical Trends

EARNINGS TRENDS IN THE UNITED STATES

Since 1974, earnings for the U.S. population have been gradually rising, with some backsliding in the early 1980s, early 1990s, and again in 2008–2009. From just over $23,000 in the mid-1970s, median earnings are nearly $30,000 today. Closer inspection (see **FIGURE 3**) reveals that, in the more than three decades that comparable records have been kept, increases in female earnings have driven this upward trend. While male earnings edged up $2,500 in inflation-adjusted dollars since 1974, female earnings doubled (from about $12,800 to $24,700) during this same period.

While the overall trend consists of rising incomes and a narrowing gap between women's and men's earnings, the gap between the richest households and the rest has not narrowed. Using the most recent available data, **the top fifth of U.S. households take home exactly half the nation's income. The bottom fifth (a total of about 23 million households) earned less than 4 percent of America's income in 2008, the latest year for which data are available** (see **FIGURE 4**).

FIGURE 3 Median Earnings for Men and Women, 1974–2008

Sources: U.S. Census Bureau, American Community Survey (Table B20017), estimates for 2005–2008. U.S. Census Bureau, Current Population Survey (Tables P-41 and P-43), estimates for 1974–2004, adjusted for comparability with ACS estimates. See Methodological Notes for more details.

For over three decades, **female earnings** have risen faster than male earnings.

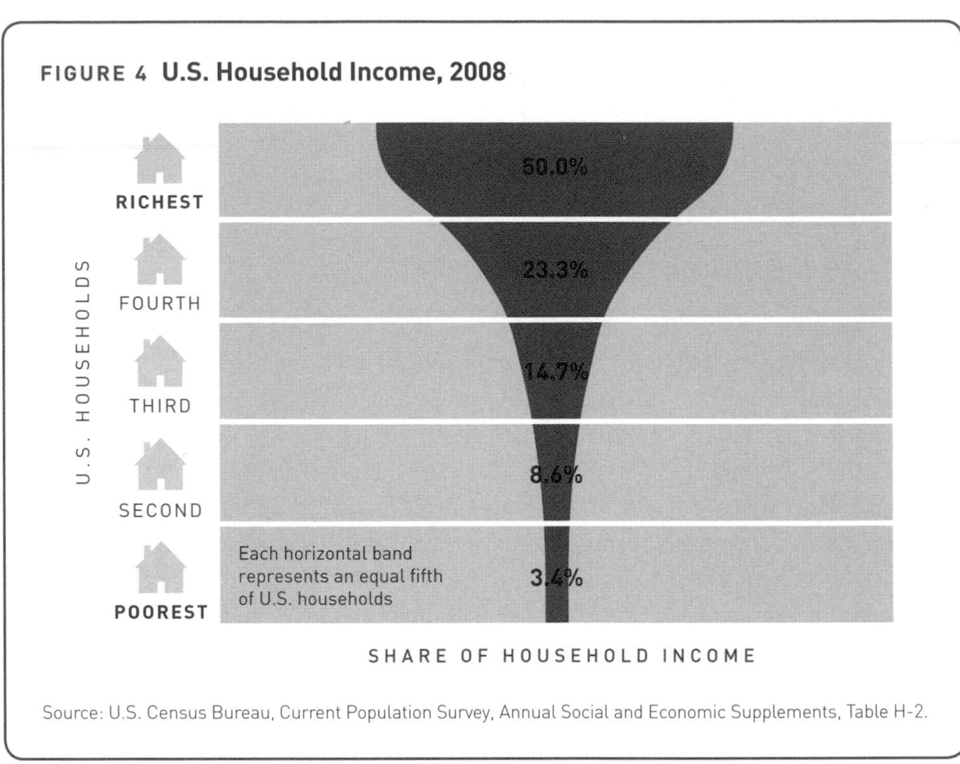

WEALTH TRENDS IN THE UNITED STATES

The United States has **one-fourth** of the world's total net worth, and the **highest overall** net worth per person among twenty-two countries studied.

The American HD Index focuses on the earnings people receive from their labor. However, wealth, sometimes called net worth, is equally crucial for understanding access to opportunities; as demonstrated in the recent recession, wealth is particularly important during rough times.

Wealth is defined as one's total financial resources amassed over a lifetime (including all assets and subtracting any debt). Wealth can be physical assets, such as real estate, or financial assets, such as stocks, bonds, dividends, retirement savings, and so forth. These assets enable families to invest in homes in safe neighborhoods with good public schools, to finance college, or to provide a down payment on a child's first home. Wealth acts as a security blanket when earnings are disrupted.

The United States has one-fourth of the world's total net worth, and the highest overall net worth per person among twenty-two countries studied. U.S. net worth per person is higher than in major European and Nordic countries, as well as in Brazil, China, India, South Africa, and other fast-growing nations.[7]

How is this tremendous wealth distributed within the United States? Using the most recent 2007 Survey of Consumer Finances, wealth expert Edward Wolff has traced the share of wealth held by different groups over time.

FIGURE 5 Change in Household Wealth over Time, 1983–2007

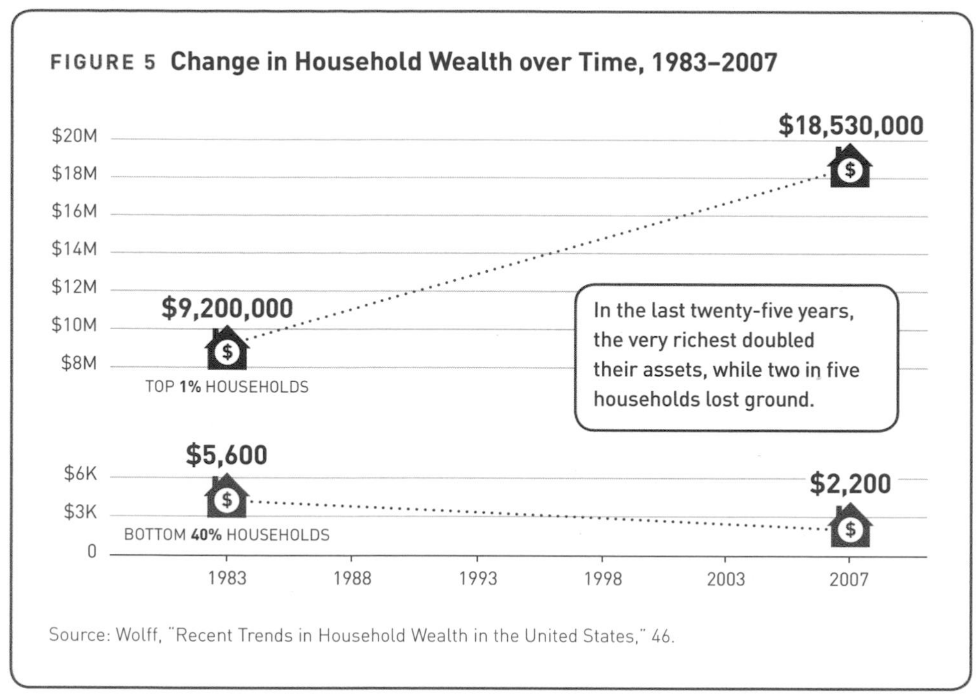

Source: Wolff, "Recent Trends in Household Wealth in the United States," 46.

FIGURE 5 shows that **while the top 1 percent of America's wealthiest households experienced a rise in their average wealth of 103 percent, to an average of $18.5 million per household, from 1983 to 2007** (the year of the most recent survey), **the poorest 40 percent of households lost 63 percent during this same period**. Average wealth among this group had fallen to $2,200 in inflation-adjusted dollars. So while the number of multimillionaires surged, nearly 19 percent of households at the bottom reported zero or negative net worth in 2007.[8] The status of these households, particularly their capacity to endure recession, natural disaster, family illness, or instability, is examined in the second part of this chapter.

Analysis by State, Congressional District, Gender, Race, and Ethnicity

COMPARISONS BY STATE

Top ranking:
1. Washington, DC
2. New Jersey
3. Maryland

Bottom ranking:
49. West Virginia
50. Montana
51. Arkansas

In *The Measure of America: American Human Development Report 2008–2009*, median earnings were presented using 2005 data, the most recent available at that time. With the wrenching changes across the nation since then, what has changed? The following observations result from comparing 2005 to 2008 earnings in inflation-adjusted figures. Census Bureau data on 2009 are not yet available, so this presents a mid-recession picture:

- Earnings for men grew in only two states: Mississippi and Wyoming. In the remaining states, earnings either declined or the change is not statistically significant.
- Men in Michigan experienced the biggest loss in earnings, which fell by more than 12 percent from about $39,000 per year to $34,000 per year.
- Women in Wyoming had the biggest gain in earnings, experiencing an increase of 14.8 percent.

On average, residents of our nation's capital have the highest earnings; indeed, Washington, DC, is the only place to break the $40,000 mark in median earnings. The remaining four top states in earnings are all along the eastern seaboard: New Jersey, Maryland, Connecticut, and Massachusetts (see **TABLE 1**).

Arkansas has the lowest median earnings of any state—$23,471—an amount typical of the United States as a whole in the late 1970s.[9] The five states at the bottom of the list, Mississippi, New Mexico, West Virginia, Montana, and Arkansas, are all located in the Mountain West and the South (see **MAP 1**).

BOX 2 explores some important factors that contribute to depressed earnings in Arkansas.

MAP 1 Median Earnings by State

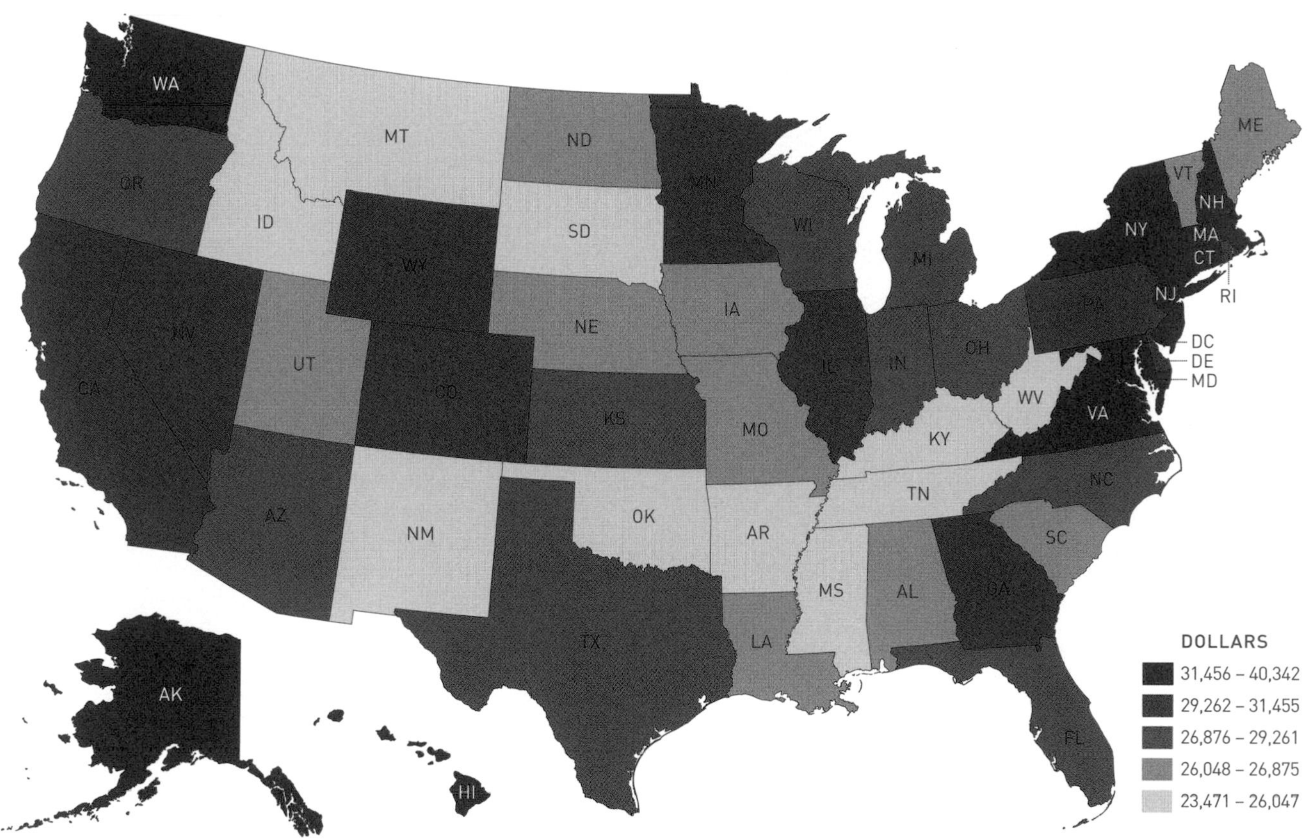

TABLE 1 Top and Bottom Five States, Median Earnings

RANK	TOP FIVE STATES	AMERICAN HD INDEX	MEDIAN EARNINGS (2009 dollars)
1	**District of Columbia**	6.21	40,342
2	**New Jersey**	6.16	37,707
3	**Maryland**	5.96	37,320
4	**Connecticut**	6.30	36,827
5	**Massachusetts**	6.24	35,533

RANK	BOTTOM FIVE STATES	AMERICAN HD INDEX	MEDIAN EARNINGS (2009 dollars)
47	**Mississippi**	3.93	24,620
48	**New Mexico**	4.56	24,495
49	**West Virginia**	3.85	24,404
50	**Montana**	4.49	24,033
51	**Arkansas**	3.87	23,471

Source: American Human Development Project calculations based on data from the American Community Survey and Centers for Disease Control and Prevention. See Methodological Notes for more details.

BOX 2 Arkansas: Caught in a Low Earnings Trap

While an affordable cost of living has helped to attract new residents and retirees to the state, particularly to Little Rock, Arkansas' median earnings are the lowest of any state, a sign of serious challenges for citizens and the state's leadership. More than one of every ten children (seventy-four thousand children under 18) in the state live in extreme poverty, compared with 8 percent in the nation as a whole.[10] **More than half a million Arkansans, one of every five residents, receives food stamps,[11] and more than 13 percent of families are living below the poverty level, a rate that is more than a third higher than the national average.**[12]

What are some factors possibly contributing to such low earnings?

Education. Arkansas ranks last on the Education Index, with rankings near or at the bottom in several categories, including the number of adults who have graduated from high school, the percentage who have attained a bachelor's or professional degree, and in the percentage of residents enrolled in school. Higher levels of educational attainment are directly linked to higher incomes, lower unemployment, and greater financial stability. Arkansas is more dependent on manufacturing, retail, and construction jobs than the country as a whole, while the percentage of residents who are professionals is significantly lower.[13] Greater education levels would likely contribute to higher earnings for Arkansas' workers.

Unionization. According to the U.S. Bureau of Labor Statistics, 12.3 percent of American workers belong to unions. In Arkansas, only 4.2 percent of wage and salary workers are union members, the second-lowest rate in the nation.[14] Wages derived from collective bargaining agreements average more than 14 percent higher than nonunion wages across the nation.[15] In addition, benefits and improved working conditions negotiated through collective bargaining have helped improve the standard of living for millions of workers and their families.

Investments in science and technology. Investment in scientific and technological research, and its conversion into commercially viable products and services, is a promising area for raising incomes and employment. Arkansas ranks near the bottom in many measures in this area. Research and development expenditures in Arkansas in math and computer science amount to $8 per person, one of the lowest investment rates of any state.[16]

Access to information. As discussed in the preceding chapter, educational investment is a critical driver of economic progress and increased earnings. Investments in other areas of information are also critical to success in a knowledge economy. In 2007 about 55 percent of individuals in Arkansas lived in households with Internet access, as compared with the national average of 67 percent. Only Alabama and Mississippi had lower rates of online access.[17]

Health coverage. Arkansas has one of the lowest rates of employer health insurance coverage in the nation, with 46 percent of residents covered by their employer (only New Mexico, Mississippi, and Texas have lower rates).[18] The total proportion of uninsured residents, at 19.2 percent of the state's population, is higher than the national average.[19] The uninsured, who often forgo preventive screening or early care, have higher rates of absence from work and face crushing financial problems in the event of serious illness. (More than half of personal bankruptcies in the United States are related to an inability to pay for illness or injury.)[20] In addition to exerting tremendous financial pressure on families, lack of health insurance also burdens state resources.

Innovative programs such as the Mid South Individual Development Accounts initiative are helping low-income families in the state increase their economic stability through savings accounts and financial management classes. Programs like this can help Arkansas' workers improve their financial prospects. But for many to obtain a decent standard of living, they will need higher earnings.

COMPARISONS BY CONGRESSIONAL DISTRICT

Earnings by congressional district range from over $60,000 in Manhattan's East Side (the highest of all 435 districts), to under $18,000 in the South Bronx of New York City (the lowest of all U.S. districts), just over two miles away (see **MAP 2**).

The twenty districts with the highest earnings all have median earnings above $40,000. They include districts in three of the four Census regions: the West (California and Washington), the South (Texas and Virginia), and the Northeast (Connecticut, New Jersey, and New York). The bottom twenty districts on the earnings scale all have earnings below $25,000. They include districts in all four Census regions: the West (California and New Mexico), the Midwest (Michigan and Missouri), the South (Alabama, Arkansas, Kentucky, Mississippi, North Carolina, Oklahoma, Texas, and Virginia), and the Northeast (New York) (see **TABLE 2**).

Another state with districts in the top and bottom twenty besides New York is Virginia. In Virginia's Ninth Congressional District, in the southwestern rural part of the state, earnings are typically under $22,000; in Virginia's Eighth Congressional District, in suburban Washington, DC, median earnings are more than $51,000. See **BOX 3** for some key differences that contribute to this sizeable gap in overall earnings.

The twenty districts with the highest earnings have median earnings **above $40,000**. The bottom twenty have earnings **below $25,000.**

TABLE 2 Top and Bottom Twenty Congressional Districts, Ranked by Earnings, 2008

RANK	TOP TWENTY	MEDIAN EARNINGS (2009 dollars)	RANK	BOTTOM TWENTY	MEDIAN EARNINGS (2009 dollars)
1	CD 14, New York	60,099	416	CD 1, Arkansas	22,153
2	CD 8, Virginia	51,260	417	CD 7, Alabama	22,125
3	CD 14, California	47,879	418	CD 1, North Carolina	21,997
4	CD 30, California	46,977	419	CD 2, Oklahoma	21,913
5	CD 7, New Jersey	46,891	420	CD 4, Arkansas	21,856
6	CD 11, New Jersey	46,761	421	CD 4, Michigan	21,798
7	CD 15, California	46,751	422	CD 9, Virginia	21,599
8	CD 11, Virginia	46,680	423	CD 27, Texas	21,394
9	CD 12, New Jersey	46,142	424	CD 34, California	21,293
10	CD 5, New Jersey	45,395	425	CD 1, Michigan	21,280
11	CD 48, California	44,803	426	CD 8, Missouri	21,103
12	CD 10, Virginia	44,732	427	CD 2, New Mexico	21,047
13	CD 8, New York	44,706	428	CD 5, Kentucky	21,031
14	CD 8, California	42,815	429	CD 2, Mississippi	20,962
15	CD 8, Washington	42,330	430	CD 16, Texas	20,621
16	CD 18, New York	42,141	431	CD 28, Texas	20,015
17	CD 4, Connecticut	42,100	432	CD 15, Texas	19,696
18	CD 12, California	41,990	433	CD 31, California	18,913
19	CD 10, California	41,868	434	CD 20, California	18,616
20	CD 7, Texas	41,838	435	CD 16, New York	17,995

Source: American Human Development Project calculations based on data from the American Community Survey, 2008. See Methodological Notes for more details.

BOX 3 A Tale of Two Districts: A $30,000 Gulf from One Corner of Virginia to Another

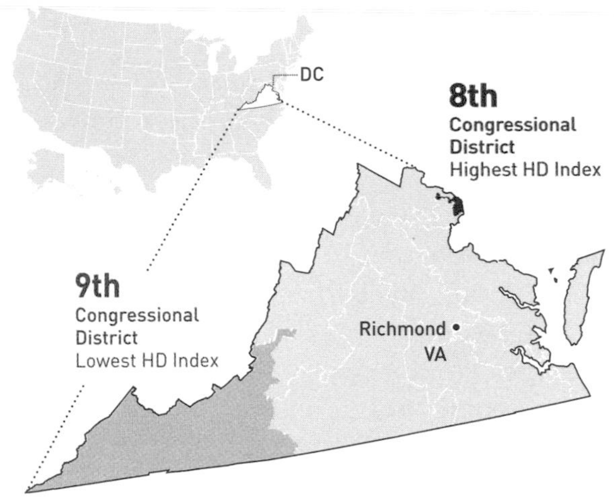

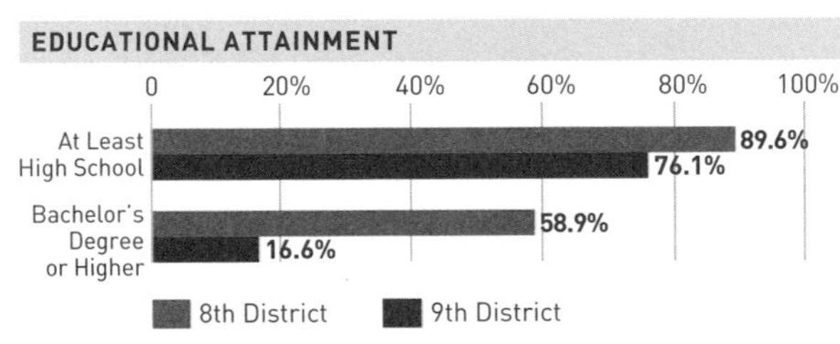

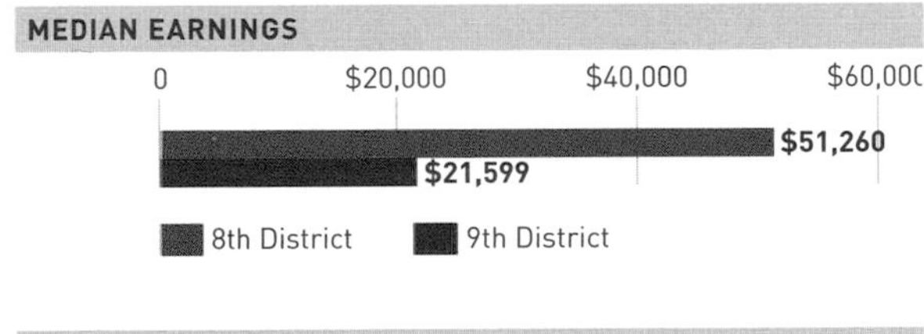

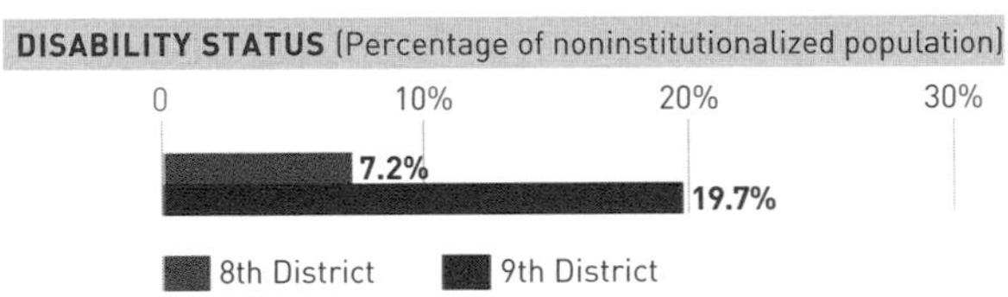

Source: U.S. Census Bureau, American Community Survey, 2008 One-year Estimates.

Northern Virginia's Eighth Congressional District (VA 8), encompassing Alexandria and other Washington suburbs, has the highest HD Index of Virginia's eleven congressional districts. The Ninth Congressional District of Virginia (VA 9), covering the southwestern end of the state, encompassing the Blue Ridge Highlands of the Appalachians, has the lowest. Judging by national trends, **almost sixty years of progress in well-being separates these two districts,** including nearly $30,000 in earnings per worker. While unemployment and homeownership rates are similar in both districts and the age distribution of their populations is comparable, other factors may contribute to earnings in VA 8 being two and a half times greater than in VA 9.

Educational attainment. The percentage of adults with a master's or professional degree in VA 8 is four and a half times higher than in VA 9, which has enabled VA 8 residents to gain higher-paid, higher-skilled employment. Twice as many adults in VA 9 have not completed high school as in VA 8.

Occupational distribution. The economies of these two districts demand, and reward, very different skill sets. More than 58 percent of the workforce in Virginia's northern suburbs, where VA 8 is located, is employed in management or professional positions; less than one-third of residents in southwestern Virginia hold such positions. By contrast, more than one-fourth of the workforce in VA 9 is employed in construction, extractive industries, repair occupations, production, or transportation, compared to about one in ten in the north. Poverty is three times greater in southwestern Virginia than in the northern suburbs.

Disability. While about 7 percent of residents of VA 8 are disabled, for VA 9, the rate is nearly 20 percent, creating severe barriers to income earning. Coal is Virginia's most valuable mineral resource, producing a vital revenue source and about half of the electricity generated in the state. VA 9 is home to coal mines, which also generate their share of damage to human health and the environment. Many residents of coal communities suffer serious respiratory ailments, asthma, emphysema, and other health conditions related to coal extraction. High disability levels in the district reflect not only the impact on miners but also on others exposed to high dust levels caused by trucks hauling coal along residential roads.[21]

MAP 2 Median Earnings by Congressional District

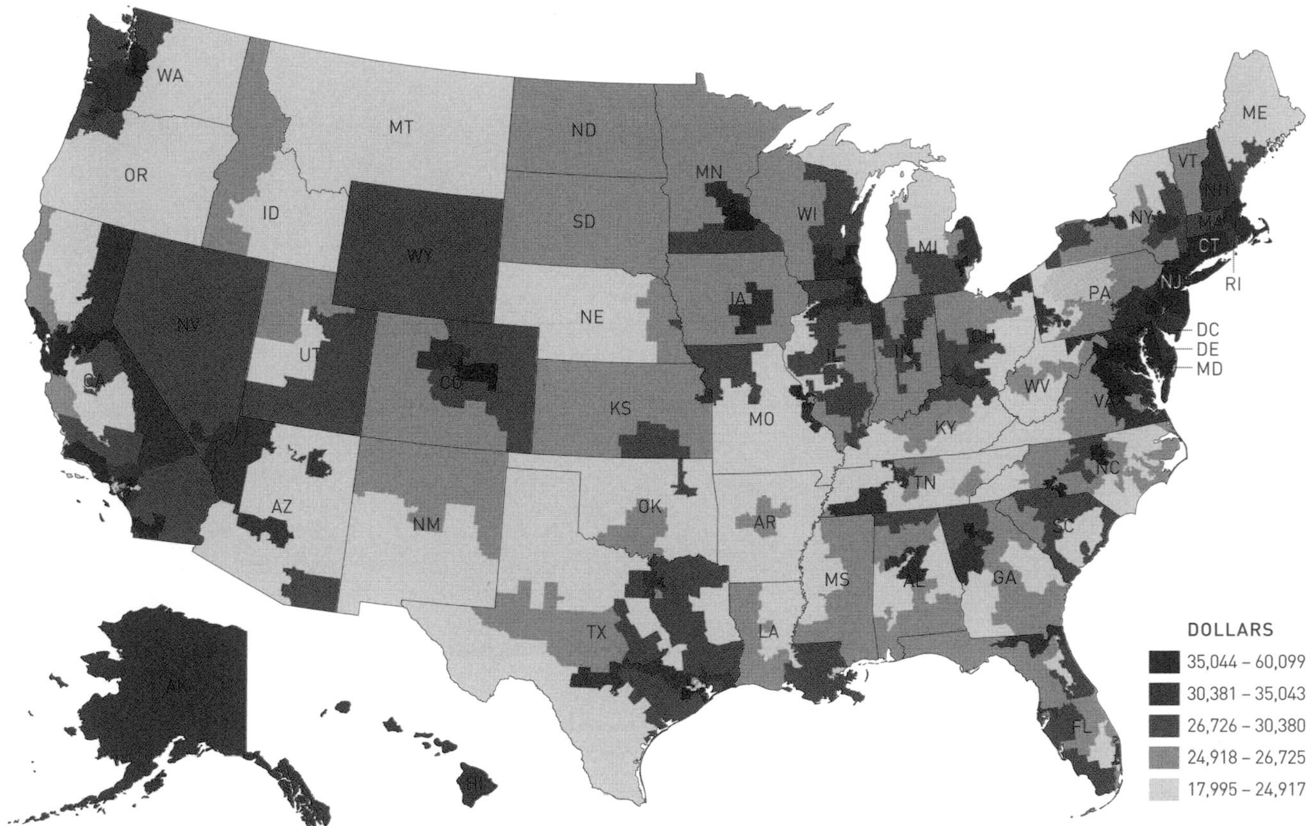

COMPARISONS BY METROPOLITAN AREAS

Looking at the ten most populous greater metro areas, which together contain about 25 percent of the country's population, one sees an enormous range in earnings (see **TABLE 3**). Within the United States, disparities in earnings are often greatest within a single city. As discussed above, nowhere is the gulf wider than in New York City, where the range in earnings ($42,104) exceeds the median annual earnings of the typical American worker (nearly $30,000). In Los Angeles, the major metro area with the second-largest earnings disparity, CA 30 (Hollywood, Beverly Hills, Santa Monica, and Malibu) is in the ballpark of $45,000. Earnings in CA 31 (downtown Los Angeles) are less than $18,000. **The metro area with the smallest variation among congressional districts is Boston.** The greater Boston metro area, which covers twelve districts and a total population of 4.5 million people, has a spread of only about $8,600 between the highest and lowest districts; income inequality in Boston is significantly less than in New York or Los Angeles.

Within the United States, **disparities in earnings** are often greatest within a single city.

TABLE 3 Highest and Lowest Earnings in the Ten Most Populous Metro Areas, by Congressional District

RANK	METRO AREA	LOCATION	MEDIAN EARNINGS (2009 dollars)
	United States		29,755
1	**Atlanta Metro Area**		
	CD 6, Georgia	Atlanta's northern suburbs	40,827
	CD 3, Georgia	South side of Atlanta metro area	25,857
2	**Boston Metro Area**		
	CD 1, Massachusetts	North-Central and western Massachusetts	30,164
	CD 9, Massachusetts	South Boston and southern suburbs	38,799
3	**Chicago Metro Area**		
	CD 4, Illinois	Most of Cook County	24,690
	CD 13, Illinois	Southwest part of Chicago	40,271
4	**Dallas Metro Area**		
	CD 3, Texas	North and northeast suburbs of Dallas	35,504
	CD 17, Texas	Suburban Fort Worth, Waco, and Brazos Valley	23,008
5	**Houston Metro Area**		
	CD 7, Texas	West Houston and western suburbs	41,838
	CD 9, Texas	Southwestern greater Houston	23,022
6	**Los Angeles Metro Area**		
	CD 30, California	Hollywood, Beverly Hills, Santa Monica, Malibu	46,977
	CD 31, California	Central and northeast LA	18,913
7	**Miami Metro Area**		
	CD 17, Florida	Northern Miami-Dade and southern Broward counties	23,237
	CD 22, Florida	Northern Broward and eastern Palm Beach counties	34,194
8	**New York City Metro Area**		
	CD 14, New York	Manhattan's East Side	60,099
	CD 16, New York	South Bronx, NYC	17,995
9	**Philadelphia Metro Area**		
	CD 1, Pennsylvania	Central and south Philadelphia, southeastern Delaware County	25,864
	CD 7, Pennsylvania	Parts of Chester, Delaware, Montgomery counties	40,026
10	**Washington, DC, Metro Area**		
	CD 6, Maryland	South of Pittsburgh to south of Philadelphia	34,857
	CD 8, Virginia	Northern Virginia	51,260

Source: American Human Development Project calculations based on data from the American Community Survey, 2008. See Methodological Notes for more details.

COMPARISONS BY GENDER

The last half century has ushered in a sea change in the way we organize work and family life. Today, 60 percent of women work for pay (and the number continues to rise) while 64 percent of small children (under age 6) have their resident parent or parents in the workforce. This is the new normal.

Fields once closed to women are now open, and laws that prohibit gender discrimination are helping to expand opportunity. Most recently, the Lilly Ledbetter Fair Pay Act was signed in early 2009—an important bill that expands workers' rights to sue for equal pay. **As FIGURE 3 shows, there has been a slow, steady march upward for women's earnings. Yet the gender earnings gap**

remains stubbornly persistent.

American women today have, on average, higher levels of educational attainment than men, and women are living, on average, five years longer. Yet Census Bureau data show that men earn $11,000 more. Looking at differences by state, Washington, DC, has the smallest earnings gap: $6,400. But in Wyoming, women's personal earnings from wages and salaries are, on average, half those of men. While women in 2008 in Wyoming typically earned about $20,000 in predominantly managerial, professional, sales, or office occupations, men more likely were earning in the $40,000 range, working in construction, extraction, maintenance, and repair operations as well as in management-related or in transportation and material-moving occupations.[22] The smaller paychecks for women mean, in turn, smaller retirement accounts, smaller pensions, and smaller Social Security checks for women later in life.

Continued progress on **narrowing the gender earnings gap** is a key to ensuring that more children get a strong start in life.

Given that one in four children today grows up in a household headed by a single mother, and that one of every three single mothers lives in poverty,[23] continued progress on narrowing the gender earnings gap is a matter of basic fairness and a key to ensuring that more children get a strong start in life, free of poverty.

What are the factors that contribute to this stubborn earnings inequality, and how can we narrow this gap?

WOMEN WHO FORGO PAID WORK FOR FAMILY CARE PAY A HIGH PENALTY

About one-third of the gender earnings gap stems from the high penalty that women pay for leaving the workforce to raise their children or care for elderly relatives. Some U.S. private companies offer family-friendly benefits, and a handful of states have enacted laws that require paid family leave and other benefits, but as **TABLE 4** shows, **many countries that have experienced a similar large-scale entry of women into the workforce have adapted to this new normal through policies and programs that help families better balance home and work responsibilities.** These policies, many of which are accessible to both men and women (see **TABLE 4**), often include

- Paid leave to care for newborns and small children or the frail elderly
- Paid leave days that can be used for teacher conferences, doctor's appointments, or a sick child
- Support for affordable child care and allowances for breastfeeding breaks during the workday

The United States is **the only OECD country** with no federally mandated paid maternity leave.

TABLE 4 Family-Friendly Policies in the Thirty OECD Countries

COUNTRY	PAID MATERNITY LEAVE (weeks entitlement)	PAID PATERNITY LEAVE (weeks entitlement)	PAID BREASTFEEDING BREAKS (Yes or No)
United States	0	0	N
Australia	*	*	N
Austria	16	0	Y
Belgium	11	1	Y
Canada	8	0	N
Czech Republic	14	0	Y
Denmark	18	2	N
Finland	17	6	N
France	16	2	N
Germany	14	0	Y
Greece	17	0	Y
Hungary	17	1	Y
Iceland	10	10	N
Ireland	18	0	Y
Italy	16	0	Y
Japan	8	0	Y
Luxembourg	16	0	Y
Mexico	12	0	Y
Netherlands	16	0	Y
New Zealand	5	0	N
Norway	9	6	N
Poland	18	4	Y
Portugal	17	2	Y
Slovak Republic	15	0	Y
South Korea	15	0	N
Spain	16	2	Y
Sweden	10	9	Y
Switzerland	13	0	Y
Turkey	8	0	Y
United Kingdom	9	0	N

Sources: OECD, Family Database 2010, Table PF7.1 for paid leave; WABA Women & Work Task Force, "Maternity Protection Chart, 2008" for breastfeeding breaks.
*Australia recently enacted a national paid parental leave scheme effective January 1, 2011; it requires eighteen weeks of pay at minimum wage.

Family-friendly policies and programs provide strong evidence of their value to individuals, to employers, and ultimately to society:

- **Workers.** Access to paid parental leave improves long-term employment prospects and earnings and can reduce infant-care expenditures.[24] Paid sick leave reduces the spread of illness and attendant low productivity from sick workers. Paternity leave has been shown to reduce marital stress, enable fathers to increase involvement in infant care, and improve gender equity at home.[25]

- **Children and health.** Research has found that breast-fed children have lower stomach, respiratory tract, and other infection rates and a 1.5- to 5-fold reduction in risk of mortality overall.[26] Parental leave also improves the chances a child gets immunized.[27] Sick children recover faster from illness and injury with parental involvement.[28]
- **Children and schooling.** When parents participate in their children's education—attending school meeting, trips, and so forth—children's achievement rises.[29]
- **Elderly.** Evidence shows that older family members who have more family support tend to live longer and to recover faster from heart attacks and strokes. Decreased use of nursing home facilities can benefit the elderly and reduce the economic burden on families caring for them.[30]
- **Employers.** Countries around the world have found that paid leave for caring responsibilities yields higher job retention, reduced costs in training new employees, better morale and employee commitment, and a sizeable decrease in unplanned absences. California's pioneering comprehensive paid family leave act found that nearly 90 percent of workers returned to their jobs after paid leave, as opposed to only 80 percent in organizations that provided just the minimum benefit.[31]
- **Society/taxpayers.** Family-friendly policies contribute to significantly lower unemployment payments, and enable employees on leave to maintain consumer spending levels.[32]

Low-wage positions traditionally held by women virtually **always pay less** than low-wage occupations dominated by men.

LOW-SKILLS JOBS PAY MEN MORE

Though women predominate in low-wage positions, such as child-care providers and home health aides, these jobs virtually always pay less than occupations dominated by men with similarly low educational attainment levels, such as security guard or parking attendant.[33]

GENDER DISCRIMINATION PERSISTS

Of more than one hundred occupations monitored by the Bureau of Labor Statistics, women's weekly earnings are higher than men's in only four (bakers, teacher assistants, food attendants and bartender helpers, and life and social science technicians). **Even in jobs where women vastly outnumber men, men still make more.** Four of five elementary and middle-school teachers are women.[34] Yet median weekly earnings for female teachers are $891, while men earn $1,040.[35] Women have been investing heavily in education to build stable financial futures for themselves and their families. These efforts deserve a more level playing field and a system that strictly enforces antidiscrimination laws.

COMPARISONS BY RACE, ETHNICITY, AND GENDER

U.S. median earnings are just under $30,000 per person, but earnings range from about $41,000 for Asian American men to just over $18,000 for Latina women (see **TABLE 5**). In every one of the five major ethnic groups, men outearn women. **The gender earnings gap is largest for white women, who earn almost $15,000 less than white men, and smallest for African American women, who earn under $4,000 less than African American men.** Latinas have median earnings today roughly equal to the average American about forty-five years ago.

Looking beyond national averages, earnings by state are presented for all five major ethnic/racial groups in **TABLE 6**. **In analyzing wages and salaries for all workers 16 and older by race, we find great variation within groups across states:**

In every one of the five major ethnic groups, men outearn women.

- White workers in Washington, DC ($60,232), typically earn $35,000 per person more than white workers in West Virginia ($24,797).
- Latinos in Hawaii earn $9,000 a year more than Latinos in Alabama.
- Typical earnings of Native Americans in California are around $24,000; in Minnesota, they are about $16,000.
- Asian Americans in New Jersey have median earnings of $50,069, more than double what the average Asian American earns in Louisiana ($22,094).
- African Americans in Maryland earn almost $16,000 a year more than African Americans in Louisiana.

TABLE 5 Earnings by Race/Ethnicity and Gender

GROUPING	MEDIAN EARNINGS (2009 dollars)	COMPARISONS WITH U.S. MEDIAN EARNINGS
United States	29,755	today's median
Asian American men	40,815	one-third higher
White men	40,157	one-third higher
Asian American women	29,133	late 1990s
African American men	26,644	early 1990s
White women	25,531	1990
Latino men	24,849	mid-1980s
Native American men	24,095	mid-1980s
African American women	22,874	1970
Native American women	19,560	mid-1960s
Latina women	18,178	early 1960s

Source: American Human Development Project calculations based on data from the American Community Survey, 2008. See Methodological Notes for more details.

What are the factors influencing these enormous earnings gaps? Many analysts and researchers seek answers, with some focusing nearly exclusively on individual drive and ambition, others on cultural values, work ethic, child-rearing practices, and social networks. Still others focus on the policies, institutions, and conditions of society that help shape what we can do and become.[36]

Research undertaken for this book reveals no magic-bullet explanation; each of these factors plays a role in explaining the stark earnings gaps we find by race, gender, and geography.

What follows is a case study of conditions and institutions that affect African Americans in two states with an enormous earnings gap between them: Maryland and Mississippi. African Americans in Maryland have the highest earnings—$34,446—approximately $5,000 above the national average. In Mississippi, earnings for African Americans are among the lowest of any state, at $18,645.

Education. The previous chapter provides ample evidence of education's role as a key determinant of income. While nearly three-quarters of African American high school students in Maryland graduate on time today, the corresponding figure for Mississippi is only 60 percent. One in four adult African Americans in Maryland has at least a bachelor's degree, and 9.4 percent have an advanced degree; the percentage of African Americans in Mississippi with bachelor's or advanced degrees is half that.

TABLE 6 Earnings by Race, by State

RANK	GROUP	AMERICAN HD INDEX	MEDIAN EARNINGS (2009 dollars)
	United States	5.17	29,755
HD Index by Ethnic Group			
1	**Asian American**	7.68	34,835
2	**White**	5.53	31,932
3	**Latino**	4.19	21,936
4	**African American**	3.91	24,792
5	**Native American**	3.24	21,744
States Where Each Racial and Ethnic Group Scores **Highest**			
	Asian American—New Jersey	9.30	50,069
	White—District of Columbia	9.03	60,232
	Latino—New Jersey	5.28	25,440
	African American—Maryland	5.09	34,446
	Native American—California	4.42	24,488
States Where Each Racial and Ethnic Group Scores **Lowest**			
	Asian America—Louisiana	5.30	22,094
	White—West Virginia	3.85	24,797
	Latino—Alabama	2.39	17,640
	African American—Louisiana	2.60	19,434
	Native American—South Dakota	1.15	16,920

Source: American Human Development Project calculations based on data from the American Community Survey and Centers for Disease Control and Prevention. See Methodological Notes for more details.

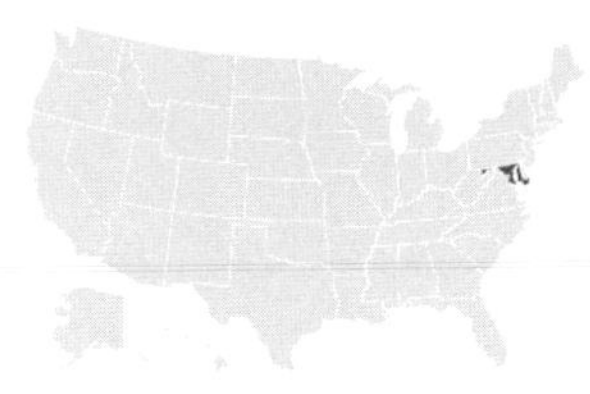

Maryland: Investing in the Future

Maryland is in the top three in the nation in median earnings and made it through the 2008–9 recession in relatively better shape than many other states. The state had one of the lowest increases in joblessness in the period April 2009 to April 2010 and the largest increase in employment of any state in March 2010, a month in which unemployment rose in seventeen states.[42]

Maryland has excelled in its aggressive efforts to create an enabling environment for research and entrepreneurship in science and technology. It is a top-five state in attainment of higher education, and has invested heavily in research and capital to build a dynamic science and technology sector. Maryland ranks first in the nation in academic research and development (R&D) dollars per person as well as in R&D spending on math, computer sciences, life science, and engineering.[43]

This investment has enabled the state to attract additional federal, industry, and academic funding, which has helped mitigate the recession and accelerate recovery in the state.

Globalization and technological innovation. Maryland has invested in skills and infrastructure to attract high-paying jobs in the technology sector (see sidebar). Mississippi ranks at or near the bottom in generating workforce skills, research, and capital to build a strong high-tech sector.[37]

Tax credits. Maryland has adopted a generous state-level Earned Income Tax Credit (EITC) of 24 percent of the federal EITC to supplement the federal tax break; Mississippi's EITC, at 4 percent of the federal credit, has limited impact in encouraging work and does little to reduce poverty among the state's lowest-earning workers, who are disproportionately African Americans.

Homeownership and foreclosures. More than half of home refinance loans are subprime in Mississippi, which tops the nation in subprime lending. In contrast, Maryland ranks thirty-sixth.[38] Subprime home refinance has higher interest rates than prevailing rates, and subprimes' typically adjustable-rate mortgages entail enormous risk for borrowers and their communities. Subprime lending has set many African American communities back decades, contributing in some cases to a downward spiral in poverty and standard of living.

Employment discrimination. Enforcement of legislation combating barriers to equal opportunity, and efforts to educate employers and the general public on the law and the value of diversity to society, have brought tremendous progress in combating racial discrimination in the United States. But studies show continued unwillingness among some employers to hire minority youth or to remove barriers to entry and advancement in the workforce, particularly for African Americans.[39] Maryland has been a leader in creating laws and practices for inclusive businesses, including being one of the only states with a commercial nondiscrimination law.[40] Mississippi lags behind in both goals and procurement programs to combat discrimination in the public and business sectors.[41]

Mississippi has made progress on some important issues for African Americans, ranging from prison reform, where Mississippi is a leading state in reducing incarceration and recidivism rates—and continued reductions in residential segregation by race. However, in many other areas, Mississippi continues to lag in providing African Americans with the tools needed to lead productive and fulfilling lives.

What Fuels These Gaps?

What are some of the factors fueling the earnings gaps among states, congressional districts, racial and ethnic groups, and men and women? Different combinations of factors contribute to the strikingly different outcomes, among them:

- **Education.** More education is the surest route to higher earnings. College graduates can expect to earn upward of $750,000 more than high school graduates over the course of a career.[44] The labor market is particularly unkind to those with low education levels: a high school dropout is over three times more likely to be unemployed than a college graduate.[45]
- **State policies and programs.** While acknowledging the many different ways to support individuals and families, policy levers such as a robust state Earned Income Tax Credit, a state minimum wage, and programs to counter deprivation, such as food stamps, can substantially increase employment and decrease poverty rates.
- **Family and work responsibilities.** The United States has been slower than peer nations to adapt to the new normal of both parents working outside the home, or to single-parent families headed by an adult in the labor force. This adjustment requires high-quality, affordable child care and mandatory polices to help parents care for children and ill or elderly family members without jeopardizing their jobs, losing income during emergencies, or placing constant stress on family life.
- **Jobs in the high-tech sector.** Investing in technology infrastructure can pay big dividends in terms of higher earnings and greater competitiveness in the global marketplace. States that have promoted technology growth by investing in R&D and capital for technology, and laid the groundwork for a skilled, educated workforce, are being rewarded with higher-paying jobs.
- **Discrimination.** Discrimination against women and people of color in employment is far less prevalent today than in the past. But it still exists. Women tend to earn less than men, $11,000 less on average, even when men and women have similar jobs and equivalent training and education. Studies have shown that employers are more likely to interview job-seekers they think are white than those they think are African American, even when their resumes list comparable levels of education and experience.[46] Discrimination based on gender and race continues to hamper efforts to draw on and fairly reward the talents and hard work of everyone in our society.

What **factors** lead to such strikingly different outcomes in earnings?

- Education
- State policies and programs
- Family and work responsibilities
- Jobs in the high-tech sector
- Discrimination

A Decent Standard of Living

Dashboard of Risks

The three indicators presented here—**young child poverty**, **marginally attached workers**, and **elderly poverty**—track risk factors that may slow or reverse human development progress and which pose direct threats to people's capability to enjoy a decent standard of living.

Children under 6 living in poverty (%), 2008[1]

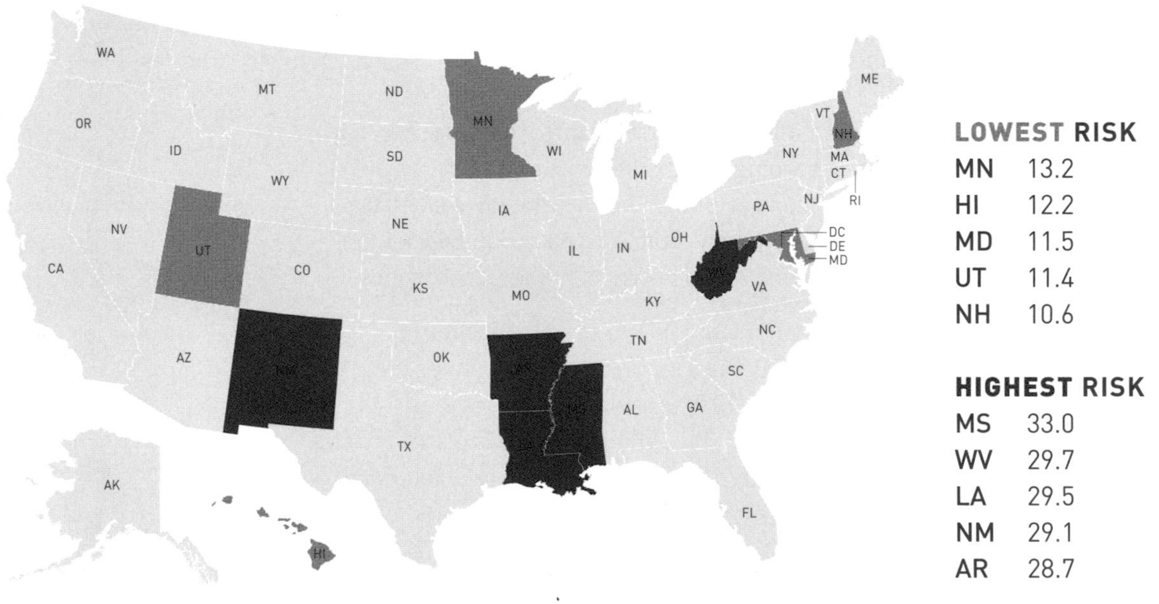

[1] American Human Development Project calculations based on data from the U.S. Census Bureau, American Community Survey 2008. Tables B17001, B17001B, B17001C, B17001D, B17001H, B17001I.

Marginally attached workers—want to work, but have stopped looking (per 10,000), 2009[2]

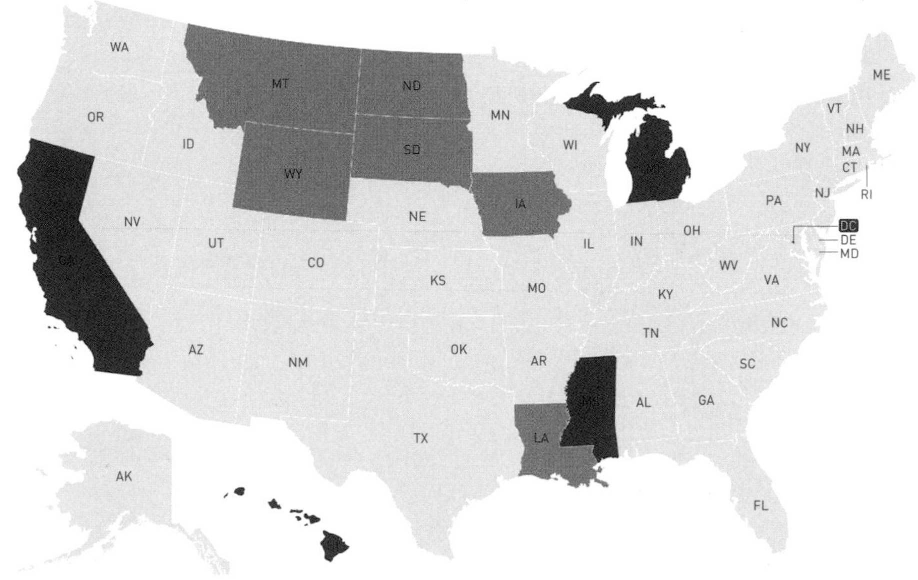

LOWEST RISK

SD	58.2
IA	57.2
WY	56.2
MT	55.0
ND	50.0

HIGHEST RISK

MS	126.7
CA	123.6
DC	120.3
MI	118.1
HI	113.8

Elderly poverty (%), 2008[3]

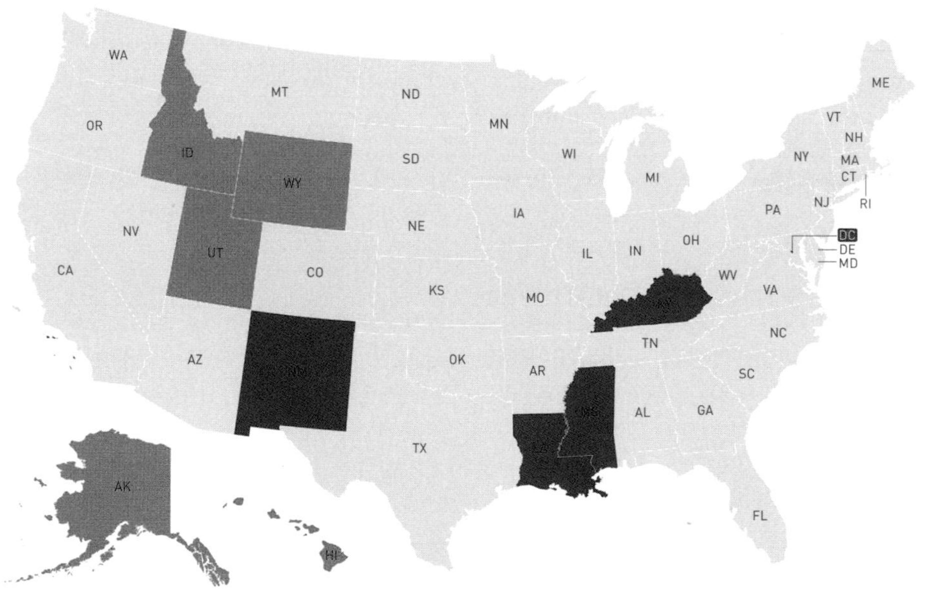

LOWEST RISK

ID	7.6
WY	7.3
UT	6.8
HI	6.8
AK	3.7

HIGHEST RISK

MS	16.9
DC	15.2
KY	13.8
LA	13.5
NM	13.4

[2] Bureau of Labor Statistics (BLS). Current Population Survey, 2009. Measures workers who have looked for work within the past year but not in the prior four weeks. These workers are not included in standard unemployment counts. These are unpublished BLS data that, due to the small survey sample size in small states, do not meet BLS standards for publication.

[3] American Human Development Project calculations based on data from the U.S. Census Bureau, American Community Survey 2008. Tables B17001, B17001B, B17001C, B17001D, B17001H, B17001I.

PART II:
Reducing Risks and Increasing Resilience in Standard of Living

Economic security enables people to seize opportunities and take risks, to make plans and investments. Without it, individuals and families struggle with a short-term vision of their lives, and communities and society are diminished by squandered opportunities and unfulfilled potential.

Building economic resilience requires an interlinked set of efforts—individual initiatives and decisions, the support of family and networks, private-sector policies, public policy instruments, and, increasingly, complementary policies and decisions made in countries beyond our borders, which have an increasingly significant impact on economic security in the United States.

Globalization—the growing interdependence of the world's economies, technologies, governance structures, cultures, and people—offers many opportunities. American consumers benefit from lower prices and a greater variety of goods, and globalized production and increased international trade offer opportunities for greater wealth and the development of competitive advantages that can benefit businesses in all fields.

Without economic security, individuals and families struggle with a **short-term vision** of their lives.

But globalization also brings new risks and insecurities. In a globalized world, the United States faces new challenges to building economic security for all Americans. Globalization has meant a new labor force of over a billion people added to the pool of job-seekers, international subcontracting introduces rapid changes to labor markets, and more open trade enables businesses to relocate to regions with cheaper labor, exerting downward pressure on U.S. wages.

Volatility has expanded with integration. The debt crisis in Greece, which first affected European nations with which it shares a currency, ultimately sent U.S. markets plunging due to fears that the crisis would spread to other banks and governments.

While the connection between household income volatility and globalization is subject to debate,[47] major changes in labor and production patterns have entailed new risks. Workers and their families, and the private and public sectors can take many steps to reduce underlying vulnerabilities and better manage these economic risks.

This section explores pervasive and acute threats across the life cycle, with a focus on reducing risks and building resilience through the three major periods of life: childhood and adolescence, the productive earning years, and retirement. This report attempts to identify groups experiencing frequent or severe deprivations in sustaining economic security during each of these three periods.

Reducing Risks for Children and Adolescents

Faced with sharp changes in economic circumstances, families can draw on savings, relatives, and other coping strategies to reduce the consequences on their children. **For the human development of young people, particularly small children, reducing the impacts of economic adversity is absolutely essential because, contrary to popular wisdom, adversity does not make most people, particularly children, stronger or more resilient.** Extreme nutritional deficits, homelessness, and other risk factors pose disproportionate harm to very young children and increase their vulnerability in the future. Prolonged exposure to stress creates nervous system reactions that damage the highly malleable brains of the youngest children, increasing their vulnerability and potentially leading to lifelong physical, mental, behavioral, and learning problems.[48] Remediation and treatment later in life are less effective and far more expensive than supporting healthy development in the critical early years.

Which groups of children and young people are at highest risk today, and what are some tools for building resilience among them?

Remediation later in life is less effective and far more expensive than supporting **healthy child development** in the early years.

CHILDHOOD POVERTY

Unlike children in many developing nations, most American children do not experience life-threatening material deprivations such as starvation or disease due to unclean water or lack of proper sanitation. Average family incomes in the United States rank near the top among our 29 peer nations.[49] Yet acute deprivations persist, costing our society dearly in terms of the chances available to children to become fulfilled, productive adults and, in turn, to raise a next generation of children who will thrive.

Poverty affects early childhood development in several ways. First, very poor families often struggle to provide nutritious food and developmentally appropriate books and toys to children, and have insufficient resources to protect their children from neighborhood violence or environmental hazards like lead paint. They cannot afford quality health services and education, and spend less time enriching children's lives with trips to the library or playground. Second, living in poverty is extremely stressful. Family stress can lead to parental depression, anxiety, and punitive, inconsistent parenting, all of which can undermine healthy early childhood development.[50]

The following conditions today threaten children's healthy physical, social, and psychological development, and their chances of developing the capabilities to pursue their ambitions and dreams:

- **Income poverty.** Children made up about one-quarter of the U.S. population in 2008, but more than one-third of the population living in poverty.[51]
- **Extreme income poverty.** In 2008, 10 percent of children under 5 years old lived in families with incomes less than 50 percent of the federal poverty level[52] ($11,000 for a family of four with two children).
- **Food insecurity.** In 2007 about 6.2 million American households with children were food insecure, meaning there was an absence of enough food for an active, healthy life for everyone in the household. In 85 percent of these households, at least one parent was working full-time.[53]
- **Homelessness.** Every year, more than 1.5 million children experience homelessness. These children have high rates of health problems and far higher rates of emotional and behavioral problems. They are also more likely to witness acts of violence.[54]
- **Family instability.** Events that disrupt a child's fundamental relationships can set the child on a less advantageous life trajectory. Such events might include the incarceration of a parent, abandonment, frequent moves within one year, homelessness, foreclosure, or a change in the adults living in the house. All these factors affect families living in poverty more often than middle-class families.[55]

Existing efforts to address **childhood poverty** are falling short for far too many children.

These deprivations often overlap within the same families, posing an urgent challenge to our nation. Efforts to help poor families today range from programs to help workers acquire higher skills and better employment, to laws regulating wages and benefits, to policies that help working parents, to direct cash assistance such as food stamps and Temporary Assistance to Needy Families. But these programs are clearly falling short for far too many children.

INCARCERATION AND CHILDREN'S LIFE CHANCES

The children of an incarcerated parent face acute risks. Some scholars estimate that the number of children in the United States with a parent who has been a prisoner, on parole, or on probation approaches 10 million.[56] The United States incarcerates at the highest rate in the world, well above the rates of Russia and China and five to nine times the rates of our peer nations in Europe, Australia, Canada, and the Nordic countries (see OECD Indicator Table on page 267). Less widely understood is how the U.S. approach to justice affects the children of imprisoned parents.

For some children, having a parent who is abusive or violent removed from the home is a net benefit. However, for most children, parental incarceration heightens risks at every turn. Arrest and imprisonment bring about family trauma, stigma, sadness, and feelings of guilt and loss. Lost income due to imprisonment creates financial hardships, often necessitating further disruptions such as relocation. The impact of a prison record on parental employment and housing upon release presents further challenges to a family. Finally the difficulties of establishing a close and positive relationship with one's mother or father within the confines of prison walls are formidable.

In 2007, 1.7 million children in the United States had an incarcerated parent.[57] While programs for imprisoned mothers and their children are increasingly common, fathers make up the vast majority of prisoners. Nearly half of those fathers lived with their children before being sent to prison. More than 70 percent of children with an imprisoned parent are children of color.[58] One in 15 African American children, one in 42 Latino children, and one in 111 white children has a parent in prison.[59]

The imprisonment of African American men at rates six and a half times higher than white men[60] has significantly hindered the creation and maintenance of stable two-parent families in some low-income neighborhoods. The prevalence of jobless men with prison records results in a shortage of role models for young men and of marriageable bachelors, in part by virtue of their inability to contribute to household finances, for women in the community. This distortion of family life has had devastating impacts on inner-city neighborhoods across the country.

African American children are **seven times more likely to have a parent in prison** than white children.

While the consequences of having an incarcerated parent vary from one child to the next, all such children are at higher risk of poverty, ill health, poor school achievement, and behavioral problems. The absence of a parent only weakens family bonds. **Program experience and research suggest the following actions can help mitigate the damage:**[61]

- **Support a continued relationship.** Supervised play areas, flexible visiting and phone calling hours, incarcerating parents near their children, improving visitation procedures to bolster the dignity of all, training prison staff on family ties, and other efforts can help children retain their bonds with an incarcerated parent. These programs and policies should be standard features of prison life.

- **Provide parenting skills instruction.** Some prisons provide parenting classes to build skills. These programs are crucial and must be made available to fathers as well as mothers.

- **Include children in reentry planning.** Beyond housing and a job, parents being released from prison need help caring for their children. In many cases, they need family counseling.

- **Reduce the debt trap.** Many fathers face child support debt upon release, creating yet another barrier to contact with their children. This debt can also drive fathers, particularly those with low skills and education levels, into illegal activities to earn more and avoid support enforcement. Some states and facilities have devised constructive ways of addressing these challenges, including temporary reprieves of support payments during incarceration, waiving arrears if families reunite, and mediated efforts to help manage arrears.

Arguably the most productive effort would be a reduction in the American incarceration rate, particularly for nonviolent offenders, many of whom serve exceedingly long sentences. **Innovative sentencing policies have shown that the criminal justice system can deter and punish crime in smarter, more humane, less socially destructive ways.**[62] Incarceration leaves a traumatic mark on millions of children, in effect punishing them for crimes they did not commit.

Working Years and Family Balance: Getting a Strong Foothold in the Job Market and Investing in the Future

A child's formative years should enable him or her to acquire the skills and behaviors necessary to lead a successful and fulfilling life. The next chapter of life involves applying those skills and behaviors and establishing careers. The working years are the period of greatest productive capacity and earnings, and thus the ideal time to save for the future.

Employment matters for social inclusion, physical health, and psychological health.

However, for many Americans, economic security is increasingly hard to come by. Rising productivity, a growing global labor pool, an exponential rate of technological innovation, and other shifts present significant challenges. Destabilized labor markets have ignited a backlash against certain groups, especially immigrants (see **BOX 4**). **This section discusses efforts to manage risks and build resilience among groups that struggle to achieve financial stability.**

EMPLOYMENT

More than 8 million jobs were lost during the Great Recession of 2007–9.[63] While employment finally started to rise in late 2009, by April 2010 nearly 45 percent of the unemployed (6.7 million people) had experienced prolonged periods of unemployment of twenty-seven weeks or more.[64] Research shows that participation in the labor force is important for reasons that go well beyond earning a paycheck and receiving benefits; employment matters for social inclusion, physical health, and psychological health. Losing a job undermines overall well-being, often leading to loss of identity, status, structure, and social support.

More than 90 percent of jobs in the United States are filled by wage and salary workers. Three-quarters of those are service jobs, ranging from health and education to finance, leisure, and government workers, with the remainder

BOX 4 Immigration and its Impacts on the Economy

Each wave of arrivals to the United States has provoked questions about American identity and potential impacts on the economy. In the nineteenth century, for example, the arrival of German and Irish immigrants sparked a nativist political party—the Know Nothings. In recent years, anxiety about both national security and the economic downturn has put immigration in the spotlight again. Some concerns center on the thorny question of American cultural identity, although most immigrant groups assimilate completely within two to three generations.[65] Others center on respect for the rule of law, still others on the impact of undocumented immigrants on the U.S. job market. These and other concerns are often highly charged and bundled together in way that hinders understanding. This box focuses on the effects of immigration on the economy in terms of living standards, jobs, use of public services, and crime—areas that have been the subject of considerable research.

Certain fears about immigration today appear misplaced against the weight of evidence. **With regard to the impact of immigration on living standards, broad consensus has emerged among economists that immigration leads to net gains in economic productivity in the long-term, including greater employment, higher wages, and higher living standards.**[66] Immigration provides new sources of labor for employers, new consumers for manufacturers and vendors, and new tax revenues for governments; it also increases trade between the United States and immigrants' home countries.[67]

The majority of immigrants are concentrated in particular economic sectors: highly skilled professions, such as engineering and medicine, and lower-skilled work, like farming and manufacturing.[68] Lower-skilled native workers who compete with immigrant laborers may face fewer opportunities and depressed wages; however, evidence indicates that this phenomenon occurs on a much smaller scale in the United States today than it does in Europe or in American history.[69] Somewhat counterintuitively, in areas with high concentrations of immigrants, low-skilled native workers can actually see greater wages than they otherwise would (although the gap between their wages and the wages of higher-skilled workers is somewhat wider).[70]

Concerns about the impact of immigration on the economy sometimes focus on lost tax revenue and a perceived drain on public services, from health care to education to law enforcement.71 A recent analysis of U.S. cities found that undocumented immigrants do, in fact, pay less in taxes on average than documented immigrants and the native-born—about $80 less per person.[72] However, they also take advantage of fewer public services, which more than offsets the lost tax revenue; they receive $600 less than native-born Americans in cash transfers (such as food stamps and unemployment insurance), and are less likely to receive Medicare or Medicaid, or to enroll in public schools (due in large part to the fact that many immigrants today are young adults without children).[73] The coffers of the Social Security Administration's earnings suspense file—where taxes paid cannot be matched to worker's names—grew by $189 billion in the 1990s and by $50 billion each year since, evidence that many undocumented immigrants contribute more in payroll taxes than they recoup in public services.[74]

Immigration has not been shown to increase crime rates, and some evidence suggests that it may even be responsible for decreasing crime in cities. [75] Indeed, several rigorous studies have found that native-born men are far more likely to be incarcerated than foreign-born men; in California, native-born men are ten times more likely to be incarcerated.[76]

When economic uncertainty is high, immigrants are a common scapegoat. Yet the evidence does not support the notion that today's economic woes stem from immigration, legal or otherwise.[77]

in sectors such as mining, construction, and manufacturing (14.2 percent), self-employed (6.2 percent), and agriculture (1.4 percent).[78]

What are the areas of greatest projected job growth? According to the Bureau of Labor Statistics, the three areas of fastest growth are professional and business services in science, technology, and management consulting to implement new technologies; health care and social assistance to cater to an aging population and keep up with new medical technologies; and state and local government, particularly schools and hospitals. The biggest losers over the next decade are projected to be manufacturing jobs, such as apparel, textiles, and footwear, due to automation and competition from cheaper imports.

Employment by Major Sector, 2008

77% Services (health care, trade, professional and business services, hospitality, public sector, etc.)

14% Goods-producing (not including agriculture)

6% Self-employed or unpaid family worker

1% Agriculture, forestry, fishing, and hunting

Source: U.S. Bureau of Labor Statistics. "Employment by major industry sector."
Note: Percentages do not equal 100 due to rounding.

The importance of education as perhaps the most valuable asset in the labor market was addressed in the preceding chapter. **But groups that face the steepest difficulties finding and retaining steady employment include:**

Youth. While youth unemployment tends to be higher than others at all times, this recession hit youth particularly hard. In January 2010, the jobless rate for workers ages 16 to 24 was nearly 19 percent, nearly double the overall unemployment rate of 9.7 percent. Those with the least work experience are often first to be let go. In addition, the huge loss of assets and home equity among older workers prompted many to postpone retirement or to return to work. As a result, many young people lost opportunities for formative work experience, instead taking jobs that undermine future wage growth, output, productivity, and in some cases, a return to higher education.[79]

African American men and economic inclusion. During the 1990s researchers found that concentrated poverty and disadvantage were declining in U.S. urban areas.[80] As a consequence, people without jobs, particularly men, grew less likely to be segregated from the employed and from the benefits that one derives from connecting to economically functioning communities. One exception, however, was jobless African American men, who tend to live in areas that are far more segregated from the working world, keeping them outside the networks of employed men. Evidence shows that this creates a severe disadvantage on many counts: joblessness limits these men's social ties to employed men and their access to informal job networks, it can mean they live farther from good jobs and adequate transport, and in the worst cases, it can lead to "jobless ghettos"[81]—areas where despair reigns and the norms of working life grow increasingly far removed.

Workers in manufacturing. After a period of extreme job loss in manufacturing from the late 1990s to the present, another 1.2 million manufacturing jobs are expected to be lost by 2018.[82] Following an already dismal decline of these jobs, this is further proof that workers today must seek the skills and training they will need in the economy of tomorrow. The issue of workforce development and training is discussed below.

WEALTH AND ASSET BUILDING

Earnings is a key component that we use to evaluate access to opportunities. In addition to being the component that the Human Development Index measures, governments most commonly use earnings to determine poverty and eligibility for social assistance. Wealth is harder to measure than earnings, but it is arguably even more important.

Earnings—salaries or wages from one's labor—allow people to meet daily needs; wealth enables them to weather downturns. Wealth can be turned into cash during lean times or crises, enabling people to buffer the effects of job loss, divorce, natural disaster, or other unexpected events.

Wealth enables families to invest in the future and in the next generation—to afford a home in a neighborhood with good schools, to pay for college or contribute to an offspring's first home, to start a business, or to leave behind an inheritance that gives family members choices they would otherwise not have.

The distribution of wealth in our society is often closely linked to the distribution of power. At last count, more than 230 millionaires were serving in the U.S. Congress, accounting for about 43 percent of the House and Senate[83]—as opposed to roughly 1 percent in the U.S. population. This is just one illustration of wealth's usefulness as a resource. At a more down-to-earth level, well-resourced groups with access to wealthy networks and sophisticated skills are more likely to set a public agenda and influence social, economic, and political processes than groups without such access.

For every $1 of white net worth, Latinos have 12 cents, and African Americans have 10 cents.

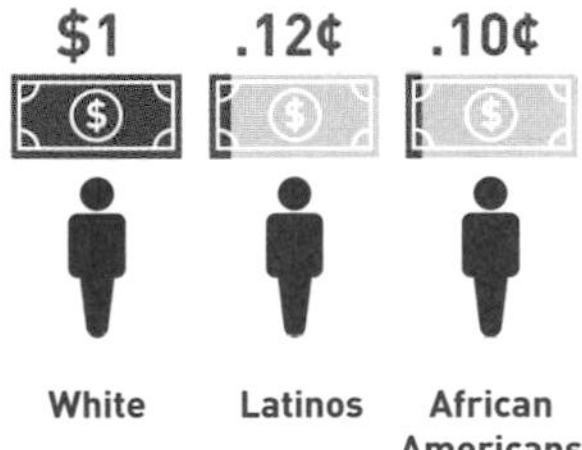

Precisely because wealth can be transferred from one generation to the next, the wealth divide is more dramatic than the earnings divide. Today, one in five households lacks the assets to sustain themselves at the federal poverty level for more than three months in the event their income is suddenly cut off.[84] African Americans have 10 cents of net worth for every dollar of white (non-Hispanic) net worth.[85] Latinos have 12 cents of net worth for every dollar of white net worth.[86] Families headed by a single mother have 53 cents to every dollar of male-headed households with children.[87]

How can families with few assets make progress in reducing risks, building resilience, and setting their children on a trajectory of opportunity and choice?

Savings accounts. More than 28 million Americans have no checking or savings account. Many cannot maintain the required minimum balance or had their accounts closed due to multiple episodes of insufficient funds to cover withdrawals. A number of state and employer programs provide excellent incentives for saving, ranging from allowing tax refunds to be directly deposited to savings accounts, to employers providing automatic payroll deductions or retirement contributions. Finally, Children's Savings Accounts are an idea whose time has come. Nearly every European country as well as Canada, Australia, and New Zealand has some form of universal cash grant for children.[88]

In the United States, various laws have been proposed at the federal, state, and municipal level, to provide incentives for saving for children from birth, though at publication time, none was yet signed into law.[89]

Safe financial services. The recent subprime mortgage crisis provided overwhelming evidence of predatory financial firms and of the extent to which cash-strapped people can fall victim to these unscrupulous services. A combination of greater consumer protections and efforts by individuals and organizations to build financial literacy skills are two low-cost measures that can help people to choose safe financial products and avoid repeating the devastating losses of the recent mortgage debacle.[90]

Homeownership. In 2007 the richest households mostly invested their wealth in stocks and investment real estate (housing was only 10 percent of their wealth). However, middle-class households (the middle three-fifths of U.S. households), invest primarily in their own homes, which accounted for nearly 66 percent of their wealth.[91]

Homeownership makes up 10 percent of the wealth of the rich. It accounts for 66 percent of the wealth of the middle class.

The foreclosure crisis further undermined many groups already struggling with low asset levels. Analysis by the U.S. Department of Housing and Urban Development, AARP, and other groups has found that the bulk of subprime victims, particularly for refinance loans, were African Americans and Latinos.[92] Subprime mortgage loans were disproportionately marketed in minority neighborhoods, particularly to older homeowners or women living alone. Analysis by the Federal Reserve and others found that the primary takers of subprime mortgages were borrowers who lacked financial knowledge. The business practices of lenders, including discrimination, predatory lending, and unregulated pricing discretion by loan officers, significantly accounted for the high proportion of minorities among victims of the subprime mortgage crisis.[93]

Jobs with benefits. Benefits such as employer-based pensions; health insurance coverage that frees workers to devote their earnings to build assets, rather than paying medical bills; and tax advantages of employer pension plans where contributions are not taxed as income and the employee pays taxes at a lower rate during retirement all contribute to the ability to build wealth. Groups facing the greatest challenges in asset building tend to be clustered in jobs that pay less and offer few or no benefits. Training programs that provide the skills and encouragement for workers to move into more secure employment with benefits, public and private policies that provide health and retirement benefits, and family-friendly policies that help remove the constraints to stable employment help working families build assets for the future.[94]

The working poor have also benefited from two recent minimum-wage increases; the former, in 2007, was the first in a decade. Twenty-four states now have a state-level Earned Income Tax Credit (EITC) (see Indicator Table on page 247), and a few municipalities have even developed local EITCs, a proven and widely endorsed method to reduce tax burdens on low- and moderate-income working families. Another success for low-income families was the strengthening of the Child Tax Credit in 2009 to make it more affordable to raise children. This credit, included in the stimulus bill, will expire in 2011 unless Congress extends it.

JOB TRAINING FOR DISPLACED WORKERS

When communities and local economies depend on a few core industries, labor market shifts can have devastating effects. The shift from manufacturing to a service-based economy that began in earnest in the 1980s left displaced workers with specialized skill sets few good employment prospects. Michigan, which accounts for 40 percent of the nation's net job loss in car manufacturing since 2003,[95] is a case in point. As discussed above, men in Michigan experienced the largest loss in median earnings of men in any state from 2005 to 2008.

Workers need to adapt to these changing labor demands, but they cannot do it alone. Both the private sector and public policy have a role to play in helping workers retool to meet the demands of a changing labor market. Today, the private sector provides the lion's share of workforce development—as much as ten times more than the public sector.[96] But private-sector training disproportionately goes to the most educated, leaving less skilled workers with fewer opportunities to adapt, advance, and become more resilient.[97]

Private-sector training disproportionately goes to the most educated, leaving less skilled workers with fewer opportunities to advance.

While federal, state, and local workforce training programs make up a small part of the training system, these modest contributions can be augmented through policies designed to leverage increased private-sector training and improve targeting of existing training. Tax credits, better job information resources, and more effective public-private collaboration could help provide the full set of services and resources workers often require to compete successfully in a transformed job market. Particularly in hard times, it is critical not to reduce workforce training as a means to close financial gaps. This short-sighted move erodes the skills workers already have, further strains public assistance, and reduces people's ability to seize new economic opportunities in a rapidly changing world.

Consider the disparate situations of two young adults interviewed for this report:

Nicky and Pedro have just graduated from the University of Michigan. They both majored in biological chemistry and have nearly straight As. Nicky's parents met at the University of Michigan. Pedro is the first person in his family to go to college.

Nicky

NO STUDENT DEBT
ASSETS VALUED AT $45,000
(CAR AND HOUSING DOWNPAYMENT)
HEALTH INSURANCE COVERAGE

Nicky finished college without student debt thanks to contributions from his parents and grandmother and a work-study job that covered his living costs. His graduation gift was a 2007 Subaru. Nicky is looking for a job anywhere in the Midwest or East Coast while also preparing to take the Graduate Record Exam to apply to graduate school. Where he lives will depend on job offers, but he has $25,000 from his grandmother for a downpayment on an apartment wherever he lands. He will have health coverage until age 26 under his parents' insurance plan.

Pedro

$22,000 IN STUDENT DEBT
ASSETS TOTALLING $500
NO HEALTH INSURANCE COVERAGE

Pedro owes $22,000 in federal and state loans for college, and so while he hopes to go to graduate school someday, it will have to wait.

He would prefer to work near his parents' home so he can live in their basement apartment to save on rent. His graduation gift of $500 will help him save for a car. Both of his parents work in restaurants with no health benefits, so he hopes to find a job with health coverage; until then, he will not have health insurance. He has decided to call himself Peter on his resume in light of the experience of several friends and of recent studies confirming the impact of race and ethnicity on job searches.

Both Nicky and Pedro are bright, twenty-one-year-old men who worked hard to get through college, and have families who have been behind them every step of the way. **Nicky's job search will be eased by the mobility a car affords him, by having health insurance, and by the considerable wealth of his family and all that it provides** in both material support and access to affluent social and employment networks. This in turn will likely have a long-lasting impact on Nicky's success in beginning to build his own wealth. **Pedro enters the world of work with strong drive and a solid educational foundation, but he faces a considerably more constrained range of choices due to economic pressures and the more limited resources and wealth of his family.**

Retirement Security: Freedom and Choices in the Golden Years

The introduction of Social Security in the 1930s and Medicare in the 1960s helped dramatically reduce poverty among the elderly. Even as recently as 1967, nearly 30 percent of elderly Americans lived in poverty. By only one decade later, that rate had been cut in half.[98] **The federal government's commitment to enhancing security in old age has been a tremendous success, and continues to be an anchor of stability in fast-changing seas.**

Social Security is one of three pillars in the U.S. retirement security system. It provides more than 70 percent of retirement income for the typical household, and 90 percent for low-income seniors. The other two pillars are private pensions, which provide about 17 percent of retirement income for the typical household, and private savings, which provide less than 10 percent.[99]

Which groups face the highest risk of poverty in old age? Those with low skills and education levels; women, who generally earn less or have earnings gaps from dropping out of the full-time workforce to care for children or elderly relatives; and older lesbian, gay, bisexual, and transgender (LGBT) Americans.

Like our government, Americans have not been saving. According to a recent Gallup Poll, 52 percent of nonretired Americans do not think they will have enough money to be able to live comfortably in retirement.[100] And many are right. A Congressional Research Service study released last year found that 47 percent of workers had no retirement savings whatsoever. Of workers 55 to 64 years old, nearly 70 percent reported retirement balances of less than $100,000.[101]

The most significant change in retirement savings, beginning in 1981, was the introduction of the 401(k) plan, often referred to as defined-contribution plans. The 401(k) was created to supplement employer-funded pensions. But now, half of the American workforce does not have access to an employer-sponsored plan,[102] and there is growing concern that the 401(k) is failing as a primary retirement savings vehicle.

A 401(k) has inherent risks. Some are human. For example, the ability to cash out of a 401(k) when you leave a job plays to many people's worst impulses—particularly if there is no new job waiting for them. In addition, many people lack the financial expertise to maximize the plan's benefits—they don't diversify their holdings, overinvesting in stocks and stock mutual funds (with tragic consequences in the recent downturn), and they don't annuitize to hedge their risk.

Finally, while 401(k)s have been a boon to Wall Street, producing more than $40.5 billion annually in fees,[103] the costs to the average worker are extremely high—the average annual fee is around $350 a year[104]—and often well hidden. Legislation was recently introduced to hinder workers' ability to cash out of a 401(k) and to foster better savings outcomes. Congress is considering other proposals as well. For families who watched their 401(k) became a "201(k)"

The introduction of Social Security in the 1930s and Medicare in the 1960s helped dramatically **reduce elderly poverty**.

in the 2007–9 market collapse, this issue requires immediate attention. **While the low personal savings rate in the United States creates risks for all but the very rich, certain groups face far higher danger of experiencing poverty in old age.**

Women. Women's lives often yield a smaller nest egg and a greater reliance on Social Security in old age. Women live more years in retirement due to a longer life span, and since they typically earn less than men, they are less likely to have well-funded pension benefits or other savings vehicles. In addition, women are more likely to take time off for caregiving, further reducing Social Security benefits and the likelihood of a vested pension.

Social Security has several features to help alleviate hardship, including inflation adjustments to protect the benefits of the longer-lived, and a higher percentage of benefits allotted to those earning lower wages. Nonetheless, elderly poverty has a distinctly female face. The poverty rate among men 65 and older is 6.7 percent; for women, it is 11.9 percent.[105] Several proposals, including some along the lines of Germany's Care Insurance Act (see **BOX 5**), have been developed to modernize Social Security to address poverty among elderly women. One idea, for instance, is to provide Social Security credit to caregivers, male or female, to compensate them for lost years of contributions.

Elderly poverty has a distinctly female face.

LGBT older adults. The lesbian, gay, bisexual, and transgender (LGBT) population faces unique barriers to financial security due to both social stigma and laws. Elderly LGBT couples contribute to Social Security but are not eligible for spousal and survivor benefits like married couples, so they are ineligible for surviving partner pension protections or tax-free health insurance benefits for spouses of an employee. As a result, lesbian couples receive, on average, nearly one-third less in Social Security than heterosexual couples, while gay male couples receive 17.8 percent less.[106]

Many good ideas are on the table for addressing today's challenges of increasing life span alongside a decrease in the ratio of workers to retirees and for reforming the retirement system. **BOX 5** looks at interesting features of retirement savings in New Zealand, Germany, and Sweden.

Despite the stress on Social Security from an aging population, several factors give cause for optimism. The first is that Americans are increasingly delaying retirement, which helps ease the strain on the Social Security fund. Second, while it has saved millions of elderly people from poverty, Social Security accounts for only 4.5 percent of GDP[107] (compared to 16 percent for health care) and has extremely low overhead costs. Social Security has previously adapted with the times and now must do so again. Efforts to privatize Social Security in 2005 failed in the face of stiff public resistance. **But a number of more moderate reform proposals advocate reductions in benefits combined with increases in revenues to restore Social Security's balance sheet for the longer term.**

BOX 5 Interesting Features of Retirement Security in Other Countries

As Americans age, fewer workers are available to support each retiree. Innovations designed in other countries facing a very similar challenge may be instructive.

New Zealand's new KiwiSaver retirement program addresses one of the greatest hurdles in retirement savings: inertia. New Zealand has had one of the lowest savings rates among the OECD countries. To counter that problem, the KiwiSaver retirement program starts saving automatically when an individual starts a job. While not mandatory, it is up to the employee to opt out of the system within the first eight weeks of employment. This automatic enrollment feature has had an enormous impact on participation, and to provide further incentive the government offers a cash bonus deposited upon enrollment. KiwiSaver accounts are designed to impose a saving culture in a country where savings had dipped into the red.[108]

Germany has taken a pioneering approach to the fate of caregivers, who end up with lower pension savings due to unpaid work caring for children and elderly or disabled family members. If an individual registers as a caregiver (for at least fourteen hours a week), the government pays their pension contribution at a rate based on their average contributions and the level of care being provided. Insurance against accident or injury that might occur during caregiving is also provided. Germany's Long Term Care Insurance Act of 1994 is funded by a small payroll tax jointly paid by employers and employees regardless of income level.[109] Germany's approach benefits those who are being cared for by loved ones and protects the caregiver as well.

In 2001, **Sweden** redesigned the pension system so that the longer citizens put off retirement after age 61, the larger their pensions.[110] In addition, the Swedish pension system has also been partially privatized, whereby 2.5 percent of a worker's salary (part of the mandatory social security tax paid jointly by workers and employers) is automatically put into a private account for individual investing.[111] Additional benefits of delayed retirement include retaining the skills of older workers in workplaces, higher productivity, and increasing worker job satisfaction.

Increasing Resilience in Standard of Living: What Will It Take?

In order to reduce Americans' **vulnerability to economic shocks**, the following actions are high priorities:

- Protect children from extreme poverty
- Create and retain jobs
- Create incentives for asset building
- Increase educational attainment
- Help families provide care
- Strengthen financial regulation and literacy
- Reform retirement systems

A central tenet of the human development approach is that money isn't everything—neither the exclusive gauge of societal progress nor the sole determinant of a person's freedom to decide what to do and be in life. Health, education, politics, personal choices and behaviors, neighborhood characteristics, bonds of love and friendship, faith, the natural environment, transportation, housing, and other factors join forces to shape the course and quality of our lives.

But money is certainly important. It provides the means to a host of ends, including the income and assets that enable us to have valuable choices and opportunities along with the capacity to blunt the impact of adverse events. In America, more than in other affluent countries, inadequate finances too often lead to a paucity of opportunities and to higher exposure to risks. Money's crucial contributions to well-being and security are reflected in the composition of the American HD Index, in which median personal earnings account for one-third of the total score.

The earnings gaps that separate states, congressional districts, racial and ethnic groups, and men and women are large. But these differences between geographic, racial, and ethnic groups, large as they are, actually fail to capture the greatest extreme: that between the ultra-rich and everyone else. Since the late 1970s, super-rich Americans—those in the top 0.1 percent of income distribution—have had a fourfold increase in their share of national earnings. Americans in the top 1 percent of the income distribution earned 18 percent of the income in 2007, and Americans in the top 0.1 percent earned 12.3 percent of income.[112] In other words, one-tenth of 1 percent of Americans pocketed one of every eight dollars earned in 2007... and asset gaps dwarf earnings gaps. The wealthiest 1 percent have assets, on average, of $18.5 million per household. Those of the bottom 20 percent of households amount to zero—or even less due to debt.[113]

For most American families, the last ten years produced little if any economic progress. Household net worth declined, median household income dropped, and the number of private-sector jobs was static even as the population increased by 9 percent.[114] The Great Recession from which we are just beginning to emerge hit those at the bottom the hardest—deferring or defeating dreams for millions. Families with next to no savings, property, or investments—some 40 percent of American households have assets of a few thousand dollars or less[115]—face extreme economic insecurity and a wide array of risks. One crisis can easily wipe them out financially. But so can more commonplace misfortune. An illness in the family, a cutback in overtime work, a disruption in childcare arrangements, even a minor fender-bender—these seemingly routine challenges can upend the shaky foundation of a life without financial assets.

The strong correlation of place, race, ethnicity, and gender to earnings challenges the meritocratic ideal that generations of Americans have held dear.

And the enormous concentration of income and assets among the very wealthiest raises a host of thorny questions. Some argue that the disproportionate ability of wealthy individuals and interest groups to influence policy outcomes in ways that solidify their economic and political power distorts the democratic process. But even many who find nothing wrong with the unprecedented concentration of wealth among the ultra-rich nevertheless agree that the extreme economic insecurity at the bottom—and, increasingly, in the middle rungs—of the economic ladder is deeply disturbing.

What can be done to improve the living standards of people in poverty, to boost the earnings of those who make the least, to reduce vulnerability to economic shocks, and to help families build assets for the proverbial rainy day and for predictable needs like retirement? **A host of actions are required; from the human development perspective, several are particularly high priorities.**

PROTECT YOUNG CHILDREN FROM THE RISKS OF EXTREME POVERTY.

Extreme poverty imperils the cognitive, social, physical, and emotional development of young children, often causing harm in the early years that reverberates across the life course of the individual and triggers high costs to society in the long term. The majority of children experiencing extreme poverty today live in single-parent households. While getting parents into the workforce is a priority, it is exceedingly difficult for some single parents to work full-time without adequate child care, stable housing, and more. To break the cycle of intergenerational poverty—and to ensure that financial hardship does not condemn children to narrow possibilities—adequate nutrition, heat, electricity, and stable housing for poor families with young children, coupled with a suite of proven programs like home visitation, parenting skills education, and intensive early childhood education[116] are essential. By easing access to existing programs through streamlining eligibility requirements and by using America's world-class marketing prowess to reach the tens of thousands of families eligible but not registered for social programs, we can help to protect children from the lasting effects of deprivation.

Extreme poverty in childhood causes harm that reverberates across the life course.

CREATE AND RETAIN JOBS.

For citizens to have the benefits of a secure livelihood, new jobs must be created and the flood of job losses in many states must be staunched. Long-term unemployment can lead to isolation, substance abuse, poor parenting, and marital difficulties; the absence of legitimate employment can increase the appeal of illegal activities. Workers with outdated or insufficient skills, limited education, or residence in an economically weak region face high hurdles in finding a job that pays a living wage. Strategies including job training and retraining along with wage subsidies, such as extending the EITC to single workers, could help low-income men, the cohort hardest hit by the current recession, to stay afloat.

CREATE INCENTIVES—AND ELIMINATE DISINCENTIVES—FOR ASSET BUILDING AMONG LOW-INCOME PEOPLE.

Middle-class and affluent Americans benefit from tax incentives to save and invest. An investment in a house is rewarded with a mortgage interest deduction; the decision to save for college or retirement is rewarded by tax-free gains through 529 savings plans, 401(k)s, or IRAs; investments in the stock market are rewarded with a lower tax rate on capital gains. Workers at companies with generous benefits are able to take advantage of matching retirement funds or subsidized life insurance coverage. The working poor seldom earn enough to benefit from these advantages and rarely have jobs that offer anything but bare-bones benefits. Their pursuit of financial security is often exploited by companies marketing shady financial products such as high-cost, low-benefit life insurance policies. People receiving certain federal or state benefits face serious disincentives to save, since having anything beyond a small sum in the bank renders them ineligible for continued services. Automatic enrollment in pension plans for all workers, matched savings accounts that allow low-income workers to build assets over the long term, children's accounts established automatically at birth, and greater asset protection, particularly related to housing, are sustainable approaches that would allow low-income households to build assets and increase self-reliance.

Given the **greater responsibility** individuals now have for their financial fate, more financial sector regulation and greater financial literacy are required.

INCREASE EDUCATIONAL ATTAINMENT.

Benjamin Franklin said that "an investment in knowledge always pays the best interest," an observation far truer today than when he wrote it many years ago. Those who fail to graduate high school are all but condemned to lifelong financial insecurity; a high school dropout is over three times more likely to be unemployed than a college graduate.[117] They also pay a high price in terms of health and psychological resilience. Boosting on-time high school graduation rates, particularly among Latino and African American men, is a vital goal, as is expanding meaningful vocational training options for those who will not graduate from college. In addition, we must expand programs that help students who begin college to obtain their bachelor's degrees.

HELP FAMILIES PROVIDE CARE.

Caring for family members doesn't register in the nation's GDP; traditional economists don't even view it as productive work. Because unpaid caring work is either invisible or perceived in sentimental terms as priceless, its actual cost only becomes apparent when it is replaced with paid services—caregivers, daycare centers, after-school programs, home health aides, and the like. Women represent half of today's workforce, and overwhelming evidence suggests that they are in it to stay. Yet people still need care—babies and children, elderly family members, and those who are ill or disabled. Paid leave for sickness and caregiving by men and women, on-site childcare at workplaces, flexible work schedules, and childcare tax credits or direct subsidies to meet the costs of providing care would help families deal with that reality.

STRENGTHEN FINANCIAL SECTOR REGULATION AND FINANCIAL LITERACY.

Americans face a financial landscape that is more complex than ever, offering them more options and entailing more risks. The shift from plain-vanilla thirty-year fixed-rate mortgages to more complex mortgage products and the move from defined-benefit pension plans to defined-contribution 401(k)s are just two examples of this trend. Individuals who would never fill a cavity in their own tooth or rewire their own house must now make financial decisions with far-reaching, and potentially grave, life consequences. Given the far greater responsibility individuals now have for their financial fate, greater regulation of the financial sector and greater financial literacy are vital. The recent passage of the Dodd-Frank Wall Street financial reform act holds promise to curtail abuses and aggressive marketing practices that contributed, in part, to 2.5 million completed foreclosures from early 2007 to the end of 2009, with communities of color experiencing disproportionate impacts.[118] Greater financial literacy at every stage of life is a requirement in order to evaluate options and avoid financially destructive transactions, whether among students taking loans, families using credit cards or buying mortgages, or elderly Americans saving for retirement.

Social and economic policies must catch up with the dramatic changes that have taken place in the economy.

REFORM RETIREMENT SYSTEMS TO ENABLE GREATER RETIREMENT SECURITY.

Major shifts in retirement systems have affected the level of retirement preparedness of all Americans, and put certain groups—particularly those with low skills and education levels, women, and LGBT households—at higher risk of elderly poverty. Sound reform proposals are on the table to make 401(k)s a stronger vehicle for retirement security, and to restore Social Security's balance sheet for the longer term in the face of an aging population. Both of these pillars of Americans' retirement must evolve with the times.

***

Globalization, deindustrialization, and other recent trends have overpowered millions of American workers, increasing their financial and social insecurity and permanently altering the economic landscape and prospects for their children. The American Dream may be unchanged, but what it takes to achieve it has been irrevocably altered. Social and economic policies must catch up with the dramatic changes that have taken place in the economy so that the vision of the American Dream, still cherished by millions of struggling workers, can become a tangible reality for larger numbers of individuals and families.

CONCLUSION

Agenda for Action: Reducing Risks, Building Resilience

Action in these areas shows great promise for boosting American Human Development Index scores for all Americans, narrowing the gaps that exist between different groups, and helping everyone build resilience to weather both the inevitable vicissitudes of life and the sudden, severe shocks that destroy capabilities years in the making.

- Prioritize prevention.
- Account for the cost of inaction.
- Make better use of economic instruments.
- Make the best choice the easiest choice.
- Beware the commonplace threat.

- Address the social and economic disparities that breed ill health.
- Minimize people's exposure to health risks, especially to the fatal four: poor diet, tobacco, physical inactivity, and excess drinking.
- Mitigate health risks through counteradvertising, treatment programs, public information campaigns, and modifications to the environment.
- Foster greater accountability for health disparities.

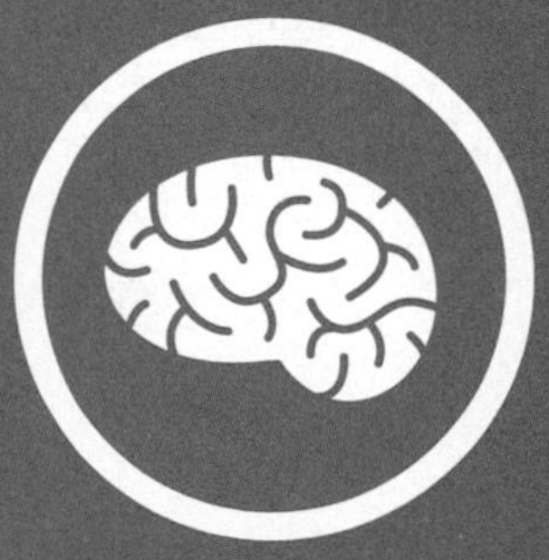

- Ensure universal, quality preschool.
- Address head-on the high school dropout crisis.
- Invest in the education of immigrant children.
- Ensure that all children have good teachers.
- Deflate ballooning college tuition costs.

- Protect young children from the risks of extreme poverty.
- Increase educational attainment.
- Create and retain jobs.
- Create incentives—and eliminate disincentives—for asset building among low-income people.
- Help families provide care.
- Strengthen financial-sector regulation and improve financial literacy.
- Reform retirement systems to enable greater retirement security and reduce elderly poverty.

Agenda for Action: Reducing Risks, Building Resilience

Hurricanes are indiscriminate in the application of force: flying and falling debris threaten life and limb, trees snap and topple, roads are rendered impassible. But while the storms themselves are indiscriminate, their effects are not. Homes set on higher ground may escape the peak storm surge and resultant flooding even as low-lying areas are inundated. New structures built to code can withstand the winds, while mobile homes are tossed about. Those with cars and credit cards can ride out the storm in hotels a few hours' drive away; families with generators and a stockpile of basic provisions can return home earlier than those without; homeowners with savings and adequate insurance can rebuild more quickly.

The planning and readiness of businesses, public utilities, municipalities, and state and federal governments are similarly important in determining how people fare. The structural integrity of dams, levies, and bridges; the enforcement of building codes; the preparations of emergency responders; the existence and promotion of emergency evacuation plans; contingency provisions for the disabled or elderly—all this and more can minimize loss of life and property damage.

Capabilities matter for expanding choices and opportunities in the future, and they **matter as much** or more when calamity strikes.

We frequently use weather metaphors to describe events in the lives of individuals, families, and the nation. We save for a rainy day, we're snowed under, we watch as businesses battle economic headwinds, and we hope that gray skies turn sunny. Sweeping financial crises like the Great Recession, the collapse of local economies in the wake of plant closings, individual crises triggered by disabling illness or injury, family dissolution from death or divorce: these types of events take people by storm. **Just as in the case of natural disasters, those people with the fewest capabilities are the hardest hit and least able to rebound.**

Human development is about the freedom ordinary people have to fulfill their potential and direct the course of their lives. It requires that people have a full toolbox of capabilities—the personal attributes, material resources, social links, and collective investments that make up the equipment people have for living a freely chosen life of value. Capabilities matter for expanding choices and opportunities in the future, and they matter as much or more when calamity strikes. People in good physical and mental health with a sound education, adequate financial resources, and strong social networks are not immune to misfortune, but they are resilient; the capabilities they possess make their recovery more likely in the face of reversals.

The current recession has emphatically underscored the fact that **education matters**. In the last quarter of 2009, Americans with graduate degrees faced a rate of unemployment or underemployment of 7 percent; those without a high school diploma experienced a rate five times higher, 35 percent.[1] **Income matters**: families with earnings in the bottom 10 percent of the income distribution registered an unemployment rate of 31 percent at the end of 2009, ten times higher than the rate of families in the top 10 percent of earners (3.2 percent).[2] **Health matters**: people in good physical and psychological health are, on average, better equipped to weather bouts of economic insecurity, find new jobs, move where there is work, and adapt in other ways to changing economic fortunes than those coping with chronic health conditions, from depression to heart disease.

The preceding chapters on health, education, and income explore the degree to which human capabilities are flourishing—or not—for different groups of Americans, and they identify severe and pervasive threats to human well-being in each of these three areas. The evidence indicates that Americans with a full toolbox of essential capabilities are able to further the goals that matter to them. But for too many, fundamental capabilities are at risk; indeed, such evidence is overwhelming. **To meet the obligations of a civilized society and realize the promise of the American Dream, we must reduce risks and build greater resilience among key populations.**

To meet the obligations of a civilized society and realize the promise of the American Dream, we must **reduce risks and build greater resilience** among key populations.

Reducing risks to fundamental capabilities requires proactive steps. People can reduce health risks by steering clear of risk behaviors, chief among them smoking, poor diet, physical inactivity, and excess drinking. State and local governments can reduce risks to educational attainment by ensuring that all children, no matter which neighborhood they live in, receive an education that prepares them for full participation in a modern, knowledge-based society. Businesses can reduce economic risks by instituting family-friendly policies—such as paid leave to care for newborns or elderly relatives and on-site childcare facilities—that put fewer men and women in the untenable position of having to choose between bringing home a needed paycheck and meeting the needs of vulnerable family members. The federal government can reduce risks to health with regulations that limit children's exposure to junk-food marketing.

Building resilience requires helping people to develop capabilities and to protect the capabilities they already have. Individuals can learn new job skills to adapt to a changing labor market. Religious institutions can help people acquire strategies for dealing with stress, and community-based organizations can teach parenting or financial management skills. Businesses can make it easier for their employees to save for the future through automatic retirement payroll deductions for all workers (with the right to opt out). The government can do more to encourage asset building among low-income people by, for instance, establishing savings accounts for newborns or enhancing tax incentives available to those with fewer assets.

The pages that follow identify priorities in the realms of health, education, and income drawn from analysis presented in this report. Evidence suggests the following recommendations have the greatest potential to raise the American Human Development Index scores for all Americans and to close the gaps separating those at the top from those at the bottom.

Stopping problems before they start is, in almost every instance, **less expensive and more effective** than delaying action until a crisis is full-blown.

Prioritize Prevention

An ounce of prevention is worth a pound of cure: this bit of homespun wisdom may sound hokey, but a wealth of research suggests it's true. Stopping problems before they start is, in almost every instance, less expensive and more effective than delaying action until a crisis is full-blown. In health, diabetes provides a case study. According to the American Diabetes Association, diabetes contributes to more than 250,000 Americans' deaths each year and costs $174 billion annually in medical expenses and lost productivity[3]—a sum that exceeds the 2009 GDP of Singapore.[4] Yet diabetes is largely preventable with appropriate diet and exercise.

In terms of education, the prison crisis provides a useful guide. Inmates in state and federal prisons are overwhelmingly men who failed to complete high school. In California, keeping a prisoner behind bars for one year costs $47,000[5]—an amount that would easily cover two years' room, board, and tuition at any campus of California State University (total costs of attendance for the school year 2010–11 ranged from a low of about $18,000 at the Bakersville campus to a high of about $22,000 at the Channel Islands campus[6]). That sum would also easily cover four years' tuition at a small, private California high school.[7] Yet campaigns to improve the quality of education tend to be long on rhetoric, short on resources. Universal preschool is much lauded as an ideal—and evidence suggests that it would significantly reduce the number of young men who end up behind bars—but in reality funds for preschool are often cut when budgets get tight.

Account for the Cost of Inaction

Proactive, preventative interventions are often rejected out of hand as too expensive. As discussed in previous chapters, other industrialized countries offer a set of benefits to everyone, including subsidies to offset child-rearing expenses, universal medical care, and comprehensive unemployment insurance. In the United States, too often we wait until a family bottoms out financially before offering a helping hand, an approach with high human and financial costs.

Washington state's farsighted paid family leave policy, approved in 2007, has been put on the shelf until 2012, a casualty of the recession.[8] Taxpayers balk at the cost of providing supportive housing—stable, affordable housing units joined with on-site mental health and social integration services—to those with persistent and severe mental illness, yet end up paying the high costs of emergency room visits and prison stays that result. Similarly, in failing to provide a quality education and a pathway toward meaningful, productive employment to young men of color, the country pays dearly in both blood and treasure, yet we focus on the cost of improving lives rather than on the costs we already pay in lives lost or wasted, in crime, imprisonment, and family and neighborhood dissolution. Our public policy is penny-wise and pound-foolish. As this book goes to press, newspapers are reporting that foundation and government funding for public health campaigns is being diverted from tobacco prevention to obesity prevention—as though the nation has sufficient resources for only one deadly health risk, but not more.[9]

Policy makers, researchers, and advocates must better enumerate and explain the costs we already pay for many social and economic ills—and the savings, as well as the social benefits, that key evidence-based interventions could bring.

Make Better Use of Economic Instruments

Expanding the use of economic instruments to induce people and institutions to make choices that are in the best interest of people and the country as a whole offers great promise for reducing risks and increasing resilience in health, education, and income. Since the 1990s, countries around the world have increasingly employed economic incentives and market-based instruments in support of environmental objectives, with considerable success.[10] Such approaches include ending harmful subsidies, effectively deploying socially beneficial taxes and subsidies, and adopting the polluter-pays principle to assign the costs of a given problem to the party that created it.

Policy makers, researchers, and advocates must **better enumerate** and explain the costs we already pay for many social and economic ills.

The $200 billion Tobacco Master Settlement Agreement of 1998, which required large tobacco companies to make annual payments to states until 2025 in order to offset Medicare costs incurred in treating smoking-related diseases, is a successful example of the polluter-pays principle applied to health rather than to the environment: tobacco companies were held responsible for the health costs their products generated. But other policies are counterproductive to health and quality of life. The United States should end agricultural aid that publicly subsidizes unhealthy snacks and soft drinks, and apply those subsidies instead to lower the cost of fruits and vegetables. Imposing a tax on sugary, fatty, and salty foods and drinks would make them less appealing, especially to children and teens, and could help curb the obesity epidemic.

Make the Best Choice the Easiest Choice

Businesses, schools, families, and governments can take many steps to help people choose options that make them better off. Improving the built environment so that walking or biking is more pleasant than driving, or selling only healthy foods and drinks in school and business vending machines are obvious examples. Offering a demanding curriculum to all students and making the college-prep track the default option rather than making students proactively select the more rigorous course of study is something schools can do to improve educational quality. Making automatic savings programs the default for new employees is something that employers can do to enhance overall economic security.

To reduce risks and build resilience, we must recognize that danger often lurks in **the familiar**.

Beware the Commonplace Threat

Few of us will die in plane crashes or terrorist attacks; our killers are more mundane—a daily lunch of a burger and fries; an unbuckled seat belt; chronic, low-level stress. The greatest danger to long-term employment prospects and the likelihood of marriage are the hundreds of small choices by children and those whose actions affect them that lead to a teen's disengagement from high school and the ultimate decision to drop out. To reduce risks and build resilience, we must recognize that danger often lurks in the familiar.

For a Long and Healthy Life

Address the social and economic disparities that breed ill health.

Low levels of income and education, discrimination and residential segregation, social exclusion, dangerous neighborhoods without places to exercise or buy healthy foods, substandard or crowded housing, the chronic stress that insecurity breeds—all these social determinants of health contribute to huge life expectancy gaps. Tackling social and economic disparities and improving the conditions in which people are born and raised hold the greatest promise for longer, healthier lives. Improvements in the other two subject areas of the American HD Index—education and income—are also critical to improvements in health.

Minimize people's exposure to health risks, especially to the fatal four: poor diet, tobacco, physical inactivity, and excess drinking.

Smoking, risky drinking, poor diet, and lack of exercise pose grave risks and are, in sum, the true leading causes of death in the United States. Minimizing these risks and the risks of trauma (homicide, suicide, and unintentional injury, including car crashes), which disproportionately affect men, especially male adolescents and men of color, is critical to lengthening the average American life span and closing gaps between groups. Priorities include improving the quality of food in daycare centers, schools, and poor neighborhoods; limiting the amounts of fat, salt, and sugar in commercially prepared food; banning advertising of such products to children; expanding bans on smoking in public places; and raising the driving age and lowering the blood alcohol limit to tackle the leading causes of car crashes.

Smoking, risky drinking, poor diet, and lack of exercise pose grave risks and are, in sum, the true leading causes of death in the United States.

Mitigate health risks through counter advertising, treatment programs, public information campaigns, and modifications to the environment.

Creating neighborhood, school, and work environments in which **healthy choices are not just possible but probable** offers great promise.

Much can be done to mitigate existing health risks. Federal, state, and local governments as well as public-interest groups should invest in counter-advertising: innovative communication campaigns to provide a counterweight to the huge, enticing marketing campaigns used by the food and beverage industries. Making mental health care more widely available, less stigmatized, and more broadly covered by health insurance would help people develop healthy approaches to dealing with stress as well as manage a range of mental health conditions. Subsidizing weight-loss programs, along with others to help people break free of tobacco, alcohol, and drug abuse, and requiring insurance plans to cover such programs would help people to improve their health. Targeting men and boys with public health campaigns that advocate healthy coping mechanisms and convey the message that asking for help is a trait of the strong, not the weak, could help mitigate the disproportionate health risks they face. Creating neighborhood, school, and work environments in which healthy choices are not just possible but probable offers great promise.

Foster greater accountability for health disparities.

We need to monitor fundamental indicators of health, such as life expectancy, the rate of low birth weight, and the diabetes rate, with the kind of intensity we apply to baseball statistics and the gyrations of the stock market.

For Access to Knowledge

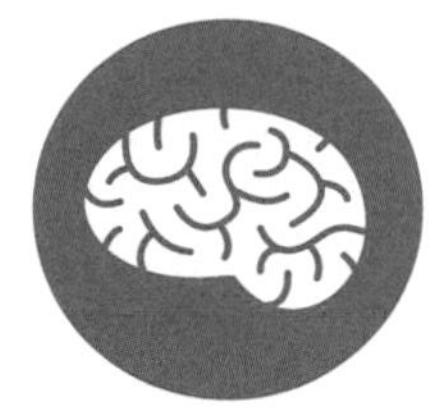

Ensure universal, quality preschool.

A quality preschool has been shown to be the single most powerful and cost-effective intervention to help disadvantaged young children learn the skills they need to succeed in school and get on the path to a life of choice and opportunity. The provision and regulation of early childhood education demands urgent attention. Despite consensus among researchers about the positive effects of preschool, many parents and policy makers have yet to recognize just how critical early childhood education is and what distinguishes a high-quality program from an inferior—and potentially harmful—one. Raising awareness of preschool among the public is crucial, because the costs of continued inaction are extraordinarily high.

Address head-on the high school dropout crisis.

Despite a rise in educational attainment over the past thirty years, the rate of on-time high school graduation has remained fundamentally unchanged. More than one-quarter of high school freshmen do not graduate in four years—if they graduate at all. Failure to graduate from high school is a harbinger of lifelong financial insecurity. Studies indicate that universal preschool would help mitigate the high school dropout crisis by helping children to develop noncognitive skills like persistence. The early warning signs that typically precede a child's dropping out of high school are now well established, allowing for the development of systems to identify, monitor, and engage at-risk youth that are being tested in states and districts across the country.

Invest in the education of immigrant children.

Whether their parents arrive in this country with high educational attainment or low literacy, with proper documentation or without, the children of immigrants deserve a fair shake from the educational system. Quality programs for English-language learners and other efforts to strengthen ties between schools, recent immigrants, and their children can help kids remain engaged in school. Immigrant children, especially Latino children, disproportionately attend large, poorly funded schools in central cities; a more equitable distribution of educational resources would help level the playing field. Latinos are the largest and fastest-growing minority group in the United States; ensuring that Latino children receive the education they need to thrive is vital not just to their futures but to the nation's.

A quality preschool has been shown to be the single most powerful and cost-effective intervention to **help disadvantaged young children** learn the skills they need to succeed in school and get on the path to a life of choice and opportunity.

Ensure that all children have good teachers.

Teacher quality is the single most decisive classroom factor influencing student achievement. It is therefore imperative that teachers bring levels of education and training to their careers—and are rewarded with salaries—commensurate with the critical importance of their jobs. In middle-class suburbs, where schools tend to have better working conditions and higher pay, there is no teacher crisis; those schools are able to attract and retain skilled professionals. But in urban and rural schools that serve children from low-income, minority families, the crisis is real. Recruiting and retaining excellent educators in high-needs schools is fundamental to educational equity.

Deflate ballooning college tuition costs.

Between 2000 and 2008, college costs for both two- and four-year colleges increased by 30 percent. A college education costs more today than ever before, with increases in tuition and fees far outpacing inflation. Sticker-shock discourages would-be first-generation college students, and high costs saddle many of the rest with increasingly unsustainable debt burdens. Increased aid would help. But the runaway cost of college suggests it might be time to reconsider the business model upon which the entire system of higher education operates. Access to knowledge is a capability, not a commodity; no one should be priced out.

For a Decent Standard of Living

Protect young children from the risks of extreme poverty.

Extreme poverty imperils the cognitive, social, physical, and emotional development of young children, often causing harm that reverberates across the life course of the individual and triggers high costs to society in the long term. To ensure that early economic hardship does not preclude a child's capacity to flourish, poor parents must have support in meeting their children's material and emotional needs.

Increase educational attainment.

Those who fail to graduate from high school are all but condemned to lifelong financial insecurity as well as more frequent health and psychological challenges. Boosting the rates of on-time high school graduation, particularly among Latino and African American males, is a critical goal. So is expanding meaningful vocational training options for the seven in ten young people who do not graduate from college. For those students who begin college but struggle to finish it, we must provide support to help them complete a bachelor's degree.

Create and retain jobs.

The flood of job loss in many states denies people the financial benefits of a secure livelihood. Less acknowledged but equally important, loss of a job too often leads to a loss of identity; it robs people of the essential psychological benefits employment confers, such as agency, self-reliance, and a sense of belonging in society. Workers with outdated or insufficient skills, limited education, or residence in a region with a weak job market will likely struggle to find a job that pays a living wage. Job training and retraining are important to retain America's global competitiveness, mitigate the damage of this recession, and ease the hardships of an economy in transition. In addition, wage subsidies, such as extending the EITC to single workers, could help low-income men, the hardest hit by the current recession, stay afloat.

Boosting the **rates of on-time high school graduation**, particularly among Latino and African American males, is a critical goal.

Both greater **regulation of the financial sector** and greater **financial literacy** are vital.

Create incentives—and eliminate disincentives—for asset building among low-income people.

The working poor seldom earn enough to benefit from government incentives that foster asset building among wealthier Americans, such as the mortgage tax deduction. In addition, they rarely have jobs providing benefits like matching 401(k) contributions. Meantime, recipients of certain federal or state benefits face serious disincentives to save; having anything beyond a small sum in the bank renders the saver ineligible for further public assistance. Automatic enrollment in pension plans for all workers, matched savings accounts that allow low-income workers to build assets over the long term, children's accounts established automatically at birth, and greater asset protection, particularly related to housing, can help low-income households to build financial security.

Help families provide care.

Women represent half of the workforce. Yet babies and children, elderly family members, and the ill and disabled still need the care that women have traditionally provided—and continue to provide—free of charge. Paid leave for sickness and caregiving by men and women, on-site childcare at more workplaces, and childcare tax credits or direct subsidies for the working poor would help families deal with today's challenges.

Strengthen financial-sector regulation and improve financial literacy.

Individuals are increasingly responsible for their financial fate; the days of defined-benefit pensions that protect workers, for example, are gone, while mortgages on property have grown increasingly exotic and difficult to comprehend. Yet most people are no more financially skilled or savvy than in the past. Recent policy reforms indicate an awareness of these risks. Both greater regulation of the financial sector and greater financial literacy are vital.

Reform retirement systems to enable greater retirement security and reduce elderly poverty.

Due to major shifts in retirement systems, certain groups, particularly those with low skills and education levels, women, and LGBT households, are at higher risk of elderly poverty. Proposals to make 401(k)s a stronger vehicle for retirement security and to strengthen Social Security's long-term balance sheet are increasingly urgent as we prepare for an aging population. The institutions of American retirement must evolve with the times.

***

Addressing our most serious problems will take a measure of sacrifice from the public and mature political leadership that does not shrink from the reality of our challenges, or attempt to exploit them for partisan and personal gain. We trust that America once again will rise to the occasion.

Human Development Indicators

The following indicator tables were prepared using, to the degree possible, official U.S. government data from the most recent available year. For cross-country comparisons, data are drawn from international organizations, such as the Organisation for Economic Co-operation and Development, the World Bank, and the United Nations, that maintain rigorous data collection standards. All data are standardized to ensure comparability.

AMERICAN HUMAN DEVELOPMENT INDEX
by Historical Trends

YEAR	HD INDEX	LIFE EXPECTANCY AT BIRTH (years)	AT LEAST HIGH SCHOOL DIPLOMA (%)	AT LEAST BACHELOR'S DEGREE (%)	GRADUATE OR PROFESSIONAL DEGREE (%)	SCHOOL ENROLLMENT (%)	MEDIAN EARNINGS (2009 dollars)	HEALTH INDEX	EDUCATION INDEX	INCOME INDEX
2008	**5.17**	78.6	85.0	27.7	10.2	87.3	29,755	5.25	5.15	5.09
2007	**5.08**	78.3	84.5	27.5	10.1	86.8	29,627	5.13	5.07	5.06
2005	**5.05**	77.9	84.2	27.2	10.0	86.8	29,994	4.96	5.04	5.14
2000	**4.67**	77.0	80.4	24.4	8.9	82.8	30,085	4.58	4.25	5.16
1990	**3.82**	75.4	75.2	20.3	7.2	80.8	25,451	3.92	3.54	4.00
1980	**2.86**	73.7	66.5	16.2	5.6	71.9	23,548	3.21	1.91	3.47
1970	**2.10**	70.8	52.3	10.7	3.6	73.3	22,648	2.00	1.10	3.20
1960	**1.23**	69.7	41.1	7.7	2.5	76.9	17,285	1.54	0.82	1.32

Note on Data Availability and Rankings

In the tables that follow, "..." denotes that the data for that particular group and indicator are either unavailable or not applicable.

In these tables, the American Human Development Index scores have been rounded to two decimal places. The resulting values may therefore appear to be tied in several instances. The rankings reflect the original values that result from calculation of the Index, not the rounded values.

When the total population of any group was less than 50,000 people, the HD Index was not calculated for that group due to the statistical instability of survey-based estimates for small populations. For example, 12 U.S. states have fewer than 50,000 African Americans living in them, and thus an HD Index value for African Americans in these states is not available.

AMERICAN HUMAN DEVELOPMENT INDEX

by Gender, Race, and Ethnicity

HD RANK		HD INDEX	LIFE EXPECTANCY AT BIRTH (years)	AT LEAST HIGH SCHOOL DIPLOMA (%)	AT LEAST BACHELOR'S DEGREE (%)	GRADUATE OR PROFESSIONAL DEGREE (%)	SCHOOL ENROLLMENT (%)	MEDIAN EARNINGS (2009 dollars)	HEALTH INDEX	EDUCATION INDEX	INCOME INDEX
	United States	**5.17**	78.6	85.0	27.7	10.2	87.3	29,755	5.25	5.15	5.09
GENDER											
1	Women	**5.15**	81.2	85.6	27.0	9.6	90.8	23,997	6.32	5.52	3.60
2	Men	**5.07**	76.0	84.3	28.4	10.8	84.0	35,170	4.15	4.81	6.25
RACE/ETHNICITY											
1	Asian American	**7.68**	87.3	85.1	49.7	19.9	102.1	34,835	8.87	7.99	6.18
2	White	**5.53**	78.7	90.1	30.7	11.4	88.6	31,932	5.31	5.72	5.58
3	Latino	**4.19**	83.5	60.8	12.9	4.0	79.7	21,936	7.28	2.31	2.97
4	African American	**3.91**	74.3	80.7	17.5	6.0	88.6	24,792	3.45	4.48	3.82
5	Native American	**3.24**	75.1	75.6	12.7	3.9	80.4	21,744	3.78	3.03	2.91
GENDER AND RACE/ETHNICITY											
1	Asian American Men	**7.81**	84.6	87.5	53.0	23.9	100.7	40,815	7.73	8.42	7.28
2	Asian American Women	**7.47**	89.7	83.0	46.8	16.4	103.2	29,133	9.86	7.61	4.92
3	White Men	**5.61**	76.2	89.7	32.1	12.2	85.3	40,157	4.23	5.43	7.17
4	White Women	**5.46**	81.2	90.4	29.4	10.6	91.9	25,531	6.34	6.01	4.03
5	African American Women	**4.45**	77.6	81.8	19.0	6.7	94.4	22,874	4.82	5.27	3.27
6	Latina Women	**4.29**	86.3	62.5	13.8	4.2	82.6	18,178	8.44	2.76	1.67
7	Latino Men	**3.94**	80.6	59.2	12.1	3.9	77.6	24,849	6.10	1.89	3.84
8	Native American Women	**3.60**	78.1	77.9	14.1	4.2	83.6	19,560	5.05	3.56	2.18
9	African American Men	**3.33**	70.7	79.2	15.8	5.2	83.4	26,644	1.95	3.72	4.32
10	Native American Men	**2.84**	72.1	73.2	11.2	3.7	76.2	24,095	2.52	2.39	3.63

AMERICAN HUMAN DEVELOPMENT INDEX

by State, Total Population

RANK	STATE	HD INDEX	LIFE EXPECTANCY AT BIRTH (years)	LESS THAN HIGH SCHOOL (%)	AT LEAST HIGH SCHOOL DIPLOMA (%)	AT LEAST BACHELOR'S DEGREE (%)	GRADUATE OR PROFESSIONAL DEGREE (%)	SCHOOL ENROLLMENT (%)	MEDIAN EARNINGS (2009 dollars)	HEALTH INDEX	EDUCATION INDEX	INCOME INDEX
1	**Connecticut**	**6.30**	80.2	11.4	88.6	35.6	15.2	92.1	36,827	5.91	6.44	6.57
2	**Massachusetts**	**6.24**	80.1	11.3	88.7	38.1	16.4	91.5	35,533	5.88	6.53	6.32
3	**District of Columbia**	**6.21**	75.6	14.2	85.8	48.2	26.7	92.7	40,342	4.00	7.44	7.20
4	**New Jersey**	**6.16**	79.7	12.6	87.4	34.4	12.8	90.8	37,707	5.69	6.07	6.73
5	**Maryland**	**5.96**	78.1	12.0	88.0	35.2	15.4	90.3	37,320	5.04	6.19	6.66
6	**New York**	**5.77**	80.4	15.9	84.1	31.9	13.8	89.7	31,963	5.98	5.74	5.58
7	**Minnesota**	**5.74**	80.9	8.4	91.6	31.5	10.0	87.0	31,442	6.19	5.58	5.47
8	**New Hampshire**	**5.73**	79.7	9.1	90.9	33.3	12.0	88.1	32,207	5.71	5.85	5.64
9	**Hawaii**	**5.73**	81.5	9.7	90.3	29.1	9.9	85.0	31,766	6.45	5.19	5.54
10	**Colorado**	**5.65**	79.9	11.1	88.9	35.6	12.7	87.5	30,853	5.80	5.81	5.34
11	**Rhode Island**	**5.56**	79.3	16.3	83.7	30.0	11.3	91.5	31,179	5.53	5.73	5.41
12	**California**	**5.56**	80.4	19.8	80.2	29.6	10.8	89.5	31,008	5.99	5.30	5.37
13	**Virginia**	**5.53**	78.5	14.1	85.9	33.7	13.8	87.8	32,467	5.22	5.68	5.69
14	**Washington**	**5.53**	79.7	10.4	89.6	30.7	10.9	85.7	31,812	5.69	5.35	5.55
15	**Illinois**	**5.39**	78.8	14.1	85.9	29.9	11.2	88.6	30,964	5.32	5.49	5.36
16	**Delaware**	**5.33**	78.3	12.8	87.2	27.5	10.8	88.4	31,320	5.13	5.40	5.44
17	**Alaska**	**5.27**	78.3	8.4	91.6	27.3	9.7	84.9	31,774	5.13	5.15	5.54
18	**Vermont**	**5.27**	79.7	9.4	90.6	32.1	12.2	87.9	26,627	5.71	5.77	4.32
19	**Wisconsin**	**5.23**	79.3	10.4	89.6	25.7	8.6	87.1	29,168	5.55	5.19	4.95
20	**Pennsylvania**	**5.12**	78.2	12.5	87.5	26.3	10.0	87.0	29,891	5.07	5.17	5.12
21	**Arizona**	**5.11**	79.9	16.2	83.8	25.1	9.2	84.2	29,049	5.80	4.61	4.92
22	**Utah**	**5.08**	80.1	9.6	90.4	29.1	9.4	85.2	26,126	5.87	5.19	4.19
23	**Florida**	**5.07**	79.7	14.8	85.2	25.8	9.0	86.9	27,366	5.71	5.00	4.51
24	**Iowa**	**5.06**	79.7	9.7	90.3	24.3	7.3	87.3	26,857	5.70	5.11	4.38
25	**Kansas**	**5.06**	78.4	10.5	89.5	29.6	10.1	87.2	27,690	5.17	5.43	4.59
26	**Nebraska**	**5.05**	79.2	9.9	90.1	27.1	8.6	87.6	26,659	5.49	5.33	4.33
27	**Oregon**	**5.03**	79.0	11.4	88.6	28.1	10.1	85.8	27,285	5.43	5.17	4.49
28	**Michigan**	**4.99**	77.9	11.9	88.1	24.7	9.4	91.2	27,125	4.95	5.57	4.45
29	**North Dakota**	**4.92**	80.1	10.4	89.6	26.9	6.6	82.8	26,224	5.88	4.67	4.21
30	**Maine**	**4.89**	78.7	10.3	89.7	25.4	8.9	87.3	26,120	5.28	5.21	4.18
31	**Ohio**	**4.87**	77.5	12.4	87.6	24.1	8.7	88.5	27,805	4.80	5.19	4.62
32	**Georgia**	**4.86**	77.1	16.1	83.9	27.5	9.7	86.1	29,453	4.62	4.95	5.02
33	**South Dakota**	**4.82**	79.9	9.7	90.3	25.1	7.3	82.5	25,717	5.77	4.62	4.08
34	**Wyoming**	**4.80**	77.6	8.3	91.7	23.6	7.9	81.6	29,507	4.84	4.54	5.03
35	**Nevada**	**4.78**	77.6	16.5	83.5	21.9	7.0	81.9	31,122	4.83	4.10	5.40
36	**Indiana**	**4.74**	77.7	13.8	86.2	22.9	8.1	85.9	27,677	4.88	4.75	4.59
37	**Missouri**	**4.68**	77.4	13.5	86.5	25.0	9.1	85.9	26,801	4.77	4.91	4.36
38	**Texas**	**4.67**	78.3	20.4	79.6	25.3	8.3	84.2	27,344	5.11	4.38	4.50
39	**Idaho**	**4.65**	79.2	12.1	87.9	24.0	7.4	83.9	24,776	5.50	4.62	3.82
40	**North Carolina**	**4.64**	77.2	16.4	83.6	26.1	8.6	86.5	26,943	4.66	4.87	4.40
41	**New Mexico**	**4.56**	78.2	17.6	82.4	24.7	10.7	86.6	24,495	5.09	4.86	3.74
42	**Montana**	**4.49**	78.4	9.1	90.9	27.1	8.4	81.8	24,033	5.15	4.71	3.61
43	**South Carolina**	**4.36**	76.6	16.8	83.2	23.7	8.5	84.1	26,247	4.40	4.47	4.22
44	**Tennessee**	**4.33**	76.2	17.0	83.0	22.9	8.0	85.7	26,044	4.25	4.58	4.16
45	**Kentucky**	**4.23**	76.2	18.7	81.3	19.7	7.9	85.5	25,861	4.25	4.34	4.12
46	**Oklahoma**	**4.15**	75.6	14.5	85.5	22.2	7.2	84.5	25,283	4.00	4.49	3.96
47	**Alabama**	**4.09**	75.2	18.1	81.9	22.0	7.7	83.6	26,112	3.83	4.25	4.18
48	**Louisiana**	**4.07**	75.4	18.8	81.2	20.3	6.5	83.3	26,357	3.91	4.05	4.25
49	**Mississippi**	**3.93**	74.8	20.1	79.9	19.4	6.8	86.7	24,620	3.67	4.35	3.77
50	**Arkansas**	**3.87**	76.1	18.0	82.0	18.8	6.3	83.0	23,471	4.20	3.98	3.44
51	**West Virginia**	**3.85**	75.2	17.8	82.2	17.1	6.7	83.7	24,404	3.82	4.02	3.71

KEY: 6.30–5.64 | 5.63–5.11 | 5.10–4.87 | 4.86–4.55 | 4.54–3.85

AMERICAN HUMAN DEVELOPMENT INDEX

by State, by Race/Ethnicity Summary

	HD INDEX	LIFE EXPECTANCY AT BIRTH (years)	LESS THAN HIGH SCHOOL (%)	AT LEAST HIGH SCHOOL DIPLOMA (%)	AT LEAST BACHELOR'S DEGREE (%)	GRADUATE OR PROFESSIONAL DEGREE (%)	SCHOOL ENROLLMENT (%)	MEDIAN EARNINGS (2009 dollars)	HEALTH INDEX	EDUCATION INDEX	INCOME INDEX
United States	**5.17**	78.6	15.0	85.0	27.7	10.2	87.3	29,755	5.25	5.15	5.09
HDI BY RACIAL AND ETHNIC GROUP											
Asian American	**7.68**	87.3	14.9	85.1	49.7	19.9	102.1	34,835	8.87	7.99	6.18
White	**5.53**	78.7	9.9	90.1	30.7	11.4	88.6	31,932	5.31	5.72	5.58
Latino	**4.19**	83.5	39.2	60.8	12.9	4.0	79.7	21,936	7.28	2.31	2.97
African American	**3.91**	74.3	19.3	80.7	17.5	6.0	88.6	24,792	3.45	4.48	3.82
Native American	**3.24**	75.1	24.4	75.6	12.7	3.9	80.4	21,744	3.78	3.03	2.91
STATES WHERE EACH RACIAL AND ETHNIC GROUP SCORE **HIGHEST**											
Asian American—New Jersey	**9.30**	91.8	8.2	91.8	66.8	27.6	98.3	50,069	10.00	9.20	8.70
White—District of Columbia	**9.03**	83.1	1.1	98.9	88.2	51.4	103.4	60,232	7.11	10.00	9.98
Latino—New Jersey	**5.28**	87.0	30.6	69.4	16.1	5.0	81.5	25,440	8.76	3.08	4.00
African American—Maryland	**5.09**	74.7	14.2	85.8	23.9	9.4	92.3	34,446	3.61	5.55	6.10
Native American—California	**4.42**	81.4	28.5	71.5	12.8	3.8	82.7	24,488	6.43	3.10	3.74
STATES WHERE EACH RACIAL AND ETHNIC GROUP SCORE **LOWEST**											
Asian American—Louisiana	**5.30**	82.3	30.7	69.3	35.4	15.9	96.4	22,094	6.80	6.07	3.02
White—West Virginia	**3.85**	75.1	17.8	82.2	16.9	6.7	82.8	24,797	3.81	3.90	3.82
African American—Louisiana	**2.60**	72.1	25.9	74.1	12.0	3.9	82.1	19,434	2.54	3.12	2.13
Latino—Arkansas	**2.49**	79.2	56.8	43.2	8.5	2.9	69.7	18,434	5.50	0.20	1.77
Native American—South Dakota	**1.15**	66.0	21.7	78.3	10.3	2.4	74.2	16,920	0.00	2.29	1.17

AMERICAN HUMAN DEVELOPMENT INDEX

by State, African American

RANK	STATE	HD INDEX	LIFE EXPECTANCY AT BIRTH (years)	LESS THAN HIGH SCHOOL (%)	AT LEAST HIGH SCHOOL DIPLOMA (%)	AT LEAST BACHELOR'S DEGREE (%)	GRADUATE OR PROFESSIONAL DEGREE (%)	SCHOOL ENROLLMENT (%)	MEDIAN EARNINGS (2009 dollars)	HEALTH INDEX	EDUCATION INDEX	INCOME INDEX
1	**Maryland**	**5.09**	74.7	14.2	85.8	23.9	9.4	92.3	34,446	3.61	5.55	6.10
2	**Massachusetts**	**5.08**	78.5	19.1	80.9	23.1	7.9	97.1	26,504	5.19	5.76	4.29
3	**Connecticut**	**5.05**	77.3	19.3	80.7	18.3	7.2	95.4	30,011	4.69	5.32	5.15
4	**New York**	**5.03**	78.6	21.1	78.9	19.5	6.9	91.1	29,589	5.23	4.80	5.05
5	**New Jersey**	**4.89**	75.4	17.3	82.7	20.6	6.6	92.1	32,132	3.93	5.12	5.62
6	**Arizona**	**4.77**	77.4	13.1	86.9	22.5	8.2	89.0	27,004	4.76	5.12	4.42
7	**Oregon**	**4.72**	77.9	14.3	85.7	22.9	6.3	90.9	25,333	4.97	5.20	3.97
8	**California**	**4.69**	74.6	13.4	86.6	20.8	7.0	91.7	30,342	3.58	5.28	5.22
9	**Colorado**	**4.65**	77.8	14.1	85.9	23.4	9.2	87.7	25,528	4.90	5.01	4.03
10	**Washington**	**4.53**	76.7	13.5	86.5	18.8	5.9	89.0	26,527	4.47	4.84	4.29
11	**Rhode Island**	**4.41**	78.8	26.1	73.9	20.0	6.3	78.5	28,202	5.32	3.18	4.72
12	**Delaware**	**4.21**	75.8	17.6	82.4	19.7	6.4	88.2	25,125	4.08	4.63	3.92
13	**Minnesota**	**4.11**	75.4	19.0	81.0	19.9	7.0	93.0	22,849	3.93	5.13	3.26
14	**District of Columbia**	**4.05**	71.0	19.2	80.8	21.6	9.5	87.6	30,911	2.08	4.70	5.35
15	**Georgia**	**4.03**	74.4	18.5	81.5	20.0	6.9	87.4	25,732	3.48	4.53	4.08
16	**Nevada**	**4.02**	75.4	15.0	85.0	15.5	5.4	80.3	27,414	3.90	3.63	4.52
17	**Texas**	**3.97**	74.2	16.4	83.6	18.6	5.8	87.3	25,389	3.43	4.50	3.99
18	**Virginia**	**3.93**	74.5	21.3	78.7	18.0	6.6	86.2	25,715	3.54	4.16	4.08
19	**Illinois**	**3.86**	72.9	18.6	81.4	19.3	6.6	88.6	25,744	2.88	4.62	4.08
20	**Kansas**	**3.85**	73.9	13.8	86.2	17.6	5.0	95.2	21,504	3.29	5.41	2.84
21	**Florida**	**3.79**	75.5	22.7	77.3	16.0	5.2	86.9	23,230	3.98	4.03	3.37
22	**Pennsylvania**	**3.69**	72.9	17.9	82.1	15.1	5.6	88.0	24,894	2.85	4.35	3.85
23	**Indiana**	**3.64**	73.6	17.4	82.6	15.9	5.0	86.9	23,590	3.18	4.26	3.48
24	**Michigan**	**3.54**	72.6	18.9	81.1	14.0	5.2	93.3	22,243	2.74	4.83	3.07
25	**North Carolina**	**3.50**	73.7	20.7	79.3	16.1	4.6	89.1	21,938	3.19	4.35	2.98
26	**Oklahoma**	**3.50**	72.5	14.4	85.6	16.6	5.2	91.3	21,546	2.73	4.92	2.85
27	**Ohio**	**3.49**	73.3	19.0	81.0	14.3	4.8	90.1	22,003	3.03	4.46	3.00
28	**Nebraska**	**3.41**	72.5	13.5	86.5	16.7	5.2	91.4	20,658	2.70	4.97	2.56
29	**Missouri**	**3.39**	72.6	18.9	81.1	15.6	5.9	88.0	22,370	2.73	4.33	3.11
30	**Iowa**	**3.36**	74.6	20.7	79.3	16.0	5.4	90.3	19,101	3.56	4.51	2.02
31	**Tennessee**	**3.29**	72.5	20.2	79.8	15.6	4.8	89.0	21,388	2.72	4.35	2.80
32	**Kentucky**	**3.28**	73.3	17.1	82.9	14.4	5.9	88.5	20,187	3.03	4.42	2.40
33	**Wisconsin**	**3.19**	72.7	21.9	78.1	14.1	5.9	85.6	21,736	2.78	3.87	2.91
34	**South Carolina**	**2.99**	73.0	23.5	76.5	12.6	4.4	83.3	20,901	2.92	3.41	2.64
35	**Alabama**	**2.88**	72.4	23.1	76.9	14.3	5.0	84.2	20,032	2.67	3.63	2.34
36	**West Virginia**	**2.86**	71.3	15.0	85.0	14.1	4.4	97.2	16,412	2.21	5.40	0.96
37	**Mississippi**	**2.78**	72.2	28.0	72.0	12.8	4.4	89.6	18,645	2.56	3.92	1.85
38	**Arkansas**	**2.64**	72.2	22.6	77.4	12.4	4.0	84.7	18,391	2.59	3.58	1.75
39	**Louisiana**	**2.60**	72.1	25.9	74.1	12.0	3.9	82.1	19,434	2.54	3.12	2.13

AMERICAN HUMAN DEVELOPMENT INDEX

by State, Asian American

RANK	STATE	HD INDEX	LIFE EXPECTANCY AT BIRTH (years)	LESS THAN HIGH SCHOOL (%)	AT LEAST HIGH SCHOOL DIPLOMA (%)	AT LEAST BACHELOR'S DEGREE (%)	GRADUATE OR PROFESSIONAL DEGREE (%)	SCHOOL ENROLLMENT (%)	MEDIAN EARNINGS (2009 dollars)	HEALTH INDEX	EDUCATION INDEX	INCOME INDEX
1	**New Jersey**	**9.30**	91.8	8.2	91.8	66.8	27.6	98.3	50,069	10.00	9.20	8.70
2	**Connecticut**	**8.83**	92.4	11.2	88.8	63.5	31.5	102.7	40,350	10.00	9.28	7.20
3	**Maryland**	**8.79**	89.9	10.8	89.2	61.7	30.0	105.8	40,548	9.98	9.15	7.23
4	**Illinois**	**8.65**	90.7	9.2	90.8	62.1	25.6	104.1	38,655	10.00	9.04	6.90
5	**Michigan**	**8.56**	89.8	12.4	87.6	60.7	32.7	107.9	36,907	9.93	9.16	6.58
6	**Massachusetts**	**8.39**	91.6	16.7	83.3	56.7	32.9	103.0	35,811	10.00	8.80	6.37
7	**Virginia**	**8.31**	88.3	12.2	87.8	55.5	23.4	105.2	39,890	9.30	8.52	7.12
8	**Texas**	**8.09**	88.8	13.2	86.8	54.1	23.5	105.6	35,845	9.48	8.42	6.38
9	**Arizona**	**7.84**	92.4	12.3	87.7	50.3	20.4	101.1	31,026	10.00	8.15	5.38
10	**Pennsylvania**	**7.72**	88.3	17.2	82.8	52.8	27.5	105.1	31,690	9.28	8.36	5.53
11	**Colorado**	**7.69**	91.8	15.7	84.3	47.5	20.4	98.8	30,836	10.00	7.74	5.34
12	**New York**	**7.66**	90.1	22.5	77.5	45.7	17.9	99.7	32,190	10.00	7.35	5.63
13	**California**	**7.61**	86.6	15.1	84.9	47.3	15.7	104.1	36,896	8.58	7.69	6.58
14	**Georgia**	**7.44**	89.0	14.4	85.6	48.6	21.7	95.2	30,267	9.60	7.51	5.21
15	**Ohio**	**7.33**	83.4	12.0	88.0	61.6	32.0	102.6	31,846	7.25	9.18	5.56
16	**Nevada**	**7.31**	88.2	8.7	91.3	38.3	9.5	100.8	31,144	9.23	7.29	5.40
17	**Washington**	**7.28**	86.7	14.6	85.4	46.3	16.7	97.1	33,142	8.63	7.39	5.84
18	**Oregon**	**7.15**	86.2	14.5	85.5	45.8	17.5	100.2	30,638	8.43	7.72	5.29
19	**Kansas**	**7.02**	84.0	14.7	85.3	53.0	29.0	108.0	29,352	7.51	8.55	4.99
20	**Utah**	**6.91**	85.3	12.9	87.1	44.7	22.0	106.6	28,387	8.03	7.95	4.76
21	**Indiana**	**6.82**	83.7	12.1	87.9	59.3	28.0	113.9	26,177	7.37	8.90	4.20
22	**Missouri**	**6.72**	83.5	16.1	83.9	50.6	28.5	99.0	27,938	7.27	8.24	4.65
23	**Florida**	**6.72**	86.0	15.5	84.5	43.9	18.0	97.0	27,547	8.32	7.28	4.55
24	**Tennessee**	**6.64**	82.7	13.7	86.3	50.9	25.3	98.5	28,525	6.94	8.17	4.80
25	**North Carolina**	**6.57**	83.3	15.3	84.7	53.3	25.2	98.0	26,858	7.20	8.13	4.38
26	**Minnesota**	**6.56**	85.3	21.2	78.8	41.0	18.3	94.4	29,561	8.02	6.63	5.04
27	**South Carolina**	**6.35**	83.2	15.3	84.7	43.7	20.4	102.2	26,035	7.16	7.73	4.16
28	**Hawaii**	**6.13**	81.7	13.5	86.5	29.0	8.5	96.5	32,214	6.53	6.23	5.64
29	**Wisconsin**	**6.11**	84.6	19.1	80.9	46.0	22.4	93.2	24,029	7.73	6.99	3.61
30	**Oklahoma**	**5.84**	82.3	19.7	80.3	45.2	20.2	109.3	22,538	6.77	7.59	3.16
31	**Louisiana**	**5.30**	82.3	30.7	69.3	35.4	15.9	96.4	22,094	6.80	6.07	3.02

AMERICAN HUMAN DEVELOPMENT INDEX
by State, Latino

RANK	STATE	HD INDEX	LIFE EXPECTANCY AT BIRTH (years)	LESS THAN HIGH SCHOOL (%)	AT LEAST HIGH SCHOOL DIPLOMA (%)	AT LEAST BACHELOR'S DEGREE (%)	GRADUATE OR PROFESSIONAL DEGREE (%)	SCHOOL ENROLLMENT (%)	MEDIAN EARNINGS (2009 dollars)	HEALTH INDEX	EDUCATION INDEX	INCOME INDEX
1	**New Jersey**	**5.28**	87.0	30.6	69.4	16.1	5.0	81.5	25,440	8.76	3.08	4.00
2	**Massachusetts**	**5.04**	87.4	35.6	64.4	15.9	5.5	81.1	23,148	8.93	2.83	3.35
3	**Nevada**	**4.99**	89.8	44.0	56.0	9.1	2.3	74.0	24,873	9.92	1.22	3.85
4	**Illinois**	**4.87**	88.0	41.3	58.7	11.7	3.5	79.2	23,251	9.16	2.08	3.38
5	**Connecticut**	**4.72**	83.9	32.4	67.6	14.8	5.2	80.4	24,914	7.48	2.83	3.86
6	**Florida**	**4.71**	83.1	26.3	73.7	21.3	6.9	82.5	23,087	7.12	3.70	3.33
7	**New York**	**4.65**	84.3	36.5	63.5	15.4	5.1	82.8	23,328	7.62	2.94	3.40
8	**Virginia**	**4.51**	81.2	33.7	66.3	23.8	7.7	78.0	26,025	6.35	3.01	4.16
9	**Washington**	**4.28**	86.1	41.8	58.2	11.4	3.7	77.4	20,779	8.38	1.86	2.60
10	**Nebraska**	**4.25**	85.0	46.5	53.5	10.6	3.2	79.0	22,209	7.93	1.76	3.06
11	**Kansas**	**4.25**	85.4	41.5	58.5	13.2	3.2	76.3	21,573	8.08	1.81	2.86
12	**California**	**4.22**	83.7	43.6	56.4	10.2	3.0	82.4	22,126	7.38	2.24	3.03
13	**Hawaii**	**4.13**	77.2	12.1	87.9	17.5	5.2	75.9	26,887	4.66	3.36	4.39
14	**Maryland**	**4.10**	80.8	38.7	61.3	20.1	8.8	76.9	23,883	6.18	2.56	3.56
15	**Rhode Island**	**4.07**	81.8	41.9	58.1	12.3	3.2	84.1	22,004	6.60	2.61	3.00
16	**Utah**	**4.07**	84.9	37.4	62.6	11.5	3.3	74.0	20,968	7.87	1.67	2.66
17	**Minnesota**	**4.04**	83.2	37.5	62.5	17.2	7.0	74.8	21,310	7.18	2.16	2.77
18	**Delaware**	**3.95**	81.2	41.5	58.5	14.1	7.3	72.3	25,251	6.31	1.58	3.95
19	**Ohio**	**3.93**	80.4	30.3	69.7	17.8	7.4	80.6	20,916	5.98	3.18	2.64
20	**Iowa**	**3.92**	82.3	41.1	58.9	12.8	4.9	79.9	21,077	6.78	2.28	2.70
21	**Pennsylvania**	**3.86**	80.9	34.0	66.0	13.6	4.9	77.8	21,855	6.22	2.41	2.95
22	**Wisconsin**	**3.81**	81.9	39.0	61.0	12.0	4.3	80.2	20,380	6.61	2.35	2.46
23	**New Mexico**	**3.73**	78.8	29.5	70.5	12.7	4.6	82.0	21,529	5.33	3.01	2.84
24	**Michigan**	**3.72**	80.7	35.2	64.8	14.3	5.8	83.5	19,043	6.11	3.05	1.99
25	**Arizona**	**3.71**	81.4	40.4	59.6	9.7	3.2	75.5	22,312	6.42	1.61	3.09
26	**Louisiana**	**3.67**	78.6	30.8	69.2	17.2	4.7	76.5	22,763	5.25	2.54	3.23
27	**Colorado**	**3.67**	80.7	36.5	63.5	11.8	3.5	76.2	21,789	6.11	1.97	2.93
28	**Texas**	**3.66**	81.4	42.8	57.2	10.9	3.1	78.9	20,939	6.40	1.93	2.65
29	**Missouri**	**3.63**	80.3	34.4	65.6	18.5	6.1	75.7	20,497	5.96	2.43	2.50
30	**Idaho**	**3.58**	84.6	50.4	49.6	6.6	2.1	72.7	19,988	7.73	0.67	2.33
31	**Oregon**	**3.41**	81.7	43.3	56.7	11.3	3.1	76.6	19,148	6.52	1.68	2.03
32	**Indiana**	**3.35**	80.6	40.7	59.3	10.2	3.7	74.5	20,293	6.07	1.53	2.43
33	**Georgia**	**3.17**	80.0	41.8	58.2	14.0	4.1	71.9	19,910	5.82	1.38	2.30
34	**Oklahoma**	**3.14**	78.7	44.4	55.6	10.4	3.1	77.3	20,355	5.30	1.66	2.46
35	**Kentucky**	**3.04**	79.2	37.4	62.6	13.0	5.6	76.6	17,698	5.50	2.12	1.49
36	**Tennessee**	**2.93**	79.2	43.2	56.8	11.9	4.0	67.9	19,840	5.51	1.01	2.28
37	**South Carolina**	**2.91**	79.7	42.3	57.7	10.7	4.0	67.2	19,178	5.70	1.00	2.04
38	**North Carolina**	**2.86**	80.1	48.3	51.7	12.8	4.6	70.5	18,523	5.87	0.90	1.80
39	**Mississippi**	**2.83**	78.1	47.1	52.9	8.4	2.1	62.9	21,574	5.05	0.60	2.86
40	**Alabama**	**2.58**	78.4	41.6	58.4	13.5	3.8	64.9	17,640	5.15	1.14	1.46
41	**Arkansas**	**2.49**	79.2	56.8	43.2	8.5	2.9	69.7	18,434	5.50	0.20	1.77

AMERICAN HUMAN DEVELOPMENT INDEX

by State, Native American

RANK	STATE	HD INDEX	LIFE EXPECTANCY AT BIRTH (years)	LESS THAN HIGH SCHOOL (%)	AT LEAST HIGH SCHOOL DIPLOMA (%)	AT LEAST BACHELOR'S DEGREE (%)	GRADUATE OR PROFESSIONAL DEGREE (%)	SCHOOL ENROLLMENT (%)	MEDIAN EARNINGS (2009 dollars)	HEALTH INDEX	EDUCATION INDEX	INCOME INDEX
1	**California**	**4.42**	81.4	28.5	71.5	12.8	3.8	82.7	24,488	6.43	3.10	3.74
2	**North Carolina**	**3.11**	73.3	30.1	69.9	12.6	4.2	88.8	20,675	3.05	3.72	2.56
3	**Arizona**	**2.85**	74.1	28.7	71.3	7.8	2.9	75.6	22,426	3.38	2.05	3.13
4	**Washington**	**2.83**	71.9	18.5	81.5	13.6	4.4	73.8	23,304	2.45	2.63	3.39
5	**New Mexico**	**2.82**	73.6	27.7	72.3	8.8	2.7	79.1	21,289	3.17	2.52	2.77
6	**Michigan**	**2.52**	69.2	16.9	83.1	11.2	3.7	81.7	21,325	1.33	3.44	2.78
7	**Oklahoma**	**2.23**	67.2	18.3	81.7	15.2	3.2	81.6	21,065	0.50	3.51	2.69
8	**Oregon**	**1.95**	74.0	41.0	59.0	9.1	2.7	70.0	17,935	3.34	0.92	1.58
9	**Alaska**	**1.55**	68.8	20.9	79.1	5.6	1.1	74.6	17,413	1.17	2.10	1.37
10	**Montana**	**1.45**	68.0	19.8	80.2	13.8	3.9	74.0	16,383	0.82	2.58	0.95
11	**Minnesota**	**1.44**	68.0	21.0	79.0	8.5	2.2	78.7	15,938	0.83	2.73	0.76
12	**South Dakota**	**1.15**	66.0	21.7	78.3	10.3	2.4	74.2	16,920	0.00	2.29	1.17

AMERICAN HUMAN DEVELOPMENT INDEX

by State, White

RANK	STATE	HD INDEX	LIFE EXPECTANCY AT BIRTH (years)	LESS THAN HIGH SCHOOL (%)	AT LEAST HIGH SCHOOL DIPLOMA (%)	AT LEAST BACHELOR'S DEGREE (%)	GRADUATE OR PROFESSIONAL DEGREE (%)	SCHOOL ENROLLMENT (%)	MEDIAN EARNINGS (2009 dollars)	HEALTH INDEX	EDUCATION INDEX	INCOME INDEX
1	**District of Columbia**	**9.03**	83.1	1.1	98.9	88.2	51.4	103.4	60,232	7.11	10.00	9.98
2	**Connecticut**	**6.77**	80.4	7.9	92.1	38.9	16.7	93.8	41,080	6.01	6.99	7.32
3	**New Jersey**	**6.63**	79.7	8.4	91.6	37.1	13.9	92.8	42,379	5.70	6.65	7.54
4	**California**	**6.60**	79.5	6.9	93.1	38.2	14.9	94.3	40,377	5.63	6.98	7.20
5	**Massachusetts**	**6.49**	80.1	8.4	91.6	39.9	16.9	91.8	38,066	5.87	6.80	6.80
6	**Maryland**	**6.45**	79.0	8.8	91.2	39.4	17.5	89.8	41,364	5.41	6.56	7.37
7	**New York**	**6.31**	80.4	9.3	90.7	36.9	16.9	90.5	36,188	6.00	6.47	6.45
8	**Colorado**	**6.24**	79.9	5.3	94.7	41.0	14.6	91.5	34,241	5.80	6.85	6.06
9	**Hawaii**	**6.23**	80.0	3.5	96.5	41.5	16.4	86.0	36,175	5.82	6.42	6.44
10	**Alaska**	**6.02**	79.1	5.1	94.9	32.2	11.9	88.6	37,015	5.44	6.02	6.60
11	**Virginia**	**6.00**	79.1	10.8	89.2	37.0	15.4	88.4	36,086	5.45	6.12	6.43
12	**Arizona**	**5.94**	80.1	7.0	93.0	30.8	11.3	91.5	32,962	5.86	6.17	5.80
13	**Illinois**	**5.92**	79.2	8.7	91.3	33.1	12.6	90.8	34,298	5.51	6.18	6.07
14	**Minnesota**	**5.92**	81.1	6.4	93.6	32.4	10.0	87.1	32,693	6.30	5.72	5.74
15	**New Mexico**	**5.86**	78.7	6.5	93.5	36.5	16.5	94.5	30,606	5.27	7.02	5.28
16	**Rhode Island**	**5.82**	79.1	12.9	87.1	32.2	12.3	93.9	32,526	5.47	6.29	5.71
17	**Washington**	**5.80**	79.5	6.9	93.1	32.0	11.4	86.6	34,513	5.60	5.69	6.12
18	**Delaware**	**5.75**	78.8	9.6	90.4	28.7	11.5	90.1	34,366	5.33	5.82	6.09
19	**New Hampshire**	**5.74**	79.5	8.7	91.3	33.0	11.8	88.1	32,704	5.62	5.84	5.74
20	**Texas**	**5.64**	77.7	8.5	91.5	33.4	10.8	87.2	35,611	4.88	5.72	6.33
21	**Florida**	**5.55**	79.6	9.8	90.2	28.5	10.1	88.5	31,161	5.68	5.56	5.41
22	**Wisconsin**	**5.45**	79.7	8.3	91.7	26.6	8.7	87.7	30,403	5.72	5.39	5.24
23	**Kansas**	**5.36**	78.6	7.6	92.4	31.2	10.5	87.9	29,831	5.25	5.73	5.11
24	**Georgia**	**5.32**	77.6	12.5	87.5	31.3	11.0	87.3	32,290	4.83	5.48	5.66
25	**Utah**	**5.32**	80.0	6.0	94.0	31.1	9.8	86.7	27,300	5.83	5.63	4.49
26	**Oregon**	**5.30**	78.7	8.1	91.9	29.3	10.6	87.3	29,772	5.27	5.55	5.09
27	**Pennsylvania**	**5.30**	78.7	10.9	89.1	27.2	10.2	87.1	30,710	5.29	5.30	5.31
28	**Nebraska**	**5.30**	79.4	7.0	93.0	28.5	8.9	88.6	27,951	5.60	5.64	4.65
29	**Nevada**	**5.29**	76.3	8.8	91.2	25.0	8.4	86.8	35,873	4.30	5.19	6.38
30	**Michigan**	**5.29**	78.8	9.8	90.2	26.0	9.6	91.1	28,722	5.31	5.71	4.84
31	**Vermont**	**5.27**	79.5	9.2	90.8	32.1	12.2	87.8	26,913	5.64	5.76	4.39
32	**North Carolina**	**5.21**	77.9	12.6	87.4	29.3	9.7	87.7	30,643	4.97	5.36	5.29
33	**Iowa**	**5.16**	79.7	8.4	91.6	24.5	7.2	87.5	27,653	5.70	5.20	4.58
34	**North Dakota**	**5.14**	80.6	9.7	90.3	27.4	6.5	84.0	27,265	6.07	4.86	4.48
35	**Ohio**	**5.09**	78.0	11.1	88.9	24.8	8.8	88.4	29,412	4.98	5.27	5.01
36	**South Dakota**	**5.08**	80.8	8.6	91.4	25.9	7.4	83.0	26,589	6.16	4.77	4.31
37	**South Carolina**	**5.06**	77.7	13.2	86.8	28.1	10.1	85.8	30,303	4.87	5.09	5.21
38	**Wyoming**	**5.00**	77.9	7.2	92.8	25.0	8.3	82.5	30,591	4.96	4.77	5.28
39	**Indiana**	**4.93**	77.9	12.2	87.8	23.6	8.3	86.4	29,057	4.94	4.92	4.92
40	**Maine**	**4.91**	78.6	10.0	90.0	25.5	8.9	87.3	26,377	5.26	5.23	4.25
41	**Missouri**	**4.88**	77.9	12.2	87.8	26.0	9.3	85.9	28,089	4.95	5.01	4.69
42	**Idaho**	**4.87**	79.1	8.8	91.2	25.4	7.7	85.7	25,851	5.46	5.05	4.11
43	**Louisiana**	**4.80**	76.5	14.8	85.2	23.7	7.5	84.1	31,600	4.36	4.52	5.51
44	**Montana**	**4.69**	78.8	8.3	91.7	28.1	8.7	82.9	24,861	5.32	4.91	3.84
45	**Mississippi**	**4.64**	76.1	15.2	84.8	23.0	8.1	85.3	29,843	4.19	4.63	5.11
46	**Alabama**	**4.61**	75.9	15.9	84.1	24.4	8.6	84.0	30,053	4.13	4.54	5.16
47	**Tennessee**	**4.59**	76.7	15.6	84.4	24.1	8.4	85.8	27,698	4.45	4.72	4.59
48	**Oklahoma**	**4.39**	75.6	11.8	88.2	23.7	7.7	84.6	27,152	4.01	4.72	4.45
49	**Kentucky**	**4.32**	76.3	18.6	81.4	19.9	7.9	85.3	26,705	4.29	4.33	4.34
50	**Arkansas**	**4.23**	76.4	15.3	84.7	20.2	6.6	84.0	25,641	4.34	4.29	4.06
51	**West Virginia**	**3.85**	75.1	17.8	82.2	16.9	6.7	82.8	24,797	3.81	3.90	3.82

AMERICAN HUMAN DEVELOPMENT INDEX

by Congressional District, Total Population

RANK	CONGRESSIONAL DISTRICT	HD INDEX	LIFE EXPECTANCY AT BIRTH (years)	LESS THAN HIGH SCHOOL (%)	AT LEAST HIGH SCHOOL DIPLOMA (%)	AT LEAST BACHELOR'S DEGREE (%)	GRADUATE OR PROFESSIONAL DEGREE (%)	SCHOOL ENROLLMENT (%)	MEDIAN EARNINGS (2009 dollars)	HEALTH INDEX	EDUCATION INDEX	INCOME INDEX
1	**CD 14, New York**	**8.79**	82.8	8.7	91.3	65.7	30.3	100.5	60,099	6.98	9.44	9.96
2	**CD 8, Virginia**	**8.30**	83.7	10.4	89.6	58.9	29.3	97.1	51,260	7.35	8.69	8.86
3	**CD 14, California**	**8.11**	82.9	9.4	90.6	57.2	28.4	99.9	47,879	7.03	8.93	8.39
4	**CD 30, California**	**7.71**	80.8	6.2	93.8	57.6	25.6	97.7	46,977	6.16	8.72	8.25
5	**CD 48, California**	**7.66**	82.1	7.1	92.9	51.7	20.4	99.0	44,803	6.72	8.33	7.93
6	**CD 15, California**	**7.60**	83.1	11.3	88.7	45.3	19.2	95.5	46,751	7.14	7.42	8.22
7	**CD 8, Maryland**	**7.57**	83.2	10.7	89.3	55.2	29.6	94.3	41,263	7.15	8.21	7.36
9	**CD 11, Virginia**	**7.51**	81.6	8.6	91.4	52.7	24.0	93.2	46,680	6.50	7.83	8.21
9	**CD 8, New York**	**7.48**	82.0	14.4	85.6	52.9	25.0	95.3	44,706	6.67	7.85	7.91
10	**CD 8, California**	**7.47**	82.6	16.8	83.2	50.0	19.4	104.3	42,815	6.90	7.89	7.61
11	**CD 12, California**	**7.44**	82.9	9.7	90.3	45.1	17.8	98.9	41,990	7.05	7.80	7.48
12	**CD 11, New Jersey**	**7.33**	80.6	8.0	92.0	47.7	19.3	95.4	46,761	6.09	7.67	8.22
13	**CD 7, New Jersey**	**7.31**	80.7	7.9	92.1	45.9	19.2	95.1	46,891	6.14	7.55	8.24
14	**CD 12, New Jersey**	**7.28**	80.0	6.8	93.2	48.0	21.9	95.6	46,142	5.85	7.87	8.13
15	**CD 46, California**	**7.17**	81.8	10.3	89.7	41.7	15.6	100.5	40,927	6.58	7.64	7.30
16	**CD 18, New York**	**7.12**	81.9	12.6	87.4	48.1	25.6	90.7	42,141	6.63	7.23	7.50
17	**CD 10, Virginia**	**7.12**	80.8	10.1	89.9	49.1	20.2	91.7	44,732	6.17	7.27	7.91
18	**CD 6, Colorado**	**7.11**	81.3	3.4	96.6	48.3	16.3	93.7	41,346	6.39	7.58	7.37
19	**CD 5, New Jersey**	**7.11**	81.0	6.4	93.6	43.2	15.7	92.6	45,395	6.24	7.06	8.02
20	**CD 4, Connecticut**	**7.06**	81.4	11.2	88.8	46.6	20.8	92.9	42,100	6.43	7.26	7.49
21	**CD 7, Washington**	**6.89**	81.1	8.0	92.0	51.5	20.6	95.1	36,564	6.30	7.85	6.52
22	**CD 42, California**	**6.87**	80.8	10.3	89.7	38.2	12.4	97.1	41,529	6.18	7.02	7.40
23	**CD 13, Illinois**	**6.84**	80.3	6.8	93.2	45.9	17.8	93.6	40,271	5.96	7.38	7.19
24	**CD 7, Massachusetts**	**6.81**	81.3	11.2	88.8	43.3	21.0	93.1	38,766	6.38	7.15	6.92
25	**CD 3, New York**	**6.79**	81.5	8.4	91.6	37.6	16.1	90.2	41,662	6.46	6.49	7.42
26	**CD 50, California**	**6.79**	80.8	10.4	89.6	46.0	18.3	92.1	39,990	6.16	7.07	7.14
27	**CD 6, Georgia**	**6.79**	79.1	6.9	93.1	51.7	17.5	93.8	40,827	5.44	7.64	7.28
28	**CD 9, Michigan**	**6.75**	79.4	6.9	93.1	47.5	21.1	93.2	39,906	5.59	7.54	7.12
29	**CD 8, Washington**	**6.72**	80.5	7.2	92.8	40.8	14.4	90.2	42,330	6.03	6.60	7.53
30	**CD 36, California**	**6.72**	80.8	13.3	86.7	41.9	15.1	97.9	37,694	6.16	7.27	6.73
31	**CD 10, California**	**6.71**	80.4	11.0	89.0	40.2	15.0	92.4	41,868	5.98	6.68	7.46
32	**CD 7, Texas**	**6.69**	78.2	8.3	91.7	51.1	19.6	92.9	41,838	5.09	7.54	7.45
33	**CD 3, Minnesota**	**6.69**	80.7	5.1	94.9	42.7	13.6	90.6	40,034	6.13	6.79	7.15
34	**CD 4, North Carolina**	**6.68**	79.4	8.2	91.8	52.9	22.3	96.3	35,601	5.59	8.12	6.33
35	**CD 9, California**	**6.59**	80.6	16.2	83.8	42.7	20.0	98.9	35,028	6.07	7.49	6.22
36	**CD 19, New York**	**6.58**	80.3	9.1	90.9	36.9	16.2	92.3	40,082	5.95	6.65	7.15
37	**CD 7, Pennsylvania**	**6.58**	78.6	7.1	92.9	41.5	16.4	95.9	40,026	5.24	7.36	7.14
38	**CD 9, New York**	**6.57**	82.4	14.7	85.3	33.9	12.7	93.4	37,079	6.85	6.24	6.61
39	**CD 4, New York**	**6.57**	81.9	14.0	86.0	36.3	15.6	91.4	37,919	6.64	6.29	6.77
40	**CD 10, Illinois**	**6.56**	79.5	10.5	89.5	50.5	21.9	91.4	37,602	5.64	7.34	6.71
41	**CD 9, Massachusetts**	**6.56**	80.3	10.0	90.0	39.0	16.4	93.0	38,799	5.96	6.80	6.93
42	**CD 24, California**	**6.56**	81.2	10.9	89.1	34.1	12.3	92.7	39,243	6.35	6.32	7.01
43	**CD 6, California**	**6.54**	81.4	10.8	89.2	41.4	16.1	92.9	35,759	6.42	6.84	6.36
44	**CD 6, Massachusetts**	**6.52**	80.1	8.9	91.1	40.7	16.2	91.8	38,693	5.86	6.78	6.91
45	**CD 1, Washington**	**6.50**	79.8	5.9	94.1	41.4	14.5	88.1	40,926	5.76	6.45	7.30
46	**CD 9, New Jersey**	**6.47**	81.5	13.7	86.3	37.0	12.6	87.3	40,478	6.44	5.75	7.22
47	**CD 5, Massachusetts**	**6.45**	80.8	12.0	88.0	38.4	16.7	90.1	38,094	6.17	6.37	6.80
48	**CD 13, California**	**6.43**	80.6	14.2	85.8	34.5	12.4	91.7	39,956	6.07	6.08	7.13
49	**CD 26, California**	**6.42**	79.5	11.5	88.5	34.9	14.7	97.8	37,263	5.62	7.01	6.65
50	**CD 1, New York**	**6.41**	80.2	9.8	90.2	32.2	14.9	90.8	39,847	5.91	6.20	7.11
51	**CD 10, Massachusetts**	**6.40**	80.7	5.4	94.6	39.4	15.0	89.6	36,384	6.13	6.58	6.48

KEY: 8.79–6.07 | 6.06–5.30 | 5.29–4.80 | 4.79–4.25 | 4.24–2.60

AMERICAN HUMAN DEVELOPMENT INDEX

by Congressional District, Total Population *continued*

RANK	CONGRESSIONAL DISTRICT	HD INDEX	LIFE EXPECTANCY AT BIRTH (years)	LESS THAN HIGH SCHOOL (%)	AT LEAST HIGH SCHOOL DIPLOMA (%)	AT LEAST BACHELOR'S DEGREE (%)	GRADUATE OR PROFESSIONAL DEGREE (%)	SCHOOL ENROLLMENT (%)	MEDIAN EARNINGS (2009 dollars)	HEALTH INDEX	EDUCATION INDEX	INCOME INDEX
52	**CD 29, California**	**6.36**	80.8	18.0	82.0	37.4	14.0	100.8	33,375	6.16	7.04	5.88
53	**CD 2, New York**	**6.33**	80.3	10.6	89.4	35.5	15.2	90.9	37,545	5.97	6.33	6.70
54	**CD 9, Illinois**	**6.32**	78.5	13.0	87.0	43.9	18.9	97.3	35,281	5.23	7.47	6.27
55	**CD 22, Florida**	**6.31**	81.1	8.0	92.0	38.9	14.1	91.3	34,194	6.28	6.58	6.05
56	**CD 5, Arizona**	**6.31**	80.2	8.4	91.6	43.0	16.1	92.2	34,211	5.93	6.93	6.06
57	**CD 5, New York**	**6.30**	82.7	20.1	79.9	37.1	14.7	93.1	32,841	6.94	6.20	5.77
58	**CD 4, Massachusetts**	**6.29**	79.9	13.3	86.7	40.5	19.6	91.1	36,282	5.78	6.64	6.46
59	**CD 6, Illinois**	**6.29**	80.8	10.8	89.2	36.8	12.3	91.4	35,896	6.17	6.30	6.39
60	**CD 4, Maryland**	**6.28**	79.6	12.4	87.6	35.8	15.3	89.9	39,244	5.67	6.15	7.01
61	**CD 5, Wisconsin**	**6.27**	80.1	5.6	94.4	38.8	13.8	90.6	35,676	5.88	6.60	6.35
62	**CD 16, California**	**6.27**	83.1	22.7	77.3	30.5	11.2	89.9	35,884	7.14	5.27	6.39
63	**CD 2, Minnesota**	**6.25**	81.2	6.2	93.8	36.6	10.2	87.0	36,579	6.32	5.92	6.52
64	**CD 20, Florida**	**6.25**	80.6	9.5	90.5	36.6	14.2	93.1	34,153	6.09	6.62	6.04
65	**CD 2, Missouri**	**6.24**	79.4	6.3	93.7	42.1	15.3	89.5	36,405	5.58	6.66	6.49
66	**CD 6, Pennsylvania**	**6.23**	80.1	10.1	89.9	40.5	16.0	89.1	36,163	5.86	6.40	6.44
67	**CD 8, Pennsylvania**	**6.23**	79.5	7.9	92.1	33.5	13.0	90.4	38,410	5.62	6.20	6.86
68	**CD 3, Kansas**	**6.22**	80.1	7.8	92.2	43.4	15.2	91.8	33,489	5.86	6.90	5.91
69	**CD 8, Massachusetts**	**6.22**	80.4	16.4	83.6	45.2	22.7	95.8	30,527	6.02	7.37	5.27
70	**District of Columbia**	**6.21**	75.6	14.2	85.8	48.2	26.7	92.7	40,342	4.00	7.44	7.20
71	**CD 3, Texas**	**6.19**	80.7	12.7	87.3	41.6	13.3	88.3	35,504	6.12	6.13	6.31
72	**CD 1, Connecticut**	**6.18**	79.6	13.0	87.0	33.1	13.7	94.2	36,274	5.68	6.41	6.46
73	**CD 2, Connecticut**	**6.18**	79.9	8.9	91.1	33.1	13.9	91.7	35,947	5.80	6.33	6.40
74	**CD 3, New Jersey**	**6.16**	79.4	8.3	91.7	31.0	10.9	90.0	39,183	5.57	5.93	7.00
75	**CD 3, Connecticut**	**6.15**	79.8	11.4	88.6	32.5	14.4	93.4	35,478	5.74	6.40	6.31
76	**CD 3, Maryland**	**6.14**	76.9	11.1	88.9	43.2	20.0	88.8	40,678	4.54	6.63	7.26
77	**CD 5, Maryland**	**6.14**	77.4	9.7	90.3	31.2	12.6	92.8	41,649	4.73	6.27	7.42
78	**CD 3, Massachusetts**	**6.14**	79.5	12.5	87.5	37.1	14.3	91.3	36,356	5.62	6.32	6.48
79	**CD 52, California**	**6.12**	80.8	10.6	89.4	30.9	11.5	90.5	35,353	6.16	5.91	6.28
80	**CD 53, California**	**6.11**	80.8	15.7	84.3	39.5	16.7	96.0	30,453	6.16	6.91	5.25
81	**CD 6, New Jersey**	**6.10**	80.3	12.4	87.6	33.8	12.0	90.3	35,906	5.95	5.96	6.39
82	**CD 2, Colorado**	**6.09**	80.0	10.0	90.0	41.8	15.0	87.5	35,027	5.82	6.24	6.22
83	**CD 13, New York**	**6.09**	80.6	17.2	82.8	26.8	10.3	90.4	38,103	6.10	5.37	6.80
84	**CD 5, Connecticut**	**6.09**	80.2	12.3	87.7	33.2	13.7	88.6	36,658	5.90	5.83	6.53
85	**CD 5, Minnesota**	**6.09**	80.7	11.0	89.0	41.1	14.3	92.2	31,442	6.12	6.67	5.47
86	**CD 8, Illinois**	**6.08**	79.8	10.1	89.9	36.0	12.7	87.4	37,111	5.75	5.87	6.62
87	**CD 1, Hawaii**	**6.07**	82.2	10.1	89.9	31.2	10.5	90.1	32,125	6.75	5.86	5.62
88	**CD 4, Minnesota**	**6.06**	80.7	9.3	90.7	37.5	14.3	90.7	32,271	6.13	6.40	5.65
89	**CD 17, New York**	**6.00**	80.6	17.5	82.5	32.1	13.9	92.0	33,901	6.08	5.93	5.99
90	**CD 40, California**	**5.99**	82.1	18.6	81.4	31.2	9.7	90.8	32,671	6.72	5.52	5.74
91	**CD 6, Minnesota**	**5.99**	81.2	6.3	93.7	29.0	8.5	87.2	34,492	6.33	5.52	6.11
92	**CD 11, New York**	**5.98**	81.3	18.4	81.6	31.4	13.9	92.3	32,299	6.38	5.90	5.66
93	**CD 11, California**	**5.97**	79.2	13.7	86.3	30.5	10.5	91.7	36,717	5.52	5.84	6.55
94	**CD 22, Texas**	**5.96**	79.0	12.9	87.1	34.9	11.6	89.0	37,248	5.42	5.83	6.65
95	**CD 3, California**	**5.96**	79.4	10.7	89.3	28.6	9.1	93.0	35,613	5.58	5.97	6.33
96	**CD 4, New Jersey**	**5.95**	79.6	12.4	87.6	30.1	10.4	90.4	36,119	5.68	5.74	6.43
97	**CD 19, Florida**	**5.91**	81.1	10.7	89.3	30.4	10.8	93.3	30,516	6.31	6.16	5.26
98	**CD 6, New York**	**5.90**	82.9	22.1	77.9	22.2	7.1	94.1	31,277	7.06	5.22	5.43
99	**CD 2, Wisconsin**	**5.90**	80.4	7.5	92.5	34.5	14.0	91.2	30,690	5.99	6.41	5.30
100	**CD 1, Oregon**	**5.89**	80.2	10.0	90.0	36.3	13.4	88.7	32,502	5.92	6.07	5.70
101	**CD 5, Illinois**	**5.89**	78.5	16.9	83.1	39.1	15.4	89.8	35,696	5.23	6.09	6.35
102	**CD 15, New York**	**5.87**	82.6	28.4	71.6	34.5	17.2	91.5	29,608	6.91	5.64	5.05

AMERICAN HUMAN DEVELOPMENT INDEX

by Congressional District, Total Population *continued*

RANK	CONGRESSIONAL DISTRICT	HD INDEX	LIFE EXPECTANCY AT BIRTH (years)	LESS THAN HIGH SCHOOL (%)	AT LEAST HIGH SCHOOL DIPLOMA (%)	AT LEAST BACHELOR'S DEGREE (%)	GRADUATE OR PROFESSIONAL DEGREE (%)	SCHOOL ENROLLMENT (%)	MEDIAN EARNINGS (2009 dollars)	HEALTH INDEX	EDUCATION INDEX	INCOME INDEX
103	**CD 9, North Carolina**	**5.82**	77.6	10.1	89.9	39.4	12.6	88.9	36,169	4.85	6.18	6.44
104	**CD 5, Georgia**	**5.82**	78.4	14.6	85.4	45.2	18.4	89.6	32,626	5.15	6.58	5.73
105	**CD 7, Virginia**	**5.79**	78.3	11.4	88.6	36.1	12.6	88.3	35,588	5.14	5.91	6.33
106	**CD 13, Pennsylvania**	**5.77**	77.3	13.1	86.9	32.6	12.6	89.6	38,130	4.69	5.83	6.81
107	**CD 12, Ohio**	**5.77**	77.8	8.0	92.0	38.3	12.9	89.0	34,661	4.90	6.25	6.15
108	**CD 8, New Jersey**	**5.76**	78.9	16.8	83.2	33.0	11.4	89.7	35,387	5.36	5.64	6.29
109	**CD 4, California**	**5.76**	80.5	8.8	91.2	28.4	8.4	88.2	32,731	6.04	5.50	5.75
110	**CD 7, Georgia**	**5.76**	79.7	12.2	87.8	34.1	10.8	90.1	32,396	5.69	5.91	5.68
111	**CD 7, Illinois**	**5.76**	78.5	16.3	83.7	38.2	17.5	86.1	35,395	5.23	5.76	6.29
112	**CD 5, Indiana**	**5.75**	78.6	8.5	91.5	35.8	12.1	88.8	33,534	5.26	6.06	5.92
113	**CD 2, New Hampshire**	**5.74**	79.6	9.1	90.9	33.1	12.6	89.3	31,736	5.68	5.99	5.54
114	**CD 1, New Hampshire**	**5.74**	79.7	9.1	90.9	33.6	11.4	87.0	32,886	5.73	5.70	5.78
115	**CD 11, Michigan**	**5.73**	76.7	9.0	91.0	33.4	12.7	93.2	35,520	4.44	6.45	6.32
116	**CD 24, Texas**	**5.73**	78.5	13.0	87.0	36.4	11.6	88.3	34,782	5.20	5.81	6.17
117	**CD 10, New York**	**5.72**	81.3	21.8	78.2	23.9	9.1	90.8	32,824	6.38	5.02	5.77
118	**CD 21, Texas**	**5.72**	79.0	9.1	90.9	39.5	14.8	89.3	31,073	5.40	6.37	5.39
119	**CD 7, California**	**5.69**	80.2	16.5	83.5	25.7	7.2	89.1	34,390	5.90	5.08	6.09
120	**CD 6, Maryland**	**5.66**	78.5	11.7	88.3	27.8	10.1	89.7	34,857	5.23	5.57	6.19
121	**CD 3, Arizona**	**5.66**	80.2	12.7	87.3	31.1	11.1	85.3	33,091	5.93	5.23	5.82
122	**CD 1, Virginia**	**5.65**	78.8	11.1	88.9	30.3	11.5	86.7	34,875	5.33	5.44	6.19
123	**CD 25, New York**	**5.64**	79.2	10.0	90.0	32.2	14.0	90.5	30,743	5.50	6.11	5.31
124	**CD 18, Pennsylvania**	**5.64**	78.1	5.9	94.1	34.5	12.5	89.2	32,409	5.05	6.18	5.68
125	**CD 2, Rhode Island**	**5.62**	79.3	14.3	85.7	30.5	11.2	91.1	31,771	5.54	5.78	5.54
126	**CD 8, Michigan**	**5.62**	79.1	7.7	92.3	31.1	11.7	93.9	29,135	5.46	6.44	4.94
127	**CD 8, Arizona**	**5.57**	80.1	8.4	91.6	32.9	13.4	89.8	28,365	5.86	6.11	4.76
128	**CD 1, Maryland**	**5.57**	77.4	10.5	89.5	29.8	11.1	88.2	35,808	4.76	5.59	6.37
129	**CD 21, New York**	**5.57**	79.0	11.4	88.6	30.6	14.6	89.8	30,971	5.42	5.93	5.37
130	**CD 6, Arizona**	**5.56**	80.2	12.0	88.0	26.4	9.1	87.4	31,899	5.92	5.21	5.57
131	**CD 10, Texas**	**5.56**	78.7	12.9	87.1	35.0	11.4	83.9	34,629	5.29	5.26	6.14
132	**CD 2, Nebraska**	**5.56**	78.8	9.4	90.6	34.3	11.7	91.2	30,045	5.32	6.20	5.16
133	**CD 14, Illinois**	**5.56**	80.0	14.7	85.3	30.2	10.4	88.5	31,169	5.84	5.42	5.41
134	**CD 27, California**	**5.56**	80.8	19.9	80.1	27.9	8.9	90.0	30,778	6.16	5.19	5.32
135	**CD 24, Florida**	**5.55**	79.3	10.2	89.8	27.2	8.8	93.4	30,011	5.54	5.97	5.15
136	**CD 14, Ohio**	**5.54**	78.4	8.6	91.4	31.1	11.4	90.9	31,201	5.16	6.05	5.42
137	**CD 2, Utah**	**5.53**	80.4	8.3	91.7	33.9	12.0	86.1	29,062	5.98	5.68	4.92
138	**CD 2, Massachusetts**	**5.53**	78.8	13.1	86.9	27.3	9.8	88.8	33,394	5.32	5.38	5.89
139	**CD 14, Florida**	**5.52**	82.0	11.6	88.4	28.5	9.7	85.4	28,478	6.67	5.12	4.78
140	**CD 1, Massachusetts**	**5.52**	79.3	10.7	89.3	29.8	11.8	90.1	30,164	5.54	5.82	5.18
141	**CD 5, Colorado**	**5.51**	79.5	9.1	90.9	33.0	12.6	90.1	28,813	5.60	6.07	4.87
142	**CD 1, Rhode Island**	**5.49**	79.2	18.3	81.7	29.6	11.5	92.0	30,624	5.51	5.68	5.29
143	**CD 3, Iowa**	**5.47**	79.7	9.0	91.0	28.6	7.9	87.2	31,012	5.69	5.35	5.38
144	**CD 15, Pennsylvania**	**5.47**	79.8	13.6	86.4	26.9	9.6	86.7	31,930	5.73	5.10	5.58
145	**CD 4, Colorado**	**5.45**	80.4	13.1	86.9	33.1	11.6	91.1	26,899	5.99	5.97	4.39
146	**CD 26, Texas**	**5.43**	78.7	15.2	84.8	30.8	9.3	88.1	32,346	5.29	5.34	5.67
147	**CD 1, Wisconsin**	**5.41**	78.8	10.6	89.4	24.7	7.7	90.4	31,300	5.35	5.45	5.44
148	**CD 2, Hawaii**	**5.41**	80.8	9.3	90.7	26.9	9.2	80.6	31,398	6.17	4.59	5.46
149	**CD 1, Colorado**	**5.41**	78.9	17.1	82.9	37.9	15.2	86.6	30,149	5.38	5.66	5.18
150	**CD 7, New York**	**5.40**	80.8	24.9	75.1	23.2	7.6	89.7	31,038	6.16	4.67	5.38
151	**CD 7, Tennessee**	**5.40**	76.4	10.2	89.8	34.5	12.5	90.7	32,548	4.33	6.16	5.71
152	**CD 2, Ohio**	**5.40**	77.3	10.4	89.6	33.7	13.2	88.5	31,836	4.73	5.91	5.56
153	**CD 12, Michigan**	**5.40**	78.6	13.1	86.9	22.5	8.1	94.7	30,138	5.26	5.75	5.18

AMERICAN HUMAN DEVELOPMENT INDEX

by Congressional District, Total Population *continued*

RANK	CONGRESSIONAL DISTRICT	HD INDEX	LIFE EXPECTANCY AT BIRTH (years)	LESS THAN HIGH SCHOOL (%)	AT LEAST HIGH SCHOOL DIPLOMA (%)	AT LEAST BACHELOR'S DEGREE (%)	GRADUATE OR PROFESSIONAL DEGREE (%)	SCHOOL ENROLLMENT (%)	MEDIAN EARNINGS (2009 dollars)	HEALTH INDEX	EDUCATION INDEX	INCOME INDEX
154	**CD 19, Pennsylvania**	**5.38**	79.4	11.7	88.3	24.1	8.2	89.6	30,421	5.59	5.32	5.24
155	**CD 7, Florida**	**5.38**	79.4	10.3	89.7	27.9	9.7	90.5	28,775	5.57	5.72	4.86
156	**CD 1, Maine**	**5.37**	79.5	8.4	91.6	31.4	11.1	87.5	28,631	5.62	5.68	4.82
157	**CD 25, California**	**5.37**	79.9	18.4	81.6	21.6	6.2	88.8	31,994	5.79	4.73	5.59
158	**CD 9, Florida**	**5.37**	78.7	11.1	88.9	29.2	10.0	87.4	31,275	5.28	5.40	5.43
159	**CD 15, Michigan**	**5.36**	77.7	11.6	88.4	29.1	13.3	98.4	27,267	4.87	6.74	4.48
160	**CD 15, Ohio**	**5.36**	76.9	11.7	88.3	35.8	12.9	90.8	31,008	4.53	6.18	5.37
161	**CD 2, Iowa**	**5.35**	80.1	8.4	91.6	27.9	9.6	91.2	26,559	5.87	5.87	4.30
162	**CD 25, Florida**	**5.34**	81.7	21.3	78.7	25.9	8.7	87.3	28,396	6.54	4.73	4.76
163	**CD 1, Minnesota**	**5.34**	81.5	10.0	90.0	25.3	8.0	85.4	27,716	6.47	4.96	4.60
164	**CD 1, New Jersey**	**5.34**	77.9	13.6	86.4	24.8	8.1	87.4	34,272	4.94	5.01	6.07
165	**CD 8, Florida**	**5.33**	80.0	11.2	88.8	28.9	9.1	88.2	28,272	5.81	5.44	4.73
166	**CD Delaware**	**5.33**	78.3	12.8	87.2	27.5	10.8	88.4	31,320	5.13	5.40	5.44
167	**CD 44, California**	**5.31**	80.0	20.1	79.9	25.7	9.1	86.2	31,241	5.83	4.68	5.43
168	**CD 10, Michigan**	**5.31**	78.1	11.6	88.4	20.9	7.2	93.5	30,790	5.03	5.56	5.33
169	**CD 6, Alabama**	**5.30**	75.7	11.1	88.9	33.6	12.0	87.2	34,912	4.05	5.67	6.20
170	**CD 26, New York**	**5.30**	78.5	9.8	90.2	29.6	13.6	89.1	28,771	5.23	5.83	4.86
171	**CD 3, Oregon**	**5.30**	78.2	11.5	88.5	32.2	11.2	87.8	30,153	5.10	5.62	5.18
172	**CD 13, Florida**	**5.30**	81.3	12.2	87.8	25.7	9.2	84.9	27,912	6.36	4.89	4.64
173	**CD 4, Pennsylvania**	**5.30**	78.0	8.0	92.0	32.2	11.5	85.5	30,919	5.00	5.53	5.35
174	**CD 10, Florida**	**5.29**	79.2	11.5	88.5	26.1	8.7	87.4	30,267	5.48	5.19	5.21
175	**CD 3, Nevada**	**5.28**	77.6	12.0	88.0	25.7	8.3	85.0	34,811	4.81	4.86	6.18
176	**CD 20, New York**	**5.28**	79.4	10.2	89.8	28.2	12.2	83.7	30,151	5.56	5.09	5.18
177	**CD 2, Illinois**	**5.27**	78.6	15.7	84.3	22.4	8.0	92.1	30,493	5.23	5.33	5.26
178	**CD Alaska**	**5.27**	78.3	8.4	91.6	27.3	9.7	84.9	31,774	5.12	5.15	5.54
179	**CD 3, Washington**	**5.27**	79.0	10.4	89.6	24.5	8.6	86.2	30,972	5.41	5.03	5.37
180	**CD 2, Virginia**	**5.27**	78.1	9.3	90.7	28.6	10.3	86.9	30,783	5.06	5.42	5.32
181	**CD Vermont**	**5.27**	79.7	9.4	90.6	32.1	12.2	87.9	26,627	5.71	5.77	4.32
182	**CD 2, Washington**	**5.25**	80.4	9.6	90.4	25.3	7.7	81.9	30,016	6.01	4.59	5.15
183	**CD 9, Washington**	**5.25**	79.7	11.2	88.8	22.0	7.0	80.7	33,064	5.71	4.20	5.82
184	**CD 2, Maryland**	**5.24**	77.0	13.6	86.4	24.4	8.9	86.6	34,925	4.58	4.95	6.20
185	**CD 13, Ohio**	**5.24**	78.1	10.3	89.7	27.1	9.8	89.8	29,630	5.05	5.61	5.06
186	**CD 33, California**	**5.23**	80.8	22.2	77.8	31.7	10.3	90.4	26,018	6.16	5.37	4.16
187	**CD 7, Maryland**	**5.22**	75.5	17.0	83.0	33.5	15.7	91.9	32,070	3.96	6.09	5.61
188	**CD 16, Illinois**	**5.22**	79.5	12.7	87.3	23.6	7.7	85.9	30,250	5.63	4.82	5.20
189	**CD 21, Florida**	**5.20**	80.9	20.7	79.3	27.9	9.4	89.4	26,470	6.22	5.12	4.28
190	**CD 3, Missouri**	**5.19**	77.2	13.2	86.8	27.2	10.7	91.0	30,568	4.65	5.65	5.27
191	**CD 1, New Mexico**	**5.18**	78.5	14.5	85.5	30.2	14.0	92.6	26,569	5.20	6.05	4.30
192	**CD 4, Indiana**	**5.18**	78.5	10.6	89.4	27.3	9.7	89.0	28,663	5.21	5.51	4.83
193	**CD 3, Illinois**	**5.18**	78.5	19.4	80.6	23.5	8.3	88.2	31,582	5.23	4.80	5.50
194	**CD 13, Georgia**	**5.18**	78.1	13.6	86.4	25.9	8.6	87.4	31,125	5.04	5.09	5.40
195	**CD 3, Michigan**	**5.15**	79.3	11.8	88.2	27.7	9.0	88.7	27,326	5.55	5.41	4.50
196	**CD 13, New Jersey**	**5.15**	79.6	25.1	74.9	26.9	9.8	84.6	31,162	5.68	4.36	5.41
197	**CD 2, New Jersey**	**5.14**	77.6	15.6	84.4	22.3	7.1	91.0	31,279	4.82	5.17	5.43
198	**CD 5, California**	**5.14**	79.3	19.0	81.0	25.1	7.8	90.1	28,609	5.53	5.07	4.82
199	**CD 10, New Jersey**	**5.13**	78.6	19.5	80.5	21.2	7.1	89.8	30,927	5.23	4.82	5.36
200	**CD 16, Pennsylvania**	**5.13**	79.9	17.1	82.9	26.5	9.2	81.6	30,540	5.80	4.33	5.27
201	**CD 1, Nebraska**	**5.13**	79.5	9.5	90.5	27.7	8.6	89.0	26,344	5.63	5.52	4.24
202	**CD 18, Florida**	**5.13**	80.6	23.1	76.9	33.9	13.4	87.8	25,474	6.09	5.28	4.01
203	**CD 6, Missouri**	**5.12**	78.3	10.5	89.5	25.0	8.4	86.1	30,302	5.13	5.02	5.21
204	**CD 5, Tennessee**	**5.12**	77.2	15.7	84.3	30.2	11.0	89.5	30,199	4.66	5.52	5.19

AMERICAN HUMAN DEVELOPMENT INDEX

by Congressional District, Total Population *continued*

RANK	CONGRESSIONAL DISTRICT	HD INDEX	LIFE EXPECTANCY AT BIRTH (years)	LESS THAN HIGH SCHOOL (%)	AT LEAST HIGH SCHOOL DIPLOMA (%)	AT LEAST BACHELOR'S DEGREE (%)	GRADUATE OR PROFESSIONAL DEGREE (%)	SCHOOL ENROLLMENT (%)	MEDIAN EARNINGS (2009 dollars)	HEALTH INDEX	EDUCATION INDEX	INCOME INDEX
205	**CD 31, Texas**	**5.11**	79.2	11.1	88.9	27.2	8.3	82.1	30,161	5.50	4.65	5.18
206	**CD 4, Georgia**	**5.10**	79.3	15.8	84.2	29.9	10.5	83.9	28,870	5.55	4.86	4.88
207	**CD 3, Kentucky**	**5.10**	76.6	11.8	88.2	28.9	12.0	90.0	29,911	4.43	5.74	5.12
208	**CD 17, California**	**5.09**	81.5	25.7	74.3	27.5	11.1	86.4	26,153	6.45	4.62	4.19
209	**CD 22, New York**	**5.09**	78.8	13.2	86.8	27.3	12.7	90.9	26,211	5.32	5.74	4.21
210	**CD 12, New York**	**5.08**	81.9	32.5	67.5	25.8	9.2	80.9	29,843	6.60	3.54	5.11
211	**CD 2, Arizona**	**5.07**	78.8	13.5	86.5	20.9	6.8	84.7	30,996	5.35	4.49	5.37
212	**CD 5, Oregon**	**5.07**	79.4	11.6	88.4	27.9	9.8	86.6	27,001	5.57	5.22	4.41
213	**CD 8, Wisconsin**	**5.06**	79.7	9.8	90.2	22.2	6.2	84.7	28,589	5.69	4.68	4.81
214	**CD 2, South Carolina**	**5.05**	77.9	11.2	88.8	31.6	11.9	84.6	29,125	4.94	5.28	4.94
215	**CD 29, New York**	**5.05**	78.7	10.7	89.3	28.3	12.3	88.8	26,242	5.29	5.64	4.22
216	**CD 15, Illinois**	**5.04**	78.2	10.8	89.2	26.9	10.5	92.3	25,980	5.07	5.89	4.15
217	**CD 1, Iowa**	**5.03**	79.8	9.5	90.5	23.0	7.3	87.6	26,303	5.75	5.10	4.23
218	**CD 15, Florida**	**5.03**	79.9	11.5	88.5	24.7	8.5	86.1	26,604	5.78	4.98	4.31
219	**CD 3, Ohio**	**5.02**	77.3	11.3	88.7	25.5	10.2	91.3	27,965	4.72	5.67	4.66
220	**CD 2, Texas**	**5.00**	76.8	15.6	84.4	23.7	6.5	86.6	32,876	4.50	4.71	5.78
221	**CD 10, Ohio**	**4.99**	77.2	13.6	86.4	25.4	8.4	88.3	30,087	4.66	5.16	5.17
222	**CD 6, Florida**	**4.99**	78.6	12.9	87.1	24.0	9.8	90.0	26,697	5.27	5.37	4.34
223	**CD 18, Illinois**	**4.98**	78.0	10.7	89.3	24.6	7.9	87.8	28,491	4.99	5.17	4.79
224	**CD 7, Colorado**	**4.98**	79.9	14.7	85.3	28.6	9.0	78.7	29,117	5.79	4.21	4.94
225	**CD 11, Illinois**	**4.97**	78.5	11.6	88.4	21.5	6.7	85.4	29,529	5.21	4.67	5.04
226	**CD 6, Wisconsin**	**4.97**	79.3	11.2	88.8	19.9	5.9	85.3	28,615	5.52	4.57	4.82
227	**CD 13, North Carolina**	**4.96**	78.0	15.2	84.8	29.9	9.3	89.1	27,257	5.00	5.41	4.48
228	**CD 1, Utah**	**4.95**	79.7	9.8	90.2	27.8	8.7	83.9	26,112	5.71	4.96	4.18
229	**CD 17, Pennsylvania**	**4.94**	78.4	14.6	85.4	19.7	6.9	85.0	30,498	5.16	4.41	5.26
230	**CD 7, Michigan**	**4.93**	77.9	10.4	89.6	22.7	8.4	90.1	27,238	4.95	5.37	4.48
231	**CD 1, California**	**4.93**	78.2	15.0	85.0	29.1	11.4	88.9	26,364	5.10	5.45	4.25
232	**CD 25, Texas**	**4.93**	79.0	19.2	80.8	31.3	10.8	86.0	26,819	5.40	5.02	4.37
233	**CD 32, Texas**	**4.93**	78.5	26.0	74.0	36.1	13.1	83.0	28,905	5.19	4.70	4.89
234	**CD North Dakota**	**4.92**	80.1	10.4	89.6	26.9	6.6	82.8	26,224	5.88	4.67	4.21
235	**CD 4, Kansas**	**4.91**	77.1	11.3	88.7	26.2	8.5	87.4	28,969	4.63	5.19	4.90
236	**CD 14, Pennsylvania**	**4.91**	78.0	10.3	89.7	27.6	11.9	90.8	25,064	5.00	5.83	3.90
237	**CD 3, Georgia**	**4.90**	76.5	13.7	86.3	24.7	8.6	87.3	30,738	4.38	5.02	5.31
238	**CD 51, California**	**4.90**	80.7	28.4	71.6	18.5	5.1	88.6	27,311	6.14	4.08	4.49
239	**CD 23, California**	**4.90**	81.4	24.5	75.5	29.4	11.9	84.3	24,518	6.40	4.57	3.75
240	**CD 27, New York**	**4.89**	78.0	12.8	87.2	22.6	9.1	87.6	27,933	5.01	5.01	4.65
241	**CD 6, Texas**	**4.89**	77.4	16.4	83.6	24.9	7.4	87.6	29,414	4.77	4.89	5.01
242	**CD 1, Ohio**	**4.88**	77.8	15.7	84.3	23.6	8.2	89.8	27,726	4.90	5.14	4.60
243	**CD 11, Ohio**	**4.88**	77.2	16.0	84.0	26.2	11.9	92.6	26,395	4.66	5.72	4.26
244	**CD 1, Missouri**	**4.87**	78.0	15.8	84.2	25.0	9.8	90.2	26,589	4.98	5.31	4.31
245	**CD 5, Missouri**	**4.87**	76.7	13.1	86.9	26.2	10.0	85.1	30,368	4.45	4.92	5.23
246	**CD 3, Wisconsin**	**4.86**	79.5	9.7	90.3	23.0	7.4	84.0	26,347	5.62	4.70	4.24
247	**CD 4, Iowa**	**4.85**	79.8	10.1	89.9	22.7	6.8	85.7	25,364	5.75	4.83	3.98
248	**CD 7, Ohio**	**4.85**	77.3	12.5	87.5	21.1	7.8	89.7	28,082	4.71	5.14	4.69
249	**CD 6, Kentucky**	**4.84**	77.2	14.9	85.1	27.8	11.5	89.9	26,660	4.68	5.52	4.33
250	**CD 41, California**	**4.84**	77.8	17.2	82.8	20.2	7.7	85.5	30,199	4.91	4.42	5.19
251	**CD 28, New York**	**4.83**	78.6	15.1	84.9	25.3	10.4	88.2	25,796	5.25	5.16	4.10
252	**CD 1, Indiana**	**4.82**	76.9	12.1	87.9	19.9	6.1	86.5	30,448	4.54	4.68	5.25
253	**CD South Dakota**	**4.82**	79.9	9.7	90.3	25.1	7.3	82.5	25,717	5.77	4.62	4.08
254	**CD 39, California**	**4.82**	80.8	31.9	68.1	16.6	4.5	87.5	27,716	6.16	3.70	4.60
255	**CD 3, Utah**	**4.81**	80.1	10.7	89.3	25.3	7.3	85.5	24,182	5.87	4.92	3.65

AMERICAN HUMAN DEVELOPMENT INDEX

by Congressional District, Total Population *continued*

RANK	CONGRESSIONAL DISTRICT	HD INDEX	LIFE EXPECTANCY AT BIRTH (years)	LESS THAN HIGH SCHOOL (%)	AT LEAST HIGH SCHOOL DIPLOMA (%)	AT LEAST BACHELOR'S DEGREE (%)	GRADUATE OR PROFESSIONAL DEGREE (%)	SCHOOL ENROLLMENT (%)	MEDIAN EARNINGS (2009 dollars)	HEALTH INDEX	EDUCATION INDEX	INCOME INDEX
256	**CD 2, Pennsylvania**	**4.81**	74.4	18.2	81.8	27.9	13.5	94.6	29,088	3.50	5.99	4.93
257	**CD 1, Illinois**	**4.81**	78.5	16.5	83.5	21.0	8.1	88.0	26,994	5.23	4.78	4.41
258	**CD 11, Georgia**	**4.81**	76.9	15.8	84.2	24.9	8.0	85.6	30,148	4.53	4.71	5.18
259	**CD Wyoming**	**4.80**	77.6	8.3	91.7	23.6	7.9	81.6	29,507	4.84	4.54	5.03
260	**CD 5, Washington**	**4.80**	78.9	9.1	90.9	25.8	9.0	87.1	24,681	5.35	5.26	3.79
261	**CD 28, California**	**4.80**	80.8	30.6	69.4	27.5	8.8	84.9	25,878	6.16	4.12	4.12
262	**CD 6, Washington**	**4.80**	78.2	11.0	89.0	23.6	8.0	83.5	28,009	5.10	4.63	4.67
263	**CD 22, California**	**4.80**	77.9	18.4	81.6	20.2	6.1	85.6	29,964	4.95	4.30	5.14
264	**CD 3, Indiana**	**4.79**	78.9	15.6	84.4	22.1	7.3	82.1	28,731	5.35	4.18	4.85
265	**CD 19, California**	**4.79**	78.8	19.6	80.4	19.6	7.0	89.1	26,867	5.34	4.66	4.38
266	**CD 14, Texas**	**4.79**	77.2	16.5	83.5	24.2	7.4	84.7	30,137	4.68	4.52	5.18
267	**CD 2, Kansas**	**4.79**	78.0	9.3	90.7	26.8	9.8	86.7	25,711	5.00	5.29	4.08
268	**CD 16, Florida**	**4.79**	80.2	16.2	83.8	22.5	8.0	83.4	25,755	5.93	4.35	4.09
269	**CD 1, Louisiana**	**4.79**	75.6	13.8	86.2	27.7	9.4	86.9	30,336	4.00	5.13	5.22
270	**CD 49, California**	**4.78**	80.3	17.6	82.4	22.8	7.6	79.1	27,616	5.97	3.80	4.57
271	**CD 4, Florida**	**4.77**	75.3	13.2	86.8	26.3	9.0	86.1	31,312	3.88	4.99	5.44
272	**CD 1, South Carolina**	**4.76**	77.6	11.3	88.7	28.0	10.7	84.9	26,844	4.82	5.09	4.37
273	**CD 19, Illinois**	**4.76**	77.5	12.3	87.7	19.7	6.8	87.3	28,240	4.78	4.78	4.73
274	**CD 2, Nevada**	**4.76**	77.7	15.7	84.3	21.4	6.8	83.1	30,134	4.86	4.24	5.18
275	**CD 7, Wisconsin**	**4.76**	79.4	11.2	88.8	19.7	6.4	83.4	26,547	5.60	4.37	4.30
276	**CD 1, Idaho**	**4.75**	79.3	12.3	87.7	22.8	6.4	85.9	25,358	5.53	4.74	3.98
277	**CD 16, Ohio**	**4.75**	78.7	11.6	88.4	21.3	7.0	87.0	25,759	5.29	4.86	4.09
278	**CD 8, Ohio**	**4.74**	77.4	13.7	86.3	20.7	7.1	89.4	27,165	4.75	5.01	4.46
279	**CD 6, North Carolina**	**4.74**	77.5	15.8	84.2	25.0	7.7	83.8	28,960	4.80	4.51	4.90
280	**CD 3, Colorado**	**4.73**	79.0	12.1	87.9	24.6	8.2	82.9	26,143	5.43	4.57	4.19
281	**CD 8, Minnesota**	**4.73**	79.4	9.2	90.8	20.8	6.4	83.2	25,835	5.59	4.48	4.11
282	**CD 6, Virginia**	**4.72**	78.0	16.4	83.6	24.5	8.9	88.0	26,009	5.01	4.98	4.16
283	**CD 6, Michigan**	**4.72**	77.7	10.9	89.1	23.8	8.6	88.9	25,342	4.89	5.28	3.98
284	**CD 9, Ohio**	**4.71**	77.0	12.1	87.9	21.3	7.8	90.5	26,475	4.60	5.25	4.28
285	**CD 5, Ohio**	**4.71**	78.4	10.9	89.1	16.5	5.6	89.4	25,814	5.15	4.87	4.10
286	**CD 4, Virginia**	**4.69**	76.5	16.6	83.4	22.8	7.5	82.8	31,388	4.35	4.26	5.46
287	**CD 11, Florida**	**4.68**	78.5	17.6	82.4	24.7	8.3	86.3	25,921	5.20	4.72	4.13
288	**CD 45, California**	**4.67**	79.7	22.1	77.9	20.3	6.0	83.7	26,854	5.70	3.93	4.38
289	**CD 4, Kentucky**	**4.67**	76.3	15.7	84.3	21.1	7.5	86.9	29,631	4.28	4.67	5.06
290	**CD 2, Florida**	**4.66**	77.4	14.9	85.1	24.2	8.9	88.9	25,860	4.73	5.14	4.12
291	**CD 2, Tennessee**	**4.66**	77.2	13.7	86.3	27.8	9.7	86.7	26,137	4.65	5.14	4.19
292	**CD 7, Minnesota**	**4.65**	80.8	11.1	88.9	19.6	5.1	79.5	25,039	6.17	3.89	3.89
293	**CD 9, Indiana**	**4.65**	77.8	15.0	85.0	20.1	8.3	88.4	26,087	4.90	4.86	4.18
294	**CD 1, Oklahoma**	**4.65**	76.0	11.8	88.2	27.3	8.4	85.7	28,289	4.17	5.03	4.74
295	**CD 12, Illinois**	**4.64**	76.3	13.3	86.7	21.0	8.3	91.8	26,584	4.28	5.35	4.31
296	**CD 37, California**	**4.64**	80.8	29.5	70.5	18.6	5.1	89.5	24,118	6.16	4.13	3.63
297	**CD 2, Michigan**	**4.63**	79.1	12.3	87.7	20.8	7.1	84.7	24,950	5.47	4.55	3.87
298	**CD 5, Iowa**	**4.62**	79.0	11.8	88.2	18.5	4.9	84.4	25,815	5.42	4.34	4.10
299	**CD 4, Oregon**	**4.60**	78.3	11.5	88.5	22.7	8.9	87.1	24,202	5.12	5.02	3.66
300	**CD 38, California**	**4.59**	80.8	33.0	67.0	14.5	3.9	86.2	26,374	6.16	3.37	4.25
301	**CD 24, New York**	**4.56**	78.8	12.7	87.3	22.5	9.1	81.9	25,339	5.33	4.39	3.97
302	**CD 12, Florida**	**4.56**	78.4	18.1	81.9	20.2	6.4	82.5	27,408	5.17	3.99	4.52
303	**CD 5, Alabama**	**4.56**	76.1	15.3	84.7	27.3	8.7	86.7	27,204	4.20	5.00	4.47
304	**CD 12, Texas**	**4.55**	77.4	21.9	78.1	22.9	7.3	81.7	29,400	4.77	3.89	5.00
305	**CD 32, California**	**4.55**	80.8	34.8	65.2	16.0	4.6	88.5	24,918	6.16	3.65	3.86
306	**CD 11, Pennsylvania**	**4.55**	77.4	13.4	86.6	19.1	6.8	87.6	25,981	4.77	4.73	4.15

AMERICAN HUMAN DEVELOPMENT INDEX

by Congressional District, Total Population *continued*

RANK	CONGRESSIONAL DISTRICT	HD INDEX	LIFE EXPECTANCY AT BIRTH (years)	LESS THAN HIGH SCHOOL (%)	AT LEAST HIGH SCHOOL DIPLOMA (%)	AT LEAST BACHELOR'S DEGREE (%)	GRADUATE OR PROFESSIONAL DEGREE (%)	SCHOOL ENROLLMENT (%)	MEDIAN EARNINGS (2009 dollars)	HEALTH INDEX	EDUCATION INDEX	INCOME INDEX
307	**CD 6, Louisiana**	**4.54**	75.5	15.4	84.6	26.3	8.5	87.2	28,003	3.97	5.00	4.67
308	**CD 5, North Carolina**	**4.54**	77.1	17.7	82.3	22.7	7.7	87.7	26,311	4.63	4.75	4.24
309	**CD 2, Idaho**	**4.53**	79.2	12.0	88.0	25.5	8.6	81.8	24,020	5.48	4.52	3.60
310	**CD 10, Pennsylvania**	**4.53**	78.2	12.7	87.3	20.1	7.7	83.5	25,832	5.09	4.40	4.11
311	**CD 4, Texas**	**4.52**	77.4	15.1	84.9	21.9	6.3	84.4	27,022	4.75	4.40	4.42
312	**CD 9, Missouri**	**4.51**	77.6	13.2	86.8	24.0	8.7	87.7	24,141	4.83	5.06	3.64
313	**CD 8, Texas**	**4.51**	76.5	15.7	84.3	21.4	6.1	81.4	29,899	4.39	4.01	5.12
314	**CD 3, New Mexico**	**4.50**	78.1	16.7	83.3	25.1	10.4	81.5	25,839	5.05	4.34	4.11
315	**CD 2, Indiana**	**4.49**	77.7	16.1	83.9	19.4	7.2	85.1	26,335	4.86	4.36	4.24
316	**CD Montana**	**4.49**	78.4	9.1	90.9	27.1	8.4	81.8	24,033	5.15	4.71	3.61
317	**CD 23, Texas**	**4.48**	79.2	25.4	74.6	23.1	8.0	86.6	24,159	5.48	4.32	3.64
318	**CD 10, Georgia**	**4.48**	76.9	18.8	81.2	24.5	10.4	86.4	25,857	4.55	4.76	4.11
319	**CD 12, North Carolina**	**4.47**	77.9	20.1	79.9	23.0	6.0	87.3	25,189	4.94	4.54	3.93
320	**CD 5, Michigan**	**4.47**	76.6	12.8	87.2	18.3	6.3	90.7	25,267	4.40	5.05	3.95
321	**CD 4, South Carolina**	**4.46**	76.7	18.9	81.1	26.0	8.9	84.5	26,840	4.47	4.54	4.37
322	**CD 5, Florida**	**4.46**	78.6	15.2	84.8	18.1	6.2	82.9	25,666	5.24	4.07	4.06
323	**CD 35, California**	**4.45**	80.8	31.7	68.3	15.9	5.5	84.2	24,909	6.16	3.34	3.86
324	**CD 3, Nebraska**	**4.44**	79.2	10.7	89.3	19.1	5.5	81.2	24,569	5.48	4.09	3.76
325	**CD 17, Florida**	**4.43**	80.9	26.2	73.8	17.3	5.8	84.6	23,237	6.20	3.71	3.37
326	**CD 6, Indiana**	**4.42**	77.2	14.6	85.4	17.8	7.0	85.1	26,288	4.67	4.35	4.23
327	**CD 2, Maine**	**4.40**	77.9	12.3	87.7	19.1	6.5	87.1	23,831	4.95	4.71	3.55
328	**CD 4, Ohio**	**4.40**	77.8	13.1	86.9	14.7	5.2	83.6	26,368	4.91	4.04	4.25
329	**CD 3, Pennsylvania**	**4.40**	78.0	11.3	88.7	20.9	7.3	83.5	24,400	5.01	4.48	3.71
330	**CD 2, Arkansas**	**4.39**	75.4	13.2	86.8	25.1	9.3	86.6	26,375	3.93	5.00	4.25
331	**CD 5, Oklahoma**	**4.39**	76.0	15.4	84.6	26.9	9.3	86.2	25,724	4.15	4.95	4.08
332	**CD 1, Kansas**	**4.39**	78.4	13.9	86.1	20.6	6.2	81.9	25,012	5.16	4.11	3.88
333	**CD 7, Arizona**	**4.38**	81.4	26.3	73.7	15.3	5.6	82.7	23,050	6.43	3.39	3.32
334	**CD 4, Michigan**	**4.36**	78.2	11.1	88.9	20.8	7.3	89.0	21,798	5.08	5.08	2.93
335	**CD 4, Wisconsin**	**4.35**	77.2	18.6	81.4	21.5	7.1	86.7	25,034	4.65	4.53	3.89
336	**CD 11, North Carolina**	**4.34**	77.5	15.6	84.4	24.8	9.0	84.8	23,776	4.80	4.68	3.53
337	**CD 8, North Carolina**	**4.34**	76.8	17.5	82.5	20.2	6.2	85.1	26,224	4.50	4.30	4.21
338	**CD 23, Florida**	**4.32**	80.8	26.5	73.5	17.4	5.4	80.9	23,707	6.18	3.27	3.51
339	**CD 9, Georgia**	**4.32**	77.3	21.7	78.3	20.1	6.7	81.2	27,555	4.72	3.69	4.56
340	**CD 17, Illinois**	**4.32**	78.1	14.5	85.5	17.6	6.0	86.0	23,665	5.05	4.40	3.50
341	**CD 16, Texas**	**4.32**	80.9	27.3	72.7	20.2	6.9	88.0	20,621	6.19	4.21	2.55
342	**CD 6, Tennessee**	**4.30**	76.6	17.2	82.8	19.7	5.7	84.2	26,701	4.41	4.16	4.34
343	**CD 8, Indiana**	**4.30**	77.1	14.6	85.4	17.3	6.2	84.5	25,558	4.64	4.23	4.03
344	**CD 9, Pennsylvania**	**4.29**	78.7	15.0	85.0	15.4	5.0	79.5	25,684	5.29	3.52	4.07
345	**CD 23, New York**	**4.29**	78.3	13.6	86.4	18.2	8.1	83.2	23,567	5.14	4.25	3.47
346	**CD 4, Oklahoma**	**4.28**	75.6	12.3	87.7	21.7	7.2	86.6	25,563	4.00	4.81	4.04
347	**CD 17, Ohio**	**4.27**	77.0	13.2	86.8	19.0	5.9	85.5	24,573	4.59	4.46	3.76
348	**CD 5, Virginia**	**4.27**	77.1	20.9	79.1	22.2	9.3	83.4	25,456	4.63	4.18	4.01
349	**CD 2, Kentucky**	**4.27**	77.4	17.3	82.7	16.0	6.3	84.4	25,418	4.77	4.04	4.00
350	**CD 1, Florida**	**4.27**	77.2	13.0	87.0	22.3	7.7	80.8	25,250	4.68	4.17	3.95
351	**CD 1, Nevada**	**4.26**	77.6	22.8	77.2	17.5	5.5	77.6	28,943	4.81	3.07	4.90
352	**CD 1, Arizona**	**4.26**	78.0	16.5	83.5	19.2	7.5	83.1	24,123	5.01	4.13	3.63
353	**CD 2, Oregon**	**4.26**	78.9	12.2	87.8	21.1	6.9	78.7	23,703	5.38	3.88	3.51
354	**CD 3, Virginia**	**4.24**	76.0	17.8	82.2	22.0	8.5	85.5	25,548	4.18	4.51	4.03
355	**CD 4, Washington**	**4.24**	79.4	21.8	78.2	19.7	7.3	80.8	23,571	5.59	3.65	3.47
356	**CD 3, Mississippi**	**4.23**	75.0	17.9	82.1	23.1	8.2	87.7	26,031	3.75	4.79	4.16
357	**CD 7, Missouri**	**4.22**	77.6	14.2	85.8	22.2	7.3	81.9	24,019	4.84	4.22	3.60

AMERICAN HUMAN DEVELOPMENT INDEX

by Congressional District, Total Population *continued*

RANK	CONGRESSIONAL DISTRICT	HD INDEX	LIFE EXPECTANCY AT BIRTH (years)	LESS THAN HIGH SCHOOL (%)	AT LEAST HIGH SCHOOL DIPLOMA (%)	AT LEAST BACHELOR'S DEGREE (%)	GRADUATE OR PROFESSIONAL DEGREE (%)	SCHOOL ENROLLMENT (%)	MEDIAN EARNINGS (2009 dollars)	HEALTH INDEX	EDUCATION INDEX	INCOME INDEX
358	CD 7, Indiana	**4.22**	76.6	18.2	81.8	23.8	8.4	82.1	25,579	4.43	4.19	4.04
359	CD 12, Pennsylvania	**4.22**	78.0	13.8	86.2	17.0	5.9	82.9	24,039	4.98	4.06	3.61
360	CD 5, Texas	**4.20**	76.6	20.8	79.2	18.8	6.2	81.7	27,213	4.43	3.70	4.47
361	CD 3, North Carolina	**4.20**	76.7	14.4	85.6	22.9	7.0	79.8	25,913	4.46	4.00	4.13
362	CD 3, South Carolina	**4.19**	76.3	19.8	80.2	19.7	6.9	85.6	25,516	4.28	4.25	4.02
363	CD 17, Texas	**4.17**	77.7	19.4	80.6	21.8	7.1	85.2	23,008	4.88	4.33	3.31
364	CD 2, West Virginia	**4.16**	75.9	16.5	83.5	19.0	7.8	83.2	26,234	4.11	4.15	4.22
365	CD 1, West Virginia	**4.15**	76.7	14.0	86.0	18.3	7.1	87.1	23,205	4.45	4.63	3.36
366	CD 1, Michigan	**4.15**	78.6	10.9	89.1	18.1	6.2	84.7	21,280	5.23	4.45	2.76
367	CD 2, North Carolina	**4.14**	76.9	18.7	81.3	18.2	5.6	82.1	25,754	4.53	3.79	4.09
368	CD 3, Tennessee	**4.13**	76.6	17.7	82.3	22.0	8.1	83.8	24,187	4.43	4.31	3.65
369	CD 10, North Carolina	**4.13**	76.7	20.8	79.2	16.7	5.2	85.5	25,267	4.44	4.00	3.95
370	CD 21, California	**4.13**	77.8	26.9	73.1	17.6	5.2	84.3	24,820	4.92	3.63	3.83
371	CD 14, Michigan	**4.13**	75.4	19.1	80.9	15.4	6.4	92.9	23,849	3.93	4.89	3.55
372	CD 2, California	**4.11**	76.9	16.7	83.3	20.0	5.8	88.2	22,456	4.55	4.65	3.14
373	CD 47, California	**4.11**	82.1	44.7	55.3	12.6	3.3	83.7	22,451	6.72	2.46	3.14
374	CD 11, Texas	**4.10**	77.7	20.0	80.0	17.5	5.2	78.6	25,923	4.88	3.30	4.13
375	CD 18, Texas	**4.10**	78.2	31.3	68.7	18.2	6.2	80.4	25,973	5.09	3.07	4.15
376	CD 7, North Carolina	**4.09**	76.0	18.6	81.4	22.0	6.6	84.9	24,702	4.15	4.32	3.80
377	CD 4, Missouri	**4.09**	77.1	13.6	86.4	17.7	5.9	82.1	24,109	4.62	4.02	3.63
378	CD 9, Tennessee	**4.08**	75.0	18.9	81.1	23.1	8.5	85.9	25,199	3.73	4.56	3.94
379	CD 1, Alabama	**4.07**	75.1	16.2	83.8	21.6	6.9	83.7	25,990	3.78	4.29	4.15
380	CD 5, South Carolina	**4.07**	75.7	19.9	80.1	18.7	6.2	82.2	26,803	4.03	3.80	4.36
381	CD 3, Arkansas	**4.06**	78.0	18.2	81.8	21.2	7.2	79.0	23,742	4.99	3.67	3.52
382	CD 8, Georgia	**4.06**	75.1	20.0	80.0	19.0	6.9	85.7	26,074	3.79	4.22	4.17
383	CD 4, Mississippi	**4.04**	75.2	17.5	82.5	18.9	7.1	85.3	25,419	3.83	4.30	4.00
384	CD 6, Ohio	**4.04**	76.2	13.5	86.5	17.6	6.1	84.5	23,907	4.26	4.29	3.57
385	CD 19, Texas	**4.01**	76.8	21.4	78.6	21.6	6.8	82.9	23,887	4.49	3.97	3.57
386	CD 1, Mississippi	**3.99**	75.4	21.7	78.3	16.9	5.7	86.5	25,377	3.90	4.10	3.98
387	CD 9, Texas	**3.99**	78.6	27.0	73.0	21.1	7.2	80.2	23,022	5.25	3.41	3.31
388	CD 4, Louisiana	**3.99**	75.3	16.7	83.3	18.1	5.9	83.3	25,702	3.88	4.03	4.07
389	CD 18, Ohio	**3.98**	77.3	17.7	82.3	12.5	4.7	81.6	24,498	4.72	3.48	3.74
390	CD 2, New Mexico	**3.95**	78.0	21.8	78.2	18.4	7.5	85.8	21,047	5.02	4.16	2.69
391	CD 3, Oklahoma	**3.95**	76.0	15.0	85.0	20.2	6.1	82.7	23,899	4.15	4.14	3.57
392	CD 2, Alabama	**3.95**	75.7	18.7	81.3	19.6	7.2	82.2	25,026	4.04	3.93	3.89
393	CD 13, Michigan	**3.95**	75.4	22.9	77.1	14.9	6.6	90.8	23,470	3.93	4.47	3.44
394	CD 3, Louisiana	**3.94**	75.7	23.7	76.3	14.0	3.6	80.5	28,055	4.03	3.11	4.68
395	CD 1, Georgia	**3.93**	75.1	17.9	82.1	18.9	6.9	82.5	25,652	3.78	3.96	4.06
396	CD 20, Texas	**3.92**	78.6	24.9	75.1	15.0	4.5	83.4	22,157	5.24	3.48	3.04
397	CD 13, Texas	**3.92**	76.4	19.0	81.0	18.1	5.4	81.3	24,506	4.33	3.68	3.74
398	CD 30, Texas	**3.90**	78.5	33.4	66.6	17.0	5.7	78.0	24,990	5.19	2.64	3.88
399	CD 1, Texas	**3.89**	76.1	18.6	81.4	19.0	5.7	82.6	23,836	4.21	3.90	3.55
400	CD 27, Texas	**3.88**	78.9	28.1	71.9	17.1	5.8	83.1	21,394	5.38	3.45	2.80
401	CD 7, Louisiana	**3.87**	74.8	21.5	78.5	18.5	5.1	82.3	26,429	3.65	3.68	4.27
402	CD 3, Florida	**3.86**	77.5	20.7	79.3	13.9	4.8	83.7	22,543	4.77	3.66	3.16
403	CD 1, Pennsylvania	**3.86**	74.5	24.9	75.1	17.5	7.6	85.1	25,864	3.55	3.91	4.12
404	CD 1, Tennessee	**3.81**	75.7	20.5	79.5	17.8	6.3	87.0	22,354	4.05	4.28	3.11
405	CD 4, Illinois	**3.80**	78.5	37.4	62.6	20.1	6.8	75.6	24,690	5.23	2.38	3.79
406	CD 43, California	**3.80**	77.6	31.9	68.1	11.7	2.8	83.8	23,957	4.83	2.98	3.59
407	CD 28, Texas	**3.78**	80.3	33.8	66.2	16.3	5.0	82.6	20,015	5.95	3.07	2.34
408	CD 31, California	**3.78**	80.8	41.6	58.4	18.4	4.9	86.4	18,913	6.16	3.23	1.95

AMERICAN HUMAN DEVELOPMENT INDEX

by Congressional District, Total Population *continued*

RANK	CONGRESSIONAL DISTRICT	HD INDEX	LIFE EXPECTANCY AT BIRTH (years)	LESS THAN HIGH SCHOOL (%)	AT LEAST HIGH SCHOOL DIPLOMA (%)	AT LEAST BACHELOR'S DEGREE (%)	GRADUATE OR PROFESSIONAL DEGREE (%)	SCHOOL ENROLLMENT (%)	MEDIAN EARNINGS (2009 dollars)	HEALTH INDEX	EDUCATION INDEX	INCOME INDEX
409	**CD 15, Texas**	**3.74**	80.7	36.0	64.0	14.7	4.7	82.2	19,696	6.13	2.85	2.23
410	**CD 18, California**	**3.73**	78.3	33.3	66.7	10.8	3.5	82.3	22,973	5.13	2.75	3.29
411	**CD 4, Arizona**	**3.70**	80.2	36.5	63.5	11.9	4.1	72.3	24,065	5.93	1.57	3.62
412	**CD 34, California**	**3.69**	80.8	46.1	53.9	11.2	2.9	82.1	21,293	6.16	2.14	2.77
413	**CD 8, Tennessee**	**3.69**	75.0	18.1	81.9	16.1	5.2	82.9	23,768	3.73	3.80	3.53
414	**CD 2, Louisiana**	**3.68**	75.9	20.6	79.4	18.4	7.0	81.6	22,601	4.13	3.73	3.18
415	**CD 12, Georgia**	**3.66**	75.4	20.0	80.0	15.5	5.6	83.0	23,150	3.91	3.72	3.35
416	**CD 3, Alabama**	**3.61**	74.7	21.4	78.6	19.4	7.7	84.3	22,560	3.61	4.06	3.17
417	**CD 2, Georgia**	**3.55**	74.6	22.0	78.0	15.4	5.6	80.8	24,296	3.58	3.38	3.68
418	**CD 1, North Carolina**	**3.53**	75.0	23.3	76.7	13.4	4.1	86.9	21,997	3.75	3.83	2.99
419	**CD 5, Louisiana**	**3.52**	75.0	21.1	78.9	17.2	5.6	80.1	23,299	3.76	3.41	3.39
420	**CD 6, South Carolina**	**3.52**	75.3	21.2	78.8	15.9	5.5	82.7	22,154	3.86	3.64	3.04
421	**CD 4, Arkansas**	**3.50**	75.1	19.7	80.3	15.0	4.3	84.1	21,856	3.78	3.78	2.95
422	**CD 9, Virginia**	**3.50**	75.7	23.9	76.1	16.6	6.3	82.6	21,599	4.06	3.58	2.87
423	**CD 4, Tennessee**	**3.50**	75.9	22.3	77.7	13.4	4.7	79.5	22,898	4.13	3.09	3.27
424	**CD 1, Kentucky**	**3.50**	75.5	21.6	78.4	13.1	5.4	80.7	22,924	3.94	3.27	3.28
425	**CD 7, Alabama**	**3.46**	74.7	20.5	79.5	16.8	5.5	82.7	22,125	3.63	3.71	3.03
426	**CD 1, Arkansas**	**3.39**	74.8	21.2	78.8	13.3	4.2	82.8	22,153	3.66	3.48	3.04
427	**CD 4, Alabama**	**3.37**	74.3	25.0	75.0	13.2	5.0	77.5	25,153	3.45	2.75	3.92
428	**CD 2, Mississippi**	**3.34**	73.6	23.6	76.4	18.6	6.1	87.2	20,962	3.17	4.19	2.66
429	**CD 2, Oklahoma**	**3.33**	74.5	18.0	82.0	14.4	4.9	80.7	21,913	3.55	3.48	2.97
430	**CD 8, Missouri**	**3.24**	75.1	22.8	77.2	14.5	5.8	80.3	21,103	3.78	3.25	2.71
431	**CD 29, Texas**	**3.23**	78.2	46.2	53.8	6.8	2.0	76.8	22,932	5.09	1.32	3.28
432	**CD 16, New York**	**3.20**	79.0	41.6	58.4	10.6	2.9	84.3	17,995	5.43	2.57	1.60
433	**CD 3, West Virginia**	**3.16**	72.9	22.8	77.2	13.8	5.3	80.6	23,206	2.89	3.24	3.36
434	**CD 5, Kentucky**	**2.82**	73.6	31.4	68.6	10.6	4.7	80.1	21,031	3.15	2.63	2.68
435	**CD 20, California**	**2.60**	77.5	46.2	53.8	7.0	1.8	75.5	18,616	4.80	1.18	1.84
436	**CD 5, Pennsylvania**	**...**	78.5	12.5	87.5	19.2	8.0	83.0	...	5.20	4.32	...

AMERICAN HUMAN DEVELOPMENT INDEX

by Top 10 Metropolitan Areas (MSAs), Total Population

RANK	METROPOLITAN AREA	HD INDEX	LIFE EXPECTANCY AT BIRTH (years)	LESS THAN HIGH SCHOOL (%)	AT LEAST HIGH SCHOOL DIPLOMA (%)	AT LEAST BACHELOR'S DEGREE (%)	GRADUATE OR PROFESSIONAL DEGREE (%)	SCHOOL ENROLLMENT (%)	MEDIAN EARNINGS (2009 dollars)	HEALTH INDEX	EDUCATION INDEX	INCOME INDEX
	United States	**5.17**	78.6	15.0	85.0	27.7	10.2	87.3	29,755	5.25	5.15	5.09
1	**Washington, DC**	**6.94**	80.3	10.7	89.3	46.8	21.9	92.4	42,556	5.97	7.29	7.57
2	**Boston**	**6.55**	80.5	10.1	89.9	41.9	18.6	92.7	37,138	6.06	6.98	6.63
3	**New York**	**6.26**	81.0	16.2	83.8	35.3	14.5	90.9	36,466	6.26	6.03	6.50
4	**Philadelphia**	**5.70**	77.7	12.4	87.6	32.1	12.6	90.4	35,523	4.87	5.93	6.32
5	**Chicago**	**5.61**	79.0	14.6	85.5	33.0	12.5	88.7	32,618	5.43	5.68	5.73
6	**Los Angeles**	**5.60**	81.1	23.2	76.8	29.9	10.5	90.6	30,349	6.29	5.27	5.23
7	**Atlanta**	**5.53**	78.5	12.7	87.4	34.6	11.9	88.4	32,173	5.20	5.77	5.63
8	**Miami**	**5.46**	81.0	17.3	82.7	29.5	10.6	88.9	28,443	6.26	5.33	4.78
9	**Dallas**	**5.11**	78.5	18.8	81.2	29.6	9.5	84.9	30,834	5.23	4.78	5.34
10	**Houston**	**5.02**	78.2	19.9	80.1	28.2	9.3	84.4	31,079	5.07	4.60	5.39

AMERICAN HUMAN DEVELOPMENT INDEX

by Top 10 Metropolitan Areas (MSAs) with Constituent CDs

METROPOLITAN AREA	HD INDEX	LIFE EXPECTANCY AT BIRTH (years)	LESS THAN HIGH SCHOOL (%)	AT LEAST HIGH SCHOOL DIPLOMA (%)	AT LEAST BACHELOR'S DEGREE (%)	GRADUATE OR PROFESSIONAL DEGREE (%)	SCHOOL ENROLLMENT (%)	MEDIAN EARNINGS (2009 dollars)	HEALTH INDEX	EDUCATION INDEX	INCOME INDEX	GINI
United States	5.17	78.6	15.0	85.0	27.7	10.2	87.3	29,755	5.25	5.15	5.09	0.469
Atlanta MSA	5.53	78.5	12.7	87.4	34.6	11.9	88.4	32,173	5.20	5.77	5.63	0.451
CD 3, Georgia	4.90	76.5	13.7	86.3	24.7	8.6	87.3	30,738	4.38	5.02	5.31	0.422
CD 4, Georgia	5.10	79.3	15.8	84.2	29.9	10.5	83.9	28,870	5.55	4.86	4.88	0.427
CD 5, Georgia	5.82	78.4	14.6	85.4	45.2	18.4	89.6	32,626	5.15	6.58	5.73	0.554
CD 6, Georgia	6.79	79.1	6.9	93.1	51.7	17.5	93.8	40,827	5.44	7.64	7.28	0.451
CD 7, Georgia	5.76	79.7	12.2	87.8	34.1	10.8	90.1	32,396	5.69	5.91	5.68	0.409
CD 8, Georgia	4.06	75.1	20.0	80.0	19.0	6.9	85.7	26,074	3.79	4.22	4.17	0.46
CD 9, Georgia	4.32	77.3	21.7	78.3	20.1	6.7	81.2	27,555	4.72	3.69	4.56	0.451
CD 11, Georgia	4.81	76.9	15.8	84.2	24.9	8.0	85.6	30,148	4.53	4.71	5.18	0.441
CD 13, Georgia	5.18	78.1	13.6	86.4	25.9	8.6	87.4	31,125	5.04	5.09	5.40	0.394
Boston MSA	6.55	80.5	10.1	89.9	41.9	18.6	92.7	37,138	6.06	6.98	6.63	0.468
CD 1, Massachusetts	5.52	79.3	10.7	89.3	29.8	11.8	90.1	30,164	5.54	5.82	5.18	0.431
CD 2, Massachusetts	5.53	78.8	13.1	86.9	27.3	9.8	88.8	33,394	5.32	5.38	5.89	0.428
CD 3, Massachusetts	6.14	79.5	12.5	87.5	37.1	14.3	91.3	36,356	5.62	6.32	6.48	0.449
CD 4, Massachusetts	6.30	79.9	13.3	86.7	40.5	19.6	91.1	36,282	5.78	6.64	6.46	0.506
CD 5, Massachusetts	6.45	80.8	12.0	88.0	38.4	16.7	90.1	38,094	6.17	6.37	6.80	0.462
CD 6, Massachusetts	6.52	80.1	8.9	91.1	40.7	16.2	91.8	38,693	5.86	6.78	6.91	0.457
CD 7, Massachusetts	6.82	81.3	11.2	88.8	43.3	21.0	93.1	38,766	6.38	7.15	6.92	0.489
CD 8, Massachusetts	6.22	80.4	16.4	83.6	45.2	22.7	95.8	30,527	6.02	7.37	5.27	0.529
CD 9, Massachusetts	6.56	80.3	10.0	90.0	39.0	16.4	93.0	38,799	5.96	6.80	6.93	0.452
CD 10, Massachusetts	6.40	80.7	5.4	94.6	39.4	15.0	89.6	36,384	6.13	6.58	6.48	0.452
CD 1, New Hampshire	5.74	79.7	9.1	90.9	33.6	11.4	87.0	32,886	5.73	5.70	5.78	0.425
CD 2, New Hampshire	5.74	79.6	9.1	90.9	33.1	12.6	89.3	31,736	5.68	5.99	5.54	0.412
Chicago MSA	5.61	79.0	14.6	85.5	33.0	12.5	88.7	32,618	5.43	5.68	5.73	0.465
CD 1, Illinois	4.81	78.5	16.5	83.5	21.0	8.1	88.0	26,994	5.23	4.78	4.41	0.477
CD 2, Illinois	5.27	78.6	15.7	84.3	22.4	8.0	92.1	30,493	5.23	5.33	5.26	0.44
CD 3, Illinois	5.18	78.5	19.4	80.6	23.5	8.3	88.2	31,582	5.23	4.80	5.50	0.436
CD 4, Illinois	3.80	78.5	37.4	62.6	20.1	6.8	75.6	24,690	5.23	2.38	3.79	0.457
CD 5, Illinois	5.89	78.5	16.9	83.1	39.1	15.4	89.8	35,696	5.23	6.09	6.35	0.468
CD 6, Illinois	6.29	80.8	10.8	89.2	36.8	12.3	91.4	35,896	6.17	6.30	6.39	0.418
CD 7, Illinois	5.76	78.5	16.3	83.7	38.2	17.5	86.1	35,395	5.23	5.76	6.29	0.57
CD 8, Illinois	6.08	79.8	10.1	89.9	36.0	12.7	87.4	37,111	5.75	5.87	6.62	0.412
CD 9, Illinois	6.32	78.5	13.0	87.0	43.9	18.9	97.3	35,281	5.23	7.47	6.27	0.486
CD 10, Illinois	6.56	79.5	10.5	89.5	50.5	21.9	91.4	37,602	5.64	7.34	6.71	0.503
CD 11, Illinois	4.97	78.5	11.6	88.4	21.5	6.7	85.4	29,529	5.21	4.67	5.04	0.402
CD 13, Illinois	6.84	80.3	6.8	93.2	45.9	17.8	93.6	40,271	5.96	7.38	7.19	0.437
CD 14, Illinois	5.56	80.0	14.7	85.3	30.2	10.4	88.5	31,169	5.84	5.42	5.41	0.421
CD 16, Illinois	5.22	79.5	12.7	87.3	23.6	7.7	85.9	30,250	5.63	4.82	5.20	0.424
CD 1, Indiana	4.82	76.9	12.1	87.9	19.9	6.1	86.5	30,448	4.54	4.68	5.25	0.42
CD 2, Indiana	4.49	77.7	16.1	83.9	19.4	7.2	85.1	26,335	4.86	4.36	4.24	0.436
CD 1, Wisconsin	5.41	78.8	10.6	89.4	24.7	7.7	90.4	31,300	5.35	5.45	5.44	0.407
Dallas MSA	5.11	78.5	18.8	81.2	29.6	9.5	84.9	30,834	5.23	4.78	5.34	0.461
CD 3, Texas	6.19	80.7	12.7	87.3	41.6	13.3	88.3	35,504	6.12	6.13	6.31	0.445
CD 4, Texas	4.52	77.4	15.1	84.9	21.9	6.3	84.4	27,022	4.75	4.40	4.42	0.445
CD 5, Texas	4.20	76.6	20.8	79.2	18.8	6.2	81.7	27,213	4.43	3.70	4.47	0.449
CD 6, Texas	4.89	77.4	16.4	83.6	24.9	7.4	87.6	29,414	4.77	4.89	5.01	0.426
CD 12, Texas	4.56	77.4	21.9	78.1	22.9	7.3	81.7	29,400	4.77	3.89	5.00	0.433
CD 17, Texas	4.17	77.7	19.4	80.6	21.8	7.1	85.2	23,008	4.88	4.33	3.31	0.476
CD 24, Texas	5.73	78.5	13.0	87.0	36.4	11.6	88.3	34,782	5.20	5.81	6.17	0.449
CD 26, Texas	5.43	78.7	15.2	84.8	30.8	9.3	88.1	32,346	5.29	5.34	5.67	0.442
CD 30, Texas	3.90	78.5	33.4	66.6	17.0	5.7	78.0	24,990	5.19	2.64	3.88	0.469

AMERICAN HUMAN DEVELOPMENT INDEX

by Top 10 Metropolitan Areas (MSAs) with Constituent CDs *continued*

METROPOLITAN AREA	HD INDEX	LIFE EXPECTANCY AT BIRTH (years)	LESS THAN HIGH SCHOOL (%)	AT LEAST HIGH SCHOOL DIPLOMA (%)	AT LEAST BACHELOR'S DEGREE (%)	GRADUATE OR PROFESSIONAL DEGREE (%)	SCHOOL ENROLLMENT (%)	MEDIAN EARNINGS (2009 dollars)	HEALTH INDEX	EDUCATION INDEX	INCOME INDEX	GINI
CD 32, Texas	4.93	78.5	26.0	74.0	36.1	13.1	83.0	28,905	5.19	4.70	4.89	0.56
Houston MSA	5.02	78.2	19.9	80.1	28.2	9.3	84.4	31,079	5.07	4.60	5.39	0.476
CD 2, Texas	5.00	76.8	15.6	84.4	23.7	6.5	86.6	32,876	4.50	4.71	5.78	0.44
CD 7, Texas	6.69	78.2	8.3	91.7	51.1	19.6	92.9	41,838	5.09	7.54	7.45	0.516
CD 8, Texas	4.51	76.5	15.7	84.3	21.4	6.1	81.4	29,899	4.39	4.01	5.12	0.461
CD 9, Texas	3.99	78.6	27.0	73.0	21.1	7.2	80.2	23,022	5.25	3.41	3.31	0.453
CD 10, Texas	5.56	78.7	12.9	87.1	35.0	11.4	83.9	34,629	5.29	5.26	6.14	0.44
CD 14, Texas	4.79	77.2	16.5	83.5	24.2	7.4	84.7	30,137	4.68	4.52	5.18	0.453
CD 18, Texas	4.10	78.2	31.3	68.7	18.2	6.2	80.4	25,973	5.09	3.07	4.15	0.468
CD 22, Texas	5.96	79.0	12.9	87.1	34.9	11.6	89.0	37,248	5.42	5.83	6.65	0.409
CD 29, Texas	3.23	78.2	46.2	53.8	6.8	2.0	76.8	22,932	5.09	1.32	3.28	0.419
Los Angeles MSA	5.60	81.1	23.2	76.8	29.9	10.5	90.6	30,349	6.29	5.27	5.23	0.487
CD 22, California	4.80	77.9	18.4	81.6	20.2	6.1	85.6	29,964	4.95	4.30	5.14	0.444
CD 25, California	5.37	79.9	18.4	81.6	21.6	6.2	88.8	31,994	5.79	4.73	5.59	0.423
CD 26, California	6.43	79.5	11.5	88.5	34.9	14.7	97.8	37,263	5.62	7.01	6.65	0.454
CD 27, California	5.56	80.8	19.9	80.1	27.9	8.9	90.0	30,778	6.16	5.19	5.32	0.452
CD 28, California	4.80	80.8	30.6	69.4	27.5	8.8	84.9	25,878	6.16	4.12	4.12	0.519
CD 29, California	6.36	80.8	18.0	82.0	37.4	14.0	100.8	33,375	6.16	7.04	5.88	0.478
CD 30, California	7.71	80.8	6.2	93.8	57.6	25.6	97.7	46,977	6.16	8.72	8.25	0.56
CD 31, California	3.78	80.8	41.6	58.4	18.4	4.9	86.4	18,913	6.16	3.23	1.95	0.473
CD 32, California	4.55	80.8	34.8	65.2	16.0	4.6	88.5	24,918	6.16	3.65	3.86	0.398
CD 33, California	5.23	80.8	22.2	77.8	31.7	10.3	90.4	26,018	6.16	5.37	4.16	0.524
CD 34, California	3.69	80.8	46.1	53.9	11.2	2.9	82.1	21,293	6.16	2.14	2.77	0.46
CD 35, California	4.45	80.8	31.7	68.3	15.9	5.5	84.2	24,909	6.16	3.34	3.86	0.476
CD 36, California	6.72	80.8	13.3	86.7	41.9	15.1	97.9	37,694	6.16	7.27	6.73	0.49
CD 37, California	4.64	80.8	29.5	70.5	18.6	5.1	89.5	24,118	6.16	4.13	3.63	0.457
CD 38, California	4.59	80.8	33.0	67.0	14.5	3.9	86.2	26,374	6.16	3.37	4.25	0.407
CD 39, California	4.82	80.8	31.9	68.1	16.6	4.5	87.5	27,716	6.16	3.70	4.60	0.405
CD 40, California	5.99	82.1	18.6	81.4	31.2	9.7	90.8	32,671	6.72	5.52	5.74	0.425
CD 42, California	6.87	80.8	10.3	89.7	38.2	12.4	97.1	41,529	6.18	7.02	7.40	0.405
CD 44, California	5.31	80.0	20.1	79.9	25.7	9.1	86.2	31,241	5.83	4.68	5.43	0.441
CD 46, California	7.17	81.8	10.3	89.7	41.7	15.6	100.5	40,927	6.58	7.64	7.30	0.46
CD 47, California	4.11	82.1	44.7	55.3	12.6	3.3	83.7	22,451	6.72	2.46	3.14	0.387
CD 48, California	7.66	82.1	7.1	92.9	51.7	20.4	99.0	44,803	6.72	8.33	7.93	0.495
Miami MSA	5.46	81.0	17.3	82.7	29.5	10.6	88.9	28,443	6.26	5.33	4.78	0.493
CD 16, Florida	4.79	80.2	16.2	83.8	22.5	8.0	83.4	25,755	5.93	4.35	4.09	0.486
CD 17, Florida	4.43	80.9	26.2	73.8	17.3	5.8	84.6	23,237	6.20	3.71	3.37	0.436
CD 18, Florida	5.13	80.6	23.1	76.9	33.9	13.4	87.8	25,474	6.09	5.28	4.01	0.57
CD 19, Florida	5.91	81.1	10.7	89.3	30.4	10.8	93.3	30,516	6.31	6.16	5.26	0.478
CD 20, Florida	6.25	80.6	9.5	90.5	36.6	14.2	93.1	34,153	6.09	6.62	6.04	0.486
CD 21, Florida	5.20	80.9	20.7	79.3	27.9	9.4	89.4	26,470	6.22	5.12	4.28	0.472
CD 22, Florida	6.31	81.1	8.0	92.0	38.9	14.1	91.3	34,194	6.28	6.58	6.05	0.538
CD 23, Florida	4.32	80.8	26.5	73.5	17.4	5.4	80.9	23,707	6.18	3.27	3.51	0.435
CD 25, Florida	5.35	81.7	21.3	78.7	25.9	8.7	87.3	28,396	6.54	4.73	4.76	0.449
New York MSA	6.26	81.0	16.2	83.8	35.3	14.5	90.9	36,466	6.26	6.03	6.50	0.503
CD 3, New Jersey	6.17	79.4	8.3	91.7	31.0	10.9	90.0	39,183	5.57	5.93	7.00	0.425
CD 4, New Jersey	5.95	79.6	12.4	87.6	30.1	10.4	90.4	36,119	5.68	5.74	6.43	0.429
CD 5, New Jersey	7.11	81.0	6.4	93.6	43.2	15.7	92.6	45,395	6.24	7.06	8.02	0.443
CD 6, New Jersey	6.10	80.3	12.4	87.6	33.8	12.0	90.3	35,906	5.95	5.96	6.39	0.435
CD 7, New Jersey	7.31	80.7	7.9	92.1	45.9	19.2	95.1	46,891	6.14	7.55	8.24	0.445
CD 8, New Jersey	5.76	78.9	16.8	83.2	33.0	11.4	89.7	35,387	5.36	5.64	6.29	0.49

AMERICAN HUMAN DEVELOPMENT INDEX

by Top 10 Metropolitan Area (MSAs) with Constituent CDs *continued*

METROPOLITAN AREA	HD INDEX	LIFE EXPECTANCY AT BIRTH (years)	LESS THAN HIGH SCHOOL (%)	AT LEAST HIGH SCHOOL DIPLOMA (%)	AT LEAST BACHELOR'S DEGREE (%)	GRADUATE OR PROFESSIONAL DEGREE (%)	SCHOOL ENROLLMENT (%)	MEDIAN EARNINGS (2009 dollars)	HEALTH INDEX	EDUCATION INDEX	INCOME INDEX	GINI
CD 9, New Jersey	**6.47**	81.5	13.7	86.3	37.0	12.6	87.3	40,478	6.44	5.75	7.22	0.432
CD 10, New Jersey	**5.14**	78.6	19.5	80.5	21.2	7.1	89.8	30,927	5.23	4.82	5.36	0.473
CD 11, New Jersey	**7.33**	80.6	8.0	92.0	47.7	19.3	95.4	46,761	6.09	7.67	8.22	0.456
CD 12, New Jersey	**7.28**	80.0	6.8	93.2	48.0	21.9	95.6	46,142	5.85	7.87	8.13	0.452
CD 13, New Jersey	**5.15**	79.6	25.1	74.9	26.9	9.8	84.6	31,162	5.68	4.36	5.41	0.497
CD 1, New York	**6.41**	80.2	9.8	90.2	32.2	14.9	90.8	39,847	5.91	6.20	7.11	0.434
CD 2, New York	**6.33**	80.3	10.6	89.4	35.5	15.2	90.9	37,545	5.97	6.33	6.70	0.406
CD 3, New York	**6.79**	81.5	8.4	91.6	37.6	16.1	90.2	41,662	6.46	6.49	7.42	0.437
CD 4, New York	**6.57**	81.9	14.0	86.0	36.3	15.6	91.4	37,919	6.64	6.29	6.77	0.423
CD 5, New York	**6.30**	82.7	20.1	79.9	37.1	14.7	93.1	32,841	6.94	6.20	5.77	0.507
CD 6, New York	**5.90**	82.9	22.1	77.9	22.2	7.1	94.1	31,277	7.06	5.22	5.43	0.406
CD 7, New York	**5.40**	80.8	24.9	75.1	23.2	7.6	89.7	31,038	7.00	4.67	5.38	0.428
CD 8, New York	**7.48**	82.0	14.4	85.6	52.9	25.0	95.3	44,706	6.67	7.85	7.91	0.612
CD 9, New York	**6.57**	82.4	14.7	85.3	33.9	12.7	93.4	37,079	6.85	6.24	6.61	0.453
CD 10, New York	**5.72**	81.3	21.8	78.2	23.9	9.1	90.8	32,824	6.38	5.02	5.77	0.497
CD 11, New York	**5.98**	81.3	18.4	81.6	31.4	13.9	92.3	32,299	6.38	5.90	5.66	0.509
CD 12, New York	**5.08**	81.9	32.5	67.5	25.8	9.2	80.9	29,843	6.60	3.54	5.11	0.513
CD 13, New York	**6.09**	80.6	17.2	82.8	26.8	10.3	90.4	38,103	6.10	5.37	6.80	0.439
CD 14, New York	**8.79**	82.8	8.7	91.3	65.7	30.3	100.5	60,099	6.98	9.44	9.96	0.564
CD 15, New York	**5.87**	82.6	28.4	71.6	34.5	17.2	91.5	29,608	6.91	5.64	5.05	0.574
CD 16, New York	**3.20**	79.0	41.6	58.4	10.6	2.9	84.3	17,995	5.43	2.57	1.60	0.477
CD 17, New York	**6.00**	80.6	17.5	82.5	32.1	13.9	92.0	33,901	6.08	5.93	5.99	0.465
CD 18, New York	**7.12**	81.9	12.6	87.4	48.1	25.6	90.7	42,141	6.63	7.23	7.50	0.548
CD 19, New York	**6.59**	80.3	9.1	90.9	36.9	16.2	92.3	40,082	5.95	6.65	7.15	0.45
CD 10, Pennsylvania	**4.53**	78.2	12.7	87.3	20.1	7.7	83.5	25,832	5.09	4.40	4.11	0.432
Philadelphia MSA	**5.70**	77.7	12.4	87.6	32.1	12.6	90.4	35,523	4.87	5.93	6.32	0.464
CD (at Large), Delaware	**5.33**	78.3	12.8	87.2	27.5	10.8	88.4	31,320	5.13	5.40	5.44	0.447
CD 1, Maryland	**5.57**	77.4	10.5	89.5	29.8	11.1	88.2	35,808	4.76	5.59	6.37	0.425
CD 1, New Jersey	**5.34**	77.9	13.6	86.4	24.8	8.1	87.4	34,272	4.94	5.01	6.07	0.416
CD 3, New Jersey	**6.17**	79.4	8.3	91.7	31.0	10.9	90.0	39,183	5.57	5.93	7.00	0.425
CD 4, New Jersey	**5.95**	79.6	12.4	87.6	30.1	10.4	90.4	36,119	5.68	5.74	6.43	0.429
CD 2, New Jersey	**5.14**	77.6	15.6	84.4	22.3	7.1	91.0	31,279	4.82	5.17	5.43	0.428
CD 1, Pennsylvania	**3.86**	74.5	24.9	75.1	17.5	7.6	85.1	25,864	3.55	3.91	4.12	0.493
CD 2, Pennsylvania	**4.81**	74.4	18.2	81.8	27.9	13.5	94.6	29,088	3.50	5.99	4.93	0.525
CD 6, Pennsylvania	**6.23**	80.1	10.1	89.9	40.5	16.0	89.1	36,163	5.86	6.40	6.44	0.464
CD 7, Pennsylvania	**6.58**	78.6	7.1	92.9	41.5	16.4	95.9	40,026	5.24	7.36	7.14	0.446
CD 8, Pennsylvania	**6.23**	79.5	7.9	92.1	33.5	13.0	90.4	38,410	5.62	6.20	6.86	0.414
CD 13, Pennsylvania	**5.77**	77.3	13.1	86.9	32.6	12.6	89.6	38,130	4.69	5.83	6.81	0.452
CD 15, Pennsylvania	**5.47**	79.8	13.6	86.4	26.9	9.6	86.7	31,930	5.73	5.10	5.58	0.43
CD 16, Pennsylvania	**5.13**	79.9	17.1	82.9	26.5	9.2	81.6	30,540	5.80	4.33	5.27	0.44
Washington DC MSA	**6.94**	80.3	10.7	89.3	46.8	21.9	92.4	42,556	5.97	7.29	7.57	0.435
District of Columbia	**6.21**	75.6	14.2	85.8	48.2	26.7	92.7	40,342	4.00	7.44	7.20	0.54
CD 4, Maryland	**6.28**	79.6	12.4	87.6	35.8	15.3	89.9	39,244	5.67	6.15	7.01	0.394
CD 5, Maryland	**6.14**	77.4	9.7	90.3	31.2	12.6	92.8	41,649	4.73	6.27	7.42	0.366
CD 6, Maryland	**5.66**	78.5	11.7	88.3	27.8	10.1	89.7	34,857	5.23	5.57	6.19	0.418
CD 8, Maryland	**7.57**	83.2	10.7	89.3	55.2	29.6	94.3	41,263	7.15	8.21	7.36	0.473
CD 1, Virginia	**5.65**	78.8	11.1	88.9	30.3	11.5	86.7	34,875	5.33	5.44	6.19	0.394
CD 7, Virginia	**5.79**	78.3	11.4	88.6	36.1	12.6	88.3	35,588	5.14	5.91	6.33	0.437
CD 8, Virginia	**8.30**	83.7	10.4	89.6	58.9	29.3	97.1	51,260	7.35	8.69	8.86	0.433
CD 10, Virginia	**7.12**	80.8	10.1	89.9	49.1	20.2	91.7	44,732	6.17	7.27	7.91	0.427
CD 11, Virginia	**7.51**	81.6	8.6	91.4	52.7	24.0	93.2	46,680	6.50	7.83	8.21	0.385

AMERICAN HUMAN DEVELOPMENT INDEX
by Top 10 Metropolitan Area (MSAs), Race/Ethnicity

RANK	METROPOLITAN AREA	HD INDEX	LIFE EXPECTANCY AT BIRTH (years)	LESS THAN HIGH SCHOOL (%)	AT LEAST HIGH SCHOOL DIPLOMA (%)	AT LEAST BACHELOR'S DEGREE (%)	GRADUATE OR PROFESSIONAL DEGREE (%)	SCHOOL ENROLLMENT (%)	MEDIAN EARNINGS (2009 dollars)	HEALTH INDEX	EDUCATION INDEX	INCOME INDEX
	United States	5.17	78.6	15.0	85.0	27.7	10.2	87.3	29,755	5.25	5.15	5.09
AFRICAN AMERICAN												
1	Washington, DC	5.53	75.6	12.3	87.7	28.3	11.6	92.4	37,307	4.02	5.93	6.66
2	Boston	5.30	79.4	19.0	81.0	23.5	8.5	97.6	27,127	5.58	5.87	4.45
3	New York	5.21	78.4	19.7	80.3	20.7	7.1	92.0	31,331	5.17	5.03	5.45
4	Atlanta	4.90	75.6	12.6	87.4	26.9	9.0	90.0	30,180	4.02	5.49	5.19
5	Los Angeles	4.87	74.7	13.2	86.8	22.4	7.8	94.3	30,775	3.63	5.67	5.32
6	Dallas	4.33	74.4	13.8	86.2	21.8	6.5	88.6	27,576	3.48	4.94	4.56
7	Houston	4.17	73.8	15.0	85.0	21.2	7.0	88.0	27,141	3.24	4.81	4.45
8	Miami	4.05	76.2	24.6	75.4	17.6	5.7	88.9	24,092	4.26	4.27	3.63
9	Philadelphia	4.04	73.1	18.1	81.9	16.5	5.9	90.1	27,358	2.97	4.65	4.51
10	Chicago	4.01	72.9	17.5	82.5	19.9	6.7	88.2	27,274	2.89	4.65	4.49
ASIAN AMERICAN												
1	Chicago	8.71	90.7	9.5	90.5	61.9	24.6	102.0	40,038	10.00	8.98	7.15
2	Washington, DC	8.69	88.9	11.5	88.5	60.7	28.9	106.3	42,116	9.54	9.03	7.50
3	Boston	8.33	91.0	16.1	83.9	56.5	32.4	102.3	34,955	10.00	8.79	6.21
4	New York	8.20	90.4	18.3	81.7	51.8	19.8	98.8	38,162	10.00	7.79	6.81
5	Dallas	8.09	87.8	12.7	87.3	54.9	25.7	103.9	37,030	9.09	8.58	6.61
6	Houston	8.03	88.2	13.6	86.4	53.1	21.3	105.3	36,881	9.25	8.25	6.58
7	Philadelphia	7.87	87.8	17.2	82.8	53.2	25.1	103.2	35,111	9.10	8.27	6.24
8	Atlanta	7.75	89.4	13.6	86.4	50.5	22.2	98.0	31,771	9.75	7.96	5.54
9	Los Angeles	7.52	86.2	14.4	85.6	48.2	14.2	105.8	36,119	8.43	7.68	6.43
10	Miami	6.78	87.0	15.0	85.0	46.2	18.8	87.7	30,180	8.74	6.41	5.19
LATINO												
1	Miami	5.12	83.3	25.4	74.6	24.9	8.1	86.4	24,658	7.19	4.39	3.79
2	New York	4.90	85.2	34.9	65.1	15.7	5.1	82.3	24,518	8.00	2.96	3.75
3	Chicago	4.89	87.9	40.8	59.2	11.5	3.3	79.3	23,536	9.12	2.10	3.46
4	Washington, DC	4.69	82.8	38.3	61.7	23.1	8.7	78.1	26,334	7.00	2.83	4.24
5	Boston	4.54	83.0	34.9	65.1	17.5	6.1	81.3	23,931	7.06	2.97	3.58
6	Philadelphia	4.39	83.2	36.0	64.0	15.2	5.7	75.3	24,979	7.15	2.14	3.88
7	Los Angeles	4.25	84.1	46.0	54.0	10.1	2.8	83.8	21,698	7.55	2.28	2.90
8	Houston	4.07	84.0	45.5	54.5	10.7	3.0	77.1	22,399	7.49	1.59	3.12
9	Dallas	3.87	84.7	51.5	48.5	9.2	2.5	74.8	21,474	7.80	0.98	2.83
10	Atlanta	3.42	81.1	40.0	60.0	16.2	4.7	72.9	19,811	6.30	1.70	2.27
WHITE												
1	Washington, DC	7.99	81.5	4.6	95.4	57.6	28.1	94.5	52,150	6.44	8.54	8.98
2	New York	7.24	81.2	8.3	91.7	43.4	19.0	93.5	46,338	6.31	7.24	8.16
3	Los Angeles	7.21	80.3	6.2	93.8	43.7	17.1	97.5	44,998	5.96	7.70	7.96
4	Boston	6.87	80.4	7.0	93.0	44.4	19.4	93.0	40,915	6.01	7.30	7.30
5	Chicago	6.58	79.8	7.1	92.9	39.6	15.4	92.5	40,104	5.73	6.86	7.16
6	Miami	6.51	81.0	7.3	92.7	37.8	14.3	92.0	37,129	6.24	6.66	6.62
7	Philadelphia	6.32	78.8	8.9	91.1	36.0	14.1	91.9	40,026	5.33	6.49	7.14
8	Atlanta	6.25	78.9	8.8	91.2	40.0	13.7	89.8	38,897	5.39	6.42	6.95
9	Dallas	6.16	78.3	7.3	92.7	37.5	11.6	89.4	39,931	5.13	6.23	7.13
10	Houston	6.14	77.3	6.7	93.3	38.1	12.3	87.6	42,737	4.70	6.12	7.60

U.S. INDICATOR TABLES

Demographics

STATES	POPULATION 2008[1]	POPULATION UNDER 18 (%) 2008[2]	POPULATION OVER 65 (%) 2008[3]	URBAN POPULATION (%) 2000[4]	RURAL POPULATION (%) 2000[5]	AFRICAN AMERICAN (%) 2008[6]	ASIAN AMERICAN (%) 2008[7]	LATINO (%) 2008[8]	NATIVE AMERICAN (%) 2008[9]	NATIVE HAWAIIAN OR PACIFIC ISLANDER (%) 2008[10]	TWO OR MORE RACES OR SOME OTHER RACE (%)[11]	WHITE (%) 2008[12]
United States	304,059,728	24.3	12.8	79.0	21.0	12.1	4.4	15.4	0.7	0.1	1.9	65.4
Alabama	4,661,900	24.1	13.8	55.4	44.6	26.1	1.0	2.8	0.5	0.0	1.2	68.4
Alaska	686,293	26.2	7.3	65.6	34.4	3.4	4.6	6.2	12.5	0.5	7.3	65.6
Arizona	6,500,180	26.3	13.3	88.2	11.8	3.5	2.3	30.1	4.1	0.1	1.7	58.2
Arkansas	2,855,390	24.6	14.3	52.5	47.5	15.5	1.0	5.5	0.5	0.1	1.8	75.6
California	36,756,666	25.5	11.2	94.4	5.6	5.9	12.2	36.6	0.4	0.3	2.5	42.0
Colorado	4,939,456	24.4	10.3	84.5	15.5	3.6	2.5	20.2	0.6	0.1	2.2	70.8
Connecticut	3,501,252	23.2	13.7	87.7	12.3	9.0	3.4	12.0	0.2	0.0	1.8	73.6
Delaware	873,092	23.6	13.9	80.1	19.9	20.2	2.9	6.8	0.3	0.0	1.7	68.2
District of Columbia	591,833	18.9	11.9	100.0	0.0	52.8	3.3	8.6	0.3	0.1	2.0	32.8
Florida	18,328,340	21.8	17.4	89.3	10.7	14.8	2.2	21.0	0.2	0.0	1.6	60.1
Georgia	9,685,744	26.3	10.1	71.6	28.4	29.6	2.8	7.9	0.2	0.0	1.5	57.9
Hawaii	1,288,198	22.1	14.8	91.5	8.5	2.3	37.6	8.7	0.1	8.6	17.9	24.8
Idaho	1,523,816	27.1	12.0	66.4	33.6	0.5	1.2	10.2	0.9	0.1	2.1	85.1
Illinois	12,901,564	24.6	12.2	87.8	12.2	14.4	4.2	15.3	0.1	0.0	1.5	64.5
Indiana	6,376,792	24.9	12.8	70.8	29.2	8.5	1.3	5.2	0.2	0.0	1.8	83.1
Iowa	3,002,557	23.7	14.8	61.1	38.9	2.5	1.5	4.1	0.2	0.1	1.3	90.2
Kansas	2,802,134	25.0	13.1	71.4	28.6	5.5	2.1	9.1	0.6	0.1	2.4	80.2
Kentucky	4,269,245	23.6	13.3	55.8	44.2	7.4	1.0	2.3	0.1	0.1	1.3	87.8
Louisiana	4,410,796	25.1	12.2	72.6	27.4	31.7	1.5	3.4	0.6	0.0	1.1	61.8
Maine	1,316,456	20.9	15.1	40.2	59.8	0.9	0.8	1.0	0.5	0.0	1.6	95.2
Maryland	5,633,597	23.8	12.1	86.1	13.9	28.5	5.0	6.6	0.2	0.0	2.1	57.5
Massachusetts	6,497,967	22.0	13.4	91.4	8.6	5.7	4.9	8.6	0.2	0.0	2.1	78.5
Michigan	10,003,422	23.9	13.0	74.7	25.3	13.8	2.3	4.1	0.5	0.0	2.0	77.3
Minnesota	5,220,393	24.0	12.5	70.9	29.1	4.4	3.5	4.1	1.0	0.0	1.7	85.3
Mississippi	2,938,618	26.1	12.6	48.8	51.2	37.4	0.8	2.0	0.4	0.0	0.8	58.6
Missouri	5,911,605	24.0	13.6	69.4	30.6	11.1	1.4	3.2	0.3	0.1	1.9	82.1
Montana	967,440	22.8	14.2	54.1	45.9	0.5	0.6	2.8	5.9	0.1	2.2	87.9
Nebraska	1,783,432	25.1	13.5	69.8	30.2	4.0	1.5	7.8	0.7	0.0	1.8	84.2
Nevada	2,600,167	25.7	11.4	91.5	8.5	7.1	5.9	25.7	1.1	0.4	2.7	57.0
New Hampshire	1,315,809	22.3	12.9	59.3	40.7	0.9	2.0	2.6	0.1	0.0	1.3	93.0
New Jersey	8,682,661	23.6	13.3	94.4	5.6	13.0	7.6	16.3	0.1	0.0	1.5	61.4
New Mexico	1,984,356	25.3	13.1	75.0	25.0	1.9	1.3	44.9	8.6	0.0	1.7	41.6
New York	19,490,297	22.6	13.4	87.5	12.5	14.7	6.9	16.7	0.3	0.0	1.7	59.7
North Carolina	9,222,414	24.3	12.4	60.2	39.8	21.0	1.8	7.4	1.0	0.0	1.6	67.1
North Dakota	641,481	22.3	14.7	55.9	44.1	0.9	0.8	2.0	5.2	0.0	1.2	89.8
Ohio	11,485,910	23.8	13.7	77.4	22.6	11.6	1.5	2.6	0.2	0.0	1.7	82.4
Oklahoma	3,642,361	24.9	13.5	65.3	34.7	7.1	1.7	7.7	6.2	0.1	6.1	71.3
Oregon	3,790,060	22.9	13.3	78.7	21.3	1.7	3.4	11.0	0.9	0.2	2.9	79.9
Pennsylvania	12,448,279	22.2	15.3	77.1	22.9	10.1	2.4	4.8	0.1	0.0	1.4	81.2
Rhode Island	1,050,788	21.7	14.1	90.9	9.1	4.7	2.8	11.6	0.4	0.0	2.1	78.4
South Carolina	4,479,800	23.8	13.3	60.5	39.5	27.9	1.1	4.1	0.2	0.0	1.6	65.1
South Dakota	804,194	24.7	14.4	51.9	48.1	0.9	0.8	2.4	7.9	0.0	2.0	86.0
Tennessee	6,214,888	23.8	13.2	63.6	36.4	16.3	1.3	3.7	0.2	0.0	1.5	77.0
Texas	24,326,974	27.6	10.2	82.5	17.5	11.2	3.4	36.5	0.3	0.1	1.3	47.2
Utah	2,736,424	31.0	9.0	88.2	11.8	1.0	1.9	12.0	1.0	0.7	1.7	81.7
Vermont	621,270	20.8	13.9	38.2	61.8	0.7	1.2	1.2	0.2	0.0	1.7	95.0
Virginia	7,769,089	23.5	12.1	73.0	27.0	19.3	4.8	6.8	0.2	0.1	2.0	66.8
Washington	6,549,224	23.5	12.0	82.0	18.0	3.3	6.4	9.8	1.2	0.4	3.6	75.3
West Virginia	1,814,468	21.3	15.7	46.1	53.9	3.3	0.5	1.1	0.1	0.0	1.4	93.5
Wisconsin	5,627,968	23.4	13.3	68.3	31.7	5.7	2.0	5.1	0.8	0.0	1.4	84.9
Wyoming	532,668	24.1	12.3	65.1	34.9	1.0	0.7	7.7	1.7	0.0	2.2	86.7

1–3. U.S. Census Bureau, American Community Survey 2008. Table B01001.

4–5. U.S. Census Bureau. 2000 Census of Population and Housing. Table 29.

6–12. U.S. Census Bureau, American Community Survey 2008. Tables B03002.

A Long and Healthy Life

GROUPING	LIFE EXPECTANCY (years) 2007[1]	INFANT MORTALITY RATE (per 1,000 live births) 2003–2005[2]	LOW-BIRTH-WEIGHT INFANTS (%) 2007[3]	CHILD MORTALITY (per 100,000 population) 2007[4]	FOOD-INSECURE HOUSEHOLDS (%) 2007[5]	CHILD IMMUNIZATION RATE (%) 2006[6]	DIABETES (% age 18 and older) 2008[7]	OBESITY (% age 20 and older) 2008[8]	BIRTHS TO TEENAGERS (per 1,000 girls age 15–19) 2006[9]
United States	78.6	6.8	8.2	28.6	11.1	84.6	8.3	26.7	41.9
GENDER									
Women	81.2	...	...	25.7	...	...	...	25.6	...
Men	76.0	...	...	31.3	...	...	...	27.4	...
RACE/ETHNICITY									
African American	74.3	13.3	13.8	43.7	22.2	80.1	...	37.4	63.7
Asian American	87.3	4.8	8.1	21.2	...	...	...	...	...
Latino	83.5	5.6	6.9	25.2	20.1	84.9	...	28.1	83.0
Native American	75.1	8.4	7.5	46.4	...	82.0	...	...	...
White	78.7	5.7	7.2	25.6	7.9	85.0	...	25.4	26.6
STATE									
Alabama	75.2	9.0	10.4	31.2	11.9	83.1	11.2	32.2	53.5
Alaska	78.3	6.5	5.7	34.8	12.4	79.2	6.7	27.1	44.3
Arizona	79.9	6.7	7.1	28.9	12.0	84.6	7.8	25.6	62.0
Arkansas	76.1	8.3	9.1	45.9	14.4	81.4	9.5	29.5	62.3
California	80.4	5.2	6.9	23.5	10.2	86.8	8.5	24.3	39.9
Colorado	79.9	6.3	9.0	21.2	11.0	86.5	6.0	19.1	43.8
Connecticut	80.2	5.5	8.1	23.0	8.8	88.2	6.8	21.4	23.5
Delaware	78.3	9.0	9.3	17.2	8.6	84.3	8.3	27.8	41.9
District of Columbia	75.6	12.2	11.1	32.6	11.9	84.6	8.0	22.3	48.4
Florida	79.7	7.2	8.7	34.8	9.0	88.5	9.5	25.2	45.2
Georgia	77.1	8.4	9.1	32.7	13.0	79.0	9.9	27.8	54.2
Hawaii	81.5	6.7	8.0	29.6	8.4	81.5	8.2	23.1	40.5
Idaho	79.2	6.1	6.5	32.8	11.4	77.6	7.0	25.2	39.2
Illinois	78.8	7.5	8.5	26.7	9.5	82.2	8.3	26.9	39.5
Indiana	77.7	7.9	8.5	30.0	10.2	85.3	9.6	27.0	43.5
Iowa	79.7	5.4	6.8	27.5	11.7	84.2	7.0	26.7	32.9
Kansas	78.4	7.1	6.0	24.3	13.0	85.7	8.1	28.1	42.0
Kentucky	76.2	6.8	9.3	28.6	12.7	86.0	9.9	30.3	56.4
Louisiana	75.4	9.8	11.0	42.4	11.7	87.7	10.7	29.0	53.9
Maine	78.7	5.9	6.3	24.6	13.3	90.3	8.3	25.9	25.8
Maryland	78.1	8.0	9.1	32.5	8.6	89.1	8.7	26.7	33.6
Massachusetts	80.1	4.9	7.9	15.5	8.0	87.2	7.2	21.5	21.3
Michigan	77.9	8.0	8.2	24.0	11.8	86.4	9.1	29.5	33.8
Minnesota	80.9	4.8	6.7	23.1	9.5	87.3	5.9	25.2	27.9
Mississippi	74.8	10.7	12.3	54.2	17.4	82.4	11.3	33.4	68.4
Missouri	77.4	7.6	7.8	35.0	12.9	82.0	9.1	29.1	45.7
Montana	78.4	6.4	7.2	36.2	9.5	74.4	6.5	24.3	39.6
Nebraska	79.2	5.9	7.0	26.2	9.5	84.9	7.8	27.2	33.4
Nevada	77.6	5.9	8.2	34.8	10.4	76.0	8.6	25.6	55.8
New Hampshire	79.7	5.0	6.3	18.0	7.7	90.0	7.2	24.9	18.7
New Jersey	79.7	5.4	8.5	20.4	8.8	80.6	8.4	23.6	24.9
New Mexico	78.2	6.1	8.7	41.5	15.0	85.2	7.9	25.7	64.1
New York	80.4	6.0	8.2	22.3	9.9	84.4	8.4	25.1	25.7
North Carolina	77.2	8.6	9.2	28.7	12.6	84.1	9.3	29.5	49.7
North Dakota	80.1	6.4	6.3	28.3	6.5	81.0	7.6	27.8	26.5
Ohio	77.5	7.8	8.7	32.3	12.2	86.1	9.9	29.3	40.0
Oklahoma	75.6	7.9	8.2	40.9	13.0	78.7	10.1	31.0	59.6
Oregon	79.0	5.7	6.1	23.9	12.4	79.7	6.9	25.0	35.7
Pennsylvania	78.2	7.3	8.4	28.2	10.0	88.1	8.8	28.4	31.0
Rhode Island	79.3	6.2	8.0	10.3	10.9	88.4	7.4	22.1	27.8

GROUPING	PRACTICING PHYSICIANS (per 10,000 population) 2007[10]	SMOKING (% age 18 and older) 2008[11]	BINGE DRINKING (% adults in past 30 days) 2008[12]	WITHOUT HEALTH INSURANCE (%) 2007–2008[13]	MEDICARE ENROLLMENT (thousands) 2007[14]	MEDICAID RECIPIENTS (thousands) 2007[15]	MEDICAID ELIGIBILITY CUTOFF (income as % of poverty line) 2009[16]	STATE MEDICAID SPENDING (per recipient) 2008[17]	CHILDREN ON MEDICAID (% age 0–18) 2008[18]
United States	hh27.4	18.4	15.6	17.4	43,259	36,118	...	...	29.7
Women	...	16.7	10.0	15.7	...	...	...	...	...
Men	...	20.3	21.0	19.1	...	...	...	...	...
African American	...	21.2	11.0	20.6	...	...	...	...	...
Asian American	...	...	...	...	...	...	...	...	...
Latino	...	15.7	13.0	32.2	...	...	...	...	...
Native American	...	...	...	...	...	...	...	...	...
White	...	17.9	16.0	12.7	...	...	...	...	...
Alabama	21.6	22.1	12.0	13.7	789	546	24	8,059	30.9
Alaska	24.2	21.5	15.9	20.8	57	69	81	15,348	21.5
Arizona	22.3	15.9	15.6	21.0	841	528	106	9,930	32.5
Arkansas	20.4	22.3	12.6	19.2	496	363	17	8,826	44.8
California	26.1	14.0	15.6	20.4	4,369	5,107	106	7,054	33.0
Colorado	26.6	17.6	16.0	17.8	558	271	66	9,528	16.4
Connecticut	36.1	15.9	16.6	11.1	537	329	191	12,964	23.9
Delaware	26.2	17.8	17.9	12.6	136	82	121	12,085	24.9
District of Columbia	73.2	16.2	17.9	10.8	74	143	207	...	41.8
Florida	25.5	17.5	13.0	23.8	3,133	1,638	53	8,773	23.3
Georgia	21.4	19.5	14.0	19.3	1,111	1,185	50	6,256	30.0
Hawaii	31.7	15.4	17.6	9.1	189	41	100	25,902	27.1
Idaho	17.9	16.9	13.1	16.9	207	119	27	10,076	22.9
Illinois	27.7	21.3	19.4	14.6	1,741	1,454	185	9,508	29.1
Indiana	22.1	26.0	16.1	13.4	941	594	25	8,842	31.1
Iowa	21.4	18.8	20.2	10.7	500	308	83	9,390	25.1
Kansas	23.6	17.9	13.8	14.1	412	251	32	9,450	26.7
Kentucky	23.0	25.2	11.3	16.9	711	641	62	7,069	34.0
Louisiana	25.5	20.5	13.5	21.9	639	778	25	6,650	35.5
Maine	31.5	18.2	15.8	11.3	247	167	206	12,521	34.3
Maryland	40.0	14.9	13.8	14.4	723	399	116	14,080	21.9
Massachusetts	43.2	16.1	17.7	6.1	997	715	133	11,534	27.3
Michigan	28.1	20.5	17.7	13.1	1,541	1,172	64	8,319	29.1
Minnesota	28.4	17.6	19.8	9.6	729	455	215	14,154	21.7
Mississippi	18.1	22.7	10.8	20.7	469	510	44	6,192	41.4
Missouri	26.2	25.0	15.3	14.4	946	636	25	11,495	28.9
Montana	22.9	18.5	17.7	18.5	156	101	56	7,089	29.3
Nebraska	24.1	18.4	19.1	14.1	268	191	58	8,084	23.1
Nevada	19.6	22.2	18.8	20.2	318	109	88	10,431	15.7
New Hampshire	27.7	17.1	16.5	11.6	204	100	49	12,500	18.3
New Jersey	33.0	14.8	14.0	16.9	1,257	714	200	13,317	17.3
New Mexico	23.8	19.4	11.4	26.0	285	318	67	8,494	35.4
New York	38.2	16.8	14.7	15.3	2,841	3,281	150	9,461	34.3
North Carolina	24.7	20.9	12.9	18.1	1,359	1,130	49	9,287	30.3
North Dakota	24.5	18.1	21.6	12.5	105	61	59	8,902	20.4
Ohio	28.0	20.1	15.8	13.2	1,805	1,478	90	8,907	27.3
Oklahoma	20.7	24.7	12.2	18.4	565	358	47	9,469	34.7
Oregon	27.3	16.3	12.8	18.9	567	450	40	7,156	25.7
Pennsylvania	32.9	21.3	16.7	11.3	2,184	1,168	34	15,227	26.4
Rhode Island	36.8	17.4	17.5	12.8	175	130	181	14,131	28.3

U.S. INDICATOR TABLES

A Long and Healthy Life *continued*

GROUPING	LIFE EXPECTANCY (years) 2007[1]	INFANT MORTALITY RATE (per 1,000 live births) 2003–2005[2]	LOW-BIRTH-WEIGHT INFANTS (%) 2007[3]	CHILD MORTALITY (per 100,000 population) 2007[4]	FOOD-INSECURE HOUSEHOLDS (%) 2007[5]	CHILD IMMUNIZATION RATE (%) 2006[6]	DIABETES (% age 18 and older) 2008[7]	OBESITY (% age 20 and older) 2008[8]	BIRTHS TO TEENAGERS (per 1,000 girls age 15–19) 2006[9]
South Carolina	76.6	9.0	10.1	40.2	13.1	84.7	10.1	30.7	53.0
South Dakota	79.9	7.2	7.0	40.1	9.7	84.3	6.6	28.1	40.2
Tennessee	76.2	8.9	9.4	33.9	12.8	87.7	10.4	31.2	54.7
Texas	78.3	6.5	8.4	31.5	14.8	83.0	9.7	28.9	63.1
Utah	80.1	4.9	6.7	30.2	12.5	83.1	6.1	23.1	34.0
Vermont	79.7	5.4	6.2	23.1	10.2	79.8	6.4	23.3	20.8
Virginia	78.5	7.5	8.6	25.3	8.0	80.3	7.9	25.8	35.2
Washington	79.7	5.4	6.3	21.1	10.1	82.7	6.9	26.0	33.4
West Virginia	75.2	7.7	9.5	36.9	10.7	84.8	11.9	31.9	44.9
Wisconsin	79.3	6.3	7.0	26.1	9.0	88.2	7.2	26.1	30.9
Wyoming	77.6	7.0	9.1	27.7	9.9	73.7	7.4	25.2	47.3

1. Life expectancy at birth calculated using mortality data from the Centers for Disease Control and Prevention, NCHS, and population data from the U.S. Census Bureau.

2. Centers for Disease Control and Prevention, Infant Mortality Statistics from the 2005 Period Linked Birth/Infant Death Data Set, 2008. Table 3.

3. Centers for Disease Control and Prevention. Births: Preliminary Data for 2007, 2009. Tables 8 and 13. Percent of live births weighing less than 2,500 grams, or 5.5 lbs.

4. Calculated using mortality data from the Centers for Disease Control and Prevention, NCHS, and population data from the U.S. Census Bureau. Mortality and population counts are for children ages 1–4.

5. U.S. Department of Agriculture. Household Food Security in the United States, 2007. Tables 5 and 7.

6. Centers for Disease Control and Prevention, National Immunization Survey 2008. Table 3, "Coverage with Individual Vaccines and Vaccination Series by State."

7–8. Centers for Disease Control and Prevention, Behavioral Risk Factor Surveillance System, 2008. National data are not directly comparable with state data.

9. Center for Disease Control and Prevention, Births: Final Data for 2006, 2009: Table 8, Table 11.

10. Centers for Disease Control and Prevention. "Health, United States, 2009 with a Special Feature on Medical Technology." Table 107.

11. Centers for Disease Control and Prevention, Behavioral Risk Factor Surveillance System, 2008. Self-reported tobacco use.

GROUPING	PRACTICING PHYSICIANS (per 10,000 population) 2007[10]	SMOKING (% age 18 and older) 2008[11]	BINGE DRINKING (% adults in past 30 days) 2008[12]	WITHOUT HEALTH INSURANCE (%) 2007–2008[13]	MEDICARE ENROLLMENT (thousands) 2007[14]	MEDICAID RECIPIENTS (thousands) 2007[15]	MEDICAID ELIGIBILITY CUTOFF (income as % of poverty line) 2009[16]	STATE MEDICAID SPENDING (per recipient) 2008[17]	CHILDREN ON MEDICAID (% age 0–18) 2008[18]
South Carolina	22.9	20.0	12.3	18.6	697	503	89	8,897	27.4
South Dakota	22.4	17.5	17.8	13.3	129	77	52	9,104	23.8
Tennessee	25.9	23.1	10.5	17.1	975	1,409	129	5,034	34.5
Texas	21.4	18.5	14.7	27.7	2,708	2,572	26	4,657	30.7
Utah	20.9	9.3	8.2	14.1	254	152	44	10,487	14.9
Vermont	36.0	16.8	17.4	11.8	102	102	191	9,833	37.5
Virginia	26.9	16.4	13.7	15.3	1,045	623	29	8,093	19.5
Washington	26.8	15.7	15.1	13.3	873	621	74	9,211	26.0
West Virginia	25.5	26.5	8.8	17.1	367	395	33	5,461	37.4
Wisconsin	26.1	19.9	22.8	10.2	854	434	200	11,237	26.1
Wyoming	19.5	19.4	15.4	15.6	74	51	52	8,863	22.8

12. Centers for Disease Control and Prevention, Behavioral Risk Factor Surveillance System, 2008. Male binge drinking is more than five drinks on one occasion; for females, more than four drinks on one occasion.

13. Kaiser Family Foundation, Kaiser State Health Facts, statehealthfacts.org. Calculated by the Urban Institute and Kaiser Commission on Medicaid and the Uninsured estimates based on the Census Bureau's March 2008 and 2009 Current Population Survey (CPS: Annual Social and Economic Supplements). Accessed May 27, 2010. Estimates do not include the elderly.

14–15. Centers for Disease Control and Prevention, "Health, United States, 2009 with a Special Feature on Medical Technology." Tables 148–149.

16. The Kaiser Family Foundation, Kaiser State Facts, statehealthfacts.org. Based on "Where Are States Today: Medicaid and State-Funded Coverage Eligibility Levels for Low-Income Adults," Kaiser Commission on Medicaid and the Uninsured analysis of state policies through program websites and contacts with state officials, December 2009. Accessed May 27, 2010.

17. Calculated using expenditure figures from the National Association of State Budget Officers, State Expenditure Report, 2008. Table 28 and Medicaid recipient totals from the Centers for Disease Control and Prevention, "Health, United States 2009 with a Special Feature on Medical Technology."

18. Kaiser Family Foundation, Kaiser State Facts, statehealthfacts.org. Calculated by the Urban Institute and Kaiser Commission on Medicaid and the Uninsured estimates based on the Census Bureau's March 2008 and 2009 Current Population Survey (CPS: Annual Social and Economic Supplements). Accessed May 27, 2010.

U.S. INDICATOR TABLES

Access to Knowledge

GROUPING	LESS THAN HIGH SCHOOL (% 25 and older) 2008[1]	AT LEAST HIGH SCHOOL DIPLOMA (% 25 and older) 2008[2]	AT LEAST BACHELOR'S DEGREE (% 25 and older) 2008[3]	PRESCHOOL ENROLLMENT (% enrolled ages 3 and 4) 2008[4]	COMBINED GROSS ENROLLMENT RATIO (% enrolled ages 3 to 24) 2008[5]
United States	15.0	85.0	27.7	49.1	87.3
GENDER					
Women	14.4	85.6	27.0	...	90.8
Men	15.7	84.3	28.4	...	84.0
RACE/ETHNICITY					
African American	19.3	80.7	17.5	...	88.6
Asian American	14.9	85.1	49.7	...	102.1
Latino	39.2	60.8	12.9	...	79.7
Native American	24.4	75.6	12.7	...	80.4
White	9.9	90.1	30.7	...	88.6
STATE					
Alabama	18.1	81.9	22.0	46.9	83.6
Alaska	8.4	91.6	27.3	43.0	84.9
Arizona	16.2	83.8	25.1	32.4	84.2
Arkansas	18.0	82.0	18.8	49.8	83.0
California	19.8	80.2	29.6	50.8	89.5
Colorado	11.1	88.9	35.6	48.9	87.5
Connecticut	11.4	88.6	35.6	64.4	92.1
Delaware	12.8	87.2	27.5	47.3	88.4
District of Columbia	14.2	85.8	48.2	73.6	92.7
Florida	14.8	85.2	25.8	51.6	86.9
Georgia	16.1	83.9	27.5	50.9	86.1
Hawaii	9.7	90.3	29.1	54.6	85.0
Idaho	12.1	87.9	24.0	36.6	83.9
Illinois	14.1	85.9	29.9	56.0	88.6
Indiana	13.8	86.2	22.9	40.2	85.9
Iowa	9.7	90.3	24.3	50.6	87.3
Kansas	10.5	89.5	29.6	47.5	87.2
Kentucky	18.7	81.3	19.7	48.5	85.5
Louisiana	18.8	81.2	20.3	55.0	83.3
Maine	10.3	89.7	25.4	39.1	87.3
Maryland	12.0	88.0	35.2	51.7	90.3
Massachusetts	11.3	88.7	38.1	62.3	91.5
Michigan	11.9	88.1	24.7	49.3	91.2
Minnesota	8.4	91.6	31.5	46.3	87.0
Mississippi	20.1	79.9	19.4	54.5	86.7
Missouri	13.5	86.5	25.0	43.0	85.9
Montana	9.1	90.9	27.1	37.2	81.8
Nebraska	9.9	90.1	27.1	45.0	87.6
Nevada	16.5	83.5	21.9	28.4	81.9
New Hampshire	9.1	90.9	33.3	51.5	88.1
New Jersey	12.6	87.4	34.4	67.3	90.8
New Mexico	17.6	82.4	24.7	42.9	86.6
New York	15.9	84.1	31.9	60.1	89.7
North Carolina	16.4	83.6	26.1	49.5	86.5
North Dakota	10.4	89.6	26.9	37.6	82.8
Ohio	12.4	87.6	24.1	46.3	88.5
Oklahoma	14.5	85.5	22.2	46.0	84.5
Oregon	11.4	88.6	28.1	43.7	85.8
Pennsylvania	12.5	87.5	26.3	49.7	87.0
Rhode Island	16.3	83.7	30.0	56.5	91.5

GROUPING	ECONOMICALLY DISADVANTAGED STUDENTS (% public K–12) 2008–2009[6]	STUDENTS WITH LIMITED ENGLISH PROFICIENCY (% public K–12) 2008–2009[7]	STUDENTS WITH DISABILITIES (% public K–12) 2008–2009[8]	4TH-GRADE NAEP READING (% at or above proficient) 2009[9]	8TH-GRADE NAEP MATH (% at or above proficient) 2009[10]
United States	44.1	8.8	13.4	33.0	33.9
Women	...	...	...	...	...
Men	...	...	...	...	...
African American	...	...	...	...	...
Asian American	...	...	...	...	...
Latino	...	...	...	...	...
Native American	...	...	...	...	...
White	...	...	...	...	...
Alabama	52.2	2.6	11.1	28.2	20.4
Alaska	34.5	9.2	13.5	27.2	33.5
Arizona	47.5	11.5	11.5	24.7	29.0
Arkansas	57.2	5.8	13.5	28.8	27.0
California	52.3	24.2	10.7	23.7	23.4
Colorado	35.4	10.9	10.2	40.2	39.7
Connecticut	30.0	5.2	12.1	42.4	39.8
Delaware	42.7	5.7	15.2	35.1	31.7
District of Columbia	68.6	8.5	14.8	16.8	11.2
Florida	49.6	8.6	14.6	35.8	29.0
Georgia	53.0	4.9	10.9	29.4	26.8
Hawaii	41.7	10.3	11.2	25.7	25.3
Idaho	39.7	6.4	10.2	32.3	38.4
Illinois	40.0	9.0	15.0	32.3	33.1
Indiana	41.8	4.4	16.8	33.7	36.2
Iowa	34.0	4.2	13.8	34.2	33.9
Kansas	42.9	7.2	14.0	35.1	39.5
Kentucky	51.6	2.2	16.1	36.2	27.2
Louisiana	65.3	1.8	12.6	18.4	20.3
Maine	37.0	2.2	17.3	35.5	35.3
Maryland	34.7	4.7	12.3	37.1	40.1
Massachusetts	30.7	5.1	17.6	47.2	51.7
Michigan	41.4	3.7	14.0	29.7	30.5
Minnesota	32.7	7.4	14.4	37.2	46.9
Mississippi	68.6	1.3	13.1	21.7	15.2
Missouri	40.7	1.8	14.5	35.7	35.5
Montana	36.8	3.2	12.4	34.6	43.6
Nebraska	38.4	6.3	15.1	34.8	34.6
Nevada	39.1	17.5	11.1	24.0	24.8
New Hampshire	20.5	2.1	15.2	41.3	43.3
New Jersey	30.0	3.9	16.2	40.3	44.4
New Mexico	61.6	16.3	13.9	19.8	20.2
New York	46.1	6.7	16.2	36.0	33.7
North Carolina	33.2	7.6	12.6	32.3	35.6
North Dakota	31.7	4.3	14.0	34.8	43.1
Ohio	37.0	2.0	14.6	35.8	35.7
Oklahoma	56.2	5.9	14.6	27.7	23.8
Oregon	45.4	11.2	14.1	30.9	36.6
Pennsylvania	33.9	2.7	16.7	36.6	39.9
Rhode Island	39.3	...	19.0	35.6	27.8

Access to Knowledge *continued*

GROUPING	LESS THAN HIGH SCHOOL (% 25 and older) 2008[1]	AT LEAST HIGH SCHOOL DIPLOMA (% 25 and older) 2008[2]	AT LEAST BACHELOR'S DEGREE (% 25 and older) 2008[3]	PRESCHOOL ENROLLMENT (% enrolled ages 3 and 4) 2008[4]	COMBINED GROSS ENROLLMENT RATIO (% enrolled ages 3 to 24) 2008[5]
South Carolina	16.8	83.2	23.7	48.9	84.1
South Dakota	9.7	90.3	25.1	38.1	82.5
Tennessee	17.0	83.0	22.9	44.5	85.7
Texas	20.4	79.6	25.3	43.0	84.2
Utah	9.6	90.4	29.1	40.5	85.2
Vermont	9.4	90.6	32.1	55.4	87.9
Virginia	14.1	85.9	33.7	49.5	87.8
Washington	10.4	89.6	30.7	43.2	85.7
West Virginia	17.8	82.2	17.1	32.2	83.7
Wisconsin	10.4	89.6	25.7	45.3	87.1
Wyoming	8.3	91.7	23.6	40.7	81.6

GROUPING	ECONOMICALLY DISADVANTAGED STUDENTS (% public K–12) 2008–2009[6]	STUDENTS WITH LIMITED ENGLISH PROFICIENCY (% public K–12) 2008–2009[7]	STUDENTS WITH DISABILITIES (% public K–12) 2008–2009[8]	4TH-GRADE NAEP READING (% at or above proficient) 2009[9]	8TH-GRADE NAEP MATH (% at or above proficient) 2009[10]
South Carolina	52.5	4.4	14.2	27.6	30.2
South Dakota	34.8	2.8	14.1	32.9	41.6
Tennessee	50.1	2.8	12.2	28.0	25.2
Texas	48.8	15.1	9.5	27.7	36.2
Utah	31.7	7.9	11.6	31.0	35.1
Vermont	28.8	1.6	15.2	41.4	43.5
Virginia	33.1	7.0	13.5	38.5	35.6
Washington	38.4	8.0	12.1	33.5	39.4
West Virginia	50.1	0.6	16.6	25.7	19.4
Wisconsin	33.5	5.5	14.3	32.8	39.3
Wyoming	31.1	2.6	16.9	32.6	34.7

Access to Knowledge *continued*

GROUPING	PUBLIC HIGH SCHOOL GRADUATION RATE (%) 2009[11]	HIGH SCHOOL GRADUATES ENROLLING IN COLLEGE (%) 2006[12]	ANNUAL COSTS OF PUBLIC 4-YEAR COLLEGE (average $) 2008–2009[13]	ANNUAL COSTS OF PRIVATE 4-YEAR COLLEGE (average $) 2008–2009[14]	ANNUAL COSTS OF PUBLIC 2-YEAR COLLEGE (average $) 2008–2009[15]
United States	73.9	62.0	14,256	31,704	2,137
GENDER					
Women	...	...	...	...	...
Men	...	...	...	...	...
RACE/ETHNICITY					
African American	...	...	...	...	...
Asian American	...	...	...	...	...
Latino	...	...	...	...	...
Native American	...	...	...	...	...
White	...	...	...	...	...
STATE					
Alabama	67.1	61.5	12,166	22,444	2,823
Alaska	69.1	45.8	12,970	28,837	3,119
Arizona	69.6	45.0	13,995	21,813	1,612
Arkansas	74.4	56.7	11,669	21,053	2,128
California	70.7	56.1	15,683	37,017	586
Colorado	76.6	63.6	14,240	29,331	2,197
Connecticut	81.8	62.9	17,364	42,268	2,982
Delaware	71.9	66.3	17,185	21,454	2,684
District of Columbia	54.9	56.3	...	37,554	...
Florida	65.0	60.2	11,506	28,185	2,099
Georgia	64.1	68.6	11,540	30,594	1,890
Hawaii	75.4	55.1	13,434	22,957	1,757
Idaho	80.4	45.8	10,408	11,724	2,242
Illinois	79.5	60.4	18,213	32,359	2,519
Indiana	73.9	63.9	14,973	31,310	2,930
Iowa	86.5	60.9	13,831	25,280	3,415
Kansas	78.9	65.6	12,012	23,842	2,091
Kentucky	76.4	61.5	13,190	23,691	2,929
Louisiana	61.3	63.9	10,384	32,013	1,713
Maine	78.5	61.1	16,112	34,784	3,272
Maryland	80.0	66.3	16,111	38,453	3,071
Massachusetts	80.8	72.6	17,112	43,522	3,255
Michigan	77.0	64.5	17,039	22,862	2,255
Minnesota	86.5	67.8	15,105	31,706	4,614
Mississippi	63.6	75.4	11,047	19,358	1,770
Missouri	81.9	57.7	14,009	26,509	2,456
Montana	81.5	56.4	11,970	22,884	3,092
Nebraska	86.3	64.3	12,641	23,722	2,220
Nevada	52.0	52.2	12,869	25,897	1,920
New Hampshire	81.7	64.6	19,242	36,786	6,001
New Jersey	84.4	70.2	20,735	37,156	3,193
New Mexico	59.1	71.1	11,266	25,458	1,272
New York	68.8	75.0	14,865	38,488	3,525
North Carolina	68.6	65.7	11,333	30,963	1,404
North Dakota	83.1	71.9	11,418	15,614	4,104
Ohio	78.7	59.5	16,582	31,611	3,150
Oklahoma	77.8	59.6	12,333	24,762	2,531
Oregon	73.8	47.7	15,179	33,763	2,937
Pennsylvania	83.0	61.6	18,124	37,964	3,308
Rhode Island	78.4	54.7	17,266	39,072	3,090

U.S. INDICATOR TABLES

GROUPING	PER PUPIL SPENDING, PUBLIC K–12 (2008–2009 $) 2006–2007[16]	STATE SPENDING ON HIGHER EDUCATION ($ per capita) 2008[17]	STATE SPENDING ON ACADEMIC RESEARCH AND DEVELOPMENT ($ per capita) FY2008[18]	INDIVIDUALS WITH HOME INTERNET ACCESS (% ages 3 and older) 2009[19]
United States	10,041	503	171	73.5
Women	...	...	...	...
Men	...	...	...	...
African American	...	...	...	...
Asian American	...	...	...	...
Latino	...	...	...	...
Native American	...	...	...	...
White	...	...	...	...
Alabama	8,709	906	152	61.7
Alaska	12,781	1,252	162	83.4
Arizona	7,610	413	128	74.3
Arkansas	8,702	962	86	63.4
California	9,283	446	191	75.6
Colorado	8,593	709	187	76.1
Connecticut	14,165	753	209	82.0
Delaware	12,196	421	153	76.5
District of Columbia	16,086	...	624	73.3
Florida	8,885	349	87	75.0
Georgia	9,439	298	157	73.0
Hawaii	11,470	875	216	78.9
Idaho	6,894	324	74	77.5
Illinois	9,951	217	153	74.2
Indiana	9,416	300	150	69.5
Iowa	9,117	1,354	176	73.2
Kansas	9,585	793	144	75.8
Kentucky	8,235	1,300	119	65.5
Louisiana	9,269	653	150	65.8
Maine	12,075	208	97	77.7
Maryland	12,418	793	488	78.7
Massachusetts	13,333	658	350	81.7
Michigan	10,290	242	159	73.8
Minnesota	9,945	584	134	77.8
Mississippi	7,735	893	138	56.6
Missouri	9,175	202	162	69.5
Montana	9,532	545	192	69.6
Nebraska	10,441	1,077	211	77.0
Nevada	8,095	390	73	76.0
New Hampshire	11,446	182	230	84.7
New Jersey	16,762	411	101	83.0
New Mexico	9,177	1,363	210	65.0
New York	16,122	421	208	76.9
North Carolina	8,170	532	215	69.1
North Dakota	8,992	1,317	282	73.2
Ohio	10,309	264	159	72.6
Oklahoma	7,705	669	91	65.2
Oregon	9,290	716	157	80.6
Pennsylvania	11,309	186	209	74.3
Rhode Island	13,951	798	225	77.0

Access to Knowledge *continued*

GROUPING	PUBLIC HIGH SCHOOL GRADUATION RATE (%) 2009[11]	HIGH SCHOOL GRADUATES ENROLLING IN COLLEGE (%) 2006[12]	ANNUAL COSTS OF PUBLIC 4-YEAR COLLEGE (average $) 2008–2009[13]	ANNUAL COSTS OF PRIVATE 4-YEAR COLLEGE (average $) 2008–2009[14]	ANNUAL COSTS OF PUBLIC 2-YEAR COLLEGE (average $) 2008–2009[15]
South Carolina	58.9	69.5	16,136	25,336	3,361
South Dakota	82.5	72.1	11,373	21,697	3,931
Tennessee	72.6	64.2	12,026	27,364	2,778
Texas	71.9	55.4	13,222	29,228	1,471
Utah	76.6	46.3	10,352	13,482	2,553
Vermont	88.6	54.5	19,661	36,101	4,684
Virginia	75.5	68.3	14,868	27,280	2,666
Washington	74.8	48.7	14,165	33,455	2,850
West Virginia	78.2	57.9	12,131	19,859	2,790
Wisconsin	88.5	61.0	12,406	30,001	3,536
Wyoming	75.8	58.0	10,556	…	2,007

1–3. U.S. Census Bureau, American Community Survey 2008. Tables B15002, B15002B, B15002C, B15002D, B15002H, B15002I.

4. U.S. Census Bureau, American Community Survey 2008. Tables B14003, C09001.

5. U.S. Census Bureau, American Community Survey 2008. Tables B14001, B14001B, B14001C, B14001D, B14001H, B14001

6–8. U.S. Department of Education. "Summer 2010 EDFacts State Profiles."

9–10. U.S. Department of Education, National Assessment of Educational Progress Data Explorer.

11. U.S. Department of Education, Digest of Education Statistics 2009. Table 105.

12. U.S. Department of Education, Digest of Education Statistics 2009. Table 203.

13–15. U.S. Department of Education, Digest of Education Statistics 2009. Table 335.

GROUPING	PER PUPIL SPENDING, PUBLIC K-12 (2008–2009 $) 2006–2007[16]	STATE SPENDING ON HIGHER EDUCATION ($ per capita) 2008[17]	STATE SPENDING ON ACADEMIC RESEARCH AND DEVELOPMENT ($ per capita) FY2008[18]	INDIVIDUALS WITH HOME INTERNET ACCESS (% ages 3 and older) 2009[19]
South Carolina	8,884	955	129	63.4
South Dakota	8,363	721	114	70.0
Tennessee	7,393	606	127	69.1
Texas	8,141	407	154	65.5
Utah	5,918	496	156	83.1
Vermont	14,134	158	189	75.4
Virginia	10,593	587	135	76.4
Washington	8,840	665	162	81.7
West Virginia	10,087	1009	94	66.9
Wisconsin	10,751	842	199	78.8
Wyoming	13,758	94	140	76.1

16. U.S. Department of Education, Digest of Education Statistics 2009. Table 185.

17. AHDP calculations based on data from the National Association of State Budget Officers, Fiscal Year 2008 State Expenditure Report, Table 12, and U.S. Census Bureau, American Community Survey 2008. Table B01003

18. National Science Foundation, "Academic R&D Expenditures FY2008." Table 17.

19. U.S. Census Bureau, "Computer Use and Ownership," October 2009. Table 3.

A Decent Standard of Living

GROUPING	MEDIAN EARNINGS (2009 $) 2008[1]	LABOR FORCE PARTICIPATION RATE (% 16 to 64) 2008[2]	STATE PER CAPITA GDP (2009 $) 2008[3]	STATE MINIMUM WAGE ($ per hour) 2010[4]	INCOME RATIO (top 20% to bottom 20%) 2001–2003[5]	STATE GINI COEFFICIENT 2008[6]	POVERTY RATE (% below federal poverty threshold) 2008[7]	CHILD POVERTY (% living in families below the poverty line) 2008[8]
United States	29,755	75.7		7.35	7.3	0.469	13.2	17.8
GENDER								
Women	23,997	70.9	...	...	...	...	14.5	...
Men	35,170	80.5	...	...	...	...	11.8	...
RACE/ETHNICITY								
African American	24,792	70.6	...	...	...	...	24.1	...
Asian American	34,835	74.7	...	...	...	...	10.5	...
Latino	21,936	74.2	...	...	...	...	21.3	...
Native American	21,744	66.5	...	...	...	...	24.2	...
White	31,932	77.3	...	...	...	...	9.3	...
STATE								
Alabama	26,112	71.6	29,299	...	7.1	0.467	15.7	21.7
Alaska	31,774	78.7	43,474	7.75	5.8	0.403	8.4	11.0
Arizona	29,049	74.1	32,220	7.25	7.7	0.453	14.7	20.8
Arkansas	23,471	71.9	27,648	6.25	6.9	0.459	17.3	24.9
California	31,008	74.0	41,904	8.00	7.6	0.473	13.3	18.5
Colorado	30,853	79.2	40,946	7.24	6.8	0.457	11.4	15.1
Connecticut	36,827	79.0	50,565	8.25	6.9	0.486	9.3	12.5
Delaware	31,320	76.9	56,187	7.25	5.8	0.447	10.0	13.6
District of Columbia	40,342	75.8	125,927	8.25	12.4	0.540	17.2	25.9
Florida	27,366	75.0	32,800	7.25	7.6	0.471	13.2	18.3
Georgia	29,453	74.5	33,888	5.15	6.4	0.467	14.7	20.1
Hawaii	31,766	78.6	38,497	7.25	6.9	0.428	9.1	10.0
Idaho	24,776	76.4	29,777	7.25	5.6	0.419	12.6	15.8
Illinois	30,964	77.1	39,854	8.25	6.8	0.467	12.2	17.0
Indiana	27,677	76.7	32,792	7.25	6.4	0.437	13.1	18.3
Iowa	26,857	82.4	36,633	7.25	5.4	0.428	11.5	14.4
Kansas	27,690	80.9	34,880	7.25	6.5	0.442	11.3	14.5
Kentucky	25,861	70.7	29,627	7.25	7.6	0.467	17.3	23.5
Louisiana	26,357	71.0	32,717	...	7.6	0.477	17.3	24.7
Maine	26,120	77.5	30,521	7.50	6.5	0.436	12.3	15.8
Maryland	37,320	79.7	39,056	7.25	7.2	0.438	8.1	10.2
Massachusetts	35,533	78.9	47,906	8.00	7.3	0.471	10.0	12.0
Michigan	27,125	74.0	32,477	7.40	6.7	0.451	14.4	19.4
Minnesota	31,442	82.7	41,415	6.15	5.8	0.445	9.6	11.4
Mississippi	24,620	70.1	24,310	...	7.1	0.478	21.2	30.4
Missouri	26,801	77.1	32,655	7.25	6.0	0.448	13.4	18.6
Montana	24,033	76.8	28,063	7.25	5.9	0.449	14.8	20.6
Nebraska	26,659	83.0	37,184	7.25	5.6	0.427	10.8	13.4
Nevada	31,122	77.7	39,536	6.55	5.9	0.431	11.3	15.0
New Hampshire	32,207	81.2	38,274	7.25	6.0	0.419	7.6	9.0
New Jersey	37,707	77.9	44,786	7.25	7.5	0.462	8.7	12.5
New Mexico	24,495	72.9	30,818	7.50	7.2	0.460	17.1	24.2
New York	31,963	74.4	49,311	7.25	8.1	0.503	13.6	19.1
North Carolina	26,943	75.8	35,583	7.25	7.4	0.463	14.6	19.9
North Dakota	26,224	82.8	37,688	7.25	5.6	0.451	12.0	15.3
Ohio	27,805	76.7	33,441	7.25	6.4	0.450	13.4	18.5
Oklahoma	25,283	73.8	29,248	7.25	6.3	0.458	15.9	22.6
Oregon	27,285	75.9	38,654	8.40	6.3	0.447	13.6	18.1
Pennsylvania	29,891	75.5	35,506	7.25	7.0	0.457	12.1	16.8
Rhode Island	31,179	77.5	36,145	7.40	6.8	0.460	11.7	15.5

GROUPING	FEDERAL REVENUE TO EACH STATE ($ per capita) 2007[9]	STATE PUBLIC ASSISTANCE SPENDING ($ per capita) 2008[10]	FOOD STAMPS USE (%) 2008[11]	UNEMPLOYMENT RATE (% ages 16 and over) May 2010[12]	UNION MEMBERSHIP (%) 2009[13]	STATE EITC (% of federal EITC) 2008[14]	BANKRUPTCIES (filings per 1,000) 2009[15]
United States	8,195	...	9.3	9.7	12.3	...	4.5
GENDER							
Women	...	...	...	10.5	11.3	...	...
Men	...	...	...	8.8	13.3	...	...
RACE/ETHNICITY							
African American	...	...	...	15.5	13.9	...	...
Asian American	...	...	...	...	11.4	...	...
Latino	...	...	...	12.4	10.2	...	...
Native American	...	...	...	...	....	...	...
White	...	...	...	8.8	12.1	...	...
STATE							
Alabama	9,571	9	12.1	10.8	10.9	...	7.3
Alaska	13,654	155	8.2	8.3	22.3	...	1.3
Arizona	7,519	18	9.5	9.6	6.5	...	5.0
Arkansas	7,655	130	13.1	7.7	4.2	...	5.5
California	7,006	271	6.0	12.4	17.2	...	5.4
Colorado	7,222	7	5.0	8.0	7.0	...	5.4
Connecticut	8,756	136	6.4	8.9	17.3	...	2.8
Delaware	6,862	27	8.4	8.8	11.9	20	3.3
District of Columbia	68,939	...	14.9	10.4	10.4	40	1.8
Florida	7,905	8	7.8	11.7	5.8	...	5.0
Georgia	6,910	55	10.4	10.2	4.6	...	7.3
Hawaii	10,555	72	7.5	6.6	23.5	...	2.3
Idaho	6,797	10	6.5	9.0	6.3	...	4.7
Illinois	6,433	10	10.1	10.8	17.5	9	5.6
Indiana	6,939	51	9.7	10.0	10.6	5	7.4
Iowa	7,344	45	8.6	6.8	11.1	7	3.3
Kansas	7,809	20	6.7	6.5	6.2	17	3.8
Kentucky	8,945	38	14.7	10.4	8.6	...	5.7
Louisiana	16,357	36	17.6	6.9	5.8	4	4.0
Maine	8,350	134	13.1	8.0	11.7	5	2.8
Maryland	12,256	98	6.3	7.2	12.6	25	4.4
Massachusetts	8,944	210	7.7	9.2	16.6	15	3.1
Michigan	6,665	49	12.6	13.6	18.8	20	6.7
Minnesota	6,189	71	5.6	7.0	15.1	33	3.9
Mississippi	14,574	9	15.1	11.4	4.8	...	4.8
Missouri	8,952	28	14.8	9.3	9.4	...	5.1
Montana	8,464	40	8.2	7.2	13.9	...	2.7
Nebraska	7,895	33	6.7	4.9	9.2	10	4.0
Nevada	5,859	22	5.5	14.0	15.7	...	10.9
New Hampshire	6,763	57	4.8	6.4	10.8	...	3.5
New Jersey	7,070	45	5.0	9.7	19.3	25	4.0
New Mexico	10,784	61	11.9	8.4	6.7	10	2.9
New York	7,932	184	10.0	8.3	25.2	30	2.8
North Carolina	6,992	26	10.1	10.3	3.1	5	2.8
North Dakota	9,903	15	7.5	3.6	6.8	...	2.4
Ohio	7,044	113	10.0	10.7	14.2	...	6.0
Oklahoma	8,130	63	11.4	6.7	5.7	5	3.7
Oregon	6,391	43	12.3	10.6	17.0	6	4.6
Pennsylvania	8,324	95	9.4	9.1	15.0	...	2.8
Rhode Island	8,255	137	8.1	12.3	17.9	25	4.7

A Decent Standard of Living *continued*

GROUPING	MEDIAN EARNINGS (2009 $) 2008[1]	LABOR FORCE PARTICIPATION RATE (% 16 to 64) 2008[2]	STATE PER CAPITA GDP (2009 $) 2008[3]	STATE MINIMUM WAGE ($ per hour) 2010[4]	INCOME RATIO (top 20% to bottom 20%) 2001–2003[5]	STATE GINI COEFFICIENT 2008[6]	POVERTY RATE (% below federal poverty threshold) 2008[7]	CHILD POVERTY (% living in families below the poverty line) 2008[8]
South Carolina	26,247	72.6	28,256	...	7.0	0.464	15.7	21.7
South Dakota	25,717	82.0	37,547	7.25	5.3	0.446	12.5	17.6
Tennessee	26,044	74.1	33,697	...	7.7	0.471	15.5	21.8
Texas	27,344	74.3	37,900	7.25	8.1	0.474	15.8	22.5
Utah	26,126	77.7	31,927	7.25	5.8	0.411	9.6	10.5
Vermont	26,627	80.2	34,791	8.06	6.0	0.434	10.6	13.2
Virginia	32,467	77.6	41,610	7.25	7.2	0.460	10.2	13.8
Washington	31,812	76.4	40,254	8.55	7.2	0.442	11.3	14.3
West Virginia	24,404	67.3	25,436	7.25	7.0	0.453	17.0	23.0
Wisconsin	29,168	81.0	35,105	7.25	5.5	0.426	10.4	13.3
Wyoming	29,507	79.9	40,682	5.15	5.2	0.441	9.4	11.6

1. U.S. Census Bureau, American Community Survey 2008. Tables B20017, B20017B, B20017C, B20017D, B20017E, B20017H, and B20017I. Earnings are the sum of wage or salary income and net income from self-employment.

2. U.S. Census Bureau, American Community Survey 2008. Tables GCT2301, B23001, B23002C, B23002E, B23002H, B23002D, B23002I, and B23002B.

3. U.S. Department of Commerce, Bureau of Economic Analysis. News Release: GDP by State 2008. Table 1–4.

4. U.S. Department of Labor, Employment Standards Administration, Wage and Hour Division.

5. Bernstein et al., "Pulling Apart" Table 2.

6. U.S. Census Bureau. American Community Survey 2008. Table B19083.

7. U.S. Census Bureau, American Community Survey 2008. Tables GCT1701, B17001, B17001B, B17001D, B17001I, B17001E, B17001C, B17001H.

8. U.S. Census Bureau, American Community Survey 2008. Table GCT1704.

9. U.S. Census Bureau, Statistical Abstract of the United States. Table 469.

10. AHDP calculations based on data from the National Association of State Budget Officers, State Expenditure Report 2008, Table 18.

GROUPING	FEDERAL REVENUE TO EACH STATE ($ per capita) 2007[9]	STATE PUBLIC ASSISTANCE SPENDING ($ per capita) 2008[10]	FOOD STAMPS USE (%) 2008[11]	UNEMPLOYMENT RATE (% ages 16 and over) May 2010[12]	UNION MEMBERSHIP (%) 2009[13]	STATE EITC (% of federal EITC) 2008[14]	BANKRUPTCIES (filings per 1,000) 2009[15]
South Carolina	7,813	16	12.9	11.0	4.5	...	2.1
South Dakota	10,135	36	7.7	4.6	5.5	...	2.2
Tennessee	8,329	18	14.5	10.4	5.1	...	8.4
Texas	7,119	4	10.2	8.3	5.1	...	2.1
Utah	6,090	31	4.8	7.3	6.9	...	5.1
Vermont	8,496	146	9.0	6.2	12.3	32	2.4
Virginia	13,489	18	6.9	7.1	4.7	20	0.0
Washington	7,602	61	8.7	9.1	20.2	5	4.6
West Virginia	8,966	45	15.2	9.1	13.9	...	3.5
Wisconsin	6,197	18	7.5	8.2	15.2	4 to 43	4.8
Wyoming	10,082	...	4.2	7.0	7.7	...	2.3

11. AHDP calculation based on usage data from the U.S. Department of Agriculture, Supplemental Nutritional Assistance Program (SNAP) State Activity Report, Table 1, and population data from U.S. Census Bureau, American Community Survey 2008, Table B01001.

12. U.S. Department of Labor, Bureau of Labor Statistics, "The Employment Situation: June 2010," Tables A-2 and A-3, and U.S. Department of Labor, Bureau of Labor Statistics, "Regional and State Employment and Unemployment: May 2010," Table 3.

13. U.S. Department of Labor, Bureau of Labor Statistics, Economic News Release, January 22, 2010. Tables 1 and 5.

14. Urban Institute—Brookings Institution, Tax Policy Center (used by permission of the Urban Institute—Brookings Institution). Minnesota EITC varies according to income; Wisconsin EITC is 4 percent with one child, and 43 percent with three children.

15. American Bankruptcy Institute, Bankruptcy Filing Statistics.

U.S. INDICATOR TABLES

Preserving the Earth for Future Generations

STATES	CARBON DIOXIDE EMISSIONS (metric tons per capita) 2007[1]	CARCINOGEN RELEASES (pounds) 2008[2]	LEAD RELEASES (pounds) 2008[3]	MERCURY RELEASES (pounds per 1,000 population) 2008[4]	DIOXIN RELEASES (grams) 2008[5]	SUPERFUND SITES, 2010[6]	PROTECTED FOREST (acres) 2010[7]	PROTECTED FARM AND RANCH LAND (acres) 2007[8]	ENERGY CONSUMPTION (BTUs per capita) 2008[9]	WATER CONSUMPTION (gallons per day, per capita) 2005[10]
United States	...	774,078,593	486,023,666	...	33,687	1,262	1,982,821	54,488	326,851	1,544
Alabama	30.5	13,507,625	4,189,437	50.90	353	13	10,127	1,309	442,952	2,464
Alaska	69.0	206,203,909	200,589,823	106.01	1	6	4,920	40	948,283	1,763
Arizona	15.1	21,492,996	17,366,164	5.37	14	9	630	0	238,886	1,172
Arkansas	21.3	3,455,259	325,555	1.00	132	9	15,923	0	393,887	4,611
California	10.8	17,906,862	8,071,051	0.78	197	94	20,620	2,015	228,027	1,433
Colorado	19.5	6,295,753	5,919,746	0.92	6	18	10,871	1,177	303,293	3,283
Connecticut	12.6	1,027,151	321,708	0.13	4	14	8,052	1,305	231,317	1,211
Delaware	20.4	592,012	73,886	18.96	968	14	2,032	280	338,223	1,357
District of Columbia	6.7	266	114	...	...	1	...	...	304,816	19
Florida	14.2	5,541,706	647,570	0.50	51	52	4,742	663	242,652	1,153
Georgia	19.3	6,934,144	950,428	0.65	445	15	22,693	176	311,324	671
Hawaii	18.1	137,191	43,593	0.10	5	3	37,055	200	220,308	1,674
Idaho	10.5	11,132,013	8,451,447	4.39	11	6	57,835	546	347,352	15,359
Illinois	19.0	7,903,629	2,324,807	0.94	141	44	493	313	316,915	1,341
Indiana	36.7	23,204,261	7,161,841	1.79	345	32	7,301	0	448,094	1,679
Iowa	26.9	2,911,959	574,438	1.56	23	11	1,986	0	471,065	1,278
Kansas	26.1	2,726,782	251,868	1.08	13	11	...	6,761	405,263	1,546
Kentucky	36.3	9,474,980	1,339,352	1.41	2,640	14	3,144	3,150	464,438	1,160
Louisiana	43.8	21,255,336	1,575,659	23.14	1,041	9	...	0	790,674	2,890
Maine	17.4	745,090	49,556	0.09	10	12	674,572	83	356,487	517
Maryland	15.0	171,767	365,272	1.37	163	18	2,014	1,116	256,834	1,505
Massachusetts	13.0	754,189	128,323	0.03	8	31	7,641	2,140	226,994	625
Michigan	18.8	6,585,369	791,632	0.74	7,239	66	120,548	463	291,730	1,298
Minnesota	19.5	2,220,721	429,970	0.36	179	25	59,531	322	379,109	887
Mississippi	21.7	6,770,072	1,094,970	0.60	1,970	4	...	0	403,455	1,131

1. U.S. Environmental Protection Agency. "CO2 Emissions from Fossil Fuel Combustion," Million Metric Tons CO_2. Includes commercial, residential, industrial, transportation, and electric power. Per capita data calculated using U.S. Census 2007 population estimates.

2–3. U.S. Environmental Protection Agency. 2008 Toxics Release Inventory Workbook. Tables B-22 and B-25.

4. AHDP calculations based on release data from the U.S. Environmental Protection Agency. 2008 Toxics Release Inventory Workbook, Table B-28 and population data from the U.S. Census Bureau, American Community Survey 2008, Table B01001.

5. U.S. Environmental Protection Agency. 2008 Toxics Release Inventory Workbook, Table B-31.

6. U.S. Environmental Protection Agency. National Priorities List. Sites as of March 2010.

U.S. INDICATOR TABLES

Preserving the Earth for Future Generations *continued*

STATES	CARBON DIOXIDE EMISSIONS (metric tons per capita) 2007[1]	CARCINOGEN RELEASES (pounds) 2008[2]	LEAD RELEASES (pounds) 2008[3]	MERCURY RELEASES (pounds per 1,000 population) 2008[4]	DIOXIN RELEASES (grams) 2008[5]	SUPERFUND SITES 2010[6]	PROTECTED FOREST (acres) 2010[7]	PROTECTED FARM AND RANCH LAND (acres) 2007[8]	ENERGY CONSUMPTION (BTUs per capita) 2008[9]	WATER CONSUMPTION (gallons per day, per capita) 2005[10]
Missouri	24.1	29,529,729	27,030,661	1.23	29	30	154	901	327,661	1,698
Montana	37.0	9,678,546	7,737,974	4.42	7	15	170,749	1,277	448,917	12,088
Nebraska	24.5	1,512,690	673,728	1.29	3	13	...	0	438,424	8,049
Nevada	19.3	153,143,381	90,940,251	2,042.52	7	1	111	579	288,481	1,108
New Hampshire	16.0	73,874	13,600	0.22	1	20	217,424	611	236,584	1,137
New Jersey	15.5	1,114,619	292,871	0.13	40	112	5,498	3,014	303,720	960
New Mexico	29.9	9,165,816	8,566,014	0.99	4	13	7,706	16	349,383	1,951
New York	11.0	2,487,402	537,896	0.39	166	86	135,820	1,444	204,620	879
North Carolina	16.9	6,510,386	1,103,298	0.61	316	35	6,696	761	293,004	1,661
North Dakota	76.7	1,547,253	131,434	5.12	18	0	...	0	687,316	2,361
Ohio	23.3	17,889,563	4,099,680	1.29	427	34	436	3,531	347,121	1,124
Oklahoma	29.3	4,447,300	1,248,558	5.59	104	8	...	0	440,209	549
Oregon	11.0	5,255,829	768,227	0.63	28	13	25	508	291,473	2,236
Pennsylvania	22.1	14,886,133	4,672,988	1.93	95	95	2,956	2,672	313,272	854
Rhode Island	10.7	95,134	23,606	0.01	...	12	3,461	339	209,462	426
South Carolina	20.0	7,901,170	1,008,818	0.53	41	26	73,428	814	370,441	2,065
South Dakota	16.5	2,351,005	2,111,644	2.61	8	2	...	0	435,467	719
Tennessee	20.7	14,220,266	6,267,216	1.24	1,956	13	40,365	125	363,820	2,018
Texas	27.9	27,761,403	2,510,761	1.07	9,488	48	13,636	250	474,872	1,316
Utah	24.7	65,422,110	55,641,374	32.90	4,406	16	64,334	234	292,133	2,292
Vermont	10.9	56,513	23,688	0.09	...	11	67,768	7,486	248,523	947
Virginia	16.7	2,836,076	699,355	0.43	44	31	5,971	428	323,551	1,573
Washington	12.2	7,528,351	5,506,956	0.13	125	48	34,115	419	313,045	1,009
West Virginia	63.0	6,362,782	844,395	6.11	64	9	764	1,625	457,875	2,988
Wisconsin	19.7	2,721,337	393,954	1.33	335	38	56,516	1,166	330,919	1,740
Wyoming	120.0	628,883	136,509	6.80	16	2	...	4,229	1,016,768	10,173

7. U.S. Department of Agriculture. Forest Service, "Forest Legacy Program." Areas protected as of February 2010.

8. U.S. Department of Agriculture. Natural Resources Conservation Service. Farm and Ranch Lands Protection Program.

9. AHDP calculations based on energy consumption data from the U.S. Energy Information Administration. Table S1—Energy Consumption Estimates by Source and End-Use Sector, 2008," and population data from the U.S. Census Bureau, American Community Survey 2008, Table B01001.

10. Kenney et al. "Estimated Water Use in the United States in 2005." U.S. Geological Survey Circular 1344. 2009. Table 1.

U.S. INDICATOR TABLES

Housing and Transportation

GROUPING	RENTERS SPENDING 30% OR MORE ON HOUSING (%) 2008[1]	OWNERS SPENDING 30% OR MORE ON HOUSING (%) 2008[2]	HOUSING UNITS OCCUPIED BY OWNER (% of all housing) 2008[3]	HOUSING UNITS WITH 1.01 OR MORE OCCUPANTS PER ROOM (%) 2008[4]	FORECLOSURE (per 10,000 homes) April 2010[5]	HOMELESS POPULATION 2007[6]	HOMELESS (% of population) 2007[7]	COMMUTE 60 MINUTES OR MORE (% of workers, 16 and over) 2008[8]	COMMUTE BY CARPOOL (% of workers) 2008[9]	STATE EXPENDITURE ON TRANSPORTATION ($ per person) 2008[10]
United States	46.1	36.9	66.6	3.2	25.9	744,313	0.30	8.2	10.7	...
GENDER										
Women	...	...	...	...	...	...	...	...	...	...
Men	...	...	...	...	...	...	...	...	...	...
RACE/ETHNICITY										
African American	...	...	45.6	...	...	...	...	...	...	...
Asian American	...	...	59.4	...	...	...	...	...	...	...
Latino	...	...	49.1	...	...	...	...	...	...	...
Native American	...	...	55.1	...	...	...	...	...	...	...
White	...	...	73.4	...	...	...	...	...	...	...
STATES										
Alabama	41.3	28.8	71.0	2.1	11.2	4,731	0.10	5.8	11.8	269
Alaska	38.0	34.2	65.0	5.7	10.1	2,749	0.41	4.5	14.4	3,230
Arizona	46.4	37.4	68.1	4.2	59.1	12,264	0.21	6.6	13.1	206
Arkansas	42.3	26.9	67.4	2.5	15.4	5,626	0.20	5.0	12.6	317
California	52.1	51.8	57.0	7.9	52.1	170,270	0.47	10.0	11.9	257
Colorado	47.3	38.5	67.5	2.5	29.7	21,730	0.47	6.4	11.3	285
Connecticut	48.2	39.6	69.0	1.9	20.2	5,357	0.15	7.8	8.8	449
Delaware	47.5	31.3	73.5	1.7	11.3	1,108	0.13	7.5	10.6	830
District of Columbia	45.5	37.8	43.4	2.5	9.0	5,518	1.00	9.3	6.6	...
Florida	53.7	44.9	69.7	2.7	55.0	60,867	0.34	7.1	10.3	423
Georgia	45.3	33.6	67.4	3.0	34.7	27,161	0.30	9.3	11.9	319
Hawaii	50.4	45.7	59.1	8.4	28.7	5,943	0.47	8.6	16.2	770
Idaho	41.3	33.9	70.9	2.2	44.2	5,424	0.38	4.9	12.9	409
Illinois	45.6	38.7	69.3	2.7	35.8	16,599	0.13	11.7	9.4	315
Indiana	43.5	26.7	71.8	1.7	20.3	9,857	0.16	5.8	10.1	375
Iowa	39.7	25.1	72.9	1.6	4.4	8,130	0.27	3.3	11.0	367
Kansas	40.3	25.8	69.4	1.8	7.4	5,278	0.19	3.5	10.3	485
Kentucky	40.7	27.7	69.5	1.5	6.0	4,934	0.12	5.5	11.3	505
Louisiana	43.5	28.7	68.5	2.7	9.8	5,476	0.12	7.8	10.9	484
Maine	47.3	33.4	72.1	1.1	5.9	2,775	0.21	6.5	10.9	425

1–2. U.S. Census Bureau, American Community Survey 2008. Tables GCT2515 and GCT2513.

3. U.S. Census Bureau, American Community Survey 2008. Tables B25003, B25003B, B25003C, B25003D, B25003H, and B25003I.

4. U.S. Census Bureau, American Community Survey 2008. Table GCT2509.

5. RealtyTrac, http://www.realtytrac.com.

U.S. INDICATOR TABLES

Housing and Transportation *continued*

GROUPING	RENTERS SPENDING 30% OR MORE ON HOUSING (%) 2008[1]	OWNERS SPENDING 30% OR MORE ON HOUSING (%) 2008[2]	HOUSING UNITS OCCUPIED BY OWNER (% of all housing) 2008[3]	HOUSING UNITS WITH 1.01 OR MORE OCCUPANTS PER ROOM (%) 2008[4]	FORECLOSURE (per 10,000 homes) April 2010[5]	HOMELESS POPULATION 2007[6]	HOMELESS (% of population) 2007[7]	COMMUTE 60 MINUTES OR MORE (% of workers,16 and over) 2008[8]	COMMUTE BY CARPOOL (% of workers) 2008[9]	STATE EXPENDITURE ON TRANSPORTATION ($ per person) 2008[10]
Maryland	46.9	35.0	69.5	1.8	23.3	7,995	0.14	13.9	10.8	613
Massachusetts	46.5	41.8	64.5	2.0	21.8	14,730	0.23	9.8	8.6	379
Michigan	48.8	35.2	74.0	1.7	42.3	26,124	0.26	6.0	9.4	346
Minnesota	46.4	33.9	74.7	1.7	14.0	7,313	0.14	5.2	9.4	507
Mississippi	43.0	33.1	70.1	2.7	2.9	1,652	0.06	6.7	12.3	527
Missouri	41.1	28.7	70.1	1.6	13.6	7,135	0.12	5.4	11.1	397
Montana	40.4	34.7	68.5	2.2	6.4	1,343	0.14	4.1	11.4	614
Nebraska	37.7	27.5	69.3	1.6	3.5	3,350	0.19	3.0	10.2	339
Nevada	47.3	45.4	59.7	4.5	143.9	16,402	0.68	5.6	12.1	572
New Hampshire	44.9	39.0	72.3	1.5	17.8	3,233	0.25	9.4	8.4	411
New Jersey	47.5	44.7	67.0	4.0	19.0	19,385	0.22	13.9	9.1	488
New Mexico	42.7	31.0	69.2	3.2	10.3	5,256	0.27	5.7	12.7	565
New York	47.9	40.9	55.3	4.7	5.5	61,094	0.32	16.6	7.7	300
North Carolina	41.8	31.3	68.2	2.1	9.3	10,765	0.12	5.4	11.5	361
North Dakota	34.4	23.0	66.6	1.6	1.7	655	0.10	3.9	10.0	687
Ohio	44.1	31.8	69.0	1.2	23.5	16,165	0.14	4.8	8.9	369
Oklahoma	40.0	26.8	67.2	2.6	12.2	4,869	0.14	4.6	11.9	265
Oregon	47.4	39.1	64.3	2.9	23.4	16,221	0.45	5.6	10.8	424
Pennsylvania	43.6	32.6	70.8	1.3	10.0	15,298	0.12	8.3	9.7	437
Rhode Island	46.5	43.5	62.4	1.5	19.1	6,866	0.64	5.4	8.0	319
South Carolina	40.8	31.8	70.6	2.3	15.3	7,958	0.19	5.1	10.9	366
South Dakota	34.9	26.8	69.2	1.7	5.1	1,029	0.13	2.6	9.8	616
Tennessee	43.0	31.5	69.8	1.8	17.4	8,066	0.14	5.5	10.6	245
Texas	43.9	33.3	64.9	4.8	13.7	43,630	0.19	7.4	12.4	333
Utah	40.2	33.1	71.7	3.7	45.2	3,104	0.13	4.7	13.1	486
Vermont	47.5	36.5	72.2	1.7	0.4	927	0.15	4.9	11.1	616
Virginia	43.7	34.2	68.7	1.7	21.4	10,346	0.14	8.9	10.9	451
Washington	45.7	39.8	65.3	2.4	15.6	23,970	0.38	8.0	12.2	334
West Virginia	38.2	24.5	73.7	1.3	1.2	1,522	0.08	9.2	10.9	533
Wisconsin	42.5	33.4	70.1	1.6	17.1	6,773	0.12	4.7	9.8	405
Wyoming	32.5	26.9	70.1	0.0	2.1	487	0.10	5.9	12.7	1,078

6–7. National Alliance to End Homelessness, Homelessness Counts. Table 2.

8–9. U.S. Census Bureau, American Community Survey 2008. Tables B08303 and B08101.

10. AHDP calculations based on data from the National Association of State Budget Officers, State Expenditure Report, 2008 Table 38, and population data from the U.S. Census Bureau, Annual Population Estimates, 2008.

Protecting Personal and Community Security

GROUPING	VIOLENT CRIME (per 100,000) 2008[1]	PROPERTY CRIME RATE (per 100,000) 2008[2]	HOMICIDE (per 100,000 age-adjusted) 2006[3]	HOMICIDE BY FIREARM (%) 2005[4]	SUICIDE (per 100,000 age-adjusted) 2006[5]	RAPE (total number) 2008[6]	RAPE (per 100,000) 2008[7]	CHILD MALTREATMENT (per 1,000 children) 2008[8]	STATE POLICE EXPENDITURE ($ per resident) 2006[9]	PRISONERS, STATE OR FEDERAL JURISDICTION* (number) 2008[10]	INCARCERATION RATE (per 100,000 inhabitants) 2008[11]	STATE EXPENDITURE ON CORRECTIONS ($ per person) 2008[12]
United States	455	3,213	6.2	...	10.9	89,000	29.3	10.3	...	2,310,984	762	...
GENDER												
Women	...	...	2.5	...	4.5	...	...	...	...	207,700	140	...
Men	...	...	9.7	...	18.0	...	...	...	...	2,103,500	1,455	...
RACE/ETHNICITY												
African American	...	...	21.6	...	5.1	...	...	...	...	913,800	2,222	...
Asian American	...	...	...	...	...	...	...	...	...	...	...	...
Latino	...	...	7.3	...	5.3	...	...	...	...	460,400	981	...
Native American	...	...	7.5	...	11.6	...	...	...	...	...	...	...
White	...	...	3.7	...	12.1	...	...	...	...	807,000	327	...
STATES												
Alabama	453	4,083	9.8	68.4	12.4	1,617	34.7	8.2	35	29,871	619	19,316
Alaska	652	2,932	6.1	59.4	20.0	441	64.3	25.1	106	5,223	357	55,524
Arizona	447	4,291	8.9	76.1	16.0	1,673	25.7	2.1	36	38,988	565	26,316
Arkansas	503	3,835	8.5	68.4	13.3	1,395	48.9	13.2	36	14,552	507	27,007
California	504	2,940	6.9	73.8	9.2	8,903	24.2	9.1	37	173,320	471	56,554
Colorado	343	2,849	3.7	64.1	15.2	2,098	42.5	9.3	23	23,130	468	32,425
Connecticut	298	2,459	3.9	48.0	8.0	674	19.3	11.9	57	21,099	411	33,461
Delaware	703	3,585	6.1	62.2	10.4	366	41.9	11.0	119	7,362	473	36,539
District of Columbia	1,438	5,105	23.3	...	5.1	186	31.4	23.6	...	...	...	...
Florida	689	4,141	7.0	...	12.6	5,972	32.6	12.8	26	100,494	548	30,649
Georgia	479	4,016	7.1	71.7	10.0	2,195	22.7	10.3	28	54,016	542	22,530
Hawaii	273	3,571	2.1	10.0	9.2	365	28.3	6.7	11	6,003	332	39,314
Idaho	229	2,101	2.6	67.6	15.6	551	36.2	4.4	31	7,338	482	33,252
Illinois	525	2,933	6.7	75.7	7.8	4,118	31.9	9.4	34	45,675	...	31,221
Indiana	334	3,336	5.9	72.2	13.0	1,720	27.0	13.8	32	27,380	429	26,808
Iowa	284	2,421	2.5	55.3	11.1	888	29.6	15.7	29	8,778	291	47,505
Kansas	411	3,377	4.1	54.7	13.8	1,190	42.5	2.4	44	8,333	308	47,162
Kentucky	296	2,584	4.6	70.1	14.6	1,408	33.0	18.1	44	21,610	488	26,469
Louisiana	656	3,823	12.8	77.4	11.6	1,232	27.9	9.2	71	38,137	858	21,344
Maine	118	2,452	1.5	36.8	11.0	375	28.5	14.7	50	2,246	133	69,902

1–2. Federal Bureau of Investigation. 2008 Crime in the United States, Table 5.

3. Centers for Disease Control and Prevention. Deaths: Final Data for 2006, 2009. Tables 13–14, and 29.

4. U.S. Department of Justice, Bureau of Justice Statistics. Crime & Justice Data Online. State-level Homicide Trends and Characteristics, 2005.

5. Centers for Disease Control and Prevention. Deaths: Final Data for 2006, 2009. Tables 13–14, and 29.

6–7. Federal Bureau of Investigation. 2008 Crime in the United States. Table 5.

8. U.S. Department of Health and Human Services. Child Maltreatment 2008. Tables 3 and 4.

9. AHDP calculations based on expenditure data from the U.S. Department of Justice, Bureau of Justice Statistics, Criminal Justice Expenditure and Employment Extracts Program, Table 9, and population data from U.S. Census Bureau, American Community Survey 2006, Table B01001.

U.S. INDICATOR TABLES

Protecting Personal and Community Security *continued*

GROUPING	VIOLENT CRIME (per 100,000) 2008[1]	PROPERTY CRIME RATE (per 100,000) 2008[2]	HOMICIDE (per 100,000 age-adjusted) 2006[3]	HOMICIDE BY FIREARM (%) 2005[4]	SUICIDE (per 100,000 age-adjusted) 2006[5]	RAPE (total number) 2008[6]	RAPE (per 100,000) 2008[7]	CHILD MALTREATMENT (per 1,000 children) 2008[8]	STATE POLICE EXPENDITURE ($ per resident) 2006[9]	PRISONERS, STATE OR FEDERAL JURISDICTION* (number) 2008[10]	INCARCERATION RATE (per 100,000 inhabitants) 2008[11]	STATE EXPENDITURE ON CORRECTIONS ($ per person) 2008[12]
Maryland	628	3,518	10.2	75.9	8.6	1,127	20.0	...	69	23,293	402	55,682
Massachusetts	449	2,400	2.9	55.0	6.7	1,736	26.7	29.1	81	11,662	252	106,671
Michigan	502	2,935	7.2	68.7	11.1	4,502	45.0	12.4	33	50,233	505	46,643
Minnesota	263	2,851	2.5	63.5	10.6	1,805	34.6	4.6	51	9,964	191	52,288
Mississippi	285	2,940	11.0	69.6	11.4	890	30.3	10.4	35	22,764	749	15,331
Missouri	504	3,664	7.1	70.1	13.5	1,615	27.3	3.9	32	30,466	515	20,121
Montana	258	2,603	3.8	29.4	19.7	294	30.4	7.4	42	3,592	368	46,771
Nebraska	304	2,879	3.1	38.5	11.2	583	32.7	10.4	44	4,419	238	50,238
Nevada	725	3,448	8.9	60.2	19.5	1,102	42.4	7.3	39	12,915	497	29,810
New Hampshire	157	2,092	1.6	37.5	11.0	391	29.7	3.8	35	2,827	213	37,496
New Jersey	327	2,293	5.3	66.0	6.5	1,122	12.9	4.4	62	26,490	305	62,892
New Mexico	650	3,909	7.0	49.6	18.0	1,139	57.4	11.3	60	6,330	307	45,972
New York	398	1,994	5.0	57.6	6.6	2,801	14.4	19.1	41	62,211	317	54,154
North Carolina	467	4,044	7.0	62.4	12.2	2,284	24.8	11.0	64	39,042	366	35,449
North Dakota	167	1,894	...	14.3	13.6	232	36.2	9.0	39	1,450	226	49,655
Ohio	348	3,412	5.9	57.3	11.2	4,419	38.5	13.2	21	51,160	445	39,777
Oklahoma	527	3,442	6.4	69.0	15.0	1,466	40.2	12.3	41	26,155	668	20,990
Oregon	257	3,282	3.1	60.8	15.2	1,156	30.5	12.7	73	14,079	370	59,308
Pennsylvania	410	2,410	6.4	71.9	10.8	3,478	27.9	1.5	53	46,313	368	42,645
Rhode Island	249	2,841	3.6	47.1	8.1	277	26.4	13.5	52	4,190	241	47,494
South Carolina	730	4,234	9.1	69.4	11.9	1,638	36.6	11.8	45	25,275	537	24,886
South Dakota	201	1,646	2.9	42.9	16.0	432	53.7	7.0	39	3,358	417	29,780
Tennessee	722	4,043	8.0	70.5	14.2	2,062	33.2	7.8	25	26,998	434	25,557
Texas	508	3,986	6.1	67.1	10.3	8,014	32.9	10.6	24	173,232	668	19,159
Utah	222	3,357	2.0	49.1	15.8	893	32.6	15.5	54	6,459	232	54,807
Vermont	136	2,539	...	62.5	12.0	127	20.4	5.3	137	2,082	250	62,920
Virginia	256	2,518	5.3	69.5	11.1	1,758	22.6	3.2	83	39,224	505	37,452
Washington	331	3,758	3.4	61.5	12.3	2,628	40.1	4.4	44	17,772	266	65,215
West Virginia	274	2,569	5.4	55.6	14.1	362	20.0	15.7	30	6,101	334	32,945
Wisconsin	274	2,756	3.5	68.0	11.9	1,120	19.9	4.4	21	23,577	386	51,618
Wyoming	232	2,717	...	50.0	21.7	180	33.8	5.7	74	2,073	389	482

10–11. U.S. Department of Justice, "Prison Inmates at Midyear 2008: Statistical Tables." Tables 10, 15, 17. National data, which also include local inmates, is not directly comparable with state data.

12. AHDP calculations based on expenditure data from the National Association of State Budget Officers, State Expenditure Report 2008, Table 32.

Political Participation

GROUPING	VOTER TURNOUT (% of eligible voters who voted) 2008[1]	CHANGE IN TURNOUT from 2004[2]	INELIGIBLE TO VOTE DUE TO FELONY CONVICTIONS (per 100,000 voting-age population) 2008[3]	SEATS IN STATE LEGISLATURE HELD BY WOMEN (%) 2010[4]	WOMEN IN CONGRESSIONAL DELEGATION 2010[5]	MEN IN CONGRESSIONAL DELEGATION 2010[6]
United States	61.7	2.7	1,457	24.4	91	446
Alabama	61.8	8.0	1,799	12.9	0	9
Alaska	68.1	-1.4	1,785	21.7	1	2
Arizona	56.2	3.9	1,635	31.1	2	8
Arkansas	53.4	-0.4	2,135	23.0	1	5
California	61.7	4.9	1,047	27.5	21	34
Colorado	69.8	4.6	817	37.0	2	7
Connecticut	67.1	3.2	858	32.1	1	6
Delaware	66.1	3.0	2,428	25.8	0	3
District of Columbia	60.6	11.6	...	...	1*	0
Florida	67.5	4.8	1,629	23.8	6	21
Georgia	61.5	9.4	4,002	19.5	0	15
Hawaii	50.5	4.8	595	32.9	1	3
Idaho	63.4	0.3	3,038	24.8	0	4
Illinois	62.9	2.3	464	27.7	4	17
Indiana	59.3	8.2	543	21.3	0	11
Iowa	70.0	0.1	1,036	23.3	0	7
Kansas	62.6	1.6	1,009	30.3	1	5
Kentucky	57.8	-1.5	1,550	15.9	0	8
Louisiana	62.2	1.8	2,410	15.3	1	8
Maine	71.3	-3.4	...	29.0	3	1
Maryland	67.6	7.5	1,741	30.9	2	8
Massachusetts	66.1	3.0	216	26.0	1	11
Michigan	68.8	3.3	677	25.0	3	14
Minnesota	78.1	-0.4	1,929	34.8	3	7
Mississippi	61.1	9.7	1,613	14.4	0	6
Missouri	67.9	4.0	1,685	22.3	2	9
Montana	66.4	3.1	476	26.0	0	3
Nebraska	62.6	-0.5	1,078	20.4	0	5
Nevada	58.5	5.8	1,185	31.7	2	3
New Hampshire	71.1	0.3	273	37.0	2	2
New Jersey	66.1	3.6	1,619	29.2	0	15
New Mexico	60.3	2.2	1,191	30.4	0	5
New York	58.2	0.3	774	24.1	7	24
North Carolina	65.8	13.8	1,364	25.9	3	12
North Dakota	64.9	0.2	273	17.0	0	3
Ohio	66.6	-0.3	560	22.0	5	15
Oklahoma	56.6	-2.9	1,612	11.4	1	6
Oregon	67.9	-5.7	467	28.9	0	7
Pennsylvania	64.0	2.2	456	14.6	2	19
Rhode Island	62.4	7.0	485	22.1	0	4
South Carolina	58.6	10.6	1,335	10.0	0	8
South Dakota	63.8	-6.5	954	20.0	1	2
Tennessee	57.3	1.8	1,275	18.9	1	10
Texas	54.7	1.9	2,769	23.2	4	30
Utah	53.6	-9.0	339	22.1	0	5
Vermont	66.7	0.6	...	37.2	0	3
Virginia	67.6	11.6	1,092	18.6	0	13
Washington	66.9	0.0	1,651	32.7	3	8
West Virginia	50.6	-6.5	768	16.4	1	4
Wisconsin	72.5	-3.1	918	22.0	2	8
Wyoming	65.3	-0.6	1,311	16.7	1	2

* non-voting

1. United States Elections Project at George Mason University. Turnout for presidential election.

2. United States Elections Project at George Mason University. Change between 2004 and 2008.

3. United States Elections Project at George Mason University.

4. National Conference of State Legislatures, "Women in State Legislatures."

5. Center for American Women and Politics, "Women Serving in the 111th Congress 2009–11." Includes members of the House of Representatives and the Senate.

6. AHDP calculation based on data from the Center for American Women and Politics, "Women Serving in the 111th Congress 2009–11."

U.S. INDICATOR TABLES

Protecting National Security

GROUPING	ARMY RECRUITS 2008[1]	ARMY RECRUITS (per 1,000 youth) 2007[2]	ARMY RECRUITS (per 1,000 youth) 2008[3]	CHANGE IN ARMY RECRUITS, 2007–2008 (%)[4]	TOTAL MILITARY CASUALTIES IN OPERATIONS ENDURING FREEDOM AND IRAQI FREEDOM, TO APRIL 2010[5]
United States	69,357	1.6	1.6	0.0	5,322
RACE/ETHNICITY					
African American	...	1.5	1.7	11.8	...
Asian American	...	...	...	...	...
Latino	...	0.9	0.9	0.0	...
Native American	...	...	...	...	...
White	...	1.7	1.7	0.0	...
STATE					
Alabama	1,630	2.5	2.5	0.0	87
Alaska	215	2.1	2.0	-5.0	21
Arizona	1,996	1.9	2.3	17.4	123
Arkansas	753	2.3	2.0	-15.0	70
California	6,087	1.1	1.1	0.0	570
Colorado	1,041	1.6	1.6	0.0	76
Connecticut	388	0.8	0.8	0.0	35
Delaware	146	0.8	1.2	33.3	16
District of Columbia	40	0.4	0.4	0.0	8
Florida	5,147	2.1	2.2	4.5	252
Georgia	3,119	2.0	2.4	16.7	171
Hawaii	260	1.7	1.5	-13.3	29
Idaho	446	1.8	2.1	14.3	34
Illinois	2,220	1.3	1.2	-8.3	207
Indiana	1,518	1.6	1.7	5.9	122
Iowa	588	1.4	1.4	0.0	56
Kansas	689	2.0	1.7	-17.6	55
Kentucky	927	1.8	1.7	-5.9	87
Louisiana	922	1.5	1.4	-7.1	99
Maine	369	2.3	2.2	-4.5	37
Maryland	952	1.2	1.2	0.0	95
Massachusetts	873	0.9	1.0	10.0	103
Michigan	2,176	1.6	1.5	-6.7	182
Minnesota	733	0.9	1.0	10.0	79
Mississippi	684	1.3	1.6	18.8	64
Missouri	1,562	2.0	1.9	-5.3	111
Montana	286	2.4	2.1	-14.3	37
Nebraska	386	1.5	1.5	0.0	51
Nevada	774	2.1	2.4	12.5	50
New Hampshire	252	1.4	1.4	0.0	33
New Jersey	999	0.8	0.9	11.1	92
New Mexico	528	1.6	1.8	11.1	48
New York	2,971	1.1	1.1	0.0	241
North Carolina	2,650	2.1	2.2	4.5	141
North Dakota	56	0.6	0.5	-20.0	18
Ohio	2,523	1.6	1.6	0.0	211
Oklahoma	1,012	2.3	1.9	-21.1	91
Oregon	867	1.7	1.8	5.6	90
Pennsylvania	2,171	1.3	1.3	0.0	239
Rhode Island	151	1.0	1.0	0.0	12
South Carolina	1,387	2.1	2.2	4.5	71
South Dakota	162	1.2	1.4	14.3	22
Tennessee	1,501	1.7	1.9	10.5	114
Texas	8,077	2.2	2.3	4.3	481
Utah	494	0.7	1.1	36.4	36

1–4. National Priorities Project. National Priorities Project Database. "Youth" recruits refer to active-duty recruits ages 15 to 24.

5. U.S. Department of Defense, "DoD Personnel and Procurement Statistics," provided by the Defense Manpower Data Center.

Protecting National Security *continued*

GROUPING	ARMY RECRUITS 2008[1]	ARMY RECRUITS (per 1,000 youth) 2007[2]	ARMY RECRUITS (per 1,000 youth) 2008[3]	CHANGE IN ARMY RECRUITS, 2007–2008 (%)[4]	TOTAL MILITARY CASUALTIES IN OPERATIONS ENDURING FREEDOM AND IRAQI FREEDOM, TO APRIL 2010[5]
Vermont	116	0.8	1.3	38.5	23
Virginia	2,103	1.8	1.9	5.3	154
Washington	1,368	1.4	1.6	12.5	120
West Virginia	448	2.0	1.9	–5.3	36
Wisconsin	1,041	1.7	1.3	–30.8	104
Wyoming	135	1.8	1.8	0.0	18

OECD INDICATOR TABLES

Demographics

COUNTRY	POPULATION (millions) 2008[1]	POPULATION 0–14 (% of total) 2008[2]	AGE 65 AND OVER (% of total) 2008[3]	POPULATION 65 AND OVER (per 100 youth under 15) 2008[4]	FOREIGN-BORN POPULATION (% of total)[5]
U.S. Rank	1st	6th	23rd	24th	7th
Australia	21.4	19.2	13.4	69.9	18.0
Austria	8.3	15.2	17.0	111.9	11.1
Belgium	10.7	16.9	17.2	102.3	9.5
Canada	33.3	16.8	13.6	81.2	16.1
Czech Republic	10.4	14.1	14.7	103.7	4.2
Denmark	5.5	18.4	15.9	86.6	5.8
Finland	5.3	16.8	16.5	98.2	2.1
France	62.0	18.4	16.6	90.3	9.0
Germany	82.1	13.7	20.0	145.7	9.5
Greece	11.2	14.2	18.2	127.9	8.9
Hungary	10.0	15.0	16.1	107.4	2.8
Iceland	0.3	20.9	11.7	55.9	...
Ireland	4.5	20.6	11.1	53.9	7.4
Italy	59.9	14.2	20.1	141.7	3.4
Japan	127.7	13.4	21.4	159.3	0.9
Luxembourg	0.5	18.0	14.0	78.0	26.0
Mexico	106.4	29.1	6.2	21.4	0.2
Netherlands	16.4	17.9	14.7	82.0	8.7
New Zealand	4.3	20.7	12.5	60.7	14.5
Norway	4.8	19.1	14.6	76.5	6.4
Poland	38.1	15.2	13.3	87.6	1.9
Portugal	10.6	15.4	17.5	113.9	5.5
Slovak Republic	5.4	15.6	12.0	76.5	2.1
South Korea	48.6	17.4	10.4	59.6	...
Spain	45.6	14.7	16.9	115.1	4.2
Sweden	9.2	16.7	17.7	106.0	10.2
Switzerland	7.6	15.5	16.7	107.5	19.1
Turkey	73.9	27.2	5.8	21.4	1.5
United Kingdom	61.4	17.5	16.3	92.9	7.3
United States	304.1	20.4	12.6	61.8	10.3

1. World Bank, World Development Indicators. Source data are from World Bank estimates from census reports, UN Population Division's World Population Prospects, national statistical offices, household surveys conducted by national agencies. Total population counts all residents regardless of legal status or citizenship.

2–3. World Bank, World Development Indicators. Source data are from World Bank estimates from census reports, UN Population Division's World Population Prospects, national statistical offices, household surveys conducted by national agencies.

4. AHDP calculations based on data in columns 2 and 3.

5. OECD StatExtract. Database on Immigrants in OECD countries. Source data are from most recent national censuses.

OECD INDICATOR TABLES

A Long and Healthy Life

COUNTRY	LIFE EXPECTANCY, TOTAL POPULATION (years) 2007[1]	LIFE EXPECTANCY, WOMEN (years) 2007[2]	LIFE EXPECTANCY, MEN (years) 2007[3]	INFANT MORTALITY (per 1,000 live births) 2008[4]	CHILD MORTALITY (under 5, per 1,000 live births) 2008[5]	TOTAL HEALTH EXPENDITURE (as % of GDP) 2008[6]	TOTAL HEALTH EXPENDITURE, PER CAPITA (PPP US$) 2007[7]
U.S. Rank	23rd	23rd	24th	3rd	4th	1st	1st
Australia	81.4	83.7	79.0	4.9	5.8	8.9	3,357
Austria	80.1	82.9	77.3	3.4	4.1	10.1	3,763
Belgium	79.8	82.6	77.1	3.9	4.8	10.2	3,595
Canada	80.7	83.0	78.4	5.7	6.4	10.1	3,895
Czech Republic	77.0	80.2	73.8	3.1	3.8	6.8	1,626
Denmark	78.0	80.6	76.2	3.7	4.4	9.8	3,512
Finland	79.5	83.1	76.0	2.7	3.4	8.2	2,840
France	80.9	84.4	77.5	3.3	3.9	11.0	3,601
Germany	80.0	82.7	77.4	3.7	4.3	10.4	3,588
Greece	79.5	82.0	77.0	3.3	4.0	9.6	2,727
Hungary	73.3	77.3	69.2	5.4	6.5	7.4	1,388
Iceland	81.2	82.9	79.4	1.9	2.8	9.3	3,319
Ireland	79.7	82.1	77.4	3.0	3.7	7.6	3,424
Italy	81.4	84.2	78.5	3.0	3.6	9.0	2,686
Japan	82.6	86.0	79.2	2.5	3.5	8.1	2,581
Luxembourg	79.4	82.2	76.7	1.9	2.6	7.3	4,162
Mexico	75.1	77.4	72.6	15.3	17.5	5.9	823
Netherlands	80.2	82.3	78.0	4.0	4.7	9.8	3,837
New Zealand	80.2	82.2	78.2	4.9	5.7	9.0	2,454
Norway	80.6	82.9	78.3	2.9	3.5	8.6	4,763
Poland	75.4	79.7	71.0	5.8	6.9	6.4	1,035
Portugal	79.1	82.2	75.9	2.9	3.6	9.9	2,150
Slovak Republic	74.3	78.1	70.5	6.6	8.0	7.7	1,555
South Korea	79.4	82.7	76.1	4.7	5.1	6.6	1,688
Spain	81.0	84.3	77.8	3.5	4.3	8.5	2,671
Sweden	81.0	83.0	78.9	2.3	3.0	9.1	3,323
Switzerland	81.9	84.4	79.5	4.0	4.6	10.8	4,417
Turkey	73.4	75.6	71.1	19.9	22.0	5.7	618
United Kingdom	79.5	81.7	77.3	4.9	5.7	8.4	2,992
United States	78.1	80.7	75.4	6.7	7.8	16.0	7,290

1–3. OECD StatExtracts, OECD Health Data 2009. Data are from 2007 or latest available year.

4–5. World Bank, World Development Indicators. Source data from the Inter-agency Group for Child Mortality Estimation (UNICEF, WHO, World Bank, UNPD, universities and research institutions).

6. OECD StatExtracts, OECD Health Data 2009. 2008 or latest available year.

7–9. OECD StatExtracts, OECD Health Data. Year cited or latest available year. Per capita expenditure data shown in purchasing power parity (PPP)-adjusted dollars.

COUNTRY	PUBLIC HEALTH EXPENDITURE (as % of total health expenditure) 2008[8]	PRIVATE HEALTH EXPENDITURE (as % of total health expenditure) 2008[9]	NEW AIDS CASES (per million population) in 2006[10]	SMOKING (% of population smoking daily) 2007[11]	PHYSICIANS (per 1,000 population) 2007[12]	SUICIDE (per 100,000 population) 2007[13]	ADULT OBESITY (%) 2008[14]
U.S. Rank	29th	2nd	1st	29th	22nd	16th	1st
Australia	67.5	32.5	10.0	16.6	2.8	9.8	21.7
Austria	76.4	23.6	6.8	23.2	3.8	12.5	12.4
Belgium	...	...	7.6	22.0	4.0	...	12.7
Canada	69.8	30.2	9.5	18.4	2.2	10.2	15.4
Czech Republic	85.2	14.8	1.6	24.3	3.6	11.1	17.0
Denmark	84.5	15.5	9.4	25.0	3.2	9.9	11.4
Finland	74.6	25.4	4.9	20.6	3.0	16.7	14.9
France	79.0	21.0	17.3	25.0	3.4	14.2	10.5
Germany	76.9	23.1	7.3	23.2	3.5	9.1	13.6
Greece	60.3	39.7	7.7	40.0	5.4	2.5	18.1
Hungary	70.6	29.4	2.2	30.4	2.8	21.0	18.8
Iceland	82.5	17.5	7.9	19.4	3.7	11.4	20.1
Ireland	80.7	19.3	8.9	29.0	3.0	10.0	15.0
Italy	77.4	22.6	19.4	22.4	3.7	4.8	9.9
Japan	81.3	18.7	3.2	26.0	2.1	19.4	3.4
Luxembourg	90.9	9.1	23.8	21.0	2.9	9.5	20.0
Mexico	45.2	54.8	45.3	26.4	2.0	4.3	30.0
Netherlands	62.5	37.5	16.7	29.0	3.9	7.1	11.2
New Zealand	78.9	21.1	5.3	18.1	2.3	12.2	26.5
Norway	84.2	15.8	6.9	22.0	3.9	10.8	9.0
Poland	70.8	29.2	4.1	26.3	2.2	13.2	12.5
Portugal	70.8	29.2	57.1	19.6	3.5	8.7	15.4
Slovak Republic	66.8	33.2	0.7	25.0	3.1	10.9	16.7
South Korea	52.7	47.3	1.6	25.3	1.7	21.5	3.5
Spain	71.8	28.2	35.3	26.4	3.7	6.3	14.9
Sweden	81.7	18.3	6.1	14.5	3.6	11.3	10.2
Switzerland	59.3	40.7	19.6	20.4	3.9	14.0	8.1
Turkey	71.4	28.6	0.5	33.4	1.5	...	12.0
United Kingdom	81.7	18.3	12.2	21.0	2.5	5.8	24.0
United States	45.4	54.6	127.0	15.4	2.4	10.1	34.3

10. OECD, Health at a Glance 2009: OECD Indicators. Table 1.13.

11–14. OECD StatExtracts, OECD Health Data 2009. Year cited or latest available year.

OECD INDICATOR TABLES

Access to Knowledge

COUNTRY	SCIENCE LITERACY (average PISA scores, out of 1,000) 2006[1]	MATH LITERACY (average PISA scores) 2006[2]	PUBLIC EDUCATION EXPENDITURE (% of GDP) 2006[3]	LESS THAN UPPER SECONDARY EDUCATION (% population 25–64) 2007[4]	AT LEAST TERTIARY EDUCATION (% population 25–64) 2007[5]	ADVANCED DEGREE (% population 25–64) 2007[6]
U.S. Rank	21st	26th	8th	28th	2nd	9th
Australia	527	520	5.2	31.8	24.1	9.6
Austria	511	505	...	19.9	10.4	7.2
Belgium	510	520	6.0	32.0	13.5	18.6
Canada	534	527	...	13.4	24.6	23.7
Czech Republic	513	510	4.6	9.3	13.7	0.0*
Denmark	498	513	7.9	24.5	25.0	7.2
Finland	563	548	6.1	19.5	20.0	16.4
France	495	496	5.6	31.3	15.3	11.5
Germany	516	504	4.4	15.6	14.4	9.9
Greece	473	459	...	40.4	15.0	7.4
Hungary	504	491	5.4	20.8	17.4	0.0*
Iceland	491	506	7.6	35.5	24.7	5.1
Ireland	508	501	4.8	32.4	20.6	11.1
Italy	475	462	4.7	47.7	12.9	0.5
Japan	531	523	3.5	...	23.1	17.9
Luxembourg	486	490	...	34.3	16.6	9.9
Mexico	410	506	4.8	66.7	14.9	0.0*
Netherlands	525	531	5.5	26.8	28.3	2.5
New Zealand	530	522	6.2	28.4	25.3	15.7
Norway	487	490	6.5	20.8	31.3	3.0
Poland	498	495	5.7	13.7	18.7	0.0*
Portugal	474	466	5.3	72.5	12.9	0.8
Slovak Republic	488	492	3.8	13.0	13.1	0.7
South Korea	522	547	4.2	22.1	24.4	10.2
Spain	488	480	4.3	49.3	19.4	9.6
Sweden	503	502	6.9	15.4	22.6	8.7
Switzerland	512	530	5.5	14.0	18.8	12.6
Turkey	424	424	...	71.3	10.8	0.0*
United Kingdom	515	495	5.6	31.5	21.8	10.0
United States	489	474	5.7	12.1	29.6	10.6

1–2. OECD PISA Country Profiles.

3. World Bank, World Development Indicators. Source data from UNESCO Institute for Statistics.

4–6. OECD, Education at a Glance 2009. Table A1.4 and Table A1.1a.

7–8. OECD StatExtracts, Education and Training—Education and Skills.

COUNTRY	PRE-PRIMARY ENROLLMENT (% enrolled ages 3 and 4) 2007[7]	GROSS ENROLLMENT (% enrolled 3–24 at any level) 2007[8]	INTERNET USERS (per 1,000 population) 2008[9]	BROADBAND SUBSCRIBERS (per 1,000 population) 2008[10]	RESEARCH AND DEVELOPMENT SPENDING (% of GDP) 2007[11]	RESEARCH AND DEVELOPMENT SPENDING (US$ per capita) 2007[12]
U.S. Rank	20th	18th	10th	15th	6th	4th
Australia	32.2	97.7	708	24.9	2.17	721
Austria	67.5	80.7	712	21.8	2.52	963
Belgium	99.7	104.1	681	28.4	1.91	664
Canada	...	71.4	753	29.7	2.03	725
Czech Republic	75.1	85.1	578	18.1	1.59	370
Denmark	94.0	97.8	833	37.0	2.57	921
Finland	46.0	100.8	825	29.7	3.47	1,196
France	99.8	85.2	679	29.1	2.10	703
Germany	89.3	87.8	755	29.3	2.55	846
Greece	27.7	82.3	431	17.0	0.50	166
Hungary	82.7	88.9	585	16.8	0.97	181
Iceland	96.0	99.9	900	32.8	2.81	1,054
Ireland	23.8	80.3	627	21.4	1.34	579
Italy	97.7	87.8	418	19.8	1.14	329
Japan	84.1	78.5	752	24.2	3.45	1,158
Luxembourg	80.6	71.4	792	31.3	1.69	1,347
Mexico	60.4	71.4	222	8.4	...	...
Netherlands	49.6	86.0	870	38.1	1.75	663
New Zealand	90.1	97.8	714	22.8	1.26	331
Norway	91.8	94.1	825	34.5	1.67	889
Poland	38.8	84.3	490	11.3	0.57	91
Portugal	72.0	83.1	421	17.0	1.19	259
Slovak Republic	68.0	78.8	660	12.6	0.46	93
South Korea	27.3	82.4	758	32.8	3.47	868
Spain	97.6	89.6	554	20.8	1.28	408
Sweden	98.4	102.0	877	31.6	3.68	1,335
Switzerland	24.1	81.0	759	33.8	...	...
Turkey	6.7	58.9	344	8.7	0.71	90
United Kingdom	85.0	81.8	760	28.9	1.84	620
United States	49.8	82.4	759	26.7	2.67	1,195

9. World Bank, World Development Indicators. Source data from International Telecommunication Union, World Telecommunication Development Report and database, and World Bank estimates.

10. OECD Directorate for Science, Technology and Industry, OECD Broadband Portal.

11–12. UNESCO Institute of Statistics. Table 12. 2007 or most recent year available.

* Advanced degree holders are counted among the population with at least a tertiary education.

A Decent Standard of Living

COUNTRY	GROSS DOMESTIC PRODUCT (PPP$ per capita) 2008[1]	GDP GROWTH (annual %) 2008[2]	INCOME RATIO OF RICHEST 10% TO POOREST 10% 1992–2007[3]	GINI INDEX, BEFORE TAXES AND TRANSFERS mid-2000s[4]	GINI INDEX, AFTER TAXES AND TRANSFERS mid-2000s[5]	POPULATION LIVING BELOW 50% OF MEDIAN INCOME (%) 2000–2006[6]	CHILD POVERTY RATE (%) 2005[7]	UNEMPLOYMENT RATE (% 15 and over) 2008[8]
U.S. Rank	3rd	19th	3rd	9th	4th	2nd	4th	16th
Australia	35,624	3.7	12.5	0.46	0.30	12.2	11.8	4.2
Austria	35,866	1.8	6.9	0.43	0.27	7.1	6.2	3.8
Belgium	33,544	1.1	8.2	0.49	0.27	8.1	10.0	7.0
Canada	36,102	0.4	9.4	0.44	0.32	13.0	15.1	6.1
Czech Republic	23,223	2.5	5.3	0.47	0.27	...	10.3	4.4
Denmark	34,005	-1.1	8.1	0.42	0.23	5.6	2.7	3.3
Finland	33,377	0.9	5.6	0.39	0.27	6.5	4.2	6.4
France	30,595	0.4	9.1	0.48	0.28	7.3	7.6	7.4
Germany	33,668	1.3	6.9	0.51	0.30	8.5	16.3	7.5
Greece	27,565	2.9	10.2	...	0.32	12.5	13.2	7.7
Hungary	18,039	0.6	5.5	...	0.29	7.4	8.7	7.8
Iceland	36,113	0.3	...	0.37	0.28	...	8.3	3.0
Ireland	39,433	-3.0	9.4	0.42	0.33	16.2	16.3	6.0
Italy	28,272	-1.0	11.6	0.56	0.35	12.1	15.5	6.7
Japan	31,464	-0.7	4.5	0.44	0.32	...	13.7	4.0
Luxembourg	72,039	-0.9	6.8	0.45	0.26	8.8	12.4	5.1
Mexico	13,407	1.8	24.6	...	0.47	18.4	22.2	4.0
Netherlands	38,048	2.1	9.2	0.42	0.27	4.9	11.5	2.8
New Zealand	25,011	-1.1	12.5	0.47	0.34	..	15.0	4.1
Norway	49,416	2.1	6.1	0.43	0.28	7.1	4.6	2.6
Poland	16,418	4.9	5.8	0.57	0.37	11.5	21.5	7.1
Portugal	21,175	0.0	15.0	0.54	0.38	...	16.6	7.6
Slovak Republic	20,515	6.2	6.8	0.46	0.27	...	10.9	9.5
South Korea	25,498	2.2	7.8	0.34	0.31	14.0	10.2	3.2
Spain	28,412	1.2	10.3	...	0.32	14.1	17.3	11.3
Sweden	33,769	-0.2	6.2	0.43	0.23	5.6	4.0	6.2
Switzerland	37,788	1.8	9.0	0.35	0.28	8.0	9.4	...
Turkey	11,932	0.9	17.4	...	0.43	..	24.6	9.4
United Kingdom	34,204	0.7	13.8	0.46	0.34	11.6	10.1	5.6
United States	42,809	0.4	15.9	0.46	0.38	17.3	20.6	5.8

1. World Bank, World Development Indicators. Source data from the World Bank International Comparisons Program database. Gross domestic product on a purchasing power parity (PPP) basis divided by population as of July 1 for the same year.

2. World Bank, World Development Indicators. Source data from World Bank national accounts data, and OECD National Accounts data files.

3. World Bank, World Development Indicators, Source data from World Bank Development Research Group and Luxembourg Income Study. Most recent year available during specified period.

4–5. OECD StatExtracts. Social and welfare statistics.

6. Luxembourg Income Study, "LISKey Figures." Most recent year available during specified period.

COUNTRY	LONG-TERM UNEMPLOYMENT (% of total unemployment) 2008[9]	UNION MEMBERSHIP (% of workforce) 2007[10]	SAVING RATE (% of household disposable income) 2008[11]	PAID MATERNITY LEAVE (weeks entitlement) 2006–2007[12]	PAID PATERNITY LEAVE (weeks entitlement) 2006–2007[13]	PAID BREASTFEEDING BREAKS (yes or no) 2008[14]	STATUTORY MINIMUM PAID ANNUAL LEAVE (days) 2007[15]
U.S. Rank	24th	15th	17th	29th	...	...	...
Australia	14.9	18.5	...	*	*	N	20
Austria	24.2	...	12.0	16.0	0.4	Y	25
Belgium	52.6	52.9	11.5	11.3	1.2	Y	20
Canada	7.1	29.4	3.8	8.3	0.0	N	10 to 20
Czech Republic	50.2	...	5.8	13.7	0.0	Y	20
Denmark	16.1	69.1	-0.3	18.0	2.0	N	25
Finland	18.2	70.3	-1.0	16.9	5.7	N	20
France	37.9	7.8	11.6	16.0	2.0	N	25
Germany	53.4	19.9	11.2	14.0	0.0	Y	20
Greece	49.6	...	...	17.0	0.4	Y	20
Hungary	47.6	16.9	3.0	16.8	1.0	Y	20
Iceland	4.1	...	4.1	10.4	10.4	N	...
Ireland	29.4	31.7	...	18.2	0.0	Y	20
Italy	47.5	33.3	8.6	16.0	0.0	Y	20
Japan	33.3	18.3	3.8	8.4	0.0	Y	10 to 20
Luxembourg	38.6	...	...	16.0	0.4	Y	25
Mexico	1.7	...	...	12.0	0.0	Y	...
Netherlands	36.3	19.8	6.8	16.0	0.4	Y	20
New Zealand	4.4	...	...	5.0	0.0	N	20
Norway	6.0	53.7	-1.2	9.0	6.0	N	21
Poland	29.0	...	7.4	18.0	4.0	Y	20
Portugal	48.3	...	-0.9	17.0	2.0	Y	22
Slovak Republic	66.1	...	1.8	15.4	0.0	Y	20
South Korea	2.7	...	2.8	15.0	0.0	N	8 to 20
Spain	23.8	...	6.1	16.0	2.0	Y	22
Sweden	12.4	70.8	12.1	9.6	9.3	N	25
Switzerland	34.3	...	12.7	12.8	0.0	Y	20 to 25
Turkey	26.9	...	...	7.9	0.0	Y	...
United Kingdom	25.5	28.0	-4.5	9.3	0.3	N	24
United States	10.6	11.6	2.7	0.0	0.0	N	0

7. OECD StatExtracts. Social and welfare statistics. Poverty is defined as less than 50 percent of median income.

8–9. International Labour Organization, Key Indicators of the Labour Market Database [KILM], Tables 8a and 10. Copyright © International Labour Organization, 1996–2010.

10. OECD StatExtracts. Labor force statistics.

11. OECD Factbook 2010. 2008 or most recent year available.

12–13. OECD Family Database 2010. Table PF2.1; reflects weeks of leave with full-time equivalent earnings.

14. World Alliance for Breastfeeding Action, "Maternity Protection Chart," 2008.

15. OECD, Society at a Glance. Table PF9.1.

* Australia recently enacted a paid parental leave law effective January 1, 2011; it requires 18 weeks of pay at minimum wage.

OECD INDICATOR TABLES

Preserving the Earth for Future Generations

COUNTRY	ELECTRICITY CONSUMPTION (kWh per capita) 2007[1]	GDP PER UNIT OF ENERGY USE (ratio of $ to kg oil equivalent in 2000 PPP$) 2007[2]	CARBON DIOXIDE EMISSIONS (% of world's total) 2006[3]	CARBON DIOXIDE EMISSIONS (tons per capita) 2006[4]	WATER CONSUMPTION (meters³ per capita) 2006[5]
U.S. Rank	7th	25th	1st	2nd	1st
Australia	11,249	6.4	1.35	19.0	930
Austria	8,033	9.2	0.27	9.3	470
Belgium	8,614	6.5	0.41	11.4	640
Canada	16,995	4.7	1.94	17.2	...
Czech Republic	6,496	5.4	0.44	12.6	190
Denmark	6,670	10.1	0.20	10.6	130
Finland	17,162	5.1	0.24	12.9	450
France	7,772	7.9	1.41	6.7	560
Germany	7,184	8.6	3.04	10.7	430
Greece	5,628	9.7	0.38	9.9	...
Hungary	3,977	7.1	0.21	6.0	580
Iceland	36,853	2.3	0.01	10.2	560
Ireland	6,263	12.9	0.16	11.2	...
Italy	5,713	10.3	1.69	8.3	...
Japan	8,474	8.4	4.40	10.0	650
Luxembourg	16,315	9.1	0.04	26.2	...
Mexico	2,036	8.1	1.51	4.1	740
Netherlands	7,097	8.0	0.60	10.5	630
New Zealand	9,622	6.9	0.13	8.8	950
Norway	24,980	9.4	0.15	9.3	540
Poland	3,662	6.4	1.14	8.7	300
Portugal	4,860	9.6	0.22	6.0	860
Slovak Republic	5,250	6.1	0.14	7.4	140
South Korea	8,502	5.8	1.64	9.9	610
Spain	6,296	9.8	1.24	8.2	890
Sweden	15,238	6.7	0.18	5.7	300
Switzerland	8,164	12.2	0.16	6.1	340
Turkey	2,238	9.4	0.95	3.7	620
United Kingdom	6,120	10.1	1.93	9.2	240
United States	13,652	5.9	20.65	19.7	1,690

1. World Bank, World Development Indicators. Source data from the International Energy Agency, Energy Statistics and Balances of Non-OECD Countries, and Energy Statistics of OECD Countries.

2. World Bank, World Development Indicators. Source data from the International Energy Agency and World Bank PPP data.

3–4. UN Statistics Division, Millennium Development Goals Database. Carbon dioxide emissions (CO2), thousand metric tons of CO2 (UNFCCC). Accessed June 22, 2010.

5. OECD Factbook 2009. Data are from 2006 or latest year available.

OECD INDICATOR TABLES

Protecting Personal and Community Security

COUNTRY	THEFTS (per 100,000 population) 2006–2008[1]	RAPE (per 100,000 population) 2006–2008[2]	HOMICIDE (per 100,000 population) 2006–2008[3]	PRISONERS (per 100,000 population) 2007–2008[4]
U.S. Rank	11th	3rd	2nd	1st
Australia	2,357	...	1.2	129
Austria	2,354	...	0.5	99
Belgium	2,056	26.3	1.8	93
Canada	1,711	1.5	1.7	116
Czech Republic	1,427	5.1	2.0	209
Denmark	3,482	7.3	1.4	63
Finland	2,266	17.2	2.5	67
France	979	16.6	1.4	96
Germany	2,399	8.9	0.8	90
Greece	760	2.0	1.1	109
Hungary	1,200	4.9	1.5	152
Iceland	2,239	21.6	0.0	44
Ireland	1,000	10.0	2.0	85
Italy	1,936	7.7	1.2	97
Japan	1,079	1.2	0.5	63
Luxembourg	1,389	11.9	1.5	97
Mexico	...	12.8	11.6	155
Netherlands	3,498	8.7	1.0	208
New Zealand	2,655	30.9	1.3	100
Norway	2,647	19.8	0.6	195
Poland	516	4.2	1.2	70
Portugal	952	3.0	1.2	225
Slovak Republic	357	2.8	1.7	104
South Korea	464	...	2.3	151
Spain	327	5.5	0.9	164
Sweden	4,256	53.2	0.9	74
Switzerland	1,602	8.1	0.7	76
Turkey	163	1.4	2.9	155
United Kingdom	...	...	...	153
United States	2,114	28.6	5.2	760

1. United Nations Office on Drugs and Crime, "UNODC Crime and Criminal Justice Statistics." UNODC Homicide Statistics.

2–3. United Nations Office on Drugs and Crime, "UNODC Crime and Criminal Justice Statistics." Source data are from United Nations Survey of Crime Trends and Operations of Criminal Justice Systems, national governments, Eurostat, and NGO estimates.

4. OECD Factbook 2010, Economic, Environmental, and Social Statistics.

OECD INDICATOR TABLES

Political Participation

COUNTRY	SEATS IN NATIONAL LEGISLATURE HELD BY WOMEN (%) 2009[1]	VOTING-AGE POPULATION WHO VOTED IN LAST PARLIAMENTARY ELECTION (%) 2008 or most recent election[2]	VOTING-AGE POPULATION WHO VOTED IN LAST PRESIDENTIAL ELECTION (%) 2008 or most recent election[3]
U.S. Rank	23rd	30th	4th
Australia	27	82.7	...
Austria	28	75.6	66.5
Belgium	35	86.0	...
Canada	22	53.6	...
Czech Republic	16	65.1	...
Denmark	38	83.2	
Finland	42	68.2	77.6
France	18	54.5	76.8
Germany	33	72.0	...
Greece	17	79.6	...
Hungary	11	41.1	...
Iceland	43	84.7	63.7
Ireland	13	68.9	47.7
Italy	21	79.1	...
Japan	11	66.6	...
Luxembourg	20	56.5	...
Mexico	28	63.6	63.3
Netherlands	41	77.5	...
New Zealand	34	77.8	...
Norway	39	76.5	...
Poland	20	54.2	51.5
Portugal	27	69.2	67.0
Slovak Republic	19	56.4	44.1
South Korea	14	46.6	64.2
Spain	36	77.2	...
Sweden	47	80.6	...
Switzerland	29	39.8	...
Turkey	9	74.0	...
United Kingdom	20	58.3	...
United States	17	37.3	58.2

1. Inter-Parliamentary Union. "Women in National Parliaments."

2–3. International Institute for Democracy and Electoral Assistance (IDEA), Voter Turnout Database©, 2010. Voting-age population includes all citizens above voting age.

OECD INDICATOR TABLES

Protecting National Security

COUNTRY	DEFENSE EXPENDITURE (% of GDP) 2008[1]	DEFENSE EXPENDITURE (PPP US$ per capita) 2008[2]	ARMED FORCES PERSONNEL (thousands) 2008[3]	MILITARY CASUALTIES IN OPERATION ENDURING FREEDOM 2010[4]	MILITARY CASUALTIES IN OPERATION IRAQI FREEDOM 2010[5]
U.S. Rank	1st	1st	1st	1st	1st
Australia	1.8	634	55	11	2
Austria	0.9	308	35	...	...
Belgium	1.1	368	39	1	...
Canada	1.3	464	64	142	...
Czech Republic	1.5	343	27	3	1
Denmark	1.3	444	30	31	7
Finland	1.3	434	32	1	...
France	2.3	703	353	41	...
Germany	1.3	431	244	42	...
Greece	3.5	978	161	...	...
Hungary	1.2	218	37	2	1
Iceland	...	...	0	...	...
Ireland	0.6	233	10	...	...
Italy	1.8	498	436	22	33
Japan	0.9	297	242	...	...
Luxembourg	...	...	2	...	...
Mexico	0.4	53	286	...	...
Netherlands	1.4	534	47	23	2
New Zealand	1.1	270	9	...	...
Norway	1.3	642	19	5	...
Poland	2.0	334	143	16	23
Portugal	2.0	418	91	2	...
Slovak Republic	1.6	319	17	...	4
South Korea	2.6	664	692	1	1
Spain	1.2	340	223	28	11
Sweden	1.3	445	18	4	...
Switzerland	0.8	311	23	...	...
Turkey	2.2	259	613	2	...
United Kingdom	2.4	837	160	281	179
United States	4.3	1,845	1,540	1,049	4,393

1. World Bank, World Development Indicators. Source data from the Stockholm International Peace Research Institute.

2. World Bank, World Development Indicators. Calculated using military expenditure, % of GDP, and GDP per capita, PPP constant 2008$.

3. World Bank, World Development Indicators. Source data from the International Institute for Strategic Studies.

4-5. icasualties.org. Current as of April 24, 2010.

References

IN THIS SECTION:

Methodological Notes[1]

Calculating the American HD Index

The American Human Development (HD) Index is calculated using a simple methodology that is replicated for each state, congressional district, metro area, and population group. First, a sub-index for each of the three components of the overall index—health, education, and income—is calculated, and each of the three components is weighted one-third in the index. This equal weighting is not arbitrary, but rather reflects a belief that these three basic building blocks of a life of freedom and opportunity are equally essential. Performance in each dimension is expressed as a value between 0 and 10 by applying the following general formula:

$$\text{Dimension Index} = \frac{\text{actual value} - \text{minimum value}}{\text{maximum value} - \text{minimum value}} \times 10$$

Goalposts for Calculating the American HD Index

For each of the three indices, goalposts are determined based on the range of the indicator observed for all possible groupings and also taking into account possible increases and decreases in years to come. In order to make the HD Index comparable over time, the health and education indicator goalposts do not change from year to year. The earnings goalposts are adjusted for inflation (please see the Income Index section below for more details). Because earnings data and the goalposts are presented in dollars of the same year, these goalposts reflect a constant amount of purchasing power regardless of the year, making Income Index results comparable over time.

INDICATOR	MAXIMUM VALUE	MINIMUM VALUE
Life expectancy at birth (years)	90	66
Educational attainment score	2.0	0.5
Combined gross enrollment ratio (%)	100	70
Median personal earnings (2009 dollars)*	$60,429	$14,283

* Earnings goalposts were originally set at $55,000 and $13,000 in 2005 dollars.

The American HD Index results from taking the simple average of the health, education, and income indices. Since all three components range from 0 to 10, the HD Index itself also varies from 0 to 10, with 10 representing the highest level of human development.

EXAMPLE:

Calculating the HD Index for the United States

HEALTH Index
Life expectancy at birth for the United States was 78.6 years in 2007. The Health Index is calculated as follows:

$$\text{Health Index} = \frac{78.6 - 66}{90 - 66} \times 10 = \mathbf{5.25}$$

EDUCATION Index
In 2008, 85 percent of U.S. adults had at least a high school diploma, 27.7 percent had at least a bachelor's degree, and 10.2 percent had a graduate degree. The Educational Attainment Score is 0.85 + 0.277 + 0.102 = 1.228. The Educational Attainment Index is then:

$$\text{Educational Attainment Index} = \frac{1.228 - 0.5}{2.0 - 0.5} \times 10 = \mathbf{4.86}$$

The combined gross enrollment ratio was 87.3 percent, and the Enrollment Index is then:

$$\text{Enrollment Index} = \frac{87.3 - 70}{100 - 70} \times 10 = \mathbf{5.76}$$

The Educational Attainment Index and the Enrollment Index are then combined to obtain the Education Index:

$$\text{Education Index} = \frac{2}{3}\mathbf{4.86} + \frac{1}{3}\mathbf{5.76} = \mathbf{5.15}$$

INCOME Index
Median earnings in 2008 were $29,755 (in 2009 dollars). The Income Index is then:

$$\text{Income Index} = \frac{\log(29{,}755) - \log(14{,}283)}{\log(60{,}429) - \log(14{,}283)} \times 10 = \mathbf{5.09}$$

HUMAN DEVELOPMENT Index
Once the dimension indices have been calculated, the HD Index is obtained by a simple average of the three indices:

$$\text{HD Index} = \frac{\mathbf{5.25} + \mathbf{5.15} + \mathbf{5.09}}{3} = \mathbf{5.17}$$

Geographic, Racial, and Ethnic Designations

Data in this book are presented for three geographic units: states, congressional districts, and Metropolitan Statistical Areas (MSAs).

Though Washington, DC, is not a state, for the purposes of this report it is treated as one. Doing so is common practice among other analyses of economic and social issues and follows the convention of the U.S. Census Bureau. Washington, DC, also has a larger population than Wyoming and is nearly as populous as Alaska, North Dakota, and Vermont.

The congressional districts in this book are those of the 111th Congress (2008–2010). Congressional districts are typically revised at the beginning of each decade based on the results of the decennial census. However, redistricting changes have occurred in both Georgia and Texas since 2005. Therefore, readers are advised not to compare congressional district data from *The Measure of America 2008–2009* to congressional district data in this volume for any of Georgia's thirteen congressional districts or for Texas Congressional Districts 15, 21, 23, 25, or 28.

MSAs are the designation for urban centers and their outlying areas as defined by the White House Office of Management and Budget. MSAs constitute counties grouped around an urban center of at least fifty thousand people plus outlying counties from which a substantial percentage of the population commute to the urban center. MSAs therefore include principal cities as well as outlying suburban and exurban areas.[2]

Racial and ethnic groups used in this analysis are based on definitions established by the White House Office of Management and Budget (OMB) and used by the Census Bureau, the Centers for Disease Control, and other government entities.[3] Since 1997 the OMB has recognized five racial groups and two ethnic categories. The racial groups include Native

Americans, Asian Americans, African Americans, Native Hawaiians and Other Pacific Islanders, and whites. The ethnic categories are Latino and not Latino. The Native American category includes Alaska Natives for the nation and in states where Alaska Natives reside. AHDP recognizes that Native Hawaiian and Other Pacific Islanders constitute one of the five racial groups recognized by the OMB. However, this group's very small population (about 428,000 in 2008 according to ACS estimates[4]) limits the availability of data for this group. We are therefore unable to provide a complete set of human development data for Native Hawaiians and Other Pacific Islanders at this time.

Health Index

The Health Index measures relative achievement in life expectancy at birth. Life expectancy at birth is calculated using data from two principal sources. Mortality data for 2007, the most recent year for which the data are available, were obtained by arrangement with the National Center for Health Statistics (NCHS) at the Centers for Disease Control and Prevention, and the National Association for Public Health Statistics and Information Systems Vital Statistics Cooperative Program. Bridged-race population estimates for the July 1, 2007, population (using Vintage 2008 data) were obtained from the CDC WONDER Database.

Life expectancy is calculated based on a widely used method developed by C. L. Chiang. This method involves the construction of abridged life tables that use population and mortality counts by age-group as inputs.

The Health Index is obtained by scaling the life expectancy at birth values using the maximum and minimum goalposts and is calculated as follows:

$$\text{Health Index}_i = \frac{LE_i - LE_{MIN}}{LE_{MAX} - LE_{MIN}} \times 10$$

where LE_i is the life expectancy at birth for unit i and LE_{MIN} and LE_{MAX} are the goalposts.

Estimation of Life Expectancy at Birth for Congressional Districts

In the mortality data received from the Centers for Disease Control and Prevention, the state and county in which each decedent lived are flagged but the congressional district of residence is not. Therefore, life expectancy for congressional districts is estimated by apportioning death and population counts by county to congressional districts.

Congressional districts contain roughly 650,000 residents each and do not cross state lines. However, congressional districts do not necessarily conform to county lines within states. In order to determine how counties match up with congressional districts, a "geographic correspondence file" is generated to determine which counties fall within each congressional district and what percentage of the population of each county lives within that district.[5] Using this data, it is possible to allocate mortality and population counts at the county level to congressional districts.

In cases where mid-decade redistricting occurred, estimating congressional district life expectancy required an additional step. Changes that occurred in Georgia and Texas between 2005 and 2008, which affected all Georgia congressional districts and Congressional Districts 15, 21, 23, 25, and 28 in Texas, were not incorporated into the existing correspondence file, requiring AHDP to generate a new correspondence file for aligning counties to congressional districts in these two states. Using the MABLE/Geocorr application, a correspondence file was generated to match counties to Census tracts for Georgia and Texas based on 2008 population estimates. This was then compared to Geographic Relationship Tables for the 110th Congressional Districts in these two states in order to see how new congressional districts map onto existing Census tracts.[6] In the cases where Census tracts were split between congressional districts during this process, the populations of those tracts were split evenly between the two districts. Census tracts contain 8,000 people or less; thus, any distortions due to this arbitrarily even division of the population of split tracts are likely to be very small. As a test of accuracy, a comparison was made between the allocation factors generated by the MABLE/Geocorr application and those generated in-house by AHDP for the Texas districts unaffected by redistricting. These two sets of allocation factors were found to correlate very strongly (r = .955). This correlation suggests that life expectancy estimates made using county-to-congressional-district allocation factors generated by AHDP should be comparable to estimates made using allocation factors generated by the MABLE/Geocorr application.

The figure below illustrates this process. It shows the Thirteenth Congressional District in Illinois, comprising parts of Cook, DuPage, and Will counties. The proportion of each county's population that lives in the congressional district is computed, based on the Census block populations, and those proportions are then used to allocate death counts and population totals for the congressional district.

The Thirteenth Congressional District, Illinois

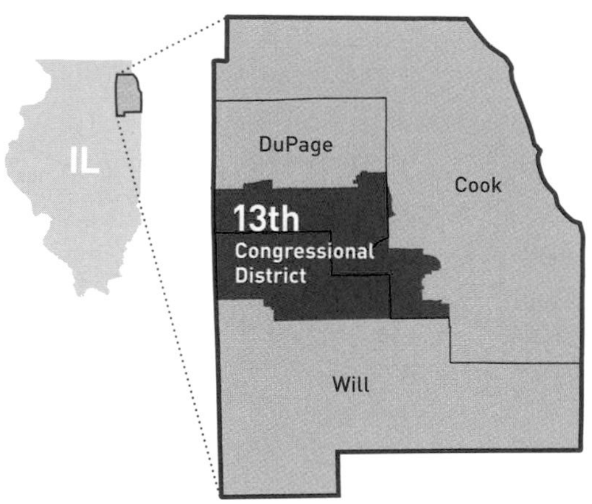

For this example, we have:

COUNTY	POPULATION	SHARE	DEATHS, <1 YEAR	POPULATION, <1 YEAR
Cook, IL	84,393	0.016	150	81,598
DuPage, IL	375,163	0.402	70	12,431
Will, IL	271,606	0.406	50	9,434

Population is the county's population residing in the congressional district; *share* is the percentage of the county's total population residing in the congressional district; *deaths* is the number of deaths of county residents in the age bracket (those are fictional numbers used for illustration purposes only, since the actual data are protected by a nondisclosure agreement); and *population* is each county's population in the age bracket. Thus, 1.6 percent of Cook County's residents, 40.2 percent of DuPage County's residents, and 40.6 percent of Will County's residents live in the Thirteenth Congressional District. The procedure then allocates 1.6 percent of the death counts in Cook County, 40.2 percent of the death counts in DuPage County, and 40.6 percent of the death counts in Will County to the target congressional district. The number of deaths in the < 1 year age bracket for the congressional district is given by

$$(0.016 \times 150) + (0.402 \times 70) + (0.406 \times 50) = 50.84$$

and the population in the same age bracket is given by

$$(0.016 \times 81{,}598) + (0.402 \times 12{,}431) + (0.406 \times 9{,}434) = 10{,}133$$

This procedure is repeated for all the age brackets, resulting in an abridged life table for the congressional district, which is then used to compute the life expectancy at birth.

In some instances, several congressional districts are entirely contained inside a single county; when this happens, the county's life expectancy at birth is assigned to all the congressional districts.

Life Expectancy Estimates for Asian Americans, Latinos, and Native Americans

One challenge in the calculation of life expectancy is the miscoding of race on death certificates, a surprisingly widespread occurrence affecting Asian Americans, Latinos, and Native Americans.[7] In order to calculate life expectancy for these groups, different methods are required to correct for errors in racial classification on death certificates.

The problem is particularly consequential for Native Americans. Drawing on studies undertaken by the National Center for Health Statistics and the Indian Health Service,[8] mortality counts have been adjusted using age group–specific correction factors based on current research about the prevalence of miscoding across the country and in specific states. Life expectancy estimates for this group are based on these adjusted mortality counts. Due to the small population size of Native Americans in the majority of states, and data inconsistencies in others, only twelve states could be included in this analysis.

For Asian Americans and Latinos, a ratio correction was applied in states in which these groups constitute a proportion of the state population that is less than half their share of the total national population. The cut-off values were thus as follows:

GROUP	% OF TOTAL POPULATION	CUT-OFF POINT BELOW WHICH CORRECTION WAS USED FOR STATES
Asian Americans	4.41% (13,413,976)	2.21%
Latinos	15.42% (46,891,456)	7.71%

Based on 2008 American Community Survey (ACS) 1-year population data, the correction was applied to mortality data for Asian Americans and Latinos in the states listed in the next column. As with state-level disaggregation in the other indices, life expectancy was not estimated for population groups smaller than 50,000 in any given state due to the statistical instability of working with survey-based estimates for small populations.

ASIAN AMERICANS	LATINOS
Florida*	Alabama
Indiana	Arkansas
Kansas	Delaware
Louisiana	Georgia*
Missouri	Indiana
North Carolina	Iowa
Ohio	Kentucky
Oklahoma	Louisiana
South Carolina	Maryland
Tennessee	Michigan
Utah	Minnesota
Wisconsin	Mississippi
	Missouri
	North Carolina
	Ohio
	Oklahoma
	Oregon*
	Pennsylvania
	Rhode Island*
	South Carolina
	Tennessee
	Virginia
	Wisconsin

* Although populations in these states are technically above the cut-off point for the application of the correction, the correction was applied nonetheless in order to ensure a plausible result.

To apply the correction method to data for Asian Americans or Latinos in a given state, for each age group, the ratio of the death rate for that group at the national level to the corresponding rate for the total population (i.e., all racial/ethnic groups combined) is calculated. Age-specific death rates for the total population in that state are then multiplied by this national ratio. In this way, for each age group, the ratio of the death rate for the state's race/ethnic group at issue to the rate for the state's total population is identical to the corresponding ratio in the national population. An identical method is used to estimate life expectancy at birth for racial and ethnic groups within certain MSAs in which Asian Americans and Latinos constitute a small percentage of the total population. This method is employed for Asian Americans in the Miami–Fort Lauderdale–Pompano Beach MSA, and for Latinos in the Atlanta–Sandy Springs–Marietta, Boston-Cambridge-Quincy, and Washington-Arlington-Alexandria MSAs. These estimates are one way to approximate life expectancies for racial and ethnic groups for which existing data are too flawed to permit actual calculations. Readers are advised to bear this in mind when comparing these estimates with life expectancy calculations for other groups.

Education Index

The Education Index is based on two sub-indices: an Educational Attainment Index and an Enrollment Index. The **Educational Attainment Index** measures the overall level of educational attainment achieved by the adult population. It takes into account the percentage of the population age 25 years and older who have earned at least a high school diploma or equivalent, at least a bachelor's degree, or an advanced degree (master's, professional, doctoral, etc.). Each category represents the percentage of the adult population who have achieved at least that level of attainment, meaning that the percentage of the population 25 and over with a master's degree necessarily includes those with a bachelor's degree and a high school diploma or its equivalent. To calculate the Educational Attainment Index, first an Attainment Sum is determined by adding the percentage of the population 25 and older with at least a high school diploma or equivalent, the percentage with at least a bachelor's degree, and the percentage with an advanced degree. Those who have earned an associate degree or those who have completed some college without earning a degree are counted in the "at least high school" category. The Educational Attainment Index is calculated as follows:

$$\text{Educational Attainment Index}_i = \frac{EAS_i - EAS_{MIN}}{EAS_{MAX} - EAS_{MIN}} \times 10$$

where EAS_i is the Educational Attainment Score for unit *i* and EAS_{MIN} and EAS_{MAX} are the goalposts.

The **Enrollment Index** is based on a gross enrollment calculation that takes into account the total number of students enrolled in school (of any age at any level) divided by the total school-aged population of 3- to 24-year-olds (inclusive). Therefore,

$$\text{Gross Enrollment Ratio}_i = \frac{ENR_i}{P3TO24_i}$$

where ENR_i is the population of any age enrolled in school at any level and $P3TO24_i$ is the population between the ages of 3 and 24. The Enrollment Index is then calculated:

$$\text{Enrollment Index}_i = \frac{GER_i - GER_{MIN}}{GER_{MAX} - GER_{MIN}} \times 10$$

where GER_i is the Educational Attainment Score for unit *i* and GER_{MIN} and GER_{MAX} are the goalposts. If the Gross Enrollment Ratios exceed 100 percent, as can happen when large numbers of older students are enrolled in school, the Gross Enrollment Ratio is capped at 100 percent for the purposes of calculating the Enrollment Index.

Finally, these two components are combined into the Education Index. In order to reflect the relative ease of enrolling students in school compared to the completion of a meaningful course of education (signified by the attainment of degrees), a two-thirds weight is applied to the Attainment Index and a one-third weight to the Enrollment Index to calculate the final Education Index as follows:

$$\text{Education Index}_i = \frac{2}{3} EAI_i + \frac{1}{3} EI_i$$

where EAI_i is Educational Attainment Index, and EI_i is Enrollment Index.

Attainment data for the United States are obtained from the ACS using attainment by education level and population from form B15002 (Sex by Educational Attainment for Population 25 Years and Over), B15002B, B15002C, B15002D, B15002H, and B15002I (same, for Black or African American Alone, Native American and Alaska Native Alone, Asian

Alone, White Non-Hispanic, and Hispanic).

Enrollment data for the United States as a whole, for individual states, and for states by race or by gender (but not by race and gender) were obtained from ACS tables B14001 (School Enrollment by Level of School for the Population 3 Years and Over), B14001B, B14001C, B14001D, B14001H, and B14001I (same, for Black or African American alone, Native American and Alaska Native Alone, Asian Alone, White Non-Hispanic Alone, and Hispanic). Enrollment data for racial and ethnic groups broken down by gender were obtained by AHDP analysis of the ACS 2008 1-year Public Use Microdata Sample (PUMS), queried using the U.S. Census Bureau DataFerrett tool.

 Income Index

The Income Index is calculated as follows:

$$\text{Income Index}_i = \frac{\log(y_i) - \log(y_{MIN})}{\log(y_{MAX}) - \log(y_{MIN})} \times 10$$

where y_i is the Median Earnings for unit i and y_{MIN} and y_{MAX} are the goalposts.

Median personal earnings data for the United States were obtained from ACS tables B20017 (Median Earnings by Sex by Work Experience for the Population 16+ Years with Earnings), B20017B, B20017C, B20017D, B20017H, and B20017I (same table for Black and African American Alone, Native American and Alaska Native Alone, Asian Alone, White Non-Hispanic Alone, and Hispanic). Median personal earnings reflect the median of the sum of wages, salaries, and net income from self-employment before deductions for taxes, and social contributions for the population age 16 and over with earnings.

Inflation adjustments. Comparing earnings from different years requires an adjustment to account for the depreciation of the purchasing power of any dollar amount due to inflation. The Consumer Price Index (CPI) as calculated by the Bureau of Labor Statistics (BLS) was used to convert dollars of different years to 2009 dollars for the purposes of this report. Following the recommendation of the U.S. Census Bureau,[9] the CPI research series using current methods (CPI-U-RS) was used to construct conversion factors for converting dollars of one year to another.

Error Margins

All of the data used to calculate the American HD Index besides life expectancy comes from the American Community Survey (ACS), an annual survey conducted by the U.S. Census Bureau that samples a small, randomly selected percentage of the population. Although the ACS is an excellent resource, as with any survey, there is some degree of sampling error. Thus, not all differences between two places or groups reflect the true difference between those places or groups. Thus, comparisons between similar values on any indicator, especially for small populations, should be made with caution since these differences may not always be statistically significant. Standard error and margin of error data for American HD Index values can be found at http://www.measureofamerica.org/report2010-11methods/. Readers interested in testing the statistical significance of estimates presented in this report are encouraged to view the supplemental web-content on error margins.

Difference between the American HD Index and the UNDP HD Index

The original HD Index was created by the United Nations Development Programme (UNDP) and is published annually in the *Human Development Report*. This composite index was created to measure human development in all countries of the world, ranging from very-low-income countries in sub-Saharan Africa to high-income countries in Europe, North America, and elsewhere. Thus, some of the indicators used are not well suited to measuring human development in an advanced industrialized economy like the United States. Nor are the goalposts for the

UNDP HD Index helpful for assessing U.S. well-being as they have been set to accommodate a very wide range of conditions—for instance, literacy rates ranging from less than 30 percent in Chad, Mali, and Burkina Faso to close to 100 percent in many other countries.

The American Human Development Project modified the UNDP HD Index to create the American HD Index. The American HD Index follows the same principles as the UNDP HD Index, and measures the same three basic dimensions of human development—a long and healthy life, access to knowledge, and a decent standard of living—but it has been adapted in order to better reflect the U.S. context.

The table below lists the indicators used in the American HD Index and the UNDP HD Index:

DIMENSION	INDICATOR AMERICAN HD INDEX	INDICATOR UNDP HD INDEX
Long and Healthy Life	Life expectancy at birth	Life expectancy at birth
Access to Knowledge	Educational attainment Gross enrollment ratio	Adult literacy rate Gross enrollment ratio
Decent Standard of Living	Median personal earnings	GDP per capita

In the health dimension, the same indicator is used (life expectancy at birth), but the goalposts are changed. The UNDP HD Index uses goalposts of 25 years (minimum) and 85 years (maximum) to accommodate the enormous gap in life expectancy found in countries around the world. For the American HD Index, the goalposts were set at 66 years and 90 years, a range that accommodates the variations across all groupings considered in *The Measure of America*. Since life span in the United States is nowhere near the lower limit of 25 years set in the standard HD Index, using the standard HD Index goalposts would cluster all Health Index values around the maximum value, providing very little differentiation among states, congressional districts, and so on.

In the knowledge dimension, adult literacy rate was replaced with an educational attainment index. Adult literacy is a relevant indicator in a global context, where low-income countries still have very high illiteracy rates, but is largely irrelevant for developed nations, where most of the adult population has basic reading and writing skills and the labor market demands increasingly sophisticated skills. Functional literacy (the ability to read, write, and speak in English, and compute and solve problems at levels of proficiency necessary to function on the job and in society, achieve one's goals, and develop one's knowledge and potential) would be a good indicator, but suffers from severe data availability problems. Thus, the educational attainment index was used. It captures the overall educational level of the population and is a good indicator of the extent to which people have the skills necessary to carry out the essential tasks of daily life in the United States, lead lives of choice and value, and meet the increasing demands of the labor market.

The other knowledge indicator, school enrollment, which is the combined gross enrollment ratio, is the same in both the American HD Index and the UNDP HD Index, with a slight modification. The enrollment ratio in the American HD Index includes nursery school and pre-kindergarten, and the age group used in the denominator of the enrollment ratio has been adjusted to accommodate this (the range begins with age 3). The goalposts were also changed, from 0 to 100 percent in the UNDP HD Index to 70 to 100 percent in the American HD Index, to reflect the ranges observed in all American HD Index groupings.

In the standard of living dimension, GDP per capita was replaced by median personal earnings. For relatively closed economies, such as those of countries, GDP per capita is a good indicator of the income appropriated by the local population. However, in smaller geographical areas within a country, such as states and congressional districts, economies are much more open, and substantial portions of the income generated within a community are used to remunerate production factors owned by persons who do not reside in that community (e.g., profits from a large manufacturing plant located in the community). Using such an indicator for states and congressional districts therefore would not adequately represent the income available to local residents. Also, there is no way to measure such an indicator for racial and ethnic groups or for men or women alone. Using median personal earnings (rather than household earnings) allows for the assessment of the difference in command over economic resources between women and men; median earnings also allow for disaggregation by race and ethnicity as well as by congressional district and state.

As a result of these modifications, the American HD Index and the UNDP HD Index are not comparable. In order to prevent any comparison attempts, the American HD Index varies from 0 to 10, whereas the UNDP HD Index varies from 0 to 1.

Balancing the American HD Index Components

In any composite index, each component of the index should contribute equally to the overall index value. The American HD Index assigns equal weights to each of the three components of the index, but how much each of these components affects the final score cannot be assumed to be equal based on this alone. If the distributions of the scores in the three components are not similar, then some components may end up having an **implicit weight** that results in one component having more of an influence on final scores than other components. How equally balanced the components of the HD Index are can be assessed by looking at the distribution of scores using box plots and also by looking at descriptive statistics and regression coefficients for these components.

A look at the distribution of scores for congressional districts on the three component indices of the American HD Index (displayed below) shows that these components are relatively well-balanced. Scores cluster around 5, and the ranges and distributions are similar. There are a few outliers, however, and the range of scores on the Health Index is narrower than the ranges of scores on the other two indices; the goalposts for the Health Index had to be set wide in order to accommodate large variations in life expectancy among racial and ethnic groups, and between women and men. As variations in life expectancy among congressional districts and states were not quite as extreme, scores on this index tend to clump closer to the midpoint.

Box Plots for the Component Indices of the American HD Index (Congressional Districts)

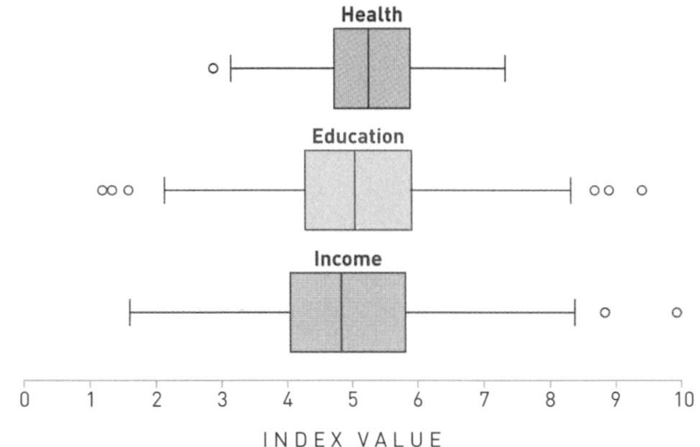

A further test of how equally each component index contributes to the final HD Index Value is to look at both the average values for each component index and also to run a simple linear regression with the final HD Index as the dependent variable and the three components as the independent variables. If the unstandardized coefficients in the resulting regression analysis are all roughly equal, each component is playing an equal role in contributing to the final HD Index score.

American HD Index Components

COMPONENT	AVERAGE COMPONENT INDEX VALUE	AVERAGE CONTRIBUTION
By State		
Health	5.15	33.4
Education	5.13	33.3
Income	4.84	33.3
By Congressional District		
Health	5.27	35.0
Education	5.15	33.0
Income	4.99	32.6

The tables above suggest that the average values and average contributions to the final HD Index of each of the component indices are roughly equal. Therefore, the HD Index is relatively well-balanced; none of the three component indices is having a disproportionately large impact on the final HD Index score.

American HD Index Historical Trends

The American HD Index for 1960, 1970, 1980, 1990, and 2000 uses different data sources, listed below.

LIFE EXPECTANCY AT BIRTH

1960–2000:

National Center for Health Statistics

Health, United States, 2007, Hyattsville, MD: 2007, Table 27. Life expectancy at birth, at 65 years of age, and at 75 years of age, by race and sex: United States, selected years 1900–2004

EDUCATIONAL ATTAINMENT

1960–1980:

U.S. Census Bureau

A Half-Century of Learning: Historical Census Statistics on Educational Attainment in the United States, 1940 to 2000, Table 1. Percent of the Population 25 Years and Over with a High School Diploma or Higher by Sex and Age, for the United States: 1940 to 2000; http://www.census.gov/population/socdemo/education/phct41/table1.xls Table 2. Percent of the Population 25 Years and Over with a Bachelor's Degree or Higher by Sex and Age, for the United States: 1940 to 2000; http://www.census.gov/population/socdemo/education/phct41/table2.xls.

1990:

U.S. Census Bureau

1990 Summary Tape File 3 (STF 3)—Sample data, DP-2. Social Characteristics: 1990

2000:

U.S. Census Bureau

Census 2000 Summary File 3 (SF 3)—Sample Data, QT-P20. Educational Attainment by Sex: 2000

SCHOOL ENROLLMENT

1960:

Population 5 to 24 years old
Enrollment 5 to 34 years old
U.S. Census Bureau,
Current Population Survey, October 1960

School Enrollment and Education of Young Adults and Their Fathers: October 1960 (P20-110), Table 3—Fall School Enrollment of the Civilian Noninstitutional Population 5 to 34 Years Old, By Age, Color, and Sex, For the United States: October 1960; http://www.census.gov/population/socdemo/education/p20-110/tab-03-04.pdf.

1970:

Population 3 to 24 years old
Enrollment 3 to 34 years old
U.S. Census Bureau,
Current Population Survey, October 1970

School Enrollment: October 1970 (P20-222), Table 1—Enrollment Status of the Population 3 to 34 Years Old, by Age, Race, Sex, and Selected Educational Characteristics, for the United States: October 1970; http://www.census.gov/population/socdemo/school/p20-222/tab01.pdf.

1980:

Population 3 to 24 years old
Enrollment 3 to 34 years old
U.S. Census Bureau,
Current Population Survey, October 1980

School Enrollment—Social and Economic Characteristics of Students: October 1980 (Advance Report) (P20-362), Table 6—Enrollment Status, for Persons 3 to 34 Years Old, by Age, Sex, Race, and Spanish Origin: October 1980; http://www.census.gov/population/socdemo/school/p20-362/tab06.pdf.

1990:

Population 3 to 24 years old
Enrollment 3 years and older
U.S. Census Bureau,
Current Population Survey, October 1990

School Enrollment—Social and Economic Characteristics of Students: October 1990 (P20-460), Table 1—Enrollment Status of the Population 3 Years Old and Over, by Age, Sex, Race, Hispanic Origin, and Selected Educational Characteristics: October 1990; http://www.census.gov/population/socdemo/school/p20-460/tab01.pdf.

2000:

Population 3 to 24 years old
Enrollment 3 years and older
U.S. Census Bureau,
Current Population Survey, October 2000

School Enrollment—Social and Economic Characteristics of Students: October 2000 (PPL-148), Table 1—Enrollment Status of the Population 3 Years Old and Over, by Age, Sex, Race, Hispanic Origin, Nativity, and Selected Educational Characteristics: October 2000; http://www.census.gov/population/socdemo/school/ppl-148/tab01.xls, Internet Release date: June 1, 2001.

MEDIAN EARNINGS

1960–2000:

U.S. Census Bureau,
Current Population Survey

Historical Income Data, Table P-43. Workers (Both Sexes Combined—All), Median and Mean Earnings: 1974 to 2005; http://www.census.gov/hhes/www/income/histinc/p43ar.html.

The income definitions on the American Community Survey (used in the current American HD Index) and the Current Population Survey are slightly different, and thus their income measures are not strictly comparable. Median earnings reported in the CPS, used in the historical American HD Index, were proportionally adjusted, based on the ratio observed between the 2005 ACS median earnings and the 2005 CPS median earnings, in order to minimize discontinuity problems between the historical series and the current HD Index values.

Notes

INTRODUCTION

Human Development in America Today

1. Ul Haq, *Reflections on Human Development*, 24.

2. Pagliani, "Influence of Regional, National, and Sub-national HDRs."

3. See Sen's writings, in particular: *The Standard of Living; Inequality Reexamined*; *Development as Freedom.*

4. See Alkire, *Valuing Freedoms*, ch. 2, for a discussion of different attempts to specify a list of basic or central capabilities. An example of such a list can be found in a U.K. government–commissioned paper. See Vizard and Burchardt, "Developing a Capability List."

5. Haycock and Gerald, "Engines of Inequality."

6. OpenSecrets.org, "Personal Finances."

7. Wolff, "Recent Trends in Household Wealth in the United States: Rising Debt and the Middle-Class Squeeze."

8 Cancian and Danziger, *Changing Poverty, Changing Policies.*

9. Nord et al., "Measuring Food Security in the United States."

10. U.S. Department of Housing and Urban Development, "2008 Annual Homeless Assessment Report to Congress," iii. Adams et al., "Summary Health Statistics for the U.S. Population," Table 15.

11. White House Office of Management and Budget, "Revisions to the Standards for the Classification of Federal Data on Race and Ethnicity."

12. U.S. Census Bureau, American Community Survey, 2008 One-Year Estimates.

13. These simplifications are to enhance accessibility of this work for a broader public. They are not intended to imply that ethnicity for Latinos is necessarily a more important identification than racial group.

14. National Data Program for the Sciences, "General Social Survey."

15 World Values Survey, "The World Values Survey."

16. Gallup, "Gallup World Poll."

17. The New Economics Foundation, "The Happy Planet Index 2.0."

18. Sen, *Idea of Justice*, 273.

19. Easterlin, "Does Rapid Economic Growth Improve the Human Lot?"

20. Diener and Biswas-Diener, "Will Money Increase Subjective Well-Being?"

21. Ibid.

22. Brickman, Coates, and Janoff-Bulman, "Lottery Winners and Accident Victims."

23. Deaton, "Income, Health, and Well-Being Around the World."

24. Oswald and Wu, "Objective Confirmation of Subjective Measures of Human Well-Being."

25. Sum and Khatiwada, "Labor Underutilization Impacts of the Great Recession of 2007–2009."

26. VanGiezen and Schwenk. "Compensation from before World War I through the Great Depression."

27. Thanks to Taylor Owen, who performed an extensive analysis of the literature on this topic for the project.

28. Social risk management was developed at the World Bank in the late 1990s. For a foundational presentation of the concept, see Holzmann and Jorgensen, "Social Protection as Social Risk Management." For a recent debate and rearticulation of these ideas, see Holzmann and Kozel, "The Role of Social Risk Management in Development," and the articles that accompany it in the same volume.

29. Kleinman and Madans, "Effects of Maternal Smoking, Physical Stature, and Educational Attainment on the Incidence of Low Birth Weight."

30. Centers for Disease Control and Prevention, National Center for Injury Prevention and Control, WISQARS Leading Causes of Death Reports.

31. Barnett, "Long-Term Effects of Early Childhood Programs on Cognitive and School Outcomes."

32. Annie E. Casey Foundation, "Early Warning! Why Reading by the End of Third Grade Matters."

33. Fernandes and Gabe, "Disconnected Youth," 23.

34. Centers for Disease Control and Prevention. Births: Preliminary Data for 2007, 2009. Tables 8 and 13.

35. Centers for Disease Control and Prevention, Behavioral Risk Factor Surveillance System 2008.

36. AHDP calculations based on mortality counts by cause of death from the Multiple Cause of Death Files for 2007 received by agreement with CDC/NCHS and NAPHSIS Vital Statistics Cooperative Program and bridged-race population estimates from the CDC WONDER Database (Vintage 2008). Trauma-related deaths include those caused by unintentional injury, homicide, and suicide. Rates are age-standardized to ensure that rates are comparable across states.

37. U.S. Census Bureau, American Community Survey 2008. Table B14001.

38. National Center for Education Statistics, National Assessment of Educational Progress (NAEP), 2009 Reading Assessment.

39. National Center for Education Statistics, Digest of Education Statistics 2009, Table 105. Averaged High School Freshman Graduation Rate.

40 and 43. AHDP calculations based on data from the U.S. Census Bureau, American Community Survey 2008. Tables B17001, B17001B, B17001C, B17001D, B17001H, B17001I.

41. AHDP calculation based on employment data from the U.S. Department of Labor, Bureau of Labor Statistics, Current Population Survey and population estimates from the U.S. Census Bureau, Population Division.

42. U.S. Census Bureau, American Community Survey 2008. Table B25070. Figures do not include home owners or renters living in group quarters. Gross rent includes average monthly utility costs.

CHAPTER 1

What the American Human Development Index Reveals

1. U.S. Census Bureau, American Community Survey, 2006–2008 Three-Year Estimates, Table S0201.

2. Ibid.

3. Ibid.

4. Sakamoto, Goyette, and Kim, "Socioeconomic Attainments of Asian Americans."

5. The Real Estate Group NY, "Manhattan Rental Market Report."

6. Basket of goods included one five-pound bag of name-brand rice, one gallon of regular milk, and a package of twenty-four name-brand diapers for babies over twenty-seven pounds. Price checks were performed in typical supermarkets in these neighborhoods in August 2010.

7. Earnings figures are not available for Pennsylvania's Fifth Congressional District for 2008. Therefore, this district is not included in the HD Index. The Index includes 434 districts plus the delegate district of Washington, DC.

8. Data disaggregated by race and ethnicity are provided by the Census Bureau and the Centers for Disease Control and Prevention, both of which use official definitions of racial and ethnic groups as defined by the Office of Management and Budget. Racial groups include African Americans, American Indians and Alaska Natives, Asian Americans, and whites. Since Alaska Natives are concentrated in Alaska, this report refers to "American Indians and Alaska Natives" as "Native Americans." Latinos are considered an ethnic group and may be of any race. The designations of "African Americans," "Asian Americans," and "Native Americans" refer to the population of these groups who self-identify as being of that race and no other. Data presented for whites do not include those who self-identify as being ethnically Latino.

9. Burd-Sharps et al., "Child Well-Being in the United States."

CHAPTER 2

A Long and Healthy Life

1. AHDP partnered with Zogby International to conduct a nationwide interactive online survey conducted on October 23, 2009. 3,767 adults responded to the survey, giving a margin of error of +/− 2.1 percentage points.

2. McGinnis et al., "The Case for More Active Policy Attention to Health Promotion."

3. Adler and Kawachi, "Reaching for a Healthier Life."

4. Wong et al., "Contribution of Major Diseases to Disparities in Mortality."

5. United Nations Development Programme, *Human Development Report 2009.*

6. Centers for Medicare and Medicaid Services, "NHE Fact Sheet."

7. Lewis and Burd-Sharps, "29 Reasons for Optimism." Health expenditure data by state were calculated by the Kaiser Family Foundation based on data from the Centers for Medicare and Medicaid Services. Data are from 2004, the most recent year available. Health expenditure data by country, including the United States, were accessed through the World Health Organization (WHO), National Health Accounts. Data are from 2006 and are expressed in purchasing power parity terms. Dollar amounts from various years were adjusted for inflation using the Consumer Price Index calculated by the Bureau of Labor Statistics and presented in constant 2008 dollars. International life expectancy data are from United Nations Development Programme, *Human Development Report 2009.*

8. Dumont and Lemaitre, "Counting Immigrants and Expatriates in OECD Countries."

9. Committee on the Consequences of Uninsurance, *Hidden Costs, Value Lost.*

10. Angrisano et al., "Accounting for the Cost of Health Care in the United States."

11. Preston and Ho, "Low Life Expectancy in the United States."

12. Ibid.

13. Centers for Disease Control and Prevention, "Cigarette Smoking among Adults and Trends in Smoking Cessation."

14. World Health Organization and the Commission on Social Determinants of Health, "Closing the Gap in a Generation."

15. Morrill and Chinn, "Obesity Epidemic in the United States."

16. United Nations Development Programme, *Human Development Report 2009.*

17. See, e.g., Marmot, *The Status Syndrome*; Wilkinson and Pickett, *The Spirit Level.*

18. Centers for Disease Control and Prevention, "The Power of Prevention."

19. Centers for Disease Control and Prevention, "Overview."

20. Danaei et al., "The Promise of Prevention."

21. Wakelee et al., "Lung Cancer Incidence in Never Smokers."

22. Kawachi, "More Evidence on the Risks of Passive Smoking."

23. Kawachi, Daniels, and Robinson, "Health Disparities by Race and Class."

24. American Cancer Society, "Questions about Smoking, Tobacco, and Health."

25. Woodward and Kawachi, "Why Reduce Health Inequalities?"

26. Centers for Disease Control and Prevention, "Cigarette Smoking among Adults: United States, 2007."

27. Centers for Disease Control and Prevention, "Cigarette Smoking among Adults and Trends in Smoking Cessation: United States, 2008."

28. Centers for Disease Control and Prevention, "Cigarette Smoking among Adults: United States, 2006."

29. Levi et al., "F as in Fat."

30. Oliver and Lee, "Public Opinion and the Politics of Obesity in America."

31. Levi et al., "F as in Fat."

32. These results are derived from an ordinary least-squares regression model that included controls for state-level median personal earnings, total health expenditure per capita, and the percentage of the population residing in rural areas. The adjusted R-square for the model was 0.679. Diabetes and smoking rates were statistically significant at the 0.05 level and uninsurance rates at the 0.10 level. State-level health risk factor data for 2008 came from the CDC Behavioral Risk Factor Surveillance System, calculated by the Kaiser Family Foundation, State Health Facts; earnings data for 2008 from the American Community Survey; and insurance coverage for 2007–8 and state health expenditure data for 2004 from the Kaiser Family Foundation, State Health Facts.

33. Lewis and Burd-Sharps, "29 Reasons for Optimism."

34. Lenton et al., *Health, Dignity, and Development.*

35. Centers for Disease Control and Prevention, "Highest Rates of Obesity, Diabetes in the South, Appalachia, and Some Tribal Lands."

36. Levi et al., "F as in Fat."

37. Organisation for Economic Co-Operation and Development, "Women and Men in OECD Countries."

38. In OECD countries, the average gender life expectancy gap is almost six years; it is smallest in the United Kingdom, Iceland, and Sweden, and largest (more than eight years) in Hungary, the Slovak Republic, and Poland (ibid.).

39. Centers for Disease Control and Prevention, *Health, United States, 2009,* 37.

40. Morning, "On Distinction."

41. Collins, Guyer, and Chakravarti, "Variations on a Theme," 1580.

42. Kaufman, "The Anatomy of a Medical Myth."

43. Centers for Disease Control and Prevention, "Cigarette Smoking among Adults: United States, 2007."

44. Centers for Disease Control and Prevention, "Racial/Ethnic Disparities in Infant Mortality: United States, 1995–2002."

45. Abraído-Lanza et al., "Latino Mortality Paradox."

46. Centers for Disease Control and Prevention, "Cigarette Smoking among Adults and Trends in Smoking Cessation: United States, 2008."

47. Abraído-Lanza et al., "Latino Mortality Paradox."

48. Centers for Disease Control and Prevention, "HIV/AIDS among Women."

49. United Nations Development Programme, *Human Development Report 2009.*

50. Shrestha, "Life Expectancy in the United States."

51. At least fifty thousand people.

52. Adler and Kawachi, "Reaching for a Healthier Life."

53. Healthy Eating Research, "Food Insecurity and Risk for Obesity among Children and Families."

54. Data Resource Center for Child and Adolescent Health, National Survey of Children's Health (NSCH), 2007.

55. Lopez-Jimenez, "Speakable and Unspeakable Facts about BMI and Mortality."

56. Levi et al., "F as in Fat."

57. Ibid.

58. Ibid.

59. Ibid.

60. Lumeng et al., "Weight Status as a Predictor of Being Bullied in Third through Sixth Grades"

61. Levi et al., "F as in Fat."

62. National Heart, Lung, and Blood Institute, "Body Mass Index Table."

63. Levi et al., "F as in Fat."

64. Ibid.

65. Conley and Glauber, "Gender, Body Mass, and Socioeconomic Status."

66. Centers for Disease Control and Prevention, "Highest Rates of Obesity, Diabetes in the South, Appalachia, and Some Tribal Lands."

67. Levi et al., "F as in Fat."

68. Halpern, "Obesity and American Indians/Alaska Natives."

69. Cossrow and Falkner, "Race/Ethnic Issues in Obesity and Obesity-Related Comorbidities."

70. Ibid.

71. Halpern, "Obesity and American Indians/Alaska Natives."

72. Centers for Disease Control and Prevention, Behavioral Risk Factor Surveillance System, 1991–2007.

73. Nestle, *Food Politics,* 13.

74. Levi et al., "F as in Fat."

75. Nestle, *Food Politics,* 199.

76. Levi et al., "F as in Fat."

77. Monsivais and Drewnowski, "The Rising Cost of Low-Energy-Density Foods."

78. Kessler, *The End of Overeating.*

79. Ibid.

80. Story, Nanney, and Schwartz, "Schools and Obesity Prevention."

81. Davis and Carpenter, "Proximity of Fast-Food Restaurants to Schools and Adolescent Obesity."

82. Young and Nestle, "Contribution of Expanding Portion Sizes to the U.S. Obesity Epidemic."

83. PepsiCo, Inc., "Pepsi Product Information."

84. Jacobson, *Liquid Candy*; Brownell and Frieden, "Ounces of Prevention."

85. Rozin et al., "Ecology of Eating."

86. Starbucks, "Explore Our Menu."

87. Wansink and Payne, "Joy of Cooking Too Much."

88. Christakis and Fowler, "Spread of Obesity in a Large Social Network over 32 Years."

89. Boardman et al., "Race Differentials in Obesity."

90. Seuss, *Cat in the Hat.*

91. Rideout et al., "Generation M2."

92. Barros et al., "School Recess and Group Classroom Behavior."

93. Levi et al., "F as in Fat."

94. Mahalik, Burns, and Syzdek, "Masculinity and Perceived Normative Health Behaviors as Predictors of Men's Health Behaviors."

95. Courtenay, "Behavioral Factors Associated with Disease, Injury, and Death among Men."

96. Ibid.

97. Morrongiello and Lasenby-Lessard, "Psychological Determinants of Risk Taking by Children."

98. Oransky and Marecek, "'I'm Not Going to Be a Girl!'"

99. Simons-Morton et al., "Observed Effects of Teenage Passengers on the Risky Driving Behavior of Teenage Drivers."

100. National Highway, Traffic, and Safety Information, "Traffic Safety Facts."

101. U.S. Department of Labor, "National Census of Fatal Occupation Injuries in 2008," Table 2: "Fatal Occupational Injuries by Industry and Selected Event or Exposure, 2008."

102. Heron, "Deaths: Leading Causes for 2006."

103 Web-based Injury Statistics Query and Reporting System (WISQARS), "Leading Causes of Death 1999-2007, by Sex."

104. Heron, "Deaths: Leading Causes for 2006."

105. Ibid.

106. Addis and Mahalik, "Men, Masculinity, and the Contexts of Help-Seeking."

107. Courtenay, "Behavioral Factors Associated with Disease, Injury, and Death among Men."

108. U.S. Department of Health and Human Services, "Stress and Your Health"; Feingold, "Gender Differences in Personality."

109. Courtenay, "Behavioral Factors Associated with Disease, Injury, and Death among Men."

110. Adler and Kawachi, "Reaching for a Healthier Life."

111. Ibid.

112. Magnuson and Votruba-Drzal, "Enduring Influences of Childhood Poverty."

113. Case and Paxon, "Causes and Consequences of Early Life Health."

114. Lleras-Muney, "The Relationship between Education and Adult Mortality in the United States."

115. Manchester and Topoleski, "Growing Disparities in Life Expectancies."

116. Kleinman and Madans, "Effects of Maternal Smoking, Physical Stature, and Educational Attainment on the Incidence of Low Birth Weight."

117. Ibid.

118. Adler and Kawachi, "Reaching for a Healthier Life."

119. Mittleman et al., "Educational Attainment, Anger, and the Risk of Triggering Myocardial Infarction Onset."

120. Centers for Disease Control and Prevention, "Cigarette Smoking among Adults and Trends in Smoking Cessation: United States, 2008."

121. Marmot and Wilkinson, *Social Determinants of Health.*

122. Parks et al., "Morbidity and Mortality in People with Serious Mental Illness."

123. Wong et al., "Contribution of Major Diseases to Disparities in Mortality."

124. Adler and Kawachi, "Reaching for a Healthier Life."

125. Iceland, Weinberg, and Steinmetz, "Racial and Ethnic Residential Segregation in the United States: 1980–2000," ch. 5.

126. Jackson et al., "Relation of Residential Segregation to All-Cause Mortality: A Study in Black and White."

127. Centers for Disease Control and Prevention, "HIV/AIDS among Women."

128. Goodarz et al., "The Promise of Prevention."

129. Buzzell and Preston, "Mortality of American Troops in Iraq."

130. U.S. Census Bureau, "American Indian, Alaska Native Tables from the Statistical Abstract of the United States: 2004–2005."

131. Ugunwole, "We the People."

132. Ibid.

133. Goodarz et al., "Promise of Prevention."

134. U.S. Census Bureau, "American Indian, Alaska Native Tables from the Statistical Abstract of the United States: 2004–2005."

135. Roubideaux et al., "Measuring the Quality of Diabetes Care for Older American Indians and Alaska Natives."

136. Goodarz et al., "Promise of Prevention."

137. Centers for Disease Control and Prevention, "Cigarette Smoking among Adults and Trends in Smoking Cessation: United States, 2008."

138. U.S. Department of Health and Human Services, "IHS Fact Sheets."

139. Klat, "State of America's Native Nations."

140. U.S. Commission on Civil Rights, "Broken Promises: Evaluating the Native American Health Care System."

141. Klat, "State of America's Native Nations."

142. Adler and Kawachi, "Reaching for a Healthier Life."

143. Centers for Disease Control and Prevention, "CDC Honors 65 Years of Community Water Fluoridation."

144. Centers for Disease Control and Prevention, "Achievements in Public Health."

145. Moss, "The Hard Sell on Salt."

146. Baker et al, "Nationwide Review of Graduated Driver Licensing."

147. Sunstein and Thaler, *Nudge.*

148. Centers for Disease Control and Prevention, *State Indicator Report on Physical Activity 2010.*

149. Kann et al., "Overview and Summary: School Health Policies and Programs Study 2006."

150. Rideout et al., "Generation M2."

151. Levi et al., "F as in Fat."

152. Singh et al., "Neighborhood Socioeconomic Conditions, Built Environments, and Childhood Obesity."

153. Bloom and Cohen, "Summary Health Statistics for U.S. Children."

154. Burdette and Whitaker, "Resurrecting Free Play in Young Children."

CHAPTER 3

Access to Knowledge

1. Sum and Khatiwada, "Labor Underutilization Impacts of the Great Recession of 2007–2009," 11.

2. Robelen, "Recession Woes Cast Pall as Schools Open."

3. Ibid.

4. Rothstein, "A Blueprint That Needs More Work."

5. Organisation for Economic Cooperation and Development (OECD), "PISA 2006."

6. See, e.g., Koretz, "How Do American Students Measure Up?"

7. Porter et al., "Is There a de Facto National Curriculum?"

8. Goertz, "National Standards: Lessons from the Past, Directions for the Future," 59.

9. Ibid., 56.

10. American Human Development Project analysis of U.S. Department of Education, *Digest of Education Statistics, 2009*, Table 185.

11. U.S. Department of Education, *Digest of Education Statistics, 2009*, Table 185. Dollar figures are expressed in 2006–7 terms.

12. American Human Development Project analysis of U.S. Department of Education, National Center for Education Statistics, Common Core of Data (CCD), "State Nonfiscal Survey of Public Elementary/ Secondary Education."

13. American Human Development Project analysis of U.S. Census Bureau, Census 2000 Summary File 1 (SF 1) 100-Percent Data, Table P2.

14. U.S. Department of Agriculture, Economic Research Service, "Rural Education at a Glance."

15. Pew Forum on Religion and Public Life, "U.S. Religious Landscape Survey."

16. Putnam, "Social Capital."

17. Pew Forum on Religion and Public Life, "U.S. Religious Landscape Survey."

18. According to an American Human Development Project analysis of the U.S. Department of Education, National Center for Education Statistics' Common Core of Data for the 2006–7 school year.

19. Ibid., 13.

20. Small and Newman, "Urban Poverty after *The Truly Disadvantaged.*"

21. Wilson, *The Truly Disadvantaged.*

22. Harding, "Counterfactual Models of Neighborhood Effects."

23. Hanushek et al., "Does Peer Ability Affect Student Achievement?"

25. New Trier was named the 2007 National Signature School by the Recording Academy, the organization behind the Grammy Awards. See Grammy.com, "2007 GRAMMY Signature Schools Named." In 2005 *Sports Illustrated* ranked New Trier among the top twenty-five high school athletics programs (Menez and Woo, "Best High School Athletic Programs").

26. According to the 2009 Illinois School Report Cards issued by the Illinois State Board of Education.

27. Ibid.

28. Iceland et al., *Racial and Ethnic Residential Segregation in the United States.*

29. Toussaint-Comeau and Rhine, "Tenure Choice with Location Selection."

30. Paral and Ready, "The Economic Progress of U.S.- and Foreign-Born Mexicans in Metro Chicago."

31. Institute for Latino Studies, "Measuring the Minority Education Gap in Metropolitan Chicago."

32. Dobbie and Fryer, "Are High Quality Schools Enough to Close the Achievement Gap?"

33. U.S. Department of Education, National Center for Education Statistics, *Digest of Education Statistics, 2008*, Table 268.

34. Goldin et al., "The Homecoming of American College Women."

35. Christopher Dougherty, "Why Are Returns to Schooling Higher for Women than for Men?"

36. Goldin et al., "The Homecoming of American College Women."

37. American Human Development Project analysis of U.S. Census Bureau, American Community Survey, 2008 One-year Estimates, Table B06004A.

38. Pew Hispanic Center, "Hispanics of Cuban Origin in the United States."

39. U.S. Census Bureau, American Community Survey, 2008 One-year Estimates, Table S0201.

40. Lopez, "Latinos and Education: Explaining the Attainment Gap."

41. For a recent study, see Lofstrom, "Why Are Hispanic and African American Dropout Rates So High?"

42. Kohler and Lazarín, "Hispanic Education in the United States."

43. Kao and Thompson, "Racial and Ethnic Stratification in Educational Achievement and Attainment."

44. Fry, "High Schools Hispanics Attend," 4.

45. Ibid., 11.

46. Bean et al., "Mexican Immigrant Political and Economic Incorporation," 311–12.

47. Erisman and Looney, "Opening the Door to the American Dream," 20.

48. Zarate and Pachon, "Perceptions of College Financial Aid among California Latino Youth."

49. OECD, *Economic Policy Reforms 2010: Going for Growth*, Fig. 5.3.

50. U.S. Department of Education, National Center for Education Statistics, *Digest of Education Statistics, 2008*, Table 3.

51. U.S. Department of Education, National Center for Education Statistics, *Digest of Education Statistics, 2009*, Table 196.

52. Ibid., Table 194.

53. U.S. Department of Education, National Center for Education Statistics, *Digest of Education Statistics, 2008*, Tables 206 and 207.

54. Dailey et al., "Broadband Adoption in Low-Income Communities."

55. Ibid.

56. Czernich et al., "Broadband Infrastructure and Economic Growth."

57. Kohn, "Benefits of Broadband in a Digital Society."

58. Kamerman and Gatenio-Gabel, "Early Childhood Education and Care in the United States," 24–25.

59. U.S. Department of Education, National Center for Education Statistics, *Digest of Education Statistics, 2008*, Table 43.

60. Barnett, "Long-Term Effects of Early Childhood Programs on Cognitive and School Outcomes."

61. Carneiro and Heckman, "Human Capital Policy," 50–55.

62. Temple and Reynolds, "Benefits and Costs of Investments in Preschool Education."

63. Barnett et al., *State of Preschool 2009*.

64. Dickens et al., "Effects of Investing in Early Education on Economic Growth."

65. American Human Development Project analysis of Barnett et al., *State of Preschool 2009*, Table 4, and U.S. Census Bureau, American Community Survey, 2008 One-year Estimates, Table B09001.

66. Kamerman and Gatenio-Gabel, "Early Childhood Education and Care in the United States," 24.

67. U.S. Department of Health and Human Services, Administration for Children and Families, "Head Start Impact Study: Final Report."

68. Barnett et al., *State of Preschool 2009*.

69. Kamerman and Gatenio-Gabel, "Early Childhood Education and Care in the United States," 30.

70. Ibid., 31.

71. Ibid., 28.

72. Heckman and LaFontaine, "American High School Graduation Rate."

73. U.S. Department of Education, *Digest of Education Statistics, 2009*, Table 107.

74. American Human Development Project analysis of U.S. Department of Education, *Digest of Education Statistics, 2009*, Table 37.

75. Tyler and Lofstrom, "Finishing High School," 93.

76. Ibid., 80.

77. Bridgeland et al., "Silent Epidemic."

78. Ibid.

79. Meara et al., "Gap Gets Bigger."

80. Singh and Siahpush, "Widening Socioeconomic Inequalities in U.S. Life Expectancy."

81. Burd-Sharps et al., "Goals for the Common Good."

82. Bridgeland, "Silent Epidemic."

83. See, e.g., Barton, "One-Third of a Nation"; Harding, "Counterfactual Models of Neighborhood Effects"; Bloom, "Programs and Policies to Assist High School Dropouts in the Transition to Adulthood."

84. Bridgeland, "Silent Epidemic."

85. See, e.g., Lopez, "Latinos and Education."

86. Swanson, "Special Education in America."

87. Pinkus, "Using Early-Warning Data to Improve Graduation Rates."

88 Princiotta and Reyna, "Achieving Graduation for All," 24.

89. Ibid., 18.

90. Ibid., 18–19.

91. Domina, "What Works in College Outreach."

92. Heinrich and Holzer, "Improving Education and Employment for Disadvantaged Young Men," 5.

93. Klima et al., "What Works?"

94. Tyler and Lofstrom, "Finishing High School," 91.

95. For recent studies of this phenomenon, see, e.g., Ainsworth, "Why Does It Take a Village?" and Card and Rothstein, "Racial Segregation and the Black-White Test Score Gap."

96. American Human Development Project analysis of data from the U.S. Census Bureau, American Community Survey, 2006–2008 Three-year Estimates, Tables B14001 and B01003.

97. Zhou, "Urban Education."

98. Harding, "Counterfactual Models of Neighborhood Effects."

99. According to American Human Development Project analysis comparing attitudes of sample respondents to integrated housing over the past four decades using data provided by the General Social Survey. The analysis examined responses to questions 127 and 128 from the GSS 1972–2008 Cumulative Datafile.

100. Cutler et al., "Rise and Decline of the American Ghetto."

101. Sohoni and Saporito, "Mapping School Segregation."

102. See, e.g., Card and Rothstein, "Racial Segregation and the Black-White Test Score Gap."

103. Echenique and Fryer, "Measure of Segregation Based on Social Interactions."

104. DeLuca and Dayton, "Switching Social Contexts."

105. Center for Research on Education Outcomes (CREDO), "Multiple Choice: Charter School Performance in 16 States."

106. See, e.g., U.S. Department of Education, Office of Planning, Evaluation and Policy Development, *ESEA Blueprint for Reform*, 37–38.

107. Hanushek et al., "Does Peer Ability Affect Student Achievement?"

108. Krueger and Whitmore, "Would Smaller Classes Help Close the Black-White Achievement Gap?"

109. Aos et al., "Benefits and Costs of K–12 Educational Policies."

110. Rivkin et al., "Teachers, Schools, and Academic Achievement."

111. Ferguson and Ladd, "How and Why Money Matters."

112. Rivkin et al., "Teachers, Schools, and Academic Achievement."

113. Clotfelter et al., "Who Teaches Whom?"

114. American Human Development Project analysis of National Center for Education Statistics, Common Core of Data (CCD), "Public Elementary/Secondary School Universe Survey."

115. Education Trust, "Funding Gap."

116. Podgursky and Springer, "Teacher Performance Pay," 909.

117. See, e.g., Rivkin et al., "Teachers, Schools, and Academic Achievement."

118. Podgursky and Springer, "Teacher Performance Pay."

119. Lavy, "Performance Pay and Teachers' Effort, Productivity, and Grading Ethics."

120. Goertz and Weiss, "Assessing Success in School Finance Litigation," 23.

121. Costrell and Podgursky, "Peaks, Cliffs, and Valleys."

122. Costrell and Podgursky, "Golden Peaks and Perilous Cliffs," 6.

123. Calculations by the American Human Development Project comparing median earnings for high school graduates (and equivalents) with median earnings for bachelor's degree holders. If a high school graduate works from age 18 to age 65 at the 2008 median of $19,989, he or she will earn $939,483 (with a margin of error of +/– $2,491). If a college graduate works from age 22 to age 65 at the 2008 median of $47,853, he or she will earn $2,057,679 (with a margin of error of +/– $3,483). The data for these estimates come from the U.S. Census Bureau, American Community Survey, 2006–8 Three-year Estimates, Table B20004.

124. Astin and Oseguera, "Degree Attainment Rates at American Colleges and Universities."

125. U.S. Department of Education, National Center for Education Statistics, Digest of Education 2009, Table 50.

126. Swanson, "Special Education in America."

127. Ibid.

128. Ibid.

129. Ibid.

130. Ibid.

131. Planty et al., *Condition of Education* 2009, Table A-22-2.

132. U.S. Department of Education, National Center for Education Statistics, *Digest of Education Statistics, 2009*, Table 196.

133. Brint, "Few Remaining Dreams," 27.

134. Bradburn et al., "Community College Transfer Rates to 4-year Institutions Using Alternative Definitions of Transfer," Figure A.

135. Provasnik and Planty, *Community Colleges: Special Supplement to the Condition of Education 2008*, Table SA-25.

136. Bradburn et al., "Community College Transfer Rates to 4-year Institutions Using Alternative Definitions of Transfer," Figure B.

137. Brint, "Few Remaining Dreams," 19.

138. Bowen et al., *Crossing the Finish Line*.

139. On this point, see Kevin Dougherty, *The Contradictory College*.

140. ACT, "Reading between the Lines."

141. Kuh et al., "What Matters to Student Success," 2.

142. National Center for Public Policy and Higher Education, "States, Schools, and Colleges."

143. Adelman, "Toolbox Revisited."

144. U.S. Department of Education, National Center for Education Statistics, *Digest of Education Statistics, 2009*, Table 334.

145. Ibid., Table 335.

146. Organisation for Economic Co-operation and Development (OECD), *Education at a Glance 2009*, Table B2.4.

147. Ibid., Table B3.2b.

148. Ibid., Table B5.1a.

149. American Human Development Project calculations based on Chronicle of Education data, "College and University Endowments, 2008–2009," accessed May 8, 2010.

150. Haycock et al., "Opportunity Adrift."

151. Domina, "What Works in College Outreach."

152. Ibid.

153. Myers et al., "Impacts of Regular Upward Bound."

154. Constantine et al., "A Study on the Effect of the Talent Search Program on Secondary and Postsecondary Outcomes in Florida, Indiana, and Texas."

155. ACT, "Using EXPLORE and PLAN Data to Evaluate GEAR UP Programs."

156. Ibid.

157. Long and Riley, "Financial Aid," 45.

158. Reed and Cheng, "Student Debt and the Class of 2008."

159. Dillon and Carey, "Charts You Can Trust."

CHAPTER 4

A Decent Standard of Living

1. Van Giezen and Schwenk, "Compensation from before World War I through the Great Depression."

2. Sum and Khatiwada, "Labor Underutilization Problems."

3. Ibid.

4. Tatlock, "Share and Share Alike: Does Income Sharing Imply Household Sharing?"

5. Centers for Disease Control and Prevention, "Marriage and Divorce."

6. Hartmann, *Poverty and Unemployment among Single Mother Families.*

7. Davies et al., "The World's Count Data Center, "Children in Extreme Poverty (%), 2008."

8. Wolff, "Recent Trends in Household Wealth in the United States."

9. U.S. Census Bureau, Current Population Survey, Annual Social and Economic Supplements for 1974–2004.

10. Annie E. Casey Foundation Kid's Count Data Center, "Children in Extreme Poverty(%), 2008."

11. Arkansas Department of Human Services. "2009 Statistical Report." Total of "unduplicated persons" participating, including those who live in a household where some member is a participant in the Supplemental Nutrition Assistance Program.

12. U.S. Census Bureau, American Community Survey, 2008 One-Year Estimates, Table DP-3.

13. U.S. Census Bureau, ACS, 2008 One-Year Estimates, Table S0101.

14. U.S. Department of Labor, Bureau of Labor Statistics. Union Membership (Annual) News Release. Table 5. "Union affiliation." http://www.bls.gov/news.release/union2.t05.htm.

15. Mishel and Bernstein, *The State of Working America, 2008/2009,* ch. 3.

16. National Science Foundation, "Academic Research and Development Expenditures: Fiscal Year 2008."

17. U.S. Census Bureau, "Computer and Internet Use in the United States: October 2007," Table 3.

18. Kaiser Family Foundation, statehealthfacts.org. "Health Insurance Coverage of the Total Population, 2007–2008."

19. Kaiser Family Foundation, statehealthfacts.org. Calculated by the Urban Institute and Kaiser Commission on Medicaid and the Uninsured estimates based on the Census Bureau's March 2008 and 2009 Current Population Survey.

20. Himmelstein et al., "Medical Bankruptcy in the United States, 2007."

21. Aneja, "Characterization of Particulate Matter in Roda, Virginia."

22. U.S. Census Bureau, American Community Survey, 2006–2008, 3-Year Estimates, Table S0201.

23. Institute for Women's Policy Research and Wellesley Centers for Women, "Achieving Equity for Women," 2.

24. Raising the Global Floor: Adult Labour, "Paid Leave from Work."

25. Ibid.

26. Ibid.

27. Grant et al., *Expecting Better*, 6.

28. Raising the Global Floor: Adult Labour, "Paid Leave from Work."

29. Ibid.

30. Ibid.

31. Applebaum, "Paid Family Leave Arrives in California."

32. Lovell, *Estimating the Benefits of Paid Family and Medical Leave.*

33. Institute for Women's Policy Research, "Fact Sheet: The Gender Wage Gap by Occupation."

34. Ibid.

35. U.S. Bureau of Labor Statistics, "Household Data Annual Averages. Table 39," 2009

36. See, e.g., Heinrich and Holzer, Improving Education and Employment for Disadvantaged Young Men, Rumbaut "Profiles in Resilience."

37. Milken Institute State Technology and Science Index, 2008.

38. Fishbein and Woodall, "Subprime Locations," 8.

39. See Giuliano et al., "Manager Race and the Race of New Hires"; Bertrand and Mullainathan, "Are Emily and Greg More Employable than Lakisha and Jamal?"

40. Insight Center for Community Economic Development, "State Inclusive Business Program Overview & Goals."

41. Ibid.

42. U.S. Department of Labor, Bureau of Labor Statistics, "Regional and State Employment and Unemployment—March 2010."

43. Milken Institute State Science and Technology Index, 2008.

44. Calculations by the American Human Development Project comparing median earnings for high school graduates (and equivalents) with median earnings for bachelor's degree holders. If a high school graduate works from age 18 to age 65 at the 2008 median of $19,989, he or she will earn $939,483 (with a margin of error of +/- $2,491). If a college graduate works from age 22 to age 65 at the 2008 median of $47,853, he or she will earn $2,057,679 (with a margin of error of +/- $3,483). The data for these estimates come from the U.S. Census Bureau, American Community Survey, 2006–2008, 3-Year Estimates, Table B20004.

45. U.S. Department of Labor, Bureau of Labor Statistics, Employment Situations News Release, Table A-4. "Employment status of the civilian population 25 years and over by educational attainment."

46. See Giuliano et al., "Manager Race and the Race of New Hires;" Bertrand and Mullainathan, "Are Emily and Greg More Employable than Lakisha and Jamal?

47. Acs and Nichols, *American Insecure*, 12–16.

48. Center on the Developing Child at Harvard University, *The Science of Early Childhood Development.*

49. Organisation for Economic Co-operation and Development, *Doing Better for Children.*

50. Adler et al., "Socioeconomic Status and Health"; Gennetian et al., *Meeting the Basic Needs of Children*.

51. DeNavas-Walt et al., "Income, Poverty, and Health Insurance Coverage in the United States: 2008."

52. U.S. Census Bureau, Current Population Survey, 2009 Annual Social and Economic Supplement, Table POV03.

53. Nord, "Food Insecurity in Households with Children."

54. National Center on Family Homelessness, "Children."

55. Karen, *Becoming Attached*.

56. Arditti, "'It's Been Hard to Be a Father.'"

57. Sentencing Project, *Incarcerated Parents and Their Children*.

58. Ibid.

59. Ibid.

60. Sabol et al., *Prisoners in 2008*.

61. Sentencing Project, *Incarcerated Parents and Their Children*; Pattillo et al. *Imprisoning America*; Nurse, "Coming Home"; Comfort, *Doing Time Together*.

62. Kleiman, "Outpatient Prison."

63. Elmendorf, "Economic and Budget Outlook."

64. Hall, Statement before the U.S. Congress Joint Economic Committee.

65. Cornelius and Rosenblum, "Immigration and Politics," 103.

66. Peri, "Impacts of Immigration in Recession and Economic Expansion."

67. Saxenian, "Brain Circulation"

68. Rumbaut, "Undocumented Immigration and Rates of Crime and Imprisonment."

69. Cornelius and Rosenblum, "Immigration and Politics," 104.

70. Card, "How Immigration Affects U.S. Cities," 20.

71. Cornelius and Rosenblum, "Immigration and Politics," 103.

72. Card, "How Immigration Affects U.S. Cities," 24.

73. Ibid.

74. Porter, "Illegal Immigrants Are Bolstering Social Security with Billions."

75. Williams Reid et al., "The Immigration-Crime Relationship: Evidence across U.S. Metropolitan Areas."

76. Butcher and Piehl, "Crime, Corrections, and California."

77. Peri, "Impacts of Immigration in Recession and Economic Expansion."

78. Woods, "Employment Outlook," 53.

79. Edwards and Hertel-Fernandez, "The Kids Aren't Alright."

80. Jargowsky and Yang, "The 'Underclass' Revisited"; Wagmiller, "Race and the Spatial Segregation of Jobless Men in Urban America."

81. Wilson, *When Work Disappears*.

82. Woods, "Employment Outlook," 55.

83. Levinthal, "Congressmen Lose Big Bucks in 2008."

84. Wiedrich et al., *Assets and Opportunity Special Report,* 1.

85. DeNavas-Walt et al., "Income, Poverty, and Health Insurance Coverage in the United States: 2008."

86. Lui, "Laying the Foundation for National Prosperity."

87. Wiedrich et al., *Assets and Opportunity Special Report,* 4.

88. Gokhale and Tanner, "KidSave."

89. See Burd-Sharps et al., *The Measure of America: American Human Development Report 2008–2009,* 135, for a full discussion of children's savings account practices in the United Kingdom and other asset-building good practices.

90. Wiedrich et al., *Assets and Opportunity Special Report,* 6–9.

91. Wolff, "Recent Trends in Household Wealth in the United States," 17.

92. Rivera et al., "Foreclosed"; Gruenstein Bocian et al. "Unfair Lending"; U.S. Department of Housing and Urban Development, *Mortgage Pricing Differentials across Hispanic, Black, and White Households;* Walters and Hermanson, "Older Subprime Refinance Mortgage Borrowers."

93. Fishbein and Woodall, "Subprime Locations."

94. Insight Center for Community Economic Development, "Lifting as We Climb."

95. Platzer and Harrison, "The U.S. Automotive Industry."

96. Mikelson and Nightingale, "Estimating Public and Private Expenditures on Occupational Training in the United States."

97. Osterman, "Employment and Training Policies"; Kletzer and Koch, "International Experience with Job Training."

98. Congressional Budget Office, *Social Security:* A Primer, Fig. 11: "Poverty Rates for Different Age Groups, 1966–1999."

99. Burtless, "Stock Market Fluctuations and Retiree Income: An Update," 10.

100. Newport, "Americans Increasingly Concerned about Retirement Income."

101. Purcell, "Retirement Savings and Household Wealth in 2007."

102. Heritage Foundation, "Protecting and Strengthening Retirement Savings"; Copeland, "Employment-Based Retirement Plan Participation," 7. An additional 16 million workers either are not eligible for their employer's plan or are eligible but fail to participate.

103. Employee Benefit Research Institute, "401(k) Plan Asset Allocation, Account Balances, and Loan Activity."

104. Deloitte and the Investment Company Institute, Defined Contribution 401(k) Study; Weller and Jenkins, "Building 401(k) Wealth One Percent at a Time," 5.

105. U.S. Social Security Administration, Income of the Aged Chartbook, 2008.

106. Goldberg, "The Impact of Inequality for Same-Sex Partners in Employer-Sponsored Retirement Plans"; Movement Advancement Project and SAGE, "Improving the Lives of LGBT Older Adults."

107. Olson in "Achieving Equity for Women: Policy Alternatives for the New Administration Symposium Report," 11.

108. Marriott, "Innovation in Retirement Savings Policy"; John and Levine, "National retirement savings systems in Australia, Chile, New Zealand and the United Kingdom."

109. Hokenstad and Curl, "Reshaping Retirement Policies in Post-Industrial Nations."

110. Swedish Ministry of Health and Social Affairs, "Old Age Pensions in Sweden."

111. Ibid.

112. Hacker and Pierson, "Winner-Take-All Politics."

113. Wolff, "Recent Trends in Household Wealth in the United States."

114. Neil Irwin, "Aughts were a lost decade for U.S. economy, workers," *Washington Post,* January 2, 2010.

115. Wolff, "Recent Trends in Household Wealth in the United States."

116. Nurse-Family Partnership evaluations have shown major positive impacts on the life courses of participating mother-infant pairs; the integrated programs of the Harlem Children's Zone, including the Baby College, the Three Year Old Journey, Get Ready for Pre-K, and Harlem Gems, help parents foster healthy development of their children.

117. U.S. Department of Labor, Bureau of Labor Statistics, Employment Situations News Release, Table A-4. "Employment status of the civilian population 25 years and over by educational attainment."

118. Gruenstein Bocian, Li, and Ernst, "Foreclosures by Race and Ethnicity."

CONCLUSION

Agenda for Action: Reducing Risks, Building Resilience

1. Sum and Khatiwada, "Labor Underutilization Impacts of the Great Recession of 2007–2009."

2. Sum and Khatiwada, "Labor Underutilization Problems."

3. American Diabetes Association, "Diabetes Statistics."

4. Central Intelligence Agency, *The World Factbook,* "Singapore."

5. California Legislative Analyst's Office, Criminal Justice and Judiciary, "How Much Does It Cost to Incarcerate an Inmate in Prison."

6. California State University 2010–2011 Cost of Attendance, Summary of Standard Student Expense Budget.

7 National Center for Education Statistics, Schools and Staffing Survey, "Number of Private Schools Charging Tuition."

8. Washington State Employment Security Department, News and Information, Legislative Resources, "Family Leave Insurance."

9. Wilson, "Tobacco Funds Shrink as Obesity Fight Intensifies."

10. United States Environmental Protection Agency, "International Experiences with Economic Incentives for Protecting the Environment."

Methodological Notes

1. Special thanks to Richard Hendra (MDRC and Milano, the New School for Management and Urban Policy) and Senior Statistical Advisor Neil Bennett (City University of New York Institute for Demographic Research and the National Bureau of Economic Research) for their guidance and support regarding data management and analysis.

2 U.S. Office of Management and Budget, "Update of Statistical Area Definitions and Guidance on Their Uses."

3 Office of Management and Budget. "Statistical Policy Directive No. 15.

4 U.S. Census Bureau. American Community Survey, Table B01001E, 2008 1-year Estimate.

5 The geographic correspondence file was generated using the MABLE/Geocorr application, developed by John Blodgett at the University of Missouri–St. Louis and jointly owned by Blodgett and CIESIN (Consortium for International Earth Science Information Network at Columbia University). Many thanks to Blodgett and CIESIN for making this tool available and for their assistance in using it.

6 U.S. Census Bureau,t 110th Congressional Districts Geographic Relationship Tables.

7 See Rosenberg et al., "Quality of Death Rates," and Arias et al. "Validity of Race and Hispanic Origin Reporting."

8 Arias et al.. "Validity of Race and Hispanic Origin Reporting," and Indian Health Service, Adjusting for Miscoding..

9 U.S. Census Bureau. "A Compass for Understanding and Using American Community Survey Data."

Bibliography

INTRODUCTION

Human Development In America Today

Adams, P. F., P.M. Barnes, and J. L. Vickerie. "Summary Health Statistics for the U.S. Population: National Health Interview Survey, 2007." *Vital and Health Statistics* 10, no. 238 (November 2008).

Alkire, Sabina. *Valuing Freedoms: Sen's Capability Approach and Poverty Reduction*. Oxford: Oxford University Press, 2002.

Brickman, P., D. Coates, and R. Janoff-Bulman. "Lottery Winners and Accident Victims: Is Happiness Relative?" *Journal of Personality and Social Psychology* 36, no. 8 (1978): 917–27.

Cancian, Maria, and Sheldon Danziger, eds. *Changing Poverty, Changing Policies*. New York: Russell Sage Foundation, 2009.

Deaton, Angus. "Income, Health, and Well-Being Around the World: Evidence from the Gallup World Poll." *Journal of Economic Perspectives* 22, no. 2 (Spring 2008): 53–72.

Deneulin, Severine, and Lila Shahani, eds. *An Introduction to the Human Development and Capability Approach: Freedom and Agency*. London: Earthscan, 2009.

Diener, Ed, and Robert Biswas-Diener. "Will Money Increase Subjective Well-Being?" *Social Indicators Research* 57, no. 2 (November 2002): 119–169.

Easterlin, R. A. "Does Rapid Economic Growth Improve the Human Lot? Some Empirical Evidence." In *Nations and Households in Economic Growth: Essays in Honor of Moses Abramovitz*. Edited by P. A. David and M. W. Reder. New York: Academic Press, 1974.

Haycock, K., and D. Gerald. "Engines of Inequality: Diminishing Equity in the Nation's Premier Public Universities." Washington, DC: The Education Trust, 2006.

Holzmann, R., and S. Jorgensen. "Social Protection as Social Risk Management: The Conceptual Underpinnings for the Social Protection Sector Strategy Paper." *Journal of International Development* 11 (December 1999): 1005–27.

Holzmann, R. and V. Kozel. "The Role of Social Risk Management in Development: A World Bank View." *IDS Bulletin* 38, no. 3 (2007): 20–22.

Nord, Mark, Margaret Andrews, and Steven Carlson. "Measuring Food Security in the United States: Household Food Security in the United States, 2008." Economic Research Report no. 83. Washington, DC: U.S. Department of Agriculture, November 2009. http://www.ers.usda.gov/Publications/ERR83/ERR83.pdf.

OpenSecrets.org. "Personal Finances: Overview." Washington, DC: Center for Responsive Politics. http://www.opensecrets.org/pfds/.

Oswald, Andrew J., and Stephen Wu. "Objective Confirmation of Subjective Measures of Human Well-Being: Evidence from the USA." *Science* 327, no. 5965 (December 2009): 576–79.

Pagliani, Paola. "Influence of Regional, National, and Sub-national HDRs." Human Development Research Paper 2010/19. New York: U.N. Human Development Report Office, July 2010. http://hdr.undp.org/es/informes/mundial/idh2010/trabajos/HDRP_2010_19.pdf.

Sen, Amartya. *Development as Freedom*. Oxford: Oxford University Press, 2001.

——. *Inequality Reexamined*. Oxford: Oxford University Press, 1992.

——. *The Idea of Justice*. Cambridge, MA: Harvard University Press, 2009.

——. *The Standard of Living*. Cambridge, U.K.: Cambridge University Press, 1987.

Sum, Andrew, and Ishwar Khatiwada. "Labor Underutilization Impacts of the Great Recession of 2007–2009: Variations in Labor Underutilization Problems across Age, Gender, Race-Ethnic, Educational Attainment and Occupational Groups in the U.S., 2009 Fourth Quarter." Boston: Northeastern University, Center for Labor Market Studies, March 2010.

Ul Haq, Mahbub. *Reflections on Human Development*. New York: Oxford University Press, 1995.

U.S. Census Bureau. American Community Survey, 2008 One-Year Estimates.

U.S. Department of Housing and Urban Development. "The 2008 Annual Homeless Assessment Report to Congress." Washington, DC: Office of Community Planning and Development, July 2009.

Van Giezen, Robert, and Albert E. Schwenk. "Compensation from before World War I through the Great Depression." Bureau of Labor Statistics. January 30, 2003. http://www.bls.gov/opub/cwc/cm20030124ar03p1.htm.

Vizard, P., and T. Burchardt. "Developing a Capability List: Final Recommendations of the Equalities Review Steering Group on Measurement." CASE Paper 121. London: London School of Economics Centre for Analysis of Social Exclusion, April 2007. http://sticerd.lse.ac.uk/dps/case/cp/CASEpaper121.pdf.

White House Office of Management and Budget. "Revisions to the Standards for the Classification of Federal Data on Race and Ethnicity." *Federal Register* 62, no. 210 (October 30, 1997): 58782–90.

Wolff, Edward N. "Recent Trends in Household Wealth in the United States: Rising Debt and the Middle Class Squeeze—An Update to 2007." Working Papers Series no. 159. Annandale-on-Hudson: Bard College Levy Economics Institute, March 2010.

Annie E. Casey Foundation. "Early Warning! Why Reading by the End of Third Grade Matters." 2010. http://eric.ed.gov/PDFS/ED509795.pdf.

Barnett, W. Steven. "Long-Term Effects of Early Childhood Programs on Cognitive and School Outcomes." *Future of Children* 5, no. 3 (1995): 25–50.

Centers for Disease Control and Prevention, National Center for Injury Prevention and Control, WISQARS Leading Causes of Death Reports, an interactive database, 2007. http://www.cdc.gov/injury/wisqars..

Fernandes, Adrienne, and Thomas Gabe. "Disconnected Youth: A Look at 16- to-24-Year-Olds Who Are Not Working or in School." U.S. Congressional Research Service, R40535. April 22, 2009.

Kleinman, Joel C., and Jennifer H. Madans. "The Effects of Maternal Smoking, Physical Stature, and Educational Attainment on the Incidence of Low Birth Weight." *American Journal of Epidemiology* 121, no. 6 (1985): 843–55.

CHAPTER 1

What the American Human Development Index Reveals

Burd-Sharps, Sarah, Patrick Guyer, Ted Lechterman, and Kristen Lewis. "Child Well-Being in the US: Proposal for the Development of a 'Tots' Index Using the Human Development Conceptual Framework," *Child Poverty: A Global Perspective*, edited by Alberto Minujin. Bristol, UK: Policy Press (forthcoming).

The Real Estate Group New York. "Manhattan Rental Market Report." New York: The Real Estate Group New York, April 2010.

Sakamoto, Arthur, Kimberly A. Goyette, and ChangHwan Kim. "Socioeconomic Attainments of Asian Americans." *Annual Review of Sociology* 35 (2009): 255–76.

U.S. Census Bureau. American Community Survey, 2006-2008 3-Year Estimates.

CHAPTER 2

A Long and Healthy Life

Abraído-Lanza, Ana F., Bruce P. Dohrenwend, Daisy S. Ng-Mak, and J. Blake Turner. "The Latino Mortality Paradox: A Test of the 'Salmon Bias' and Healthy Migrant Hypotheses." *American Journal of Public Health* 89, no. 10 (October 1999): 1543–48.

Addis, Michael E., and James R. Mahalik. "Men, Masculinity, and the Contexts of Help-Seeking." *American Psychologist* 58 (2003): 5–14.

Adler, Nancy, and Ichiro Kawachi. "Reaching for a Healthier Life: Facts on Socioeconomic Status and Health in the U.S." Presentation made to the National Health Policy Forum. Washington, DC. March 14, 2008.

Ahmedin, Jemal, Michael J. Thun, Elizabeth E. Ward, S. Jane Henley, Vilma E. Cokkinades, and Taylor E. Murray. "Mortality from Leading Causes by Education and Race in the United States, 2001." *American Journal of Preventative Medicine* 34, no. 1 (2008): 1-8.

American Cancer Society. "Questions about Smoking, Tobacco and Health." Fact Sheet. Atlanta, GA. July 7, 2010. http://www.cancer.org/acs/groups/cid/documents/webcontent/002974-pdf.pdf.

Angrisano, Carlos, Diana Farrell, Bob Kocher, Martha Laboissiere, and Sara Parker. "Accounting for the Cost of Health Care in the United States." McKinsey Global Institute. January 2007. http://www.mckinsey.com/mgi/reports/pdfs/healthcare/MGI_US_HC_fullreport.pdf.

Baker, S. P., Chen, L., & Li, G. "Nationwide Review of Graduated Driver Licensing," Washington DC: AAA Foundation for Traffic Safety, 2007.

Barros, Romina, Ellen J. Silver, and Ruth E. K. Stein. "School Recess and Group Classroom Behavior." *Pediatrics* 123, no. 2 (February 1, 2009): 431–36.

Basch, Charles E. "Healthier Students Are Better Learners: A Missing Link in School Reforms to Close the Achievement Gap." *Equity Matters* 6. New York: Campaign for Educational Equity, March 2010.

Bloom, B., and R. A. Cohen. "Summary Health Statistics for U.S. Children: National Health Interview Survey, 2006." *Vital and Health Statistics* 10, no. 234 (September 2007): 1–79.

Boardman, Jason D., Jarron M. Saint Onge, Richard G. Rogers, and Justin T. Denney. "Race Differentials in Obesity: The Impact of Place." *Journal of Health and Social Behavior* 46 (September 2005): 229–43.

Brownell, Kelly D., and Thomas R. Frieden. "Ounces of Prevention: The Public Policy Case for Taxes on Sugared Beverages." *New England Journal of Medicine* 360, no. 18 (April 30, 2009): 1805–8.

Burdette H. L., and R. C. Whitaker. "Resurrecting Free Play in Young Children: Looking beyond Fitness and Fatness to Attention, Affiliation, and Affect." *Archives of Pediatrics and Adolescent Medicine* 159, no. 1 (January 2005): 46–50.

Buzzell, Emily, and Samuel H. Preston, "Mortality of American Troops in Iraq." PSC Working Paper Series 06-01. Philadelphia: University of Pennsylvania Population Studies Center, August 26, 2006. http://repository.upenn.edu/psc_working_papers/1/.

Case, Anne, and Christina Paxon. "Causes and Consequences of Early Life Health." Working Paper 15637. Cambridge, MA: National Bureau of Economic Research, January 2010. http://www.nber.org/papers/w15637.

Centers for Disease Control and Prevention. "Achievements in Public Health, 1900–1999: Fluoridation of Drinking Water to Prevent Dental Caries." *MMWR Weekly* 48, no. 41 (October 22, 1999): 933–40. http://www.cdc.gov/mmwr/preview/mmwrhtml/mm4841a1.htm

———. "Behavioral Risk Factor Surveillance System, 1991–2007." http://www.cdc.gov/brfss/.

———. "CDC Honors 65 Years of Community Water Fluoridation." Atlanta, GA: Division of Oral Health, January 25, 2010. http://www.cdc.gov/fluoridation/65_years.htm.

———. "Cigarette Smoking among Adults and Trends in Smoking Cessation: United States, 2008." *MMWR Weekly* 58, no. 44 (November 13, 2009): 1227–32. http://www.cdc.gov/mmwr/preview/mmwrhtml/mm5844a2.htm.

———. "Cigarette Smoking among Adults: United States, 2006." *MMWR Weekly* 56, no. 45 (November 9, 2007): 1221–26.

———. "Cigarette Smoking among Adults: United States, 2007." *MMWR Weekly* 57, no. 45 (November 14, 2008): 1221–26. http://www.cdc.gov/mmwr/preview/mmwrhtml/mm5745a2.htm.

———. *Health, United States, 2009: With Special Feature on Medical Technology*. Hyattsville, MD: National Center for Health Statistics, 2010.

———. "Highest Rates of Obesity, Diabetes in the South, Appalachia, and Some Tribal Lands." Press Release. Atlanta, GA: Office of the Associate Director for Communication, November 19, 2009. http://www.cdc.gov/media/pressrel/2009/r091119c.htm.

———. "HIV/AIDS among Women." Fact Sheet. Atlanta, GA: Divisions of HIV/AIDS Prevention, August 3, 2008. http://www.cdc.gov/hiv/topics/women/resources/factsheets/pdf/women.pdf.

———. "Overview." Atlanta, GA: National Center for Chronic Disease Prevention and Health Promotion. July 7, 2010. http://www.cdc.gov/chronicdisease/overview/index.htm.

———. "Racial/Ethnic Disparities in Infant Mortality: United States, 1995–2002." *MMWR Weekly* 54, no. 22 (June 10, 2005): 553–56. http://www.cdc.gov/mmwr/preview/mmwrhtml/mm5422a1.htm.

———. "State Indicator Report on Physical Activity 2010." Atlanta, GA: U.S. Department of Health and Human Services, 2010. http://www.cdc.gov/physicalactivity/downloads/PA_State_Indicator_Report_2009.pdf.

Centers for Medicare and Medicaid Services. "NHE Fact Sheet." February 3, 2010. http://www.cms.gov/NationalHealthExpendData/25_NHE_Fact_Sheet.asp.

Christakis, Nicholas A., and James H. Fowler. "The Spread of Obesity in a Large Social Network over 32 Years." *New England Journal of Medicine* 357, no. 4 (2007): 370–79.

Collins, Francis S., Mark S. Guyer, and Aravinda Chakravarti. "Variations on a Theme: Cataloging Human DNA Variation." *Science* 278, no. 5343 (November 28, 1997): 1580–81.

Committee on the Consequences of Uninsurance. *Hidden Costs, Value Lost: Uninsurance in America, 2003.* Board on Health Care Services, Institute of Medicine of the National Academies. Washington, DC: National Academies Press, 2003.

Conley, Dalton, and Rebecca Glauber. "Gender, Body Mass, and Socioeconomic Status: New Evidence from the PSID." *Economics of Obesity: Advances in Health Economics and Health Services Research* 17 (2007): 253–75.

Cossrow, Nicole, and Bonita Falkner. "Race/Ethnic Issues in Obesity and Obesity-Related Comorbidities." *Journal of Clinical Endocrinology and Metabolism* 89, no. 6 (2004): 2590–94.

Courtenay, Will. "Behavioral Factors Associated with Disease, Injury, and Death among Men: Evidence and Implications for Prevention." *Journal of Men's Studies* 9, no. 1 (2000): 81–142.

Data Resource Center for Child and Adolescent Health. National Survey of Children's Health, 2007. Portland, OR: Child and Adolescent Health Measurement Initiative. http://www.nschdata.org.

Davis, B., and C. Carpenter. "Proximity of Fast-Food Restaurants to Schools and Adolescent Obesity." *American Journal of Public Health* 99, no. 3 (March 2009): 1–6.

Dumont, Jean-Christophe, and George Lemaitre. "Counting Immigrants and Expatriates in OECD Countries: A New Perspective." OECD Social, Employment and Migration Working Papers 25. June 22, 2005. http://www.oecd.org/dataoecd/34/59/35043046.pdf.

"The Elephant in the Room: Evolution, Behavioralism, and Counteradvertising in the Coming War against Obesity." Editorial. *Harvard Law Review* 116, no. 4 (February 2003): 1161–84.

Feingold, Alan. "Gender Differences in Personality: A Meta-Analysis." *Psychological Bulletin* 116, no. 3 (November 1994): 429–56.

Ferriman, Annabel. "*BMJ* Readers Choose the 'Sanitary Revolution' as Greatest Medical Advance since 1840." *British Medical Journal* 334 (January 20, 2007): 111.

Frieden, Thomas R. "Asleep at the Switch: Local Public Health and Chronic Disease." *American Journal of Public Health* 94, no. 12 (December 2004): 2059–61.

Goodarz, Danaei, Eric B. Rimm, Shefali Oza, Sandeep C. Kulkarni, Christopher J. L. Murray, and Majod Ezzati. "The Promise of Prevention: The Effects of Four Preventable Risk Factors on National Life Expectancy and Life Expectancy Disparities by Race and County in the United States." *PLoS Medicine* 7, no. 3 (2010): 1–13.

Halpern, Peggy. "Obesity and American Indians/Alaska Natives." Washington, DC: U.S. Department of Health and Human Services, Office of the Assistant Secretary for Planning and Evaluation, April 2007. http://aspe.hhs.gov/hsp/07/AI-AN-obesity/report.pdf.

Harper, Sam, and John Lynch. "Trends in Socioeconomic Inequalities in Adult Health Behaviors among U.S. States, 1990–2004." *Public Health Reports* 122, no. 2 (March-April 2007): 177–89.

Hayes-Bautista, David. "The Latino Health Research Agenda for the Twenty-first Century." In *Latinos: Remaking America*, edited by Marcelo Suárez-Orozco and Mariela Páez, 215–35. Berkeley: University of California Press and the David Rockefeller Center for Latin American Studies, 2008.

Healthy Eating Research. "Food Insecurity and Risk for Obesity Among Children and Families: Is There a Relationship?" Minneapolis: Robert Wood Johnson Foundation, April 2010. http://www.rwjf.org/files/research/herfoodinsecurity20100504.pdf.

Heron, Melanie. "Deaths: Leading Causes for 2006." *National Vital Statistics Reports* 58, no. 14 (March 31, 2010).

——, Donna L. Hoyert, Sherry L. Murphy, Jiaquan Su, Kenneth Kochanek, and Betzaida Tejada-Vera. "Deaths: Final Data for 2006." *National Vital Statistics Reports* 57, no. 14 (April 17, 2009).

Iceland, John, Daniel H. Weinberg, and Erika Steinmetz. "Racial and Ethnic Residential Segregation in the United States: 1980–2000." *Census 2000 Special Reports.* Washington, DC: U.S. Census Bureau, August 2002. http://www.census.gov/hhes/www/housing/resseg/pdf/front_toc.pdf.

Jackson, Sharon A., Roger T. Anderson, Norman J. Johnson, and Paul D. Sorlie. "The Relation of Residential Segregation to All-Cause Mortality: A Study in Black and White." *American Journal of Public Health* 90, no. 4 (April 2000): 615–17.

Jacobson, Michael F. *Liquid Candy: How Soft Drinks are Harming American's Health.* Washington, DC: Center for Science in the Public Interest, 2005.

Kann, L., N. Brener, and H. Wechsler. "Overview and Summary: School Health Policies and Programs Study 2006." *Journal of School Health* 77, no. 8 (September 2007): 385–95.

Kaufman, Jay. "The Anatomy of a Medical Myth." In *Is Race "Real"?* Social Science Research Council online essay forum. Brooklyn, NY: Social Science Research Council, 2006. http://raceandgenomics.ssrc.org/Kaufman/.

Kawachi, Ichiro. "More Evidence on the Risks of Passive Smoking." *British Medical Journal* 330 (February 5, 2005): 265–66.

Kawachi, Ichiro, and L. F. Berkman, eds. *Neighborhoods and Health*. New York: Oxford University Press, 2003.

Kawachi, Ichiro, Norman Daniels, and Dean E. Robinson. "Health Disparities by Race and Class: Why Both Matter." *Health Affairs* 24, no. 2 (2005): 343–52.

Kessler, David A. *The End of Overeating: Taking Control of the Insatiable American Appetite*. Emmaus, PA: Rodale, 2009.

Klat, Joseph P. "The State of America's Native Nations." Testimony before the U.S. House of Representatives, March 13, 2008. http://hpaied.org/images/resources/publibrary/KaltHOUSEApprop03-13-07.pdf.

Kleinman, Joel C., and Jennifer H. Madans. "The Effects of Maternal Smoking, Physical Stature, and Educational Attainment on the Incidence of Low Birth Weight." *American Journal of Epidemiology* 121, no. 6 (1985): 843–55.

Lee, M. A., and K. F. Ferraro. "Neighborhood Residential Segregation and Physical Health among Hispanic Americans: Good, Bad, or Benign?" *Journal of Health and Social Behavior* 48, no. 2 (June 2007): 131–48.

Lenton, Robert, Albert Wright, and Kristen Lewis. *Health, Dignity, and Development: What Will It Take?* United Nations Millennium Project Task Force on Water and Sanitation, Final Report. London: Earthscan, 2005.

Levi, Jeffrey, Serena Winter, Liz Richardson, Rebecca St. Laurent, and Laura M. Segal. "F as in Fat: How Obesity Policies Are Failing in America." Washington, DC: Trust for America's Health, July 2009. http://healthyamericans.org/reports/obesity2009/Obesity2009Report.pdf.

Levin, Henry M. "The Economic Payoff to Investing in Educational Justice." *Educational Researcher* 38, no. 1 (2009): 5–20.

Levine, Robert S., James E. Foster, Robert E. Fullilove, Mindy T. Fullilove, and Nathaniel C. Briggs. "Black-White Inequalities in Mortality and Life Expectancy, 1933–1999: Implications for Healthy People 2010." *Public Health Reports* 116, no. 5 (September–October 2001): 474–83.

Lleras-Muney, Adriana. "The Relationship between Education and Adult Mortality in the United States." *Review of Economic Studies* 72, no. 1 (2005): 189–221.

Lopez-Jimenez, Francisco. "Speakable and Unspeakable Facts about BMI and Mortality." *Lancet* 373, no. 9669 (March 28, 2009): 1055–56.

Lumeng, Julie C., Patrick Forrest, Danielle P. Appugliese, Niko Kaciroti, Robert F. Corwyn, and Robert H. Bradley. "Weight Status as a Predictor of Being Bullied in Third through Sixth Grades." *Pediatrics* 12, no. 6 (June 2010): 1301–7.

Magnuson, Katherine, and Elizabeth Votruba-Drzal. "Enduring Influences of Childhood Poverty." In *Changing Poverty, Changing Policies*, edited by Maria Cancian and Sheldon Danziger. New York: Russell Sage Foundation, 2009.

Mahalik, James R., Shaun M. Burns, and Matthew Syzdek. "Masculinity and Perceived Normative Health Behaviors as Predictors of Men's Health Behaviors." *Social Science & Medicine* 64 (March 26, 2007): 2201–9.

Manchester, Joyce, and Julie Topoleski. "Growing Disparities in Life Expectancies." Economic and Budget Issue Brief. Congressional Budget Office, April 17, 2008. http://www.cbo.gov/ftpdocs/91xx/doc9104/LifeExpectancy_Brief.1.1.shtml.

Marmot, Michael G. *The Status Syndrome: How Social Standing Affects Our Health and Longevity.* New York: Henry Holt, 2004.

——, and Richard Wilkinson, eds. *The Social Determinants of Health: The Solid Facts.* 2nd ed. Oxford: Oxford University Press, 2006.

McGinnis, J. Michael et al. "The Case for More Active Policy Attention to Health Promotion," *Health Affairs* 21, no.2 (2002): 78–93.

Meara, Ellen, Seth Richards, and David Cutler. "The Gap Gets Bigger: Changes in Mortality and Life Expectancy by Education, 1981–2000." *Health Affairs* 27, no. 2 (2008): 350–60.

Mittleman, Murray A., Malcolm Maclure, Manesh Nachnani, Jane B. Sherwood, and James E. Muller. "Educational Attainment, Anger, and the Risk of Triggering Myocardial Infarction Onset." *Archive of Internal Medicine* 157, no. 7 (1997): 769–75.

Mokdad, Ali H., James S. Marks, Donna F. Stroup, and Julie L. Gerberding. "Actual Causes of Death in the United States, 2000." *Journal of the American Medical* Association 291, no. 10 (March 10, 2004): 1238–45.

Monsivais, P., and A. Drewnowski. "The Rising Cost of Low-Energy-Density Foods." *Journal of the American Dietetic Association* 107, no. 12 (2007): 2017–76.

Morning, Ann. "On Distinction." In *Is Race "Real"?* Social Science Research Council online essay forum. Brooklyn, NY: Social Science Research Council, June 2006. http://raceandgenomics.ssrc.org/Morning/.

Morrill, Allison C., and Christopher D. Chinn. "The Obesity Epidemic in the United States." *Journal of Public Health Policy* 25, nos. 3/4 (2004): 353–66.

Morrongiello, Barbara A., and Jennifer Lasenby-Lessard. "Psychological Determinants of Risk Taking by Children: An Integrative Model and Implications for Interventions." *Journal of Injury Prevention* 13, no. 1 (2007): 20–25.

Moss, M. "The Hard Sell on Salt," *The New York Times*, May 29, 2010.

National Heart, Lung, and Blood Institute. "Body Mass Index Table." Bethesda, MD. http://www.nhlbi.nih.gov/guidelines/obesity/bmi_tbl.pdf.

National Highway, Traffic, and Safety Information. "Traffic Safety Facts: 2007 Traffic Safety Annual Assessment—Alcohol-Impaired Driving Fatalities." Research Note. Washington, DC: National Center for Statistics and Analysis, August 2008. http://www-nrd.nhtsa.dot.gov/Pubs/811016.pdf.

Nestle, Marion. *Food Politics: How the Food Industry Influences Nutrition and Health.* Berkeley: University of California Press, 2007.

Oliver, J. Eric, and Taeku Lee. "Public Opinion and the Politics of Obesity in America." *Journal of Health Politics, Policy and Law* 30 (2005): 923–54.

Oransky, Matthew, and Jeanne Marecek. "'I'm Not Going to Be a Girl!' Masculinity and Emotions in Boys' Friendships and Peer Groups." *Journal of Adolescent Research* 24, no. 2 (2009): 218–41.

Organisation for Economic Co-Operation and Development. "Women and Men in OECD Countries." Paris: OECD Publications, 2006. http://www.oecd.org/dataoecd/44/52/37962502.pdf.

Parks, Joe, Dale Svendsen, Patricia Singer, and Mary Ellen Foti, eds. "Morbidity and Mortality in People with Serious Mental Illness." Technical Report. Alexandria, VA: National Association of State Mental Health Program Directors, October 2006. http://www.nasmhpd.org/general_files/publications/med_directors_pubs/technical%20report%20on%20morbidity%20and%20mortaility%20-%20final%2011-06.pdf.

PepsiCo, Inc. "Pepsi Product Information." http://pepsiproductfacts.com/infobyproduct.php.

Plescia, Marcus, Harry Herrick, and LaTonya Chavis. "Improving Health Behaviors in an African American Community: The Charlotte Racial and Ethnic Approaches to Community Health Project." *American Journal of Public Health* 98, no. 9 (September 2008): 1678–84.

Preston, Samuel H., and Jessica Ho. "Low Life Expectancy in the United States: Is the Health Care System at Fault?" PSC Working Paper Series 09-03. Philadelphia: University of Pennsylvania Population Studies Center, July 2009. http://repository.upenn.edu/psc_working_papers/13.

Rideout, Victoria A., Ulla G. Foehr, and Donald F. Roberts. "Generation M^2: Media in the Lives of 8- to 18-Year-Olds." Menlo Park, CA: Henry J. Kaiser Family Foundation, January 2010. http://www.kff.org/entmedia/upload/8010.pdf.

Roubideaux, Yvette, et al. "Measuring the Quality of Diabetes Care for Older American Indians and Alaska Natives." *American Journal of Public Health* 94, no. 1 (2004): 60.

Rozin, Paul, Kimberly Kabnick, Erin Pete, Claude Fischler, and Christy Shields. "The Ecology of Eating: Smaller Portion Sizes in France than in the United States Help Explain the French Paradox." *Psychological Science* 14, no. 5 (September 2003): 450–54.

Schalkwyk, Joanna. "Culture, Gender Equality, and Development Cooperation." Québec, Canada: Canadian International Development Agency, June 2000. http://www.oecd.org/dataoecd/2/9/1896320.pdf.

Seuss, Dr. *The Cat in the Hat.* New York: Random House, 1957.

Shrestha, Laura B. "Life Expectancy in the United States." Congressional Research Service Report for Congress. August 16, 2006. http://aging.senate.gov/crs/aging1.pdf.

Silka, Linda, Robin Toof, and Dorcas Grigg-Saito. "Eight Americas: Differences in Asian Communities Are Important." *PLoS Medicine* 4, no. 1 (2007): e41.

Simons-Morton, Bruce, Neil Lerner, and Jeremiah Singer. "The Observed Effects of Teenage Passengers on the Risky Driving Behavior of Teenage Drivers." *Accident Analysis and Prevention* 37 (2005): 973–82.

Singh, G. K., M. Siahpush, and M. D. Kogan. "Neighborhood Socioeconomic Conditions, Built Environments, and Childhood Obesity." *Health Affairs* 29, no. 3 (March 2010): 501–12.

Starbucks Corporation. "Explore Our Menu." http://www.starbucks.com/menu/catalog/nutrition/food.

Story, Mary, Marilyn S. Nanney, and Marlene B. Schwartz. "Schools and Obesity Prevention: Creating School Environments and Policies to Promote Healthy Eating and Physical Activity." *Milbank Quarterly* 87, no. 1 (2009): 71–100.

Sunstein, C. R., and R. H. Thaler. *Nudge: Improving Decisions about Health, Wealth and Happiness.* New York: Penguin, 2008.

Trasande, Leonardo, Chris Cronk, Maureen Durkin, Marianne Weiss, Dale A. Schoeller, Elizabeth A. Gall, Jeanne B. Hewitt, Aaron L. Carrel, Philip J. Landrigan, and Matthew W. Gillman. "Environment and Obesity in the National Children's Study." *Environmental Health Perspectives* 117, no. 2 (February 2009): 159–66.

Ugunwole, Stella. "We the People: American Indians and Alaska Natives in the United States." *Census 2000 Special Reports.* Washington, DC: U.S. Census Bureau, February 2006. http://www.census.gov/population/www/socdemo/race/censr-28.pdf.

United Nations Development Programme. *Human Development Report 1990.* New York: Oxford University Press, 1990.

——. *Human Development Report 2006.* New York: Palgrave Macmillan, 2006.

——. *Human Development Report 2009.* New York: Palgrave Macmillan, 2009.

U.S. Census Bureau. "American Indian, Alaska Native Tables from the Statistical Abstract of the United States: 2004–2005." *Statistical Abstract of the United States: 2004–2005.* Washington, DC, 2004. http://www.census.gov/statab/www/sa04aian.pdf.

U.S. Commission on Civil Rights. "Broken Promises: Evaluating the Native American Health Care System." Washington, DC, 2004. http://www.usccr.gov/pubs/nahealth/nabroken.pdf.

U.S. Department of Health and Human Services. "American Indian/Alaska Native Profile." Rockville, MD: Office of Minority Health, October 21, 2009. http://minorityhealth.hhs.gov/templates/browse.aspx?lvl=2&lvlID=52.

——. "IHS Fact Sheets: Indian Health Disparities." Rockville, MD: Indian Health Service, January 2010. http://info.ihs.gov/Disparities.asp.

——. "Stress and Your Health." Washington, DC: Office on Women's Health, March 17, 2010. http://www.womenshealth.gov/faq/stress-your-health.pdf.

U.S. Department of Labor. "National Census of Fatal Occupation Injuries in 2008." News Release. Washington, DC: Bureau of Labor Statistics, August 20, 2009. http://www.bls.gov/news.release/cfoi.htm.

Wakelee, Heather A., Ellen T. Chang, Scarlett L. Gomez, Theresa H. Keegan, Diane Feskanich, Christina A. Clarke, Lars Holmberg, Lee C. Yong, Laurence N. Kolonel, Michael K. Gould, Dee W. West, et al. "Lung Cancer Incidence in Never Smokers." *Journal of Clinical Oncology* 25, no. 5 (February 10, 2007): 472–78.

Wansink, Brian, and Collin R. Payne. "The Joy of Cooking Too Much: 70 Years of Calorie Increases in Classic Recipes." *Annals of Internal Medicine* 150, no. 4 (February 17, 2009): 291–92.

Web-based Injury Statistics Query and Reporting System (WISQARS). Leading Causes of Death 1999–2007. Atlanta, GA: Centers for Disease Prevention and Control, National Center for Injury Prevention and Control. http://webappa.cdc.gov/sasweb/ncipc/leadcaus10.html.

WHO Global Strategy on Diet, Physical Activity, and Health. "Chronic Disease." Geneva, Switzerland: World Health Organization, 2003. http://www.who.int/dietphysicalactivity/media/en/gsfs_chronic_disease.pdf.

Wilkinson, Richard, and Kate Pickett. *The Spirit Level: Why Greater Equality Makes Societies Stronger.* New York: Bloomsbury Press, 2010.

Wong, Mitchell D., Martin F. Shapiro, W. John Boscardin, and Susan L. Ettner. "Contribution of Major Diseases to Disparities in Mortality." *New England Journal of Medicine* 347 (November 14, 2002): 1585–92.

Woodward, Alistair, and Ichiro Kawachi. "Why Reduce Health Inequalities?" *Journal of Epidemiology and Community Health* 54, no. 12 (December 2000): 923–29.

World Health Organization. "Closing the gap in a generation" Geneva, Switzerland: Commission on Social Determinants of Health, 2003. http://www.who.int/social_determinants/.

Young, L. R., and M. Nestle. "The Contribution of Expanding Portion Sizes to the U.S. Obesity Epidemic." *American Journal of Public Health* 92, no. 2 (2002): 246–49.

CHAPTER 3

Access to Knowledge

ACT. "Reading between the Lines: What the ACT Reading Test Reveals about College Readiness." Iowa City: ACT Inc., 2006.

——. "Using EXPLORE and PLAN Data to Evaluate GEAR UP Programs." Washington, DC: National Council for Community and Education Partnerships, 2007.

Adelman, Clifford. "The Toolbox Revisited: Paths to Degree Completion from High School through College." Washington, DC: U.S. Department of Education, 2006.

Ainsworth, James W. "Why Does It Take a Village? The Mediation of Neighborhood Effects on Educational Achievement." *Social Forces* 81, no. 1 (September 2002): 117–52.

Aos, Steve, Marna Miller, and Jim Mayfield. "Benefits and Costs of K–12 Educational Policies: Evidence-Based Effects of Class Size Reductions and Full-Day Kindergarten." Document No. 07-03-2201. Olympia,WA: Washington State Institute for Public Policy, 2007.

Astin, Alexander W., and Leticia Oseguera. "Degree Attainment Rates at American Colleges and Universities." Rev. ed. Los Angeles: UCLA Higher Education Research Institute, January 2005.

Balfanz, Robert, and Nettie Legters. "Locating the Dropout Crisis: Which High Schools Produce the Nation's Dropouts? Where Are They Located? Who Attends Them?" Baltimore: Center for Research on the Education of Students Placed at Risk (CRESPAR), September 2004.

Barnett, W. Steven. "Long-Term Effects of Early Childhood Programs on Cognitive and School Outcomes." *Future of Children* 5, no. 3 (1995): 25–50.

——, Dale J. Epstein, Allison H. Friedman, Rachel A. Sansanelli, and Jason T. Hustedt. *The State of Preschool 2009: State Preschool Yearbook*. New Brunswick, NJ: National Institute for Early Education Research, 2009.

Barton, Paul E. "One-Third of a Nation: Rising Dropout Rates and Declining Opportunities." Princeton,NJ: Educational Testing Service Policy Evaluation and Research Center, February 2005.

Bean, Frank D., Susan K. Brown, and Ruben G. Rumbaut. "Mexican Immigrant Political and Economic Incorporation." *Perspectives on Politics* 4 (2006): 309–13.

Bloom, Dan. "Programs and Policies to Assist High School Dropouts in the Transition to Adulthood." *Future of Children* 20, no. 1 (2010): 89–108.

——, and Ron Haskins. "Helping High School Dropouts Improve Their Prospects." Policy Brief. Princeton-Brookings *The Future of Children*, Spring 2010.

Bound, John, Michael Lovenheim, and Sarah Turner. "Why Have College Completion Rates Declined? An Analysis of Changing Student Preparation and Collegiate Resources." NBER Working Paper 15566. Cambridge, MA: National Bureau of Economic Research, December 2009.

Bowen, William G., Matthew M. Chingos, and Michael S. McPherson. *Crossing the Finish Line: Completing College at America's Public Universities*. Princeton,NJ: Princeton University Press, 2009.

Bradburn, Ellen M., David G. Hurst, and Samuel Peng. "Community College Transfer Rates to 4-year Institutions Using Alternative Definitions of Transfer." NCES 2001-197. Washington, DC: U.S. Department of Education, National Center for Education Statistics, 2001.

Bridgeland, John, John J. Dilulio, and Karen Burke Morison. "The Silent Epidemic: Perspectives of High School Dropouts." Washington, DC: Civic Enterprises, 2006.

Brint, Steven. "Few Remaining Dreams: Community Colleges since 1985." *The Annals of the American Academy of Political and Social Science* 586 (March 2003): 16–37.

——, and Jerome Karabel. *The Diverted Dream: Community Colleges and the Promise of Educational Opportunity in America, 1900–1985*. New York: Oxford University Press, 1989.

Burd-Sharps, Sarah, Jeff Elder, Kristen Lewis, and Eduardo Martins. "Goals for the Common Good: Exploring the Impact of Education." New York: American Human Development Project, 2009.

Card, David, and Jesse Rothstein. "Racial Segregation and the Black-White Test Score Gap." *Journal of Public Economics* 91, nos. 11–12 (December 2007): 2158–84.

Carneiro, Pedro, and James J. Heckman. "Human Capital Policy." IZA Discussion Paper No. 821. Bonn, Germany: Institute for the Study of Labor, July 2003.

Center for Research on Education Outcomes (CREDO). "Multiple Choice: Charter School Performance in 16 States." Palo Alto,CA: Stanford University, June 2009.

Chang Wei, Christina, Lutz Berkner, Shirley He, Stephen Lew, and James Griffith. "Web Tables: Undergraduate Financial Aid Estimates by Type of Institution in 2007–08." NCES 2009-201. Washington, DC: U.S. Department of Education, National Center for Education Statistics, May 2009.

Chronicle of Education. "College and University Endowments, 2008–2009." http://chronicle.com/stats/endowments.

Clotfelter, Charles T., Helen F. Ladd, and Jacob Vigdor. "Who Teaches Whom? Race and the Distribution of Novice Teachers." *Economics of Education Review* 24, no. 4 (August 2005): 377–92.

Committee for Economic Development. *The Economic Promise of Investing in High-Quality Preschool: Using Early Education to Improve Economic Growth and the Fiscal Sustainability of States and the Nation*. Washington, DC: Committee for Economic Development, 2006.

Constantine, J. M., N. Seftor, E. S. Martin, T. Silva, and D. Myers. "A Study on the Effect of the Talent Search Program on Secondary and Postsecondary Outcomes in Florida, Indiana, and Texas." Washington, DC: U.S. Department of Education, Office of Planning, Evaluation, and Policy Development, 2006.

Costrell, Robert M. and Michael Podgursky. "Golden Peaks and Perilous Cliffs: Rethinking Ohio's Teacher Pension System." Washington, DC: Thomas B. Fordham Institute, June 2007.

——. "Peaks, Cliffs, and Valleys: The Peculiar Incentives in Teacher Retirement Systems and Their Consequences for School Staffing." *Education Finance and Policy* 4, no. 2 (Spring 2009): 175–211.

Cutler, David M., Edward L. Glaeser, and Jacob L. Vigdor. "The Rise and Decline of the American Ghetto." *Journal of Political Economy* 107, no. 3 (1999): 455–506.

Czernich, Nina, Oliver Falck, Tobias Kretschmer, and Ludger Wößmann. "Broadband Infrastructure and Economic Growth." CESifo Working Paper Series No. 2861. Munich: CESifo Group, December 2009.

Dailey, Dharma, Amelia Bryne, Alison Powell, Joe Karaganis, and Jaewon Chung. "Broadband Adoption in Low-Income Communities." Report commissioned by the Federal Communications Commission. Brooklyn,NY: Social Science Research Council, March 2010.

DeLuca, Stefanie, and Elizabeth Dayton. "Switching Social Contexts: The Effects of Housing Mobility and School Choice Programs on Youth Outcomes." *Annual Review of Sociology* 35 (2009): 457–91.

Dickens, William T., Isabel Sawhill, and Jeffrey Tebbs. "The Effects of Investing in Early Education on Economic Growth." Policy Brief 153. Washington, DC: Brookings Institution, April 2006.

Dillon, Erin, and Kevin Carey. "Charts You Can Trust: Drowning in Debt—The Emerging Student Loan Crisis." Washington, DC: EducationSector, July 9, 2009.

Dobbie, Will, and Roland G. Fryer Jr. "Are High Quality Schools Enough to Close the Achievement Gap? Evidence from a Social Experiment in Harlem." NBER Working Paper No. 15473. Cambridge, MA: National Bureau of Economic Research, November 2009.

Domina, Thurston. "What Works in College Outreach: Assessing Targeted and Schoolwide Interventions for Disadvantaged Students." *Educational Evaluation and Policy Analysis* 31, no. 2 (2009): 127–52.

Dougherty, Christopher. "Why Are Returns to Schooling Higher for Women than for Men?" *Journal of Human Resources* 40, no. 4 (2005): 969–88.

Dougherty, Kevin. *The Contradictory College: The Conflicting Origins, Impacts, and Futures of the Community College*. Albany: State University of New York Press, 1994.

Echenique, Federico, and Roland G. Fryer Jr. "A Measure of Segregation Based on Social Interactions." *Quarterly Journal of Economics* 122, no. 2 (May 2007): 441–85.

Education Trust. "The Funding Gap, 2006." Washington, DC: Education Trust, 2006.

Erisman, Wendy, and Shannon Looney. "Opening the Door to the American Dream: Increasing Higher Education Access and Success for Immigrants." Washington, DC: Institute for Higher Education Policy, April 2007.

Ferguson, Ronald F., and Helen F. Ladd. "How and Why Money Matters: A Study of Alabama Schools." In *Holding Schools Accountable: Performance-based Reform in Education*, edited by Helen F. Ladd, 265–98. Washington, DC: Brookings Institution, 1996.

Fry, Richard. "The High Schools Hispanics Attend: Size and Other Key Characteristics." Washington, DC: Pew Hispanic Center, November 1, 2005.

General Social Survey. GSS 1972–2008 Cumulative Datafile. Chicago: National Opinion Research Center, 2008.

Goertz, Margaret E. "National Standards: Lessons from the Past, Directions for the Future." In *Mathematics Curriculum: Issues, Trends, and Future Directions* (2010 National Council of Teachers of Mathematics Yearbook), edited by R. Reys and B. Reys, 51–63. Reston, VA: National Council of Teachers of Mathematics, 2009.

——, and Michael Weiss. "Assessing Success in School Finance Litigation: The Case of New Jersey." *Education, Equity, and the Law*, No. 1. New York: Campaign for Educational Equity, November 2009.

Goldin, Claudia, Lawrence F. Katz, and Ilyana Kuziemko. "The Homecoming of American College Women: The Reversal of the College Gender Gap." *Journal of Economic Perspectives* 20, no. 4 (Fall 2006): 133–56.

Grammy.com. "2007 GRAMMY Signature Schools Named." News Release. April 5, 2007. http://www2.grammy.com/GRAMMY_Awards/News/Default.aspx?newsID=2443&newsCategoryID=11.

Hanushek, Eric A., John F. Kain, Jacob M. Markman, and Steven G. Rivkind. "Does Peer Ability Affect Student Achievement?" *Journal of Applied Econometrics* 18 (2003): 527–44.

Harding, David J. "Counterfactual Models of Neighborhood Effects: The Effect of Neighborhood Poverty on Dropping Out and Teenage Pregnancy." *American Journal of Sociology* 109, no. 3 (November 2003): 676–719.

Haycock, Kati, Mary Lynch, and Jennifer Engle. "Opportunity Adrift: Our Flagship Universities Are Straying from Their Public Mission." Washington, DC: Education Trust, January 2010.

Heckman, James J., and Paul A. LaFontaine. "The American High School Graduation Rate: Trends and Levels." IZA Discussion Paper No. 3216. Bonn, Germany: Institute for the Study of Labor, December 2007.

Heinrich, Carolyn J., and Harry J. Holzer. "Improving Education and Employment for Disadvantaged Young Men." National Poverty Center Working Paper Series, No. 10-04. Ann Arbor: University of Michigan, April 2010.

Hoxby, Caroline M., and Andrew Leigh. "Wage Distortion." *Education Next* 4, no. 2 (Spring 2005): 51–56.

Iceland, John, Daniel H. Weinberg, and Erika Steinmetz. *Racial and Ethnic Residential Segregation in the United States: 1980–2000*. Series CENSR-3. Washington, DC: U.S. Census Bureau, 2002.

Illinois School Report Card. "J. Sterling Morton East High School." 14-016-2010-17-0001. Springfield, IL: Illinois State Board of Education, 2009.

——. "New Trier Township H.S. Winnetka." 14-016-2030-17-0001. Springfield, IL: Illinois State Board of Education, 2009.

Institute for Latino Studies. "Measuring the Minority Education Gap in Metropolitan Chicago." Notre Dame, IN: University of Notre Dame, July 2005.

Kamerman, Sheila B., and Shirley Gatenio-Gabel. "Early Childhood Education and Care in the United States: An Overview of the Current Policy Picture." *International Journal of Child Care and Education Policy* 1, no. 1 (2007): 23–34.

Kao, Grace, and Jennifer S. Thompson. "Racial and Ethnic Stratification in Educational Achievement and Attainment." *Annual Review of Sociology* 29 (2003): 417–42.

Klima, T., M. Miller, and C. Nunlist. "What Works? Targeted Truancy and Dropout Programs in Middle and High School." Document No. 09-06-2201. Olympia: Washington State Institute for Public Policy, June 2009.

Kohler, Adriana D. and Melissa Lazarín. "Hispanic Education in the United States." Statistical Brief No. 8. Washington, DC: National Council of La Raza, 2007.

Kohn, Elise. "Benefits of Broadband in a Digital Society." Blogband: The Official Blog of the National Broadband Plan. Washington, DC: Federal Communications Commission, May 26, 2010. http://blog.broadband.gov/?entryId=464954.

Koretz, Daniel. "How Do American Students Measure Up? Making Sense of International Comparisons." *Future of Children* 19, no. 1 (Spring 2009): 37–51.

Krueger, Alan B., and Diane M. Whitmore. "Would Smaller Classes Help Close the Black-White Achievement Gap?" Working Paper no. 451. Princeton,NJ: Princeton University Industrial Relations Section, March 2001.

Kuh, George D., Jillian Kinzie, Jennifer A. Buckley, Brian K. Bridges, and John C. Hayek. "What Matters to Student Success: A Review of the Literature." Commissioned Report for the National Symposium on Postsecondary Student Success: Spearheading a Dialog on Student Success. Washington, DC: U.S. Department of Education, National Postsecondary Education Cooperative, July 2006.

Lareau, Annette. *Unequal Childhoods: Class, Race, and Family Life*. Berkeley: University of California Press, 2003.

Lavy, Victor. "Performance Pay and Teachers' Effort, Productivity, and Grading Ethics." *American Economic Review* 99, no. 5 (2009): 1979–2011.

Lofstrom, Magnus. "Why Are Hispanic and African American Dropout Rates So High?" IZA Discussion Paper No. 3265. Bonn, Germany: Institute for the Study of Labor, December 2007.

Long, Bridget Terry, and Erin Riley. "Financial Aid: A Broken Bridge to College Access?" *Harvard Educational Review* 77, no. 1 (Spring 2007): 39–63.

Lopez, Mark Hugo. "Latinos and Education: Explaining the Attainment Gap." Washington, DC: Pew Hispanic Center, October 7, 2009.

Meara, Ellen R., Seth Richards, and David M. Cutler. "The Gap Gets Bigger: Changes in Mortality and Life Expectancy, by Education, 1981–2000." *Health Affairs* 27, no. 2 (2008): 350–60.

Menez, Gene, and Andrea Woo. "Best High School Athletic Programs." *Sports Illustrated*, May 16, 2005.

Myers, D., R. Olsen, N. Seftor, J. Young, and C. Tuttle. "The Impacts of Regular Upward Bound: Results from the Third Follow-up Data Collection." Washington, DC: Mathematica Policy Research, 2004.

National Center for Public Policy and Higher Education. "States, Schools, and Colleges: Policies to Improve Student Readiness for College and Strengthen Coordination between Schools and Colleges." National Center Report No. 09-2. San Jose: National Center for Public Policy and Higher Education, November 2009.

Organisation for Economic Co-operation and Development (OECD). *Economic Policy Reforms 2010: Going for Growth*. Paris: OECD Publishing, 2010.

———. *Education at a Glance 2009: OECD Indicators*. Paris: OECD Publishing, 2009.

———. "PISA 2006: Science Competencies for Tomorrow's World." OECD Briefing Note for the United States. December 4, 2007. http://www.oecd.org/dataoecd/16/28/39722597.pdf.

Paral, Rob, and Timothy Ready. "The Economic Progress of U.S.- and Foreign-Born Mexicans in Metro Chicago: Indications from the United States Census." *Research Reports* 5, no. 4. Notre Dame, IN: University of Notre Dame, Institute for Latino Studies, May 2005.

Pew Forum on Religion and Public Life. "U.S. Religious Landscape Survey: February 2008." Washington, DC: Pew Research Center, 2008.

Pew Hispanic Center. "Hispanics of Cuban Origin in the United States, 2007, Fact Sheet." Washington, DC, September 16, 2009.

———. "Statistical Portrait of Hispanics in the United States, 2008." Washington, DC: Pew Hispanic Center, 2008.

Pew Research Center's Internet & American Life Project. November 30–December 27, 2009 Tracking Survey. Washington, DC, 2010.

Pinkus, Lyndsay. "Using Early-Warning Data to Improve Graduation Rates: Closing Cracks in the Education System." Policy Brief. Washington, DC: Alliance for Excellent Education, August 2008.

Planty, M., W. Hussar, T. Snyder, G. Kena, A. KewalRamani, J. Kemp, K. Bianco, and R. Dinkes. *The Condition of Education 2009*. NCES 2009-081. Washington, DC: National Center for Education Statistics, 2009.

Podgursky, Michael J., and Matthew G. Springer. "Teacher Performance Pay: A Review." *Journal of Policy Analysis and Management* 26, no. 4 (2007): 909–49.

Porter, Andrew C., Morgan S. Polikoff, and John Smithson. "Is There a de Facto National Curriculum? Evidence from State Content Standards." *Educational Evaluation and Policy Analysis* 31, no. 3 (2009): 238–68.

Prieger, James, and Wei-Min Hu. "The Broadband Digital Divide and the Nexus of Race, Competition, and Quality." *Information Economics and Policy* 20, no. 2 (2008): 150–67.

Princiotta, Daniel, and Ryan Reyna. "Achieving Graduation for All: A Governor's Guide to Dropout Prevention and Recovery." Washington, DC: National Governors Association Center for Best Practices, 2009.

Provasnik, S., and M. Planty. *Community Colleges: Special Supplement to the Condition of Education 2008*. NCES 2008-033. Washington, DC: U.S. Department of Education, National Center for Education Statistics, Institute of Education Sciences, 2008.

Putnam, Robert. "Social Capital: Measurement and Consequences." Paper presented at the Contribution of Human and Social Capital to Sustained Economic Growth and Well-being conference, Québec City, Canada, March 20, 2000. http://www.oecd.org/dataoecd/25/6/1825848.pdf.

Rampey, B. D., G. S. Dion, and P. L. Donahue. *NAEP 2008 Trends in Academic Progress*. NCES 2009–479. Washington, DC: U.S. Department of Education, National Center for Education Statistics, Institute of Education Sciences, 2009.

Reed, Matthew, and Diane Cheng. "Student Debt and the Class of 2008." Oakland: Project on Student Debt, Institute for College Access and Success, December 2009.

Rivkin, Steven G., Eric A. Hanushek, and John F. Kain. "Teachers, Schools, and Academic Achievement." *Econometrica* 73, no. 2 (March 2005): 417–58.

Robelen, Erik W. "Recession Woes Cast Pall as Schools Open." *Education Week* 29, no. 1 (August 25, 2009): 15, 18.

Rothstein, Richard. "A Blueprint That Needs More Work." Policy Memorandum #162. Washington, DC: Economic Policy Institute, March 27, 2010.

Salzman, Hal, and Lindsay Lowell. "Making the Grade." *Nature* 453 (May 1, 2008): 28–30.

Singh, Gopal K., and Mohammad Siahpush. "Widening Socioeconomic Inequalities in U.S. Life Expectancy, 1980–2000." *International Journal of Epidemiology* 35, no. 4 (2006): 969–79.

Small, Mario Luis, and Katherine Newman. "Urban Poverty after *The Truly Disadvantaged*: The Rediscovery of the Family, the Neighborhood, and Culture." *Annual Review of Sociology* 27 (2001): 23–45.

Sohoni, Deenesh, and Salvatore Saporito. "Mapping School Segregation: Using GIS to Explore Racial Segregation between Schools and Their Corresponding Attendance Areas." *American Journal of Education* 115 (August 2009): 569–600.

Sum, Andrew, and Ishwar Khatiwada. "Labor Underutilization Impacts of the Great Recession of 2007–2009: Variations in Labor Underutilization Problems across Age, Gender, Race-Ethnic, Educational Attainment and Occupational Groups in the U.S., 2009 Fourth Quarter." Boston: Northeastern University, Center for Labor Market Studies, March 2010.

Swanson, Christopher B. "Cities in Crisis 2009: Closing the Graduation Gap." Bethesda, MD: Editorial Projects in Education Research Center, April 2009.

———. "Special Education in America." Baltimore: Editorial Projects in Education Research Center, November 3, 2008.

Temple, Judy A., and Arthur J. Reynolds. "Benefits and Costs of Investments in Preschool Education: Evidence from the Child-Parent Centers and Related Programs." *Economics of Education Review* 26, no. 1 (February 2007): 126–44.

Toussaint-Comeau, Maude, and Sherrie L. W. Rhine. "Tenure Choice with Location Selection: The Case of Hispanic Neighborhoods in Chicago." *Contemporary Economic Policy* 22, no. 1 (January 2004): 95–110.

Tyler, John H., and Magnus Lofstrom. "Finishing High School: Alternative Pathways and Dropout Recovery." *Future of Children* 19, no. 1 (Spring 2009): 77–103.

———. "Is the GED an Effective Route to Postsecondary Education for School Dropouts?" IZA Discussion Paper No. 3297. Bonn, Germany: Institute for the Study of Labor, January 2008.

U.S. Census Bureau. American Community Survey, 2008 One-Year Estimates.

———. American Community Survey, 2006-8 Three-Year Estimates.

———. Census 2000 Summary File 1 (SF 1) 100-Percent Data.

U.S. Department of Agriculture. Economic Research Service. "Rural Education at a Glance." Rural Development Research Report 98. Washington, DC, November 2003.

U.S. Department of Education. National Center for Education Statistics. *Digest of Education Statistics, 2008*. NCES 2009-020. Washington, DC, 2009.

———. *Digest of Education Statistics, 2009*. NCES 2010-013. Washington, DC, 2010.

———. *Preschool: First Findings from the Third Follow-up of the Early Childhood Longitudinal Study, Birth Cohort (ECLS-B)*. NCES 2008-025. Washington, DC, 2007.

U.S. Department of Education. National Center for Education Statistics. Common Core of Data (CCD). "National Public Education Financial Survey (State Fiscal)," 2006–07 (FY 2007) v.1a.

———. "Public Elementary/Secondary School Universe Survey," 2006–07 v.1c.

———. "State Nonfiscal Survey of Public Elementary/Secondary Education," 2006–7 v.1c.

U.S. Department of Education. Office of Planning, Evaluation and Policy Development. *ESEA Blueprint for Reform*. Washington, DC, March 2010.

U.S. Department of Health and Human Services. Administration for Children and Families. "Head Start Impact Study: Final Report." Washington, DC, January 2010.

Wilson, William Julius. *The Truly Disadvantaged: The Inner City, the Underclass, and Public Policy*. Chicago: University of Chicago Press, 1987.

World Bank. *Information and Communication for Development 2009: Extending Reach and Increasing Impact*. Washington, DC, 2009.

Zarate, Maria Estela, and Harry P. Pachon. "Perceptions of College Financial Aid among California Latino Youth." Policy Brief. Los Angeles: Tomás Rivera Policy Institute, June 2006.

Zhou, Min. "Urban Education: Challenges in Educating Culturally Diverse Children." *Teachers College Record* 105, no. 2 (2003): 208–25.

CHAPTER 4
A Decent Standard of Living

Acs, Gregory, and Austin Nichols. *American Insecure: Changes in the Economic Security of American Families, Low-Income Working Families.* Paper 16. Washington, DC: Urban Institute, February 2010.

Adler, N. E., T. Boyce, M. A. Chesney, S. Cohen, S. Folkman, R. L. Kahn, and S. L. Syme. "Socioeconomic Status and Health: The Challenge of the Gradient." *American Psychologist* 49, no. 1 (January 1994): 15–24.

Alemayehu, Bishaw, and Jessica Semega. "Income, Earnings, and Poverty Data from the 2007 American Community Survey: American Community Survey Reports." Washington, DC: U.S. Census Bureau, August 2008. http://www.census.gov/prod/2008pubs/acs-09.pdf.

Aneja, Viney P. "Characterization of Particulate Matter in Roda, Virginia." Raleigh: North Carolina State University, 2009. http://www.sierraclub.org/coal/downloads/2009-VA-particulates.pdf.

Annie E. Casey Foundation Kids Count Data Center. Data by State. Baltimore, MD. http://datacenter.kidscount.org/data/bystate.

Applebaum, Eileen. "Paid Family Leave Arrives in California." Washington, DC: Center for American Progress, July 12, 2004. http://www.americanprogress.org/issues/2004/07/b117048.html.

Applied Research and Consulting LLC. "Financial Capability in the United States: National Survey." New York: FINRA Investor Education Foundation, December 1, 2009. http://www.finrafoundation.org/web/groups/foundation/@foundation/documents/foundation/p120536.pdf.

Arditti, J. A., S. A. Smock, and T. S. Parkman. "'It's Been Hard to Be a Father': A Qualitative Exploration of Incarcerated Fatherhood." *Fathering: A Journal of Theory, Research, and Practice about Men as Fathers* 3, no. 3 (Fall 2005): 267–88.

Arkansas Department of Human Services. "2009 Statistical Report." Little Rock, Arkansas, 2009. http://www.state.ar.us/dhs/AnnualStatRpts/ASR%202009.pdf.

Bell, Kate, Jared Bernstein, and Mark Greenberg. "Lessons for the United States from Other Advanced Economies in Tackling Child Poverty." In *First Focus, Big Ideas for Children: Investing in Our Nation's Future*, edited by First Focus: Making Children and Families the Priority, 81–92. Washington, DC: First Focus, 2008.

Bernstein, Jared, Elizabeth McNichol, and Karen Lyons. "Pulling Apart: A State-by-State Analysis of Income Trends." Economic Policy Institute (January 2006).

Bertrand, Marianne, and Sendhil Mullainathan. "Are Emily and Greg More Employable than Lakisha and Jamal? A Field Experiment on Labor Market Discrimination." *American Economic Review* 94, no. 4 (September 2004): 991–1013.

Besharov, Douglas J., and Douglas M. Call. "Income Transfers Alone Won't Eradicate Poverty." *Policy Studies Journal* 37, no. 4 (2009): 599–631.

Boushey, Heather. *Family-Friendly Policies: Boosting Mothers' Wages.* Briefing Paper. Washington, DC: Center for Economic and Policy Research, 2005. http://www.cepr.net/publications/labor_markets_2005_04_06.pdf.

———. *Tag Team Parenting.* Washington, DC: Center for Economic and Policy Research, 2006. http://www.cepr.net/documents/work_schedules_2006_08.pdf.

Bucks, Brian K., et al. "Changes in U.S. Family Finances from 2004 to 2007: Evidence from the Survey of Consumer Finances." *Federal Reserve Bulletin.* February 2009. http://www.federalreserve.gov/pubs/bulletin/2009/pdf/scf09.pdf.

Burd-Sharps, Sarah, Kristen Lewis, and Eduardo Borges Martins. *The Measure of America: American Human Development Report 2008–2009.* New York: Columbia University Press. 2008.

Burtless, Gary. "Stock Market Fluctuations and Retiree Income: An Update." Washington, DC: Brookings Institution, October 31, 2008. http://www.brookings.edu/papers/2008/1031_market_burtless.aspx.

Butcher, Kristin F., and Anne Morison Piehl. "Crime, Corrections, and California: What Does Immigration Have to Do with It?" San Francisco: Public Policy Institute of California, February 2008.

Capps, Randy, and Michael Fix. "Undocumented Immigrants: Myths and Reality." Washington, DC: Urban Institute, 2005. http://www.urban.org/publications/900898.html.

Card, David. "How Immigration Affects U.S. Cities." CReAM Discussion Paper Series No. 11/07, University College London: Centre for Research and Analysis of Migration (CReAM), June 2007.

Center on the Developing Child at Harvard University. *The Science of Early Childhood Development.* Cambridge, MA: National Scientific Council on the Developing Child, 2007.

Centers for Disease Control and Prevention. National Center for Health Statistics. FastStats. "Marriage and Divorce." December 22, 2009. http://www.cdc.gov/nchs/fastats/divorce.htm.

Cohen, Rick. *A Structural Racism Lens on Subprime Foreclosures and Vacant Properties.* Columbus,OH: Kirwan Institute, September 2008.

Comfort, Megan. *Doing Time Together: Love and Family in the Shadow of Prison.* Chicago: University of Chicago Press, 2008.

Conley, Dalton. "Capital for College: Parental Assets and Postsecondary Schooling." *Sociology of Education* 74, no. 1 (January 2001): 59–72.

Copeland, Craig. "Employment-Based Retirement Plan Participation: Geographic Differences and Trends, 2006." EBRI Issue Brief 311 (November 2007). Washington, DC: Employee Benefit Research Institute. http://www.ebri.org/pdf/briefspdf/EBRI_IB_11-20074.pdf.

Cornelius, Wayne A. and Marc R. Rosenblum. "Immigration and Politics." *Annual Review Political Science* 8 (2005): 99-119.

Davies, James B., et al. "The World Distribution of Household Wealth." Working Paper. Helsinki, Finland: UNUĐWIDER, December 5, 2006. http://www.iariw.org/papers/2006/davies.pdf.

De la Garza, Rodolfo O. "Understanding Contemporary Immigration Debates: The Need for a Multidimensional Approach." In *Border Battles: The U.S. Immigration Debates of the Social Science Research Council*. Brooklyn, NY: Social Science Research Council, July 31, 2006. http://borderbattles.ssrc.org/de_la_Garza/.

Deloitte and the Investment Company Institute. *Defined Contribution/401(k) Study—Inside the Structure of Defined Contribution/401(k) Plan Feeds: A Study Assessing the Mechanics of What Drives the "All-In" Fee*. Washington, DC: Investment Company Institute, June 2009. http://www.ici.org/pdf/rpt_09_dc_401k_fee_study.pdf.

DeNavas-Walt, Carmen, Bernadette D. Proctor, and Jessica C. Smith. "Income, Poverty, and Health Insurance Coverage in the United States: 2008." P60-236 (RV). Washington, DC: U.S. Census Bureau, September 2009. http://www.census.gov/prod/2009pubs/p60-236.pdf.

Diamond, Peter A., and Peter R. Orszag. *Saving Social Security: A Balanced Approach*. Washington, DC: Brookings Institution Press, 2003.

Edelman, Peter. "Welfare and the Poorest of the Poor." *Dissent* 56, no. 4 (Fall 2009): 36–41.

——. *Social Security: A Primer*. Washington, DC, September 2001. http://www.cbo.gov/ftpdocs/32xx/doc3213/EntireReport.pdf.

Edwards, Kathryn Anne, and Alexander Hertel-Fernandez. "The Kids Aren't Alright: A Labor Market Analysis of Young Workers." Briefing Paper no. 258. Washington, DC: Economic Policy Institute, April 7, 2010. http://www.epi.org/publications/entry/bp258/.

Elmendorf, Douglas W. "Economic and Budget Outlook." Presentation to the 35th Annual AAAS Forum on Science and Technology Policy. Washington, DC: Congressional Budget Office, May 13, 2010. http://www.cbo.gov/ftpdocs/110xx/doc11047/05-13-CBO_Presentation_to_AAAS.pdf.

——. *Social Security: A Primer*. Washington, DC: Congressional Budget Office, September 2001.

Employee Benefit Research Institute. "401(k) Plan Asset Allocation, Account Balances, and Loan Activity: An Information Sheet from the Employee Benefit Research Institute." Washington, DC, October 23, 2007. http://www.ebri.org/pdf/InfSheet.QDIA.23Oct07.Final.pdf.

Federal Reserve Board. Survey of Consumer Finances, 2007. http://www.federalreserve.gov/pubs/oss/oss2/scfindex.html.

Fishbein, Allen J., and Patrick Woodall. "Subprime Locations: Patterns of Geographic Disparity in Subprime Lending." Washington, DC: Consumer Federation of America, September 5, 2006. http://www.consumerfed.org/pdfs/SubprimeLocationsStudy090506.pdf.

Gennetian, Lisa A., Nina Castells, and Pamela Morris. "Meeting the Basic Needs of Children: Does Income Matter?" Working Paper Series no. 09-11. Ann Arbor, MI: National Poverty Center, August 2009.

Giuliano, Laura, David I. Levine, and Jonathan Leonard. "Manager Race and the Race of New Hires." *Journal of Labor Economics* 27, no. 4 (October 2009): 589–631.

Gokhale, Jagadeesh, and Michael Tanner. "KidSave: Real Problem, Wrong Solution." Policy Analysis no. 562. Washington, DC: Cato Institute, January 2006.

Goldberg, Naomi G. "The Impact of Inequality for Same-Sex Partners in Employer-Sponsored Retirement Plans." Los Angeles: UCLA Williams Institute, October 2009. http://askmerrill.ml.com/publish/mkt/pdfs/RetirementAnalysis_Final.pdf.

Graham, Mary E., and Julie L. Hotchkiss. "A More Proactive Approach to Addressing Gender-Related Employment Disparities in the United States." *Gender in Management: An International Journal* 24, no. 8 (2009): 577–95.

Grant, Jodi, Taylor Hatcher, and Nirali Patel. *Expecting Better: A State-by-State Analysis of Parental Leave Programs*. Washington, DC: National Partnership for Women & Families, 2005.

Gruenstein Bocian, Debbie, Wei Li, and Keith S. Ernst. "Foreclosures by Race and Ethnicity: The Demographics of a Crisis." Durham, NC: Center for Responsible Lending, June 18, 2010.

Gruenstein Bocian, Debbie, Keith S. Ernst, and Wei Li. "Unfair Lending: The Effect of Race and Ethnicity on the Price of Subprime Mortgages." Durham, NC: Center for Responsible Lending, May 31, 2006.

Hacker, Jacob, and Paul Pierson. "Winner-Take-All Politics: Public Policy, Political Organization, and the Precipitous Rise of Top Incomes in the United States." *Politics & Society* 38, no. 2 (2010): 158–204.

Hall, Keith. Statement before the U.S. Congress Joint Economic Committee. May 7, 2010. http://www.bls.gov/news.release/pdf/jec.pdf.

Hartmann, Heidi. *Poverty and Unemployment among Single Mother Families*. Washington, DC: Institute for Women's Policy Research, 2009.

——, Ariane Hegewisch, and Vicky Lovell. "An Economy That Puts Families First: Expanding the Social Contract to Include Family Care." Briefing Paper no. 190. Washington, DC: Economic Policy Institute, May 2007.

Heinrich, Carolyn J., and Harry J. Holzer. "Improving Education and Employment for Disadvantaged Young Men: Proven and Promising Strategies." Washington, DC: Urban Institute, May 6, 2010. http://www.urban.org/url.cfm?ID=412086.

Himmelstein, David U., et al. "Medical Bankruptcy in the United States, 2007: Results of a National Study." *American Journal of Medicine* 122, no. 8 (August 2009): 741–46.

Hokenstad, M. C., and Angela C. Curl. "Reshaping Retirement Policies in Post-Industrial Nations: The Need for Flexibility." *Journal of Sociology and Social Welfare* 33, no. 2 (2006): 85–106.

Holzer, Harry. *Better Workers for Better Jobs: Improving Worker Advancement in the Low-Wage Labor Market.* Washington, DC: Urban Institute, December 12, 2007. http://www.urban.org/url.cfm?ID=1001118.

——, Steven Raphael, and Michael A. Stoll. "Perceived Criminality, Criminal Background Checks and the Racial Hiring Practices of Employers." *Journal of Law and Economics* 49, no. 2 (2006): 451–80.

Insight Center for Community Economic Development. "Lifting as We Climb: Women of Color, Wealth, and America's Future." Oakland, CA. Spring 2010. http://www.insightcced.org/uploads/CRWG/LiftingAsWeClimb-WomenWealth-Report-InsightCenter-Spring2010.pdf.

——. "State Inclusive Business Program Overview & Goals." http://www.insightcced.org/communities/inbiz/programgoals.html (accessed May 13, 2010).

Institute for Women's Policy Research. "Fact Sheet: The Gender Wage Gap by Occupation." No. C350a. Washington, DC, April 2010. http://www.iwpr.org/pdf/C350a.pdf.

Institute for Women's Policy Research and Wellesley Centers for Women. "Achieving Equity for Women: Policy Alternatives for the New Administration Symposium Report." Washington, DC. April 2, 2009. http://iwpr.org/pdf/Symposiump09.pdf.

Jargowsky, Paul A., and Rebecca Yang. "The 'Underclass' Revisited: A Social Problem in Decline." *Journal of Urban Affairs* 28 (2006): 55–70.

John, David C., and J. Mark Iwry. "Protecting and Strengthening Retirement Savings: Strategies to Reduce Leakage in 401(k)s and Expand Saving through Automatic IRAs." Testimony of David C. John and J. Mark Iwry before the Special Committee on Aging, U.S. Senate, July 16, 2008. http://aging.senate.gov/events/hr198dj.pdf.

John, David C., and Ruth Levine. "National Retirement Savings Systems in Australia, Chile, New Zealand and the United Kingdom: Lessons for the United States." Washington, DC: Brookings Institution, July 2009.

Johnson, Simon. "The Quiet Coup." *The Atlantic* (May 2009).

Kaiser Family Foundation. statehealthfacts.org Database. "Health Insurance Coverage of the Total Population, 2007–2008." http://www.statehealthfacts.org.

Karen, Robert. *Becoming Attached: First Relationships and How They Shape Our Capacity to Love.* New York: Oxford University Press, 1998.

Kleiman, Mark A. R. "The Outpatient Prison." *American Interest* (March–April 2010). http://www.the-american-interest.com/article.cfm?piece=786.

Kletzer, Lori G. and William L. Koch. "International Experience with Job Training: Lessons for the United States." Kalamazoo, Michigan: W.E. Upjohn Institute, 2004.

Lechterman, Ted. "Risks and Resilience in the American Human Development Report: Conceptual and Methodological Issues." Background paper commissioned for *The Measure of America 2010–2011: Mapping Risks and Resilience*. American Human Development Project, June 2010.

Levinthal, Dave. "Congressmen Lose Big Bucks in 2008, But Still Rank among Nation's Richest." OpenSecrets. November 4, 2009. http://www.opensecrets.org/news/2009/11/congressmen-lose-big-bucks-in.html.

Lovell, Vicky. *Estimating the Benefits of Paid Family and Medical Leave: A Colloquium Report.* Washington, DC: Institute for Women's Policy Research, 2003. http://www.iwpr.org/pdf/A130.pdf.

Lui, Meizhu. "Laying the Foundation for National Prosperity: The Imperative of Closing the Racial Wealth Gap." Oakland, CA: Insight Center for Community Economic Development, March 2009. http://www.insightcced.org/uploads/CRWG/Executive%20Summary.pdf.

Marriott, Lisa. "Innovation in Retirement Savings Policy: The New Zealand Experience." *Journal of Comparative Policy Analysis: Research and Practice* 12, nos. 1 and 2 (2010): 197–212.

Meschede, Tatjana, Thomas M. Shapiro, and Jennifer Wheary. *Living Longer on Less: The New Economic (In)Security of Seniors.* Waltham, MA: Brandeis University Institute on Assets and Social Policy, 2009.

Mikelson, Kelly S. and Demetra Smith Nigntingale. "Estimating Public and Private Expenditures on Occupational Training in the United States." Washington, DC: U.S. Department of Labor, December 2004.

Milken Institute State Technology and Science Index. June 2008. http://www.milkeninstitute.org/tech/.

Mishel, Lawrence, and Jared Bernstein. *The State of Working America, 2008/2009.* Washington, DC: Economic Policy Institute, 2008.

Movement Advancement Project and SAGE (Services & Advocacy for Gay, Lesbian, Bisexual and Transgender Elders). "Improving the Lives of LGBT Older Adults." Denver, CO, March 2010. http://www.lgbtmap.org/file/advancing-equality-for-lgbt-elders.pdf.

Munnell, Alicia H. "Retirements at Risk." In *Pensions, Social Security and the Privatization of Risk*. Edited by Mitchell A. Orenstein. New York: Columbia University Press, 2009.

Munnell, Alicia H., Francesca Golub-Sass, and Dan Muldoon. "An Update on 401(k) Plans: Insights from the 2007 SCF." Boston: Boston College Center for Retirement Research, March 2009. http://crr.bc.edu/images/stories/Briefs/ib_9_5.pdf.

National Center on Family Homelessness. "Children." Newton, MA. http://www.familyhomelessness.org/Children.

National Immigration Forum. "Top 10 Immigration Myths and Facts." Washington, DC. June 2003. http://www.immigrationforum.org/images/uploads/MythsandFacts.pdf.

National Science Foundation. "Academic R&D Expenditures FY 2008." NSF 10-311. Washington, DC: Division of Science Resources Statistics. http://www.nsf.gov/statistics/rdexpenditures/.

Newport, Frank. "Americans Increasingly Concerned about Retirement Income." Washington, DC: Gallup, April 20, 2009. http://www.gallup.com/poll/117703/Americans-Increasingly-Concerned-Retirement-Income.aspx.

Nord, Mark. "Food Insecurity in Households with Children: Prevalence, Severity, and Household Characteristics." Economic Information Bulletin no. EIB-56. Washington, DC: U.S. Department of Agriculture, September 2009. http://www.ers.usda.gov/Publications/EIB56/EIB56.pdf.

Nurse, A. M. "Coming Home: The Transition from Incarcerated to Paroled Young Father." In *Contemporary Perspectives in Family Research*. Vol. 2: *Families, Crime and Criminal Justice*. Edited by Greer Litton Fox and Michael L. Benson. New York: Elsevier Science Inc., 2000.

Orenstein, Mitchell A., ed. *Pensions, Social Security, and the Privatization of Risk*. New York: Columbia University Press and Social Science Research Council, 2009.

Organisation for Economic Co-Operation and Development. *Doing Better for Children*. Paris: OECD Publishing, 2009.

Osterman, Paul. "Employment and Training Policies: New Directions for Less-Skilled Adults," in Reshaping the American Workforce in a Changing Economy. Harry J. Holzer and Demetra Smith Nightingale (Editors). Washington, DC: The Urban Institute Press, 2007.

Passel, Jeffrey S., and D'Vera Cohn. "A Portrait of Unauthorized Immigrants in the United States." Pew Hispanic Center. Washington, DC: Pew Research Center, April 14, 2009. http://pewresearch.org/pubs/1190/portrait-unauthorized-immigrants-states.

Pattillo, Mary, David F. Weiman, and Bruce Western, eds. *Imprisoning America: The Social Effects of Mass Incarceration*. New York: Russell Sage Foundation, 2004.

Platzer, Michaela and Glennon Harrison. "The U.S. Automotive Industry: National and State Trends in Manufacturing Employment." U.S. Congressional Research Service, R40746. August 3, 2009.

Peri, Giovanni. "Impacts of Immigration in Recession and Economic Expansion." Washington, DC: Migration Policy Forum, June 2010.

Porter, Eduardo. "Illegal Immigrants Are Bolstering Social Security with Billions." *New York Times*, April 5, 2005.

Purcell, Patrick. "Retirement Savings and Household Wealth in 2007." Washington, DC: Congressional Research Service, April 8, 2009. http://www.policyarchive.org/handle/10207/bitstreams/19203.pdf.

Raising the Global Floor: Adult Labour. "Paid Leave from Work." Montréal, Canada: McGill Institute for Health and Social Policy, 2010. http://raisingtheglobalfloor.org.

Ray, Rebecca. "A Detailed Look at Parental Leave Policies in 21 OECD Countries." Washington, DC: Center for Economic and Policy Research. September 2008. http://www.lisproject.org/publications/parentwork/parent-leave-details.pdf.

The Real Estate Group New York. "Manhattan Rental Market Report." New York, NY. April 2010. http://www.tregny.com/manhattan_rental_market_report.

Rivera, Amaad, Brenda Cotto-Escalera, Anisha Desai, Jeannette Huezo, and Dedrick Muhammad. "Foreclosed: State of the Dream." Boston: United for a Fair Economy, January 15, 2008. http://www.faireconomy.org/files/StateOfDream_01_16_08_Web.pdf.

Roemer, John E. "Equality and Responsibility." *Boston Review* 20, no. 2 (April/May 1995). http://www.bostonreview.net/BR20.2/roemer.html.

Rosenberg, Jennifer. "Children Need Dads Too: Children with Fathers in Prison." Geneva, Switzerland: Quaker United Nations Office (QUNO), July 2009. http://www.quno.org/geneva/pdf/humanrights/women-in-prison/CNDT%20internet-1.pdf.

Rumbaut, Ruben G. "Profiles in Resistance: Educational Achievement and Ambition among Children of Immigrants in Southern California." In *Resilience across Contexts: Family, Work, Culture and Community*, edited by Ronald D. Taylor and Margaret C. Wang, 252–92. Mahwah, NJ: Lawrence Erlbaum and Associates, 2000.

——. "Undocumented Immigration and Rates of Crime and Imprisonment: Popular Myths and Empirical Realities." In *The Role of Local Police: Striking a Balance between Immigration Enforcement and Civil Liberties*. Edited by Mary Malina. Washington, DC: Police Foundation, 2009.

Sabol, William J., Heather C. West, and Matthew Cooper. *Prisoners in 2008*. Washington, DC: U.S. Department of Justice, Bureau of Justice Statistics, April 2010.

Saxenian, AnnaLee. "Brain Circulation: How High-Skill Immigration Makes Everyone Better Off." Washington, DC: Brookings Institution, 2002. http://www.brookings.edu/articles/2002/winter_immigration_saxenian.aspx.

Sen, Amartya. *The Standard of Living: The Tanner Lectures*. Cambridge: Cambridge University Press, 1987.

The Sentencing Project. *Incarcerated Parents and Their Children: Trends 1991–2007*. Washington, DC. February 2009. http://www.sentencingproject.org/doc/publications/publications/inc_incarceratedparents.pdf.

Small, Mario Luis, and Katherine Newman. "Urban Poverty after *The Truly Disadvantaged*: The Rediscovery of the Family, the Neighborhood and Culture." *Annual Review of Sociology* 27 (2001): 23–45.

Sum, Andrew, and Ishwar Khatiwada. "Labor Underutilization Problems of U.S. Workers across Household Income Groups at the End of the Great Recession: A Truly Great Depression among the Nation's Low Income Workers amidst Full Employment among the Most Affluent." Boston: Northeastern University Center for Labor Market Studies, February 2010.

Swedish Ministry of Health and Social Affairs. "Old Age Pensions in Sweden." Fact Sheet no. 4. July 2000. http://www.globalaging.org/pension/world/sweden.pdf.

Tatlock, Anne. "Share and Share Alike: Does Income Sharing Imply Household Sharing?" Unpublished master's thesis. Irvine: University of California-Irvine, 2010.

U.S. Census Bureau. American Community Survey, 2006–2008 3-Year Estimates.

——. "Computer and Internet Use in the United States: October 2007." Table 3. "Reported Internet Usage for Individuals 3 Years and Older, by State: 2007." http://www.census.gov/population/www/socdemo/computer/2007.html.

——. Current Population Survey. Annual Social and Economic Supplements for 1974–2004. http://www.census.gov/cps/.

——. Current Population Survey. 2009 Annual Social and Economic Supplement. POV03: "People in Families with Related Children Under 18 by Family Structure, Age, and Sex, Iterated by Income-to-Poverty Ratio and Race: 2008." http://www.census.gov/hhes/www/cpstables/032009/pov/new03_50_01.htm.

——. Historical Income Tables. Table H-2: "Share of Aggregate Income Received by Each Fifth and Top 5 Percent of Households, All Races: 1967 to 2008." http://www.census.gov/hhes/www/income/data/historical/household/index.html.

U.S. Department of Housing and Urban Development. *Mortgage Pricing Differentials across Hispanic, Black, and White Households: Evidence from the American Housing Survey.* February 2006. http://www.huduser.org/Publications/PDF/hisp_homeown5.pdf.

U.S. Department of Labor. Bureau of Labor Statistics. Employment Situation News Release. USDL-10-0886. July 2, 2010. http://www.bls.gov/news.release/empsit.htm.

——. "Household Data Annual Averages. Table 39." http://www.bls.gov/cps/cpsaat39.pdf.

——. "Regional and State Employment and Unemployment—March 2010." News Release. April 16, 2010. http://www.bls.gov/news.release/pdf/laus.pdf.

——. "Union Membership (Annual) News Release." USDL-10-0069. January 22, 2010. http://www.bls.gov/news.release/union2.htm.

U.S. Social Security Administration. *Income of the Aged Chartbook, 2008.* April 2010. http://www.ssa.gov/policy/docs/chartbooks/income_aged/.

——. *Women and Social Security.* Fact Sheet. February 2002.

Van Giezen, Robert, and Albert E. Schwenk. "Compensation from before World War I through the Great Depression." Bureau of Labor Statistics. January 30, 2003. http://www.bls.gov/opub/cwc/cm20030124ar03p1.htm.

Wagmiller, Robert L. "Race and the Spatial Segregation of Jobless Men in Urban America." *Demography* 44, no. 3 (August 2007): 539–62.

Walters, Neal, and Sharon Hermanson. "Older Subprime Refinance Mortgage Borrowers." Washington, DC: AARP Public Policy Institute, July 2002. http://www.aarp.org/money/credit-loans-debt/info-2002/aresearch-import-184-DD74.html.

Weller, Christian E., and Shana Jenkins. "Building 401(k) Wealth One Percent at a Time: Fees Chip Away at People's Retirement Nest Eggs." Washington, DC: Center for American Progress, March 2007. http://www.americanprogress.org/issues/2007/03/pdf/401k_report.pdf.

Wiedrich, Kasey, Stephen Crawford, and Leigh Tivol. *Assets and Opportunity Special Report: The Financial Security of Households with Children.* Washington, DC: CFED, May 2010. http://cfed.org/assets/pdfs/SpecialReport_Children.pdf.

Williams Reid, Lesley, Harald E. Weiss, Robert M. Adelman, and Charles Jaret. "The Immigration-Crime Relationship: Evidence across U.S. Metropolitan Areas." Social Science Research 34, Issue 4 (December 2005): 757-780

Wilson, William Julius. *When Work Disappears: The World of the New Urban Poor.* New York: Vintage, 1997.

Wolff, Edward N. "Recent Trends in Household Wealth in the United States: Rising Debt and the Middle Class Squeeze—An Update to 2007." Working Papers Series no. 159. Annandale-on-Hudson, NY: Bard College Levy Economics Institute, March 2010. http://papers.ssrn.com/sol3/papers.cfm?abstract_id=1585409.

Woods, Rose A. "Employment Outlook: 2008–2018—Industry Output and Employment Projections to 2018." *Monthly Labor Review* (November 2009): 52–81.

CONCLUSION

Agenda for Action: Reducing Risks, Building Resilience

American Diabetes Association. "Diabetes Statistics." http://www.diabetes.org/diabetes-basics/diabetes-statistics/ (accessed August 1, 2010).

Brunkard, Joan, Gonza Namulanda, and Raoult Ratard. "Hurricane Katrina Deaths, Louisiana, 2005." Disaster Medicine and Public Health Preparedness. August 28, 2008. http://www.dhh.louisiana.gov/offices/publications/pubs-192/KatrinaDeaths_082008.pdf.

California Legislative Analyst's Office. Criminal Justice and Judiciary. "How Much Does It Cost to Incarcerate an Inmate in Prison." http://www.lao.ca.gov/laoapp/laomenus/sections/crim_justice/6_cj_inmatecost.aspx?catid=3.

California State University. 2010–2011 Cost of Attendance. Summary of Standard Student Expense Budget. http://www.calstate.edu/SAS/documents/2010-11COA.pdf.

Central Intelligence Agency. *The World Factbook*. "Singapore." https://www.cia.gov/library/publications/the-world-factbook/geos/sn.html (accessed August 18, 2010).

Klinenberg, E. *Heat Wave: A Social Autopsy of Disaster in Chicago*. Chicago: University of Chicago Press, 2003.

National Center for Education Statistics. Schools and Staffing Survey. "Number of Private Schools Charging Tuition and the Median Highest Annual Private School Tuition, by Community Type and Religious Orientation: 2003–04." http://nces.ed.gov/surveys/sass/tables/affil_2004_whs.asp.

Sum, Andrew, and Ishwar Khatiwada. "Labor Underutilization Impacts of the Great Recession of 2007–2009: Variations in Labor Underutilization Problems across Age, Gender, Race-Ethnic, Educational Attainment and Occupational Groups in the U.S., 2009 Fourth Quarter." Boston: Northeastern University, Center for Labor Market Studies, March 2010.

———. "Labor Underutilization Problems of U.S. Workers across Household Income Groups at the End of the Great Recession: A Truly Great Depression among the Nation's Low Income Workers amidst Full Employment among the Most Affluent." Boston: Northeastern University Center for Labor Market Studies, February 2010.

United States Environmental Protection Agency. "International Experiences with Economic Incentives for Protecting the Environment." November 2004. http://yosemite.epa.gov/ee/epa/eerm.nsf/vwAN/EE-0487-01.pdf/$file/EE-0487-01.pdf.

Van Giezen, Robert, and Albert E. Schwenk. "Compensation from before World War I through the Great Depression." Bureau of Labor Statistics. January 30, 2003. http://www.bls.gov/opub/cwc/cm20030124ar03p1.htm.

Washington State Employment Security Department. News and Information, Legislative Resources. "Family Leave Insurance." http://www.esd.wa.gov/newsandinformation/legresources/family-leave-insurance.php (accessed August 18, 2010).

Wilson, Duff. "Tobacco Funds Shrink as Obesity Fight Intensifies." *New York Times*, July 27, 2010.

Human Development Indicators

American Bankruptcy Institute. Bankruptcy Filing Statistics. Alexandria, VA. http://www.abiworld.org.

Bernstein, Jared, Elizabeth McNichol, and Karen Lyons. "Pulling Apart: A State-by-State Analysis of Income Trends." Washington, DC: Center on Budget and Policy Priorities, 2006. http://www.cbpp.org/files/1-26-06sfp.pdf.

Center for American Women and Politics. "Women Serving in the 111th Congress 2009–11." New Brunswick, NJ: Rutgers University Eagleton Institute of Politics. http://www.cawp.rutgers.edu/fast_facts/levels_of_office/Congress-Current.php.

Centers for Disease Control and Prevention. Behavioral Risk Factor Surveillance System. Atlanta, GA: National Center for Chronic Disease Prevention and Health Promotion. http://apps.nccd.cdc.gov/brfss/.

———. "Births: Final Data for 2006." *National Vital Statistics Reports* 57, no. 7 (January 7, 2009).

———. "Births: Preliminary Data for 2007." *National Vital Statistics Reports* 57, no. 12 (March 18, 2009).

———. Bridged-Race Population Estimates, United States: July 1st Resident Population by State, Age, Sex, Bridged-Race, and Hispanic Origin, 2007, on CDC WONDER Online Database, Vintage 2008. Atlanta, GA: National Center for Health Statistics. http://wonder.cdc.gov/bridged-race-V2008.html.

———. "Deaths: Final Data for 2006." *National Vital Statistics Reports* 57, no. 14 (April 17, 2009).

———. Health Data Interactive. http://www.cdc.gov/nchs/hdi.htm.

———. "Health, United States, 2009: With a Special Feature on Medical Technology." Washington, DC: National Center for Health Statistics, 2010.

———. "Infant Mortality Statistics from the 2005 Period Linked Birth/Infant Death Data Set." *National Vital Statistics Reports* 57, no. 2 (July 30, 2008).

———. "Multiple Cause of Death Files for 2007 with All Counties Coded by NCHS Identified." Compiled from data provided by the 57 vital statistics jurisdictions through the Vital Statistics Cooperative Program. Washington, DC: National Center for Health Statistics, 2009.

———. National Immunization Survey. National Center for Immunization and Respiratory Diseases. http://www.cdc.gov/vaccines/stats-surv/imz-coverage.htm.

———. National Vital Statistics System. Mortality Data. http://www.cdc.gov/nchs/deaths.htm.

———. Web-based Injury Statistics Query and Reporting System (WISQARS). National Center for Injury Prevention and Control. http://www.cdc.gov/injury/wisqars/index.html.

Federal Bureau of Investigation. 2008 Crime in the United States. September 2009. http://www.fbi.gov/ucr/cius2008/index.html.

George Mason University. United States Election Project. http://elections.gmu.edu.

iCasualities.org. "Coalition and Afghanistan Coalition Deaths by Nationality." Iraq Coalition Casualty Count. http://www.icasualties.org.

International Institute for Democracy and Electoral Assistance (IDEA). Voter Turnout Database. Stockholm, Sweden. http://www.idea.int/vt/viewdata.cfm.

International Labour Organization. Key Indicators of the Labour Market Database (KILM). Geneva, Switzerland. http://kilm.ilo.org.

Inter-Parliamentary Union. "Women in National Parliaments." Geneva, Switzerland. http://www.ipu.org/wmn-e/classif.htm.

Kaiser Family Foundation statehealthfacts.org. Washington, DC. http://www.statehealthfacts.org.

Kenny, Joan F., Nancy L. Barber, Susan S. Hutson, Kristin S. Linsey, John K. Lovelace, and Molly A. Maupin. "Estimated Water Use in the United States in 2005." U.S. Geological Survey Circular 1344. Reston, VA: U.S. Geological Survey, 2009. http://pubs.usgs.gov/circ/1344/pdf/c1344.pdf.

Luxembourg Income Study. "LIS Key Figures." Luxembourg. http://www.lisproject.org/key-figures/key-figures.htm.

National Alliance to End Homelessness. Homelessness Counts. Washington, DC, January 2007. http://www.endhomelessness.org/content/article/detail/1440.

National Association of State Budget Officers. State Expenditure Report 2008. Washington, DC, 2009. http://www.nasbo.org/LinkClick.aspx?link=79&tabid=106.

National Conference of State Legislatures. "Women in State Legislatures: 2010." Women's Legislative Network. Denver, CO. http://www.ncsl.org/default.aspx?tabid=19481.

National Priorities Project. National Priorities Project Database. Northampton, MA. http://www.nationalpriorities.org/nppdatabase_tool.

National Science Foundation. "Academic R&D Expenditures FY 2008." NSF 10-311. Washington, DC: Division of Science Resources Statistics. http://www.nsf.gov/statistics/rdexpenditures/.

Organisation for Economic Co-operation and Development (OECD). Directorate for Science, Technology and Industry. Paris. OECD Broadband Portal. http://www.oecd.org/sti/ict/broadband.

——. Education at a Glance 2009: OECD Indicators. Paris. http://www.oecd.org/edu/eag2009.

——. Health at a Glance 2009: OECD Indicators. Paris. http://www.oecdilibrary.org/content/book/health_glance-2009-en.

——. OECD Factbook 2007: Economic, Environmental and Social Statistics. Paris. http://www.oecd-ilibrary.org/factbook.

——. OECD Factbook 2009: Economic, Environmental and Social Statistics. Paris. http://www.oecd-ilibrary.org/factbook.

——. OECD Factbook 2010: Economic, Environmental and Social Statistics. Paris. http://www.oecd-ilibrary.org/factbook.

——. OECD Family Database. "PF2.1: Key characteristics of parental leave systems." Social Policy Division. Directorate of Employment, Labour and Social Affairs. Paris, January 7, 2010. http://www.oecd.org/dataoecd/45/26/37864482.pdf.

——. OECD StatExtracts. Paris. http://stats.oecd.org.

——. PISA Country Profiles. Programme for International Student Assessment (PISA). Paris. http://pisacountry.acer.edu.au/.

——. Society at a Glance 2009: OECD Social Indicators. Paris. http://www.oecd.org/els/social/indicators/SAG.

RealtyTrac. National Real Estate Trends. Irvine, CA. http://www.realtytrac.com.

UNESCO (United Nations Educational, Scientific, and Cultural Organization). Institute for Statistics. Montreal. http://www.uis.unesco.org.

United Nations Office on Drugs and Crime. "UNODC Crime and Criminal Justice Statistics." Vienna. http://www.unodc.org/unodc/en/data-and-analysis/crimedata.html.

United Nations Statistics Division. New York. http://unstats.un.org.

Urban Institute–Brookings Institution Tax Policy Center. Washington, DC. http://www.taxpolicycenter.org.

U.S. Census Bureau. American Community Survey. 2008 One-Year Estimates. http://factfinder.census.gov.

——. "Computer Use and Ownership: Current Population Survey Reports." Population Division. http://www.census.gov/population/www/socdemo/computer.html.

——. "Population Estimates: Estimates Data." http://www.census.gov/popest/estimates.html.

——. *Statistical Abstract of the United States: 2010* (129th Edition) Washington, DC, 2009. http://www.census.gov/compendia/statab/2010edition.html.

——. 2000 Census of Population and Housing. Population and Housing Unit Counts. PHC-3-1, United States Summary. Washington, DC, 2004. http://www.census.gov/prod/cen2000/phc3-us-pt1.pdf.

U.S. Department of Agriculture. Household Food Security in the United States, 2007. By Mark Nord, Margaret Andrews, and Steven Carlson. Economic Research Report no. ERR-66 (November 2008). http://www.ers.usda.gov/Publications/ERR66/ERR66b.pdf.

——. Farm and Ranch Lands Protection Program. Natural Resources Conservation Service. http://www.nrcs.usda.gov/programs/frpp/.

——. Forest Service. "Forest Legacy Program: Funded and Completed Projects." http://www.fs.fed.us/spf/coop/programs/loa/flp_projects.shtml.

——. State Activity Report: Federal Fiscal Year 2008. Alexandria, VA: Supplemental Nutritional Assistance Program (SNAP), 2010. http://www.fns.usda.gov/snap/qc/pdfs/2008_state_activity.pdf.

U.S. Department of Commerce. Bureau of Economic Analysis. News Release: GDP by State 2008. Table1–4.

——. Regional Economic Accounts. http://www.bea.gov.

U.S. Department of Defense. "DoD Personnel and Procurement Statistics." http://siadapp.dmdc.osd.mil.

U.S. Department of Education. Common Core of Data. National Center for Education Statistics. http://nces.ed.gov/ccd/.

——. Digest of Education Statistics 2009. Washington, DC: National Center for Education Statistics, 2010. http://nces.ed.gov/pubsearch/pubsinfo.asp?pubid=2010013.

———. National Assessment of Educational Progress Data Explorer. National Center for Education Statistics. http://nces.ed.gov/nationsreportcard/naepdata/.

———. "Summer 2010 EDFacts State Profiles." EDFacts Initiative. July 2010. http://www2.ed.gov/about/inits/ed/edfacts/state-profiles/index.html.

U.S. Department of Health and Human Services. Child Maltreatment 2008. Washington, DC: Administration for Children and Families Children's Bureau, 2010. http://www.acf.hhs.gov/programs/cb/pubs/cm08/index.htm.

U.S. Department of Justice. Bureau of Justice Statistics. Crime and Justice Data Online. http://bjsdata.ojp.usdoj.gov/dataonline/.

———. "Prison Inmates at Midyear 2008: Statistical Tables." Office of Justice Programs. http://bjs.ojp.usdoj.gov/index.cfm?ty=pbse&sid=38.

U.S. Department of Labor. Bureau of Labor Statistics. http://www.bls.gov.

———. "The Employment Situation: June 2010." News Release. USDL-10-0886 (July 2, 2010). http://www.bls.gov/news.release/pdf/empsit.pdf.

———. "Regional and State Employment and Unemployment: May 2010." News Release. USDL-10-0992 (July 20, 2010). http://www.bls.gov/news.release/pdf/laus.pdf.

———. "Alternative Measures of Labor Underutilization for States, Second Quarter of 2009 through First Quarter of 2010." Local Area Unemployment Statistics. April 23, 2010. http://www.bls.gov/lau/stalt10q1.htm.

U.S. Department of Labor. Employment Standards Administration. Wage and Hour Division. http://www.dol.gov.

U.S. Energy Information Administration. http://www.eia.doe.gov/.

U.S. Environmental Protection Agency. "CO2 Emissions from Fossil Fuel Combustion." State and Local Climate and Energy Program. 2007. http://www.epa.gov/climatechange/emissions/downloads/CO2FFC_2007.pdf.

———. National Priorities List. "NPL Site Status Information." http://www.epa.gov/superfund/sites/npl/status.htm.

———. 2008 Toxic Release Inventory Program. http://www.epa.gov/tri/tridata/tri08/national_analysis/.

World Alliance for Breastfeeding Action. "Maternity Protection Chart." Penang, Malaysia, August 2008. http://www.waba.org.my/whatwedo/womenandwork/pdf/MaternityProtectionChartAug2008.pdf.

World Bank. World Development Indicators Online Database. Washington, DC. http://data.worldbank.org.

Methodological Notes

Arias, Elizabeth, William Schauman, Karl Eschbach, Paul Sorlie, and Eric Backlund. "The Validity of Race and Hispanic Origin Reporting on Death Certificates in the United States." *Vital and Health Statistics* Series 2, no. 18 (October 2008). http://www.cdc.gov/nchs/data/series/sr_02/sr02_148.pdf.

Burd-Sharps, Sarah, Patrick Guyer, Ted Lechterman, and Kristen Lewis. "Child Well-Being in the US: Proposal for the Development of a 'Tot's Index' Using the Human Development Conceptual Framework." *Child Poverty: A Global Perspective* (Bristol, UK: Policy Press, forthcoming).

Chiang, C. L. *The Life Table and Its Applications.* Malabar, FL: Krieger, 1984.

Indian Health Service. *Adjusting for Miscoding of Indian Race on State Death Certificates.* Washington, DC: Indian Health Service, 1996.

MABLE/Geocorr2k. "Geographic Correspondence Engine with Census 2000 Geography." http://mcdc2.missouri.edu/websas/geocorr2k.html.

Meara, Ellen R., Seth Richards, and David M. Cutler. "The Gap Gets Bigger: Changes in Mortality and Life Expectancy, by Education, 1981–2000." *Health Affairs* 27, no. 2 (2008): 350–60.

National Center for Health Statistics. *Bridged-Race Population Estimates, United States.* July 1st Resident Population by State, Age, Sex, Bridged-Race, and Hispanic Origin, 2007. Accessed through CDC WONDER Online Database, Vintage 2008.

———. *Multiple Cause of Death Files for 2007 with All Counties Coded by NCHS Identified,* 2009 [received by agreement with NCHS and NAPHSIS Vital Statistics Cooperative Program].

Real Estate Group New York, The. "Manhattan Rental Market Report," April 2010. http://www.tregny.com/pdf/market_report_may_10.pdf.

Rosenberg, Harry M., Jeffrey D. Maurer, Paul D. Sorlie, Norman J. Johnson, Mariam F. MacDorman, Donna L. Hoyert, James F. Spitler, and Chester Scott. "Quality of Death Rates by Race and Hispanic Origin: A Summary of Current Research, 1999," *Vital and Health Statistics—Data Evaluation and Methods Research.* No. 128. September 1999. http://wonder.cdc.gov/wonder/help/CMF/sr02_128.pdf.

Toson, Barbara, and Alan Baker. "Life Expectancy at Birth: Methodological Options for Small Populations." National Statistics Methodological Series No. 33. London: Office for National Statistics, 2003.

U.S. Census Bureau.American Community Survey. 2008 Estimates. 2009. On American FactFinder Online Database, 1-year Estimates. http://factfinder.census.gov/servlet/DatasetMainPageServlet?_program=ACS&_submenuId=datasets_2&_lang=en.

———. "A Compass for Understanding and Using American Community Survey Data." 2008. www.census.gov/acs/www/Downloads/ACSGeneralHandbook.pdf.

———. DataFerrett, American Community Survey Public Use Microdata Sample, 2008 1-year Estimates.

———. 110th Congressional Districts Geographic Relationship Tables; http://www.census.gov/geo/www/cd110th/tables110.html.

U.S. Office of Management and Budget. "Statistical Policy Directive No. 15, Race and Ethnic Standards for Federal Statistics and Administrative Reporting." Federal Register Notice, October 30, 1997. http://www.whitehouse.gov/omb/rewrite/fedreg/ombdir15.html.

———."Update of Statistical Area Definitions and Guidance on Their Uses." OMB Bulletin No. 10-02. December 1, 2009. http://www.whitehouse.gov/omb/assets/bulletins/b10-02.pdf.

Index to Indicators

H

I

L

M

O

P

R

S

T

U

V

W

Maps At-A-Glance

AMERICAN HUMAN DEVELOPMENT INDEX 2008

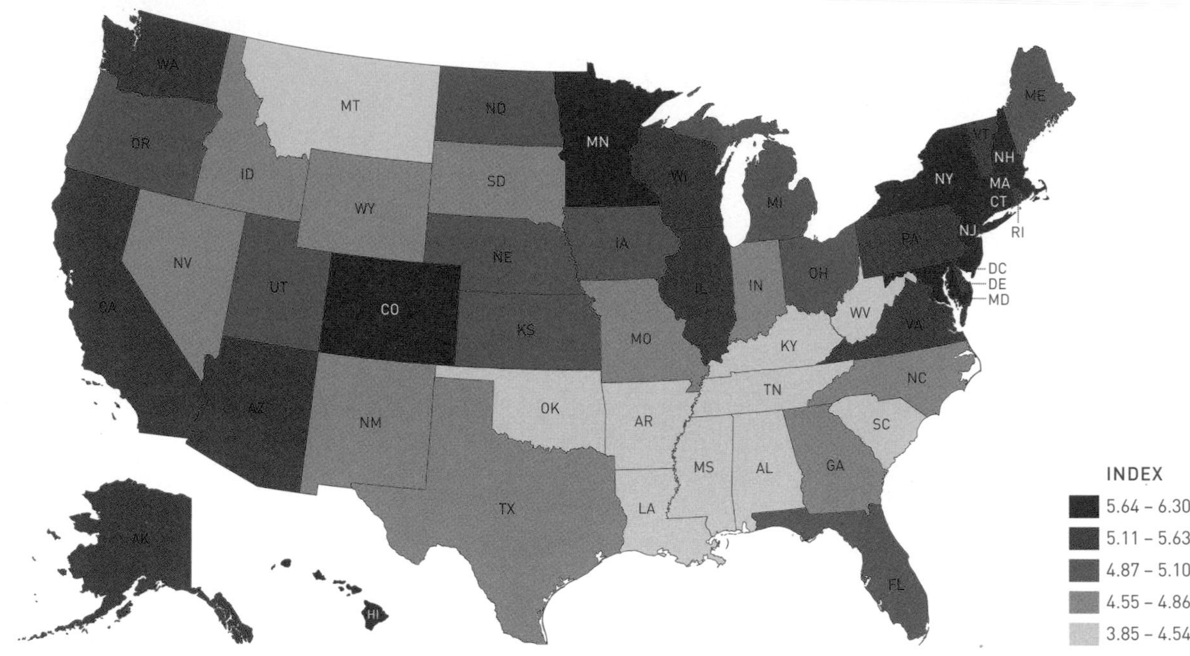

HEALTH INDEX 2008: Life Expectancy at Birth

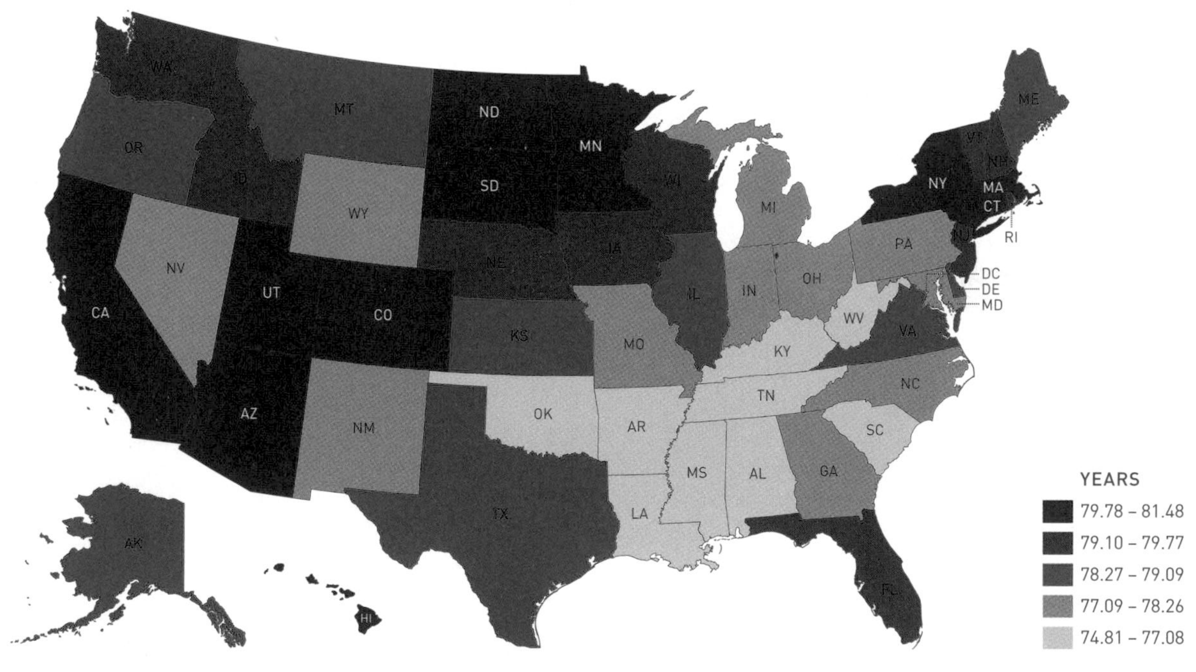

EDUCATION INDEX 2008: Educational Attainment and School Enrollment

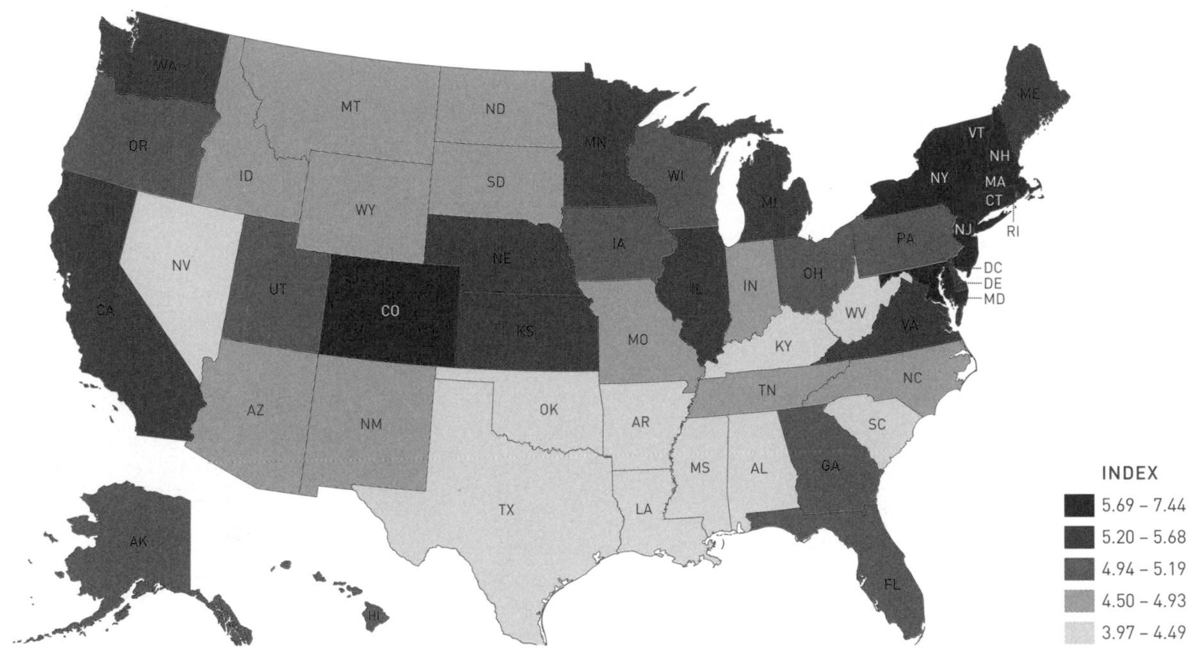

INCOME INDEX 2008: Median Earnings for the Population 16 and Older

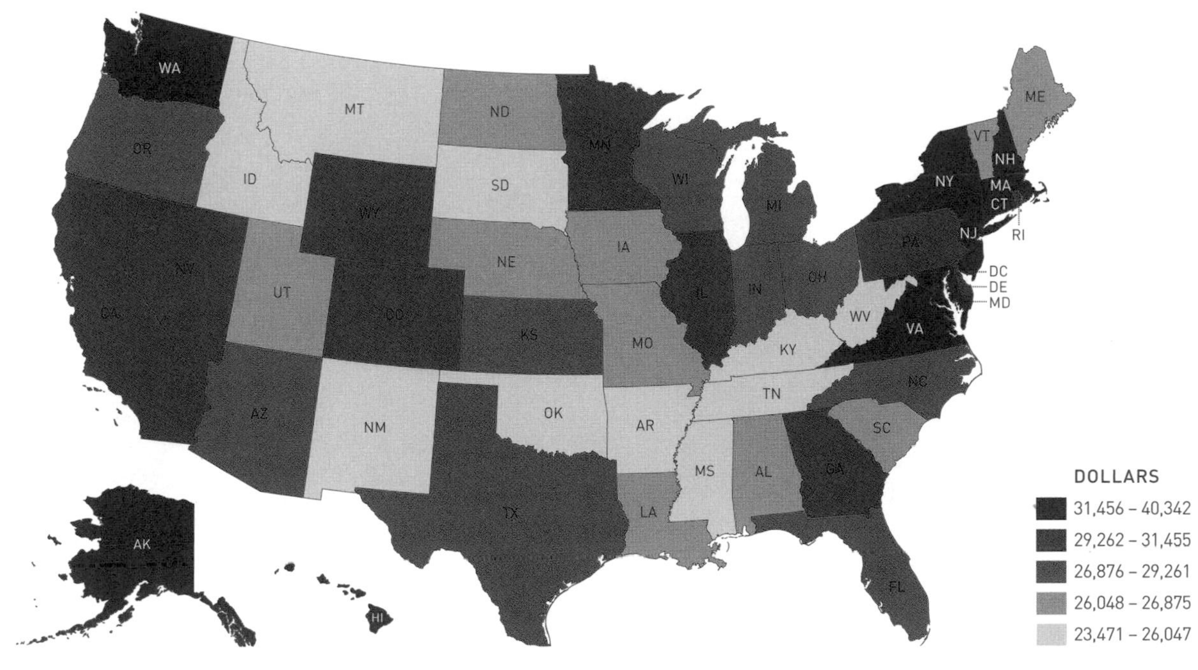

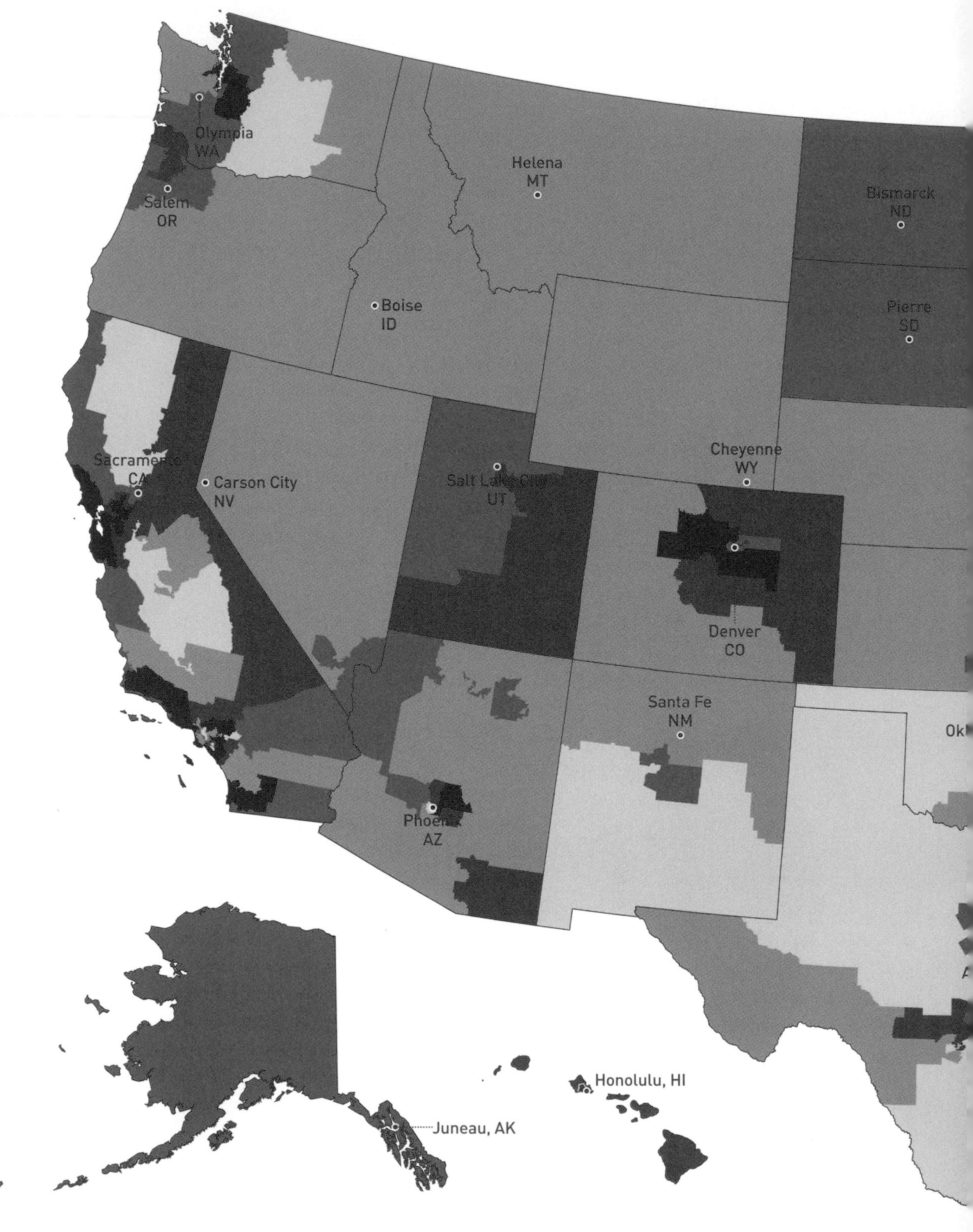
Olympia
WA
Salem
OR
Helena
MT
Bismarck
ND
Boise
ID
Pierre
SD
Sacramento
CA
Carson City
NV
Salt Lake City
UT
Cheyenne
WY
Denver
CO
Santa Fe
NM
Phoenix
AZ
Honolulu, HI
Juneau, AK

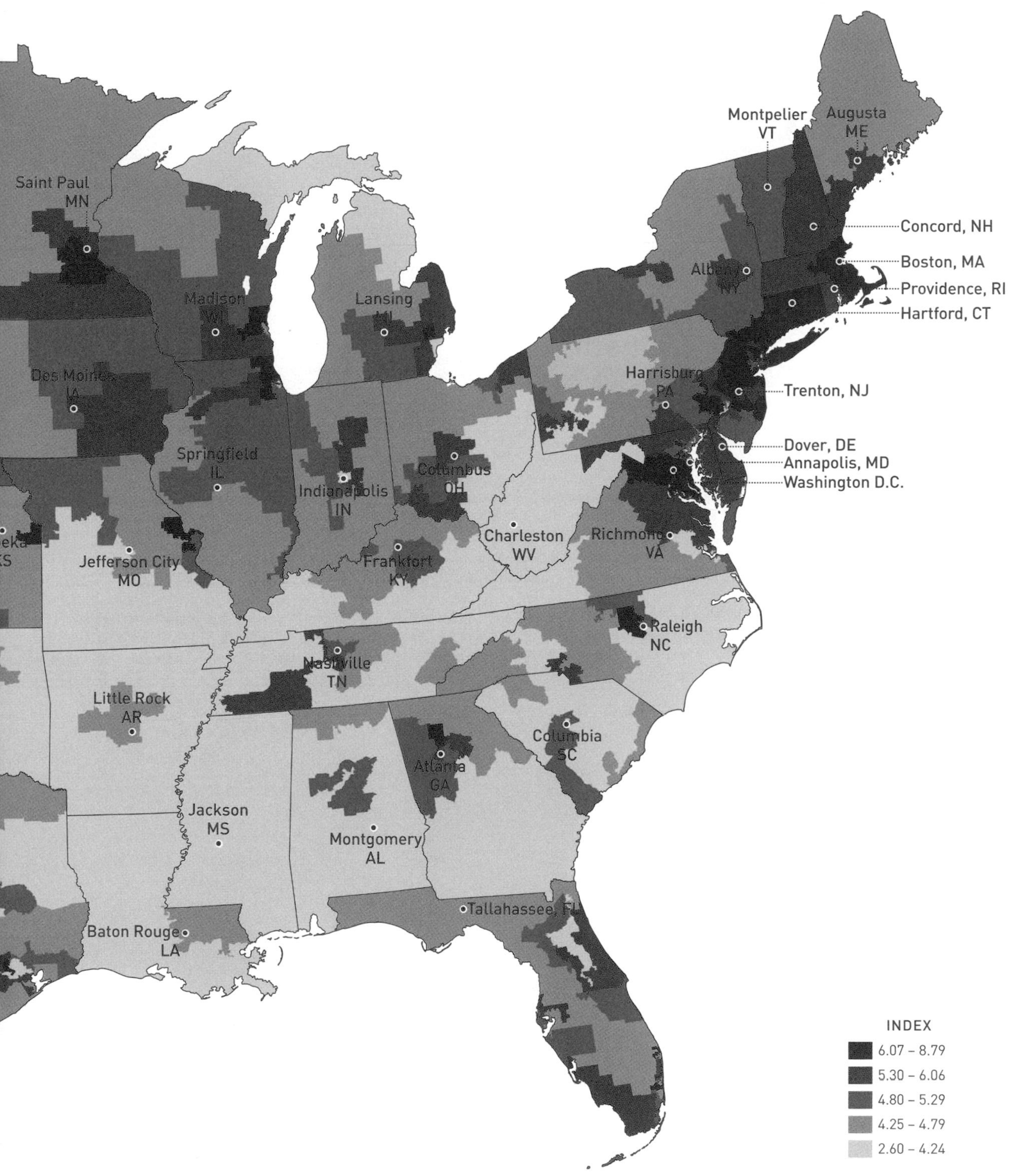

Montpelier
VT
Augusta
ME
Saint Paul
MN
Concord, NH
Boston, MA
Providence, RI
Hartford, CT
Madison
WI
Lansing
MI
Harrisburg
PA
Trenton, NJ
Springfield
IL
Indianapolis
IN
Columbus
OH
Dover, DE
Annapolis, MD
Washington D.C.
Jefferson City
MO
Frankfort
KY
Charleston
WV
Richmond
VA
Raleigh
NC
Nashville
TN
Little Rock
AR
Columbia
SC
Atlanta
GA
Jackson
MS
Montgomery
AL
Tallahassee, FL
Baton Rouge
LA
INDEX
6.07 – 8.79
5.30 – 6.06
4.80 – 5.29
4.25 – 4.79
2.60 – 4.24

A Day in the Life

8:10 am

Brush teeth

Jennifer brushes her teeth and showers in water pumped via underground pipes into her home. The water is monitored at the source for contaminants, and added fluoride helps to prevent cavities.

8:40 am

Drive to work

Jennifer wears a seatbelt, as required by law, to reduce auto injuries. Her car was manufactured according to automobile safety standards and is inspected annually for emissions levels to protect air quality.

12:20 pm

Make ATM withdrawal

Jennifer's bank accounts are insured by the Federal Deposit Insurance Corporation, created by Congress to ensure that people do not lose their savings if their bank fails.

12:30 pm

Buy lunch

Jennifer buys a salad from her favorite deli. The local health department inspects the deli for cleanliness and makes sure employees practice hygienic food handling.

4:00 pm

Take son to park after school

Jennifer's 4-year-old son plays and learns at their local public preschool. Jennifer's county government maintains parks, pools, skating rinks, and more, keeping them clean, safe, and fun.

7:30 pm

Put baby to bed

Their daughter wears flame-retardant pajamas, cuddles a teddy bear appropriate for a child her age, and sleeps in a safe crib, all thanks to consumer protection and safety regulations.

A walk through the day of a typical American woman reveals an array of public investments that help us build capabilities, decrease risks, and increase resilience. The legacy of such investments are all around us—so much so that we tend to take them for granted.

9:15 am

Cross the street

Jennifer parks her car in a municipal lot, drops a birthday card for her brother in the mailbox, and crosses to her office building. She has to walk around some construction workers filling potholes.

9:25 am

Take elevator to office

To get to her office, Jennifer takes the elevator. It has been built to comply with safety regulations. Her building is reinforced to protect against injury during earthquakes, hurricanes, and other natural disasters.

11:00 am

Work on the Internet

In her office, Jennifer uses the Internet to communicate, get information, and conduct business. The Internet was first developed by researchers at the Department of Defense.

5:10 pm

Take mother to the doctor

Jennifer picks up her mother to get her a flu shot, as recommended by health officials, who coordinate flu vaccine development each year. Since she's over 65, she qualifies for Medicare to help pay her medical bills.

6:30 pm

Cook dinner

Jennifer and her husband prepare a meal. The variety of food products available to Americans has been expanded by new trade treaties. Food quality, safety, and labeling are monitored upon entry into the U.S.

7:20 pm

Recycle trash

Jennifer sorts her garbage for curbside pickup. Her town provides sanitation services, such as garbage collection and sewerage systems, that protect public health and ensure a pleasant living environment.

WHO ARE WE?

KEY FACTS ABOUT THE U.S. POPULATION

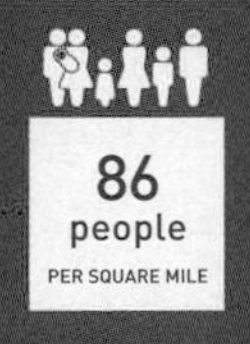

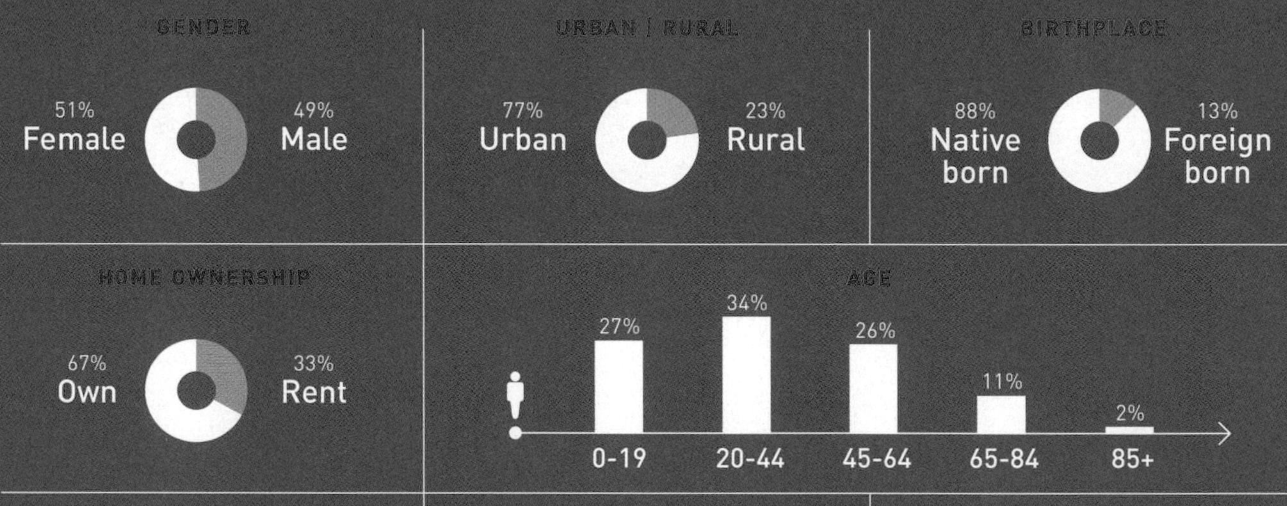

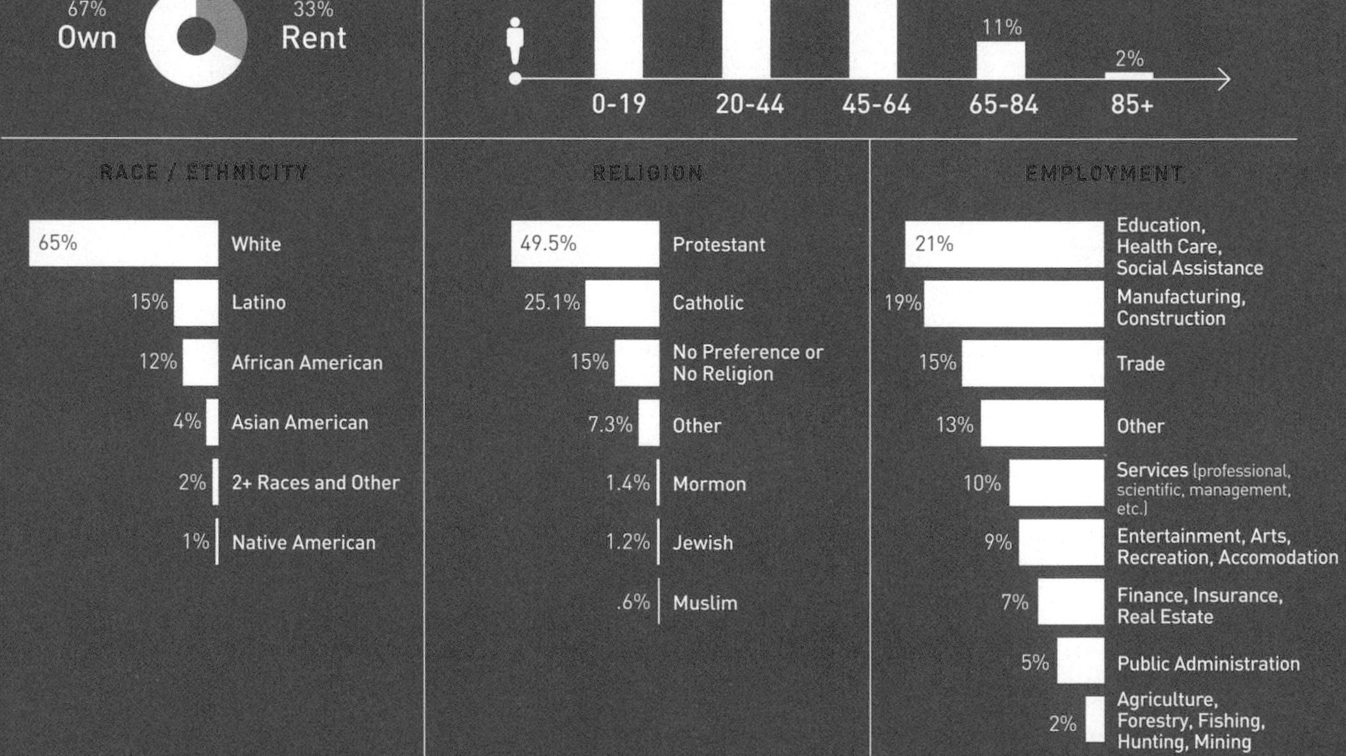

Note: All data are from 2008. Percentages may exceed 100 due to rounding.

Sources: U.S. Census Bureau USA QuickFacts; U.S. Census Bureau, American Community Survey, 2008. Tables S0201 and C0300; religious affiliation: Kosmin & Keysar, American Religious Identification Survey 2009, Table 3 "Self-Identification of U.S. Adult Population by Religious Tradition, 2008."